Online resources to take you further

Every **DIRECTIONS** book comes complete with **additional online resources** to enhance your learning

www.oxfordtextbooks.co.uk/orc/directions/

 online resource centre

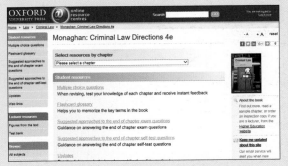

www.oxfordtextbooks.co.uk/orc/monaghan4e/

Visit the website for access to the specific resources.

FOR STUDENTS

* Updates on legislation and case law

* Annotated web links

* Guidance on answering all end-of-chapter questions

* Over 120 multiple-choice questions to test your knowledge

* Flashcard glossary

FOR LECTURERS

* A test bank of approximately 150 questions with answers and feedback

* A selection of figures and tables from the text

See the Guide to the Online Resource Centre on p. viii for full details.

Criminal Law

DIRECTIONS

4th Edition

NICOLA MONAGHAN

OXFORD
UNIVERSITY PRESS

OXFORD
UNIVERSITY PRESS

Great Clarendon Street, Oxford, OX2 6DP,
United Kingdom

Oxford University Press is a department of the University of Oxford.
It furthers the University's objective of excellence in research, scholarship,
and education by publishing worldwide. Oxford is a registered trade mark of
Oxford University Press in the UK and in certain other countries

© Oxford University Press 2016

The moral rights of the author have been asserted

First edition 2010
Second edition 2012
Third edition 2014

Impression: 1

Public sector information reproduced under Open Government Licence v2.0
(http://www.nationalarchives.gov.uk/doc/open-government-licence/open-government-licence.htm)

Published in the United States of America by Oxford University Press
198 Madison Avenue, New York, NY 10016, United States of America

British Library Cataloguing in Publication Data
Data available

Library of Congress Control Number: 2015957843

ISBN 978–0–19–875327–8

Printed in Italy by
L.E.G.O. S.p.A.

To my parents Nick and June

Guide to using the book

Criminal Law Directions is enriched with a range of features designed to help support and reinforce your learning. This guided tour shows you how to fully utilise your textbook and get the most out of your study.

Learning objectives

Each chapter begins with a list of learning objectives. These serve as a helpful signpost to what you can expect to learn by reading the chapter.

 LEARNING OBJECTIVES

By the end of this chapter, you should be able to:

- distinguish between conduct, consequences, and circumstances *actus reus* of an offence;
- understand the circumstances in which one can be criminally lia

Thinking points

Thinking points allow you to pause and reflect on what you are reading. They give you the opportunity to form your own views and provide valuable practice in critical thinking.

 THINKING POINT

Do you agree with Lord Diplock's statement? Can you think of any reaso *actus reus* ('guilty act') should not be used?

Hint: refer back to the definition of theft in chapter 1. Can all the *actus r* that definition be classed as guilty 'acts'?

Case close-ups

Summaries of key cases are boxed throughout so you can easily pick out the significant facts and details.

 CASE CLOSE-UP

Gibbins and Proctor (1918) 13 Cr App R 134

In the case of *Gibbins and Proctor*, the defendants lived wi ter, who they neglected to feed. The child died as a result o

Tables and figures

Tables and figures are presented across the book. These will help with your learning and revision, graphically presenting some of the key cases, concepts, and principles of the criminal law.

Figure 1.2 The criminal process

Cross references

Connections between topics are cross-referenced so you can see how they interlink. Links are highlighted to aid quick and accurate navigation through the book.

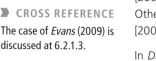 **CROSS REFERENCE**

The case of *Evans* (2009) is discussed at 6.2.1.3.

[2003] EWCA Crim 122, alth Other examples of the applic [2003] EWHC 2908 (Admin)

In *DPP v Santana-Bermudez* lawful search of the defenda

Statutes

Boxed extracts or summaries of key pieces of legislation are provided throughout for ease of reference and recall.

 STATUTE

Section 8, Criminal Justice Act 1967

A court or jury, in determining whether a person has committed an offer

  (a) shall not be bound in law to infer that he intended or foresaw actions by reason only of its being a natural and probable conse

End-of-chapter summaries

A list of summary points is included at the end of each chapter. These lists provide an overview of the main concepts and principles discussed across the chapter.

Summary

- The law does not punish individuals' 'evil thoughts' alone: some e required. If there is no *actus reus*, there is no crime.
- The *actus reus* of an offence may involve an act or omission (cc consequences being caused (result crimes); or the existence of surr

The bigger picture

A selection of pointers show you how you can deepen and contextualise your new legal understanding.

The bigger picture

- For an authoritative analysis of the philosophy of causation, yo Honoré (1985).
- As part of the foundations of liability for many offences, on both topics which feature again in later chapters in this book. T

Self-test questions

A selection of self-test questions is provided at the end of each chapter with answer guidance available on the Online Resource Centre. These will help you to recognise any gaps in your understanding.

? Questions

Self-test questions

1. Name the three different types of *actus reus* ele
2. What does the phrase 'there is no duty of easy r

Exam questions

End-of-chapter problem and essay-style questions help you to develop analytical and problem-solving skills. The Online Resource Centre provides answer guidance to each question.

Exam questions

1. Answer *all* parts below:

   (a) Jo is a lifeguard at the local swimming pool. While o difficulty in the pool. Does she have a duty to act to answer with reference to case law.

Further reading

Selected further reading is included at the end of each chapter to provide a springboard for further study. This will help you to take your learning further and guide you to some of the key academic literature in the field.

☰ Further reading

Books

Alexander, L. 'Criminal Liability for Omissions: An Inventory of Issues' in S. Shute and A. Simester (eds), *Criminal Law Theory: Doctrines of the General Part* (2002), Oxford: Oxford University Press, pp. 121–142

Hart, H. L. A. and Honoré, T. *Causation in the Law* (2nd edn, 1985), Oxford: Oxford University Press

Guide to the Online Resource Centre

The Online Resource Centre that accompanies this book provides students and lecturers with ready-to-use teaching and learning resources. The resources are intended to be used alongside the book and are designed to maximise the learning experience.

 www.oxfordtextbooks.co.uk/orc/monaghan4e/

For students

Accessible to all, with no registration or password required, enabling you to get the most from your textbook.

Updates to the law

An indispensable resource providing access to recent cases and developments in the law that have occurred since publication of the book.

> Updates
>
> Updates covering recent developments in the law since book publication will be added to this page. Sign up to be alerted when a new update is added by clicking on the link below.
> ✉ Keep me updated

Guidance on answering the end-of-chapter exam questions

All the end-of-chapter questions are supplemented with notes from the author indicating how they should be approached, so you can check your answers. Where relevant, the author points out the difficulties and controversies you will need to be aware of when tackling these questions.

> **Question 2**
>
> Critically evaluate the approach of English law towards imposing criminal liability for an omission to act.
>
> **Bullets**
>
> - This question covers the law on omissions. Students are expected to explore the law on omissions using case law as examples. Good students will discuss the theoretical debate on omissions.
>
> - Students should point out the general rule that there is no criminal liability for omissions; a person can only usually be subject to criminal sanction where he has performed a positive act. It is often said that under English law there is no duty of "easy rescue".
>
> - However, this is subject to a number of exceptions where there is a specific duty

Web links

A selection of annotated web links chosen by the author allows you to easily research those topics that are of particular interest to you. These links are checked regularly to ensure they remain up to date.

Multiple-choice questions

A selection of multiple-choice questions, arranged by chapter, allows you to quickly assess your knowledge of the various topics in criminal law.

Flashcard glossary

A series of interactive flashcards containing key terms and concepts enables you to test your understanding of criminal law terminology.

For lecturers

Password protected to ensure only lecturers can access the resource; each registration is personally checked to ensure the security of the site.

Registering is easy: click on the 'Lecturer Resources' on the Online Resource Centre, complete a simple registration form which allows you to choose your own username and password.

Test bank

Comprising of approximately 150 multiple-choice questions with answers and feedback, this is a fully customisable resource containing ready-made assessments.

Figures and tables

All of the figures and tables from the book are available to lecturers for use in their teaching.

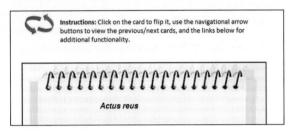

Web links

The Courts
The Courts Service
http://www.courtservice.gov.uk/
Executive agency of the Ministry of Justice

Judiciary of England and Wales
http://www.judiciary.gov.uk/

Instructions
Choose your answer by clicking the radio button next to your choice and then press 'Submit' to get your score.

Question 1

Which of the following describes the conduct requirement of a criminal offence?

○ a) Transferred malice

○ b) Doctrine of joint enterprise

Instructions: Click on the card to flip it, use the navigational arrow buttons to view the previous/next cards, and the links below for additional functionality.

Actus reus

Peggy fails to feed her 3 year old daughter, Lisa. Lisa dies due to starvation. Under which of the following categories of duty is liability most likely to be imposed upon Peggy for her failure to act?

○ a. Contractual duty and statutory duty
○ b. Public duty and special relationship
○ c. Danger to avert danger created and contractual duty
○ d. Special relationship and statutory duty

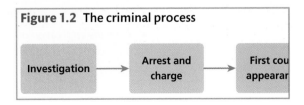

Figure 1.2 The criminal process

Investigation → Arrest and charge → First cou appearan

New to this edition

Below are some of the key updates in this edition:

- A new chapter on drugs offences which incorporates the offences of possession of a controlled drug under s.5(2), Misuse of Drugs Act 1971; possession of a controlled drug with the intention to supply that drug to another under s.5(3), Misuse of Drugs Act 1971; production of a controlled drug under s.4(2), Misuse of Drugs Act 1971; supplying or offering to supply a controlled drug under s.4(3), Misuse of Drugs Act 1971; and the liability of an occupier for knowingly permitting premises to be used for certain drug-related activities under s.8, Misuse of Drugs Act 1971. This chapter also covers the defences under ss.5(4) and 28, Misuse of Drugs Act 1971.

- A new section on child sex offences, covering rape of a child under 13 contrary to s.5, Sexual Offences Act 2003; assault of a child under 13 by penetration, contrary to s.6, Sexual Offences Act 2003; sexual assault of a child under 13, contrary to s.7, Sexual Offences Act 2003; causing or inciting a child under 13 to engage in sexual activity, contrary to s.8, Sexual Offences Act 2003; sexual activity with a child, contrary to s.9, Sexual Offences Act 2003; causing or inciting a child to engage in sexual activity, contrary to s.10, Sexual Offences Act 2003; engaging in sexual activity in the presence of a child, contrary to s.11, Sexual Offences Act 2003; causing a child to watch a sexual act, contrary to s.12, Sexual Offences Act 2003.

Recent cases and legislation such as:

- *Gurpinar; Kojo-Smith* (2015), *Jewell* (2014), *Workman* (2014), and *Barnsdale-Quean* (2014) on the partial defence of loss of control;

- *Brennan* (2014), *Golds* (2014), *Williams* (2013), and *Bunch* (2013) on the partial defence of diminished responsibility;

- *JF and NE* (2015), and *Webster v Crown Prosecution Service* (2014) on unlawful act manslaughter;

- *Hutchinson v UK* (2015) on whole life sentences;

- *Golding* (2014) on the transmission of sexually transmitted diseases;

- *W* (2015), *Tambedou* (2014), and *Kamki* (2013) on consent in sexual offences;

- *Waters* (2015) on intention to permanently deprive in theft;

- *Agrigoroaie and Savoae* (2015), *Valujevs* (2015), *Rouse* (2014), *Sakalauskau* (2014), and *Montague* (2013) on fraud and related offences;

- *Ankerson* (2015) on threats to destroy or damage property;

- *R (on the application of Nicklinson and another) v Ministry of Justice and others* (2015) on necessity and assisted suicide;

- *Pace* (2014) on attempts;

- The Anti-social Behaviour, Crime and Policing Act 2014 which abolishes marital coercion.

New academic papers of note include:

- Antrobus, S. 'The Criminal Liability of Directors for Health and Safety Breaches and Manslaughter' [2013] Crim LR 309.

- Arenson, K. 'The Paradox of Disallowing Duress as a Defence to Murder' (2014) 78 JCL 65.

- Ashworth, A. 'Manslaughter by Omission and the Rule of Law' [2015] Crim LR 563.

- Bleasdale-Hill, L. ' "Our Home is our Haven and Refuge—A Place Where We have Every Right to Feel Safe": Justifying the Use of up to "Grossly Disproportionate Force" in a Place of Residence' [2015] Crim LR 407.

- Child, J. J. and Sullivan, G. R. 'When Does the Insanity Defence Apply? Some Recent Cases' [2014] Crim LR 788.

- Crewe, B., Liebling, A., Padfield, N., and Virgo, G. 'Joint Enterprise: The Implications of an Unfair and Unclear Law' [2015] Crim LR 252.

- Dyson, M. 'The Future of Joint-Up Thinking: Living in a Post-Accessory Liability World' (2015) 79 JCL 181.

- Green, A. and McGourlay, C. 'The Wolf Packs in our Midst and other Products of Criminal Joint Enterprise Prosecutions' (2015) 79 JCL 280.

- Jarvis, P. and Bisgrove, M. 'The Use and Abuse of Conspiracy' [2014] Crim LR 261.

- Laird, K. 'Rapist or Rogue? Deception, Consent and the Sexual Offences Act 2003' [2014] Crim LR 492.

- Leahy, S. ' "No Means No", But Where's the Force? Addressing the Challenges of Formally Recognising Non-Violent Sexual Coercion as a Serious Criminal Offence' (2014) 78 JCL 309.

- Mawhinney, G. 'To be Ill or to Kill: The Criminality of Contagion' (2013) 77 JCL 202.

- Mirfield, P. 'Intention and Criminal Attempts' [2015] Crim LR 142.

- Padfield, N. 'Reform of Offences Against the Person' [2015] Crim LR 175.

- Parsons, S. 'The Loss of Control Defence—Fit for Purpose?' (2015) 79 JCL 94.

- Sjolin, C. 'Ten Years On: Consent Under the Sexual Offences Act 2003' (2015) 79 JCL 20.

Late news

The following change in the law occurred during the production of this book and so could not be inserted in the main chapter.

Important update for Chapter 16 Accessorial Liability

R v Jogee [2016] UKSC 8; *Ruddock v The Queen* [2016] UKPC 7

On 18th February 2016, the Supreme Court (sitting as both the Supreme Court and Privy Council) gave judgment in the case of *R v Jogee* [2016] UKSC 8; *Ruddock v The Queen* [2016] UKPC 7. This landmark decision alters the law relating to accessorial liability, reversing a legal principle which has been applied for the past 30 years. The Court was asked to consider the *mens rea* required in order to be convicted as an accessory to a crime under the 'doctrine of joint enterprise'. The Court unanimously held that the law relating to 'parasitic accessorial liability' (or the doctrine of joint enterprise) had been erroneously stated by the Privy Council in *Chan Wing-Siu* [1985] AC 168 and applied in later decisions, including by the House of Lords in *R v Powell and Daniels; R v English* [1999] 1 AC 1.

Prior to *Chan Wing-Siu*, the courts had recognised that where an accessory merely foresees that the principal might kill with the requisite intention for murder, he should be convicted of manslaughter rather than murder: '[o]nly he who intended that unlawful and grievous bodily harm should be done is guilty of murder. He who intended only that the victim should be unlawfully hit and hurt will be guilty of manslaughter if death results' (*R v Smith (Wesley)* [1963] 1 WLR 1200, p.1206, as cited in *R v Jogee* [2016] UKSC 8 at [28] and [70]). The Supreme Court held that a new and contrary principle of law had been introduced by the Privy Council in *Chan Wing-Siu* which provided that 'if two people set out to commit an offence (crime A), and in the course of that joint enterprise one of them (D1) commits another offence (crime B), the second person (D2) is guilty as an accessory to crime B if he had foreseen the possibility that D1 might act as he did' (at [2]). After an extensive review of the authorities, the Supreme Court held that the Privy Council had made an error in *Chan Wing-Siu* by equating foresight with an intention to assist as a matter of law. The Court held that 'the correct approach is to treat [foresight] as evidence of intent' from which the jury can infer intention (at [87]) and stated that foresight and intention are not synonymous (at [73]). Thus, a defendant can only be convicted as an accessory to murder if he 'intended to assist the intentional infliction of grievous bodily harm at least' and this 'will often … be answered by asking simply whether he himself intended grievous bodily harm at least' (at [98]). The Supreme Court gave five reasons for the decision:

1. The Court had the benefit of a much fuller analysis of the authorities than the Privy Council did in *Chan Wing-Siu*.

2. '[I]t cannot be said that the law is now well established and working satisfactorily. It remains highly controversial and a continuing source of difficulty for trial judges. It also led to a large number of appeals' (at [81]).

3. The law relating to secondary liability is important and any error should be corrected.

4. Murder already has a low *mens rea* threshold and the principle in *Chan Wing-Siu* extends that threshold further in the case of accessories. This is an 'over-extension of the law of murder and reduction of the law of manslaughter'. It is a 'serious and anomalous departure' from the law on murder (at [82]).

5. The law requires a lower mental threshold of liability for accessories than for principals (at [83]).

The principle from *Chan Wing-Siu* had been based on an incomplete and erroneous reading of previous case law along with 'generalised and questionable policy arguments' (at [79]). The Court commented that altering long-standing general principles of law relating to as difficult and serious a subject as homicide 'requires caution' and noted that neither the Privy Council in *Chan Wing-Siu* nor the House of Lords in *R v Powell and Daniels; R v English* gave any consideration to 'whether and why it was necessary and appropriate to reclassify such conduct as murder rather than manslaughter' (at [74]). The Court stated that the expression 'joint enterprise' was 'not a legal term of art' (at [77]) and that there was no separate form of secondary liability as formulated in *Chan Wing-Siu*. The Court confirmed that the ordinary principles of secondary liability are of general application (at [76]). The Supreme Court took the opportunity to restate the essential principles of accessorial liability:

- The prosecution does not have to prove that the defendant was a principal offender or an accessory.

- '[I]t is sufficient to be able to prove that he participated in the crime in one way or another' (at [88]).

- A defendant is a participant if he assisted or encouraged the commission of the crime (at [89]).

- It must also be proved that the accessory 'intended to encourage or assist D1 to commit the crime, acting with whatever mental element the offence requires of D1…. If the crime requires a particular intent, D2 must intend … to assist D1 to act with such intent' (at [90]).

- Where the defendant is party to a violent attack but he does not have the intention to assist in the causing of death or grievous bodily harm, but the victim dies as a result of an escalation of the violence, the defendant will be guilty of manslaughter rather than murder.

- If the defendant encourages or assists an unlawful act which all sober and reasonable people would recognise carried the risk of some harm and death results, the defendant will be guilty of unlawful act manslaughter (at [96]).

- There is one qualification to this, namely that 'it is possible for death to be caused by some overwhelming supervening act by the perpetrator which nobody in the defendant's shoes could have contemplated might happen and is of such character as to relegate his acts to history', then the defendant will not be guilty of a criminal offence (at [97]).

NOTE: An extended update on this case will be added to the Online Resource Centre in advance of the 2016/17 academic year.

Preface

This fourth edition of *Criminal Law Directions* has been expanded to include a new chapter on drugs offences under the Misuse of Drugs Act 1971 (chapter 12), and a new section on child sexual offences under the Sexual Offences Act 2003 (which can be found within chapter 8). This edition also incorporates some exciting legal developments in criminal law, including further recent cases from the Court of Appeal on consent in sexual offences, the defences of loss of control and diminished responsibility, and other recent cases which illustrate the operation of the Fraud Act 2006.

I hope that the pedagogic features in this textbook continue to offer an accessible and student-friendly approach to the study of criminal law, and will help students to get to grips with the more complex substantive principles of law. One new feature to this edition, 'the bigger picture', aims to contextualise the subject, for instance by highlighting how topics in various chapters are interlinked, and providing references to further research in particularly topical areas. I hope that this feature will encourage students to engage further with some of the academic research in the various areas of criminal law. In addition to these features, the book covers the standard substantive topics that one would expect to see in a typical criminal law module. These include murder and manslaughter, non-fatal offences against the person (including sexual offences), theft, fraud, and other property offences, general defences, and principles such as inchoate liability and accessories.

I am grateful to the team at Oxford University Press who have been involved in the editorial process, design, and production of this edition. Particular thanks are due to my editor, John Carroll, and production editor, Elisa Cozzi, who have both been supportive, encouraging, and patient throughout the writing and production processes, and to Deborah Hey for her meticulous copy-editing of this edition. I would also like to thank the anonymous reviewers who provided feedback on the previous edition of the book and who suggested some of the new content that features in this edition. Finally, my thanks are also due (as always) to my husband, Chris, for his unwavering support.

As always, all errors are my own.

The law is stated as at 1 October 2015.

Nicola Monaghan
Hertfordshire, November 2015

Outline contents

Detailed contents

Table of cases

Bold page entries refer to text in a 'case close-up' box

Table of legislation

Statutory Instruments

Foreign legislation

International conventions

1 Introduction to criminal law

LEARNING OBJECTIVES

By the end of this chapter, you should be able to:

- distinguish between criminal law and other areas;
- understand the nature and function of the criminal law;
- explain the criminal process;
- outline the hierarchy of the criminal courts;
- understand the burden and standard of proof; and
- identify the *actus reus* and *mens rea* of a criminal offence.

Introduction

Criminal law is a subject which affects us all. Consider for a moment whether you have ever committed a criminal offence. Have you ever exceeded the speed limit whilst driving? Used your mobile phone while waiting in a traffic jam? Jumped a red light? Eaten loose cherries or grapes whilst shopping in a supermarket and before paying for them? Noticed that you've been given too much change in a shop or been overpaid by your employers, but said nothing? 'Borrowed' a friend's CD without returning it? Been in possession of cannabis? Drawn graffiti on property belonging to another person? Given somebody an unwanted kiss? Touched somebody when they did not want you to? Each of these might amount to a criminal offence and carry a sanction. The vast majority of people have, at some stage in their lives, been a victim of a crime, witnessed a criminal offence or committed one (quite possibly without being caught and prosecuted). Indeed, many people are able to claim experience from all three perspectives. The scope of criminal law is vast, encompassing an enormous range of offences. This book focuses on the criminal offences commonly covered on criminal law modules, including murder and manslaughter (chapters 5 and 6), non-fatal offences against the person (chapters 7 and 8), property offences such as theft, fraud, and burglary (chapters 9 to 11), and drugs offences (chapter 12). The general principles of criminal law are also covered, including the elements of an offence (chapters 1 to 3), general defences (chapters 13 and 14), and principles of liability, including inchoate and accessorial liability (chapters 4, 15, and 16).

1.1 Crime statistics

The Office for National Statistics publishes a statistical bulletin on crime in England and Wales. The bulletin provides statistics from the annual Crime Survey for England and Wales (CSEW, formerly known as the British Crime Survey) as well as statistics on police reported crime. The statistics from both sources have shown a decrease in crime in England and Wales over the year 2013–14. The statistics from the Crime Survey for England and Wales for the year ending December 2014 show a 7% decrease in crime compared to the survey from the previous year, and 'the lowest estimate since the CSEW began in 1981'. This figure is in contrast to the statistic for police reported crime, which increased by 2% compared with the previous year. Victim-based crime (as opposed to other crimes against society) accounts for 83% of all police reported crime and there were large increases in offences of violence against the person (up 21%), sexual offences (up 32%), and public order offences (up 14%). However, these statistics have been affected by improved compliance with recording standards. The figures also show that there have been increases in offences of fraud and sexual offences, and these are also due to other factors. In particular, there have been changes to the way in which offences of fraud are recorded with a move towards a centralised system of recording and this may have caused the statistics for fraud to show an increase of 9% compared to the previous year, so this figure must be treated with caution. The Office for National Statistics suggests that the significant increase in sexual offences is due to both improvements in recording offences and a greater willingness of complainants to come forward to report sexual offences. Despite apparent increases in these categories of offences, the statistics published demonstrate that, contrary to the sensationalist headlines which feature in most tabloid newspapers from time to time, crime is not significantly on the increase. However, the accuracy of any official statistical analysis can always be criticised. The extent of the Crime Survey for England and Wales is limited in the sense that it only covers crimes against those aged 10 and above who are resident in households, and the statistics of police recorded crime only present data from crimes which have actually been reported to the police which may be influenced by other factors. It is difficult to conduct an accurate and comprehensive analysis of all crimes.

 THINKING POINT

Think of as many criminal offences as you can. Consider why such conduct is regarded as criminal. If you were writing the next criminal statute, what other conduct would you criminalise, and why?

1.2 What is criminal law about?

Criminal law is a fascinating subject which students find highly enjoyable. During your criminal law module, you will come across cases which you will remember for years; ask any lawyer or law graduate about *Brown* [1994] 1 AC 212 or *Collins* [1973] QB 100, and you will probably be regaled with the glorious facts of these cases. There exists a very wide range of criminal offences, which has increased substantially in recent years. Examples range from the obvious offences against property, such as theft and burglary; offences against the person, such as murder, rape, and assault; to drug offences, road traffic offences, pollution offences, offences against the administration of justice, offences against public order, and offences against public morals. On your criminal law module you will be introduced to only a fraction of these. Nevertheless, you will explore the law relating to some of the most serious and/or common criminal offences, including murder, manslaughter, non-fatal offences against the person, and theft. In addition to these offences, you will explore a range of both specific and general defences, such as loss of control, self-defence, duress, and automatism. You will also encounter a number of key concepts and fundamental principles of criminal liability, for example *actus reus* and *mens rea*, the doctrine of transferred malice, liability for inchoate offences, and the doctrine of joint enterprise.

1.3 Criminalisation

What constitutes criminal behaviour varies from country to country and from era to era. For example, homosexuality is a criminal offence in Saudi Arabia, although it is not in England and Wales. Similarly, behaviour which historically amounted to a criminal offence, may not amount to a crime today. For example, suicide constituted a criminal offence in England and Wales up until 1961, when the offence was abolished by the Suicide Act 1961. Rape of a woman by her husband was once not deemed to be an offence, but the House of Lords recognised this conduct to be a criminal offence in the case of *R v R (Rape: Marital Exemption)* [1992] 1 AC 599.

So, how is a crime defined? Although we are able to provide many examples of criminal offences, defining what constitutes criminal conduct is a difficult task. In *Principles of Criminal Law*, Professor Ashworth and Professor Horder state that:

> There are certain serious wrongs which are criminal in most jurisdictions, but in general there is no straightforward moral or social test of whether conduct is criminal. The most reliable test is the formal one: is the conduct prohibited, on pain of conviction and sentence? (7th edn, p.5)

A crime is conduct which the law deems to be criminal under statute (an Act of Parliament) or common law (case law). Such conduct is prohibited because it involves the threatening or causing of harm to individuals or to public interests. Conduct may be deemed to be criminal due to moral and/or social reasons. Although a crime may be committed against a specific individual, a crime is classed as a public wrong as it affects the public at large by making society feel less secure and safe from harm.

1.3.1 **The harm principle**

The question of whether conduct constitutes a criminal offence is usually relatively easy to determine; criminal offences are prescribed by statute or common law and, in theory, the law should be clear and accessible in accordance with the rule of law. However, the question of whether conduct *should* constitute a criminal offence is often more difficult to determine. The rationale for criminalising offences such as murder, manslaughter, and offences against the person is straightforward; these are crimes because of the harm that is caused to others. State interference with the liberty of an individual can be justified on the basis that it is necessary to prevent harm to others in society. The harm principle was espoused by John Stuart Mill in 1859 in his book, *On Liberty*: 'the only purpose for which power can be rightfully exercised over any member of a civilized community, against his will, is to prevent harm to others' (Mill 2008: 14). This principle is often relatively straightforward to apply because it relies on an objective standard of whether harm is caused to others. However, it is not sufficient on its own as a barometer of whether conduct should be criminalised as it does not justify the criminalisation of conduct which does not cause harm, such as attempted offences or regulatory offences.

It is useful to consider the scope of the term 'harm'; for instance, a narrow interpretation of harm which is based solely on physical harm would fail to justify the criminalisation of offences such as hate speech and harassment. Criminal law needs to strike a balance between protecting the autonomy/freedom of individuals and social welfare (Wilson 2002: 20). Thus, the harm principle formed the basis of the 'offence principle' put forward by Joel Feinberg in 1987. This principle looks more broadly at the criminalisation of conduct that causes offence to others. Feinberg argues that the prevention of shock, disgust, or revulsion justifies the criminalisation of certain conduct. This principle might be used as the rationale for criminalising hate speech, harassment, and some social media offences.

1.3.2 **Enforcing morality**

Lord Devlin famously argued that morality should play a part in the criminalisation of conduct, such that conduct which was deemed by the reasonable man to be morally wrong should be criminalised in order to prevent the breakdown of society, irrespective of whether that conduct actually caused harm to others (Devlin 1965). This view was opposed by Hart (1968 and 1965).

 THINKING POINT

- Consider the offence of possession of cannabis with intent to supply. What harm is caused as a result of this offence? Does the offence affect only one or two individuals or society as a whole?
- Who is affected by the conduct of hooligans at a football match?
- Imagine that your room in the university halls of residence is burgled. How do you think this offence might affect the public at large?

1.4 Distinguishing criminal law, the law of tort, and contract law

Criminal law can be distinguished from other areas of law such as the law of tort and contract law. However, there are areas in which these subjects overlap. Criminal law is a branch of public law in that it affects society at large. By contrast, the law of tort and contract law are branches of private law in that they affect individuals. Different terminology is used in criminal proceedings to that which is used in civil proceedings. For example, in criminal proceedings, a prosecution is brought by the *State* (the Crown), whereas in tort and contract an *individual* sues another individual or a body. In criminal law, the State *prosecutes* a defendant, whereas in tort and contract an individual *sues* another person. Criminal law is concerned with the prosecution of individuals whose behaviour or conduct has not met the standards of acceptable behaviour expected of citizens. These individuals have committed a *public* wrong. The law of tort and contract law govern the law relating to *private* wrongs.

In criminal proceedings, a *verdict* is delivered at the end of the trial, according to which the defendant will usually either be found *guilty* or *not guilty*. Criminal law is concerned with the *punishment* of offenders and a defendant who has been found guilty (*convicted*) of a criminal offence will be *sentenced*. Sentences range from terms of *imprisonment* to community sentences, such as community punishment orders and community rehabilitation orders, and fines. A defendant who is found not guilty is *acquitted*. By contrast, at the conclusion of a civil trial, there will be a *finding* that the defendant was either *liable* or *not liable*. Civil law is concerned with *compensating* the wronged individual through the payment of *damages*.

1.5 The function of criminal law

The criminal law has a number of functions:

- The law sets standards of behaviour which citizens must meet and these standards reflect the values of society (such as morality or religion).
- Criminal law prohibits conduct which threatens or causes harm to individuals or to the wider public.
- The criminal justice system is punitive, punishing defendants for criminal conduct.
- Another argument often put forward in favour of criminalising certain conduct is that of deterrence. It is argued that if certain behaviour is deemed to be criminal, then members of society will refrain from such conduct. By punishing offenders, the criminal justice system seeks to encourage other members of society to comply with the law.

 THINKING POINT

- Do you agree with the decision to reclassify cannabis as a Class B drug in January 2009? Why?
- Should fox hunting be a criminal offence?
- Do you think the deterrent theory is effective?

1.6 Sources of criminal law

1.6.1 **Statute and common law**

Whilst studying criminal law, you will meet two main sources of law: statute and common law. Some criminal offences have been created over the years by case law. These offences are called common law offences. Murder is a common law offence, as is manslaughter. These offences have been defined by judges in previous cases and the current definitions of these offences are still to be found in case law. Other offences are set down in statute (Acts of Parliament); these offences are called statutory offences. Examples include: theft, which is charged contrary to s.1 of the Theft Act 1968; rape, which is charged contrary to s.1 of the Sexual Offences Act 2003; and wounding or causing grievous bodily harm with intent, which is charged contrary to s.18 of the Offences Against the Person Act 1861. The definitions of these offences are found in statute, although the elements of such offences may be further defined by case law. Occasionally, offences are charged contrary to statute, but the definition of the offence is found in common law. Examples include assault and battery, which are charged contrary to s.39 of the Criminal Justice Act 1988, but are defined in the case of *Fagan v Metropolitan Police Commissioner* [1969] 1 QB 439.

1.6.2 **A Criminal Code?**

Some countries have a Criminal Code, which is a comprehensive document setting out the definitions for all criminal offences and defences. For many years, the Law Commission has given consideration to the adoption of such a Criminal Code in England and Wales, and in 1989, the Commission proposed a Draft Criminal Code. However, the Government has yet to adopt any such Code.

The advantages of having a Criminal Code are: the law would be much more readily accessible. In addition, there would be clear definitions for all offences and defences, avoiding the ambiguity which sometimes arises under the common law. One major disadvantage with a Criminal Code is its inflexibility. A key advantage of the common law is that it changes as attitudes in society do. As seen in 1.3, it was the common law which in 1991 confirmed rape by a husband of his wife to be a criminal offence. At present, such changes can be made relatively quickly as the judiciary can define or clarify key elements of our criminal offences. A Criminal Code would be less flexible as such alterations to the law would have to go through a lengthy administrative procedure before taking effect.

1.7 The classification of offences

Offences are often classified by their seriousness. There are three categories of offences:

- indictable only offences;
- either way offences;
- summary only offences.

Indictable only offences are the most serious offences and include murder, manslaughter, rape, robbery, and wounding or causing grievous bodily harm with intent. These offences carry high penalties upon conviction, sometimes with a maximum sentence of life imprisonment. These offences must always be tried in the Crown court with a jury.

Summary offences are the least serious offences. They include driving offences, assault, and battery. These offences carry much lighter penalties, which may be anything from an endorsement (points) on a driving licence, to a fine or a short term of imprisonment. Summary offences are tried in the magistrates' court without a jury. The magistrates' court may only sentence an offender to a maximum of 6 months in prison (or 12 months in total where the offender is sentenced for more than one offence). A defendant charged with a summary offence does not have a right to trial by jury.

Either way offences are offences of medium seriousness, where the facts of the particular incident will usually determine the severity of the offence. These include theft, assault occasioning actual bodily harm, wounding or inflicting grievous bodily harm, burglary. Where a defendant is charged with an either way offence, he may be tried either in the Crown court (with a jury) or in the magistrates' court (without a jury). A mode of trial hearing will take place in the magistrates' court in order to determine where the defendant will be tried. If the magistrates consider the offence to be too serious for the magistrates' court, they will commit (send) the defendant to the Crown court for trial. The defendant will have no choice in this. On the other hand, if the magistrates consider the case to be suitable for summary trial, they will accept jurisdiction over the case. The defendant then has a choice to make: he can either elect to be tried in the magistrates' court, or he may choose to be tried in the Crown court by a jury (this is often referred to as the 'right to trial by jury'). It will be noted, therefore, that a right to a trial by jury is not always available: the defendant has no such right if he is charged with a summary only offence. For a classification of offences, see figure 1.1.

Figure 1.1 The classification of offences

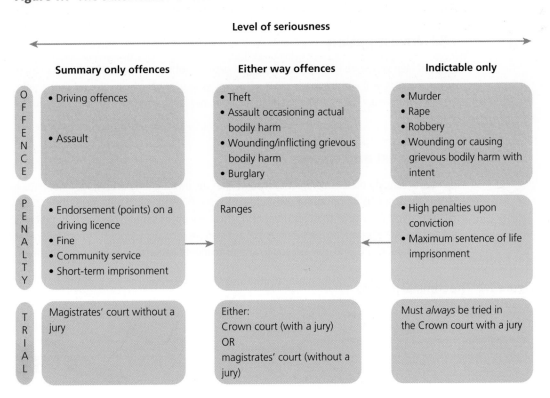

1.8 The criminal justice process

In order to get the most out of your criminal law module, you will need to have some understanding of criminal procedure and the process by which a case proceeds through the criminal justice system. There are various sources of law which govern the criminal justice process from investigation to trial and sentencing. The most important for you to be aware of at this stage in your studies are the Police and Criminal Evidence Act 1984 which governs police powers and the admissibility of evidence gathered during the investigation, as well as the Codes of Practice which provide the police with guidance on the exercise of their powers. The Criminal Procedure Rules 2014 govern the management of a criminal case within the courts and provide that there is an overriding objective that criminal cases be dealt with justly (see rule 1.1). Finally, the Criminal Justice Act 2003 is a major piece of legislation governing most aspects of the criminal justice system, from procedural matters to the law of evidence and the sentencing of offenders. You may delve into these Acts of Parliaments and Rules in much greater detail in your future studies. For now it is sufficient to briefly run through the criminal justice process in very general terms.

When a criminal offence occurs, it is usual practice for the police to investigate the alleged offence and for the State (more specifically, the Crown Prosecution Service (CPS)) to prosecute the alleged offender. However, it is also possible (although rare) for an individual to bring a private prosecution in criminal law. Let us take a practical example. Imagine that one day, a person takes your iPod out of your bag without your knowledge and keeps it. Presumably, you would make a phone call to the police in order to report the offence. On reporting the offence, the criminal process begins (figure 1.2).

1.8.1 Investigation

The next step would be for the police to investigate this offence. They would take a witness statement from you and from any other witnesses who may have been around at the time, they would seize any CCTV footage which might be available, and they would try to find the offender.

1.8.2 Arrest and charge

In order to simplify our example, let us assume that the investigating officer, PC Plod, finds a person (the suspect), whom he believes is the offender. PC Plod would next arrest the suspect for the criminal offence of theft and interview him at the police station (be aware that there is law and guidance governing the treatment of arrested persons and various other procedures at the police station). PC Plod may ask you to attend an identification parade at the police station

Figure 1.2 The criminal process

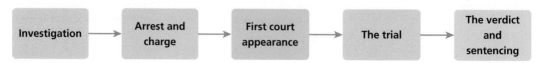

in order that you to try to pick out the offender. If there is enough evidence, PC Plod would then (after consulting the CPS) charge the suspect with the offence of theft and send the case papers to the CPS. The CPS is the body responsible for the decision to bring a criminal prosecution against an individual. If the CPS decides not to prosecute the suspect (now referred to as the accused), it will not proceed with the case.

An option open to you would then be to privately prosecute the accused. The major disadvantages of a private prosecution are that you would then bear all the costs inherent in bringing a prosecution and you would have limited access to scientific resources and expert witnesses, and again, these cost money. Consequently, the vast majority of criminal prosecutions are brought by the State.

1.8.3 **First court appearance**

The next stage in the criminal process is the first court appearance. The accused (or defendant) would appear at court as soon as possible after he has been charged with the offence. The case would be called *R v [Defendant]* or *Regina v [Defendant]*. The 'R' or 'Regina' refers to the Queen (the State), who brings the case against the defendant. The first court appearance always takes place at a local magistrates' court. At this hearing, the charge would be read to the defendant and he would simply be required to confirm details, such as his name and address. At this stage, the date for the next court hearing will be set.

After a number of pre-trial hearings (depending upon the offence charged), the case will be given a date for trial. The trial will take place either at the magistrates' court or at the Crown court. The court at which the trial takes place will depend upon the classification of the offence with which a defendant is charged. In our example, the defendant has been charged with theft, which is an either way offence. Mode of trial proceedings will take place to determine whether the defendant will be tried in the Crown court or in the magistrates' court.

CROSS REFERENCE
Refer back to 1.7 for an explanation of mode of trial proceedings.

1.8.4 **The trial**

As the prosecution bring the case against the defendant, the prosecution must prove that the defendant committed a criminal offence. The prosecution will, therefore, present their case and call their witnesses first (figure 1.3). When the prosecution have finished calling all of their witnesses, it is open to the defence to make a submission of no case to answer. This is often called a 'half-time submission': the defence argue either that the prosecution have failed to prove the elements of the offence, or that the evidence that they have put forward is so weak that a jury (or magistrates) properly directed could not convict on it. If this submission is successful, the judge will direct an acquittal and the trial is over. If the submission fails, the trial continues with the defence presenting their case and calling their witnesses. At the conclusion of the defence case, both the prosecution and defence will give closing speeches.

At this stage in the magistrates' court, the judge (usually three Justices of the Peace or one District Judge) will retire to consider their verdict. On the other hand, if the trial took place in the Crown court, the trial judge would give a summing up speech to the jury (summarising the evidence they heard and directing them on the law) and the jury would retire to consider its verdict. When the magistrates or jury reach their verdict, they will deliver it in open court.

Figure 1.3 The trial

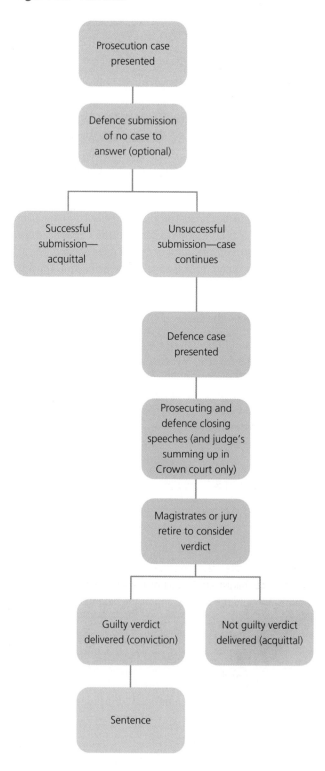

1.8.5 **The verdict and sentencing**

If the jury or magistrates return a not guilty verdict, the defendant is acquitted and is free to leave court. If the jury or magistrates return a guilty verdict, the defendant is convicted of a criminal offence and the court will sentence him. The sentencing hearing may not take place straightaway. It is quite usual for the trial judge to adjourn proceedings for four weeks in order to obtain a Pre-Sentence Report (PSR) on the offender. A PSR is written by a probation officer who has regular meetings with the offender during the adjournment. The report will recommend certain types of sentence for the offender and the judge will take this into account in sentencing. At the sentencing hearing, after hearing representations from both the prosecution and the defence, the judge may impose one of a variety of sentences on the offender, depending upon the offence for which he has been convicted.

There is an enormous range of sentences available. These include: imprisonment; suspended sentences of imprisonment; community rehabilitation orders; community punishment orders; curfew orders; supervision orders; attendance centre orders; drug treatment and testing orders; drug abstinence orders; reparation orders; action plan orders; parenting orders; fines; endorsements; conditional discharges; absolute discharges; bind overs; forfeiture orders; compensation orders; restitution orders; confiscation orders; hospital orders; and anti-social behaviour orders. However, these do not form the subject of this book and you will need to refer to a textbook on criminal procedure or sentencing for further information on sentencing.

1.9 The hierarchy of the criminal courts

As mentioned in 1.8.3, a defendant's first appearance at court is always at the magistrates' court. This is the lowest of the criminal courts in the hierarchy and is where trials for summary offences take place. There is no jury in a magistrates' court. Defendants are tried either by one judge who is legally qualified, a District Judge, or a bench of three lay (not legally qualified) judges, Justices of the Peace. The Crown court is a higher court in the hierarchy. This is where trials for indictable only offences must take place. Trials for either way offences may take place in either the magistrates' court or the Crown court, depending upon the seriousness of the circumstances of the offence and/or the defendant's wishes. Trial in the Crown court involves a judge and a jury. Each has different roles to play. The jury is the tribunal of fact and decides whether or not the defendant is guilty of the offence charged. The judge in a Crown court is legally qualified and is called a circuit judge. The judge is the tribunal of law: it is his job to make rulings on the law, decide upon the admissibility of evidence, and summarise the case to the jury and direct them on the law.

Where a defendant has been tried and convicted in the magistrates' court, he has a right of appeal against conviction and/or sentence. The appeal will be heard in the Crown court. Where a defendant has been tried and convicted in the Crown court, he also has a right of appeal against conviction and/or sentence. The appeal will be heard in the Court of Appeal

(Criminal Division). Another option potentially available to defendants convicted in the magistrates' court or the Crown court, or even to the prosecution, is to appeal to the High Court by way of case stated. This procedure applies to appeals on a point of law. Alternatively, an application for judicial review of the magistrates' or trial judge's decision may be made to the High Court.

Appeals from the Court of Appeal may be made to the Supreme Court by either the prosecution or the defence. Prior to 1 October 2009, appeals from the Court of Appeal were made to the House of Lords. A case will only proceed to the Supreme Court if the Court of Appeal certifies a question of law of public importance and grants leave to appeal. If leave to appeal is refused by the Court of Appeal, an application for leave can be made directly to the Supreme Court.

Under s.58 of the Criminal Justice Act 2003, the prosecution may appeal against an acquittal to the Court of Appeal. This may occur where the prosecution think that the trial judge has made an error in a legal ruling which results in the case collapsing before the jury have a chance to deliver a verdict. The Attorney General may also refer a case to the Court of Appeal if clarification on the law is required. You will notice such cases throughout this book, they are referred to as *Attorney General's Reference (No. [x] of [Year])*. (For the process of appealing against conviction and/or sentence from the Crown court, see figure 1.4; for appealing from the magistrates' court, see figure 1.5.)

Figure 1.4 Appealing from the Crown court

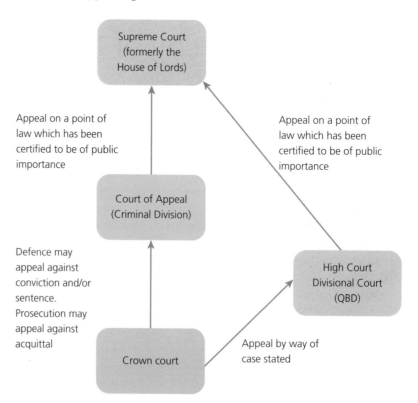

Figure 1.5 Appealing from the magistrates' court

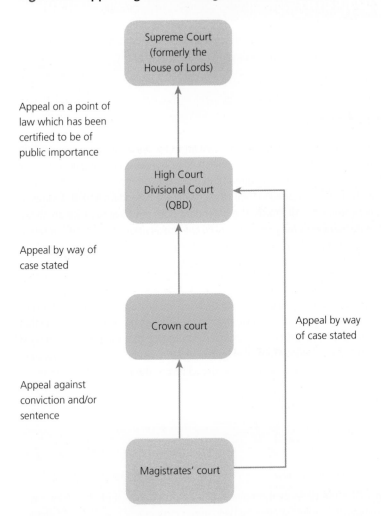

1.10 The burden and standard of proof

You will no doubt have heard phrases such as 'innocent until proven guilty' and 'beyond reasonable doubt'. These phrases relate to the burden and standard of proof in criminal law. This area is really a topic which is studied in greater detail on modules on the law of evidence. However, in studying criminal law, it is important to have some understanding of what these concepts actually mean. Students often confuse the terms 'burden of proof' and 'standard of proof', but these are distinct concepts which should be considered and applied separately.

THINKING POINT

Consider the meaning of the fundamental principle that a defendant is presumed inno-cent until proven guilty. What is the rationale behind this principle?

1.10.1 Burden of proof

Generally, where a person (the defendant) is prosecuted for a criminal offence, the prosecution is brought by the State. As the State (with all its powers and resources) is accusing an individual (who lacks such powers and resources) of committing a criminal offence, the law states that the prosecution bear the burden of proving their case against the defendant and of disproving any defence that the defendant might raise. The defendant does not have to prove anything, as he is presumed to be innocent until proven guilty by the prosecution. This is often referred to as the 'presumption of innocence'. This is enshrined within Article 6.2 of the European Convention on Human Rights and has been incorporated into the law of England and Wales by the Human Rights Act 1998.

The job of defence counsel in a criminal case is to undermine the prosecution's case and to put forward his client's defence, but he has no obligation to prove anything. The general rule that the burden of proof is on the prosecution in criminal cases, means that the prosecution must prove each and every element of the offence charged in order to establish that the defendant is guilty. This fundamental principle of evidence is derived from the case of *Woolmington v DPP* [1935] AC 462.

 CASE CLOSE-UP

Woolmington v DPP [1935] AC 462

In *Woolmington v DPP*, the defendant, Reginald Woolmington, had separated from his wife, Violet Woolmington. Violet had moved back to her mother's house. Reginald went to visit her in order to persuade her to come back to him. In pursuance of this, he decided to take a loaded shotgun with him and hid it under his coat. He claimed that he was going to threaten to kill himself with the shotgun. Arriving at his mother-in-law's house, Reginald removed the shotgun, which accidentally went off, killing Violet. Reginald was charged with her murder. At trial, the trial judge misdirected the jury in relation to the burden of proof. He stated that it was for the prosecution to prove that the defendant had killed Violet, and that once they had done this, the offence of murder was to be presumed unless the defence could satisfy the jury that the defendant did not have the necessary guilty state of mind for murder or that he had another defence.

▶ CROSS REFERENCE

Look at 1.11 for an explanation of the elements of an offence.

The House of Lords held that this was a misdirection and Viscount Sankey LC pronounced:

> Throughout the web of English Criminal Law one golden thread is always to be seen, that it is the duty of the prosecution to prove the prisoner's guilt…No matter what the charge or where the trial, the principle that the prosecution must prove the guilt of the prisoner is part of the common law of England and no attempt to whittle it down can be entertained.

Finally, it should be noted that there are some exceptions to the general rule that the burden of proof is on the prosecution. The burden of proving the elements of the *offence* will always be on the prosecution. However, in certain circumstances, the burden of proving the *defence* may lie with the defence. Whether or not this occurs depends on the defence raised and to some degree on the offence charged, however, such detail is beyond the scope of this book. It is only necessary at this stage to explain that where a defendant pleads the defences of insanity or diminished responsibility, the burden of proving that defence will be on the defendant. It should also be noted that where the burden of proof is on the defence, the standard of proof is different.

1.10.2 **Standard of proof**

When the burden of proof is on the prosecution, the standard of proof is 'beyond reasonable doubt'. This is an intentionally high standard of proof because (in contrast to civil cases such as contract and tort) there is potentially much at stake for a defendant. In civil matters, a defendant who is held liable will only have to pay an amount of money in compensation (albeit a large amount of money may be payable in some cases). By contrast, in criminal cases, a convicted defendant may lose his liberty through a sentence of imprisonment. Another reason for the higher criminal standard of proof lies with the fact that criminal cases are usually brought by the State, which has many resources and much money at its disposal. Hence, a criminal case is quite unbalanced as it involves a battle between the State and an individual. By contrast, civil cases involve disputes between two individuals, who are usually on much more of a level playing field (although there are exceptions to this, for example where an individual sues a company). The standard of proof in criminal proceedings is such that the jury can only convict the defendant if the prosecution have proved beyond reasonable doubt that the defendant is guilty. If the jury think that a reasonable doubt remains, they must acquit. This phrase has been the subject of much criticism, but no satisfactory alternative has been found yet. In the case of *Miller v Minister of Pensions* [1947] 2 All ER 372, Denning J explained the meaning of the criminal standard of proof:

> Proof beyond reasonable doubt does not mean proof beyond a shadow of a doubt... If the evidence is so strong as to leave only a remote possibility in the defendant's favour, which can be dismissed with the sentence, 'Of course it is possible, but not in the least probable', the case is proved beyond reasonable doubt. But nothing short of that would suffice.

The common explanation of the standard of proof which is usually given to juries by the trial judge is, 'you must be satisfied so that you are sure' and the Court of Appeal has confirmed that 'beyond reasonable doubt' and 'to be sure' are synonymous (see *Folley* [2013] EWCA Crim 396 at [12]). Occasionally, the trial judge might explain to the jury that they have to be as sure as they would be if they were making a decision about something important in their lives, such as a mortgage. If the jury are 'satisfied so that they are sure' about the defendant's guilt, then they must convict. If they are not sure, then they must acquit.

Occasionally, in criminal proceedings, the burden of proving a defence is on the defendant. Where this is the case, the standard of proof is 'on a balance of probabilities', a lower standard. Incidentally, this is also the standard of proof applied in civil proceedings. When something is judged on a balance of probabilities, the jury (or magistrates) only need to be 51% sure of the facts put forward. As an example, suppose that a defendant, X, is charged with murder. At trial, the prosecution bear the burden of proving the elements of murder: that X killed the victim (the *actus reus* of murder) and that he intended to kill or cause grievous bodily harm to the victim (the *mens rea* for murder). They will have to prove these elements beyond reasonable

Table 1.1 Burden and standard of proof

	On the prosecution	On the defence
Burden of proof	• To prove all the elements of the offence • To disprove the defence	• Occasionally to prove the defence (e.g., if pleading insanity or diminished responsibility)
Standard of proof	Beyond reasonable doubt	Balance of probabilities

CROSS REFERENCE

For a detailed discussion of the defence of diminished responsibility, see chapter 5. For a detailed discussion on insanity, see chapter 13.

doubt, so that the jury are satisfied that they are sure that the elements of murder are satisfied. Suppose that the prosecution achieve this; so far, the defendant is guilty of murder. However, if the defendant raises the defence of insanity or, as is more likely, the defence of diminished responsibility, the defendant will bear the burden of proving the elements of insanity or diminished responsibility. He will have to prove his defence on a balance of probabilities, so that the jury are 51% sure that he was legally insane or that his responsibility was diminished. If the jury are 51% sure that the defence is made out, they must acquit the defendant (table 1.1).

1.10.3 Evidential burden

Another concept which we have yet to discuss is the 'evidential burden'. An evidential burden is not a burden of proof—it does not require a party to *prove* anything. In fact, Lord Devlin once stated that 'it is misleading to call it a burden of proof...when it can be discharged by the production of evidence that falls short of proof' (*Jayasena v R* [1970] AC 618 at 624). As such, it does not have a corresponding standard of proof. Students often confuse the legal burden of proof with the evidential burden. An evidential burden is simply a burden to raise some evidence in order to make an issue a 'live one': 'a party may be required to adduce some evidence in support of his case, whether on the general issue or on a particular issue, before that issue is left to the jury' (*per* Lord Devlin in *Jayasena v R* [1970] AC 618 at 624). The evidential burden in a criminal trial only really becomes significant where the defendant relies upon certain defences such as self-defence, loss of control, automatism, and duress. In such cases, the defendant will bear the evidential burden, i.e., he/she will have to raise 'enough evidence to suggest a reasonable possibility' that he acted in accordance with the relevant defence (*per* Lord Devlin in *Jayasena v R* [1970] AC 618 at 624). The legal burden remains with the prosecution to prove beyond reasonable doubt that the elements of the defence are not satisfied.

1.11 The elements of an offence

As we approach the end of this chapter, we need to focus on the substantive criminal law which is the subject of this textbook. In this section, we will explore the elements which need to be proved by the prosecution in order to establish liability for a criminal offence. The Latin maxim, *actus non facit reum nisi mens sit rea*, is fundamental to criminal liability. In the case of *Haughton v Smith* [1975] AC 476, Lord Hailsham stated that it meant that, 'an act does not make a man guilty of a crime, unless his mind be also guilty'.

Figure 1.6 Elements of an offence

Consequently, criminal offences are generally made up of three key elements: *actus reus*, *mens rea*, and the absence of a defence. The Latin terms, **actus reus** and **mens rea**, are fundamental to the study of criminal law and you will come across them in most chapters in this book. The term *actus reus*, literally translated, means 'guilty act'. The term *mens rea*, literally translated, means 'guilty mind'. So, criminal liability involves a defendant committing a guilty act with a guilty mind. If either the guilty act or the guilty mind is missing, no offence will have been committed (with the exception of strict liability offences which do not require *mens rea*).

In order to prove that a defendant is guilty of a criminal offence, the prosecution will need to break down the definition of the offence and identify the parts of it which constitute the *actus reus* and the parts which constitute the *mens rea*. They will then need to prove that the defendant did the *actus reus* of the criminal offence, and that *at that time*, he also had the *mens rea* of the offence (this is often referred to as the requirement of coincidence of *actus reus* and *mens rea*). However, their job does not end there. Criminal liability is only established if, in addition to the *actus reus* and *mens rea*, it is proved that the defendant has no defence in law. This is conveniently summarised in figure 1.6.

If we now refer back to our defendant who has been charged with theft in the earlier example (see 1.8), we can explore the elements of the offence charged. The offence of theft is defined in s.1 of the Theft Act 1968:

> **actus reus**
> *actus reus* is a guilty act

> **mens rea**
> *mens rea* is a guilty mind

> ❯ CROSS REFERENCE
> For a discussion on strict liability, see chapter 4.

 STATUTE

Section 1, Theft Act 1968

A person is guilty of theft if he dishonestly appropriates property belonging to another with the intention of permanently depriving the other of it . . .

This definition sets down the five elements of the offence of theft:

- Dishonestly
- Appropriates
- Property
- Belonging to another
- With the intention to permanently deprive

The easiest way to differentiate between the *actus reus* elements and the *mens rea* elements is to first identify the *mens rea* elements and then subtract these from the definition. Everything remaining in the definition is part of the *actus reus*. The elements which relate to the guilty mind (the *mens rea*) of the defendant are 'dishonesty' and 'intention to permanently deprive', as these are states of mind. The remaining elements, 'appropriation', 'property', and 'belonging to another', are part of the *actus reus* of theft. Consequently, before our defendant can be convicted of theft, the prosecution will need to prove (burden of proof) beyond reasonable doubt (standard of proof) that: the defendant committed the *actus reus* of theft (appropriated property belonging to another), at the same time as having the *mens rea* of theft (a dishonest intention to permanently deprive), and that the defendant had no defence in law to this offence. The next two chapters will explore the concepts of *actus reus* and *mens rea* in more detail.

 ## Summary

- Criminal behaviour varies from country to country and from era to era.

- A crime is classed as a public wrong as it affects the public at large.

- The criminal law is punitive and seeks to act as a deterrent.

- In criminal proceedings, a prosecution is brought by the State (the Crown Prosecution Service (CPS)).

- There are two sources of criminal law: statute and common law.

- Offences may be classified as: indictable only, either way, or summary only.

- Criminal trials will take place either in the magistrates' court (with three Justices of the Peace or one District Judge) or in the Crown court (with a judge and jury).

- The prosecution bear the burden of proving that the defendant committed the offence.

- The standard to which they must prove this is 'beyond reasonable doubt'.

- Criminal liability requires *actus reus* (a guilty act) and *mens rea* (a guilty mind) and the absence of a defence.

The bigger picture

- For the latest crime statistics and more detail regarding these, you could refer to the Crime Survey for England and Wales published by the Office for National Statistics: http://www.crimesurvey.co.uk.

- For more information on criminalisation, the harm principle, and morality, you should refer to the following authoritative works:

  Lord Devlin, *The Enforcement of Morals* (1965), Oxford: Oxford University Press

  Joel Feinberg, *The Moral Limits of the Criminal Law, Volume 2 Offense to Others* (1987), Oxford: Oxford University Press

  H. L. A. Hart, *The Morality of the Criminal Law* (1965), Oxford University Press

  H. L. A. Hart, *Law, Liberty and Morality* (1968), Oxford: Oxford University Press

  John Stuart Mill, *On Liberty and Other Essays* (2008), Oxford: Oxford University Press

- You might want to consider the operation of the legal burden and evidential burden in relation to some of the defences that feature in this book. For instance, 5.5.1 and 13.4.2 respectively cover the reversal of the legal burden in cases involving defences of diminished responsibility and insanity, and 14.2.1, 14.3, and 5.4.1 cover the reversal of the evidential burden only for the defences of self-defence, duress, and loss of control respectively.

? Questions

Self-test questions

1. Outline the main differences between criminal law and civil law.

2. What is the distinction between indictable only offences, either way offences, and summary offences?

3. In which court is each offence in question 2 tried?

4. Briefly describe the criminal justice process and the hierarchy of the criminal courts.

5. What is the 'golden thread' in English criminal law? How is the 'golden thread' justified?

6. What is the meaning of the maxim, *actus non facit reum nisi mens sit rea*?

7. Define and distinguish between the terms *actus reus* and *mens rea*.

8. Explain the requirement of coincidence.

For suggested approaches, please visit the Online Resource Centre.

≡ Further reading

Books

Ashworth, A. and Horder, J. *Principles of Criminal Law* (7th edn, 2013), Oxford: Oxford University Press

Devlin, P. *The Enforcement of Morals* (1965), Oxford: Oxford University Press

Feinberg, J. *The Moral Limits of the Criminal Law, Volume 2 Offense to Others* (1987), Oxford: Oxford University Press

Hart, H. L. A. *The Morality of the Criminal Law* (1965), Oxford: Oxford University Press

Hart, H. L. A. *Law, Liberty and Morality* (1968), Oxford: Oxford University Press

Mill, J. S. *On Liberty and Other Essays* (2008), Oxford: Oxford University Press

Wilson, W. *Central Issues in Criminal Theory* (2002), Oxford: Hart Publishing

Journal articles

Ashworth, A. and Blake, M. 'The Presumption of Innocence in English Criminal Law' [1996] Crim LR 306

Lord Bingham, 'A Criminal Code: Must We Wait Forever?' [1999] Crim LR 694

Lamond, G. 'What is a Crime?' (2007) 27 OJLS 609

Roberts, P. 'Taking the Burden of Proof Seriously' [1995] Crim LR 783

Williams, G. 'The Definition of a Crime' (1955) 13 CLJ 107

2 Actus reus

LEARNING OBJECTIVES

By the end of this chapter, you should be able to:

- distinguish between conduct, consequences, and circumstances within the *actus reus* of an offence;
- understand the circumstances in which one can be criminally liable for an omission to act;
- explain the rules on causation; and
- identify 'state of affairs' offences.

Introduction

In chapter 1, you were introduced to the Latin maxim *actus non facit reum nisi mens sit rea* ('an act does not make a man guilty of a crime unless his mind be also guilty'), and to the concepts of *actus reus* ('guilty act') and *mens rea* ('guilty mind'). As mentioned in chapter 1, these Latin phrases will be used throughout your criminal law module and throughout this textbook. Despite their common usage among criminal lawyers, these terms have been subject to judicial criticism. In the case of *Miller* [1983] 2 AC 161 in the House of Lords, Lord Diplock stated:

> My Lords, it would I think be conducive to clarity of analysis of the ingredients of a crime that is created by statute, as are the great majority of criminal offences today, if we were to avoid bad Latin and instead to think and speak...about the conduct of the accused and his state of mind at the time of that conduct, instead of speaking of *actus reus* and *mens rea*.

THINKING POINT

Do you agree with Lord Diplock's statement? Can you think of any reasons why the term *actus reus* ('guilty act') should not be used?

Hint: refer back to the definition of theft in chapter 1. Can all the *actus reus* elements in that definition be classed as guilty 'acts'?

This chapter is concerned primarily with the *actus reus* elements of an offence and we will consider issues such as whether there are any circumstances in which a defendant can be held criminally liable for an *omission* to act, such as where he fails to rescue a person who is drowning in a lake and who ultimately dies. We will also consider when a defendant can be said to have *caused* a result, such as the death of the victim. Imagine that the defendant shoots the victim in the arm, but the victim refuses all medical treatment and bleeds to death. Can the defendant be said to have caused the victim's death? Should the defendant be held criminally responsible for the victim's death? What if instead, the victim was stabbed in the chest and accepted medical treatment, but a doctor treating him negligently failed to realise that the victim's lung had been pierced, and the victim died when he could have been saved had he been treated appropriately? Should the defendant be held criminally responsible for the victim's death in these circumstances? This chapter will consider these issues relating to omissions liability and causation, as well as other general principles of *actus reus*.

2.1 No liability for 'evil thoughts' alone

The law does not punish a person for simply having 'evil thoughts'. A person may think about committing a criminal offence. In fact, they may even decide or intend to do so (i.e., they may have the *mens rea* of the criminal offence). However, the law will not punish an individual unless they act upon these thoughts (they must also have the corresponding *actus reus* for the criminal offence). For example, you might decide to steal a shot glass from a pub or a criminal law textbook from the library. If you dishonestly intend to steal the glass or the book, you have the *mens rea* of the crime of theft, but you will not be guilty of theft unless you commit the physical aspect of the offence, i.e., do the *actus reus* or 'guilty act' (appropriate the glass or book which belongs to another). Sometimes, the physical aspect of a criminal offence is minimal, such as conspiracy to commit an offence. The *actus reus* for this requires only an agreement between two or more people to commit an offence. Despite the minimal degree of conduct involved, some physical aspect is required.

The law punishes individuals for criminal conduct. Although certain evil thoughts may be morally reprehensible, the criminal law considers it morally inappropriate to convict a person for merely having evil thoughts. Practically speaking, convicting individuals for having 'evil thoughts' would also be very difficult to police. Without the ability to read minds, it would be very difficult to prove at any one time that a person had the necessary *mens rea* of a criminal offence. Referring back to the example used above, if you decide to steal a textbook from your law library, nobody would know. Consequently, unless you physically do something about your intention to steal, such as communicate your intention to another person, proving such an offence would be almost impossible.

2.2 The elements of *actus reus*

Every criminal offence must contain *actus reus* elements. A defendant will not be liable for a criminal offence unless the *actus reus* of the offence is proved: *Deller* (1952) 36 Cr App R 184. Although the vast majority of criminal offences consist of both *actus reus* elements and *mens rea* elements, some criminal offences do not require a *mens rea* element for every element of the *actus reus*. Such offences are called strict liability offences and these will be discussed further in chapter 4. However, it is essential that every criminal offence contains elements of *actus reus*. This chapter will focus on the physical aspect of criminal offences.

The *actus reus* of every offence is different. The *actus reus* elements of an offence are every element within the definition of the offence which is not related to the state of mind of the defendant. Consequently, the simplest way to identify the *actus reus* of a criminal offence is to subtract the *mens rea* elements—which relate to the defendant's state of mind—from the definition of the offence. The remaining elements are the *actus reus* elements. The phrase 'guilty act' is misleading as it implies that the *actus reus* of an offence must involve an 'act'. This is not strictly true. In fact, the *actus reus* of an offence is wider and more complex than this. The *actus reus* of an offence may involve:

- an act or omission (conduct);
- the occurrence of a result (consequences);
- the existence of surrounding circumstances.

Some criminal offences may contain just one of these elements (conduct, consequences, or surrounding circumstances). Other offences may contain two of these elements, or even all three. As you discovered in chapter 1, the prosecution must prove that the defendant had committed the *actus reus* with the relevant *mens rea* of the criminal offence in question. In order to establish the guilt of the defendant, the prosecution must prove each and every element of the *actus reus* of the offence. If one element of the *actus reus* is not established, then the *actus reus* cannot be proved and there is no criminal liability. This is irrespective of whether or not the defendant had the *mens rea* of the offence. For example, take the offence of murder. If the death of the victim cannot be proved by the prosecution, then the defendant is not guilty of murder, even if it is established that the defendant had the *mens rea* for the offence (table 2.1).

2.3 The voluntariness requirement

The *actus reus* of an offence must be voluntarily performed. This means that the defendant must have been in control of his movements at the time that he performed the conduct element of the *actus reus* (or at the time that he omitted to act if liability is based upon an omission to act). Where the defendant's conduct is involuntarily performed, no criminal offence has been committed. For instance, a defendant will not be guilty of a criminal offence where he performs the *actus reus* of the offence due to a muscle spasm, a reflex, or some other uncontrollable movement, such as physical compulsion by another person, or if he was rendered unconscious by an external factor (with the exception of unconsciousness due to voluntary intoxication).

Table 2.1 Conduct, consequences, circumstances

Conduct	Consequences	Circumstances
• Conduct elements involve either **an act or an omission** to act by the defendant (see 2.4 for further detail on liability for omissions to act). • Conduct offences are 'doing' offences, although this term is misleading, as a conduct offence can involve an omission to act. • Perjury contains a conduct element. The conduct is simply making a statement on oath in judicial proceedings which is known to be false. (The fact that the statement must be made 'in judicial proceedings' is a surrounding circumstance.)	• Consequence elements involve a result which must have been **caused** by the conduct of the defendant. • Proof of causation is required. • Murder is also a 'result crime': the result is the death of a human being and it must be established that the defendant caused the victim's death. (There is obviously also a conduct element to murder; act or omission which causes death is required.) • See 2.5 for further detail on the rules of causation.	• Circumstance elements involve the existence of a set of circumstances or **'state of affairs'**. • The *actus reus* of theft requires the existence of certain circumstances: the property stolen must belong to another. • The *actus reus* of rape also involves surrounding circumstances: the absence of consent to sexual intercourse. • Some offences have no conduct or consequence elements, but simply depend upon the existence of a set of circumstances; these are often referred to as 'state of affairs' crimes. • See 2.6 for further detail on 'state of affairs' crimes.

An often cited example is that given by Lord Goddard CJ and Pearson J in *Hill v Baxter* [1958] 1 QB 277: a driver's conduct in driving dangerously might be involuntary if he was stunned by a blow on the head from a stone, or if he was attacked by a swarm of bees. Under these circumstances, the *actus reus* of the offence of dangerous driving would not be voluntary and the driver would escape criminal liability.

Where the conduct is involuntary, the defendant is deemed to be an automaton and will have the defence of automatism available to him. Lord Denning defined automatism in *Bratty v Attorney General for Northern Ireland* [1963] AC 386 as:

> an act which is done by the muscles without any control by the mind, such as a spasm, a reflex action or a convulsion; or an act done by a person who is not conscious of what he is doing, such as an act done whilst suffering from concussion.

Automatism is a defence of general application, meaning that it can be raised in relation to any offence, and it is a complete defence, which means that if pleaded successfully it leads to a complete acquittal. While automatism is said to be a defence (and it is dealt with in the defences chapter of most criminal law textbooks), in reality the defendant is seeking to deny an element of the offence. Academics tend to disagree as to whether a defendant who claims that his conduct was involuntary is answering the offence charged by denying that the *actus reus* of the offence has been committed (see Wilson 2014: 203–4) or whether the voluntary or involuntary nature of the defendant's conduct is part of the *mens rea*. As Professor David Ormerod and Karl Laird state:

> Writers dispute whether the voluntariness of D's conduct should be regarded as part of the *actus reus* or as part of the *mens rea*. On the one hand, it is a mental element; on the other, it is said that it is an essential constituent of the act, which is part of the *actus reus* (Ormerod and Laird 2015: 62–3).

In order for the defence of automatism to be successful, the defendant must suffer a total loss of voluntary control: *Broome v Perkins* (1987) 85 Cr App R 321. Where a defendant has some voluntary control over his actions, the defence will fail: *Attorney General's Reference (No. 2 of 1992)* [1994] QB 91.

▶ CROSS REFERENCE

See chapter 13 for a more detailed discussion of the defence of automatism.

2.4 Omissions

So far, you have been introduced to the three different types of *actus reus* elements. Conduct offences usually require the defendant to perform a positive act if the defendant is to be guilty of the offence. This section deals with the question of whether a defendant can be criminally liable for an omission (a failure) to act.

Imagine that you are driving on your way to university, when a car pulls out in front you and you collide with it. You are under a legal obligation to stop and exchange your name, address, and registration number with the driver of the other car. If there are reasonable grounds for not stopping, you must report the accident to the police within 24 hours. Failure to do so would render you guilty of a criminal offence under s.170 of the Road Traffic Act 1988. Similarly, if you are stopped by the police and fail to provide a breath specimen without reasonable excuse, then you will be guilty of an offence under s.6(4) of the Road Traffic Act 1988. These are examples of offences in which the *actus reus* is not an act, but is an omission to act.

Thus, although the *actus reus* element of conduct offences will usually involve the performance of a positive act, a defendant may sometimes be criminally liable for an omission to act. There are a number of criminal offences which are capable of being committed by omission. This section of the chapter will focus predominantly on the offences of murder and manslaughter.

2.4.1 General rule

The general rule is that there is no liability for an omission to act. Thus, conduct offences require a positive act by the defendant in order to establish liability. This general rule is often expressed by the phrase that 'there is no duty of easy rescue'. In 1887, Fitzjames Stephen gave us a classic example to illustrate this general rule. Over 120 years later, his example is still being used in lectures and seminars on criminal law.

> A sees B drowning and is able to save him by holding out his hand. A abstains from doing so in order that B may be drowned, and B is drowned. A has committed no offence.
>
> Stephen, *Digest of Criminal Law* (1887)

Conduct offences require a positive act, so A would be guilty of murder if he deliberately and actively drowns B, such as by physically holding B's head under water. However, generally speaking, A will not be guilty of any offence if he leaves B to drown, even if he desires B's death, because omitting to act carries no liability in English criminal law (note that there are exceptions to this general rule which are set out at 2.4.2). Although A might have failed to save B by a simple task such as holding out his hand, A has performed no positive act, and thus is not criminally liable for B's death. English law dictates that there is no requirement that A saves B, irrespective of how easy such a rescue might be (i.e., 'no duty of easy rescue'). In many European countries, such as France and Germany, the position is very different: there is a duty of 'easy rescue' and a failure to act will amount to a criminal offence (French Penal Code: Article 63; German Penal Code: Article 323c).

THINKING POINT

Do you think there should be a general duty of 'easy rescue' in England and Wales?

Would your answer be different if:

- B was a child?
- Or A was unable to swim and afraid of water?
- Or A was a strong swimmer who had gained lifeguard badges?
- Or A was standing with 50 other people?
- Or B was A's child?

Two different approaches are taken to the question of whether there should be a general duty of 'easy rescue', and these are compared in table 2.2. Professor Williams favours the conventional view, which states that A should not be obliged to save B. Professor Ashworth advocates the social responsibility view, which is in favour of a general duty of 'easy rescue'.

There are a number of exceptions to the general rule that there is no criminal liability for an omission to act. Such liability will be imposed upon the defendant where the defendant has a legal duty to act and fails to do so. This raises the question: when does the law impose a duty on an individual to act?

Table 2.2 Conventional view vs social responsibility view

Conventional view	Social responsibility view
• A should not be compelled to serve B	• A should be under a duty to help a stranger B
• A should not be encouraged to interfere in B's life—the law values individual autonomy and liberty	• Society recognises a duty of mutual support
• Doing a positive criminal act with bad consequences is morally more blameworthy than omitting to act and causing the same consequences	• The whole of society will benefit from a duty to rescue
	• Liability should be limited to those who had a greater opportunity to save B
• Such a duty would increase the possibility of mass liability (e.g., if 50 people watch B drown, they would all be liable)	• Liability should be limited to cases where the danger to B far outweighs the inconvenience or cost to A

2.4.2 **Exceptions**

There are five instances where the law imposes a duty on an individual to act. If there is such a duty on the defendant to act and he fails to do so, he will be guilty of a criminal offence by omission (figure 2.1). The categorisation of the exceptions set out in the sections that follow has been constructed by academics seeking a clear framework for omissions liability, but as you will see from the cases discussed, these categories are not clearly defined by the courts and they overlap heavily.

2.4.2.1 **Special relationship**

The common law imposes a duty on an individual to act where there is a special relationship between the parties. The closer the relationship, the more likely it is that the law will impose a duty on an individual to act. Examples of special relationships include relationships between parent and child, married couples, and doctor–patient relationships (a doctor has a duty to keep a patient alive).

The case of *Downes* (1875) 13 Cox CC 111 is an early authority in which a duty was imposed upon a parent to act to provide medical assistance for his child. In this case, the defendant was a member of a religious sect which prohibited all medical treatment because they believed that prayer would heal the sick. The defendant failed to call a doctor to attend to his 2-year-old child who had been very ill. The child died and the defendant was convicted of manslaughter. In this case, the duty to act was imposed upon the defendant by statute (s.37 of the Poor Law Amendment Act 1868). Lord Coleridge CJ deliberately did not express an opinion as to whether such a duty to act would have been imposed upon the defendant at common law, had the statute not been in existence. Although this case does demonstrate a duty of a parent to provide medical treatment for his child, the duty was imposed by statute. Consequently, this case could also fall under the heading of statutory duty at 2.4.2.5.

Figure 2.1 Duties to act

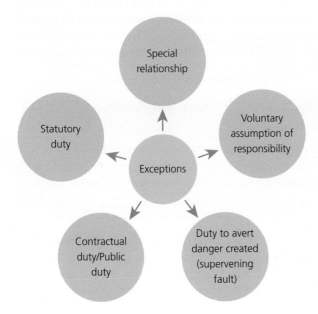

The common law duty to act due to the existence of a special relationship was firmly established by the twentieth century.

CASE CLOSE-UP

***Gibbins and Proctor* (1918) 13 Cr App R 134**

In the case of *Gibbins and Proctor*, the defendants lived with Gibbins's 7-year-old daughter, who they neglected to feed. The child died as a result of starvation. Gibbins had been in employment and he provided Proctor with money to buy food. Both defendants were convicted of murder. As the child's father, Gibbins had a special relationship with the deceased and therefore owed her a duty to care for her. His failure to do so rendered him guilty of her murder. Proctor was also guilty of murder as she had voluntarily assumed responsibility for the child by taking money from Gibbins in order to buy food (see voluntary assumption of responsibility at 2.4.2.2).

The case of *Smith* [1979] Crim LR 251 suggests that spouses also have a special relationship, and, as such, owe each other a duty to act to aid each other. The defendant's wife refused to go into hospital to give birth to her child due to her phobia of doctors. The baby was stillborn and the wife became ill. When she eventually did permit the defendant to call a doctor, she died before the doctor arrived. The defendant was charged with her manslaughter. There was medical evidence to suggest that had she received medical attention earlier, she might not have died. The jury in this case were directed to consider whether it was reasonable for the defendant to abide by his wife's request that he not call a doctor, if, indeed, the wife had the capacity to make rational decisions at the time of her request. The jury were unable to agree on a verdict and were eventually discharged. However, the authority does suggest that spouses may have a special relationship. It might be argued that this suggestion is supported by the case of *Hood* [2004] 1 Cr App R (S) 73, in which the defendant was the sole carer for his wife and he was convicted of gross negligence manslaughter after he failed to call her an ambulance after she suffered an accident. There was also evidence that she had been neglected: she was very thin and debilitated and she had pressure sores. While the defendant was convicted on the basis of his omissions, it is not clear from the case whether he was convicted on the basis that he had a special relationship with the victim, as her husband, or whether he was deemed to have voluntarily assumed responsibility for her, as her sole carer (see 2.4.2.2). It is suggested that the latter seems more likely.

THINKING POINT

It is unclear whether the law permits a person to discharge the other from their duty/special relationship. Do you think that the wife in *Smith* had released her husband from his duty to obtain medical assistance for her? Or should his duty to care for her remain, despite her protestations?

The scope of a special relationship is not entirely clear. We know that parent–child relationships are covered within this category and it would appear that spouses may also fall under this heading, but it is unlikely that separated spouses have a special relationship. It would appear that a blood relationship does not automatically result in a special relationship; the precise nature and closeness of the relationship would need to be explored. Similarly, separated spouses and cohabiting couples will not necessarily be in a special relationship for the purposes of omissions to act. Nonetheless, even where there is no clear special relationship, there may be a duty to act imposed due to a voluntary assumption of responsibility (discussed at 2.4.2.2).

2.4.2.2 Voluntary assumption of responsibility

A duty to act may be imposed on a defendant where the defendant has voluntarily assumed responsibility for another person. Hence, where the defendant undertakes to care for a helpless or infirm relative, any omission to do so resulting in death will render the defendant guilty of murder or manslaughter. Such an undertaking to care for another may arise as a result of an express or implied act. For example, in the case of *Nicholls* (1874) 13 Cox CC 75, the defendant took her grandchild into her home and expressly undertook to care for the child. The child died as a result of neglect and the defendant was charged with manslaughter. The trial judge, Brett J, directed the jury as follows:

> If a grown-up person chooses to undertake the charge of a human creature helpless either from infancy, simplicity, lunacy, or other infirmity, he is bound to execute that charge without (at all events) wicked negligence; and if a person who has chosen to take charge of a helpless creature lets it die by wicked negligence, that person is guilty of manslaughter.

An implied undertaking of care was found in the case of *Instan* [1893] 1 QB 450. In this case, the defendant, Kate Instan, went to live with her 73-year-old aunt. The aunt became ill and bedridden and the only person who knew of her aunt's condition was Kate Instan. The defendant failed to feed her aunt or to summon any medical assistance. Nevertheless, she continued to live in her aunt's house and was maintained by her aunt's money. When her aunt died, the defendant was charged with manslaughter. She was convicted on the basis that there was an implied undertaking that she would care for her aunt. The defendant's conviction was upheld by the Court for Crown Cases Reserved. Lord Coleridge CJ stated:

> It would not be correct to say that every moral obligation involves a legal duty; but every legal duty is founded on a moral obligation ... There can be no question in this case that it was the clear duty of the prisoner to impart to the deceased so much as was necessary to sustain life of the food from which she from time to time took in, and which was paid for by the deceased's own money for the purpose of maintaining herself and the prisoner; it was only through the instrumentality of the prisoner that the deceased could get food. There was, therefore, a common law duty imposed upon the prisoner which she did not discharge.

We have already seen that in the case of *Gibbins and Proctor*, the defendant Proctor was held to have voluntarily assumed responsibility towards her partner's daughter because she lived with her partner and his daughter, and he gave her money with which she was to buy food. From this case, we can see that even without a blood relationship, it is possible for a person to voluntarily assume responsibility for another. This was also confirmed in the leading authority of *Stone and Dobinson* [1977] QB 354.

 CASE CLOSE-UP

Stone and Dobinson [1977] QB 354

In *Stone and Dobinson*, Stone, who was a partially deaf and almost totally blind man of low to average intelligence, lived with his mistress, Dobinson, who was described as 'ineffectual' and 'inadequate' and his son, who was of low intelligence. Stone's sister, Fanny, came to live with Stone as a lodger, paying a small sum towards the rent. She suffered from the psychological disorder anorexia nervosa and thus she would not eat and she shut herself away in her room for days at a time. One day, in 1975, Fanny was found wandering in the street in a confused state. The defendants decided to try to find Fanny's doctor, but their efforts were unsuccessful. Fanny's condition deteriorated. A neighbour, Mrs Wilson, volunteered to help Dobinson to wash Fanny. Further efforts were then made to find a local doctor for Fanny and a neighbour volunteered to phone a doctor (the defendants were unable to use the telephone themselves). These attempts were unsuccessful. Over the next couple of weeks, Fanny's condition deteriorated further and she was found dead in her bed.

The defendants were charged with her manslaughter. Evidence was adduced from the pathologist that had Fanny gone into hospital two weeks earlier, there was 'a distinct possibility that they may have saved her; and three weeks earlier the chances would have been good'. The defendants were convicted of manslaughter and the convictions were upheld by the Court of Appeal. The defendants were held to have accepted responsibility for Fanny as her carers, and once she became bed-bound, they had a duty to help her. Although they made some efforts to seek medical assistance, their actions were entirely inadequate.

Lord Lane CJ stated:

> Whether Fanny was a lodger or not she was a blood relative of the appellant Stone; she was occupying a room in his house; the appellant Dobinson had undertaken the duty of trying to wash her, of taking such food to her as she required. There was ample evidence that each appellant was aware of the poor condition she was in . . . This was not a situation analogous to the drowning stranger. They did make efforts to care. They tried to get a doctor; they tried to discover the previous doctor. The appellant Dobinson helped with the washing and the provision of food . . . The jury were entitled to find that the duty had been assumed . . . that once Fanny became helplessly infirm . . . the appellants were, in the circumstances, obliged either to summon help or else to care for Fanny themselves.

 THINKING POINT

Do you think it right that the defendants, Stone and Dobinson, were convicted in spite of their extremely limited intelligence?

Should the defendants have refused to take Fanny into their home in order to avoid such liability?

Could it be said that Fanny had released the defendants from their duty to help her by refusing to tell them who her doctor was?

In the more recent case of *Ruffell* [2003] EWCA Crim 122, the defendant was convicted of manslaughter. He and the victim had taken a cocktail of drugs (heroin and cocaine) together at the defendant's house. The victim became very ill and fell unconscious. The defendant tried to revive the victim, but when he could not rouse him, the defendant left the victim outside the house, on the front doorstep, and went to bed. The victim died of hypothermia and intoxication from the drugs. The trial judge directed the jury that the defendant assumed a duty of care over the victim because they were friends, the victim was a guest in the defendant's house, and because the defendant had made some efforts to revive the victim. The defendant appealed against his conviction on the grounds that this was a misdirection, but the Court of Appeal approved the trial judge's direction. It is not entirely clear whether the duty to act in this case was imposed on the defendant because he had voluntarily assumed responsibility for the victim, or whether the case falls under the heading of the '*Miller* principle' (i.e., the defendant had created a dangerous situation by placing his unconscious friend outside, and he therefore had a duty to avert the danger of death, see 2.4.2.3).

This category could also be applied to a babysitter who is taking care of a small child as the babysitter can be said to have voluntarily assumed responsibility for the welfare of the child. Since a babysitter may very well be paid for his/her services, there could also be said to be a contractual duty here; however, where a grandmother is the babysitter for her grandson, she will probably be said to have voluntarily assumed responsibility for the child, especially since it is unclear whether a grandmother and grandson could be said to have a special relationship (this may depend upon the individual relationship between the particular grandmother and grandson and would probably be decided on a case-by-case basis).

2.4.2.3 Duty to avert danger created (the '*Miller* principle')

The common law imposes a duty on a defendant to act to avert a danger that he has created. Where the defendant innocently does an act which creates a risk of personal injury or damage to property and the defendant becomes aware of that risk, the law imposes a duty on the defendant to act to avert or minimise the danger. For instance, this principle might be applied to an electrician carrying out some work on a person's property and who fails to adequately cover cabling he installs if in the event someone is killed after touching an exposed cable (there might also be a contractual duty here). This category is best illustrated by the case of *Miller* [1983] 2 AC 161.

> ### 🔍 CASE CLOSE-UP
>
> **Miller [1983] 2 AC 161**
>
> The defendant in *Miller* was a squatter in a building. He was lying on a mattress in a room and lit a cigarette. He then fell asleep and dropped the cigarette on the mattress, setting it on fire. He awoke and realised that the mattress was on fire, but he simply got up, walked into the next room, and fell asleep in there. The fire spread and caused £800 worth of damage to the house. The defendant was convicted of arson, contrary to s.1(1) and s.1(3) of the Criminal Damage Act 1971. His appeals to the Court of Appeal and House of Lords were dismissed.
>
> Lord Diplock stated that:
>
> > conduct of the accused that is causative of the result may consist not only of his doing physical acts which cause the fire to start or spread but also of his failing to take measures that lie within his power to counteract the danger that he himself has created.

The *actus reus* of the offence is committed by the original act (setting the mattress on fire, in this case). However, as this act was committed innocently, the *mens rea* of the offence is not present at this point in time. Hence, there is no coincidence of *actus reus* and *mens rea* and no offence.

The defendant becomes liable when the defendant realises the danger that he has created (i.e., the defendant forms the *mens rea*) and he then fails to act to avert that danger (this

> **CROSS REFERENCE**
> See 3.7.1 for an explanation of the principle of coincidence of *actus reus* and *mens rea*.

omission is sufficient *actus reus*). At this point in time, the *actus reus* and *mens rea* coincide, resulting in the criminal liability of the defendant. How might a defendant in Mr Miller's situation satisfactorily discharge his duty to avert the danger? What exactly is expected of him? Clearly, a defendant is not expected to extinguish a dangerous fire. However, he is at least expected to call the fire brigade in such a situation. Where the fire is smaller and the risk a lesser one, the defendant might be expected to tackle the fire himself.

The '*Miller* principle' might also have been the basis for the liability of the defendant in *Ruffell* [2003] EWCA Crim 122, although this is not entirely clear from the judgment (see 2.4.2.2). Other examples of the application of this principle are the cases of *DPP v Santana- Bermudez* [2003] EWHC 2908 (Admin) and *Evans* [2009] EWCA Crim 650.

CROSS REFERENCE

The case of *Evans* (2009) is discussed at 6.2.1.3.

In *DPP v Santana-Bermudez* (2003), a female police officer was injured after carrying out a lawful search of the defendant whom she suspected was in possession of controlled drugs. She asked the defendant to empty his pockets, at which point he produced some syringes. The police officer then asked the defendant if he had any needles or 'sharps'; he replied that he didn't. The officer then put her hand into one of the defendant's pockets and her finger was pierced by a hypodermic needle. The defendant was charged with assault occasioning actual bodily harm, contrary to s.47 of the Offences Against the Person Act 1861. The trial judge dismissed the case after a defence submission of no case to answer and the Director of Public Prosecutions (DPP) appealed to the High Court by way of case stated. The High Court allowed the appeal and held that the defendant could be liable for an assault by omission. It was held that 'where someone (by act or word or a combination of the two) creates a danger and thereby exposes another to a reasonably foreseeable risk of injury which materialises, there is an evidential basis for the *actus reus* of an assault occasioning actual bodily harm'. Applying the principle in *Miller*, by creating a dangerous situation, the defendant owed the police officer a duty of care to avert that danger to her. His failure to do so was sufficient to constitute the *actus reus* of an assault and liability would then be dependent on the *mens rea* of assault being proved.

2.4.2.4 Contractual duty or public duty

A contract may give rise to duty to act which may then lead to criminal liability if the defendant fails to meet his contractual obligations and this leads to a fatality or serious harm being caused to a person. This type of duty usually arises in the context of an employment contract where the employee has failed to do what he is contractually obliged to do, and it may be owed to people who are not necessarily party to the contract, but who are likely to be injured by a failure to perform the contract (as in the example at 2.4.2.3 involving the electrician who leaves cabling exposed causing a fatality). For instance, if a lifeguard notices a person drowning and does not attempt to save them, or if she fails to notice a person drowning in the swimming pool because she has become distracted by checking her mobile phone for messages, she could be held criminally liable for the death of the victim if she is deemed to have failed to perform her contractual duty. Similarly, if a school nurse fails to give basic medical attention to a child who has fallen head first from a climbing frame, he could be criminally liable for the child's death if he has failed to perform his contractual duty. However, the extent of this duty is not particularly clear: for instance, would the school nurse have a duty to act if he leaves school at the conclusion of his contractual hours and notices a child with a serious injury in the playground, or if he sees an injured child on his way home and not on school property?

The leading authority on contractual duties to act is *Pittwood* (1902) 19 TLR 37. In this case, the defendant was a railway gatekeeper, who was employed to operate a level crossing. His job involved ensuring that the gate was shut whenever a train was passing along the line. One day, he went off to lunch and left the gate open. A cart crossed the railway line and was hit by a train; the cart driver was killed. The defendant was convicted of gross negligence manslaughter due to his failure to fulfil his contractual obligation of closing the gate. It was held that his duty arose under his contract of employment.

Similarly, a defendant may be under a public duty to act if, for example, he holds a position of public authority or responsibility. An example of such a duty arising is evident in the case of *Dytham* [1979] QB 722. The defendant in this case was a police officer who, while on duty in uniform, saw a man being ejected from a nightclub and beaten to death by a 'bouncer'. The defendant did not intervene; he drove away without calling for any assistance or summoning an ambulance. He was convicted of the common law offence of misconduct of an officer of justice and fined £150. His conviction was upheld by the Court of Appeal, which relied on Stephen's *Digest of Criminal Law*:

> Every public officer commits a misdemeanour who wilfully neglects to perform any duty which he is bound either by common law or statute to perform provided that the discharge of such duty is not attended with greater danger that a man of ordinary firmness and activity may be expected to encounter.

THINKING POINT

Do you think the defendant should have been charged with manslaughter?

Why do you think the prosecution chose not to charge him with manslaughter?

Professor Hogan argues that the law should not punish a defendant like Dytham for the harmful consequences that he might have prevented, but did not cause. He should only be punished for his actual dereliction of duty:

> public officers who neglect without reasonable cause to perform the obligations of their offices may be convicted of an offence but the offence lies in the neglect and the office holder does not become a party to the harm he might have prevented.

(See Hogan 1987.)

THINKING POINT

On 3 May 2007, a 10-year-old boy, Jordon Lyon, jumped into a pond in order to save his younger stepsister who had got into difficulties in the water. Two men who were nearby jumped in and saved the stepsister. However, by this time, Jordon had disappeared out of sight.

Two police community support officers arrived at the scene after the alarm was raised. They could see no sign of Jordon, so they radioed trained officers for assistance. Unfortunately, Jordon drowned. The community support officers were criticised in the press for failing to jump into the water (BBC News, 'Police Defend Drowning Death Case', reported 21 September 2007 available at: http://news.bbc.co.uk/1/hi/england/manchester/7006412.stm).

Do you think the officers had a duty to jump into the water?

2.4.2.5 **Statutory duty**

The law may impose a statutory duty on a defendant to act in a particular way. Failure to act in accordance with the statute will render a defendant liable for a criminal offence. We have already come across two such examples in 2.4: failing to report an accident contrary to s.170 of the Road Traffic Act 1988 and failing to provide a breath specimen contrary to s.6(4) of the Road Traffic Act 1988.

Under s.1 of the Children and Young Persons Act 1933, it is an offence for a person to wilfully neglect a child. In the case of *Sheppard* [1981] AC 394, the defendants' 16-month-old child died from malnutrition and hypothermia. The defendants were convicted of causing cruelty to the child by wilful neglect.

2.4.3 **Act or omission?**

It is often difficult to distinguish between a positive act and an omission. Imagine that when your student loan is paid into your bank account, you realise that you have been overpaid by £200. If you realise this and keep the money, you may be guilty of theft. In this example, does keeping the money amount to a positive act, or is failing to disclose the overpayment an omission? Consider also a driver who accidentally reverses into a wall, causing damage to the wall. The driver may be guilty of criminal damage, but did driving into the wall amount to a positive act, or was the failure to brake in time an omission? The law generally regards these as positive acts. Now suppose that whilst walking your inebriated friend home from the Student Union, you have an argument and you abandon your friend by the river to make his own way home. In attempting to make it home, your friend falls into the river and drowns. Does abandoning your friend amount to a positive act or an omission? This would amount to an omission in law, but this does not necessarily mean that you will not be liable in respect of your friend's death as the offences of murder and manslaughter are offences which can be committed by omission (see 2.4.4).

The distinction between positive acts and omissions becomes most apparent in medical cases involving the withdrawal of treatment from a patient. Where a doctor ends a patient's life through the positive act of administering a drug which has the effect of accelerating death, the doctor will be guilty of murder or manslaughter. In the case of *Dr Arthur* (1981) 12 BMLR 1, a baby suffering from Down's syndrome was rejected by his mother, who told the doctor that she did not want the baby to survive. Dr Arthur directed that the baby should receive 'nursing care only' (water but no food). The baby was also given a drug, the purpose of which was allegedly sedative, to stop the baby seeking sustenance. The baby died less than 3 days after birth and Dr Arthur was charged with murder (later dropped to attempted murder because there may have been an alternative cause of death). The jury acquitted the defendant after the trial judge directed them that they should consider whether 'there was an act properly so-called on the part of Dr Arthur, as distinct from simply allowing the child to die'. Withholding food from the child and, consequently, allowing the child to die would not be unlawful. This is a 'negative' act, a mere omission for which no criminal liability can be imposed on the doctor. However, it is clear that the law will impose criminal liability on a doctor for a positive act.

 THINKING POINT

Is a doctor criminally liable if the doctor turns off the patient's life support machine, resulting in the death of the patient? Is switching off the machine a positive act (incurring liability) or an omission (and thus lawful)?

This important issue was determined in the well-known case of *Airedale NHS Trust v Bland* [1993] 2 WLR 316.

 CASE CLOSE-UP

Airedale NHS Trust v Bland [1993] 2 WLR 316

Tony Bland was a victim of the disaster at Hillsborough Stadium in 1989. He suffered irreversible brain damage as a result of the incident, and spent over three years in hospital in a persistent vegetative state (PVS), unable to see, hear, feel, or communicate. Nevertheless, his brain stem, controlling his heartbeat and breathing, was still functioning; as such, Tony Bland was not clinically dead. He was fed and his condition maintained by artificial means. Doctors agreed that there was no hope of recovery or improvement in Tony Bland's condition, but that he could maintain his state of existence for years provided his medical treatment continued. Tony Bland's family and the NHS Trust wished to turn off the life-support machine maintaining Tony Bland's existence. An application was made to the High Court for a declaration that turning off the life support would not amount to a criminal offence or a civil wrong. The High Court granted the declaration and this was upheld on appeal to the House of Lords. The House (acting in its civil capacity) held that switching off the life-support machine amounted to an omission, not a positive act. Consequently, there would be no resulting liability.

Lord Goff stated:

> the law draws a crucial distinction between cases in which a doctor decides not to provide, or to continue to provide, for his patient treatment or care which could or might prolong his life and those in which he decides, for example by administering a lethal drug, actively to bring his patient's life to an end. . . . [T]he former may be lawful. . . But it is not lawful for a doctor to administer a drug to his patient to bring about his death, even though that course is prompted by a humanitarian desire to end his suffering, however great that suffering might be.

Thus, a doctor will be liable for murder or manslaughter where the doctor does a positive act which brings about the death of the patient. The doctor also owes a patient a duty to act to provide medical treatment in order to preserve the life of the patient. However, the courts have taken a liberal approach insofar as doctors are concerned, so as to protect doctors from criminal prosecution for murder when they withdraw treatment from a patient where it is in the best interests of the patient to do so.

2.4.4 Offences which may be committed by omission

It is clear from the authorities cited earlier, that murder and manslaughter can be committed by omission. The authority of *DPP v Santana-Bermudez* also suggests that an assault can be committed by omission, but this decision would seem to conflict with the case of *Fagan v Metropolitan Police Commissioner* [1969] 1 QB 439. In *Fagan*, a police officer asked the defendant to move his car. When he accidentally drove onto the police officer's foot, the officer shouted, 'Get off, you are on my foot.' The defendant refused to move the car and turned off the ignition. He was convicted of assaulting a police officer in the execution of his duty. He appealed, arguing that he had been convicted on the basis of an omission to act, but that an assault required a positive act. The Divisional Court dismissed his appeal. The Court agreed with the defendant that an assault could not be committed by omission, but they interpreted the defendant's conduct of driving onto the officer's foot and remaining there as one continuing act, as opposed to a separate act and omission. This is referred to as the 'continuing act' theory. In order for a defendant to be guilty of an offence using this theory, he must form the *mens rea* for the relevant offence at some point during the continuing act. In the present case, the defendant formed the *mens rea* of an assault when he realised he was on the officer's foot and refused to move. At this point in time, his conduct was still continuing, thus the *actus reus* and *mens rea* of assault coincided and the defendant was guilty.

The cases of *Fagan* and *DPP v Santana-Bermudez* reach the same conclusion by different means. In *Fagan*, the Divisional Court got round their refusal to accept that an assault could be committed by omission with some inventive interpretation. However, the High Court in *DPP v Santana-Bermudez* was content to apply the *Miller* principle and accepted the idea that an assault can be committed by omission. The continuing act theory has also been applied in relation to the offence of rape in *Kaitamaki v R* [1985] AC 147, and this has now been put onto a statutory footing by the Sexual Offences Act 2003.

2.5 Causation

We noted earlier that the *actus reus* of an offence may comprise a number of different types of *actus reus* elements: conduct, consequences, and circumstances. This part of the chapter will explore the way in which the law deals with offences which require proof of a consequence. These are referred to as 'result crimes'. Where a defendant is charged with a result crime, the prosecution must prove that the defendant caused the result in order for the *actus reus* to be satisfied. For example, in order to establish the *actus reus* of murder, the prosecution need to prove that the defendant caused the death of the victim. There must be a chain of causation between the act or omission of the defendant and the result. It is for the jury to decide whether or not the prosecution have proved beyond reasonable doubt that the defendant caused the necessary result. In *Clarke and Morabir* [2013] EWCA Crim 162, the Court of Appeal confirmed that in a murder case, the question of whether the defendant had caused the death of the victim is a question for the jury to determine (at [67]).

There are two main rules of causation: the prosecution must prove that the defendant was the factual cause of the result and that he was the legal cause of the result. Both tests are described in greater detail at 2.5.1 and 2.5.2. The test for factual causation is the 'but for' test: it must be established that but for the defendant's actions, the result would not have occurred. Legal causation is referred to as the 'chain of causation': the prosecution must prove that there was no *novus actus interveniens* ('new intervening act'), which broke the chain of causation. If the chain of causation is established, then the defendant will have caused the result and may be guilty of an offence if the remaining elements of the *actus reus* and the *mens rea* of the offence can be proved. However, if the chain of causation is not established due to the existence of an intervening event which breaks the chain, the defendant cannot be said to have caused the result. Hence, there is no *actus reus* and he will not be guilty of an offence (figure 2.2).

It may be the case that causation is simple to establish. For example, if A shoots V in the head and V dies as a result, it will be clear that A caused V's death. However, there may be a number of events which each contribute to the result. Where such multiple causes of a result exist, the

Figure 2.2 Causation

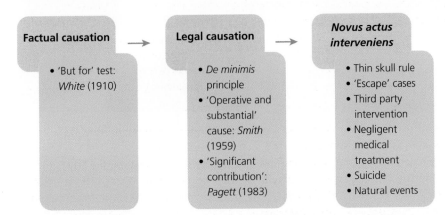

Factual causation	→	Legal causation	→	*Novus actus interveniens*
• 'But for' test: *White* (1910)		• *De minimis* principle • 'Operative and substantial' cause: *Smith* (1959) • 'Significant contribution': *Pagett* (1983)		• Thin skull rule • 'Escape' cases • Third party intervention • Negligent medical treatment • Suicide • Natural events

judge must determine which of these causes may contribute in law to the result. Consider first an example with two possible causes: imagine that B shoots V in the leg. V is taken to hospital, where he is informed that he needs a blood transfusion which will save his life. V refuses to have the blood transfusion and dies as a result. In such a situation, can it still be said that B has caused V's death? Or has V caused his own death? Does V's refusal of treatment absolve B of any criminal liability for V's death? In this case, B is the factual cause of V's death because V's death would not have occurred were it not for B's act in shooting V. However, it is more difficult to determine whether or not B was the legal cause of V's death as V's refusal of treatment may amount to an intervening act which breaks the chain of causation, absolving B of liability for murder or manslaughter.

Let us now increase the number of contributing factors in our example. Imagine that C points a gun at V. V is so frightened, that he jumps out of a second-floor window in order to escape the threat. In doing so, he sustains a serious head injury. An ambulance is called, but arrives an hour late because the driver got lost. At the hospital, V is attended to by a junior doctor who misdiagnoses the severity of V's injuries and sends V home. V returns to hospital a week later as his head injury worsens. This time, a female doctor attends to V, but V refuses to allow her to treat him. V dies from the head injury. Who has caused V's death? Can it be said that C caused V's death? Or do the actions of V, the ambulance driver, or the junior doctor break the chain of causation? Could it be argued that the ambulance driver or the junior doctor have caused V's death? Applying the rules of causation to this scenario, it is again clear that C was the factual cause of V's death: were it not for C's conduct in pointing the gun at V, V would not have jumped out of the window and sustained head injuries, an ambulance would not have been required, the junior doctor would not have misdiagnosed V, V would not have had the opportunity to refuse treatment, and he would not have ultimately died. However, legal causation also needs to be established and there are multiple causes in this scenario. It must be ascertained whether any of these contributory factors will break the chain of causation and release the defendant from liability. We must now examine the rules of causation in more detail.

2.5.1 Factual causation

The prosecution must initially establish that the defendant's conduct was a factual cause of the result. His conduct (act or omission) must be a *sine qua non* ('without which not') of the

Figure 2.3 Factual causation

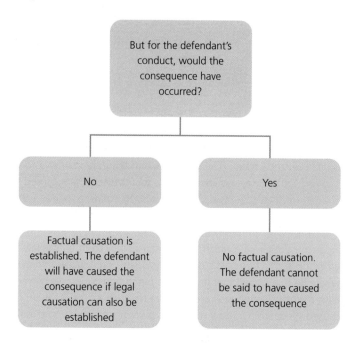

> But for the defendant's conduct, would the consequence have occurred?
>
> **No** → Factual causation is established. The defendant will have caused the consequence if legal causation can also be established
>
> **Yes** → No factual causation. The defendant cannot be said to have caused the consequence

result. This is referred to as the 'but for' test. This test is applied by asking the question: but for the defendant's conduct, would the consequence have occurred? If the result would have occurred irrespective of the defendant's conduct, then factual causation is not established. The defendant cannot be said to have caused the result and he will not have the *actus reus* for any offence requiring proof of causation of that result. If the result would not have occurred but for the defendant's conduct, then factual causation is established. However, this does not automatically lead to liability. In order to establish the *actus reus* of the offence, the prosecution would also have to prove that the defendant was the legal cause of the result and that there is no *novus actus interveniens* which breaks the chain of causation (figure 2.3).

The case most commonly associated with the test for factual causation actually gives us an example of a situation where the 'but for' test was not satisfied. This is the case of *White* [1910] 2 KB 124.

🔍 CASE CLOSE-UP

White [1910] 2 KB 124

In *White*, the defendant laced his mother's drink with potassium cyanide, intending to kill her. His mother drank about a quarter of the drink. She was found dead the following morning and the defendant was charged with her murder. In order to establish the *actus reus* of murder, the prosecution had to prove that the defendant had caused his mother's death. However, medical evidence showed that she died from heart failure and not from poisoning. The defendant was acquitted of murder, as it could not be shown that he was the factual cause of his mother's death. Evidence showed that she would have died anyway, irrespective of the defendant's conduct. Factual causation could not be established as 'but for' the defendant's conduct, the result would have occurred anyway.

As causation could not be proved, the *actus reus* of murder was not established, hence the defendant was not guilty of murder. He was, however, convicted of attempted murder because he took steps which were more than merely preparatory towards killing his mother (the *actus reus* of attempted murder) and he intended to kill her (the *mens rea* of attempted murder).

Similarly, in *Dalloway* (1847) 2 Cox CC 273, factual causation could not be established. The defendant in this case was driving a horse and cart negligently, without holding onto the reins of the horse. A child ran in front of the horse and cart and the defendant was unable to stop in time. The child died and the defendant was charged with manslaughter. The prosecution was required to prove that the defendant caused the child's death. Applying the 'but for' test, the question which had to be determined was: but for the defendant's negligence in failing to hold the horse's reins, would the child have died? The jury acquitted the defendant, suggesting that the jury thought that the child would have died even if the driver had been driving carefully. Hence, the driver's negligence was not the factual cause of the child's death.

An example of the successful application of the 'but for' test is the case of *Mitchell* [1983] QB 741. In this case, the defendant became impatient whilst in a queue in the post office. He pushed the person in front of him, a 72-year-old man, who fell forwards onto the next person in the queue, an 89-year-old woman. The woman fell and broke her hip. She later developed a blood clot and died. The defendant was convicted of manslaughter. Applying the 'but for' test here, factual causation can be easily established: but for the defendant pushing the man in front of him, that man would not have fallen into the 89-year-old woman, who in turn would not have fallen, broken her hip, developed a blood clot, and ultimately, died. If it is established that the defendant was a factual cause of the result in any given case, the next question is whether the defendant was the legal cause of the result.

2.5.2 Legal causation

As we have seen already, there may be more than one factual cause of a result. However, not all factual causes will amount to legal causes; otherwise the concept of causation would be ludicrously wide. For example, it could be argued that but for the defendant's mother giving birth to the defendant, he would not have acted as he did. The defendant's grandmother could be another factual cause, as could her mother and her grandmother, and so on. Clearly, this would be a nonsensical approach for the law to take. Consequently, the principles relating to legal causation act as a commonsense filter, limiting the number of factual causes which the jury can take into account by law.

The prosecution must prove that the defendant's conduct was a more than minimal cause of the prohibited consequence (see *Cato* [1976] 1 WLR 110, *Notman* [1994] Crim LR 518, and *Kimsey* [1996] Crim LR 35). This is referred to as the *de minimis* principle, through which the law seeks to disregard any negligible or trifling causes. However, the cases in this area have developed further terminology which is often used in reference to legal causation. A defendant will be the legal cause of the consequence if his conduct was the 'operating and substantial cause' of that result (*Smith* [1959] 2 QB 35 and *Malcherek; Steel* [1981] 2 All ER 422). In *Pagett* (1983) 76 Cr App R 279, it was held that a defendant's conduct must 'contribute significantly' to the prohibited result (see also *Mellor* [1996] Crim LR 743). It is a matter for the jury to decide whether or not the conduct of the defendant has a sufficient link to the end result to justify attaching blame to the defendant. As such, the jury are tasked with making a value judgement. As we have seen already, there may be multiple causes of a particular result. This does not preclude liability, as Goff LJ stated in *Pagett* (1983):

> the accused's act need not be the sole cause, or even the main cause, of the victim's death, it being enough that his act contributed significantly to that result.

The case of *Benge* (1865) 4 F & F 504 demonstrates that the accused's act need not be the sole cause of the result. In this case, third parties also contributed to the result, but this did not absolve the defendant of criminal liability. The defendant was employed to take up part of a railway line. He misread the train timetable and removed part of a railway line at a time when a train was due. He placed a signalman with a flag further up the line to warn the oncoming train, but the signalman was not at a sufficient distance up the line, in violation of company regulations. The ensuing accident resulted in the death of a person and the defendant was convicted of manslaughter. The defendant's argument that the accident would not have happened were it not for the conduct of the signalman and train driver was rejected. It was held that provided the defendant's negligence was the 'substantial cause' of the accident, then he was criminally liable for the death.

 THINKING POINT

The two defendants in the case of *Lane and Lane* (1985) 82 Cr App R 50 were charged with the manslaughter of their baby. The baby was taken to hospital with severe bruises over her body and died in hospital. It was clear that the baby had been beaten. Medical evidence pinpointed a specific time when the injuries had taken place, but the parents lied, covering up for each other. The baby was with her mother for part of the time, with the father for part of the time, and with both parents the rest of the time.

Can the prosecution prove that the defendants were the legal cause of the baby's death?

We have already seen that the defendant's conduct does not need to be the sole cause, or even the main cause, of the result, but it must be a cause. Where there are alternative causes of a result, the prosecution need to prove that the defendant in question was actually a cause of the result. The case of *Dyos et al.* [1979] Crim LR 660 involved a fight between two groups of youths. One of the youths was injured and died as a result of his wounds. He had two main wounds, one of which (a wound to the head) was caused by the defendant. The source of the other wound was unknown, but both wounds were potentially fatal, and either one could have caused the death of the victim. There was no evidence as to which wound was caused first. The trial judge discharged the jury from reaching a verdict and directed an acquittal, because the prosecution had failed to show that the wound from an unknown source was not the cause of death. Consequently, the prosecution were not able to prove that the wound caused by the defendant was the cause of the victim's death.

Similarly, in *Lane and Lane* (mentioned in the thinking point), the defendants could not be guilty of the manslaughter of their baby as the prosecution were unable to prove who caused the injuries which led to the death of the baby. The Court of Appeal quashed the defendant's convictions. There were three possible scenarios in this case: either the mother had inflicted the injuries on the baby, or the father had done so, or both of them had a part in injuring the baby. As the defendants had lied about the events and covered up for each other, there was no way of proving who caused the death of the baby. This would appear to be a highly unsatisfactory result and this case highlighted a loophole in the law. This issue has now been resolved with the enactment of s.5 of the Domestic Violence, Crime and Victims Act 2004 (as amended by s.1 of the Domestic Violence, Crime and Victims (Amendment) Act 2012). Today, defendants such as those in *Lane and Lane* would be guilty under s.5 of the Act, which provides that it is an offence to cause or allow the death of or serious physical harm to a child or vulnerable adult.

2.5.3 *Novus actus interveniens* ('New intervening act')

Where the defendant's conduct is a more than minimal or 'operating and substantial' cause of the result, the defendant will be the legal cause of that result, unless there is a *novus actus interveniens* which breaks the chain of causation (figure 2.4).

If an intervening act does break the chain of causation, the defendant will not be the cause of the result and will be absolved of liability for that result. The types of intervening event which might break the chain of causation are: an unforeseeable escape, a voluntary act by a third party or the victim, negligent medical treatment, or a natural event. Policy considerations often play a part in the courts' decisions in relation to *novus actus interveniens*.

2.5.3.1 The 'thin skull' rule

The thin skull rule is neatly summarised by the statement 'you take your victim as you find them'. A defendant who causes some injury to the victim must take his victim as he finds him.

Figure 2.4 Causation flowchart

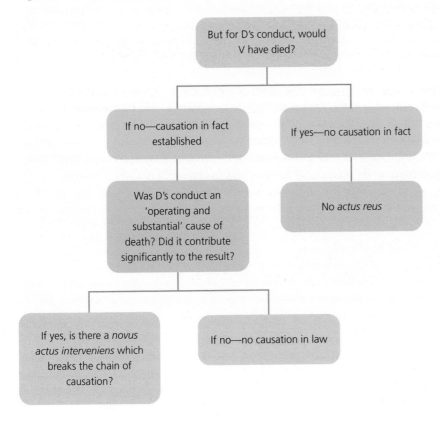

This means that where the victim suffers from some latent, pre-existing physical condition, which renders him unusually susceptible to injury, the defendant remains liable for the consequences of his conduct, no matter how unusually serious they are. For example, if a defendant strikes the victim on the head in a manner which would normally cause no injury to a person, but the victim has an unusually thin skull which breaks (or is a haemophiliac which means that a defendant may bleed to death as a result of a small cut which would usually cause no serious injury), then the defendant is liable for the full consequences of his act and will be liable for the victim's death should he die. Hence, a victim's particular susceptibility due to a pre-existing condition does not break the chain of causation.

An example of the application of the thin skull rule is the case of *Hayward* (1908) 21 Cox CC 692. In this case, the defendant was heard saying that he would 'give his wife something' when she returned home. He seemed to be in a state of 'violent excitement'. On his wife's return home, he chased her into the street and threatened her with violence. She had been suffering from a latent, pre-existing thyroid condition, such that any physical exertion or fright might cause her death. She collapsed suddenly and died. The defendant was convicted of her manslaughter. He had to take his victim as he found her, even though his wife's thyroid condition was unforeseen.

This rule extends not only to unusual physical conditions, but also covers the 'whole man'.

 CASE CLOSE-UP

Blaue [1975] 1 WLR 1411

In *Blaue*, the defendant stabbed a young woman, piercing her lung. She was taken to hospital, where she was informed that she required a blood transfusion. The woman was a Jehovah's Witness and she refused a blood transfusion due to her religious beliefs. She was told that she would die if she did not receive the transfusion, but she still refused to have it. She died from loss of blood and the defendant was convicted of her manslaughter. The Court of Appeal was satisfied that the thin skull rule should apply in this case, and that the defendant should be liable for the consequences of his actions (the victim's death), even though those consequences were unusual or unforeseeable. The defendant was deemed to be the cause of the victim's death, even though she refused a blood transfusion which would probably have saved her life.

Lawton LJ stated:

It has long been the policy of the law that those who use violence on other people must take their victims as they find them. This in our judgment means the whole man, not just the physical man. It does not lie in the mouth of an assailant to say that his victim's religious beliefs which inhibited him from accepting certain kinds of medical treatment were unreasonable. The question for decision is what caused her death. The answer is the stab wound. The fact that the victim refused to stop this end coming about, did not break the causal connection between the act and death.

As a result of *Blaue*, the thin skull rule extends beyond mere physical conditions and encompasses religious beliefs. Lawton LJ took the view that the thin skull rule extended to 'the whole man'. It is not entirely clear what this means, nor how far beyond religious beliefs the thin skull rule will reach. As yet, no other authorities have tested the scope of this rule.

THINKING POINT

How far should the thin skull rule be applied beyond religious beliefs?

Should it encompass the psychological state of the victim? Should it encompass other beliefs? Should it cover phobias or irrational decisions? (See *Holland* (1841) and *Dear* (1996) at 2.5.3.3.)

2.5.3.2 'Escape' cases

The chain of causation may be broken by the actions of the victim in effecting an unforesee-able escape. This means that the defendant will not be liable for any injuries that the victim sustains as a result of his escape from the defendant if that escape was unforeseeable. The law distinguishes between the acts of the victim which are reasonably foreseeable and involuntary, and those which are unforeseeable and voluntary. Professors Hart and Honoré (1985) define a voluntary act as one which is 'free, deliberate and informed'. Such an act breaks the chain of causation. A victim who is forced to escape from the defendant as a direct result of his conduct effects a reasonably foreseeable and involuntary escape. This will not break the chain of causation and the defendant will be liable for any resultant injuries to the victim. The cases discussed in this paragraph are often also referred to as 'fright and flight' cases (figure 2.5).

Early authorities in this area made reference to the unlawful conduct of the defendant which caused the death of the victim. We have already come across the case of *Hayward* (1908), in which the defendant's wife collapsed and died while fleeing from her husband. The wife's escape in this case was not an intervening event sufficient to break the chain of causation

Figure 2.5 Act of the victim: escape cases

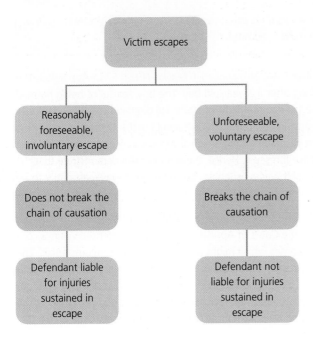

and the defendant's unlawful conduct in threatening and chasing his wife was regarded as having caused the death of the victim. The same approach was adopted a year later, in the case of *Curley* (1909) 2 Cr App R 109. The defendant had an argument with the woman with whom he lived. The argument had taken place in the bedroom. Evidence was adduced that she had shouted 'Let me out', 'Murder', and 'Police'. The defendant admitted that he ran towards the victim to hit her, but he didn't actually touch her. The victim jumped out of the bedroom window and died as a result of the fall. The defendant's conviction for manslaughter was upheld in the Court of Appeal. Jelf J stated that: 'The jumping out of the window was contributed to by the appellant's unlawful act.'

Later authorities focused on the foreseeability of the victim's conduct in escaping.

 CASE CLOSE-UP

Roberts (1971) 56 Cr App R 95

The defendant in *Roberts* made sexual advances towards a woman while driving her home from a party. He tried to pull her coat off and told her that he had previously beaten up women who had refused his advances. The woman jumped out of the moving car as a result of the defendant's conduct and was injured. The Court of Appeal dismissed the defendant's appeal against conviction for assault occasioning actual bodily harm, contrary to s.47 of the Offences Against the Person Act 1861.

The Court held that it had been established that the defendant caused the victim's injuries. Although the injuries had been caused in part by the victim's own conduct in escaping, her escape was reasonably foreseeable in the circumstances.

Stephenson LJ stated:

> The test is: was it the natural result of what the alleged assailant said and did, in the sense that it was something that could reasonably have been foreseen as the consequence of what he was saying or doing?

His Lordship explained that if the victim's act in escaping was 'so daft as to make it [the victim's] own voluntary act' the chain of causation is broken.

The test of 'reasonable foreseeability' was also applied in *Mackie* (1973) 57 Cr App R 453. The defendant in this case was looking after a 3-year-old boy. The boy, fearful of being harmed by the defendant, ran away and fell down a flight of stairs. He died and the defendant was convicted of manslaughter. Dismissing his appeal, Stephenson LJ in the Court of Appeal held that 'the attempt to escape must be . . . something which any reasonable and responsible man in the assailant's shoes would have foreseen'. Hence, these authorities demonstrate that the test is not whether the escape itself was reasonable, but whether it was reasonably to be expected, i.e., foreseeable.

However, other authorities focus on the reasonableness of the victim's escape. In *Williams and Davies* (1992) 95 Cr App R 1, the Court of Appeal questioned whether the victim's conduct was within the 'range of responses which might be expected' in the circumstances. The two defendants in this case threatened a hitchhiker with violence unless he handed over his money. The hitchhiker jumped out of the defendant's car, which was travelling at about 30 mph. He died as a result of serious head injuries sustained during his escape. The Court of Appeal quashed both defendants' convictions for manslaughter and robbery because the trial judge had failed to direct the jury on the issue of causation. Stuart-Smith LJ stated that the victim's act must be:

> proportionate to the threat, that is to say that it was within the ambit of reasonableness and not so daft as to make it his own voluntary act which amounted to a *novus actus interveniens* and consequently broke the chain of causation.

The test is:

> whether the deceased's reaction…was within the range of responses which might be expected from a victim placed in the situation which he was. The jury should bear in mind any particular characteristic of the victim and the fact that in the agony of the moment he may act without thought and deliberation…

The test in *Williams and Davies* was applied by the Court of Appeal in *Lewis* [2010] EWCA Crim 151, where it also held that the nature of the escape by the victim must be a foreseeable consequence of the unlawful act. Although the trial judge in *Lewis* did not make reference to the words 'proportionate' or 'daft' during his summing up to the jury, he had used ordinary language in directing them. The Court of Appeal held that the jury 'could not have been in doubt that they were being asked to measure the nature of the threat posed by the unlawful act with the form of escape adopted by the deceased' (at [40]). Having considered this, the jury were then to decide whether the victim's escape might have been expected.

Williams and Davies introduced a subjective element into the objective 'reasonable foreseeability' test: the jury should consider what might be expected from a person in the same situation as the victim, taking into account the characteristics of the victim. This approach was followed in *Corbett* [1996] Crim LR 594, a case involving an escape by a drunk, mentally handicapped man. The victim's characteristics were to be taken into account by the jury in deciding whether the response was within the range of foreseeable responses. In the case of *Marjoram* [2000] Crim LR 372, it was argued that the reasonable person shares the defendant's age and sex. The Court of Appeal rejected this argument that the characteristics of the defendant be taken into account. The characteristics and circumstances surrounding the victim may be relevant, but those of the defendant are not. Hence, the test to be applied is: whether the victim's response was one within a range of responses to be expected of a person in the victim's situation, bearing the victim's characteristics.

2.5.3.3 Victim's self-neglect

As we have seen already, there are circumstances in which the conduct of the victim may break the chain of causation.

In *Holland* (1841) 2 Mood & R 351, the defendant cut the victim on the finger. The wound became infected and the victim was advised that he should have his thumb amputated, but he refused to agree to this. He was warned that he was endangering his life through his refusal as he could develop tetanus. The victim died from tetanus and the defendant was convicted of murder. The defendant would not be absolved of liability on the basis that the victim could have done more to minimise the risk of death. In this particular case, refusing an amputation would not appear to be unreasonable as such an operation was likely to carry a high degree of risk in 1841.

The Court of Appeal has more recently reiterated the principle that self-neglect by the victim does not release the defendant of liability. The defendant in *Dear* [1996] Crim LR 595 had been told that the victim had sexually abused his 12-year-old daughter. The defendant slashed the victim repeatedly with a Stanley knife and the victim died 2 days later from loss of blood. There was evidence to suggest that the bleeding had stopped at some point and it was not clear how or why the wounds had begun to bleed again. The defendant appealed against this conviction for murder, arguing that the victim had attempted to commit suicide by reopening the healing wounds or by failing to stem the blood flow if the wounds reopened naturally. The Court of Appeal held that the correct approach in directing a jury would be to explain to them that the defendant would be liable if his conduct 'made an operative and significant contribution to the death'. As long as the defendant's act was a cause of the victim's death, it did not matter that it was not the sole cause. Rose LJ considered a submission put forward by counsel for the appellant that the law should be re-expressed such that gross self-neglect by the deceased (as he submitted had occurred in this case) should break the chain of causation, thus absolving the defendant of liability, while mere self-neglect would not. His Lordship took the view that the conduct of the victim in such cases was not to be subjected to 'analysis of whether a victim had treated himself with mere negligence or gross neglect'.

The Court of Appeal in *Dear* avoided dealing directly with the issue of whether or not a suicide could break the chain of causation. The courts could take a number of approaches to such a situation. It could be argued that the rules relating to the 'escape cases' should apply, such that the chain of causation is not broken where the victim's act was reasonably foreseeable; or, it could be said that the thin skull rule in *Blaue* applies and that the defendant in *Dear* was effectively forced to take his victim as he found him, inclusive of any phobias and irrational judgements that he made. This rule would then appear to encompass a defendant's psychological make-up as well as his physical condition. Alternatively, it could be argued that suicide amounts to a free and voluntary act of the victim which breaks the chain of causation.

2.5.3.4 **The drugs cases**

There are a string of 'drugs cases' on unlawful act manslaughter in which the issue arises of whether a free and voluntary act by the victim precludes causation from being established. These cases will be discussed in detail in 6.1.5. The most recent authority in this area is *Kennedy (No. 2)* [2007] UKHL 38, in which the defendant prepared a syringe of heroin and handed it to the victim. The victim injected himself with the drugs and later died. The defendant appealed against his conviction for unlawful act manslaughter. The House of Lords held that a defendant was not to be treated as causing the victim to act in a certain way if the victim made a voluntary and informed decision to act in that way. It could not be shown that the defendant had caused the victim to administer the drugs. The victim's free and voluntary act of administering the drugs to himself was fatal to any argument that the defendant had caused the drugs to be administered to the victim.

2.5.3.5 **Third party intervention**

An act by a third party might break the chain of causation if that act is a voluntary one which contributes to the result. If the act of the third party does break the chain of causation, then the original defendant is absolved of liability. The separate issue of the third party's potential liability could also be considered. However, an involuntary act of a third party will not break the chain of causation, and the chain of causation will remain intact.

 CASE CLOSE-UP

Pagett (1983) 76 Cr App R 279

The defendant in *Pagett* took his pregnant girlfriend as hostage, held her as a shield in front of him, and shot at the police who were trying to arrest him. Instinctively, the police shot back in self-defence, wounding the girlfriend, who died from these wounds. The defendant was convicted of the manslaughter of his girlfriend. As we saw earlier, the Court of Appeal held that the defendant's act need not be the sole or even the main cause of the victim's death, provided that it 'contributed significantly' to that result. The question which arose on appeal was whether the act of the police officers in shooting the girlfriend was capable of breaking the chain of causation and releasing the defendant from liability. If the act of the police in shooting back was a voluntary one, then the defendant would not be liable. However, if the act was an involuntary one, the defendant would still have caused the death of his girlfriend. Goff LJ cited Professors Hart and Honoré's definition of a voluntary act as one which is 'free, deliberate and informed'. The Court of Appeal held that the conduct of the police was reasonably foreseeable; they were acting instinctively in self-defence. This was an involuntary act which had been caused by the conduct of the defendant and did not release the defendant from liability. So, the chain of causation was not broken by this third party act of self-defence.

2.5.3.6 Negligent medical treatment

A subset of intervention by a third party is negligent medical treatment provided to a victim who requires medical treatment as a result of the defendant's conduct. The cases discussed in this section deal with whether subsequent negligent medical treatment can break the chain of causation, absolving the defendant from liability. The courts have taken a strict approach here and the general rule is that the conduct of a doctor, even if negligent, does not release the defendant from liability. A negligent doctor may himself be liable civilly for negligence, or may even be criminally liable for gross negligent manslaughter where the victim dies as a result of his negligent conduct. However, any such liability on the part of the doctor is a separate issue entirely to that of the defendant's liability. Policy considerations largely govern this area of causation: the court does not desire an original attacker to escape criminal sanction simply because a doctor who arrives on the scene as a result of that defendant's conduct is negligent.

The case of *Smith* [1959] 2 QB 35 illustrates the current approach of the courts. In this case, the defendant was a soldier who stabbed another soldier during a fight in their barracks. The victim sustained two stab wounds. The victim was carried to the medical station by another soldier, but he dropped the victim twice on the way. The medics failed to realise how severe the victim's injuries were and that a stab wound to his back had pierced a lung and caused a haemorrhage. The victim was given inappropriate medical treatment and died. Medical evidence showed that had he received adequate treatment, he might not have died. The defendant (the original attacker) was convicted of the victim's murder. The issue on appeal was whether the negligent medical treatment was sufficient to break the chain of causation and absolve the defendant of liability. The Court Martial Appeal Court held that in order for the defendant to be liable, the original wound need not be the sole cause of death, as long as it was still an 'operating and substantial' cause of death. Causation in this case was established and the conviction upheld. However, Lord Parker CJ stated that there would have been no causation if the defendant's act could be said to have merely provided the setting in which some other cause operated:

> It seems to the court that if at the time of death the original wound is still an operating cause and a substantial cause, then the death can properly be said to be the result of the wound, albeit that some other cause of death is also operating. Only if it can be said that the original wounding is merely the setting in which another cause operates can it be said that the death does not result from the wound. Putting it another way, only if the second cause is so overwhelming as to make the original wound merely part of the history can it be said that the death does not flow from the wound.

> ## CASE CLOSE-UP
>
> ### *Cheshire* (1991) 93 Cr App R 93
>
> This approach was also followed in the case of *Cheshire*. The defendant in this case shot the victim in the leg and the stomach. He was given a tracheotomy at the hospital, but 2 months after the incident, his windpipe became blocked and he died. The victim's wounds were no longer life-threatening at this time, yet the original attacker was charged with murder and convicted. There was evidence to suggest that medical staff had not realised quickly enough the severity of the blockage. Nevertheless, the Court of Appeal held that the original attacker's conduct was an operating and substantial cause of death.
>
> Beldam LJ stated that:
>
>> [T]he accused's acts need not be the sole cause or even the main cause of death it being sufficient that his acts contributed significantly to that result. Even though negligence in the treatment of the victim was the immediate cause of his death, the jury should not regard it as excluding the responsibility of the accused unless the negligent treatment *was so independent of his acts, and in itself so potent in causing death, that they regard the contribution made by his acts as insignificant.* (Author's emphasis.)

Hence, the chain of causation may be broken where the doctor's conduct was 'so independent' of the original attacker's act and 'so potent in causing death' that it rendered the contribution made by the original attacker's act as 'insignificant'. It would appear then that conduct more than mere negligence is required to break the chain of causation.

It has previously been held that grossly negligent or 'palpably wrong' medical treatment will break the chain of causation: *Jordan* (1956) 40 Cr App R 152. However, this case has been distinguished on its own facts and is not generally applicable today. The case involved a victim who was stabbed by the defendant and died after medical treatment. At the time of death, the wound had mainly healed, but negligent medical treatment had contributed to the death of the victim. The victim had been given an antibiotic to which he had previously shown intolerance and he was intravenously given large quantities of liquid which led to his lungs becoming waterlogged. He ultimately died from broncho-pneumonia. The defendant's conviction for murder was quashed on appeal because the medical treatment had been 'palpably wrong' and had broken the chain of causation between the defendant's original act of stabbing the victim, and the victim's death. This case suggests that there is scope for negligent treatment to break the chain of causation, but the case is an extreme example which is limited to its own facts and is unlikely to be applied again.

2.5.3.7 Natural events

A natural event which was not reasonably foreseeable (an 'Act of God') will break the chain of causation. As with 'escape' cases, the foreseeability of the subsequent event is the determining factor for liability. For example, imagine that the defendant strikes the victim, knocking him unconscious, and then leaves him in a park on a sunny afternoon, where he is later struck by lightning during a sudden storm, and dies. If the original injury did not directly lead to the death of the victim, the defendant will not be liable for his death as the bolt of lightning was objectively not foreseeable. Consequently, it will break the chain of causation. However, where

Figure 2.6 What amounts to an intervening act?

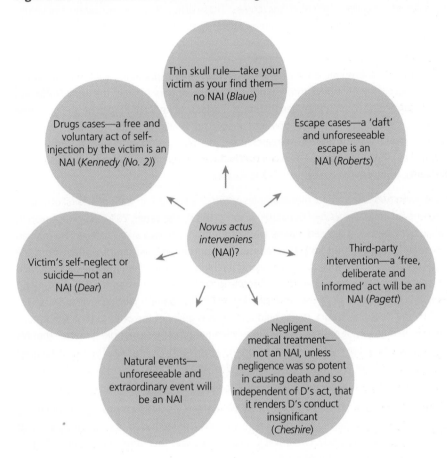

the natural event is reasonably foreseeable—for example, if the defendant leaves the victim on a railway track or on a beach when the tide is coming in, and the victim dies—the natural event will not break the chain of causation (figure 2.6).

2.6 Surrounding circumstances/'state of affairs' crimes

So far in this chapter we have explored conduct offences and result offences. This section of the chapter will examine offences which require 'surrounding circumstances' as part of the *actus reus*. The *actus reus* of some crimes includes elements of conduct, consequences, and surrounding circumstances (or just two of these elements). The example given earlier was that of the offence of theft, which has a conduct element (appropriation) and two surrounding circumstances (property, belonging to another).

The *actus reus* of some offences require proof only of the existence of surrounding circumstances. These are called 'state of affairs' crimes. These offences require no conduct or voluntary act to be proved, and as such, are an exception to the general rule that the *actus reus* of an offence must be voluntary. The defendant will be guilty of the offence if the prosecution prove simply that a specific set of circumstances exists. These offences are 'being' crimes, not 'doing' crimes. One example is the offence of being in charge of a motor vehicle on a road or public place whilst unfit to drive through drink or drugs, contrary to s.4 of the Road Traffic Act 1988. The offence is committed when this state of affairs, of *being* unfit to drive and in charge of the vehicle, exists. The defendant does not need to physically *do* anything. Another example is the offence of *having* an offensive weapon in a public place, contrary to s.1 of the Prevention of Crime Act 1953. This offence is committed if the defendant simply *has* the weapon; he is not required to do anything, such as use the weapon.

The following two cases are further examples of the prosecution of 'state of affairs' offences. The defendant in *Winzar v Chief Constable of Kent* (1983), *The Times*, 28 March, was taken to hospital, but when staff realised that he was merely drunk, he was asked to leave. He refused to do so and was found on hospital premises. The police removed the defendant from the hospital and took him in their patrol car along the highway. They then left him at a point on the highway. He was later picked up by another patrol car and arrested for being drunk on a highway, contrary to s.12 of the Licensing Act 1872. His appeal against conviction was dismissed by the Divisional Court. It was held that he was guilty of the offence if he simply *was* drunk on the highway. It did not matter how he came to be there, nor did it matter that his act was involuntary, having been dumped on the highway by the police. The Court focused on the purpose of the offence, which it was said was to deal with the nuisance of drunkenness in public places.

Similarly, in *Larsonneur* (1933) 24 Cr App R 74, the defendant, a French citizen, was deported from the UK. She travelled to Ireland, where she was arrested as an illegal immigrant and returned to the UK in custody. On arrival in the UK, she was then arrested for *being* illegally in the country, contrary to the Aliens Order 1920. Her conviction was upheld by the Court of Appeal. It did not matter that she had not actually performed a voluntary act as this was a state of affairs offence. The offence simply requires the existence of certain circumstances.

> **THINKING POINT**
>
> Do you think that these decisions are fair? Are the defendants' convictions justifiable? Did the defendants in each case have the *actus reus* of the respective offences?
>
> In both cases, the offences were procured by the authorities. Can it be said that the *actus reus* in each case was voluntary?

The results of these cases seem unfair. The defendants in both cases were convicted because the *actus reus* of each respective offence was present. These offences are unique in that they require no *mens rea* element to be present. Such offences are called 'absolute liability' offences. It could be argued that the *actus reus* in each case was not voluntarily brought about (refer back to 2.3). In fact, the authorities in each case procured the commission of the relevant offence by placing the defendants in such a position as to render them guilty of an absolute liability offence. The extent to which convictions in such circumstances can be fair must be questioned.

Summary

- The law does not punish individuals' 'evil thoughts' alone: some element of *actus reus* is required. If there is no *actus reus*, there is no crime.

- The *actus reus* of an offence may involve an act or omission (conduct crimes); certain consequences being caused (result crimes); or the existence of surrounding circumstances ('state of affairs' crimes).

- The *actus reus* of an offence must be voluntarily performed.

- The general rule is that there is no liability for an omission to act.

- There are five exceptions to this: special relationship; voluntary assumption of responsibility; duty to avert danger created; contractual duty or public office; and statutory duty.

- Causation is an *actus reus* element: where the defendant is charged with a 'result' crime, the prosecution must prove that he caused the result in order to establish the *actus reus* of the offence.

- The test for factual causation is the 'but for' test: *White* (1910). It must be established that but for the defendant's conduct, the result would not have occurred.

- Legal causation is the 'chain of causation': the defendant's conduct must be a more than minimal cause of the result, or an 'operating and substantial cause': *Smith* (1959); or it must 'contribute significantly' to the result: *Pagett* (1983).

- If there is a *novus actus interveniens*, the chain of causation will be broken and the *actus reus* will not be established.

- The types of intervening event which might break the chain of causation are: an unforeseeable escape: *Roberts* (1971); a voluntary act by the victim: *Kennedy (No. 2)* (2007); a voluntary act by a third party: *Pagett* (1983); negligent medical treatment which was 'so independent of the defendant's act' and 'so potent in causing death' that the contribution made by the defendant was rendered insignificant: *Cheshire* (1991); and a natural event which was not reasonably foreseeable.

- The thin skull rule states that the defendant must 'take his victim as he finds him'. This means 'the whole man, not just the physical man': *Blaue* (1975). The chain of causation is not broken by the existence of a latent, physical, or psychological condition which renders the victim particularly susceptible to unusual consequences.

The bigger picture

- For an authoritative analysis of the philosophy of causation, you should refer to Hart and Honoré (1985).

- As part of the foundations of liability for many offences, omissions and causation are both topics which feature again in later chapters in this book. To gain a greater appreciation of the application of these topics in the context of some of the substantive offences to which they apply, you should read 5.2 on murder (paying particular attention to

5.2.2.2), 6.1 on unlawful act manslaughter (particularly 6.1.2, 6.1.4, and 6.1.5), 6.2 on gross negligent manslaughter (particularly 6.2.1.3), and 7.3 on assault occasioning ABH (particularly 7.3.2).

- Liability for an omission to act often features as an examinable topic or as the subject of a coursework assignment.

@ For some guidance on how you might approach an essay question on omissions, you should visit the Online Resource Centre for this book.

? Questions

Self-test questions

1. Name the three different types of *actus reus* elements.

2. What does the phrase 'there is no duty of easy rescue' mean?

3. Explain when a defendant is criminally liable for an omission to act.

4. Explain the legal principle derived from the case of *Stone and Dobinson* (1977).

5. What is the test for factual causation? Cite an authority to support your answer.

6. What test(s) is/are applied in relation to legal causation? Cite authorities to support your answer.

7. Explain when the chain of causation is broken.

8. What is the thin skull rule? Cite an authority for this.

9. Explain the relevance of the case of *Cheshire* (1991). What is the test arising from this case?

10. What is a 'state of affairs' crime?

@ For suggested approaches, please visit the Online Resource Centre.

Exam questions

1. Answer *all* parts below:

    (a) Jo is a lifeguard at the local swimming pool. While on duty she notices a child in difficulty in the pool. Does she have a duty to act to help the child? Explain your answer with reference to case law.

    (b) Would your answer to part (a) differ if Jo was on her lunch break at the time? Or if she had finished her shift?

    (c) Rob visits his friend, Andy, once a week. Andy is bed-bound. Rob occasionally cooks for Andy and does his shopping every week. Rob goes away on holiday for two weeks. On his return, he finds that Andy died due to starvation. Does Rob have the *actus reus* of murder/manslaughter re Andy's death?

2. Critically evaluate the approach of English law towards imposing criminal liability for an omission to act.

For suggested approaches, please visit the Online Resource Centre.

Further reading

Books

Alexander, L. 'Criminal Liability for Omissions: An Inventory of Issues' in S. Shute and A. P. Simester (eds), *Criminal Law Theory: Doctrines of the General Part* (2002), Oxford: Oxford University Press, pp. 121–142

Hart, H. L. A. and Honoré, T. *Causation in the Law* (2nd edn, 1985), Oxford: Oxford University Press

Hogan, B. 'Omissions and the Duty Myth' in P. Smith (ed.), *Criminal Law: Essays in Honour of J. C. Smith* (1987), London: Butterworths, pp. 85–91

Ormerod, D. and Laird, K. *Smith and Hogan's Criminal Law* (14th edn, 2015), Oxford: Oxford University Press

Wilson, W. *Criminal Law* (5th edn, 2014), Harlow: Pearson

Journal articles

Ashworth, A. 'The Scope of Criminal Liability for Omissions' (1989) 105 LQR 424

Baker, D. 'Omissions Liability for Homicide Offences: Reconciling *R v Kennedy* with *R v Evans*' (2010) 74 JCL 310

Elliot, C. 'Liability for Manslaughter by Omission: Don't Let the Baby Drown!' (2010) 74 JCL 163

Norrie, A. 'A Critique of Criminal Causation' (1991) 54 MLR 685

Sannard, J. 'Criminal Causation and the Careless Doctor' (1992) 55 MLR 577

Shute, S. 'Causation: Foreseeability v Natural Consequences' (1992) 55 MLR 584

Williams, G. 'Criminal Omissions—The Conventional View' (1991) 107 LQR 86

3 Mens rea

LEARNING OBJECTIVES

By the end of this chapter, you should be able to:

- identify the *mens rea* elements of a criminal offence;
- explain the difference between direct and oblique intent;
- explain the subjective test for recklessness;
- understand the principle of coincidence of *actus reus* and *mens rea*; and
- discuss the application of the doctrine of transferred malice.

Introduction

The *mens rea* is the mental element or 'fault' element of a criminal offence. Literally translated from the Latin, *mens rea* means 'guilty mind'. As we saw in chapter 1, in order to be convicted of a criminal offence, the prosecution must prove that the defendant had the requisite *mens rea* for the particular offence charged. This raises questions such as: How can the prosecution prove that the defendant intended to kill or cause GBH? How do we know what was in the mind of the defendant at the time that he committed the offence? The only exception to this rule requiring proof of *mens rea* lies with the prosecution of strict liability offences, which are offences where one or more of the *actus reus* elements does not require a *mens rea* element (see chapter 4 for a more detailed discussion on strict liability).

There may be more than one element of *mens rea* in a criminal offence. For example, the offence of theft contains two *mens rea* elements: dishonesty and an intention to permanently deprive. The *mens rea* elements of an offence are identified by words such as: intentionally, recklessly, maliciously, knowingly, believing, dishonestly. The two most common categories of *mens rea* are intention and recklessness, and it is these states of mind which will make up a significant part of this chapter.

Other fault elements which less frequently make up the *mens rea* of a criminal offence, such as knowledge and belief, will be briefly discussed. Some criminal offences require an element of negligence. Negligence is arguably not a state of mind as it requires inadvertence, and, therefore, it is not really a *mens rea* element. Nevertheless, negligence is often covered in the *mens rea* chapter of criminal law textbooks and, consequently, there will be discussion of it in this chapter.

3.1 Subjectivity and objectivity

Intention and recklessness are regarded as subjective concepts. A subjective approach examines what the *defendant himself* saw or perceived as a consequence of his actions. Negligence is an objective concept. An objective approach compares the defendant's actions with those of a hypothetical *reasonable person*.

In convicting a defendant of a criminal offence, we are usually concerned to know what *the defendant's* state of mind was. In deciding whether or not a defendant has the *mens rea* of murder, we ask: did the defendant have malice aforethought (i.e., did the defendant intend to kill or cause grievous bodily harm (GBH))? Thus, intention is a subjective concept.

Recklessness has traditionally been regarded as a subjective concept, with the exception of criminal damage, which included an objective standard of fault for many years. However, since the House of Lords' decision in *R v G and another* in 2003, recklessness in relation to criminal damage has also reverted to being an essentially subjective concept. Subjective recklessness involves the conscious taking of an unjustified risk, which means that the defendant must recognise an unjustified risk and go on to take that risk.

>> CROSS REFERENCE
For further discussion of these cases and the law on recklessness see 3.4.2.

Although the House of Lords stated in *R v G and another* that their Lordships' definition of recklessness related specifically to criminal damage, the Court of Appeal in *Attorney General's Reference (No. 3 of 2003)* [2004] 2 Cr App R 367 later held that *R v G and another* laid down general principles. In practice, it seems likely that the definition of recklessness adopted in *R v G and another* will be applied to other statutory offences, unless the contrary is stated within the relevant statute.

3.2 Motive

Students often confuse motive with intention, but a defendant's motive is not normally relevant to his criminal liability. As Lord Bridge stated in *Moloney* [1985] 1 AC 905, 'intention is something quite distinct from motive or desire'. A defendant might intend to commit an offence, yet have a good, even admirable motive for doing so. Lord Bridge explained this statement with a useful example:

> A man who at London Airport, boards a plane which he knows to be bound for Manchester, clearly intends to travel to Manchester, even though Manchester is the last place he wants to be and his motive for boarding the plane is simply to escape pursuit. The possibility that the plane may have engine trouble and be diverted to Luton does not affect the matter. By boarding the Manchester plane, the man conclusively demonstrates his intention to go there, because it is a moral certainty that that is where he will arrive.

This example demonstrates that a person's intention may be different to their desire or motive. The man's motive in the above example is to escape pursuit (and this is also his intention). He has no desire to go to Manchester (no motive), yet he demonstrates his intention to go there by boarding the plane.

THINKING POINT

Sandra's husband is terminally ill. His condition deteriorates daily and he suffers a great deal of pain. He tells Sandra that he wishes he could die and begs her to help him. One evening, while her husband is asleep, Sandra covers his face with a pillow until he stops breathing and dies.

Is Sandra guilty of murder? Did she intend to kill her husband or to cause him GBH? What was her motive?

Motive becomes relevant after conviction as it might be used in mitigation to reduce the sentence which might be imposed on the offender. It is not usually relevant to the question of intention, i.e., whether the defendant had the appropriate *mens rea* for murder.

CASE CLOSE-UP

Steane [1947] KB 887

The defendant in this case was a British actor who lived and worked in Germany. During the Second World War, as a result of threats to himself and his family, he broadcast the news on German radio over several months. His conviction for doing acts likely to assist the enemy with intent to assist the enemy was quashed on appeal. The Court of Appeal placed much reliance on the fact that the defendant acted in order to save his family from the concentration camps in concluding that he did not intend to assist the enemy. The reasoning in this case is questionable. It would appear that the Court of Appeal confused motive with intention in this case in an attempt to be sympathetic to the defendant.

THINKING POINT

Do you think that the Court of Appeal were right to quash the defendant's conviction in *Steane*? What was the defendant's intention? What was his motive?

As you read 3.3.1 and 3.3.2, consider whether the defendant had a direct intent, an oblique intent, or no intention to assist the enemy.

3.3 Intention

In this section of the chapter, we will explore the meaning that the criminal law gives to the word 'intention' and the development of the common law in this area. However, it is first important to consider why the courts have found it necessary to devote so much attention to determining the meaning of intention. The precise meaning of the elements of criminal offences must be accessible and unambiguous. The law must be clear so that any person is able to understand (albeit with legal advice) what is and what is not permitted by law. A defendant charged with a criminal offence must be able to understand the essence of and rationale behind the charge against him. It is also important to ensure the accessibility of the law so that a trial judge can explain the defining elements of criminal offences to a jury.

Intention is an ordinary word in everyday usage. It has a commonly understood meaning and one which is seldom scrutinised. However, when used in the context of criminal law, the precise meaning of the word 'intention' becomes highly significant and somewhat confusing.

Intention is the most culpable form of *mens rea*, as it involves acting with the objective of bringing about a consequence or with the desire to bring about that consequence and foresight that those actions are virtually certain to do so. A defendant who is charged with a serious criminal offence, such as murder, has his liberty at stake. If convicted, he will be sentenced to imprisonment for life with a tariff recommended by the trial judge. A tariff is the minimum period to be served in order to satisfy the sentencing objectives of deterrence and retribution before the prisoner is eligible for parole. Where such a conviction and severe penalty turns on whether or not the defendant had the necessary intention to kill or cause GBH (i.e., the *mens rea* for murder), clarity and precision in the law is clearly of the utmost importance.

Criminal law recognises two types of intention: direct intent and oblique (or indirect) intent. These concepts will be explored in detail in the following sections. Over the past 60 years, the courts (and even Parliament) have attempted to explain the concept of oblique intention. The key cases on oblique intention will be explored at 3.3.2.

3.3.1 Direct intent

Direct intent is one's aim or purpose. Direct intention may be explained in basic terms: when you or I state that we have an intention to do an act, such as go to the cinema, we mean that it is our aim or purpose to go to the cinema, or that we have a desire to go to the cinema. This is our direct intention. In the vast majority of cases, where the intention of the defendant is in question, the court is concerned with direct intent. In such cases, the everyday meaning of intention is applied. Consequently, the judge does not need to give the jury any specific direction on intention, but asks the jury to apply their common sense to its meaning.

3.3.2 Oblique intent

3.3.2.1 The current law

Oblique intent is a less common form of intention. It does not involve a person's aim or purpose, nor does it involve the desire to do an act. It does, however, require the consequences of the defendant's actions to be virtually certain to occur along with the defendant's appreciation that they are so (table 3.1).

Table 3.1 Direct and oblique intent

Direct intent	Oblique intent
Defendant's aim or purpose	Not defendant's aim or purpose
Consequences desired but not necessarily foreseen as certain	No desire but consequences are virtually certain and D appreciates this

> ## THINKING POINT
>
> What type of intention do I have:
>
> **(1)** If, wanting to kill Sam, I point my gun at him and pull the trigger?
>
> **(2)** In relation to damaging the window if Sam is standing behind a window?
>
> **(3)** In relation to the building if I throw a petrol bomb into an office late at night?
>
> **(4)** In relation to Matthew who was working late in the office in (3) and sustained severe burns as a result of the petrol bomb?

The precise meaning of oblique intention has caused much consternation and confusion in the courts. There are two issues which have proved problematic for the courts over the years:

(1) *What degree of foresight is required for oblique intent?*

The courts have held that the defendant must foresee the consequences as virtually certain to occur: *Woollin* (1999).

(2) *Does foresight of the consequences equate to intention in law or evidence of intention?*

If the defendant does foresee the consequences as virtually certain to occur, is he to be taken to have intended those consequences or is his foresight merely evidence from which the jury *may* find intention? The courts have held that foresight of the consequences is a 'rule of evidence'. This means that a defendant's foresight of the consequences as virtually certain to occur is evidence from which the jury may find that he intended those consequences. The jury are not bound by law to find that he did intend those consequences, but they *may* find that he did.

These two issues have resulted in a string of cases on oblique intent which will be explored in 3.3.2.2. The current law on oblique intent is derived from the Court of Appeal decision in *Nedrick* [1986] 1 WLR 1025, which was approved by the House of Lords in *Woollin* [1999] 1 AC 82 and is referred to as the 'virtual certainty' test. As most of the authorities on oblique intent are murder cases, it is necessary at this stage to remind ourselves briefly that the *mens rea* for murder is malice aforethought, commonly expressed today as an intention to kill or cause GBH (figure 3.1).

> **The current law: *Woollin* [1999] 1 AC 82, HL**
>
> According to Lord Steyn in *Woollin*, where a person charged with murder performs an act and does not desire the consequence (i.e., the death of the victim), but death or serious bodily harm is virtually certain to occur and the defendant appreciates this, the jury are entitled to find that the defendant had the necessary intention and, thus, the *mens rea* for murder. *Woollin* will be discussed further in 3.3.2.2.

Notably, the case of *Woollin* and the other cases on oblique intention (that feature in 3.3.2.2) all involved charges of murder. In *Woollin*, Lord Steyn sought to limit the 'virtual certainty' test to murder cases only: 'it does not follow that "intent" necessarily has precisely the same meaning in every context in the criminal law' (at 90). However, no such limitation was specified in *Nedrick* [1986] 1 WLR 1025, which is the case from which the 'virtual certainty' test is

Figure 3.1 Did the defendant have the requisite intention (e.g., to kill or cause GBH)?

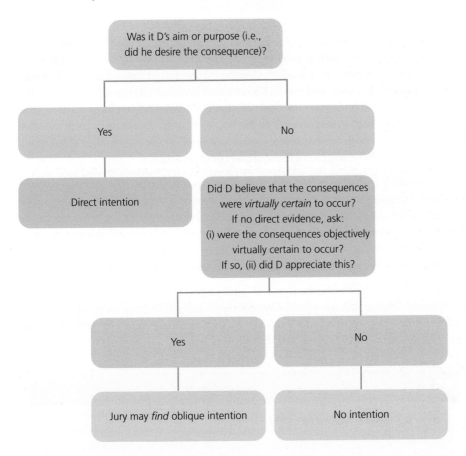

derived. It has been argued that 'if, as generally accepted, *Woollin* is interpreted as not defining intention, but simply confirming *Nedrick* . . . then this limitation is unimportant' (Keating et al. 2014: 163). The earlier test for oblique intent from *Moloney* [1985] 1 AC 905 (the full test is set out in 3.3.2.2) was applied to the offence of wounding with intent under s.18 of the Offences Against the Person Act 1861 in *Bryson* [1985] Crim LR 669. It is submitted that it would be wholly unsatisfactory if the meaning of intention was not applied in a consistent fashion across all criminal offences.

3.3.2.2 The development of the law

The degree of foresight required for oblique intention has not always been clear (it is worth noting that Professor Alan Norrie argues that the law after *Woollin* remains unclear: see Norrie (1999). This paragraph explores the historical development of the law through the cases which have sought to define the concept of oblique intention. While the current law is most relevant to the application of the law in a given factual scenario today, the development of the law is still significant as it assists us in understanding why the 'virtual certainty' test exists today and in evaluating whether/why the current law is satisfactory. You may be expected to draw upon the development of the law in an essay-style question, such as in the exam question which features at the end of this chapter, and thus you should be able to offer a critical evaluation of the various cases on oblique intention.

In 3.1 we learnt that intention is a subjective concept. This is clear today. However, in the case of *DPP v Smith* [1961] AC 290, the court confusingly used an objective presumption to conclusively identify what the defendant's intention was. In this case, the defendant was driving a car containing stolen property. He was asked to pull over by a police officer. Instead, the defendant accelerated. The officer clung to the side of the car and the defendant drove erratically, causing the officer to fall into the path of another car. As a result of this, the officer died. At trial, the defendant raised the defence of accident, claiming that he did not realise that the officer was hanging onto the car. He claimed that he intended only to escape and not to kill or cause GBH, but he was convicted of murder. The Court of Appeal substituted a verdict of manslaughter, but the murder conviction was restored by the House of Lords. The House of Lords held that intention should be objectively assessed, approving an irrebuttable presumption of law that a man intends the natural and probable consequences of his acts.

Thus, after *DPP v Smith*, the defendant's state of mind was no longer a factor in determining intention. Consideration was, instead, to be given to what a reasonable person would have foreseen as the natural and probable consequences of the defendant's act. If the reasonable person would have foreseen death or serious injury as a natural and probable consequence of his actions, then the defendant was, as a matter of law, presumed to have intended that consequence, and he would have the requisite *mens rea* of murder.

This unsatisfactory decision of the House of Lords caused Parliament to intervene to reverse this objective irrebuttable presumption. Accordingly, s.8 of the Criminal Justice Act 1967 was enacted, confirming intention as a subjective concept and the 'natural and probable consequences' rule as one of evidence rather than a rule of law.

 STATUTE

Section 8, Criminal Justice Act 1967

A court or jury, in determining whether a person has committed an offence—

(a) shall not be bound in law to infer that he intended or foresaw a result of his actions by reason only of its being a natural and probable consequence of those actions; but

(b) shall decide whether he did intend or foresee that result by reference to all the evidence, drawing such inferences as appear proper in the circumstances.

The issue of intention was again considered in the case of *Hyam v DPP* [1975] 1 AC 55, although this case focused more specifically on the meaning of *mens rea* of murder and the judgment is confusing. The defendant, Mrs Hyam, poured petrol through the letterbox of her ex-lover's fiancée, Mrs Booth, and then ignited it. Two children died in the fire. At her trial for murder, the defendant claimed that she had only intended to frighten Mrs Booth and that she had not intended to kill or cause GBH. The defendant was convicted and she appealed, the case eventually reaching the House of Lords. The House upheld the convictions by a majority of 3:2. It was held that the defendant would have the *mens rea* for murder if she foresaw that death or GBH was a likely or highly probable consequence of placing petrol-soaked newspaper through the letterbox and igniting it.

Hyam v DPP was a case dealing with the broader issue of the *mens rea* of murder (rather than the specific issues of the meaning of intention). The House of Lords took the view that a person intends the consequence of his actions when he foresees that consequence to be a highly probable result of his actions. Hence, the meaning of oblique intent was couched in terms of probability, a word usually reserved for describing **recklessness**. The House also seemingly equated foresight with intention.

This decision caused much confusion for two main reasons. First, confusion was largely due to the lack of consistency in the opinions of the Law Lords. Secondly, the meaning of intention after *Hyam v DPP* was very broad and too close to the concept of recklessness. This effectively meant that the *mens rea* for murder, one of the most serious criminal offences, which carries a mandatory sentence of life imprisonment, could be satisfied by something akin to reck- lessness. The idea that a defendant was deemed by law to have intended consequences that he foresaw was also criticised. The approach currently taken by the courts is that foresight is merely evidence of intention and this view was clearly expressed by the Court of Appeal in the case of *Mohan* [1976] 1 QB 1. In this case, the defendant was convicted of attempting (by wanton driving) to cause bodily harm to a police officer when he accelerated and drove straight at a police officer who ordered him to stop his car. In the Court of Appeal, James LJ stated that:

> evidence of knowledge of likely consequences, or from which likely consequences can be inferred, is evidence by which intent may be established but it is not, in relation to the offence of attempt, to be equated with intent. If the jury find such knowledge established they may and, using common sense, they probably will find intent proved, but it is not the case that they must do so.

Ten years after the confusing decision in *Hyam v DPP*, the House of Lords was once again given the opportunity to revisit its position in relation to the meaning of intention. In the case of *Moloney* [1985] 1 AC 905, the House of Lords recognised that its decision in *Hyam v DPP* had caused confusion and that clarity and simplicity were of paramount importance in this area of the law.

> **recklessness**
>
> recklessness is foreseeing a consequence as possible or probable yet going ahead and taking that risk, where the risk was unjustifiable or unreasonable

🔍 CASE CLOSE-UP

Moloney [1985] 1 AC 905

The defendant shot and killed his stepfather. The defendant's case was that his stepfather claimed that he could 'outshoot, outload and outdraw' the defendant. The defendant claimed that he was the first to load his shotgun, which he then pointed at his stepfather who then said, 'You wouldn't dare pull the trigger.' He then shot his stepfather in the head. He stated, 'I didn't aim the gun. I just pulled the trigger and he was dead.' At trial, the defendant stated that he 'never conceived that what [he] was doing might cause injury to anybody. It was just a lark.' The trial judge directed the jury that foresight that a consequence will probably happen is sufficient to amount to intention. The defendant was convicted of murder. However, the House of Lords substituted a verdict of manslaughter.

The House of Lords retreated from the 'probability' test relied upon in *Hyam v DPP*. Lord Bridge laid down new guidelines (which His Lordship conceded were *obiter*) on the *mens rea* of murder. His Lordship asserted that when directing the jury on the mental element in a crime of specific intent (i.e., an offence which requires proof of intention), the trial judge should avoid any elaboration or paraphrase of what is meant by intent. The trial judge should leave it to the jury's good sense, unless the judge is convinced that some further explanation is necessary to avoid any misunderstanding.

His Lordship criticised the irrebuttable presumption laid down by the House of Lords in *DPP v Smith*, which he stated had elevated what should be a rule of evidence to the status of a rule of substantive law.

His Lordship confirmed that foresight is merely evidence of intention which 'belongs, not to the substantive law, but to the law of evidence'.

Finally, Lord Bridge stated that where a direction on intention to the jury was necessary, the trial judge should invite the jury to consider two questions:

- First, was death or really serious injury in a murder case (or whatever relevant consequence must be proved to have been intended in any other case) a natural consequence of the defendant's voluntary act?
- Secondly, did the defendant foresee that consequence as being a natural consequence of his act? The jury should then be told that if they answer yes to both questions it is a proper inference for them to draw that he intended that consequence.

The first question is objective, and was arguably inconsistent with s.8 of the Criminal Justice Act 1967.

 THINKING POINT

Consider the following question posed by Lord Bridge in *Moloney* (1985):

> Suppose a terrorist plants a bomb which is timed to go off 12 hours later. The terrorist informs the police so that the building may be cleared. A bomb disposal expert trying to defuse the bomb is killed. Is the terrorist . . . guilty of murder?

Would your answer be different if the bomb was planted in a busy shopping centre and timed to explode at midday on a Saturday?

Would your answer be different if the terrorist gives his warning 5 minutes before the bomb is timed to explode?

The House of Lords had to revise its views on oblique intention just under a year after *Moloney*. The case of *Hancock and Shankland* [1986] AC 455 involved two striking miners who pushed a concrete block from a bridge over a highway on which a miner was travelling to work in a taxi. The block hit the windscreen and the driver was killed. At their trial for murder, the defendants argued that they had intended merely to block the road or frighten the miner, and that they had not intended to kill or cause really serious injury. The trial judge directed the jury in accordance with the guidelines laid down by Lord Bridge in *Moloney*.

On appeal against their convictions for murder, both the Court of Appeal and the House of Lords held that the trial judge's direction was inadequate and that the *Moloney* guidelines were potentially misleading. In the House of Lords, Lord Scarman held that the *Moloney* guidelines were 'defective' and lacked reference to probability. His Lordship stated that the phrase 'natural consequences' referred to by Lord Bridge was not the same as 'probable consequences' and that the jury needed guidance:

> the *Moloney* guidelines as they stand are unsafe and misleading. They require a reference to probability. They also require an explanation that the greater the probability of a consequence

the more likely it is that the consequence was foreseen and that if that consequence was foreseen the greater the probability is that that consequence was also intended.

His Lordship further commented on the complexity of Lord Bridge's *Moloney* guidelines:

> I fear that their elaborate structure may well create difficulty. Juries are not chosen for their understanding of a logical and phased process leading by question and answer to a conclusion but are expected to exercise practical common sense.

The case of *Nedrick* [1986] 1 WLR 1025 reached the Court of Appeal in the same year. The facts of *Nedrick* are similar to those of *Hyam v DPP*. The defendant poured paraffin through a woman's letterbox. He set the paraffin alight, burning down the house and killing the woman's child. The defendant claimed that he didn't want anyone to die and that he did it '[j]ust to wake her up and frighten her'. The jury convicted him of murder and the defendant appealed on the ground that the trial judge had misdirected the jury on the intent necessary to establish murder. As the trial took place prior to the House of Lords' decision in *Moloney*, the trial judge directed the jury in accordance with *Hyam v DPP*, equating foresight of consequences as highly probable with intention.

The Court of Appeal, whilst acknowledging that the trial judge was in no way to blame, stated that this direction was 'plainly wrong' in light of *Moloney*. The Court quashed the defendant's conviction for murder, substituting one for manslaughter. Lord Lane CJ gave the leading judgment. His Lordship stated that, in the majority of cases where the issue is intention, the simple direction will be sufficient. This will usually apply in cases where the defendant made a direct attack on the victim, where the defendant's motive or desire is clear. In such cases, the meaning of intention should not be explained and the jury must pay regard to 'all the relevant circumstances, including what the defendant himself said and did' in deciding whether the defendant has the requisite intention to kill or cause serious bodily harm. However, the Court of Appeal recognised that in cases where the defendant does a manifestly dangerous act resulting in the victim's death and his primary desire or motive is not to cause harm, further direction is required.

The direction suggested by Lord Lane CJ in the Court of Appeal was:

> Where the charge is murder and in the rare cases where the simple direction is not enough, the jury should be directed that they are not entitled to infer the necessary intention, unless they feel sure that death or serious bodily harm was a virtual certainty (barring some unforeseen intervention) as a result of the defendant's actions and that the defendant appreciated that such was the case.

Thus, in this case, the jury could infer that the defendant had the necessary intention if they were sure that death or serious bodily harm was virtually certain to occur as a result of the defendant setting the house on fire, and that the defendant had appreciated this.

This authority marked a clear move away from the word 'probability' and towards a greater degree of 'certainty'. The 'virtual certainty' test in *Nedrick* is a much narrower test than the 'highly probable' test applied in *Hyam*. This ensures a clearer distinction between the concepts of oblique intent and recklessness. With the use of the phrase 'entitled to infer', the Court of Appeal in *Nedrick* was also concerned to emphasise that foresight of a result as a virtually certain consequence is merely evidence of intention. It does not equate to intention as a matter of law (as was seemingly suggested in *Hyam v DPP*). In any event, in the vast majority of cases, no direction on intention is given to the jury as jurors are left to apply their common sense to the question of whether or not the defendant had the requisite intention. The jury need only be given further direction in cases where the consequence was not desired by the defendant, but may have been foreseen.

The direction proposed by the Court of Appeal in *Nedrick* was later approved by the House of Lords in *Woollin* [1999] 1 AC 82.

 CASE CLOSE-UP

Woollin [1999] 1 AC 82

In this case, the defendant lost his temper when his baby began to choke. He shook the baby and then, in a fit of rage or frustration, he threw the baby across the room. The baby struck a wall and died. The defendant claimed that he had not intended to throw the baby against the wall, but he did accept that in throwing the baby there was a risk of serious injury. At his trial for murder, the trial judge directed the jury in accordance with *Nedrick*, however, he later added:

> If you…are quite satisfied that he was aware of what he was doing and must have realised and appreciated when he threw that child that there was a substantial risk that he would cause serious injury to it, then it would be open to you to find that he intended to cause injury to the child and you should convict him of murder.

The defendant was convicted of murder and appealed. The House of Lords allowed the appeal, quashing the murder conviction, and substituting one of manslaughter. The House held that the trial judge was correct to use the *Nedrick* direction, but that he had later misdirected the jury when he departed from *Nedrick* by using the wider phrase 'substantial risk'. Lord Steyn, giving the leading judgment of the House of Lords, stated that:

> By using the phrase 'substantial risk' the judge blurred the line between intention and recklessness, and hence between murder and manslaughter. The misdirection enlarged the scope of the mental element required for murder. It was a material misdirection.

Although it approved the *Nedrick* direction, the House of Lords altered one word in the direction, changing 'infer' to 'find'. The direction now reads:

> Where the charge is murder and in the rare cases where the simple direction is not enough, the jury should be directed that they are not entitled to *find* the necessary intention, unless they feel sure that death or serious bodily harm was a virtual certainty (barring some unforeseen intervention) as a result of the defendant's actions and that the defendant appreciated that such was the case. (Author's emphasis.)

Thus, in this case, the jury could find that the defendant had the necessary intention if they were sure that death or serious bodily harm was virtually certain to occur as a result of the defendant throwing the baby, and that the defendant had appreciated this.

 SUMMARY

Accordingly, if the jury:

(1) feel sure that death or serious bodily harm was a virtual certainty as a result of the defendant's actions; and

(2) that the defendant appreciated this,

then the jury is entitled to find that the defendant has the *mens rea* for murder (intention to kill or cause GBH).

It is clear from the *Nedrick/Woollin* direction that a defendant will have oblique intent where the consequence is actually virtually certain to occur (objectively), and the defendant appreciates this. However, a defendant will also have oblique intent where he believes that the consequence is virtually certain, although it is actually unlikely to occur in reality, and then it does occur. For instance, imagine that I believe that it is virtually certain that I will be able to shoot my friend who is standing a distance away from me. In fact, the chances of me actually hitting my friend are unlikely from such a distance. If I do manage to shoot my friend, surely I must have oblique intent in relation to that result. The first objective question is only relevant where there is no other evidence of the defendant's state of mind (i.e., whether he foresaw the consequences as virtually certain), so this has to be inferred.

However, it is worth remembering that the *Nedrick/Woollin* direction will not be given in every case in which the issue of intention arises. The direction itself specifies that it should only be given 'in the rare cases where the simple direction is not enough'. In *R v Royle* [2013] EWCA Crim 1461, the defendant was convicted of murder after the death of a woman that he robbed. He was said to have inflicted head injuries on her during the course of the robbery and she died 2 days later from a heart attack. At trial, the defendant's case was 'not that this was a robbery that went wrong', but rather he completely denied his involvement in the incident. Thus, both the trial judge and the Court of Appeal held that a *Nedrick/Woollin* direction was not necessary. The trial judge directed the jury on intention in the following way, '[y]ou must be sure that he did not just realise that it could happen but acted on the basis that it would or that he intended that it would'. The Court of Appeal dismissed the defendant's appeal and held that in fact the trial judge had 'arguably set a hurdle higher than that in *Woollin* and *Nedrick*. It contemplates not virtual certainty but certainty. We find it difficult to see how it can be a misdirection since it is to the benefit of the appellant' (at [27]).

3.3.2.3 Rule of evidence or law?

What is the significance of the decision of the House of Lords to change the word 'infer' to 'find'? It is questionable whether this modification made any real difference to the direction. The Court of Appeal in *Nedrick* was clear in its opinion that foresight of a consequence was a piece of evidence from which intention could be inferred by the jury. By replacing the word 'infer' with 'find' it is unclear whether Lord Steyn elevated a rule of evidence to one of substantive law.

If this were a rule of evidence, a defendant's foresight of the consequences as virtually certain to occur would only be one piece of evidence from which the jury could infer that he intended those consequences. However, if the rule were one of substantive law, the defendant's foresight would (in law) amount to an intention to bring about that consequence.

Arguably, the fact that His Lordship did not abandon the word 'entitled' (such that a jury are 'entitled to find' intention where the defendant foresaw the consequence as virtually certain) implies that the rule remains one of evidence. However, at another point in His Lordship's opinion, Lord Steyn made a puzzling remark whilst referring to the unmodified *Nedrick* direction. He stated that, '[t]he effect of the critical direction is that a result foreseen as virtually certain is an intended result'. This statement removes a degree of discretion from the jury and elevates the direction to one of substantive law. This issue was further considered by the Court of Appeal in *Matthews and Alleyne* [2003] 2 Cr App R 30.

The defendants attacked the victim and threw him off a bridge into a river. He drowned. The defendants appealed against their convictions for murder on the ground that the trial judge had misdirected the jury on intention. The trial judge had directed the jury to find the necessary intent proved provided they were satisfied that the defendants appreciated that death was virtually certain. This elevated the *Woollin* direction from a rule of evidence (where the defendant's foresight is one piece of evidence from which the jury *may* find that he had the necessary intention) to a rule of substantive law (where they *must* find that he intended the consequences if they are satisfied that he foresaw them as a virtually certain to occur).

The Court of Appeal held that the trial judge had misdirected the jury. Rix LJ stated, 'we do not regard *Woollin* as yet reaching or laying down a substantive rule of law'. This authority states that *Woollin* lays down a rule of evidence—the defendant's foresight of a consequence as virtually certain to occur is evidence from which the jury could find that the defendant had the necessary intention. However, Rix LJ added, 'there is very little to choose between a rule of evidence and one of substantive law'. The Court considered that on the facts of the case, a finding that there was the necessary intention was inevitable. (For a summary of cases on oblique intent, see table 3.2.)

Table 3.2 Summary of cases on oblique intent

Case	Test
DPP v Smith (1961)	Objective irrebuttable presumption of law. A man intends the natural and probable consequences of his acts.
s.8, CJA 1967	Subjective rule of evidence restored.
Hyam v DPP (1975)	Confusing decision. A person intends the consequence of his actions when he foresees that consequence to be a highly probable result of his actions.
Mohan (1976)	Knowledge of likely consequences is evidence of intention.
Moloney (1985)	Foresight of consequence as a natural consequence is evidence of intention.
Hancock and Shankland (1986)	The greater the probability of a consequence, the more likely it is that the consequence was foreseen and that if that consequence was foreseen the greater the probability is that that consequence was also intended.
Nedrick (1986)	The jury are not entitled to infer intention, unless death or serious bodily harm was a virtual certainty as a result of the defendant's actions and that the defendant appreciated that such was the case.
Woollin (1999)	Confirmed *Nedrick* direction. Changed 'infer' to 'find', resulting in confusion over whether *Nedrick/Woollin* laid down a rule of evidence or one of substantive law.
Matthews and Alleyne (2003)	Confirmed *Nedrick/Woollin* direction as a rule of evidence.

3.3.3 **Reform**

In 2006, the Law Commission published its report, *Murder, Manslaughter and Infanticide* (Law Com. No. 304, 2006). The Law Commission proposed that the meaning of intention should be put on a statutory footing as follows:

(1) A person should be taken to intend a result if he or she acts in order to bring it about.

(2) In cases where the judge believes that justice may not be done unless an expanded understanding of intention is given, the jury should be directed as follows: an intention to bring about a result may be found if it is shown that the defendant thought that the result was a virtually certain consequence of his or her action.

The first statement refers to direct intent and is uncontroversial. The second relates to oblique intent. The Law Commission evidently took the view that the 'virtual certainty' test should be applied with respect to oblique intent (in accordance with *Nedrick* and *Woollin*). It is also clear that the Law Commission propose that this should be a rule of evidence, rather than one of substantive law. The defendant's foresight of a result as a virtually certain consequence is evidence from which the jury *may* find intention.

3.3.4 **Intoxication and intention**

A defendant's intention may be relevant where he is charged with committing a criminal offence while voluntarily intoxicated. For the purposes of voluntary intoxication, offences have been loosely categorised into offences of 'specific intent' and offences of 'basic intent' (although this categorisation has been criticised, see 13.6.2.2 for more detail). A crime of 'specific intent' is one which requires intention as the *mens rea* (e.g., murder, wounding or causing GBH with intent (s.18), theft, and robbery). A crime of 'basic intent' is one which can be committed with a lesser form of *mens rea* than intention, such as recklessness (e.g., manslaughter, maliciously wounding, or inflicting GBH (s.20), assault occasioning ABH (s.47), assault, battery, and criminal damage). A voluntarily intoxicated defendant will have no defence to a 'basic intent' offence, but he may be able to use evidence of his voluntary intoxication to negate the *mens rea* of a 'specific intent' offence by arguing that due to his intoxication he did not, in fact, form the necessary intention and thus is not liable: *DPP v Majewski* [1977] AC 443.

3.4 Recklessness

Recklessness involves the taking of an unjustified or unreasonable risk. Recklessness is a less culpable form of *mens rea* than intention as it involves foresight of possible or probable consequences, instead of desire or foresight of virtually certain consequences. Subjective or advertent recklessness is foreseeing the risk of a consequence occurring as a result of one's actions and going ahead to take that (unjustified or unreasonable) risk.

The current law on recklessness is relatively straightforward: there is one subjective standard of recklessness which applies to most criminal offences requiring recklessness as part of the *mens rea*. However, the history of the law on recklessness is less simple. For over 20 years, there existed two tests of recklessness, one subjective (advertent recklessness) and the other containing an additional objective limb (inadvertent recklessness). Each test applied to different offences.

The subjective standard of recklessness is referred to as *Cunningham* recklessness. This test applied to most offences. The House of Lords' decision in *Metropolitan Police Commissioner v Caldwell* in 1981 provided a second test of recklessness which applied to criminal damage. In *R v G and another* in 2003, the House of Lords overruled its earlier decision in *Caldwell* and restored a subjective standard of recklessness to the offence of criminal damage. The House was keen to emphasise that the decision in *R v G and another* applied only to the offence of criminal damage, but it seems likely that the subjective standard set down in this authority will be applied to all offences. This has been confirmed by the Court of Appeal in *Attorney General's Reference (No. 3 of 2003)* [2004] 2 Cr App R 367, where it was stated that *R v G and another* laid down general principles. As a result, we now seem to have one, universally applied, subjective test of recklessness. This section of the chapter will explore both the current position and the development of the law on recklessness.

3.4.1 **The current law**

In *R v G and another* [2003] UKHL 50, Lord Bingham adopted the definition of recklessness proposed by the Law Commission and set out in clause 18 of the Draft Criminal Code 1989. His Lordship stated that:

> A person acts 'recklessly' within the meaning of section 1 of the Criminal Damage Act 1971 with respect to—
>
> (i)   a circumstance when he is aware of a risk that it exists or will exist;
>
> (ii) a result when he is aware of a risk that it will occur;
>
> and it is, in the circumstances known to him, unreasonable to take the risk.

Although recklessness is subjective in requiring awareness of the existence of the risk, there is an objective element to the definition: the separate issue of whether or not the risk is justified or reasonable. This question is assessed by balancing the social utility in taking the risk against the likelihood or severity of harm resulting and questioning whether the risk was one that a reasonable person might take. It is unreasonable to take a risk where the social utility in taking it is outweighed by the harm it is likely to cause. The more severe the harm is likely to be, the higher the social utility in taking the risk must be in order for the risk to be justified. For instance, the conduct of a homeowner in entering her burning house to save a piece of treasured jewellery is more reckless than that of a lifeguard jumping into a swimming pool to save a person from drowning. The latter act carries more social utility and less danger than the former. The homeowner in the former example is taking an unreasonable risk, whereas the lifeguard in the latter example is not.

3.4.2 **The development of the law**

Prior to 2003, the leading authority on recklessness was *Cunningham* [1957] 2 QB 396, in which a subjective standard was applied to the concept of recklessness.

 CASE CLOSE-UP

Cunningham [1957] 2 QB 396

The defendant broke a gas meter and cracked a gas pipe, causing gas to leak into the house next door. A woman living there inhaled the gas and the defendant was convicted of maliciously administering a noxious thing so as to endanger life, contrary to s.23 of the Offences Against the Person Act 1861. He appealed on the basis that the trial judge had misdirected the jury by stating that the word 'maliciously' meant 'wickedly', doing 'something which he has no business to do and perfectly well knows it'. The Court of Appeal quashed the defendant's conviction and held that this was a misdirection and that 'maliciously' meant intentionally or recklessly.

The Court applied a subjective standard to recklessness, such that in order to be reckless the defendant must have foreseen that the harm might occur but had gone ahead and acted anyway. Thus, in this case, the defendant would have been reckless if he had realised that there was a risk of gas escaping and endangering someone as a result of his breaking into the gas meter, but had gone ahead with the act anyway.

The Court of Appeal approved this subjective test of recklessness in *Stephenson* [1979] 1 QB 695. The defendant crawled into a haystack and lit a fire in order to keep warm. The fire spread, causing £3,500 worth of damage. The defendant was charged with arson contrary to s.1(1) and (3) of the Criminal Damage Act 1971. The defence argued that as the defendant suffered from schizophrenia, he might not have had the same ability to foresee or appreciate risks as the mentally normal person and adduced medical evidence to support this. The trial judge directed the jury that the defendant was reckless if the risk of damage would have been obvious to the reasonable person, attaching an objective standard to recklessness. The defendant's conviction was quashed on appeal as the trial judge had misdirected the jury. The Court of Appeal confirmed that recklessness was subjectively assessed. Lane LJ stated that:

> A man is reckless when he carries out the deliberate act appreciating that there is a risk that damage to property may result from his act. It is however not the taking of every risk which could properly be classed as reckless. The risk must be one which it is in all the circumstances unreasonable for him to take.

 ## SUMMARY

Hence, there are two elements of subjective recklessness:

(1) Did the defendant foresee the possibility of the consequence occurring?

(2) Was it unjustifiable or unreasonable to take the risk?

In this particular case, the defence argued that due to his schizophrenic state, the defendant himself had not foreseen the possibility of the fire causing damage to property, and as such, that he was not subjectively reckless. Whether or not the risk would have been obvious to the reasonable person, was not a relevant consideration. The key question was whether or not the defendant himself actually foresaw the risk of damage to property. Lane LJ continued:

> The appellant, through no fault of his own, was in a mental condition which might have prevented him from appreciating the risk which would have been obvious to any normal person ... The schizophrenia was on the evidence something which might have prevented the idea of danger entering the appellant's mind at all. If that was the truth of the matter, then the appellant was entitled to be acquitted.

This represents the current position of the law because the House of Lords decided in *R v G and another* (2003) to revert to the law as it stood after *Stephenson*. Nevertheless, it is important to understand something of the following cases in order to assess whether the law is satisfactory as it stands. The House of Lords' opinions in the cases of *Metropolitan Police Commissioner v Caldwell* [1982] 1 AC 341 and *Lawrence* [1982] 1 AC 510 were handed down on the same day and drastically changed the law on recklessness. *Caldwell* involved a defendant who started a fire in a hotel. He was tried for arson, contrary to s.1(2) and (3) of the Criminal Damage Act 1971 and claimed that he was so drunk that it never occurred to him that he might be endangering the lives of people in the hotel. The Court of Appeal allowed the defendant's appeal against conviction on the basis that the trial judge had mis-directed the jury. The Crown then appealed to the House of Lords. The issue in this case was really one of intoxication: the House confirmed that intoxication was no defence to a crime of basic intent, such as arson.

CROSS REFERENCE

See chapter 13 (Defences I) for a detailed discussion on the defence of intoxication and the meaning of 'basic intent'.

The House of Lords also took the opportunity to review the law on recklessness. The majority of the House held that when used in a statute, the word 'reckless' is 'an ordinary English word'. Lord Diplock gave the leading opinion and stated that:

> a person charged with an offence under section 1(1) of the Criminal Damage Act 1971 is 'reckless as to whether any such property would be destroyed or damaged' if (1) he does an act which in fact creates an obvious risk that property will be destroyed or damaged and (2) when he does the act he either has not given any thought to the possibility of there being any such risk or has recognised that there was some risk involved and has nonetheless gone on to do it.

Thus, under *Caldwell*, there are really two different tests (or limbs) of recklessness. Under the first test (or limb), a defendant would be reckless if:

(1) he does an act which creates an obvious risk of damage; and

(2) he does not give any thought to the possibility of there being any such risk.

Under the second test (or limb), a defendant would be reckless if he recognises that there is some risk involved and, nonetheless, goes on to do it.

The first limb is inadvertent recklessness, often referred to as the 'objective limb'. This definition of recklessness is wider than the test set out in *Cunningham* as it encompasses an inadvertent state of mind. Under *Caldwell*, a defendant would be reckless if he failed to give any thought to the risk of a consequence occurring if that risk would have been obvious to the reasonable person.

The second alternative test (or limb) is one of advertent, subjective recklessness. This is similar to that in *Cunningham*, but crucially, this did not have to be proved under *Caldwell*, the first (objective) limb being sufficient.

Lawrence was a case involving a charge of causing death by reckless driving, contrary to the Road Traffic Act 1972 (an offence which no longer exists and which was replaced by the offence of causing death by dangerous driving under the Road Traffic Act 1991). The House of Lords applied the *Caldwell* test of recklessness to this offence. For over 20 years, *Caldwell* and *Lawrence* were applied where a statutory offence required recklessness as part of the *mens rea*.

These cases were heavily criticised by academics, practitioners, and the judiciary. Criticisms related to the fact that the objective limb in the test rendered the law particularly harsh towards defendants who were incapable of recognising the risk in question (such as children, the mentally ill, or persons of low intelligence). The harsh application of the objective limb and the criticisms of *Caldwell* by academics ultimately led to the restoration of the law prior to *Caldwell* in the House of Lords' decision of *R v G and another* [2003] UKHL 50. This landmark authority decided that a subjective test of recklessness should apply to the offence of criminal damage, overruling the earlier House of Lords' decision in *Caldwell*.

Q CASE CLOSE-UP

R v G and another [2003] UKHL 50

The two young defendants, aged 11 and 12, were 'camping' in a yard behind a shop. They set fire to some newspapers which they threw under a wheelie bin. The fire spread to the shop and caused £1 million worth of damage. The defendants were charged with causing damage to property by fire, being reckless as to whether such property would be damaged, contrary to s.1(1) and (3) of the Criminal Damage Act 1971.

It was accepted that the defendants had not appreciated the risk that the fire might spread to the buildings. The defendants claimed that they thought the newspapers would extinguish themselves on the concrete floor. The trial judge, bound by *Caldwell*, directed the jury that the boys would be reckless if there was a risk of damage to property which would have been obvious to the reasonable bystander and the boys did not give any thought to the possibility of such a risk. He stated that 'no allowance is made by the law for the youth of these boys or their lack of maturity'. The defendants appealed against their convictions and the Court of Appeal certified a point of law of public importance for the House of Lords.

The House of Lords quashed the defendants' convictions and overruled *Caldwell*, restoring the law to its position as understood prior to *Caldwell*. In respect of criminal damage, the House adopted the test of recklessness proposed by the Law Commission in the Draft Criminal Code 1989 (set out in 3.4.1). The leading opinion was given by Lord Bingham, who gave four reasons for overruling *Caldwell*:

(1) Liability for a serious criminal offence should be dependent upon proof of a culpable state of mind. Lord Bingham took the view that the *mens rea* of a serious offence should be subjective. A defendant should only be held criminally liable if he intended the consequence or he knowingly disregarded an appreciated and unacceptable risk of the consequence occurring. A defendant must perceive the risk himself. If he does not, he 'may fairly be accused of stupidity or lack of imagination, but neither of those failings should expose him to conviction of serious crime or the risk of punishment' (*per* Lord Bingham).

(2) *Caldwell* led to 'obvious unfairness' and it was clear from notes that the jury sent to the trial judge that the direction in *Caldwell* 'offended the jury's sense of fairness'. Lord Bingham further stated that, 'It is neither moral nor just to convict a defendant (least of all a child) on the strength of what someone else would have apprehended if the defendant himself had no such apprehension.'

(3) Lord Bingham stated that the reasoned and outspoken criticisms of *Caldwell* expressed by leading academics, judges, and practitioners should not be ignored.

(4) The majority in *Caldwell* had misinterpreted the meaning of 'recklessness' in s.1 of the Criminal Damage Act 1971. The majority had been wrong to decide that

> the Act had redefined 'recklessness' such that it should not be given the same subjective meaning that it had been given in *Cunningham*. Lord Bingham took the view that this misinterpretation was 'offensive to principle' and 'apt to cause injustice'.
>
> His Lordship acknowledged the problem that the House of Lords attempted to deal with in the case of *Caldwell*. Lord Diplock in *Caldwell* was concerned that a purely subjective approach to recklessness would 'lead to the acquittal of [defendants] whom public policy would require to be convicted' (*per* Lord Bingham in *R v G and another*). The House of Lords in *Caldwell* drew attention to the ease with which a defendant could simply plead in defence that the risk had never occurred to him, thus escaping liability. However, in *R v G and another*, Lord Bingham refused to accept this view. His Lordship stated that there was no evidence that this was a problem prior to *Caldwell* and expressed his faith in juries to use their common sense in their deliberations to reject such a defence when they are of the view that it is unrealistic.

In *Brady* [2006] EWCA Crim 2413, the Court of Appeal held that in order to be reckless, a defendant only needs to foresee 'a' risk of harm occurring, it is not necessary to prove that the defendant foresaw 'an obvious and significant risk'. In this case, the defendant fell from a balcony in a nightclub onto the dance floor whilst drunk. He landed on the victim, causing her serious injury and was charged with inflicting grievous bodily harm contrary to s.20 of the Offences Against the Person Act 1861. His conviction was quashed on appeal because the trial judge had directed the jury on recklessness in unclear terms.

3.4.3 **The problems with *Caldwell***

 THINKING POINT

Why, in your opinion, was *Caldwell* a problematic authority?

We have touched very briefly upon one of the problems with the *Caldwell* test of recklessness. The law under *Caldwell* failed to provide any protection to a defendant who, due to his age, lack of maturity, or limited intellect, was incapable of appreciating a risk that would be obvious to the reasonable person. Under *Caldwell*, such a defendant would be convicted. This harsh and unsatisfactory result was heavily criticised by proponents of a subjective approach to *mens rea*.

One example of the harsh operation of *Caldwell* is the case of *Elliott v C* [1983] 1 WLR 939. The defendant was a 14-year-old girl of low intelligence. She poured white spirit on the floor of a shed and then threw two lighted matches on the spirit. The shed was destroyed and she was charged with causing damage to property by fire, being reckless as to whether such property would be damaged, contrary to s.1(1) and (3) of the Criminal Damage Act 1971.

The justices in the magistrates' court acquitted the defendant because, due to her age, lack of understanding, lack of experience, and exhaustion (she had been up all night), she would not have been capable of appreciating the risk of destroying the shed. The Crown appealed to the Divisional Court, which allowed the appeal. The Court held, reluctantly, that the first limb of the *Caldwell* test was objective. Hence, the fact that she was not capable of recognising the risk was irrelevant: the risk only had to be obvious to a reasonably prudent person. The Court directed the justices to convict the defendant.

This decision was confirmed and strictly applied in *R (Stephen Malcolm)* (1984) 79 Cr App R 334, *Bell* [1984] 3 All ER 842, and *Coles* [1995] 1 Cr App R 157. Some attempt was made to modify this harsh test in *Reid* (1992) 95 Cr App R 393 and *R v R (Rape: Marital Exemption)* [1992] 1 AC 599, but this was largely unsuccessful as the lower courts were bound by *Caldwell* until it was formally overruled in 2003.

Caldwell was an unsatisfactory authority because it rather confusingly left us with two different tests of recklessness. Each test was applied in relation to different offences, but there was no clear reason why one test applied in a certain scenario instead of the other. This arbitrary distinction was also presumably confusing for the jury, who would be directed that 'reckless' had different meanings, depending upon the offence charged. The wider, objective, limb of the *Caldwell* test of recklessness applied to criminal damage and other statutory offences involving recklessness. The narrower, subjective, *Cunningham* test of recklessness applied to all other offences, including non-fatal offences against the person. Thus, a defendant who failed to consider a risk which would have been obvious to the reasonable person would be convicted if he was charged with an offence under the Criminal Damage Act 1971, but acquitted if charged with assault or battery. *Caldwell* was also problematic because the objective limb was not easy to reconcile with the traditional subjective approach to *mens rea* in criminal law. Objectivity or unconscious risk-taking is more akin to negligence than recklessness. Thus *Caldwell* drew the law on recklessness uncomfortably close to negligence.

Academics were also critical of *Caldwell* as it appeared to leave a loophole in the law where a defendant did consider whether or not there was a risk, but ruled it out completely or took action to minimise it. It was suggested that in such a scenario, the defendant would not be reckless under *Caldwell* and this became known as the *Caldwell* lacuna. In *Chief Constable of Avon and Somerset Constabulary v Shimmen* (1987) 84 Cr App R 7, the defendant was a martial arts expert who kicked out at a window and broke it. He was charged with criminal damage contrary to s.1(1) of the Criminal Damage Act 1971. He argued that he had not acted recklessly because he had concluded that there was no risk of the window breaking due to his high level of muscular control and skill in martial arts. The Divisional Court held that the defendant was reckless because he recognised the risk involved, however slight.

The Court did not deal directly with the issue of whether or not the lacuna existed. However, a distinction was drawn between a defendant who mistakenly concludes that there is no risk (see *Reid* (1992)), and a defendant who recognises a risk but thinks that it no longer exists because he has taken steps to eliminate it. The Court took the view that the former would not be reckless, while the latter would. This distinction is difficult to justify on a moral basis. There is no difference between a defendant who mistakenly decides that there is no risk and one who takes insufficient steps to eliminate a risk.

The issue was dealt with *obiter* by the House of Lords in *Reid* (1992) 95 Cr App R 393. The House held that the lacuna existed, but that it was very narrow. The lacuna would only apply to a defendant who considered whether there was a risk and, due to an honest and reasonable mistake, decided that there was none. The Law Lords seemed content to leave the lacuna as it only applied to a special category of cases in which it would be inappropriate to characterise

Table 3.3 Summary table: level of *mens rea* relative to degree of foresight of consequence X

Degree of foresight	Intention or recklessness?	Relevant authority
Want or desire X to happen	Direct intention	
X is virtually certain to happen	Evidence of oblique intention	*Woollin* (1999), HL *Nedrick* (1986), CA
X is highly probable to occur	Not sufficient for oblique intent Amounts to recklessness (if the risk taken was unreasonable)	*Hyam v DPP* (1975), HL
X is likely or will probably occur	Not sufficient for oblique intent Amounts to recklessness (if the risk taken was unreasonable)	*Mohan* (1976), CA *Hancock and Shankland* (1986), HL
X might possibly happen	Recklessness (if the risk taken was unreasonable).	*Cunningham* (1957), CA *R v G and another* (2003), HL

the conduct of the defendant as reckless. (For a summary on the level of *mens rea* relative to the degree of foresight, see table 3.3.)

3.5 Knowledge and belief

Some criminal offences require knowledge or belief as the *mens rea* element. For instance, the offence of handling stolen goods under s.22 of the Theft Act 1968 requires the defendant to know or believe that the goods are stolen. The new offences under the Serious Crime Act 2007 (which came into force on 1 October 2008) of encouraging or assisting an offence or offences, under ss.45 and 46, require the defendant to believe that one or more offences will be committed. Knowledge is also a necessary element of offences involving possession (such as possession of a controlled drug under the Misuse of Drugs Act 1971): see *Warner v MPC* [1969] 2 AC 256. Knowledge and belief are both subjective concepts.

Actual knowledge involves a person being certain that a circumstance exists, whereas belief requires less certainty. Knowledge may also encompass 'wilful blindness', where a defendant closes his eyes to his suspicion of the truth. Although suspicion alone does not constitute knowledge, a deliberate or wilful failure to ascertain the truth may elevate such suspicion to 'wilful blindness'.

In relation to belief, the Court of Appeal stated in *Hall* (1985) 81 Cr App R 260, that:

> Belief . . . is something short of knowledge. It may be said to be the state of mind of a person who says to himself: 'I cannot say I know for certain that these goods are stolen, but there can be no other reasonable conclusion in the light of all the circumstances, in the light of all that I have heard and seen'.

3.6 Negligence

Negligence is regarded by some as not really a type of *mens rea* because it does not require consideration of the state of mind of the defendant, which it is said that *mens rea* does. Negligence imposes an objective standard on a defendant and can be satisfied by inadvertence to an obvious risk. The defendant's conduct is judged against the conduct of the hypothetical reasonable person. This means that the characteristics of the defendant are not to be taken into account when assessing his fault. It is irrelevant that a defendant was unable to understand or did not know of the risk. Negligence is a much wider fault element than intention or recklessness.

A person is negligent when:

(1) he fails to foresee a risk that a reasonable person would have foreseen; or

(2) he does foresee the risk, but either does not take steps to avoid the risk or takes inadequate steps, thereby falling below the standard to be expected of the reasonable person.

There are various degrees of negligence, and thus, culpability. In (1), negligence is satisfied by inadvertence to a risk that would have been obvious to a reasonable person. The defendant is more culpable in (2), where the defendant is aware of the risk but fails to take adequate steps to prevent it, falling below the objective standard. The more obvious the risk would have been to the reasonable person, the higher the degree of negligence (or culpability) of the defendant who failed to recognise that risk.

At common law, negligence is rarely sufficient for criminal liability. The offence of gross negligence manslaughter, which requires a much higher degree of fault than ordinary tortious negligence, will be discussed in chapter 6. The concept of negligence is used much more readily in statutory offences, although most of these are regulatory in nature.

Some examples of statutory offences involving negligence include offences under the Road Traffic Act 1988. Section 3 of the Act provides for the offence of driving without due care and attention. This offence requires the defendant to drive in a way which falls below the standard of driving to be expected of the reasonable person. Section 1 of the Act provides for the offence of causing death by dangerous driving and s.2 provides for dangerous driving. 'Dangerous driving' is defined in s.2A as falling far below what would be expected of a competent and careful driver, when it would be obvious to a competent and careful driver that driving in such a way would be dangerous.

Another notable example is the offence of causing or allowing the death of or serious physical harm to a child or vulnerable adult under s.5 of the Domestic Violence, Crime and Victims Act 2004 (as amended by s.1 the Domestic Violence, Crime and Victims (Amendment) Act 2012).

3.7 The relationship between *actus reus* and *mens rea*

In this chapter and in chapter 2, we have explored the fundamental elements of a criminal offence. Although *actus reus* and *mens rea* have been dealt with in this textbook in two separate chapters, these elements are inextricably linked in criminal liability. We already know that criminal liability generally depends upon proof of the *actus reus* of a criminal offence and the corresponding *mens rea* of that same offence. However, this general rule is occasionally loosely interpreted and applied. The following section deals with two common law doctrines developed in order to circumvent the strict general rule. It begins with an explanation of the principle of coincidence of *actus reus* and *mens rea* and concludes with a discussion of the doctrine of transferred malice.

3.7.1 **Coincidence of *actus reus* and *mens rea***

The principle of coincidence requires that the *actus reus* and *mens rea* coincide in time in order for a defendant to be guilty of a criminal offence. This means that the defendant must form the *mens rea* for the requisite offence at some point during the *actus reus* of the offence. However, case law demonstrates that the courts are willing to stretch the concept of an act in order to ensure that cases fall within the principle of coincidence. For instance, in chapter 2, we came across the case of *Fagan v Metropolitan Police Commissioner* (1969) in which the continuing act theory was adopted in order to satisfy the principle of coincidence.

> **CROSS REFERENCE**
>
> Remind yourself of the facts of *Fagan v Metropolitan Police Commissioner* (1969) in 2.4.4.

If the *actus reus* and *mens rea* do not coincide, no offence will have been committed. For example, if I pick up a tin of beans in a supermarket, I have the *actus reus* of theft (as I have appropriated property belonging to another). If, once I have put the tin of beans back on the shelf, I then decide dishonestly to permanently deprive the supermarket of the beans (i.e., I form the *mens rea* of theft), I will not be guilty of any offence. In this example, the *actus reus* and *mens rea* occur at different times and thus no liability arises. However, if, after forming the *mens rea* and whilst continuing to have that *mens rea*, I then pick up the tin of beans again (i.e., I perform the *actus reus* of theft), I will be guilty of theft because at this point the *actus reus* and *mens rea* coincide.

The continuing act theory was also followed in the case of *Kaitamaki* [1985] AC 147, in which the Privy Council held that sexual intercourse was a continuing act in relation to a charge of rape. Thus, where a defendant penetrates the complainant in the belief that he has such consent when in fact he doesn't, he has the *actus reus* of rape but not the *mens rea*. On realising that the complainant is not consenting, the defendant will be guilty of rape if he fails to withdraw. At this point, he will have formed the requisite *mens rea* and the *actus reus* is continuing. If the defendant penetrates the complainant with consent and in the belief that he has such consent, he has neither the *actus reus* nor the *mens rea* of rape. If the complainant then withdraws consent, the defendant has the *actus reus* of rape which will continue throughout the duration of the intercourse. If the defendant then realises that the complainant no longer consents, he will form the *mens rea* of rape if he fails to withdraw, and will incur liability for rape at this point in time. The continuing act theory in respect of rape has now been placed on a statutory footing: s.79(2) of the Sexual Offences Act 2003 states that, '[p]enetration is a continuing act from entry to withdrawal'.

> **CROSS REFERENCE**
>
> Remind yourself of the facts of *Miller* (1983) and *DPP v Santana-Bermudez* (2003) in 2.4.2.3.

In other cases, the courts have also sought to circumvent the principle of coincidence in order to impose liability on a defendant. In the case of *Miller* (1983), the House of Lords avoided a strict application of the principle of coincidence through the 'duty' principle. The House held that where the defendant performs an act without the relevant *mens rea*, and that act creates a danger to property (or to another person), he has a duty to avert the danger when he realises that he has caused it. His advertent failure to avert the danger (the *mens rea*) coincides with the *actus reus* at this point. This approach was also adopted in *DPP v Santana-Bermudez* (2003).

Another method by which the courts have circumvented the principle of coincidence is through the inventive interpretation of a number of consecutive events as a 'single transaction'.

 CASE CLOSE-UP

Thabo Meli v R [1954] 1 WLR 288

In this case, the defendants struck the victim on the head, intending to kill him. Believing the victim to be dead, the defendants then rolled the body over a cliff. In fact, the victim died from exposure at the bottom of the cliff. The defendants were convicted of murder. On appeal, they argued that there was no coincidence of *actus reus* and *mens rea* as although they had the *mens rea* for murder when they initially struck the victim, they did not have it when they rolled his body over the cliff as they had assumed that the victim was already dead. The defendants' convictions for murder were upheld by the Privy Council. Lord Reid stated that it was 'impossible to divide up what was really one series of acts'. His Lordship held that rolling the body over the cliff was part of a preconceived plan and just one of a series of acts which essentially amounted to a single transaction. The defendants would be guilty of murder provided they had the *mens rea* for murder at some stage during this transaction.

The same principle was applied by the Court of Appeal in the case of *R v Church* [1966] 1 QB 59, where, unlike in *Thabo Meli*, there was no preconceived plan. The defendant was mocked by the victim after he was unable to satisfy her sexually. He knocked the victim unconscious. Assuming that she was dead, he threw her body into a river. In fact, she drowned. The defendant's conviction for manslaughter was upheld by the Court of Appeal, irrespective of whether the defendant thought that she was dead or alive when he threw her in the river. The series of acts which led to the victim's death amounted to a single transaction, and if the *mens rea* for manslaughter was present at some point during that transaction, the defendant would be liable.

Similarly, in *Le Brun* [1991] 4 All ER 673, the 'single transaction' principle was again applied. In this case, the defendant struck his wife, knocking her unconscious. Believing her to be dead, he then attempted to drag her into their house. He dropped her, fracturing her skull and killing her. Applying *Church*, the Court of Appeal upheld the defendant's conviction for manslaughter. Lord Lane CJ held that the fact that there was no preconceived plan of killing the victim was immaterial. As long as the defendant had the *mens rea* for the offence during the series of acts (i.e., at the beginning, when he struck his wife), liability would be imposed. The fact that there was an interval of time between the initial act of striking her and the act which eventually causes death is no barrier to conviction where both acts are part of the same transaction. This is especially so since the latter act was performed in an attempt to conceal the original unlawful act. Lord Lane CJ stated:

> In short, in circumstances such as the present, . . . the act which causes death and the necessary mental state to constitute manslaughter need not coincide in point of time.

A difficulty of proof arose in the case of *Attorney General's Reference (No. 4 of 1980)* [1981] 1 WLR 705, in which the prosecution could not prove which act in a series of acts caused the death of the victim. In this case, the defendant slapped his girlfriend. She fell backwards, down a flight of stairs and lay unconscious. The defendant placed a rope around her neck which he used to drag her body upstairs. He slit her throat and cut up the body and disposed of it. As the precise cause of death could not be determined, the trial judge withdrew the case from the jury. The Court of Appeal held that the prosecution did not need to prove which act caused the death of the victim. The defendant could still be guilty of manslaughter provided that the prosecution proved that each of the defendant's acts was performed with the requisite *mens rea* for manslaughter.

This case does not seem to be entirely reconcilable with the authorities noted earlier. The Court of Appeal could have decided that the defendant would be guilty if he had the requisite *mens rea* at the time of the first act. As the law stands, where the precise cause of death is uncertain, the prosecution bear a high burden of proving the *mens rea* at the time of each and every act. It is difficult to see why this authority should be any different in this respect to *Thabo Meli* and *Church*.

3.7.2 The doctrine of transferred malice

The doctrine of transferred malice is best explained by an example. Imagine that you decide to shoot and kill X. You point your gun at X and pull the trigger, but you are a poor shot and the bullet misses X, instead striking and killing Y. Are you guilty of the murder of Y? You clearly have performed the *actus reus* of murder in relation to Y. However, you only had the *mens rea* of murder in relation to X. You did not intend to kill or cause GBH to Y. In fact, you may not have even noticed that Y was present. Strictly speaking, then, you do not have the *mens rea* of murder in respect of Y and, consequently, you should not be guilty of his murder. However, the law would be absurd and inadequate if it allowed such a defendant to escape criminal liability for his actions simply due to his own incompetence. If he intended to kill X but actually killed Y, he should be punished for the consequence of his actions. The doctrine of transferred malice is employed in such a scenario. The doctrine provides that the defendant's intention in relation to X be transferred to the crime committed against Y. As such, the *actus reus* of the offence against Y is matched by the transferred *mens rea* and the defendant is criminally liable for Y's murder.

The leading authority on the application of the doctrine of transferred malice is *Latimer* (1886) 17 QBD 359.

Q CASE CLOSE-UP

Latimer (1886) 17 QBD 359

During a quarrel, the defendant aimed a blow at a man with his belt. The belt struck the man, but then bounced off and struck a woman who was standing nearby, causing a severe wound to her face. The defendant was convicted of unlawfully and maliciously wounding the woman. On appeal, the Court for Crown Cases Reserved held that the jury's finding that the defendant's striking of the woman was purely accidental and not a consequence that he ought to have expected, did not entitle the defendant to an acquittal. Lord Coleridge stated that:

> It is common knowledge that a man who has an unlawful and malicious intent against another, and, in attempting to carry it out, injures a third person, is guilty of what the law deems malice against the person injured, because the offender is doing an unlawful act, and has that which the judges call general malice, and that is enough.

THINKING POINT

D throws a stone intending to strike X. However, she misses and strikes V, who was standing nearby. Apart from the doctrine of transferred malice, can you think of another basis upon which a conviction for battery could be based?

A more recent example of the doctrine of transferred malice can be seen on the facts of *Gnango* [2011] UKSC 59. In this case, the defendant, Gnango, and another man, X, had been engaged in a gunfight. X fired a shot aimed at Gnango, but the bullet struck and killed a passer-by. By law, X was guilty of the murder of the passer-by since his intention to kill or cause grievous bodily harm to Gnango was transferred to the passer-by. X was clearly the principal offender since he fired the shot that killed the passer-by. In relation to the liability of Gnango, the Supreme Court held that by agreeing to the gunfight, he had aided and abetted X in committing attempted murder; thus he was a secondary party to the attempted murder. The Court took this further and held that the doctrine of transferred malice could be applied in respect of Gnango, so that he was also guilty of the murder of the passer-by, albeit as a secondary party.

However, the law would be too onerous if a defendant were to be held criminally liable for every unintended consequence and, as such, a limitation is placed on the doctrine of transferred malice. For example, imagine that you decide to throw a brick at your friend's window, intending to break it. Let's say that you miss your friend's window and accidentally break the window of his neighbour. We know that under the doctrine of transferred malice, your intention in relation to your friend's window would be transferred and you would consequently be guilty of criminal damage in relation to the neighbour's window. However, imagine further that after breaking the window the brick strikes the neighbour on the head, killing him. Are you also guilty of the neighbour's murder? In such a scenario, where the *actus reus* and *mens rea* relate to different types of offences, the doctrine of transferred malice does not operate and you would not be guilty of murder (unless an intention to kill or cause GBH to the neighbour could be proved, for example by establishing oblique intent in accordance with *Woollin* (see 3.3.2.2)). The inapplicability of the doctrine of transferred malice in such a scenario is illustrated by the case of *Pembliton* (1874) 2 CCR 119, which was distinguished in *Latimer*. In *Pembliton*, the defendant threw a stone at a group of people. He missed and the stone broke a window. The jury found that whereas the defendant had intended to strike the group of people, he had not intended to break the window. His conviction for unlawfully and maliciously damaging property was quashed on appeal as it had not been proved that he had the *mens rea* for the offence in question. On appeal, the Court for Crown Cases Reserved considered that the result may have been different had the jury found that the defendant had been reckless in relation to the damage to the window. It is not always necessary to employ the doctrine of transferred malice in order to secure a conviction. Where the *mens rea* of an offence includes recklessness, a defendant could be convicted if the prosecution prove that he foresaw a risk of the consequence and ran that risk (see the thinking point).

A further authority in which the doctrine of transferred malice was unsuccessfully relied upon is that of *Attorney General's Reference (No. 3 of 1994)* [1998] AC 245. In this case, the House of Lords held that the *mens rea* could only be transferred once and that a double transfer of intent was not permitted.

CASE CLOSE-UP

Attorney General's Reference (No. 3 of 1994) [1998] AC 245

The defendant stabbed his pregnant girlfriend in the abdomen. The knife penetrated the uterus and the abdomen of the foetus. The woman prematurely gave birth to the baby, which died 120 days later. The defendant pleaded guilty to wounding the woman with intent to cause her GBH, contrary to s.18 of the Offences Against the Person Act 1861. After the death of the baby, the defendant was further charged with the murder of the child. The trial judge directed an acquittal, and the case subsequently found its way to the House of Lords, where Lord Mustill reluctantly confirmed the existence of the doctrine of transferred intent. His Lordship displayed a clear lack of enthusiasm for the doctrine and also expressed his dislike of the 'fiction' that an intention to cause GBH is sufficient *mens rea* for murder. Disagreeing with the decision in the Court of Appeal, His Lordship held that a foetus is a separate organism to its mother and that in this case, a murder conviction would not be possible as this would require a double transfer of intent, 'first from the mother to the foetus and then from the foetus to the child as yet unborn'. Lord Hope considered, however, that a conviction for unlawful act manslaughter might be possible in such a case.

 ## Summary

- Intention is a subjective concept. There are two types of intention: direct intent and oblique intent.

- A person has direct intention in relation to a consequence where it is his aim or purpose to achieve that consequence (i.e., where he desires that consequence).

- Where a person does not desire the consequence, but appreciates that it is virtually certain to occur as a result of his actions, this appreciation is evidence from which a jury may find that he intended the consequence: *Woollin* (1999). This is referred to as oblique intent.

- There is now one subjective test of recklessness from *Cunningham* (1957) and *R v G and another* (2003).

- Subjective recklessness requires two questions to be asked: *(a)* did D foresee the possibility of the consequence occurring; and *(b)* was it unreasonable to take the risk?

- The *actus reus* and *mens rea* of an offence must coincide in time in order for the defendant to be guilty of that offence. The continuing act theory might be employed in order to establish coincidence: *Fagan v MPC* (1969). An alternative approach would be the 'single transaction' theory: *Thabo Meli v R* (1954) and *Church* (1966).

- Under the doctrine of transferred malice, the defendant's intention in relation to X can be transferred to Y where he commits the *actus reus* of that same offence in respect of Y: *Latimer* (1886).

- The doctrine does not apply where the *actus reus* committed in respect of Y relates to a different offence: *Pembliton* (1874). Neither does the doctrine of transferred malice extend to a double transfer of intent: *Attorney General's Reference (No. 3 of 1994)* (1998).

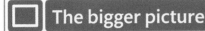 **The bigger picture**

- For a more detailed discussion on the terrorist question posed by Lord Bridge in *Moloney* [1985] 1 AC 905, see Duff (1986), Williams (1987), and Pedain (2003).

- For more information on the reforms to the meaning of intention proposed by the Law Commission, see the Law Commission Report, *Murder, Manslaughter and Infanticide* (Law Com. No. 304, 2006).

- Both intention and recklessness are topics which might feature on an exam paper or as the subject of a coursework assignment.

  For some guidance on how you might approach essay questions on these topics, you should visit the Online Resource Centre.

? Questions

Self-test questions

1. Explain the difference between direct intent and oblique intent.

2. X puts some cyanide in tea that she thinks V is highly likely to drink. If V does drink the tea and dies, does X have sufficient *mens rea* for murder? Support your answer with case law.

3. What is the test for oblique intent? Support your answer with case law.

4. Y plants a bomb in a lecture hall and then sets off the fire alarms. The bomb explodes while the building is being evacuated and V dies. Does Y have the *mens rea* for murder?

5. What is the test for recklessness? Support your answer with case law.

6. Explain the problems with *Caldwell* recklessness.

7. Z thinks that he can shoot an apple on V's head without hitting V. He shoots and hits V in the ear. Is Z reckless? Support your answer with case law.

8. How have the courts sought to circumvent the principle of coincidence of *actus reus* and *mens rea*?

9. Using authorities, explain the doctrine of transferred malice.

   For suggested approaches, please visit the Online Resource Centre.

Exam questions

1. The law on intention has caused much confusion in the courts. To what extent is the law now certain and clear? Refer to case law in your answer.

2. To what extent has the case of *R v G and another* [2003] UKHL 50 clarified the law on recklessness? Refer to case law in your answer.

   For suggested approaches, please visit the Online Resource Centre.

Further reading

Books

Keating, H. M. et al. *Clarkson and Keating: Criminal Law* (8th edn, 2014), London: Sweet & Maxwell

Journal articles

Amirthalingam, K. '*Caldwell* Recklessness is Dead, Long Live *Mens Rea*'s Fecklessness' (2004) 67 MLR 491

Arenson, K. '*Thabo Meli* Revisited: The Pernicious Effects of Result-Driven Decisions' (2013) 77 JCL 41

Coffey, G. 'Codifying the Meaning of "Intention" in the Criminal Law' (2009) 73 JCL 394

Duff, R. A. 'The Obscure Intentions of the House of Lords' [1986] Crim LR 771

Haralambous, N. 'Retreating from *Caldwell*: Restoring Subjectivism' (2003) 153 NLJ 1712

Horder, J. 'Intention in the Criminal Law—A Rejoinder' (1995) 58 MLR 678

Kaverny, M. C. 'Inferring Intention from Foresight' (2004) 120 LQR 81

Kugler, I. 'The Definition of Oblique Intention' (2004) 68 JCL 79

Lacey, N. 'A Clear Concept of Intention: Elusive or Illusory?' (1993) 56 MLR 621

Norrie, A. 'After *Woollin*' [1999] Crim LR 532

Pedain, A. 'Intention and the Terrorist Example' [2003] Crim LR 579

Simester, A. 'Moral Certainty and the Boundaries of Intention' (1996) 16 OJLS 445

Williams, G. 'Oblique Intention' (1987) 46 CLJ 417

Williams, G. 'The *Mens Rea* of Murder: Leave it Alone' (1989) 105 LQR 387

4 Strict, vicarious, and corporate liability

LEARNING OBJECTIVES

By the end of this chapter, you should be able to:

- distinguish between strict liability and absolute liability offences;
- explain the presumption of *mens rea*;
- evaluate the arguments for and against strict liability;
- understand the nature of vicarious liability; and
- understand the nature of corporate liability.

Introduction

Before we look at specific criminal offences in chapters 5 to 12, this chapter explores three special forms of criminal liability: strict liability, vicarious liability, and corporate liability. Where an offence does not require proof of a fault element (i.e., where the prosecution need not prove an element of *mens rea* in order for the defendant to be found liable), the offence is said to be one of strict liability. This goes against the usual requirement (which we explored in chapter 2) of both *actus reus* and *mens rea* elements of an offence to be proved in order for a defendant to be held criminally liable. This chapter will consider when a defendant can be convicted of a criminal offence without proof of an element of *mens rea*, and whether it is right that a defendant can be held criminally liable and punished for an offence when an element of *mens rea* (or his 'guilty mind') has not been established. This chapter also deals with vicarious liability, which is liability imposed upon a defendant for the acts of another person, and corporate liability, which relates to the liability of a company for a criminal offence.

4.1 Strict liability

It is often stated that strict liability offences do not require proof of fault. This simplistic statement does not accurately represent the notion of strict liability, nor does it distinguish between strict and absolute liability. It is more accurate to define strict liability offences as offences which do not require proof of *mens rea* in respect of at least one element of the *actus reus*. However, proof of *mens rea* may be required for some of the elements of the *actus reus*.

The majority of strict liability offences are regulatory offences. They are usually provided for by statute and govern issues such as health and safety, pollution, food safety, road traffic, and licensing. Although some strict liability offences carry the possibility of a sentence of imprisonment upon conviction, many of these offences are relatively minor and may be dealt with by the imposition of a fine. However, there are also some very serious offences of strict liability, such as rape of a child under the age of 13 under s.5 of the Sexual Offences Act 2003. Assault occasioning actual bodily harm (s.47, Offences Against the Person Act 1861) can also be described as a strict liability offence. This is because the only element of *mens rea* required is that relating to the assault or battery and no *mens rea* is required in relation to the degree of harm actually caused (the actual bodily harm).

Strict liability offences permit a defendant to be convicted of a criminal offence without proof of some element of fault. It is important to understand the justifications for imposing criminal liability in the absence of clear blameworthiness. We will take a more detailed look at some of the arguments for and against strict liability offences in 4.1.5.

4.1.1 Absolute liability

Absolute liability is a form of strict liability. Absolute liability offences do not require proof of any *mens rea* element, but are satisfied by proof of the *actus reus* only. Offences of absolute liability are very rare and are often referred to as 'state of affairs' crimes. A defendant will be guilty of such an offence if a certain 'state of affairs' (or set of circumstances) is proved to exist. In addition, an absolute liability offence does not even require proof of a voluntary act, so the fact that the defendant committed the offence involuntarily is irrelevant and no defence.

One example of an offence of absolute liability is drink-driving under s.4(1) of the Road Traffic Act 1988. This offence simply requires a defendant to be driving or attempting to drive a mechanically propelled vehicle in a public place when unfit to drive through drink or drugs. There is no *mens rea* element.

⟩ CROSS REFERENCE

For a discussion of 'state of affairs' offences and the cases of *Larsonneur* and *Winzar v Chief Constable of Kent* refer to 2.6.

In *Larsonneur* (1933) 24 Cr App R 74, the defendant was convicted of being illegally in the country, contrary to the Aliens Order 1920, after she was brought back to the UK in custody. As this is an offence of absolute liability, no proof of her state of mind was necessary. The defendant's involuntariness in entering the UK was also not relevant to her liability. Similarly, in *Winzar v Chief Constable of Kent* (1983), *The Times*, 28 March, the defendant was convicted of being drunk on the highway, contrary to s.12 of the Licensing Act 1872. The defendant had been placed on the highway by the police, but his involuntariness was no defence. The Divisional Court stated that how the defendant came to be on the highway whilst drunk was not relevant to his liability. The offence was committed because he actually was drunk on the highway. The rationale for imposing liability for such an offence was in order to deal with the nuisance of drunkenness in public places.

4.1.2 **Identifying offences of strict liability**

Although the majority of strict liability offences are found in statute, there are some common law offences of strict liability. Examples include contempt of court and libel. There are a greater number of statutory offences of strict liability.

It is often difficult to identify offences of strict liability as Acts of Parliament creating criminal offences do not specify which offences are ones of strict liability. Where the statute uses a *mens rea* word, such as intentionally, recklessly, negligently, knowingly, or wilfully, such that the *mens rea* in the offence is clear, the offence is not one of strict liability. However, where a statute is not clear on the *mens rea* of the offence, it is left to the courts to determine whether the offence is one of strict liability or not. In doing so, the courts have held that there is a general presumption in favour of the requirement of *mens rea* in a criminal offence. This means that criminal offences are presumed to contain *mens rea* elements, even where the statute is silent as to the *mens rea*. However, this presumption may be displaced, rendering the offence one of strict liability.

4.1.3 **The presumption of *mens rea***

The existence of a presumption of *mens rea* was confirmed in the case of *Sherras v De Rutzen* [1895] 1 QB 918. The defendant in this case was a landlord of a pub who served alcohol to a police constable, believing him to be off duty. The police officer was in fact on duty and the defendant was convicted of unlawfully supplying liquor to a constable on duty, contrary to s.16(2) of the Licensing Act 1872. The Divisional Court quashed the defendant's conviction. Wright J stated that:

> There is a presumption that *mens rea*, an evil intention, or a knowledge of the wrongfulness of the act, is an essential ingredient in every offence; but that presumption is liable to be displaced either by the words of the statute creating the offence or by the subject-matter with which it deals, and both must be considered . . .

The presumption in favour of *mens rea* was adopted by the House of Lords in the case of *Sweet v Parsley* [1970] AC 132. The defendant in this case was a schoolmistress. She let out the rooms in a farmhouse and occasionally returned to collect the rent. The defendant was arrested after quantities of cannabis resin were found in the farmhouse. She had no idea that the premises were being used for smoking cannabis. Nevertheless, she was convicted of being concerned in the management of premises used for the purpose of smoking cannabis resin, contrary to s.5(b) of the Dangerous Drugs Act 1965. The House of Lords quashed her conviction and held that this was not a strict liability offence. The House held that the presumption of *mens rea* meant that the wording of the section should be read so as to require *mens rea*. Lord Reid stated that:

> Sometimes the words of the section which creates a particular offence make it clear that *mens rea* is required in one form or another. Such cases are quite frequent. But in a very large number of cases there is no clear indication either way. In such cases there has for centuries been a presumption that Parliament did not intend to make criminals of persons who were in no way blameworthy in what they did. That means that whenever a section is silent as to *mens rea* there is a presumption that, in order to give effect to the will of Parliament, we must read in words appropriate to require *mens rea*.

In particular, the House stated that the word 'purpose' should be read so as to require proof that the defendant's purpose was that the premises be used for smoking cannabis. As the defendant had no such purpose, she could not be guilty of the offence. Lord Reid set out some guidelines to be applied where a statutory provision is silent as to *mens rea*.

Guidelines

1. When a section is silent as to the *mens rea*, there is a presumption that we must read in words appropriate to require *mens rea*.

2. The fact that other sections of the Act expressly require *mens rea* is not in itself sufficient to justify a decision that a section which is silent as to *mens rea* creates a strict liability offence.

3. In the absence of a clear indication in the Act that an offence is intended to be a strict liability offence, it is necessary to go outside the Act and examine all relevant circumstances in order to establish that this must have been the intention of Parliament.

4. If the provision is reasonably capable of two interpretations, that interpretation which is most favourable to the accused must be adopted.

In considering 'all relevant circumstances' to establish the intention of Parliament, the court should take into account the wording of the Act, and the character and seriousness of the mischief which constitutes the offence. Lord Reid held that where the offence is 'truly criminal', it would also be proper to take into account: whether 'the public interest really requires that an innocent person should be prevented from proving his innocence in order that fewer guilty men may escape', and the fact that 'every manifestly unjust conviction made known to the public tends to injure the body politic by undermining public confidence in the justice of the law and of its administration'.

 CASE CLOSE-UP

Gammon (Hong Kong) Ltd v Attorney General of Hong Kong [1985] AC 1

In *Gammon (Hong Kong) Ltd v Attorney General of Hong Kong*, the Privy Council reaffirmed the presumption of *mens rea*. The appellants were a building contractor, project manager, and site agent carrying out works on a site in Hong Kong. Part of a lateral support system collapsed after a deviation from the plans approved by the building authority. The contractor was charged with deviating in a material way from approved plans and with carrying out the works in a manner likely to cause risk of injury or damage. The magistrate dismissed the case and held that actual or constructive knowledge was necessary and had not been proved. The Court of Appeal of Hong Kong remitted the case to the magistrate and held that proof of knowledge was not necessary. The appellants were convicted and appealed to the Privy Council.

The Privy Council reaffirmed the presumption of *mens rea* and Lord Scarman set out guidance to be followed in determining whether an offence is one of strict liability.

Lord Scarman stated that:

(1) there is a presumption of law that *mens rea* is required before a person can be held guilty of a criminal offence;

(2) the presumption is particularly strong where the offence is 'truly criminal' in character;

(3) the presumption applies to statutory offences, and can be displaced only if this is clearly or by necessary implication the effect of the statute;

(4) the only situation in which the presumption can be displaced is where the statute is concerned with an issue of social concern, and public safety is such an issue;

(5) even where a statute is concerned with such an issue, the presumption of *mens rea* stands unless it can also be shown that the creation of strict liability will be effective to promote the objects of the statute by encouraging greater vigilance to prevent the commission of the prohibited act.

Taking into account the fact that the offence is designed to prevent danger to public safety and the need to promote greater vigilance in construction work, the Privy Council held that the offence in this case was one of strict liability.

The presumption of *mens rea* was more recently confirmed by the House of Lords in the cases of *B (A minor) v DPP* [2000] 2 AC 428 and *K* [2002] 1 AC 462. In *B (A minor) v DPP*, the defendant was a 15-year-old boy who repeatedly asked a 13-year-old girl to perform oral sex on him. He was charged with inciting a girl under the age of 14 to commit an act of gross indecency, contrary to s.1(1) of the Indecency with Children Act 1960. He maintained that he honestly believed that she was over 14. At first instance, the offence was held to be one of strict liability in respect of the complainant's age, so the defendant pleaded guilty and appealed. The House of Lords allowed the appeal and held that the defendant's state of mind, i.e., his honest belief that the complainant was over 14, was relevant to liability. The House held that the presumption of *mens rea* required that even where the statute was silent as to *mens rea*, *mens rea* would have to be proved unless Parliament indicated otherwise, either expressly or by implication.

The House took into consideration the nature of the offence as a serious sexual offence which carries a severe penalty of up to 10 years' imprisonment. Lord Nicholls stated:

> The more serious the offence, the greater is the weight to be attached to the presumption, because the more severe is the punishment and the graver the stigma which accompany a conviction.

Thus, the seriousness of the offence required that *mens rea* be established before liability could be imposed. Lord Steyn also greatly emphasised the importance of the presumption of *mens rea* by deeming it a constitutional principle.

This House of Lords' decision conflicted with the older authority of *Prince* (1875) LR 2 CCR 154. In this case, the Court for Crown Cases Reserved held that the defendant's mistake as to a girl's age was not relevant. The defendant was convicted of taking a girl under the age of 16 out of her father's possession against his will, contrary to s.55 of the Offences Against the Person Act 1861. The defendant had reasonable grounds for believing that the girl was 18 years old. However, this was held not to be a valid defence. There was no requirement of *mens rea* in respect of the girl's age, so knowledge that she was under 16 was not a requirement of the offence. Although it has not been expressly overruled, this decision would appear to be incorrect in light of the House of Lords' decision in *B (A minor) v DPP* (2000).

> ## 🔍 CASE CLOSE-UP
>
> ### *K* [2002] 1 AC 462
>
> In the case of *K*, the House of Lords affirmed the decision in *B (A minor) v DPP* (2000). *K* involved the conviction of a defendant for indecent assault, contrary to s.14(1) of the Sexual Offences Act 1956 (which has since been repealed by the Sexual Offences Act 2003). The complainant was a 14-year-old girl. The defendant claimed that she had consented to the touching and that she had informed him that she was 16 years old. Under s.14(2) of the Act, a girl under 16 years of age could not consent to indecent assault.
>
> The Court of Appeal upheld the defendant's conviction and held that this was an offence of strict liability in respect of the complainant's age.
>
> However, the House of Lords overruled the Court of Appeal and held that the presumption of *mens rea* required the prosecution to prove that the defendant had no genuine belief that the girl was 16 or over.
>
> Once again, the serious nature of this offence and the severity of the penalty upon conviction led to the House affirming the presumption of *mens rea*.
>
> It should be noted that the Sexual Offences Act 2003 has superseded these decisions. This Act created a new framework of sexual offences, thus the offence of indecent assault no longer exists.

In *Brown (Richard)* [2013] UKSC 43, the Supreme Court reiterated that the presumption of *mens rea* in determining criminal liability was both a 'constitutional principle' and 'a strong one' which could only be displaced by 'clear statutory language or unmistakably necessary implication' (at [26]). Lord Kerr further acknowledged that the presumption was even stronger in cases where the offence is '"truly criminal" and carries a heavy penalty or a substantial social stigma' (at [26]). The Court applied the decision in *B (A minor) v DPP* in relation to the offence in Northern Ireland of unlawful carnal knowledge of a girl under the age of 14 under the Criminal Law Amendment Acts (Northern Ireland) 1885–1923. The Court held that while the presumption was a strong one and was not easily displaced, the legislation clearly intended to impose strict liability. Consequently, there was no requirement of proof of any *mens rea* of the defendant in relation to the age of the complainant. The Court was keen to emphasise that the policy approach of protecting young females by ensuring that the defendant cannot rely on a defence of reasonable belief has been 'unswerving' (at [37]).

4.1.4 **Factors to be considered**

4.1.4.1 **'Truly criminal' vs regulatory offences**

Gammon (Hong Kong) Ltd v Attorney General of Hong Kong (1985) established that 'truly criminal' offences are more likely to require proof of *mens rea*. Regulatory offences are more likely to be offences of strict liability than 'truly criminal' offences. The seriousness of the offence charged and the severity of the penalty imposed upon conviction are important considerations in determining whether an offence is one of strict liability (see figure 4.1). This has been followed in the later cases of *B (A minor) v DPP* (2000) and *K* (2002). In *Sheldrake v DPP*

Figure 4.1 'Truly criminal' offences vs regulatory offences

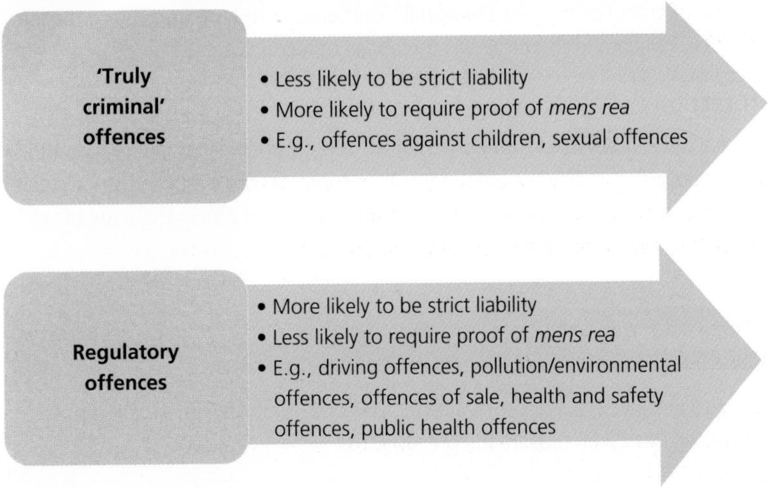

'Truly criminal' offences
- Less likely to be strict liability
- More likely to require proof of *mens rea*
- E.g., offences against children, sexual offences

Regulatory offences
- More likely to be strict liability
- Less likely to require proof of *mens rea*
- E.g., driving offences, pollution/environmental offences, offences of sale, health and safety offences, public health offences

[2005] 1 AC 264, Lord Bingham held that the more serious the criminal offence and the more severe the potential sentence, the less likely it is that the presumption in favour of *mens rea* will be displaced, and in *Brown (Richard)* (2013), Lord Kerr reiterated that 'where the statutory offence is grave or "truly criminal" and carries a heavy penalty or a substantial social stigma, the case is enhanced against implying that *mens rea* of any ingredient of the offence is not needed' (at [26]).

4.1.4.2 **Social concern**

Regulatory offences are more likely to be offences of strict liability. According to *Gammon (Hong Kong) Ltd v Attorney General of Hong Kong* (1985), the presumption of *mens rea* can only be displaced if this is clearly or by implication the effect of the statute and the statute is one which deals with an issue of social concern.

Protection of children

The policy consideration of protecting children in relation to offences of sexual activity with a young girl was recently reaffirmed by the Supreme Court in *Brown (Richard)* (2013). Lord Kerr held that this policy approach had been 'unswerving' historically. His Lordship referred to a comment made by Baroness Hale in *R v G* [2009] AC 92 in which Her Ladyship stated that the defendant must take responsibility for what he chooses to do and so he bears the risk if he has sexual intercourse with someone who is younger than he thinks she is. The case of *R v G* involved the offence of rape of a child under the age of 13 under s.5 of the Sexual Offences Act 2003. The House of Lords held that this is a strict liability offence: while the offence requires proof of intentional penetration, no other elements of *mens rea* are required. Thus, it is no defence to say that the defendant believed the child to be over the age of 13: *R v G* [2009] 1 AC 92. The rationale for making this offence one of strict liability is clearly the protection of children.

▶ CROSS-REFERENCE

For a more detailed discussion of *R v G* [2009] 1 AC 92 see 8.6.1.1 and 8.6.1.2.

Alcohol abuse

For instance, *Cundy v Le Cocq* (1884) 13 QBD 207 was a case involving the sale of alcohol to a person who was drunk. The defendant was the landlord of a pub. He was convicted of selling intoxicating liquor to a person who was drunk, contrary to s.13 of the Licensing Act 1872. The defendant's claim that he did not know that the person was drunk was not held to be relevant. The offence was one of strict liability. The Divisional Court considered the purpose of the statute. The issue of social concern in this case was the abuse of alcohol.

Consumer protection

Similarly, in the case of *Smedleys Ltd v Breed* [1974] AC 839, a small caterpillar was found in one of millions of tins of peas sold by the defendant. The House of Lords imposed strict liability on the defendant after a prosecution under the Food and Drugs Act 1955. The issue of social concern in this case was the protection of consumers.

THINKING POINT

Is the decision in *Smedleys Ltd v Breed* a satisfactory one? Should liability be imposed where the defendant has taken reasonable precautions?

Although the House of Lords justified their decision on the basis of consumer protection, this authority imposes an extremely heavy burden on the manufacturer or supplier of food products. In order to avoid liability, the defendant would have had to inspect every single pea, and even then there is no certainty that the caterpillar would have been found and the incident prevented. It is surely not practicable to expect a defendant to go to such lengths.

Misuse of drugs

The first case on strict liability to be considered by the House of Lords was *Warner v Metropolitan Police Commissioner* [1969] 2 AC 256. The defendant was found in possession of a box containing a controlled drug. He was convicted of being in unlawful possession of a controlled drug, contrary to s.1(1) of the Drugs (Prevention of Misuse) Act 1964. The defendant knew that he was in possession of the box, but claimed that he thought it contained perfume. This offence was held to be an offence of strict liability. Thus, the prosecution did not have to prove that the defendant knew that he was in possession of a controlled drug. It was enough that he knew he was in possession of the box and he knew that the box contained something. The issue of social concern in this case was the prevention of misuse of drugs.

Road safety

The offence of driving or being in charge of a motor vehicle whilst over the prescribed alcohol limit, contrary to s.5 of the Road Traffic Act 1988, is also an offence of strict liability. This was confirmed in the case of *DPP v Harper* [1997] 1 WLR 1406. The issue of social concern here is maintaining road safety and the protection of other road users.

Prevention of pollution

In the case of *Alphacell Ltd v Woodward* [1972] AC 824, the appellants were convicted of causing or knowingly permitting polluted matter to enter a river, contrary to s.2(1)(a) of the Rivers (Prevention of Pollution) Act 1951. The appellant pumped large quantities of a polluted effluent into a tank near a river. The pumps became blocked and the tank overflowed, causing the effluent to enter the river without the knowledge of the appellants. The House of Lords upheld the appellants' conviction on the basis that strict liability was justified here for the prevention of pollution and there was a need to encourage greater vigilance. More recent examples of a similar rationale being employed can be found in the Court of Appeal case of *Ezeemo (Godwin Chukwnaenya) v R* [2013] Env LR 15 and the decision of the Queen's Bench Division of the High Court in *R (on the application of Thames Water Utilities Ltd) v Bromley Magistrates' Court* [2013] Env LR 25. In *Ezeemo (Godwin Chukwnaenya) v R*, the defendant and others were convicted of a number of offences of transporting hazardous waste to Nigeria, a country which was not a member of the Organisation for Economic Co-operation and Development, contrary to regulation 23 of the Transfrontier Shipment of Waste Regulations 2007. The Court of Appeal held that the offences were strict liability offences: 'the offences created by the regulations are truly regulatory in nature, not aimed at the public in general but at those who operate in the business of collection and disposal of waste. They are designed to protect the environment and public health' (at [75]). In *R (on the application of Thames Water Utilities Ltd) v Bromley Magistrates' Court*, the defendant was a sewerage undertaker. He sought to judicially review his conviction in the magistrates' court for offences relating to the escape of sewage from his network into surrounding properties, contrary to s.33(1)(a) of the Environmental Protection Act 1990. It was held that the presumption of *mens rea* was displaced by an issue of social concern, namely 'the protection of human health and the environment' (at [49]).

Underage gambling

The issue of social concern in the case of *London Borough of Harrow v Shah and Shah* [1999] 3 All ER 302 was underage gambling. The defendants were charged with selling a National Lottery ticket to a boy under 16 years of age, contrary to s.13(1)(c) of the National Lottery Act 1993. The Divisional Court did not regard this as a 'truly criminal' offence, despite the sentence of 2 years' imprisonment that it carries. It was held to be a strict liability offence.

4.1.4.3 **Encouraging greater vigilance**

The guidelines in *Gammon (Hong Kong) Ltd v Attorney General of Hong Kong* (1985) also require that before the presumption of *mens rea* is displaced, 'the creation of strict liability will be effective to promote the objects of the statute by encouraging greater vigilance to prevent the commission of the prohibited act'. This was echoed by the High Court in *R (on the application of Thames Water Utilities Ltd) v Bromley Magistrates' Court*, in which Gross LJ held that strict liability would be effective '"to promote the objects of the statute by encouraging greater vigilance" to prevent the escape of sewerage from the network'. While acknowledging that technical faults may occur from time to time in even the best systems, Gross LJ stated that 'strict liability will serve to concentrate minds at senior management levels' (at [50]).

4.1.4.4 **No-fault defences**

Where an offence provides for a defence of 'due diligence', the offence is one of strict liability. Where it is a defence to show 'due diligence', the defendant must prove that he has taken reasonable care in preventing the commission of the offence by acting with due diligence.

THINKING POINT

Before reading the next section, consider what you think are the advantages and disadvantages of strict liability.

4.1.5 Justifying strict liability

Strict liability is a controversial issue. The imposition of criminal liability without proof of *mens rea* requires justification. The following paragraphs deal with the arguments for and against strict liability.

4.1.5.1 Arguments for strict liability

Protection of the public

The imposition of strict liability is necessary for the protection of the public. It generally relates to regulatory offences, encouraging greater vigilance and safety, and deterring incompetence and unsafe behaviour. For example, see *Ezeemo (Godwin Chukwnaenya) v R* [2013] Env LR 15.

Easier to prove

Strict liability offences are easier to prosecute as they do not require the prosecution to spend time and effort proving the *mens rea* element.

Small penalty

As most strict liability offences are regulatory only and not 'truly criminal', they carry only a minor penalty of, perhaps, a fine. The imposition of strict liability for imprisonable offences is rare and, as such, there is generally no danger of sacrificing an individual's liberty without proof of *mens rea*.

4.1.5.2 Arguments against strict liability

Violation of 'actus non facit reum nisi mens sit rea'

Criminal liability generally requires proof of both an *actus reus* and a *mens rea*. One of the fundamental principles of criminal liability is derived from the Latin maxim *actus non facit reum nisi mens sit rea*. This means 'an act does not make a man guilty of a crime unless his mind be also guilty': as stated by Lord Hailsham in *Haughton v Smith* [1975] AC 476. Strict liability, which does not require proof of *mens rea* in respect of at least one element of *actus reus*, surely violates this principle.

Punishing reasonable behaviour

The imposition of strict liability can be unjust and contrary to principles of fairness. In some situations, a defendant who has taken all reasonably practicable steps to avoid liability may be strictly liable. It is questionable whether it is in the interests of justice to convict and punish a defendant who has acted reasonably. Consider the case of *Smedleys Ltd v Breed* (1974) at 4.1.4.2. Thus, the deterrence argument put forward to justify imposing strict liability must also be doubted.

Stigma of a conviction

Although the penalty may be small in most cases of strict liability, a defendant may still be 'punished' by the stigma which goes with being convicted of a criminal offence. In some cases, such a conviction may also damage the reputation of the defendant, potentially also affecting his livelihood.

Alternatives to strict liability

As an alternative to imposing criminal liability in the absence of fault, offences could contain a requirement of negligence. This would ensure that a defendant is only convicted if he fails to meet the objective standard of the reasonable man. Another possibility is that statutes contain a defence of due diligence (discussed at 4.1.4.4). Either of these alternatives would remove some of the harshness of strict liability.

4.2 Vicarious liability

Generally, a person may only be held liable for their own acts. Vicarious liability is an exception to this, as it imposes liability on the defendant for the acts or omissions of another person. Vicarious liability is prevalent in the law of tort: employers can be held liable for any torts committed by their employees in the course of their employment. However, although the concept of vicarious liability applies in civil law, it does not usually extend to criminal law. There are two exceptions to this. A person may be criminally liable for the acts or omissions of another under: *(a)* the delegation principle, or *(b)* the attribution principle.

4.2.1 **The delegation principle**

Under this principle, a person may be held criminally liable for the acts of another person where he delegated duties imposed on him by law to that other person. In order for the delegation principle to apply, there must be a complete delegation of authority to another person: *Vane v Yiannopoullos* [1965] AC 486.

An example of the application of the delegation principle is the case of *Allen v Whitehead* [1930] 1 KB 211. The defendant in this case was the occupier and licensee of a café which he employed a manager to run. He instructed the manager not to permit any prostitutes to gather on the premises. However, a number of prostitutes did gather at the premises and the defendant was convicted of knowingly permitting prostitutes to remain in a place of refreshment, contrary to s.44 of the Metropolitan Police Act 1839. The defendant had visited the café once or twice a week and there was nothing to suggest that the women gathered on the premises in his presence. The Divisional Court held that the defendant was guilty of the offence and that his ignorance was no defence. The defendant had delegated management of the café and the responsibility of ensuring that prostitutes did not gather on the premises to the manager. The *actus reus* of the offence was present because the women were allowed to gather on the premises. The *mens rea* of the manager, who knew that the women were prostitutes, was imputed to the defendant.

4.2.2 **The attribution principle**

Under this principle, an employer may be held liable for the acts of his employee. This principle applies to strict liability offences. The unlawful act of the employee may be attributed to the employer. An example is in the case of *London Borough of Harrow v Shah and Shah* (1999) (discussed at 4.1.4.2). The defendants in this case were held liable for the actions of their employee in selling a National Lottery ticket to a person under the age of 16. The defendants had done everything that they reasonably could to ensure that they complied with the law. However, the act of their employee was attributed to them, resulting in their liability.

4.3 Corporate liability

A corporation (such as a limited company, whether public or not) has legal personality independent of its members (such as the board of directors, managers, etc.). A corporation may sue or be sued in its own name, it may enter into a contract, and commit a tort or a criminal offence.

Corporate liability for criminal offences has been topical in recent years in light of various disasters, such as the Southall train crash and the Zeebrugge disaster. Although a company may be held vicariously liable for a strict liability offence in the same way that an employer is held vicariously liable for the acts of his employee, it is difficult to envisage how a corporation can commit the *actus reus* and *mens rea* required for other criminal offences and be punished accordingly.

A corporation may be convicted of a criminal offence through the application of the identification doctrine. Liability for a criminal offence must be found against an individual on the board of directors or senior management in order for the corporation to be convicted of an offence. In *HL Bolton (Engineering) Co Ltd v PJ Graham and Sons Ltd* [1957] 1 QB 159, Lord Denning explained that:

> A company may in many ways be likened to a human body. It has a brain and nerve centre which controls what it does. It also has hands which hold the tools and act in accordance with directions from the centre. Some of the people in the company are mere servants and agents who are nothing more than hands to do the work and cannot be said to represent the mind or will. Others are directors and managers who represent the directing mind and will of the company, and control what it does. The state of mind of these managers is the state of mind of the company and is treated by the law as such.

It is not enough that a subordinate employee had the *actus reus* and *mens rea* of the offence. In *Tesco Supermarkets Ltd v Nattrass* [1972] AC 153, the House of Lords held that the company could be liable for criminal offences committed by those individuals who control the company, whereas those committed by mere servants (employees) could not be (except by vicarious liability: see 4.2). Lord Reid stated that:

> A living person has a mind which can have knowledge or intention or be negligent and he has hands to carry out his intentions. A corporation has none of these: it must act through living persons, though not always one or the same person. Then the person who acts is not speaking or acting for the company. He is acting as the company and his mind which directs his acts is the mind of the company. There is no question of the company being vicariously liable. He is not acting as a servant, representative, agent or delegate. He is an embodiment of the company or, one could say, he hears and speaks through the persona of the company, within his appropriate sphere, and his mind is the mind of the company. If it is a guilty mind then that guilt is the guilt of the company.

> **CROSS REFERENCE**
>
> Refer to chapter 6 on involuntary manslaughter for a more detailed discussion of corporate manslaughter and the Corporate Manslaughter and Corporate Homicide Act 2007.

However, despite many public disasters over the past 30 years, there have been few successful prosecutions against corporations. Recommendations for reform aimed at holding corporations to account for negligence which leads to loss of life have culminated in the enactment of the Corporate Manslaughter and Corporate Homicide Act 2007, which came into force on 6 April 2008. The Act abolished the common law liability of organisations for gross negligence manslaughter and created a new offence of corporate manslaughter in England and Wales.

Summary

- A strict liability offence is an offence which does not require proof of at least one *mens rea* element.

- An offence of absolute liability is an offence which does not require proof of any fault, and does not require that the act be voluntary.

- There is a presumption that every criminal offence requires proof of *mens rea* before a defendant can be convicted. This is so even where the statute is silent as to the *mens rea*. The presumption is particularly strong where the offence is 'truly criminal' in nature: *Gammon (Hong Kong) Ltd v Attorney General of Hong Kong* (1985).

- In relation to statutory offences, the presumption can only be displaced where this is clearly or implicitly the effect of the statute. The statute must deal with an issue of social concern (e.g., public safety). Strict liability must be necessary to promote the aims of the statute by encouraging greater vigilance to prevent the prohibited act: *Gammon (Hong Kong) Ltd v Attorney General of Hong Kong* (1985).

- Strict liability is a controversial area and there are a number of arguments both in favour of strict liability and against it.

- Vicarious liability imposes liability on the defendant for the acts or omissions of another person.

- Under the delegation principle, a person may be held criminally liable for the acts of another person where he delegated duties imposed on him by law to that other person.

- Under the attribution principle, an employer may be held liable for the acts of his employee.

- A corporation is regarded as a separate person in law and can be convicted of a criminal offence under the identification doctrine: *Tesco Supermarkets Ltd v Nattrass* (1972).

- The Corporate Manslaughter and Corporate Homicide Act 2007 created a new offence of corporate manslaughter. This came into force on 6 April 2008.

The bigger picture

- For a more detailed discussion of *R v G* [2009] 1 AC 92 and strict liability in relation to child sex offences, you should refer to 8.6.1.2 for a case close-up box and extracts from the case.

- For a more detailed discussion of corporate liability in the context of corporate manslaughter, you should refer to 6.4.

- If you are answering a coursework question or exam question on strict liability, you might want to read the following authorities:

  Woodrow (1846) 153 ER 907 (Exch)

  Lim Chin Aik v The Queen [1963] AC 160, PC

  Pharmaceutical Society of Great Britain v Storkwain [1986] 2 All ER 635, HL

  Muhamad v R [2003] 2 WLR 1050, CA

? Questions

Self-test questions

1. Explain the difference between strict liability and absolute liability.

2. Give examples of absolute liability offences.

3. When may the presumption of *mens rea* be displaced? Cite case law.

4. What types of offences are usually strict liability offences? Give examples.

5. What issues of social concern might an offence of strict liability deal with? Cite case law.

6. Consider the advantages and disadvantages of strict liability.

7. When may a person be vicariously liable for a criminal offence?

8. What is the delegation principle? Cite an authority as an example.

9. What is the attribution principle? Cite an authority as an example.

10. What is the identification doctrine? Cite an authority.

 For suggested approaches, please visit the Online Resource Centre.

Exam questions

1. To what extent, if at all, do you think that strict liability is justified?

2. Section 1 of the Law Library (Modernisation) Act 2012 (fictitious) provides that it is a criminal offence 'to be in possession of a hardback or paperback law textbook, law report or law journal'.

   Ellie, a librarian, removes all law books from the library in preparation for a library inspection. Paul, a law lecturer, gives her a wrapped present, which she places on her desk, planning to open it later. The present is a limited edition of *Smith and Hogan: Criminal Law*.

   Discuss Ellie's criminal liability.

 For suggested approaches, please visit the Online Resource Centre.

≡ Further reading

Books

Gobert, J. and Punch, M. *Rethinking Corporate Crime* (2003), London: Butterworths LexisNexis

Matthews, R. *Blackstone's Guide to the Corporate Manslaughter and Corporate Homicide Act 2007* (2008), Oxford: Oxford University Press

Simester, A. (ed.) *Appraising Strict Liability* (2005), Oxford: Oxford University Press

Wells, C. *Corporations and Criminal Responsibility* (2001), Oxford: Oxford University Press

Journal articles

Campbell, K. 'New Directions in Strict Liability' (2000) 11 Kings College Law Journal 261

Horder, J. 'Strict Liability, Statutory Construction, and the Spirit of Liberty' (2002) 118 LQR 458

Manchester, C. 'Knowledge, Due Diligence and Strict Liability in Regulatory Offences' [2006] Crim LR 213

Ormerod, D. and Taylor, R. 'The Corporate Manslaughter and Corporate Homicide Act 2007' [2008] Crim LR 589

Salako, S. 'Strict Criminal Liability: A Violation of the Convention?' (2006) 70 JCL 531

Stanton-Ife, J. 'Strict Liability: Stigma and Regret' (2007) 27 OJLS 151

5 Murder and voluntary manslaughter

Introduction

Homicide is the killing of another human being. 'Homicide' is an umbrella term which encompasses both lawful and unlawful killings. Homicide may be lawful where it is justified, for example where a person kills using reasonable force in self-defence (see 14.2). Unlawful acts of homicide include criminal offences such as murder, manslaughter, causing death by dangerous driving, and infanticide. Murder is the most serious offence of homicide. Manslaughter is a less serious offence of homicide. There are two types of manslaughter: voluntary manslaughter and involuntary manslaughter. The difference between these types of manslaughter will be explored in this chapter.

This chapter and the next chapter cover some of the main criminal offences relating to unlawful homicide. In this chapter, we will explore the elements of murder and the partial defences which reduce a defendant's liability to voluntary manslaughter (with particular focus on loss of control and diminished responsibility), as well as the offence of infanticide. We will consider questions such as: Is a defendant who kills someone who is terminally ill in order to end their suffering guilty of murder? Will a husband who snaps after finding his wife in bed with another man, killing both his wife and her lover, be able to rely on the partial defence of loss of control?

In chapter 6, we will explore the three main types of involuntary manslaughter: unlawful act manslaughter, gross negligence manslaughter, and reckless manslaughter, as well as the offence of corporate manslaughter.

5.1 The offences of unlawful homicide

It is important to understand the relationship between murder, voluntary manslaughter, and involuntary manslaughter (figure 5.1). All offences of homicide share a common *actus reus*: that the defendant unlawfully causes the death of another human being. Murder is the most serious of these offences and requires the highest form of *mens rea*: an intention to kill or cause GBH. Where a defendant has both the *actus reus* and *mens rea* for murder, but also has one of three special partial defences available to him, his liability for murder is reduced to that of manslaughter. This type of manslaughter (where the defendant did intend to kill or cause GBH) is termed voluntary manslaughter. The special defences which will reduce a defendant's liability in this way are: loss of control, diminished responsibility, and suicide pact. Involuntary manslaughter arises where the defendant unlawfully causes the death of the victim, but does not have the *mens rea* for murder, i.e., he has no intention to kill or cause GBH (figure 5.2).

Figure 5.1 Relationship between murder, voluntary manslaughter, and involuntary manslaughter

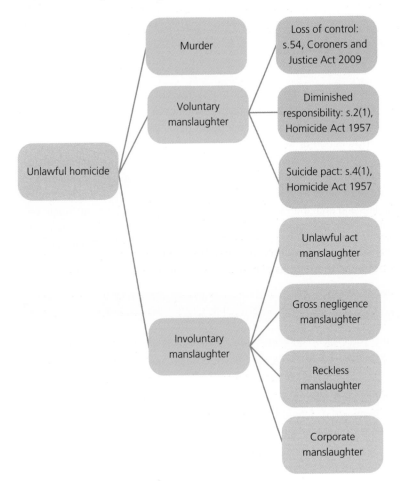

Figure 5.2 The elements of murder, voluntary manslaughter, and involuntary manslaughter

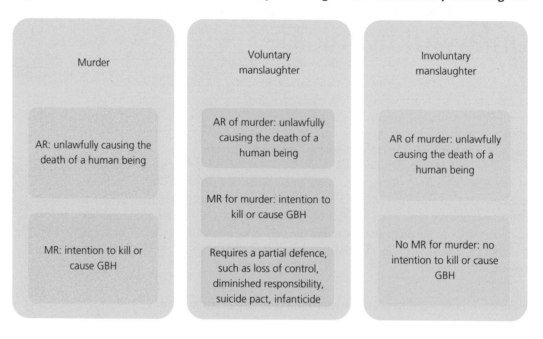

5.2 Murder

Murder is a common law offence. It is one of the most serious offences in our criminal justice system. Its seriousness is reflected in the mandatory sentence of life imprisonment imposed upon offenders. Previously, murder carried the death penalty, but this was abolished by s.1(1) of the Murder (Abolition of the Death Penalty) Act 1965. Under the current system, when a defendant is convicted of murder, the sentencing judge will impose the mandatory sentence of life imprisonment. The judge will also set a 'tariff', which is the minimum term that the defendant must serve in prison. After this period, the defendant will continue to serve in prison unless and until the Parole Board considers the defendant to no longer be a danger to the public. Once the defendant has been released, he will remain 'on licence' for the rest of his life. This means that the defendant can be recalled to prison if he commits a further offence.

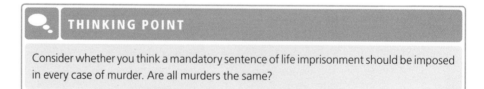

THINKING POINT

Consider whether you think a mandatory sentence of life imprisonment should be imposed in every case of murder. Are all murders the same?

While murder carries a mandatory sentence of life imprisonment, manslaughter carries a discretionary life sentence. A defendant who is convicted of manslaughter may be given a maximum sentence of life imprisonment; this is merely a maximum sentence and is not a mandatory one.

Murder carries a higher penalty than manslaughter to reflect the severity of the offence. However, in 2013 the European Court of Human Rights considered the lawfulness of using whole life sentences. In *Vinter others v UK* [2013] ECHR 645, the Grand Chamber of the European Court of Human Rights ruled that a whole life sentence would breach Article 3 (inhuman or degrading treatment or punishment) of the European Convention on Human Rights if there was no possibility that the sentence might be reviewed or reduced. In *Hutchinson v UK* [2015] ECHR 111, the European Court of Human Rights held that there was no violation of Article 3 in respect of the applicant's whole life sentence because domestic law now provided the possibility of review of such a sentence. The European Court referred to the Court of Appeal decision in *Newell; McLoughlin* [2014] EWCA Crim 188 in which the Court of Appeal stated that a whole life sentence might be reviewed by the Secretary of State in exceptional circumstances. Thus, in *Hutchinson v UK*, the European Court of Human Rights was satisfied that the Court of Appeal had sufficiently clarified the law since *Vinter v UK*; however, Hutchinson will now appeal to the Grand Chamber of the Court and we await the outcome of that appeal.

5.2.1 Definition

Murder is committed when a defendant unlawfully causes the death of a person with an intention to kill or cause GBH. The classic definition of murder is given by the English jurist Sir Edward Coke (Coke, 3 Inst. 47):

> Murder is when a man of sound memory, and of the age of discretion, unlawfully killeth within any county of the realm any reasonable creature in rerum natura under the king's peace, with malice aforethought, either expressed by the party or implied by law, [so as the party wounded, or hurt, etc. die of the wound or hurt, etc. within a year and a day after the same].

Using Coke's definition, the *actus reus* of murder is unlawfully causing the death of a human being under the Queen's peace. The *mens rea* is 'malice aforethought'; according to the case of *Vickers* [1957] 2 QB 664, this means an intention to kill or cause GBH (see 5.2.3 and table 5.1). The section of the quotation in square brackets has now been repealed (see 5.2.2.5).

5.2.2 *Actus reus*

The *actus reus* of murder is unlawfully causing the death of a human being under the Queen's peace. This *actus reus* is common to all forms of homicide.

Table 5.1 The elements of murder

Murder

Actus reus	*Mens rea*
• unlawfully	• with malice aforethought (intention to kill or cause GBH)
• causes death	
• of a human being	
• under the Queen's peace	

5.2.2.1 Unlawfully

The offence of murder requires that the death of the victim is unlawfully caused. Where the defendant lawfully causes the death of another person, he will not be guilty of a criminal offence.

> ### THINKING POINT
>
> Consider when a killing might be justified by law.

A killing will be lawful where it is justified. For instance, where the defendant kills another person whilst acting in self-defence or in the defence or another, the killing will be lawful. The defence of self-defence negates the unlawfulness of the killing. Authority seems to suggest that a killing may also be rendered lawful through the defence of necessity which justifies the killing. Necessity was relied upon to this effect in the case of *Re A (Children) (Conjoined Twins: Surgical Separation)* [2001] Fam 147. This case required the court to decide upon the legality of an operation to separate conjoined twins which would inevitably lead to the death of one of the twins. The defence of necessity was relied upon by Brooke LJ to justify the operation, and, thus, the killing. However, it is important to note that, whilst the other judges in the Court of Appeal accepted the arguments relating to necessity, their Lordships adopted different reasoning in reaching their conclusions. Thus, their judgments are not clearly based upon necessity.

> **CROSS REFERENCE**
>
> Refer to 14.4 for further details on *Re A (Children) (Conjoined Twins: Surgical Separation)* (2001).

Equally, where a patient requiring medical treatment dies as a result of a surgical procedure, the death will not be unlawful. The bona fide surgical procedure will negate the unlawfulness of any death which results.

5.2.2.2 Causes death

The prosecution must prove that the defendant caused the death of the victim. The usual rules of causation apply. This means that the prosecution must prove that the defendant was both the factual cause and the legal cause of the victim's death. The question of whether the defendant had caused the death of the victim is a question for the jury to determine (*Clarke and Morabir* [2013] EWCA Crim 162 at [67]).

> **CROSS REFERENCE**
>
> Refer to 2.5 for a more detailed explanation of the rules on causation and intervening events which break the chain of causation.

The test for factual causation is the 'but for' test: *White* [1910] 2 KB 124. The prosecution must establish that but for the defendant's act or omission, the death would not have occurred. Factual causation is usually easy to prove. The prosecution must also prove that the defendant was the legal cause of the victim's death. The defendant's conduct need not be the sole cause of death, but it must make a significant contribution to the death of the victim: *Pagett* (1963) 76 Cr App R 279. The defendant will be the legal cause of death if his act or omission was a more than minimal cause of the prohibited consequence (*Cato* [1976] 1 WLR 110), or if it was the 'operating and substantial cause' of death (*Smith* [1959] 2 QB 35). Where this is the case, the defendant will be the legal cause of death, unless there is a *novus actus interveniens* which breaks the chain of causation. If an intervening act does break the chain of causation, the defendant will be absolved of liability for the death of the victim.

5.2.2.3 Reasonable creature in being

The defendant will only be guilty of murder (or manslaughter) if the victim is a reasonable creature *in rerum natura* (or a reasonable creature in being). This means that the victim must be a human being in order to be capable of being murdered. It is clearly not possible to be guilty of the murder of an animal, such as a dog. The killing of an animal would usually amount to criminal damage, contrary to s.1(1) of the Criminal Damage Act 1971, provided it could be shown that the animal was property which belonged to another.

⟩ CROSS REFERENCE

Refer to 10.6 for a discussion of the elements of criminal damage.

The issue of whether the victim is a reasonable creature in being is usually not problematic; difficulty only arises at each of the ends of the spectrum of life. The law needs to be clear on when an individual becomes, and ceases to be, a human being.

According to the case of *Poulton* (1832) 5 C & P 329, a baby is a reasonable creature in being when the whole body of the child is brought alive into the world. Once the child has completely left the mother's womb and has lived outside the womb, it is capable of being a victim of murder. The case of *Reeves* (1839) 9 C & P 25 further adds that the child is in being even if the umbilical cord has not been cut. A foetus in its mother's womb is not a reasonable creature in being and, thus, is not capable of being murdered. This is supported by the case of *Attorney General's Reference (No. 3 of 1994)* [1998] AC 245 (see 3.7.2 for the facts of this case). There are specific offences which cover the unlawful killing of a foetus which is in the mother's womb. Where an abortion is unlawfully procured outside the scope of the terms of the Abortion Act 1967, the offence of procuring a miscarriage is available under s.58 of the Offences Against the Person Act 1861. Another offence of child destruction under s.1 of the Infant Life (Preservation) Act 1929, applies to the destruction of a foetus which was capable of being born alive.

At the other end of the spectrum, the law does not define 'death'. A patient who is on a life-support machine is a reasonable creature in being and capable of being murdered: *Malcherek; Steel* [1981] 2 All ER 422. This raises the question of whether a doctor is criminally liable if he turns off his patient's life-support machine, resulting in the death of the patient. If switching off the machine is a positive act, then the doctor is criminally liable for the death of the patient, but if it is deemed to be an omission to act, it is lawful. The House of Lords decided this issue in the case of *Airedale NHS Trust v Bland* [1993] 2 WLR 316.

⟩ CROSS REFERENCE

Refer to 2.4.3 for the facts of *Airedale NHS Trust v Bland* [1993] 2 WLR 316.

The House of Lords held that switching off the life-support machine amounted to an omission rather than a positive act, so a doctor would not be criminally liable for the patient's death by withdrawing treatment. This decision is largely a policy one to avoid the imposition of liability upon doctors for the withdrawal of treatment. However, if a doctor deliberately performs a positive act in relation to a patient on a life-support machine, such as administering a lethal drug, in order to end the patient's life, the doctor would be liable for the murder of the patient. The patient is a reasonable creature in being and capable of being murdered.

5.2.2.4 Under the Queen's peace

The killing must take place under the Queen's peace in order for the offence of murder to be satisfied. Where the defendant kills an enemy combatant during times of war, he has a defence to a charge of murder.

5.2.2.5 The year and a day rule

Under the common law, there used to exist a rule that the death must occur within a year and a day of the act or omission of the defendant. This rule was abolished by the Law Reform (Year and a Day Rule) Act 1996, due to the advances which had been made in the medical sphere, for example we currently have life-support machines which can keep a person alive for longer than a year and a day after the defendant's conduct. However, where the death occurs 3 years after the act or omission of the defendant, the permission of the Attorney General must be sought before a prosecution for murder can be brought (s.2, Law Reform (Year and a Day Rule) Act 1996).

5.2.3 *Mens rea*

The *mens rea* for murder is an intention to kill or cause GBH: *Vickers* (1957). Recklessness is not sufficient for murder.

5.2.3.1 **Malice aforethought**

According to Coke's definition of murder, the defendant must cause the death of the victim 'with malice aforethought'. This term is no longer used in the courts as it is misleading and not entirely accurate.

> **THINKING POINT**
>
> Before reading the next paragraph, consider why the term 'malice aforethought' is misleading today.

First, it is clear that there is no requirement of 'malice' in the offence of murder. A defendant who has a benevolent motive and no malice when he kills another person, is still guilty of murder. Take, for instance, a mercy killing, where the defendant kills his child who is in a lot of pain and suffering from a terminal condition. The defendant has no malice towards the child, in fact he carries out the killing in order to end the child's suffering. Nevertheless, the defendant is guilty of murder because he intended to kill the child. The Court of Appeal has confirmed that mercy killing is no defence in English law: *Inglis* [2011] 1 WLR 1110 and *R (Nicklinson) v Ministry of Justice* [2012] EWHC 2381 (Admin). 'Malice' is also misleading because it has been defined as 'intention or recklessness' in respect of the non-fatal offences against the person: *Cunningham* [1957] 2 QB 396. Secondly, the word 'aforethought' is misleading. It implies that a degree of premeditation is required in the offence, but a murder may be committed on the spur of the moment without any planning or premeditation.

5.2.3.2 **The abolition of constructive malice**

Prior to 1957, criminal law acknowledged the existence of three different types of malice aforethought:

(1) express malice—intention to kill;

(2) implied malice—intention to cause GBH; and

(3) constructive malice.

Constructive malice arose where the defendant killed the victim in the course of committing a felony involving violence or resisting arrest, even if he did not intend to kill or cause GBH. Hence, the defendant may not have even considered the possibility of killing the victim, yet he may have been deemed to have constructive malice and, thus, the *mens rea* of murder. However, constructive malice was abolished by s.1 of the Homicide Act 1957.

5.2.3.3 **The *mens rea* for murder: intention to kill or cause GBH**

As stated already, the *mens rea* for murder is an intention to kill or cause GBH. According to the case of *DPP v Smith* [1961] AC 290, GBH means 'really serious harm'. Thus, the *mens rea* for murder is an intention to kill or cause really serious harm.

The case of *Vickers* [1957] 2 QB 664 is an important authority on the *mens rea* of murder. In this case, the defendant broke into a house intending to steal. He was confronted by the owner of the house, an elderly woman. In order to prevent her from recognising him, the defendant struck the elderly woman many times, killing her. He was convicted of her murder. He appealed, arguing that as s.1 of the Homicide Act 1957 abolished constructive malice, the prosecution had failed to prove that the defendant had the *mens rea* for murder where the defendant killed the victim in the course of a burglary. The Court of Appeal upheld his conviction for murder. The Court held that although s.1 of the Homicide Act 1957 abolished constructive malice, it expressly preserves both express malice (an intention to kill) and implied malice (an intention to cause GBH). As the defendant in this case struck the victim intending to cause her GBH, he had sufficient *mens rea* to support a murder conviction. Thus, *Vickers* is authority for the principle that the *mens rea* of murder is an intention to kill or cause GBH.

5.2.3.4 Direct and oblique intent

A further issue which requires consideration at this stage is the meaning of intention. There are two forms of intention in criminal law: direct intent and oblique intent. Direct intent is a person's aim or purpose. A person has direct intent in relation to something which he desires and foresees. Thus, if the defendant desires the death of the victim and foresees that the victim's death will be a consequence of his actions, he has direct intent in relation to the death. Oblique intent does not involve a person's aim or purpose, nor does it involve the desire to do an act. It does, however, require the defendant to foresee the consequences of his actions as virtually certain to occur: *Nedrick* [1986] 1 WLR 1025 and *Woollin* [1999] 1 AC 82. Thus, if the defendant does not desire the death of the victim, but does foresee that the victim's death is virtually certain to occur as a result of the defendant's conduct, he will have oblique intent in relation to the death.

> **CROSS REFERENCE**
>
> Refer to 3.3 for a more detailed discussion of intention, the distinction between direct and oblique intent, and the cases of *Nedrick* (1986) and *Woollin* (1999).

 SUMMARY

The defendant will have the *mens rea* for murder if he:

(1) desires and foresees the death of the victim; or

(2) desires and foresees that the victim will suffer GBH; or

(3) does not desire the death of the victim but foresees it as virtually certain to occur; or

(4) does not desire to cause the victim GBH but foresees it as virtually certain to occur.

5.2.4 Reform

In November 2006, the Law Commission published its report, *Murder, Manslaughter and Infanticide* (Law Com. No. 304). In this report, the Law Commission reviewed the law relating to homicide and made some major recommendations to reform the current system. The Commission recommended replacing the current two-tier structure of murder and manslaughter with a new three-tier structure of general homicide offences: first degree murder, second degree murder, and manslaughter. The report states (at paragraph 2.4) that:

> To bring greater order, fairness and clarity to the law of homicide, the scope of and distinctions between individual homicide offences must be made clearer and more intelligible, as well as being morally more defensible.

5.2.4.1 **First degree murder**

The offence of first degree murder carries a mandatory life sentence. It would be committed where the defendant:

(1) kills intentionally; or

(2) kills with an intention to do serious injury, coupled with an awareness of a serious risk of causing death.

The *mens rea* of this offence requires the prosecution to prove either that the defendant intended to kill or that he intended to cause serious injury. If the latter is proved, there is an additional requirement that the defendant recognised that there was a serious risk of causing death. If the defendant is not aware of a serious risk of causing death, he will not be liable for first degree murder, but will be liable for second degree murder.

5.2.4.2 **Second degree murder**

The maximum sentence for second degree murder is a discretionary life sentence. This offence would be committed where the defendant:

(1) kills and intends to do serious injury; or

(2) kills with an intention to cause some injury or a fear or risk of injury, and was aware of a serious risk of causing death; or

(3) kills and there is a partial defence to what would otherwise be first degree murder.

The offence of second degree murder is a lesser offence than first degree murder. It is much wider than the current offence of murder. Second degree murder can be committed where the defendant kills and intends to do serious injury. There is no need to prove that the defendant was aware of a serious risk of causing death. Second degree murder can alternatively be committed where the defendant kills and intends to cause either some injury or a fear or risk of injury. It must also be proved that the defendant was aware of a serious risk of causing death. The final way in which second degree murder can be committed is where the defendant kills and has a partial defence.

5.2.4.3 **Manslaughter**

The maximum sentence for manslaughter is a discretionary life sentence. This offence would be committed where the defendant:

(1) kills through gross negligence as to a risk of causing death; or

(2) kills through a criminal act:

    (a) intended to cause injury; or

    (b) where there was an awareness that the act involved a serious risk of causing injury;

(3) participates in a joint criminal venture in the course of which another participant commits first or second degree murder, in circumstances where it should have been obvious that first or second degree murder might be committed by another participant.

Manslaughter is a lesser offence than second degree murder. This offence encompasses forms of gross negligence manslaughter and unlawful act manslaughter. It also encompasses liability on the basis of a joint venture, where the perpetrator commits first or second degree murder and it should have been obvious that first or second degree murder might be committed.

5.3 Voluntary manslaughter

As stated already, there are two different types of manslaughter: voluntary manslaughter and involuntary manslaughter. It is important to be able to distinguish between these types of manslaughter. A quick and simple way to determine whether a scenario is one of voluntary or involuntary manslaughter is to look for an intention to kill or cause GBH (the *mens rea* of murder). If the *mens rea* for murder is present and the defendant is able to plead a special defence, his liability may be reduced to voluntary manslaughter. Where the *mens rea* for murder is absent, the different types of involuntary manslaughter require discussion. The flowchart at figure 5.3 seeks to aid this process.

Where a defendant charged with murder successfully pleads one of three special, partial defences: loss of control, diminished responsibility, or suicide pact, he will be acquitted of murder and convicted of manslaughter. This type of manslaughter is known as voluntary manslaughter. In such cases, the defendant accepts that he did cause the victim's death (i.e., he had the *actus reus* of murder), and that he intended to kill or cause GBH to the victim (i.e., he had the *mens rea* of murder).

5.4 Loss of control

Loss of control is a partial defence to murder which is found within the Coroners and Justice Act 2009. Sections 54–56 of the Coroners and Justice Act 2009 came into force on 4 October 2010 and these provisions set out the defence of loss of control. The defence of loss of control replaced the old common law defence of provocation; s.56 abolished the common law on provocation and repealed s.3 of the Homicide Act 1957. Since the enactment of s.54, the Court of Appeal has clearly stated that the defence of loss of control is 'self-contained' within the statute and that '[i]ts common law heritage is irrelevant' (Lord Judge CJ in *Clinton; Parker; Evans* [2012] EWCA Crim 2 at [2]). More recently, Lord Thomas CJ reiterated that 'it should rarely be necessary to look at cases decided under the old law of provocation' (*Gurpinar; Kojo-Smith* [2015] EWCA Crim 178 at [4]). However, while the old defence of provocation is no longer applicable in practice, this chapter will refer to aspects of the old law by way of comparison between the old law of provocation and the new defence of loss of control. This is because some knowledge of the law of provocation is necessary from an academic perspective in order to understand why the defence of loss of control was introduced in its current form.

Loss of control is a special defence in the sense that it may only provide a defence to murder. Students should not make the mistake of applying loss of control as a defence to other offences, such as the non-fatal offences against the person. Loss of control is not a general defence and will not absolve a defendant of liability for any offence other than murder. It may, however, be pleaded in mitigation after conviction in order to obtain a reduced sentence.

As stated earlier, loss of control is a partial defence. Thus, a defendant who pleads loss of control successfully will be absolved of liability for murder, but will still be convicted of manslaughter (s.54(7)).

Figure 5.3 Flowchart to distinguish between voluntary manslaughter and involuntary manslaughter

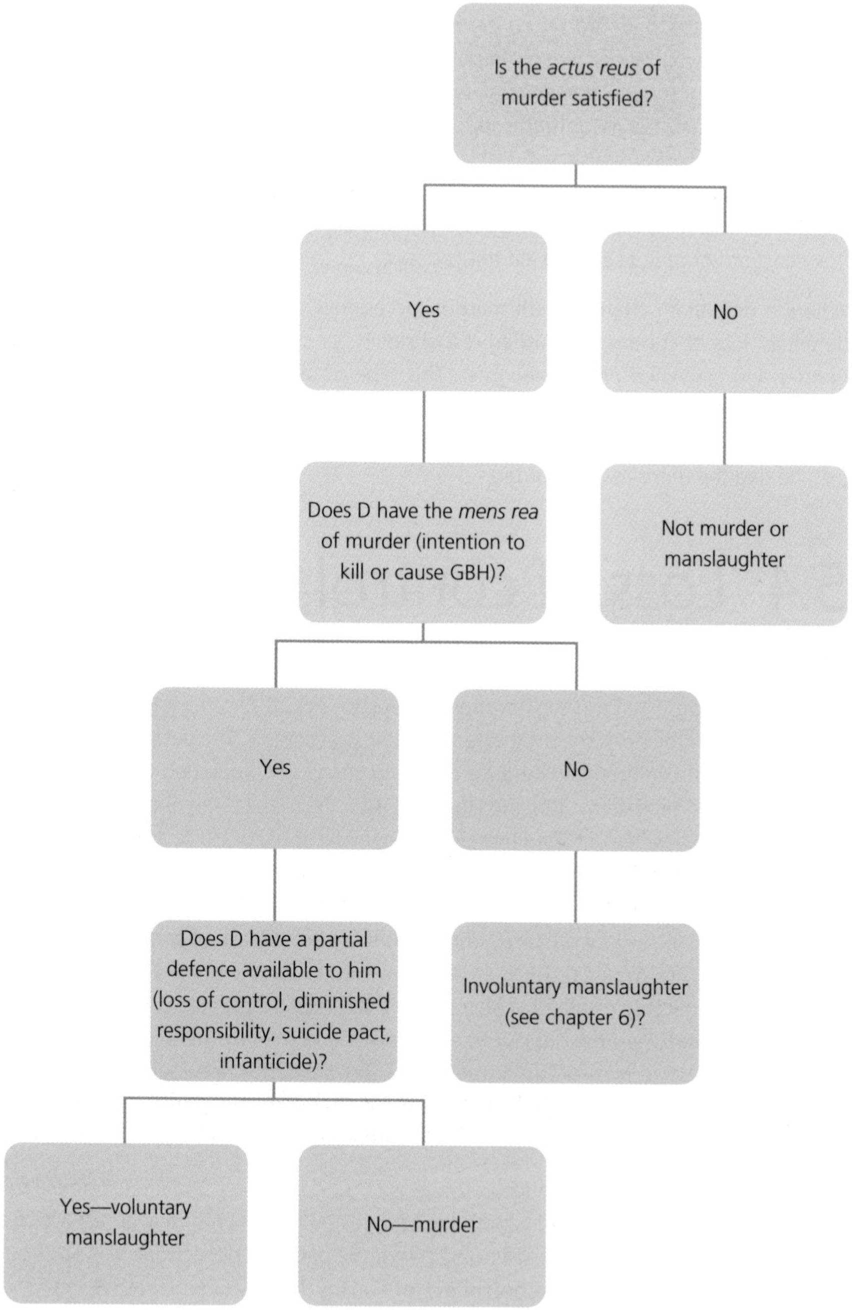

CROSS REFERENCE
Refer to 1.8.1 and 1.8.3 to ensure that you are fully aware of the distinction between a legal burden of proof and an evidential burden.

5.4.1 Evidential issues

5.4.1.1 Burden and standard of proof

Section 54(5) of the Coroners and Justice Act 2009 provides that the legal burden of disproving loss of control remains with the prosecution (this reflects the previous position in respect of the common law defence of provocation). The prosecution must prove beyond reasonable doubt that the elements of loss of control are not satisfied.

5.4.1.2 Sufficiency of evidence

The defence of loss of control can only be left to the jury if 'sufficient evidence is adduced to raise an issue with respect to the defence' (s.54(5)). Section 54(6) goes on to provide that 'sufficient evidence is adduced...if evidence is adduced on which, in the opinion of the trial judge, a jury, properly directed, could reasonably conclude that the defence might apply'. Where sufficient evidence is raised then the defence of loss of control must be left to the jury. The issue of whether 'sufficient evidence' has been raised has been the subject of several recent cases in the Court of Appeal. At the conclusion of the evidence, the trial judge should consider whether sufficient evidence has been raised in respect of all of the components of the defence: *Dawes; Hatter; Bowyer* [2013] EWCA Crim 322. Each component should be considered sequentially and separately, and if one component is missing the defence should not be left to the jury (*Clinton; Parker; Evans* [2012] EWCA Crim 2 at [9] and *Gurpinar; Kojo-Smith* [2015] EWCA Crim 178 at [5]). Where there is insufficient evidence of the first component (that the defendant lost control), then the trial judge need not consider the other components (*Gurpinar; Kojo-Smith* [2015] EWCA Crim 178 at [13], following *Clinton; Parker; Evans* [2012] EWCA Crim 2 and *Dawes; Hatter; Bowyer* [2013] EWCA Crim 322). Provided that the trial judge gives a reasoned ruling on the issue, it is unlikely that the Court of Appeal would interfere with the decision (*Gurpinar; Kojo-Smith* [2015] EWCA Crim 178 at [16]).

Even if loss of control has not been raised by the defence or the defendant did not give evidence, or gave evidence but this did not support the defence of loss of control, the trial judge should consider (on an objective assessment of the evidence) whether the defence should be left to the jury (*Gurpinar; Kojo-Smith* [2015] EWCA Crim 178 at [10]).

The following cases provide examples of the courts' approach to the issue of sufficiency of evidence. In *Jewell* [2014] EWCA Crim 414, the trial judge held that there was insufficient evidence to leave the defence of loss of control to the jury. In this case, the defence of loss of control was based upon the defendant's assertions that he had lost control. The trial judge stated, 'the defendant recited, as if reciting a mantra from legal textbooks: "I did it because I lost control. I could not control my actions..." ' (at [19]). The trial judge held that a mere assertion by the defendant that he had lost control was not on its own sufficient evidence upon which a jury could reasonably conclude that the defence might apply (at [19]). The trial judge ruled that there was insufficient evidence to leave the first limb of the defence under s.54(1)(a) to the jury and the Court of Appeal approved of the trial judge's approach to the defence and reiterated that 'if any one of the components is absent the partial defence fails' (at [50]).

Where there is no evidence of a loss of control, the defence should not be left to the jury. For example, in the case of *Workman* [2014] EWCA Crim 575, the defendant killed his wife with a single stab wound to the chest. The defendant claimed that his wife had been holding the knife and that she was stabbed accidentally when he tried to restrain her and he lost his grip on her arm. On appeal against his conviction for murder, the defendant claimed that the trial judge should have left the defence of loss of control to the jury (even though he did not raise this defence at trial). The Court of Appeal held that the trial judge had been right not to leave loss of control to the jury as there was insufficient evidence to raise it as an issue. Similarly, in *Barnsdale-Quean* [2014] EWCA Crim 1418, the Court of Appeal held that the defendant, who was charged with the murder of his wife, could not rely on the defence of loss of control where his defence was that his wife had attacked him and then killed herself.

5.4.2 The components of loss of control

A defendant may plead this defence where he lost his self-control as a result of a qualifying trigger, and a person of the defendant's sex and age, with a normal degree of tolerance and self-restraint and in the circumstances of the defendant, might have reacted in the same or in a similar way as the defendant did.

As stated already, this defence is found under s.54 of the Coroners and Justice Act 2009.

STATUTE

Section 54, Coroners and Justice Act 2009

(1) Where a person ('D') kills or is a party to the killing of another ('V'), D is not to be convicted of murder if—

  (a) D's acts and omissions in doing or being a party to the killing resulted from D's loss of self-control,

  (b) the loss of self-control had a qualifying trigger, and

  (c) a person of D's sex and age, with a normal degree of tolerance and self-restraint and in the circumstances of D, might have reacted in the same or in a similar way to D.

(2) For the purposes of subsection (1)(a), it does not matter whether or not the loss of control was sudden.

(3) In subsection (1)(c) the reference to 'the circumstances of D' is a reference to all of D's circumstances other than those whose only relevance to D's conduct is that they bear on D's general capacity for tolerance or self-restraint.

From s.54, we can identify three main components:

(1) the defendant must lose self-control;

(2) the loss of control must have a qualifying trigger; and

(3) a person of the defendant's sex and age, with a normal degree of tolerance and self-restraint and in the circumstances of the defendant, might have reacted in the same or in a similar way as the defendant did.

These components are illustrated in figure 5.4 and each of these three components will be examined in turn in 5.4.3 to 5.4.5.

Figure 5.4 The elements of loss of control

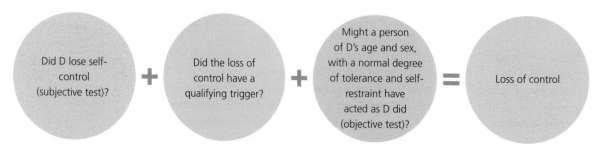

5.4.3 Defendant's loss of control

The first requirement under s.54(1)(a) is that the defendant lost self-control. In line with the old common law defence of provocation, this is subjectively assessed: the defendant himself must have actually lost self-control. It is not enough that the reasonable man would have lost control but the defendant actually did not. In *Jewell* [2014] EWCA Crim 414, the Court of Appeal considered the meaning of 'loss of control'.

Q CASE CLOSE-UP

Jewell [2014] EWCA Crim 414

The defendant in this case drove to the victim's house to collect the victim for work, but he shot and killed the victim outside his house. Twelve hours before driving to the victim's house, the defendant had armed himself with firearms, a tent, spare clothing, a passport, driving licence, and cash. He drove to the victim's house armed with loaded guns and shot and killed the victim without warning.

The defendant was charged with murder and sought to rely on the defence of loss of control on the basis that he was intimidated by the victim and his associates. He claimed that the victim had threatened him the previous evening and that he had armed himself for his protection. He claimed that when he saw the victim, he could not control himself and he just shot him.

The trial judge refused to leave the defence of loss of control to the jury since the defendant's mere assertion that he had lost control was not on its own sufficient evidence of the defence. The defendant was convicted of murder and appealed. The Court of Appeal approved the meaning of loss of control provided by Professor Ormerod in *Smith and Hogan's Criminal Law* (13th edn, 2011): 'a loss of the ability to act in accordance with considered judgment or a loss of normal powers of reasoning' (at [24]).

The Court also approved the trial judge's approach to the defence of loss of control and held that the defendant's claims that he was afraid of the victim 'must be seen in context', which included his failure to seek help from his family and friends and the fact that he drove alone to the victim's house. The Court cited with approval Lord Chief Justice Judge in *Clinton; Parker; Evans* [2012] EWCA Crim 2:

> We remind ourselves of the words of the Lord Chief Justice in *Clinton*: 'In reality, the greater the level of deliberation, the less likely it will be that the killing followed a true loss of self control.' In our view, the 12-hour cooling off period, as the judge in his ruling labelled it, reflects exactly this analysis. The evidence that this was a planned execution is best described as overwhelming (at [46] to [48]).

The Court of Appeal held that the trial judge's conclusion that there was insufficient evidence to leave the defence of loss of control to the jury was 'unimpeachable' (at [55]).

5.4.3.1 Loss of control need not be sudden

The Coroners and Justice Act 2009 contains no requirement that the loss of control be sudden. In fact, s.54(2) states that it does not matter whether the loss of control was sudden. This provision has been criticised by L. H. Leigh who states that 'the notion of loss of self-control as such does rather suggest a sudden point of explosion' (Leigh 2010). The position under s.54(2) is also in direct contrast to the old common law which required a 'sudden and temporary loss of control': see *Duffy* (1949). The classic definition of provocation was found in this case: 'Provocation is some act, or series of acts, done by the dead man to the accused which would cause in any reasonable person, and actually causes in the accused, a sudden and temporary loss of self-control, rendering the accused so subject to passion as to make him or her for the moment not master of his mind' (Lord Goddard CJ, approving the direction given by Devlin J (later Lord Devlin) to the jury).

5.4.3.2 No loss of control if acted in considered desire for revenge

However, the defence of loss of control will not apply if, in doing or being a party to the killing, the defendant acted in a considered desire for revenge (s.54(4)). This reflects the position under the old common law defence of provocation. It also reflects the recommendation put forward by the Law Commission in its Report *Partial Defences to Murder* (Law Com. No. 290, 2004), in which the Law Commission recommended that '[a] defendant who acts in a considered desire for revenge is to be distinguished from a defendant who acts on impulse or in fear or both' (at [35]).

One criticism of the 2009 Act is that there is no guidance as to the meaning of what degree of 'consideration' will preclude the application of the defence. Professor Ormerod and Karl Laird question whether arming oneself with a weapon, as in *Pearson* [1992] Crim LR 193, would be regarded as a considered desire for revenge and thus preclude the operation of the defence (Ormerod and Laird 2015: 582). Presumably this question will be left to be determined by the jury.

Evidence of planning and a significant delay between the provoking words or conduct and the killing negated the spontaneity which was essential for the old defence of provocation. This was recognised in the case law on provocation. In *Duffy* (1949), Lord Devlin stated that:

> circumstances which induce a desire for revenge are inconsistent with provocation, since the conscious formulation of a desire for revenge means that a person has had time to think, to reflect, and that would negative a sudden temporary loss of self-control which is of the essence of provocation.

This was further confirmed in the old case of *Ibrams and Gregory* (1981). While this is a pre-Coroners and Justice Act 2009 case, it is worth looking at as an illustration of the type of case which might fall under s.54(4) today.

 CASE CLOSE-UP

Ibrams and Gregory (1981) 74 Cr App R 154

The defendants in this case planned their attack on the victim. Ibrams lived with his fiancée, X. The victim was X's former boyfriend, who had been terrorising the couple in their home. The second defendant, Gregory, had also been present on occasions when the victim had used violent and threatening behaviour towards the defendants and X. One week after the victim last terrorised the defendants, they attacked him with an axe and a knife when he was sleeping. The victim died and the defendants were charged with his murder.

The trial judge refused to leave the defence of provocation to the jury and the defendants appealed against their convictions for murder. The Court of Appeal upheld the defendants' convictions. Lawton LJ gave the leading judgment of the Court. His Lordship stated that there was nothing which happened on the night of the killing which caused the defendants to lose self-control. The fact that there had been a plan to attack the victim negated any defence of provocation.

5.4.3.3 Problems with the old common law: cooling-off periods

This previous law on provocation caused problems in cases where there was a lapse of time between the provoking words or conduct and the killing, i.e., a 'cooling off' period.

The requirement of a sudden and temporary loss of control was criticised as favouring men, who may typically be more likely to react spontaneously to provoking words or conduct. The old common law defence of provocation was not always available to those whose reaction was not spontaneous upon the provoking words or conduct and where the provocation accumulated, ultimately leading to the defendant killing the victim. Thus, the common law defence of provocation was criticised for disadvantaging women, who may typically be more likely to react in this 'slow burn' manner.

Evidence that the defendant has had time to think and 'cool off' was evidence which went towards negating the sudden loss of control necessary for the defence of provocation. Evidence that the defendant took the time to arm himself with a weapon before killing also went towards negating the spontaneity requirement. However, a cooling-off period would not necessarily have precluded a defendant from relying upon the defence of provocation. Where there was a delay between the provoking words or conduct and the killing, the defendant might still have relied on provocation, provided that at the time that he did kill, he suddenly and temporarily lost control.

There are several cases involving a time lapse. The defence of provocation was still available to the defendant where there was a delay between the provoking words or conduct and the killing. However, the leading authority of *Ahluwalia* (1993) 96 Cr App R 133 confirmed that the longer the delay and the stronger the evidence of deliberation, the more likely it was that the defence of provocation would be negated.

One of the first significant cases in this area was *Thornton* (1993) 96 Cr App R 112. The defendant was charged with murder after killing her husband. Their marriage had been a violent one, the defendant having been subjected to violent abuse over a period of 2 years. One night, when the defendant returned home, the victim called her 'a whore' and accused her of selling her body. She went into the kitchen to try to calm down, where she picked up and sharpened a carving knife. She returned to where the victim was lying on the sofa and tried to persuade him to come up to bed. The victim responded by saying that he would kill her when she was asleep. She then stabbed him in the stomach and phoned for an ambulance and the police. When the paramedics tried to resuscitate the victim, the defendant told them to 'let him die'. The trial judge left the defence of provocation to the jury despite the time lapse between the provoking words and the killing. The defendant was convicted of murder and appealed.

The Court of Appeal confirmed that the 'sudden and temporary loss of self-control' test was appropriately left to the jury. The Court also held that where there were provocative words and/or conduct which did not cause a sudden and temporary loss of control, the defence of provocation was not available. In this case, the defendant's behaviour suggested that she had 'cooled off' before the killing, despite the earlier threats of violence. Thus, the defence of provocation was held not to be available to the defendant.

> ## 🔍 CASE CLOSE-UP
>
> ### *Ahluwalia* (1993) 96 Cr App R 133
>
> The leading authority on cooling-off periods pre-Coroners and Justice Act 2009 was *Ahluwalia* (1993). The defendant in this case was raped and violently abused by her husband for more than 10 years. Her religious beliefs prevented her from leaving him. One night, after he had beaten her, the defendant waited for her husband to fall asleep and then poured petrol over him and set him alight. He died from his burns. The defendant was charged with his murder. The trial judge refused to leave the defence of provocation to the jury because the time delay during which the defendant waited for the victim to fall asleep amounted to evidence of a cooling-off period. The defendant was convicted of murder and appealed.
>
> The Court of Appeal held that provocation could be left to the jury where there was evidence of a time lapse between the provoking words or conduct and the killing. However, the longer the delay and the stronger the evidence of deliberation, the more likely it will be that the defence of provocation will be negated.

Hence, although evidence of a delay did not automatically preclude a defendant from relying upon the defence of provocation, such evidence meant that the defence was less likely to succeed.

Section 54(2) removes the confusion over whether a sudden loss of control can be reconciled with a delay between the provocation and the killing. Instead, the issue of whether a delay precludes the defence of loss of control will be an issue for the judge (in deciding to leave the defence to the jury) and the jury (in deciding whether there was a loss of control).

5.4.4 Qualifying trigger

fear trigger

applies where the defendant has a fear of serious violence

anger trigger

applies where something is said and/or done which amounted to circumstances of an extremely grave character and caused the defendant to have a justifiable sense of having been seriously wronged

Another new addition to the law is the requirement of a qualifying trigger under s.55. Section 54(1)(b) of the Coroners and Justice Act 2009 requires that the loss of control was the result of one of two qualifying triggers: the **fear trigger** or the **anger trigger**, or indeed both. The old common law defence of provocation required provoking words and/or conduct, but the phrase 'qualifying trigger' is a new addition to the law. In fact, the 2009 Act restricts the scope of the defence of loss of control by excluding cases such as *Doughty* (1986) 83 Cr App R 319, in which the defendant killed a baby after it cried persistently. The Court of Appeal held that this may amount to provocation, since there was no requirement that the provoking words or conduct be illegal, and the defence should be left to the jury. If this case were to come before the courts today, the defendant would not be able to avail himself of the defence of loss of control as it would not fall under either of the two qualifying triggers. Consequently, Professor Norrie questions 'if moral progress has been made here' (Norrie 2010: 284).

Section 55 of the Act deals with the meaning of 'qualifying trigger'. The 'fear trigger' under s.55(3) is attributable to the defendant's fear of serious violence. The 'anger trigger' under s.55(4) is attributable to something said and/or done which amounted to circumstances of an extremely grave character and which caused the defendant to have a justifiable sense of having been seriously wronged. Section 55(5) states that the loss of control may be attributable to a combination of both triggers.

5.4.4.1 **The fear trigger: fear of serious violence**

The fear trigger under s.55(3) is a new addition to the law and it extends the remit of the defence to cover situations in which previously only the complete defence of self-defence was available. The defendant's fear of serious violence is subjectively assessed such that the defendant must have a genuine fear of serious violence; his fear need not be reasonable. The fear of serious violence must be from the victim against the defendant or another identified person (s.55(3)). Thus, it may not be from an unidentified person or group. The inclusion of this new trigger also inevitably results in a degree of overlap between the defences of loss of control and self-defence. However, the defence of loss of control is precluded where the defendant was the initial aggressor (see s.55(6)(a)), whereas the same is not true of self-defence.

5.4.4.2 **The anger trigger: justifiable sense of being seriously wronged**

The anger trigger under s.55(4) applies where the defendant's loss of control is attributable to things said and/or done which amounted to circumstances of an extremely grave character and caused the defendant to have a justifiable sense of having been seriously wronged. Anger was a sufficient basis for a loss of control under the old common law, the only requirement then being that the loss of control was 'sudden and temporary' (*Duffy* (1949)). One problem with the 2009 Act is that terms such as 'extremely grave character' and 'justifiable sense of having been seriously wronged' have not been defined. These issues are for the judge to consider at the end of the evidence, and if the defence is left to the jury, the jury will then determine them: *Dawes; Hatter; Bowyer* [2013] EWCA Crim 322. Whether the defendant's sense of being seriously wronged was justifiable will be objectively assessed. The Explanatory Notes to the Bill cite an example of the application of the defence given by the Law Commission, where a parent arrives home to find that his child has just been raped and kills the offender after losing control. In *Zebedee* [2013] 1 Cr App R (S) 37, the defendant's defence of loss of control was rejected by the jury and he was convicted of the murder of his 94-year-old father who suffered from senile dementia and incontinence. The defendant killed his father by punching and strangling him. He claimed that he had lost control as a result of the frustration and anger he suffered through looking after his father. The jury presumably decided that this did not constitute 'circumstances of an extremely grave character' which caused the defendant to have a justifiable sense of having been seriously wronged.

Prior to the Homicide Act 1957, it was held that words alone could not amount to provocation: *Holmes v DPP* [1946] AC 588. However, the Homicide Act 1957 expanded the scope of the defence so as to include provocation by words, as well as by acts and this has been retained in the Coroners and Justice Act 2009. Similarly, the old common law requirement that provocation is something 'done by the dead man to the accused' was dispensed with by the Homicide Act 1957. Indeed, s.3 of the Homicide Act 1957 did not require the provocation to be directed at the defendant. In *Davies* [1975] QB 691, the Court of Appeal held that the provoking act could come from a third party provocation. In this case, the defendant's wife had left him for another man. He killed her and was charged with her murder. The Court of Appeal held that the acts of the wife's lover could amount to provocation. In *Pearson* [1992] Crim LR 193, the Court of Appeal held that provocation may include acts by the deceased to a third party. In this case, the defendant and his brother had been violently bullied by their father for years. The defendant killed his father as a result of the violence which his father had inflicted on the defendant's brother.

Where the defendant himself has incited the thing said or done which caused the fear of serious violence or the sense of being seriously wronged in order to provide an excuse to use violence, there will be no qualifying trigger (see s.55(6)(a) and (b)). This change does not reflect the old common law position in respect of provocation, which could be self-induced. In *Johnson* [1989] 1 WLR 740, the Court of Appeal held that the fact that the defendant did something to cause a reaction in another person which then provoked the defendant to lose his self-control, did not preclude the defendant from relying on the defence. In *Dawes; Hatter; Bowyer* [2013] EWCA Crim 322, the Court of Appeal held that reference to *Johnson* was now inappropriate since it no longer fully reflects the law.

5.4.4.3 **Sexual infidelity**

A controversial addition to the Act is s.55(6)(c), which states that 'the fact that a thing done or said constituted sexual infidelity is to be disregarded'. Thus, something done or said constituting sexual infidelity will not amount to a 'qualifying trigger'. This provision was introduced by the House of Commons, but was removed from the Bill at Report stage in the House of Lords. However, the provision was reinstated in the Bill during the consideration of amendments (the 'ping pong' stage). Thus, under the 2009 Act the defence of loss of control will not be available to a defendant who kills as a result of a loss of control triggered by the discovery that his partner has been unfaithful. L. H. Leigh describes the justification for the inclusion of this provision as 'incoherent' (Leigh 2010). Professor Norrie questions how the law will deal with the 'difficult cases'; he asks: 'where a taunt of infidelity is part of a range of taunts and the taunting is systematic, should it be the case that one somehow excludes the one taunt and admits the others?' (Norrie 2010: 289).

The case of *Clinton; Parker; Evans* [2012] EWCA Crim 2 was the first significant Court of Appeal judgment on sexual infidelity and the defence of loss of control.

 CASE CLOSE-UP

Clinton; Parker; Evans [2012] EWCA Crim 2

The case involved three separate appeals against convictions for murder. The key issue which arose in the appeals was whether or not s.55(6)(c) of the Coroners and Justice Act 2009 provides that sexual infidelity is wholly excluded from consideration in a case involving other potential qualifying triggers.

The Court concluded that where there was no other potential qualifying trigger, evidence of sexual infidelity must be excluded. However, ruling that 'context is critical' in order to avoid potential injustice, the Court held that sexual infidelity is 'not subject to a blanket exclusion' and that where it 'is integral to and forms an essential part of the context in which to make a just evaluation whether a qualifying trigger properly falls within the ambit of subsections 55(3) and (4), the prohibition in section 55(6)(c) does not operate to exclude it' (at [39]).

The effect of this decision is that sexual infidelity may be considered as part of the contextual background to a case where there is another potential qualifying trigger, but it may not be considered as a potential qualifying trigger in itself. Judge LCJ, who delivered the judgment of the Court, stated that this approach was supported by s.54(1)(c) and (3) which provides that the circumstances of the defendant may be taken into account. His Lordship was also satisfied that this was consistent with the views of both those who proposed the enactment of s.55(6)(c) as well as those who were opposed to it. He cited Claire Ward who, speaking for the Government, stated that '[i]f something else is relied on as the qualifying trigger, any sexual infidelity that forms part of the background can be considered, but it cannot be the trigger' (9 November 2009). This decision is welcomed for carving out some clarity in relation to what was described by counsel appearing for the prosecution in the appeal as a 'formidably difficult provision'.

5.4.5 Reaction of a person of normal tolerance and self-restraint

Finally, under s.54(1)(c), the defendant's reaction is to be compared to that of a person with a 'normal degree of tolerance and self-restraint' sharing the age and sex of the defendant. This follows the approach taken in the cases of *Camplin* [1978] AC 705 and *Attorney General for Jersey v Holley* [2005] UKPC 23 before the implementation of the Coroners and Justice Act 2009. Professor Norrie questions 'the role that "sex" should play in the new law' and also criticises the use of age: 'Capacity for self-control is indeed an aspect of maturity, but age is not then the main issue, maturity is. Age is no more than a rough and ready way of marking maturity' (Norrie 2010: 281).

Section 54(1)(c) also states that the circumstances of the defendant may be taken into account. Section 54(3) elaborates on what is meant by 'the circumstances of D'. This section allows for a history of abuse or any gravity characteristic to be taken into account in assessing whether a person of the defendant's age and sex, with a normal degree of tolerance and self-restraint, might have reacted in the same way.

In the case of *Asmelash* [2013] 1 Cr App R 33, the Court of Appeal held that voluntary intoxication is not a factor to be taken into account in determining whether a person of the defendant's age and sex, with a normal degree of tolerance and self-restraint and in the circumstances of the defendant, might have reacted in the same or in a similar way to the defendant under s.54(1)(c) of the Coroners and Justice Act 2009. This does not mean that a drunk defendant cannot plead loss of control, but rather, such a defendant is to be assessed against a sober person in the defendant's circumstances, with normal levels of tolerance and self-restraint. However, where a defendant was not merely voluntarily intoxicated, but suffered from alcoholism or an addiction to drugs and he was taunted about that condition to the extent that it constituted a qualifying trigger, then the alcoholism or addiction would be a relevant factor to take into account (see 13.6.4.5).

Under the common law, where there was a history of abuse which ultimately led to the defendant losing control and killing, the background of provocative conduct was taken into account. In the case of *Humphreys* [1995] 4 All ER 1008, the defendant was a 17-year-old girl who was subjected to abuse by her boyfriend. On one evening, the defendant cut her wrists because she feared that her boyfriend would come home drunk, beat her, and force her to have sex with him and other men. When her boyfriend came home, he taunted her about cutting her wrists, telling her that she hadn't done a very good job of it. At this point, the defendant stabbed and killed her boyfriend. She was charged with murder and relied upon the defence of provocation and the history of her relationship with her boyfriend. The defence also adduced evidence that the defendant had been suffering from an abnormal mentality with a tendency to attention-seeking behaviour, such as immaturity and wrist slashing.

The defendant was convicted of murder and appealed. The Court of Appeal allowed the appeal and held that the history of the defendant's relationship with her boyfriend could be taken into account. The Court substituted a verdict of manslaughter by provocation. The trigger or 'last straw' in this case was the taunt about the defendant not doing a very good job of cutting her wrists. However, the judge should direct the jury that previous cumulative acts of provocation might also provide evidence to support the contention that the defendant suffered a loss of self-control at the time of the killing.

A similar approach to cumulative provocation was also taken in the case of *Thornton (No. 2)* [1996] 2 All ER 1023, in which Lord Taylor CJ stated that 'battered women syndrome' may be relevant because:

> it may form an important background to whatever triggered the *actus reus*. A jury may more readily find there was a sudden loss of control triggered by even a minor incident if the defendant has endured abuse over a period, on the 'last straw' basis...

Thus, where there is a history of provocative conduct and the killing was triggered by a relatively minor incident, the 'last straw', the jury should be told to consider the cumulative background of provocation in considering whether the defendant did lose control. This reflects the position under s.54(3) of the Coroners and Justice Act 2009.

5.4.6 The old common law: the reasonable man test

Notably, the Coroners and Justice Act 2009 Act does away with the phrase 'reasonable man' from s.3 of the Homicide Act 1957 which was used in respect of the old common law defence of provocation.

Under the old common law, there was a requirement that the provocation was enough to make the reasonable man do as the defendant did. This was an objective test which asked the jury to consider whether a reasonable man would have acted as the defendant did under such provocation. The test is a controversial one and has occupied much of the courts' time for more than half a century. Although it is clear that the reasonable man would not kill, even when provoked, the test ensured that some objectivity was retained in order that a defendant with a short temper might not be able to excuse his behaviour by relying upon a purely subjective defence of provocation. The defendant was expected to be able to exercise the same level of self-control as the reasonable man.

However, there was a series of cases which cast doubt over the objectivity of the test. In *Camplin* [1978] AC 705, the House of Lords held that the defendant's age and sex could be taken into account in assessing whether the reasonable man would have acted as the defendant did. Thus, the House added a degree of subjectivity to the objective test. The jury would be required to consider whether a reasonable person with the same age and sex of the defendant would have acted as the defendant did. In the case of *Smith (Morgan James)* [2001] 1 AC 146, the House of Lords held, by a 3:2 majority, that both the circumstances and the characteristics of the defendant should be taken into account. This resulted in a wholly subjective approach under which the jury should determine whether, in light of the circumstances and the defendant's characteristics, his conduct was 'sufficiently excusable'. However, in the later authority of *Attorney General for Jersey v Holley* [2005] UKPC 23, the Privy Council held that the law should revert back to the position before the House of Lords' decision in *Smith* (2001). The approach in *Holley* (2005) is preferred. This *Smith/Holley* debate will be considered in more detail at 5.4.6.3.

The reasonable man test was criticised by the House of Lords in the case of *Smith (Morgan James)* [2001] 1 AC 146. Section 54(1)(c) of the Coroners and Justice Act 2009 reflects the law as preferred by the Privy Council in *Attorney General for Jersey v Holley* [2005] UKPC 23, namely a reversion to the position on the law after the case of *Camplin* [1978] AC 705. Thus, the only control characteristics which may be considered are the age and sex of the defendant.

5.4.6.1 The development of the law

The courts originally took an objective approach to the defence of provocation. In *Lesbini* [1914] 3 KB 1116, the Court of Appeal held that the reasonable man is not unusually excitable. Similarly, in *McCarthy* [1954] 2 QB 105, the Court of Appeal held that the reasonable man is not drunk and in *Bedder v DPP* [1954] 1 WLR 1119, the House of Lords held that the reasonable man is not impotent. In this case, the House of Lords confirmed that the jury should only consider whether the reasonable man would have reacted as the defendant did to the taunts and violence; they should not consider whether the reasonable impotent man would have reacted as the defendant did. In this sense, the objective approach does not take into account the defendant's actual characteristics. The case of *Bedder v DPP* (1954) was disapproved by Lord Diplock in the House of Lords in *Camplin* (1978).

Q CASE CLOSE-UP

Camplin [1978] AC 705

The defendant in this case was a 15-year-old boy who was raped by his employer. The employer then began to gloat and laugh about the rape, at which point the defendant struck him on the head with a chapati pan, killing him. The defendant was charged with his murder and pleaded provocation. The trial judge directed the jury that in relation to the second element of provocation, the defendant should be judged according to the reasonable man, and not the reasonable 15-year-old boy. The defendant was convicted of murder and appealed. The Court of Appeal allowed the appeal and substituted a verdict of manslaughter. The Director of Public Prosecutions appealed to the House of Lords.

The House upheld the decision of the Court of Appeal and held that the defendant should have been judged according to the standard of the reasonable 15-year-old boy. Thus, the defendant's age and sex should have been taken into account in determining whether the reasonable man would have acted as the defendant did. According to Lord Diplock in *Camplin* (1978):

> the reasonable man...is a person having the power of self-control to be expected of an ordinary person of the sex and age of the accused, but in other respects sharing such of the accused's characteristics as they think would affect the gravity of the provocation to him;...the question is not merely whether such a person would in like circumstances be provoked to lose his self-control but also whether he would react to the provocation as the accused did.

5.4.6.2 'Control' characteristics and 'gravity' characteristics

In *Camplin* (1978), Lord Diplock drew a distinction between characteristics which affect the level of self-control to be expected of the defendant ('control' characteristics) and characteristics which affect the gravity of the provocation to the defendant ('gravity' characteristics) (see figure 5.5). After *Camplin* (1978), the age and the sex of the defendant were the only 'control' characteristics which could be taken into account, whereas there was no limit on the 'gravity' characteristics which might be considered relevant. This position is also reflected under s.54(3) of the Coroners and Justice Act 2009.

In the case of *Humphreys* [1995] 4 All ER 1008, it was held that in deciding whether a reasonable person would have lost self-control, the defendant's abnormal immaturity and

Figure 5.5 'Control' and 'gravity' characteristics

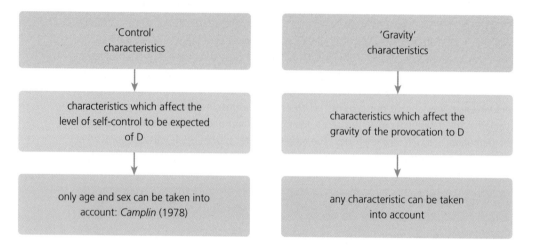

attention-seeking behaviour were relevant characteristics which could be taken into account by the jury. In *Dryden* [1995] 4 All ER 987, the Court of Appeal held that the defendant's eccentric and obsessional personality could be taken into account as a control characteristic in assessing whether a reasonable man would have acted as the defendant did. In *Thornton (No. 2)* [1996] 2 All ER 1023, the Court of Appeal held that 'battered women syndrome' was also a characteristic which could be taken into account in considering whether the reasonable man would have exercised the same degree of control as the defendant did.

An addiction to glue sniffing was held not to be a relevant control characteristic in the case of *Morhall* [1996] AC 90. The defendant in this case was addicted to sniffing solvents. He killed a man who had nagged him about his addiction. The defendant was convicted of murder and appealed. The Court of Appeal upheld his conviction, but the House of Lords substituted a conviction for manslaughter. The House held that the addiction to sniffing solvents was a relevant characteristic insofar as the gravity of the provocation was concerned. Lord Goff stated that:

> the judge should have directed the jury to take into account the fact of the defendant's addiction to glue-sniffing when considering whether a person with the ordinary person's power of self-control would have reacted to the provocation as the defendant did.

The addiction was not a 'control' characteristic: it did not affect the level of self-control to be expected from the defendant. The defendant is expected to exercise the same level of self-control as a reasonable person without such an addiction. However, it was a 'gravity' characteristic. Thus, it could be considered by the jury in deciding the effect that the taunts or nagging would have on a person with ordinary powers of control, who shares such characteristics of the defendant as the jury think would affect the gravity of the provocation.

Similarly, in *Luc Thiet Thuan v R* [1997] AC 131, the Privy Council held that the defendant's mental disability which reduced the defendant's power of self-control was not a relevant characteristic for the purposes of the reasonable man test. The defendant in this case killed his former girlfriend after she taunted him about her new boyfriend and the defendant's sexual inadequacy. Medical evidence was adduced to show that the defendant was suffering from brain damage which made it difficult for him to control his behaviour. The defendant was convicted of murder and appealed on the ground that the trial judge had not directed the jury in relation to his mental disability. The appeal was dismissed by the Court of Appeal and the Privy Council. The Privy Council distinguished between 'control' characteristics and 'gravity' characteristics. The defendant's mental disability was a 'control' characteristic which could not be taken into account in relation to the reasonable man test. The defendant was still expected to exercise the same level of control as the reasonable man.

If the courts had allowed the consideration of mental disabilities as part of the reasonable man test, the distinction between the defences of provocation and diminished responsibility would have become unclear. Had the victim in this case taunted the defendant about his mental disability, then it would have been relevant as a 'gravity' characteristic.

5.4.6.3 The *Smith/Holley* debate

Two cases caused a conflict in the law between the House of Lords and the Privy Council. The House of Lords' decision in *Smith* [2001] 1 AC 146 conflicted with the Privy Council decision in *Attorney General for Jersey v Holley* [2005] UKPC 23.

In July 2000, the House of Lords' decision in *Smith* (2001) radically changed the law relating to provocation. The defendant in this case suffered from a severe depressive illness which impaired his ability to exercise self-control. He was also an alcoholic. The defendant had an argument with the victim about a set of tools which he believed that the victim had stolen from him. During the argument, the defendant stabbed the victim, killing him. He was charged with murder and raised three defences: *(a)* that he did not have the *mens rea* for murder as he did not intend to kill him or cause him GBH; *(b)* that he was suffering from diminished responsibility; and *(c)* that he was provoked. The defence adduced psychiatric evidence that the defendant's depression made him less able to exercise self-control.

The trial judge directed the jury that the defendant's depression was relevant in relation to the subjective question of whether the defendant lost self-control, but was not relevant in relation to the objective question. The jury convicted the defendant of murder and he appealed. The Court of Appeal allowed the appeal and held that the defendant's depression was relevant to the question of whether the reasonable man would have acted as the defendant did. The jury should have been directed to attribute the defendant's depression to the reasonable man. The Court substituted a conviction of manslaughter. The prosecution appealed to the House of Lords.

The House of Lords dismissed the appeal by a 3:2 majority, agreeing with the decision of the Court of Appeal. The majority held that it was for the jury to decide whether the defendant's depression was a relevant characteristic for the purposes of the objective test or not. Lord Hoffmann rejected the use of the term 'reasonable man'. Instead, the jury should consider the degree of control that 'everyone is entitled to expect that his fellow citizens will exercise in society as it is today' (Lord Hoffmann in *Smith* (2001), citing Lord Diplock in *Camplin* (1978)). It was held that the jury should be left to decide which of the defendant's characteristics to take into account in determining whether the defendant's conduct was sufficiently excusable. Lord Hoffmann held that:

> The law expects people to exercise control over their emotions. A tendency to violent rages or childish tantrums is a defect in character rather than an excuse. The jury must think that the circumstances were such as to make the loss of self-control sufficiently *excusable* to reduce the gravity of the offence from murder to manslaughter . . . In deciding what should count as a sufficient excuse, they have to apply what they consider to be appropriate standards of behaviour; on the one hand making allowance for human nature and the power of the emotions but, on the other hand, not allowing someone to rely upon his own violent disposition.

Thus, the jury should be able to decide what should and what should not be taken into account. A judge should leave this to the jury's discretion and should not tell a jury to exclude certain characteristics from their deliberations. Lord Hoffmann added the exception that characteristics such as male possessiveness, jealousy, obsession, and a tendency to violent rages or childish tantrums should be ignored. His Lordship also rejected the distinction between 'control' characteristics and 'gravity' characteristics, taking the view that *Camplin* (1978) did not provide support for such a distinction.

In the later case of *Weller* [2003] EWCA Crim 815, the Court of Appeal interpreted the decision in *Smith* (2001) and held that the question of 'whether the defendant should reasonably have controlled himself is to be answered by the jury taking all matters into account'. Mantell LJ stated:

> That includes matters relating to the defendant, the kind of man he is and his mental state, as well as the circumstances in which the death occurred. The judge should not tell the jury that they should, as a matter of law, ignore any aspect. He may give them some guidance as to the weight to be given to some aspects, provided he makes it clear that the question is one which, as the law provides, they are to answer, and not him.

However, in June 2005, the Privy Council reconsidered the law relating to the second element of provocation in *Attorney General for Jersey v Holley* (2005).

 CASE CLOSE-UP

Attorney General for Jersey v Holley [2005] UKPC 23

This case occurred in Jersey. The defendant was a chronic alcoholic who killed his girl-friend with an axe after she told him that she had slept with another man. The defendant was charged with her murder and relied upon the defence of provocation. In relation to the question whether the provocation was enough to make a reasonable man act as the defendant had done, the jury were invited to consider whether any particular characteristic reduced the defendant's power of self-control so as to excuse his action. However, the jury were directed that the defendant's drunkenness at the time of the killing could not be taken into account. The defendant was convicted of murder and appealed. The Court of Appeal of Jersey allowed the appeal and ruled that while the defendant's drunkenness could not be taken into account, his chronic alcoholism could be considered when determining whether his loss of self-control was excusable. The Court substituted a conviction of manslaughter due to provocation. The Attorney General for Jersey appealed to the Privy Council.

An enlarged bench of nine Lords of Appeal in Ordinary presided over this appeal in the Privy Council. The decision of the Privy Council was a majority one of 6:3. The six Law Lords in the majority decided that the defendant's alcoholism was not a characteristic which could be taken into account. The majority disapproved the House of Lords' decision in *Smith* (2001), taking the view that the House had departed from the law as declared under s.3 of the Homicide Act 1957 and significantly relaxed the objective standard adopted by Parliament. Lord Nicholls stated that 'it is not open to judges now to change ("develop") the common law and thereby depart from the law as declared by Parliament'. Lord Nicholls held that:

> Under the statute the sufficiency of the provocation ('whether the provocation was enough to make a reasonable man do as [the defendant] did') is to be judged by one stand-ard, not a standard which varies from defendant to defendant. Whether the provocative act or words and the defendant's response met the 'ordinary person' standard prescribed by the statute is the question the jury must consider, not the altogether looser question of whether, having regard to all the circumstances, the jury consider the loss of self-con-trol was sufficiently excusable. The statute does not leave each jury free to set whatever standard they consider appropriate in the circumstances by which to judge whether the defendant's conduct is 'excusable'.

The majority in the Privy Council favoured reverting back to the position in *Camplin* (1978). Lord Nicholls justified this approach:

> The powers of self-control possessed by *ordinary* people vary according to their age and, more doubtfully, their sex. These features are to be contrasted with abnormalities, that is, features not found in a person having ordinary powers of self-control. The former are relevant when identifying and applying the objective standard of self-control, the latter are not. (Author's emphasis.)

The Privy Council also drew a distinction between 'control' characteristics and 'gravity' characteristics. Thus, only the defendant's age and sex may be taken into account in determining whether a reasonable person would have acted as the defendant did. No other characteristics may be taken into account in relation to the level of self-control to be expected of the defendant. Any characteristic may be taken into account in relation to the gravity of the provocation to the defendant.

Although *Holley* (2005) was the more recent decision relating to the law on provocation, it was unclear whether *Holley* (2005) or *Smith* (2001) reflected the true state of the law after this decision. This was because decisions of the Privy Council are merely persuasive, whereas decisions of the House of Lords are binding. Thus, *Holley* (2005) was merely persuasive, while *Smith* (2001) was technically binding. The decision in *Holley* (2005) was especially persuasive due to the enlarged bench of nine Lords of Appeal in Ordinary. It should be noted that there were only ever 12 House of Lords judges at any one time. Thus, the six Law Lords in the majority in *Holley* (2006) represented half of the Lords of Appeal in Ordinary at that time.

Lord Nicholls also stated that the Privy Council was 'concerned to resolve this conflict and clarify definitively the present state of English law'. This statement highlights the intention of the Privy Council to rule definitively upon the issue of the objective element of the law relating to provocation. In *Mohammed (Faqir)* [2005] EWCA Crim 1880 and *Karimi and James* [2006] EWCA Crim 14, the Court of Appeal did not follow *Smith* (2001), instead confirming that *Holley* (2005) should be followed. The bench in *Karimi and James* (2006) consisted of five Lords Justices of Appeal, instead of the usual bench of three.

As a result of s.54(1)(c) of the Coroners and Justice Act 2009, it is quite clear now that Parliament favoured the approach in *Holley* (2005) and *Camplin* (1978). Thus only the age and sex of the defendant can be taken into account in assessing the degree of tolerance and self-control to be expected of the defendant.

5.5 Diminished responsibility

The defence of diminished responsibility was introduced by the Homicide Act 1957 as a result of criticism of the defence of insanity. In *Brown* [2012] 2 Cr App R (S) 27, the Court of Appeal noted that '[o]ne purpose of the 2009 amendments was to ensure a greater equilibrium between the law and medical science'. Diminished responsibility differs from insanity in that it is a special defence, available in relation to murder only. It is no defence to attempted murder: *Campbell* [1997] Crim LR 495. By contrast, insanity is a defence to any offence. Diminished responsibility is also a partial defence, so a successful plea of diminished responsibility will reduce the defendant's liability to manslaughter.

5.5.1 **Evidential issues**

As with insanity, the legal burden of proving diminished responsibility is on the defendant: s.2(2) of the Homicide Act 1957. This defence provides one of the rare circumstances in which the burden of proof rests on the defence. The defence must prove all of the elements of diminished responsibility on a balance of probabilities: *Dunbar* [1958] 1 QB 1.

 THINKING POINT

Consider whether placing the burden of proof for the defence of diminished responsibility on the defendant violates the presumption of innocence under Article 6(2) of the ECHR.

In the case of *Lambert, Ali and Jordan* [2001] 2 WLR 211, the Court of Appeal confirmed that placing the legal burden of proving diminished responsibility on the defendant did not violate the presumption of innocence under Article 6.2 of the European Convention on Human Rights because diminished responsibility is a defence and does not form part of the elements of the offence of murder. This was confirmed more recently in the case of *Foye* [2013] EWCA Crim 475.

5.5.2 **The elements of diminished responsibility**

The defence is provided for by s.2(1) of the Homicide Act 1957. Note that s.52 of the Coroners and Justice Act 2009 has amended s.2 of the Homicide Act 1957, replacing the previous definition of diminished responsibility with a more modern version. Part of the rationale for this was to ensure 'a greater equilibrium between the law and medical science' (*Brown* [2012] 2 Cr App R (S) 27 at [23]).

 STATUTE

Section 2, Homicide Act 1957 (as amended)

(1) A person ('D') who kills or is a party to the killing of another is not to be convicted of murder if D was suffering from an abnormality of mental functioning which—

  (a) arose from a recognised medical condition,

  (b) substantially impaired D's ability to do one or more of the things mentioned in subsection (1A), and

  (c) provides an explanation for D's acts and omissions in doing or being a party to the killing.

(1A) Those things are—

  (a) to understand the nature of D's conduct;

  (b) to form a rational judgment;

  (c) to exercise self-control.

(1B) For the purposes of subsection (1)(c), an abnormality of mental functioning provides an explanation for D's conduct if it causes, or is a significant contributory factor in causing, D to carry out that conduct.

Figure 5.6 The elements of diminished responsibility

The original section was 'broadly phrased and rather more obviously couched in terms of a value judgment', while the amended section is 'more tightly structured' (*Brennan* [2014] EWCA Crim 2387 at [49]). Under the amended section, the old phrase 'abnormality of mind' has been replaced with 'abnormality of mental functioning'. The defendant's abnormality of mental functioning must arise from a 'recognised medical condition' (s.2(1)(a)) and it must substantially impair the defendant's ability to understand the nature of his conduct, form a rational judgement, or exercise self-control (s.2(1)(b) and s.2(1A)). The abnormality of mental functioning must also provide an explanation for the defendant's conduct (s.2(1)(c)), which it will do if it causes, or is a significant contributory factor in causing, the defendant to carry out that conduct (s.2(1B)).

The defence must prove that the defendant:

(1) was suffering from an abnormality of mental functioning;

(2) arising from a recognised medical condition;

(3) which substantially impaired the defendant's ability to understand the nature of his conduct, form a rational judgement, or exercise self-control; and

(4) which provides an explanation for the defendant's acts and omissions in doing or being party to the killing.

This is illustrated in figure 5.6.

5.5.3 **Abnormality of mental functioning**

The first element of diminished responsibility which must be proved by the defendant is that the defendant was suffering from an abnormality of mental functioning at the time of the killing.

Prior to the amendments made by s.52 of the Coroners and Justice Act 2009, this was expressed as an 'abnormality of mind'. The leading authority on abnormality of mind is *Byrne* [1960] 2 QB 396. The defendant in this case killed a young girl by strangling her. He then committed 'horrifying mutilations upon her dead body'. He was charged with her murder and pleaded diminished responsibility. The defence adduced psychiatric evidence that the defendant was a sexual psychopath who experienced 'violent perverted sexual desires' which he found difficult to control. The defendant appealed against his conviction for murder on the ground that the trial judge had misdirected the jury in relation to diminished responsibility. The Court of Appeal allowed the appeal, quashing the defendant's conviction for murder and substituting one for manslaughter by diminished responsibility. Lord Parker CJ stated that 'abnormality of mind':

> means a state of mind so different from that of ordinary human beings that the reasonable man would term it abnormal. It appears to us to be wide enough to cover the mind's activities in all its aspects, not only the perception of physical acts and matters, and the ability to form a rational judgment as to whether an act is right or wrong, but also the ability to exercise will power to control physical acts in accordance with that rational judgment.

The definition of the term 'abnormality of mind' given by Lord Parker CJ was very wide. It encompassed all aspects of the mind's activities and not just the defendant's brain. An abnormality of mind might simply involve an inability to exercise control over acts which the defendant knows to be wrong. The phrase 'abnormality of mental functioning' replaced 'abnormality of mind' when s.52 of the Coroners and Justice Act 2009 came into force. It is likely that 'abnormality of mental functioning' will be interpreted equally widely by the courts.

 THINKING POINT

Compare and contrast the defences of diminished responsibility and insanity. Why didn't the defendant in *Byrne* plead insanity instead?

By contrast, the term 'disease of the mind', which is an element of the defence of insanity under the *M'Naghten Rules* (1843), is very narrow in scope. It is a requirement of insanity that the defendant did not know what he was doing or that he did not know that it was wrong. The defendant in *Byrne* would not have been able to successfully plead insanity because he did know what he was doing and that it was wrong, he was simply unable to control his impulses. These are not requirements of diminished responsibility. A defendant may plead diminished responsibility even though he appreciated what he was doing in killing the victim and knew that it was wrong. Thus, the defence of diminished responsibility is much wider than that of insanity.

Diminished responsibility and insanity must remain distinct defences. Diminished responsibility is wider in scope and does not require a defendant to be insane or partially insane. In the case of *Seers* (1984) 79 Cr App R 261, the Court of Appeal held that when directing the jury in relation to diminished responsibility, terms such as 'partial insanity' or 'borderline insanity' should be avoided as they may confuse a jury. In this case, the defendant was suffering from chronic reactive depression. He was charged with the murder of his estranged wife. The defendant pleaded diminished responsibility and the trial judge directed the jury to consider whether the defendant was partially insane or on the border of insanity. This was held to be a misdirection and the defendant's conviction for murder was substituted for one of manslaughter by diminished responsibility.

5.5.4 **Recognised medical condition**

The abnormality of mental functioning must arise from a recognised medical condition. This means that the abnormality of mental functioning must be supported by medical evidence; in *Bunch* [2013] EWCA Crim 2498 it was held that medical evidence is a practical necessity if the defence is to succeed. This reflects the position prior to the amendments by the Coroners and Justice Act 2009 (see *Dix* (1981) 74 Cr App R 306). The Court of Appeal has recently stated that 'most, if not all, of the aspects of the new provisions relate entirely to psychiatric matters', and conclude that it would therefore be 'both legitimate and helpful . . . for an expert psychiatrist to include in his or her evidence a view on all four stages' (*Brennan* [2014] EWCA Crim 2387 at [51]).

Prior to the amendments made by the 2009 Act, the causes from which the abnormality of mind arose were widely construed. Consequently, diminished responsibility was available where the defendant was suffering from battered women syndrome (*Hobson* [1998] 1 Cr App R 31), depression (*Ahluwalia* (1993) 96 Cr App R 133), pre-menstrual syndrome (*Smith* [1982] Crim LR 531), morbid jealousy (*Vinagre* (1979) 69 Cr App R 104), or paranoid psychosis and functional mental illness as well as organic or physical injury or disease of the body, including the brain (*Sanderson* (1994) 98 Cr App R 325).

Since the 2009 Act, any recognised medical condition which causes an abnormality of mental function will suffice.

5.5.5 Substantial impairment of the defendant's ability

The defendant must also prove that the abnormality of mental functioning substantially impaired his ability to do one of the things listed in subsection (1A). These are: to understand the nature of his conduct, form a rational judgement, or exercise self-control. It must also provide an explanation for the defendant's acts and omissions in killing or being a party to the killing. This involves consideration of the extent to which the defendant is answerable for his acts in light of his state of mind and ability to exercise self-control. In *Byrne* (1960), Lord Parker CJ commented that:

> The expression 'mental responsibility for his acts' points to a consideration of the extent to which the accused's mind is answerable for his physical acts which must include a consideration of the extent of his ability to exercise will power to control his physical acts.

Whether or not the defendant's ability to do one of the things listed was substantially impaired is a question for the jury to determine (*Lloyd* [1967] 1 QB 175) and trial judges should refuse to give any further direction on the meaning of the term 'on the premise that the meaning is obvious' (*Golds* [2014] EWCA Crim 748). The word 'substantially' is an ordinary English word intended to ensure that the defence of diminished responsibility is not available to a defendant whose impairment of mental responsibility was only trivial or insignificant.

In recent years, case law has conflicted on the meaning of the word 'substantially' in this context. While some cases take a narrow approach (see *Brown* [2012] 2 Cr App R (S) 27, in which the impairment had to be more than minimal), more recently a wide approach has been preferred. In *Golds* [2014] EWCA Crim 748, it was held that 'substantially impairs' refers to an abnormality of mental functioning which 'significantly or appreciably impairs [the defendant's ability to do the things specified in s.2(1A)], beyond something that is merely more than trivial or minimal' (at [55]). While no direction should be given on the meaning of 'substantially', where the jury does ask for help, a judge should not adopt the narrow meaning given in *Brown* [2012] 2 Cr App R (S) 27.

5.5.6 Diminished responsibility and intoxication

This paragraph addresses the effect of intoxication on the defence of diminished responsibility. In *Fenton* (1975) 61 Cr App R 261, the Court of Appeal held that self-induced intoxication cannot produce an abnormality of mind (as it then was) for the purposes of s.2(1) of the Homicide Act 1957. This was confirmed by the Court of Appeal in *Wood* [2008] EWCA Crim 1305, in which Sir Igor P (as he then was) stated, 'the consumption of alcohol . . . cannot, without more, bring his actions within the concept of diminished responsibility'. More recently the Court of Appeal has also confirmed the position post-Coroners and Justice Act 2009 in the case of *Dowds* [2012] 1 WLR 2576 in which Hughes LJ stated that, '[v]oluntary acute intoxication, whether from alcohol or other substance, is not capable of founding diminished responsibility', and this was confirmed in *Bunch* [2013] EWCA Crim 2498 and *Williams* [2013] EWCA Crim 2749. In *Williams* the Court of Appeal stated that the concept of mental responsibility 'describes . . . the extent to which a person's act are the choice of a free and rational mind . . . Such a choice may be inhibited by many things. The effect of drink is plainly one. But the effect of drink on its own will not necessarily bring the case within s.2(1) of the Homicide Act 1957 for of itself the use of drink, even excessive use, is not an abnormality of mind' (at [21]). Thus, intoxication alone may not amount to one of the inherent causes under s.2(1). However, a condition such as alcoholism (alcohol dependency syndrome) might amount to an abnormality of mental functioning as it is a recognised medical condition.

5.5.6.1 Alcohol dependency syndrome

In the case of *Tandy* [1989] 1 WLR 350, the Court of Appeal held that the disease of alcoholism could amount to an abnormality of mind for the purposes of s.2(1) of the Homicide Act 1957. However, in order for alcoholism to amount to an abnormality of mind, the defendant's craving must render his consumption of alcohol involuntary. Where the defendant's consumption of alcohol was voluntary and he simply did not resist an impulse to drink, diminished responsibility would not be available. However, in *Woods* [2008] 2 Cr App R 34, the Court of Appeal held that alcoholism could be regarded as an abnormality of mind for the purposes of diminished responsibility, even where there had been no brain damage resulting from the alcohol dependency syndrome. The Court held that it was no longer appropriate to draw a distinction between cases where brain damage had and had not occurred. Thus, even where the defendant voluntarily consumed alcohol, he may still rely on the defence of diminished responsibility. According to the case of *Stewart* [2009] 2 Cr App R 30, whether the alcoholism would amount to an abnormality of mind would be a matter for the jury and would depend on the nature and extent of the alcohol dependency syndrome and whether the defendant had an irresistible craving for drink.

5.5.6.2 Multiple causes

Recent case law has explored the effect of intoxication on the defence where the defendant is suffering from an abnormality of mind caused by an inherent cause and is also intoxicated at the time of the killing. In such cases, the jury must be directed to disregard the defendant's intoxication. If the jury is satisfied that, despite the intoxication, the abnormality did substantially impair the defendant's mental responsibility for his acts, the defence of diminished responsibility will be successful. See *Gittens* [1984] QB 698, in which the defendant killed his wife and stepdaughter. His abnormality of mind had been caused partly by his depression and partly by his consumption of alcohol and medication for his depression.

 CASE CLOSE-UP

Dietschmann [2003] UKHL 10

In this case the House of Lords held that the abnormality of mind did not have to be the sole cause of the defendant's acts in killing the victim. Where, at the time of the killing, the defendant acted in part due to the abnormality of mind and in part due to his intoxication, the jury should be directed to disregard the effect of the intoxication and consider whether the defendant's abnormality of mind substantially impaired his mental responsibility for his acts when killing the victim. The defendant in this case suffered from depression and was taking anti-depressants and sleeping tablets. His aunt, with whom he had had a relationship, had recently died. He had an argument with a friend about a watch which the defendant's aunt had left him. The defendant killed his friend and pleaded diminished responsibility to the murder. The defence adduced evidence that he had been suffering from an adjustment disorder caused by grief. The defendant appealed against his conviction for murder. The Court of Appeal dismissed his appeal, but the appeal was allowed by the House of Lords. In the House of Lords, Lord Hutton read s.2(1) of the Homicide Act 1957 to mean that:

> if the defendant satisfies the jury that, notwithstanding the alcohol he had consumed and its effect on him, his abnormality of mind substantially impaired his mental responsibility for his acts in doing the killing, the jury should find him not guilty of murder but…guilty of manslaughter. I take this view because I think that in referring to substantial impairment of mental responsibility the subsection does not require the abnormality of mind to be the sole cause of the defendant's acts in doing the killing. In my opinion, even if the defendant would not have killed if he had not taken drink, the causative effect of the drink does not necessarily prevent an abnormality of mind suffered by the defendant from substantially impairing his mental responsibility for his fatal acts.

Thus, where a defendant is intoxicated and suffering from an abnormality of mind (mental functioning), the jury must ask whether, despite the alcohol, the abnormality of mind substantially impaired the defendant's responsibility for the killing.

5.6 Suicide pact

Suicide pact is also a special defence, available to murder only. Like loss of control and diminished responsibility, it is a partial defence which reduces liability to manslaughter if pleaded successfully. A suicide pact arises where two or more people agree to kill each other. If one party to the suicide pact survives, he may be charged with murder and may have the defence available to him. If he successfully pleads suicide pact, he will be convicted of manslaughter.

5.6.1 Evidential issues

The legal burden of proving that the defendant was acting under a suicide pact with the victim rests with the defence: s.4(2) of the Homicide Act 1957. The standard of proof is on a balance of probabilities.

5.6.2 The elements of suicide pact

The defence of suicide pact is provided for under s.4(1) of the Homicide Act 1957.

 STATUTE

Section 4(1), Homicide Act 1957

It shall be manslaughter, and shall not be murder, for a person acting in pursuance of a suicide pact between him and another to kill the other or be a party to the other…being killed by a third person.

The term 'suicide pact' is explained under s.4(3) of the Act. It requires all persons who are party to the pact to have a 'common agreement' which has as its object the death of all parties to the pact. Only acts committed while the defendant has a 'settled intention of dying' may be treated as acts done in pursuance of the suicide pact.

5.6.3 Encouraging or assisting suicide

It is no longer an offence to commit suicide. The offence of suicide was abolished by s.1 of the Suicide Act 1961. However, it is an offence to encourage or assist suicide or encourage or assist attempted suicide under s.2(1) of the Suicide Act 1961 (as amended by s.59 of the Coroners and Justice Act 2009).

 CROSS REFERENCE

Refer to chapter 15 on inchoate offences for a more detailed discussion of these provisions.

Thus, where a defendant helps or encourages another person to kill themselves, he may be charged with this offence instead. This offence carries a maximum sentence of 14 years' imprisonment. In *R (on the application of Purdy) v DPP* [2009] UKHL 45, the House of Lords ruled that the guidance in the Code for Crown Prosecutors was not sufficiently clear on how decisions should or were likely to be taken as to whether, in a given case, it would be in the public interest to prosecute. As a result of this case, the DPP published an interim policy on prosecuting assisted suicide to clarify the factors of public interest which influence the decision to prosecute. The finalised policy was published in February 2010 and is available online at http://www.cps.gov.uk/publications/prosecution/assisted_suicide_policy.html.

The language used in the amendments corresponds to the offences of encouraging or assisting the commission of offence(s) under ss.44–46 of the Serious Crime Act 2007.

5.7 Infanticide

Infanticide is provided for under s.1(1) of the Infanticide Act 1938. It arises where a woman kills her child, who is under the age of 12 months, by any wilful act or omission and, at the time, the balance of her mind was disturbed due to the birth. A woman may be tried for the offence of infanticide, or may be tried for murder and raise the defence of infanticide under s.1(2) of the Infanticide Act 1938. Infanticide is treated like a conviction for manslaughter, and thus carries a maximum sentence of life imprisonment. The defendant bears an evidential burden, but the prosecution bears the legal burden of proving that infanticide does not apply.

> **STATUTE**
>
> **Section 1(1), Infanticide Act 1938**
>
> Where a woman by any wilful act or omission causes the death of her child being a child under the age of twelve months, but at the time of the act or omission the balance of her mind was disturbed by reason of her not having fully recovered from the effect of giving birth to the child or by reason of the effect of lactation consequent upon the birth of the child, then, notwithstanding that the circumstances were such that but for this Act the offence would have amounted to murder, she shall be guilty of felony, to wit of infanticide, and may for such offence be dealt with and punished as if she had been guilty of the offence of manslaughter of the child.

Note that s.57 of the Coroners and Justice Act 2009 also made some minor amendments to s.1 of the Infanticide Act 1938.

Summary

- Murder is a common law offence. It is committed when a defendant unlawfully causes the death of a person with an intention to kill or cause GBH.

- There are two types of manslaughter: voluntary manslaughter and involuntary manslaughter.

- Where a defendant has both the *actus reus* and *mens rea* for murder, but also has one of three special, partial defences available to him, his liability for murder is reduced to that of manslaughter (voluntary manslaughter).

- Loss of control is a statutory defence under s.54 of the Coroners and Justice Act 2009. It is a defence to murder only. A successful plea of loss of control will reduce the defendant's liability to voluntary manslaughter.

- There are three components to the defence of loss of control: (1) the defendant loses self-control (the subjective test); (2) the loss of control had a qualifying trigger; and (3) a person of the defendant's sex and age, with a normal degree of tolerance and self-restraint and in the circumstances of the defendant, might have reacted in the same or in a similar way (the objective test).

- Diminished responsibility is a defence under s.2 of the Homicide Act 1957. It is a defence to murder only. A successful plea of diminished responsibility will reduce the defendant's liability to voluntary manslaughter.

- There are three elements to the defence of diminished responsibility: (1) the defendant must suffer an abnormality of mental functioning; (2) which arises from a recognised medical condition; and (3) which substantially impairs the defendant's ability to understand the nature of his conduct, form a rational judgement, or exercise self-control, and which explains the defendant's acts and omissions in doing the killing.

 ## The bigger picture

- For more information on sentencing in murder cases, you might want to look at: *R (on the application of Anderson) v Secretary of State for the Home Department* [2002] 4 All ER 1089; s.269 and Schedule 21, Criminal Justice Act 2003; *R v Sullivan and others* [2004] EWCA Crim 1762; Criminal Practice Directions, Sentencing L and Sentencing M [2013] EWCA Crim 1631; and CPS guidance on sentencing in murder cases: http://www.cps.gov.uk/legal/s_to_u/sentencing_-_mandatory_life_sentences_in_murder_cases/.

- For a detailed discussion on the issue of sexual infidelity and gender imbalance, see S. Edwards 'Loss of Self-Control: When His Anger is Worth More than Her Fear' in Reed and Bohlander (2001), pp.79–95.

- For more information on diminished responsibility and the requirement of a causal link between the killing and the abnormality of mental functioning, see Mackay (2010).

? Questions

Self-test questions

1. Define murder.

2. What is the *mens rea* for murder? Cite an authority for this.

3. Explain the difference between voluntary manslaughter and involuntary manslaughter.

4. What is the subjective element of the defence of loss of control?

5. Explain what a qualifying trigger is.

6. Explain the difference between 'gravity characteristics' and 'control characteristics'.

7. Can any of the defendant's characteristics be taken into account in relation to the last element of loss of control?

8. What are the elements of diminished responsibility?

9. Who bears the legal burden for: *(a)* loss of control; *(b)* diminished responsibility; *(c)* suicide pact?

10. What are the requirements of the defence of suicide pact?

 For suggested approaches, please visit the Online Resource Centre.

Exam questions

1. Jack and Kate have been unhappily married for several years. They argue continually and many of their arguments have turned violent. Jack suffers from depression and is impotent. He has also started drinking heavily. One evening, Jack returns home after a night in the pub and finds Kate in her dressing gown, in a passionate embrace with another man. When Jack confronts Kate, she admits to having an affair and taunts Jack, telling him that he fails to satisfy her in bed. Jack waits for Kate to turn around and start to climb the stairs, then he strikes her on the head with a wine bottle, killing her.

    Discuss Jack's liability for Kate's death.

2. The defence of loss of control introduced by the Coroners and Justice Act 2009 greatly clarifies the law.

    To what extent, if at all, do you agree with the above statement?

 For suggested approaches, please visit the Online Resource Centre.

☰ Further reading

Books

Ashworth, A. and Mitchell, B. *Rethinking English Homicide Law* (2000), Oxford: Oxford University Press

Horder, J. (ed.) *Homicide Law in Comparative Perspective* (2007), Oxford: Hart Publishing

Ormerod, D. and Laird, K. *Smith and Hogan: Criminal Law* (14th edn, 2015), Oxford: Oxford University Press

Reed, A. and Bohlander, M. (eds) *Loss of Control and Diminished Responsibility Domestic, Comparative and International Perspectives* (2011), Farnham: Ashgate

Journal articles

Allen, M. 'Provocation's Reasonable Man: A Plea for Self-Control' (2000) 64 JCL 216

Ashworth, A. 'Principles, Pragmatism and the Law Commission's Recommendations on Homicide Law Reform' [2007] Crim LR 333

Baker, D. and Zhao, L. 'Contributory Qualifying and Non-Qualifying Triggers in the Loss of Control Defence: A Wrong Turn on Sexual Infidelity' (2012) 76 JCL 254

Clough, A. 'Loss of Self-Control as a Defence: The Key to Replacing Provocation' (2010) 74 JCL 118

Edwards, S. 'Anger and Fear as Justifiable Preludes for Loss of Self-Control' (2010) 74 JCL 223

Fitz-Gibbon, K. 'Replacing Provocation in England and Wales: Examining the Partial Defence of Loss of Control' (2013) 40 Journal of Law and Society 280

Gibson, M. 'Intoxicants and Diminished Responsibility: The Impact of the Coroners and Justice Act 2009' [2011] Crim LR 909

Holton, R. and Shute, S. 'Self-Control in the Modern Provocation Defence' (2007) 27 OJLS 49

Leigh, L. H. 'Two New Partial Defences to Murder' (2010) 174 CL&J 53

Mackay, R. 'The Coroners and Justice Act 2009—Partial Defences to Murder (2) The New Diminished Responsibility Plea' [2010] Crim LR 290

Mackay, R. and Mitchell, B. 'But is this Provocation? Some Thoughts on the Law Commission's Report on Partial Defences to Murder' [2005] Crim LR 85

Mitchell, B. and Mackay, R. 'Loss of Control and Diminished Responsibility: Monitoring the New Partial Defences' (2011) 3 Archbold Review 5

Morgan, C. 'Loss of Self-Control: Back to the Good Old Days' (2013) 77 JCL 119

Norrie, A. 'The Coroners and Justice Act 2009—Partial Defences to Murder (1) Loss of Control' [2010] Crim LR 275

Parsons, S. 'The Loss of Control Defence—Fit for Purpose?' (2015) 79 JCL 94

Wake, N. 'Recognising Acute Intoxication as Diminished Responsibility? A Comparative Analysis?' (2012) 76 JCL 71

Wake, N. 'Battered Women, Startled Householders and Psychological Self-Defence: Anglo-Australian Perspectives' (2013) 77 JCL 433

Withey, C. 'Loss of Control, Loss of Opportunity?' [2011] Crim LR 263

Reports

Law Commission Report, *Murder, Manslaughter and Infanticide* (Law Com. No. 304, 2006)

Law Commission Report, *Partial Defences to Murder* (Law Com. No. 290, 2004)

6 Involuntary manslaughter

☐ **LEARNING OBJECTIVES**

By the end of this chapter, you should be able to:

● define unlawful act manslaughter and explain the elements of the offence;

● explain the development of the law relating to the 'drugs cases';

● define gross negligence manslaughter and explain the elements of the offence;

● understand the offence of subjectively reckless manslaughter; and

● understand the offence of corporate manslaughter.

Introduction

This chapter deals predominantly with situations where a defendant kills the victim but does not have the requisite *mens rea* for murder (see chapter 5). Imagine that a defendant punches the victim once in the chest, causing the victim to fall back and strike his head, and resulting in his death (such a defendant is known colloquially as a 'one-punch killer'). One punch to the chest is unlikely to be sufficient to prove an intention to kill or cause GBH, so the defendant will not be guilty of murder, but surely this cannot mean that the defendant escapes liability. What about a defendant who takes drugs together with the victim, injecting the victim with a dose of heroin that kills him? If the object of the injection was not to kill or cause GBH, the defendant will not be guilty of murder, but having injected the heroin into the victim's body, surely the defendant must be held criminally liable for the death of the victim. In fact, the defendant in each of these examples is likely to be convicted of unlawful act manslaughter, a form of involuntary manslaughter.

This chapter explores the main types of involuntary manslaughter and the offence of corporate manslaughter. A defendant will be guilty of involuntary manslaughter where he unlawfully causes the death of the victim but has no intention to kill or cause GBH (i.e., the defendant does not have the requisite *mens rea* for murder). The three main types of involuntary manslaughter are unlawful act manslaughter, gross negligence manslaughter, and reckless manslaughter. These will be discussed in detail in this chapter. The final section of this chapter will then cover two further offences of involuntary manslaughter: the offence of corporate manslaughter under s.1 of the Corporate Manslaughter and Corporate Homicide Act 2007 and the offence of causing or allowing the death of or serious harm to a child or vulnerable adult under s.5 of the Domestic Violence, Crime and Victims Act 2004.

6.1 Unlawful act manslaughter

Unlawful act manslaughter arises where the defendant intentionally commits an unlawful act which a reasonable person would recognise exposes the victim to the risk of some harm and the victim dies as a result. Unlawful act manslaughter is also known as 'constructive manslaughter' because the defendant's liability for manslaughter is constructed out of his liability for a lesser offence. The offence of unlawful act manslaughter was defined by the Court of Criminal Appeal in the case of *Larkin* (1944) 29 Cr App R 18. The defendant in this case killed his girlfriend when she fell on a razor he was holding. When he saw her at a party with another man, the defendant brandished a razor to scare the man. However, the victim drunkenly swayed towards him and fell on the razor, which cut her throat and killed her. The defendant was convicted of manslaughter. The Court of Criminal Appeal dismissed the appeal. Humphreys J explained how liability for manslaughter arises through an unlawful act:

> Where the act which a person is engaged in performing is unlawful, then if at the same time it is a dangerous act, that is, an act which is likely to injure another person, and quite inadvertently the doer of the act causes the death of that other person by that act, then he is guilty of manslaughter.

This type of manslaughter was also defined in the House of Lords' authority of *DPP v Newbury and Jones* [1977] AC 500.

🔍 CASE CLOSE-UP

DPP v Newbury and Jones [1977] AC 500

The defendants in this case were two 15-year-old boys who were on a railway bridge. They pushed a paving stone over the bridge onto an oncoming train. The stone went through the glass window of the driver's cab, killing the guard. The defendants were convicted of manslaughter. Their appeals to the Court of Appeal and House of Lords were dismissed. Lord Salmon defined unlawful act manslaughter:

> an accused is guilty of manslaughter if it is proved that he intentionally did an act which was unlawful and dangerous and that that act inadvertently caused death . . . [I]t is unnecessary to prove that the accused knew that the act was unlawful or dangerous.

However, the House did not specify what the unlawful act was in this case. Lord Salmon identified four ingredients of unlawful act manslaughter which must be proved by the prosecution in order to secure a conviction:

  (i) the defendant must intentionally do an act;

 (ii) the act must be unlawful;

(iii) the act must be dangerous;

(iv) the act must cause death.

Figure 6.1 The elements of unlawful act manslaughter

An intentional act **+** The act is unlawful **+** The act is objectively dangerous **+** The act causes death **=** Unlawful act manslaughter

THINKING POINT

What do you think the unlawful act was in *DPP v Newbury and Jones* (1977)?

Unlawful act manslaughter involves the commission of an unlawful act which inadvertently causes death. The defendant need not intend to kill (as this would amount to murder), in fact, he need not even foresee the death of the victim. There is no requirement that the defendant knows that the act is unlawful and dangerous. The offence is objectively assessed in this regard—the reasonable person must merely recognise the risk of some harm (see 6.1.3). The only elements of subjectivity in the offence lie in the intentional commission of an act (see 6.1.1) and the *mens rea* of the unlawful act which must be proved (see 6.1.2). As such, the offence of unlawful act manslaughter punishes an offender for the consequences of their conduct, even though there is no corresponding *mens rea* (see figure 6.1).

These four elements will be explored in 6.1.1 to 6.1.4.

6.1.1 **Intentional act**

The first element that the prosecution must prove is that the defendant intentionally did an act. The intention in this element relates to the act committed by the defendant and not the resultant death. Where the death is intentionally caused, the defendant is guilty of murder, not manslaughter.

It appears that in order to be guilty of unlawful act manslaughter, the defendant must intentionally engage in a positive act. A negligent omission will not suffice. In the case of *Lowe* [1973] QB 702, the defendant wilfully neglected his child, contrary to s.1(1) of the Children and Young Persons Act 1933, resulting in the child's death. This was not sufficient for a conviction for unlawful act manslaughter. It remains unclear whether a defendant might be convicted of unlawful act manslaughter on the basis of an intentional or deliberate omission. It is difficult to identify any rationale for distinguishing between deliberate acts and deliberate omissions which both lead to the same result, the death of a person.

6.1.2 **Unlawful act**

The second requirement is that the act be unlawful. This means that it must be a criminal offence. The prosecution must prove both the *actus reus* and the *mens rea* of the offence. Historically, a civil wrong was held to be sufficient as the unlawful act. In the case of *Fenton* (1830) 1 Lewin 179, it was held that liability for manslaughter could be constructed out of the tort of trespass to the person. However, *Fenton* (1830) was rejected in *Franklin* (1883) 15 Cox CC 163. The defendant in this case took a box from a refreshment stall on Brighton Pier and threw it into the sea. The box struck a swimmer in the sea, killing him. It was held that the tort of trespass to the property of the stall keeper was not sufficient for constructive manslaughter. Field J stated that a civil tort should not form the basis of liability for a criminal offence. The unlawful act must be a criminal offence. Thus, the defendant was convicted of gross negligence manslaughter, rather than unlawful act manslaughter.

The unlawful act must amount to a criminal offence in law. The prosecution must prove both the *actus reus* and *mens rea* of the crime and the absence of a defence. If these basic elements of criminal liability cannot be established, there is no unlawful act and, thus, there can be no liability for unlawful act manslaughter.

 CASE CLOSE-UP

Lamb [1967] 2 QB 981

The case of *Lamb* involved an unfortunate accident which occurred during a practical joke. The defendant pointed a loaded revolver at his friend, the victim. Although the defendant and victim knew that there were bullets in the cylinder of the revolver, there was no bullet opposite the barrel of the gun, and they did not realise that the cylinder rotated when the trigger was pulled. Thus, both the defendant and the victim believed that no bullet would be fired from the gun if the defendant pulled the trigger. Unfortunately, they were wrong. The defendant did pull the trigger and killed his friend. The defendant was charged with manslaughter. He argued that the killing was an accident.

The trial judge directed the jury that the defendant pointing the gun at the victim could be an unlawful act for the purposes of unlawful act manslaughter. The defendant was accordingly convicted of unlawful act manslaughter and appealed.

The Court of Appeal allowed the appeal and quashed the defendant's conviction. The Court held that unlawful act manslaughter required proof of a criminal offence. In this case, there was no criminal offence. There was no assault because the *mens rea* of assault was not present. The defendant did not intend to cause the victim to apprehend immediate and unlawful violence because the killing was an accident. He could not intend to cause such apprehension when neither he nor the victim thought that a bullet would be fired from the gun. The Court held that the trial judge had misdirected the jury, effectively withdrawing the defence of accident from their consideration.

 THINKING POINT

The Court of Appeal in *Lamb* (1967) focused on the absence of the *mens rea* of assault. Was the *actus reus* present?

Was there any other offence of which the defendant could have been convicted?

Why would this not be sufficient as a basis for a conviction for unlawful act manslaughter?

It should also be noted that recklessness is sufficient *mens rea* for an assault. It is enough that the defendant recognised the risk that the victim would apprehend immediate and unlawful violence and went on to take that risk. However, it is clear that the defendant in this case did not recognise such a risk as he did not believe that a bullet would be fired from the gun if he pulled the trigger. Similarly, it could be argued that the *actus reus* of assault is also absent in this case. As the unfortunate events of this case originated as a practical joke, it is most unlikely that the victim apprehended immediate and unlawful violence. It was not necessary for the court to consider whether the *actus reus* of assault was present or not because the trial judge had clearly misdirected the jury and the *mens rea* of assault was absent.

▶ CROSS REFERENCE

Refer to 7.1 to ascertain the elements of an assault.

There will be no liability for unlawful act manslaughter where the defendant has a defence to the unlawful act, such as where he is lawfully using self-defence in applying force to the victim: 'if the application of force is committed in lawful self-defence, it does not constitute an assault and it is not unlawful. Accordingly . . . there will be no conviction for manslaughter' (see *Webster v Crown Prosecution Service* [2014] EWHC 2516 (Admin) at [21]).

The cases discussed in this paragraph and those discussed in 6.1.3 and 6.1.4 illustrate that the criminal offence which constitutes the unlawful act may vary. An assault may amount to an unlawful act for the purposes of unlawful act manslaughter (e.g., see *Lewis* [2010] EWCA Crim 151), as may robbery under s.8 of the Theft Act 1968, burglary under s.9(1) of the Theft Act 1968, or maliciously administering poison or a noxious thing so as to endanger life or inflict grievous bodily harm under s.23 of the Offences Against the Person Act 1861. In the case of *Carey* [2006] EWCA Crim 17, it was held that the minor affray committed in this case did not amount to an unlawful act for the purposes of unlawful act manslaughter because there was no evidence that the affray was objectively dangerous. Nevertheless, the Court acknowledged that there could be circumstances in which an affray could constitute an unlawful act for the purposes of unlawful act manslaughter, and in the recent case of *M* [2013] 1 WLR 1083, the Court of Appeal confirmed that an affray could constitute an unlawful act for the purposes of unlawful act manslaughter. The victim in this case was a nightclub doorman who, unbeknown to anyone, suffered from a heart condition. He became involved in a verbal altercation with the defendants outside the nightclub and the altercation resulted in the death of the doorman after he suffered shock and collapsed. The Court held that the question of dangerousness was one of fact for the jury to determine.

It has even been held that the offence of interference with a motor vehicle under s.22A(1)(b) of the Road Traffic Act 1988 could constitute an unlawful act for the purposes of unlawful act manslaughter. In *Meeking* [2012] 1 WLR 3349, the Court of Appeal upheld the defendant's conviction for unlawful act manslaughter. The defendant was the passenger in a car which her husband was driving. She pulled on the handbrake when the car was moving and without warning. The car spun across the road and collided with another car, killing her husband. The act of pulling on the handbrake constituted an offence of inference with a motor vehicle and this was sufficient to found a conviction of unlawful act manslaughter. The Court commented *obiter* that it might have been easier for the prosecution to rely on gross negligence manslaughter instead of unlawful act manslaughter.

6.1.3 **Dangerous act**

The third ingredient of the offence requires that the act be dangerous. In the case of *Larkin* (1944), Humphreys J held that 'a dangerous act' is 'an act which is likely to injure another person'. The act is dangerous if it presents a risk of physical injury to another person. An objective test is applied to the meaning of 'dangerous': the act must be dangerous from the point of view of the reasonable man. It is not necessary for the prosecution to show that the defendant himself realised that the act was dangerous.

The objective test for dangerousness is derived from the case of *Church* [1966] 1 QB 59.

🔍 CASE CLOSE-UP

Church [1966] 1 QB 59

The victim in this case mocked the defendant for failing to satisfy her sexually. A fight ensued and the defendant struck the woman, knocking her unconscious. Believing her to be dead, the defendant then threw her in the river. She died from drowning. The defendant was convicted of manslaughter and appealed. The Court of Appeal held that the trial judge had misdirected the jury in relation to unlawful act manslaughter. Edmund Davies J held that:

> the unlawful act must be such as all sober and reasonable people would inevitably recognise must subject the other person to, at least, the risk of some harm resulting therefrom, albeit not serious harm. . . .

The reasonable person does not need to recognise a risk of serious injury or death resulting from the unlawful act; he/she must merely recognise the risk of *some* harm. The test is clearly objective. Thus, it does not matter that the defendant in this case did not recognise a risk of harm to the victim when he threw her body into the river, because he believed her to be dead. What is relevant is whether or not the reasonable person would have recognised a risk of some harm.

▶ CROSS REFERENCE

The case of *Church* (1966) was also discussed at 3.7.1 in relation to the coincidence of *actus reus* and *mens rea*.

The objective nature of the test can be criticised because it fails to reflect the moral culpability of the defendant to convict him in the absence of proof that he foresaw a risk of some harm. This is best illustrated by the famous example of the 'one-punch killer' in which a drunk defendant punches the victim, who falls over and sustains a fatal head injury. Such a defendant could be convicted of unlawful act manslaughter even if he did not foresee the risk of death, or even harm to the victim (see Mitchell 2008 and Mitchell 2009).

The objective nature of the test was confirmed in the case of *DPP v Newbury and Jones* (1977). Lord Salmon approved the test from *Church* (1966) and stated that:

> The test is still the objective test. In judging whether the act was dangerous the test is not did the accused recognise that it was dangerous but would all sober and reasonable people recognise its danger.

More recently, the objective nature of the test was confirmed in the case of *JF and NE* [2015] EWCA Crim 351, in which the appellants argued that the objective test should be adapted to take into account the ages and mental capacity of the appellants (in a similar vein to the subjective test of recklessness restored by the House of Lords in *R v G and another* [2003] UKHL 50). However, this argument was rejected by the Court of Appeal on the basis that the law on dangerousness in unlawful act manslaughter is 'clear and well established', and while the Law Commission has recommended a subjective test of foresight of the risk causing some injury (Law Commission Reports, *Legislating the Criminal Code: Involuntary Manslaughter* (Law Com. No. 237, 1996) and *Murder, Manslaughter and Infanticide* (Law Com. No. 304,

2006)), Parliament has not sought to carry this recommendation forward (at [32]). Thus, the test remains objective for now.

In determining whether the reasonable man would have recognised a risk of some harm, the reasonable man is deemed to have the knowledge that the defendant had, or should have had, at the time of the offence. An authority for this principle is the case of *Dawson* (1985) 81 Cr App R 150. The defendants in this case attempted to rob an attendant at a petrol station. Two defendants entered the kiosk at the petrol station. They covered their faces with a balaclava and a stocking and were carrying pickaxe handles and imitation firearms. The attendant at the petrol station was a 60-year-old man who had a severe heart condition. When the men entered the kiosk, the attendant suffered a heart attack and died. The three men were convicted of unlawful act manslaughter. The Court of Appeal quashed their convictions and held that the defendants could not be guilty of manslaughter because the victim's heart condition would not have been obvious to the reasonable person if he were present at the scene. The defendants did not know that the victim had a heart condition and they could not be expected to know this. Watkins LJ stated that:

> This test can only be undertaken upon the basis of the knowledge gained by a sober and reasonable man as though he were present at the scene of and watched the unlawful act being performed and who knows that, as in the present case, an unloaded replica gun was in use, but that the victim may have thought it was a loaded gun in working order. In other words, he has the same knowledge as the man attempting to rob and no more. It was never suggested that any of these appellants knew that their victim had a bad heart. They knew nothing about him.

It is apparent from this decision that an act creating shock may amount to a dangerous act: 'injury to the person through the operation of shock emanating from fright' is sufficient for the purposes of unlawful act manslaughter.

The reasonable man is attributed with the same knowledge as the defendant at the scene of the crime. Where the risk of harm becomes obvious to the reasonable person present at the scene of the crime, the defendant's unlawful act becomes dangerous. Thus, in the case of *Watson* [1989] 1 WLR 684, the risk of harm to the victim would have become obvious to the reasonable man when he saw the victim who was elderly and frail.

CASE CLOSE-UP

Watson [1989] 1 WLR 684

In this case, the defendant and another man burgled the house of an 87-year-old man who had a serious heart condition. They threw a brick and entered the house. When they confronted the victim, they verbally abused him and then left the house, without stealing anything. The victim suffered a heart attack and died an hour and a half later. The defendant pleaded guilty to burglary, contrary to s.9(1)(a) of the Theft Act 1968, but was tried for manslaughter. The defence argued that the defendant was not the cause of the victim's death because any adverse effect of the burglary would have ceased long before the death, which occurred an hour and a half later. The defence further suggested that the victim's heart condition meant that he could have died at any time, and that two events after the burglary might have caused the heart attack: *(a)* the arrival of the police, and *(b)* the arrival of council workmen to fix the broken window.

The trial judge directed the jury that the reasonable man would have the knowledge which the defendant gained whilst in the house. The defendant was convicted of manslaughter and appealed. The Court of Appeal held that the trial judge's direction to the jury was correct. The sober and reasonable person is attributed with the knowledge of the defendant as gained in the house. Lord Lane CJ agreed with the view of the trial judge that:

> the jury were entitled to ascribe to the bystander the knowledge which the appellant gained during the whole of his stay in the house ...

Thus, the act will be dangerous if the sober and reasonable person, sharing the knowledge the defendant gained during the commission of the unlawful act, would have recognised a risk of some harm to the victim. Nevertheless, the Court of Appeal allowed the appeal and quashed the defendant's conviction because the prosecution had failed to prove that the shock from the burglary caused the death of the victim.

In the case of *Ball* [1989] Crim LR 730, the Court of Appeal held that the dangerousness of the act is assessed by the appreciation of the sober and reasonable man. The defendant's mistaken belief that the act was not dangerous could not be attributed to the reasonable man. The defendant in this case shot and killed the victim. He mistakenly believed that he had loaded the gun with blank cartridges. The defendant appealed against his conviction, arguing that the test for dangerousness must be based on the act which the defendant believed himself to be committing. However, the Court of Appeal dismissed the appeal and held that the sober and reasonable man is not to be judged by the defendant's appreciation of the mistaken belief. Instead, the sober and reasonable man did not have knowledge of the defendant's mistaken belief that his act was not dangerous.

In the case of *Bristow* [2013] EWCA Crim 1540, the Court of Appeal held that a burglary could constitute an unlawful act for the purposes of unlawful act manslaughter because the burglary was objectively dangerous. The defendants in this case were convicted of unlawful act manslaughter after they executed a burglary of a vehicle-repair business and then ran over the victim in vehicles that they were using to get away. The Court held that the burglary was objectively dangerous for several reasons, including the fact that there was a risk of someone intervening to prevent the defendants' escape, they were using vehicles to escape, and due to the nature and geography of the site which was in a remote location on a farm and the only escape route from the scene was a single track. The unlawful act was objectively dangerous from the outset because the burglary was capable of being an unlawful act which a reasonable and sober person would inevitably recognise must subject a person intervening to the risk of some harm; it did not only become dangerous at the point where the burglars were disturbed by the victim (as in *Dawson* and *Watson*).

 SUMMARY

Dawson (1985): the reasonable man is deemed to have the knowledge that the defendant had, or should have had, at the time of the offence.

Watson (1989): where the risk of harm becomes obvious to the reasonable person present at the scene of the crime, the defendant's unlawful act becomes dangerous.

Ball (1989): the defendant's mistaken belief that the act was not dangerous could not be attributed to the reasonable man.

6.1.4 **Causes death**

⟫ CROSS REFERENCE

Refer to 2.5 to remind yourself of the rules of causation.

The final requirement of unlawful act manslaughter is that the unlawful act causes the death of the victim. The usual rules of causation apply. This means that the prosecution must prove that the defendant was both the factual and legal cause of the victim's death. There will be no liability for manslaughter where there is an intervening act which breaks the chain of causation.

It was once thought that the unlawful act must be aimed at the victim: *Dalby* [1982] 1 WLR 425. However, although the defendant's unlawful act must cause the death of the victim, the act does not need to be directed towards the victim: *Goodfellow* (1986) 83 Cr App R 23. The defendant in *Goodfellow* set fire to his council house in order to be rehoused. He set fire to the house while his wife, three children, and his girlfriend were in the house. He intended that the adults would rescue the children once the fire had started. However, the fire became too intense and the defendant's wife, girlfriend, and one child died. The defendant was convicted of three counts of manslaughter, as well as counts of arson, and appealed. The Court of Appeal held that the unlawful act did not have to be aimed at the victim.

6.1.5 **The 'drugs cases'**

> **THINKING POINT**
>
> Consider whether the defendants are liable for unlawful act manslaughter in the following scenarios:
>
> (1) Marcus asks Chris to prepare a syringe with heroin and to inject him with it. Chris does so and Marcus dies as a result.
>
> (2) Yasmin supplies Nadia with a syringe of heroin. Nadia injects herself with the drug and dies as a result.

The element of causation has attracted much judicial attention over the past 10 years. In particular, there have been a number of 'drugs cases' involving defendants who inject the victim with a Class A drug or supply such drugs to the victim who self-injects and then dies. The difficulty lies in identifying the unlawful act which causes the death of the victim.

6.1.5.1 **Defendant injects the victim**

Where the defendant injects the victim, the unlawful act may be the malicious administration of a poison or noxious thing so as to endanger life or inflict grievous bodily harm, contrary to s.23 of the Offences Against the Person Act 1861. This act is certainly unlawful, objectively dangerous, and causes the death of the victim.

In the case of *Cato* [1976] 1 WLR 110, the defendant and the victim were both heroin addicts. They each prepared their own syringes with a mixture of heroin and water which they then handed to each other. They then injected each other with heroin. The victim died and the defendant was convicted of unlawful act manslaughter and maliciously administering poison or a noxious thing so as to endanger life or inflict grievous bodily harm, contrary to s.23 of the Offences Against the Person Act 1861. He appealed against his convictions. The Court of Appeal dismissed the appeal and upheld the convictions. The Court held that the administration of heroin to the victim by the defendant was a criminal offence under s.23 of the Offences Against the Person Act 1861 which could amount to an unlawful act for the purposes of unlawful act manslaughter. Lord Widgery CJ stated that:

> we think that the unlawful act here would be described as injecting the deceased…with a mixture of heroin and water which at the time of the injection and for the purposes of the injection the accused had unlawfully taken into his possession.

For a conviction of unlawful act manslaughter to succeed, the prosecution must prove that the injection was a cause of death, and not merely *de minimis*. The fact that the victim consented to the injection is no defence to manslaughter.

CROSS REFERENCE

Further reference to *Cato* (1976) and the offence under s.23 of the Offences Against the Person Act 1861 is made in 7.6.1.2.

6.1.5.2 Defendant supplies the drugs, victim self-injects

However, where the defendant does not inject the victim but merely supplies the drugs, proving the unlawful act element of unlawful act manslaughter becomes problematic. Although both the possession of controlled drugs and the act of supplying a controlled drug to another person are offences under the Misuse of Drugs Act 1971, the courts have struggled to justify convictions for unlawful act manslaughter because of the difficulty of proving that the supply of the drug caused the death of the victim.

The current law

The law was clarified by the House of Lords in the leading case of *Kennedy (No. 2)* [2007] UKHL 38, in which it was held that the supplier of the drug is not guilty of unlawful act manslaughter because the free and voluntary act of self-administration breaks the chain of causation. Before discussing this case further, it is prudent to explore the authorities which preceded the House of Lords' decision in *Kennedy (No. 2)* in 2007.

> **The current law: *Kennedy (No. 2)* [2007] UKHL 38**
>
> According to the House of Lords in *Kennedy (No. 2)*, where a person charged with unlawful act manslaughter has supplied the victim with an illicit drug which the victim has self-injected, the defendant is not guilty of manslaughter because the free and voluntary act of self-administration by the victim breaks the chain of causation. *Kennedy (No. 2)* will be discussed further in 6.1.5.3.

The development of the law

In the case of *Dalby* [1982] 1 WLR 425, the defendant supplied the victim with a prescription drug in tablet form. The victim then made up a solution with which he injected himself. The defendant was not present on two occasions when the victim self-injected. The victim died and the defendant was convicted of unlawful act manslaughter. The Court of Appeal held that the act of supplying a controlled drug to the victim was not a sufficient basis for a conviction for unlawful act manslaughter and quashed the defendant's conviction. This conclusion is in line with the conclusion reached by the House of Lords in *Kennedy (No. 2)*. However, the Court of Appeal in *Dalby* (1982) reached this conclusion in a different way to the House of Lords in *Kennedy (No. 2)*. The Court of Appeal reasoned that the unlawful act must be directed at the victim (a point now disapproved in *Goodfellow*

(1986), see 6.1.4) and the act of supplying a controlled drug did not cause direct harm. Waller LJ stated that:

> In this case, the supply of drugs would itself have caused no harm unless the deceased had subsequently used the drugs in a form and quality which was dangerous.

However, the Court did not then go on to discuss the possibility of the victim's voluntary act of self-injection breaking the chain of causation.

The leading case of *Kennedy* has been mentioned earlier. There are three different reports relating to the case of *Kennedy*. The first was the Court of Appeal decision in *Kennedy* in 1999 (reported as *Kennedy* [1999] Crim LR 65). In 2005, the Criminal Cases Review Commission referred the case back to the Court of Appeal. This case report is referred to as *Kennedy (No. 2)* [2005] EWCA Crim 685. Then, in 2007, the case came before the House of Lords. All of these case reports refer to the same case. The facts of *Kennedy* are discussed at 7.6.1.1 but are also worth setting out briefly here.

The victim asked the defendant for something to make him sleep. The defendant prepared a syringe of heroin and the victim injected himself with it. The victim died within an hour. The defendant was convicted of both supplying a Class A drug and manslaughter. *Kennedy* [1999] Crim LR 65 involved the defendant's initial appeal to the Court of Appeal against the manslaughter conviction. The defendant argued that the case of *Dalby* was authority for the proposition that the supply of drugs cannot amount to the unlawful act for the purposes of unlawful act manslaughter. The Court of Appeal dismissed the appeal and held that the unlawful act of the defendant was not limited to supply of the drugs. Rather confusingly, the Court held that the unlawful act committed by the defendant could have been one of two offences: *(a)* causing the administration of a poison or noxious thing under s.23 of the Offences Against the Person Act 1861; or *(b)* assisting and wilfully encouraging the unlawful self-injection of the victim (as a secondary party).

 THINKING POINT

Consider whether this judgment is a satisfactory one. Is it against the law to self-inject drugs?

The Court of Appeal considered the act of the victim in injecting himself to be an unlawful act. Thus, by preparing and handing the syringe to the victim, the defendant was an accomplice to the victim's unlawful act.

The flaw with this judgment was that self-injection is not in fact unlawful. Whilst it is unlawful to be in possession of or to supply a controlled drug and to inject a drug into another person, it is not unlawful to take drugs yourself. If self-injection is not a criminal offence, then the defendant cannot be an accomplice to it. It is also the case that liability for manslaughter could not be constructed out of the offences of possession and supply because these offences do not cause death. This decision faced strong criticism from academics and the case was referred back to the Court of Appeal by the Criminal Cases Review Commission in 2005 (discussed in 6.1.5.3).

With similar facts to *Kennedy*, in the case of *Dias* [2001] EWCA Crim 2986, the trial judge ruled that the victim's self-injection was unlawful, thus, by aiding and abetting the self-injection of the victim, the defendant was liable as secondary party to that offence. The defendant was convicted of manslaughter and appealed. However, the Court of Appeal held that neither stat-ute nor the common law provided for an offence of injecting oneself with a controlled drug and thus the defendant could not be a secondary party to this. The Court held that '[n]o one could be charged with injecting himself with heroin, only with possession of it'.

> **THINKING POINT**
>
> Could the offence of possession amount to the unlawful act for the purposes of unlawful act manslaughter?

However, the Court also dismissed the offence of possession of the drugs because '[t]he causative act (the act causing death) was essentially the injection of the heroin rather than the possession of it'.

In *Rogers* [2003] EWCA Crim 945, the Court of Appeal also agreed that self-injection did not amount to an offence. Thus, the defendant could not be liable as a secondary party to that injection. However, the Court held that the defendant could be guilty of manslaughter where he played a part in the mechanics of the injection which caused the victim's death by applying and holding a tourniquet for the victim. The defendant in this case did exactly that and was charged with the offence of administering a poison or noxious thing under s.23 of the Offences Against the Person Act 1861 and manslaughter. The trial judge ruled that the defendant's application of the tourniquet to the victim's arm was part of the unlawful act of administering a noxious thing. The defendant changed his plea to guilty and appealed against the ruling of the trial judge. The Court of Appeal confirmed that self-injection did not amount to a criminal offence, thus, the defendant could not be liable as a secondary party to it. However, the Court dismissed the appeal because the defendant had played a part in the injection by holding the tourniquet for the victim. Rose LJ stated that:

> The purpose and effect of the tourniquet, plainly, was to raise a vein in which the deceased could insert the syringe. Accordingly, by applying and holding the tourniquet, the defendant was playing a part in the mechanics of the injection which caused death.

Rogers was overruled by the House of Lords in *Kennedy (No. 2)* and is no longer good law.

The next case to address self-injection was that of *Finlay* [2003] EWCA Crim 3868. It was unclear in this case whether the defendant had injected the victim or simply prepared the syringe and handed it to the victim for self-injection. Nevertheless, the Court of Appeal took the view that the defendant could have caused the death of the victim, even if the victim had self-injected because such self-injection was foreseeable. In doing so, the Court applied the House of Lords' decision in *Empress Car Co. (Abertillay) Ltd v National River Authority* [1999] 2 AC 22, a case which concerned an offence relating to causing pollution to a river under the Water Resources Act 1991. However, this approach was rejected by the House of Lords in *Kennedy (No. 2)* and the case of *Empress* was restricted to its con-text. The case of *Finlay* returned to the Court of Appeal in 2009 after the House of Lords' decision in *Kennedy (No. 2)*, and the defendant's conviction was quashed posthumously.

6.1.5.3 The House of Lords' decision in *Kennedy (No. 2)*

The case of *Kennedy* was referred back to the Court of Appeal by the Criminal Cases Review Commission. The Court of Appeal certified a point of law for the House of Lords to decide in a further appeal.

> **Certified question in *Kennedy (No. 2)* [2007] UKHL 38:**
>
> When is it appropriate to find someone guilty of manslaughter where that person has been involved in the supply of a Class A controlled drug, which is then freely and voluntarily self-administered by the person to whom it was supplied and the administration of the drug then causes his death?

The House of Lords restored clarity to the law by responding: 'In the case of a fully informed and responsible adult, never.' The House took a different approach to that in *Rogers* and focused on the free and voluntary decision of the victim to inject. The House held that where the defendant supplies a drug to a fully informed and responsible adult victim of sound mind who injects himself and dies, the defendant may not be convicted of manslaughter. The House of Lords held that supplying controlled drugs to the victim will not amount to an unlawful act for the purposes of unlawful act manslaughter. The unlawful supply of the drugs does not cause the death of the victim where the victim made a voluntary and informed decision to inject himself with the drugs. In such a situation, the self-injection by the victim breaks the chain of causation and the defendant will not be liable for manslaughter. The defendant's conviction was quashed. Lord Bingham stated that:

> The criminal law generally assumes the existence of free will.... [I]nformed adults of sound mind are treated as autonomous beings able to make their own decisions how they will act...Thus D is not to be treated as causing V to act in a certain way if V makes a voluntary and informed decision to act in that way rather than another.

This decision from the House of Lords has added much clarity to a somewhat confused string of prior authorities and is expected to be the final word on the matter. *Kennedy (No. 2)* (2007) has since been applied by the Court of Appeal in *Burgess; Byram* [2008] EWCA Crim 516, *Keen* [2008] EWCA Crim 1000, and *Craven; McGovern* [2008] EWCA Crim 1742.

One further *obiter* point was made by Lord Bingham in *Kennedy (No. 2)* about joint administration of an injection. Lord Bingham suggested that where the defendant and victim acted together to administer an injection so that the drug was jointly administered, the defendant could be convicted of unlawful act manslaughter: 'it is possible to imagine factual scenarios in which two people could properly be regarded as acting together to administer an injection' (at [24]). This was later considered in *Burgess; Byram* [2008] EWCA Crim 516, in which the Court of Appeal stated that it followed that a defendant who laid the tip of the needle against the skin of the deceased over the vein is not automatically entitled to an acquittal if the deceased ultimately physically pressed the plunger on the syringe and caused the drug to enter his body (at [12]).

6.1.6 **Reform**

In a Report in 1996 (*Legislating the Criminal Code: Involuntary Manslaughter*, Law Com. No. 237), the Law Commission recommended the abolition of the current law on involuntary manslaughter. The Commission proposed that involuntary manslaughter should be replaced by two offences of reckless killing and killing by gross carelessness.

CROSS REFERENCE

Refer to 5.2.4.3 to see the proposed offences.

The 2006 Law Commission Report, *Murder, Manslaughter and Infanticide* (Law Com. No. 304) proposed major reforms to the law relating to homicide.

The proposed offence of manslaughter would incorporate forms of unlawful act manslaughter. This offence requires the killing to take place through an unlawful act which was either intended to cause injury, or where the defendant was aware that the act involved a serious risk of injury. Thus, unlike the current offence of unlawful act manslaughter, the proposed offence is subjectively assessed.

6.2 Gross negligence manslaughter

Negligence is a tort (a civil wrong). A defendant is negligent if his conduct falls below that expected of a reasonable person. Negligence is an objective concept, judged against the standard of the reasonable man. Thus, there is no need to prove that the defendant was aware of the risk that his conduct might fall below the standard of the reasonable person, merely that it did. If the defendant negligently causes the death of a person, he may be prosecuted for the criminal offence of gross negligence manslaughter and be subject to punishment if convicted. As gross negligence manslaughter is a criminal offence which carries a maximum sentence of life imprisonment, it requires a much higher degree of negligence than is sufficient for the tort of negligence.

Gross negligence manslaughter arises where the defendant causes the death of the victim through the breach of a duty of care owed to that victim. The defendant's act or omission must be grossly negligent in order for the elements of the offence to be satisfied. This means that the conduct of the defendant must be sufficiently bad as to warrant criminal sanction.

Gross negligence manslaughter

The prosecution must prove that:

(1) The defendant owed the victim a duty of care.

(2) The defendant breached that duty of care (i.e., was negligent).

(3) The breach of duty caused the death of the victim.

(4) The defendant's conduct was grossly negligent.

The leading authority on gross negligence manslaughter is the House of Lords' decision in *Adomako* [1995] 1 AC 171. In order to prove gross negligence manslaughter, the prosecution must prove four elements (figure 6.2). These four elements will be explored in 6.2.1 to 6.2.4.

Figure 6.2 The elements of gross negligence manslaughter

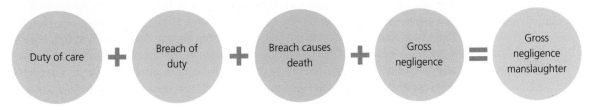

6.2.1 **Duty of care**

The first element that the prosecution must prove is that the defendant owed the victim a duty of care. The authorities are unclear on whether the civil meaning of duty of care applies in relation to gross negligence manslaughter and whether duty of care is a question of law to be decided by the judge, or a question of fact to be determined by the jury. Until recently, duty of care in gross negligence manslaughter had failed to attract much attention and the law was confusing and in need of clarification. The recent case of *Evans* [2009] EWCA Crim 650 (discussed in 6.2.1.2), confirmed that duty of care is a question of law.

6.2.1.1 **The civil meaning**

'Duty of care' is traditionally a civil concept; however, it is not clear whether or not the civil meaning is applied for the purposes of gross negligence manslaughter. In the leading House of Lords' decision of *Adomako* (1995), Lord Mackay held that 'the ordinary principles of the law of negligence apply to ascertain whether or not the defendant has been in breach of a duty'. If this statement accurately reflects the approach adopted by the criminal law, it is necessary to consider briefly the meaning of duty of care in the law of tort. The modern approach to establishing a duty of care is the incremental approach. Under this approach, the court will look at established categories of recognised duty situations in order to determine whether there is an existing precedent governing the particular case in question. For example, a duty exists between doctor and patient, occupier and visitor, employer and employee, driver and passenger, and driver and other road users. Where there is no such precedent, the court will consider three main factors:

(1) the reasonable foreseeability that the claimant would be harmed;

(2) the proximity of the relationship; and

(3) whether it would be fair, just, and reasonable to impose a duty (see *Caparo Industries plc v Dickman and others* [1990] 2 AC 605).

In the case of *Wacker* [2002] EWCA Crim 1944, the Court of Appeal held that the defendant owed the victims a duty of care because it was reasonably foreseeable that they would be injured by his breach. However, the Court refused to allow the defendant to rely upon the tortious defence of *ex turpi causa non oritur actio* (illegality). The defendant in *Wacker* (2002) drove a lorry from Rotterdam to Dover. Hiding on the lorry were 60 illegal immigrants. The container was sealed but for a small air vent. The vent was closed while the lorry was on the ferry to Dover and 58 of the immigrants suffocated to death. The defendant was charged with 58 counts of manslaughter. The trial judge ruled that the principles of negligence applied to the offence of gross negligence manslaughter in order to determine whether the defendant owed the victims a duty of care. The defendant was convicted and appealed. The Court of Appeal held that the defence of illegality (expressed by the Latin maxim *ex turpi causa non oritur actio*) would not preclude a finding that the defendant owed a duty of care to the victims for the purposes of gross negligence manslaughter. The defendant's convictions for manslaughter were upheld.

The Court of Appeal in *Wacker* (2002) gave 'duty of care' the civil meaning by applying the 'reasonable foreseeability' test—the first of these three factors from *Caparo*. However, the Court gave no consideration to the other factors from *Caparo*. Kay LJ held that Lord Mackay in *Adomako* had not intended all of the complexities of the tort of negligence to be applicable. It remains unclear to what degree the principles of negligence are followed in respect of gross negligence manslaughter. However, it is evident from *Wacker* (2002) that the defence of illegality may not be relied upon to negate a duty of care.

6.2.1.2 The roles of judge and jury

In the case of *Willoughby* [2004] EWCA Crim 3365, the Court of Appeal stated that where a duty of care is already well established or provided for by statute (e.g., in a doctor–patient relationship), the trial judge can direct the jury that a duty of care exists. This suggests that duty of care is a question of law. The Court also stated that it is for the jury to decide whether the defendant owed the victim a duty of care. The issue should be left to the jury once the judge has decided that there is evidence capable of establishing such a duty. This, rather confusingly, suggests that duty of care is a question of fact, not law, and that the general principles of negligence do not apply.

The Court of Appeal attempted to clarify the law in the case of *Evans* [2009] EWCA Crim 650. An enlarged bench of five Lords Justices in the Court of Appeal confirmed that duty of care is a question of law. Thus, the trial judge should direct the jury as to the law and explain to them that a duty would exist if they find certain facts to be established, but that a duty would not exist if they find certain other facts to be established. The Court of Appeal drew support from s.2(5) of the Corporate Manslaughter and Corporate Homicide Act 2007, which provides that, in the context of corporate manslaughter, the question of whether a duty of care exists is a matter of law. It is for the judge to direct the jury on the law and it is for the jury to find certain facts established in accordance with the judge's direction before they find a legal duty of care.

6.2.1.3 Omissions

Unlike unlawful act manslaughter, gross negligence manslaughter can be committed by omission, as well as by a positive act. The subject of omissions was discussed in detail in chapter 2. It was explained at 2.4.1 that there is generally no liability for an omission to act. However, there are a number of exceptions to this rule, where a duty to act is imposed upon the defendant by law (e.g., where there is a special relationship, a voluntary assumption of responsibility, a contractual duty or public duty, a statutory duty, or a duty to avert a danger created by the defendant).

CROSS REFERENCE
Refer to 2.4.2 to remind yourself of the instances when a duty to act is imposed upon a defendant.

In *Evans* [2009] EWCA Crim 650, the Court of Appeal acknowledged that previous authorities were inconsistent and the Court expressed an intention to clarify the law. The defendant supplied the 16-year-old victim, a drug addict, with some heroin. The victim took the heroin and began to display symptoms of overdose. The defendant and her mother were afraid of getting into trouble and so did not call an ambulance. The victim died. At trial, it was accepted that the defendant and her mother believed that they were responsible for looking after the victim after she had taken the heroin. The issue in the case was whether the defendant owed the victim a duty of care when their relationship was not one which imposed a familial duty or responsibility. The defendant was convicted of manslaughter by gross negligence and appealed. The Court of Appeal dismissed the appeal and held that even though there was no familial relationship between the defendant and victim, the defendant was 'under a duty to take reasonable steps for the safety of the deceased once she appreciated that the heroin she procured for her was having a potentially fatal impact on her health'. Lord Judge CJ held that:

> The duty necessary to found gross negligence manslaughter is plainly not confined to cases of a familial or professional relationship between the defendant and the deceased... [F]or the purposes of gross negligence manslaughter, when a person has created or contributed to the creation of a state of affairs which he knows, or ought reasonably to know, has become life threatening, a consequent duty on him to act by taking reasonable steps to save the other's life will normally arise.

CROSS REFERENCE
Refer to 2.4.2.3 for a more detailed discussion of the 'Miller' principle.

Thus, the Court of Appeal applied the 'Miller' principle: where a defendant becomes liable when he realises the danger that he has created and he then fails to take reasonable steps to avert that danger.

There was a duty of care in this case due to the combined effect of three factors: *(a)* the defendant's act of supplying heroin to the victim; *(b)* the fact that there was a reasonably foreseeable danger to the life of the victim; and *(c)* the fact that the defendant knew that the victim was reliant upon her and her mother taking care of her.

The Court stated that the judge may direct the jury that there is a duty to act where the existence of such a duty is not in dispute, such as in a doctor–patient relationship. However, if the facts of the case did not fall into a pre-existing duty situation or where the issue of whether a duty of care exists is otherwise in dispute, the judge may direct the jury:

> that if facts a + b and/or c or d are established, then in law a duty will arise, but if facts x or y or z were present, the duty would be negatived. In this sense, of course, the jury is deciding whether the duty situation has been established. In our judgment this is the way in which Willoughby should be understood...

The Court further held that there was no violation of Article 6 (right to a fair trial) and Article 7 (no punishment without law) of the European Convention on Human Rights (ECHR).

6.2.2 **Breach of duty**

The prosecution must also prove that the defendant breached his duty of care towards the victim. According to Lord Mackay in *Adomako* (1995), 'the ordinary principles of negligence apply to ascertain whether or not the defendant has been in breach of a duty'. A defendant will breach his duty of care to the victim where his conduct falls below that expected of a reasonable person. Where the defendant has special knowledge or expertise, he will be expected to meet the standard of care expected of a reasonable person with that knowledge or expertise: *Adomako* (1995).

The defendant might breach his duty of care by the performance of a positive act or by an omission to act. Contrast this to the offence of unlawful act manslaughter which cannot be committed by omission (see 6.1.1 and the case of *Lowe* (1973)).

6.2.3 **Causation**

CROSS REFERENCE
Refer to 2.5 to remind yourself of the rules of causation.

It must be shown that the defendant's breach of duty caused the death of the victim. The usual rules of causation will apply here. These have been discussed in detail in chapter 2.

6.2.4 **Gross negligence**

The final element that the prosecution must prove is that the defendant's breach of duty was grossly negligent. In *Andrews v DPP* [1937] AC 576, the House of Lords held that a very high degree of negligence is required for the offence of manslaughter. The standard of negligence required for liability in the law of tort would not be sufficient. In the case of *Bateman* [1925] All ER 25, Lord Hewart CJ stated that:

> in order to establish criminal liability the facts must be such that, in the opinion of the jury, the negligence of the accused went beyond a mere matter of compensation between subjects and showed such disregard for the life and safety of others as to amount to a crime against the State and conduct deserving punishment.

The leading case on gross negligence manslaughter is the House of Lords' decision in *Adomako* (1995).

 CASE CLOSE-UP

***Adomako* [1995] 1 AC 171**

The defendant in this case was an anaesthetist in charge of a patient who was undergoing an eye operation. The patient died after a tube which supplied oxygen to the patient became disconnected from the ventilator. The defendant failed to check the tube when an alarm sounded on a machine which monitored the patient's blood pressure. He was convicted of manslaughter by gross negligence and appealed. The House of Lords dismissed the appeal and confirmed gross negligence as a head of involuntary manslaughter. The House set out the four elements which need to be established for a conviction for gross negligence manslaughter: that the defendant owed the patient a duty of care, that he breached that duty of care, that the breach caused the death of the victim, and that the breach was grossly negligent and therefore a crime. In relation to the question of whether the defendant's breach was grossly negligent, Lord Mackay stated that the jury should consider:

> whether having regard to the risk of death involved, the conduct of the defendant was so bad in all the circumstances as to amount in their judgment to a criminal act or omission.

In deciding whether the defendant's conduct was so bad as to warrant criminal sanction, the jury will take into account the risk of death involved in the defendant's conduct. His conduct is judged according to the standard of the reasonable man, so there is no need to prove that the defendant himself was aware of such a risk of death, or that his conduct was negligent. In *Attorney General's Reference (No. 2 of 1999)* [2000] 2 Cr App R 207, the Court of Appeal held that evidence of the defendant's state of mind was not necessary in order to secure a conviction for gross negligence manslaughter.

The test from *Adomako* (1995) may be criticised for being circular. Lord Mackay himself acknowledged that the test involved 'an element of circularity'. The jury are asked to decide whether the defendant's conduct was 'so bad' that it warrants criminal sanction, i.e., whether the defendant's conduct constitutes a crime. Thus, the jury are left to decide what constitutes gross negligence manslaughter. This should be a question of law.

The compatibility of the test from *Adomako* (1995) with Article 7 of the ECHR (no punishment without law) was challenged in the case of *Misra and Srivastava* [2003] EWCA Crim 2375. Article 7 of the ECHR provides that a person may not be punished for an act that was not a criminal offence at the time of its commission. The Court of Appeal held that there was no violation of Article 7. This case involved two doctors who were convicted of gross negligence manslaughter after a patient in their care died from toxic shock syndrome. The prosecution case was that the doctors had failed to treat the victim as they failed to appreciate how seriously ill he was. The defendants appealed against conviction, arguing that the circularity and uncertainty of the test in *Adomako* (1995) violated Article 7 because the jury were left to decide upon a matter of law, namely the criminality of the defendant's conduct. The Court of Appeal dismissed the appeal and held that there was no breach of Article 7. The Court reasoned that the test in *Adomako* (1995) clearly identified the ingredients of manslaughter by gross negligence and that the degree of negligence required for a conviction was a question of fact, not law. Lord Judge CJ explained the test in *Adomako* (1995):

> The decision whether the conduct was criminal is described not as 'the' test, but as 'a' test as to how far the conduct in question must depart from accepted standards to be 'characterised as criminal'. On proper analysis, therefore, the jury is not deciding whether the particular defendant ought to be convicted on some unprincipled basis. The question for the jury is not whether the defendant's negligence was gross, and whether, *additionally*, it was a crime, but whether his behaviour was grossly negligent and *consequently* criminal. This is not a question of law, but one of fact, for decision in the individual case. (Author's emphasis.)

It must be remembered that gross negligence manslaughter is a serious offence which carries a discretionary sentence of life imprisonment. The law must be accessible and the offence must be clearly defined so that an individual may ensure that his conduct conforms to the law. The extent to which the explanation proffered by Lord Judge CJ satisfies the criticisms of circularity (which was, in fact, conceded by Lord Mackay himself in the House of Lords) and clarity must be questioned. It must be accepted that the role of the jury in the criminalisation of a defendant's behaviour is a highly significant one. It is submitted that gross negligence manslaughter is essentially a jury-prescribed offence.

6.2.5 Reform

As stated at 6.1.6, in 1996, the Law Commission proposed the abolition of the current law on involuntary manslaughter and the creation of two new offences of reckless killing and killing by gross carelessness. The 2006 Report of the Law Commission incorporates killing through gross negligence as to a risk of causing death into the proposed offence of manslaughter.

6.3 Subjectively reckless manslaughter

The third head of involuntary manslaughter is subjectively reckless manslaughter. For many years, it was accepted that there were only two heads of involuntary manslaughter. The first was unlawful act manslaughter, but it was unclear whether the second head of involuntary manslaughter could be committed by gross negligence or if recklessness was required. It is now generally accepted that there are, indeed, three heads of involuntary manslaughter.

In the case of *Lidar* (unreported, 11 November 1999), the Court of Appeal held that a defendant could be convicted of manslaughter if he foresaw death or serious harm as highly probable. The defendant in this case ran over the victim in his car. The victim had been clinging onto the defendant's car as they fought, but he fell off and was run over. The defendant appealed against his conviction for manslaughter. The Court of Appeal dismissed the appeal and held that subjective reckless manslaughter was a valid head of involuntary manslaughter. Thus, a defendant can be convicted of manslaughter where he recognises that death or serious injury is highly probable to occur, but he goes ahead and takes that risk.

6.3.1 Reform

Reckless manslaughter is also incorporated into the proposed reforms in the 2006 Report of the Law Commission. This type of liability may fall under the head of second degree murder, which requires the defendant to kill with an intention to cause some injury or a fear of injury or a risk of injury, plus an awareness that there was a serious risk of causing death.

6.4 Corporate manslaughter

The Corporate Manslaughter and Corporate Homicide Act 2007 abolished the common law liability of organisations for gross negligence manslaughter and created an offence of corporate manslaughter in England and Wales. The Act came into force on 6 April 2008. The long overdue Act was enacted after a series of public disasters which failed to result in successful prosecutions for gross negligence manslaughter:

- In 1987, the *Herald of Free Enterprise* capsized, killing 193 people.
- In the same year, 31 people died in the King's Cross Fire.
- In 1988, 167 people died in the Piper Alpha oil rig fire.
- In the same year, the Clapham train crash killed 35 people.
- In 1989, the *Marchioness* pleasure boat sank, killing 51 people.
- In 1997, six people were killed in the Southall rail disaster.
- In 1999, 31 people were killed in the Ladbroke Grove (Paddington) rail disaster.
- In 2000, the Hatfield rail disaster killed four people.
- In 2002, seven people died in the Potters Bar rail disaster.

The failure of these prosecutions was largely due to the identification doctrine, which requires proof of liability of an individual who was part of the 'brains' of the company in order for there to be a conviction of gross negligence manslaughter against the company.

6.4.1 The offence

The offence of corporate manslaughter is found under s.1(1) of the Corporate Manslaughter and Corporate Homicide Act 2007. An organisation may be convicted of corporate manslaughter if the management or organisation of its activities by senior management causes the death of a person and amounts to a gross breach of a duty of care owed to the victim.

> **CROSS REFERENCE**
> Refer to 4.3 for a brief discussion on corporate liability and the identification doctrine.

 STATUTE

Section 1, Corporate Manslaughter and Corporate Homicide Act 2007

(1) An organisation to which this section applies is guilty of an offence if the way in which its activities are managed or organised—

    (a) causes a person's death, and

    (b) amounts to a gross breach of a relevant duty of care owed by the organisation to the deceased.

(2) The organisations to which this section applies are—

    (a) a corporation;

    (b) a department or other body listed in Schedule 1;

(c) a police force;

(d) a partnership, or a trade union or employers' association, that is an employer.

(3) An organisation is guilty of an offence under this section only if the way in which its activities are managed or organised by its senior management is a substantial element in the breach referred to in subsection (1).

(4) For the purposes of this Act—

(a) 'relevant duty of care' has the meaning given by section 2, read with sections 3 to 7;

(b) a breach of a duty of care by an organisation is a 'gross' breach if the conduct alleged to amount to a breach of that duty falls far below what can reasonably be expected of the organisation in the circumstances;

(c) 'senior management', in relation to an organisation, means the persons who play significant roles in—

(i) the making of decisions about how the whole or a substantial part of its activities are to be managed or organised, or

(ii) the actual managing or organising of the whole or a substantial part of those activities.

Section 1(2) details the organisations to which this offence applies. Section 1(3) provides that the liability of an organisation is dependent upon a substantial element of the breach of duty being due to the way in which the activities of the organisation are managed or organised by senior management. As such, the liability of the company is not dependent upon proof of liability of an individual on the board of directors or senior management. Thus, the identification doctrine has no application. The Act is aimed at 'senior management', i.e., those persons who play a significant role in deciding how activities are to be managed or organised or actually manage or organise those activities: s.1(4)(c).

The organisation must owe a 'relevant duty of care' to the victim. These duties of care are set out under s.2(1) of the Act and encompass any of the following duties owed under the law of negligence.

 STATUTE

Section 2(1), Corporate Manslaughter and Corporate Homicide Act 2007

(a) a duty owed to its employees or to other persons working for the organisation or performing services for it;

(b) a duty owed as occupier of premises;

(c) a duty owed in connection with—

(i) the supply by the organisation of goods or services (whether for consideration or not),

(ii) the carrying on by the organisation of any construction or maintenance operations,

> **(iii)** the carrying on by the organisation of any other activity on a commercial basis, or
>
> **(iv)** the use or keeping by the organisation of any plant, vehicle or other thing;
>
> **(d)** a duty owed to a person who, by reason of being a person within subsection (2), is someone for whose safety the organisation is responsible.

Section 2(5) of the Act provides that duty of care is a question of law.

The definition of a 'gross' breach is given in s.1(4)(b) and requires the conduct of the organisation to fall 'far below' what is reasonably expected of an organisation in the circumstances. There are a number of factors for the jury to consider in deciding whether the conduct of the defendant organisation amounts to a gross breach of duty. These are set out under s.8 of the Act and include whether the evidence shows that the organisation failed to comply with any health and safety legislation that relates to the alleged breach and, if so, how serious that failure was and how much of a risk of death it posed. The jury may also consider the extent to which attitudes, policies, systems, or accepted practices within the organisation encouraged the failure or produced tolerance of it, and may have regard to any health and safety guidance that relates to the alleged breach. Under s.8(4), the jury may have regard to any other matters they consider relevant.

6.4.2 **Convictions**

There have been a handful of convictions for corporate manslaughter since the Corporate Manslaughter and Corporate Homicide Act 2007 came into force. However, to date these cases all seem to involve prosecutions against small business which are owner-managed, thus the Act has not been tested against a large company which has several layers of management. Even though there is the potential for an unlimited fine upon conviction, all of the sentences handed down to date have been relatively low fines, although this is probably due to the nature and size of the companies prosecuted.

The first conviction for corporate manslaughter under the Act occurred in February 2011. In *Cotswold Geotechnical Holdings Ltd* [2012] 1 Cr App R (S) 26, Cotswold Geotechnical Holdings Ltd became the first company to be convicted of corporate manslaughter in relation to the death of Alexander Wright who was a geologist working for the company. Mr Wright had been left working alone in a deep trench when the trench collapsed and Mr Wright died. The company was sentenced to a fine of £385,000.

In July 2012, Lion Steel Equipment Ltd pleaded guilty to a charge of corporate manslaughter after an employee of the defendant company died at the company premises (*Lion Steel Equipment Ltd* (Manchester Crown Court, unreported, 20 July 2012) (T20117411)). The employee climbed a roof to repair a leak and he fell 13 metres through a skylight in the roof. The defendant company was sentenced to a fine of £480,000 and a costs order of £84,000 was imposed.

More recently, in December 2014, Peter Mawson Ltd was convicted of corporate manslaughter after an employee fell through a skylight onto a concrete floor and died (*Peter Mawson Ltd* (Preston Crown Court, unreported, December 2014)). The company had failed to ensure that the employee was safe while working on the roof by providing equipment such as scaffolding or netting. The defendant company was fined £200,000 for the offence of corporate man-slaughter and its owner, Peter Mawson, was personally convicted of a health and safety breach and sentenced to 8 months' imprisonment suspended for 2 years, 200 hours of unpaid work, a publicity order, and a costs order of £31,504.77.

6.5 Causing or allowing the death of or serious harm to a child or vulnerable adult

The offence of causing or allowing the death of or serious harm to a child or vulnerable adult is found under s.5 of the Domestic Violence, Crime and Victims Act 2004 (as amended by the Domestic Violence, Crime and Victims (Amendment) Act 2012). This offence is committed where two or more people share a household and have frequent contact with a child or vulnerable adult who dies or suffers serious injury as a result of an unlawful act by one member of the household. The defendant will be guilty of this offence if he was the person who caused the death or serious injury, or if he did not cause the death or serious injury but he ought to have been aware of the significant risk of serious harm being caused to the victim by another person in the household and he failed to take reasonable steps to protect the victim from the risk. This offence was intended to avoid situations such as that which occurred in *Lane and Lane* (1985) 82 Cr App R 50, where the defendants could not be convicted of the manslaughter of their baby as the prosecution were unable to prove who caused the injuries which led to the death of the baby.

⟲ Summary

- Involuntary manslaughter arises when a defendant unlawfully causes the death of the victim but has no intention to kill or cause GBH (i.e., he does not have the requisite *mens rea* for murder).

- The three main types of involuntary manslaughter are unlawful act manslaughter, gross negligence manslaughter, and subjectively reckless manslaughter. Unlawful act man-slaughter requires proof of four ingredients (*DPP v Newbury and Jones* (1977)):

  (1) The defendant intentionally did an act.

  (2) The act was unlawful.

  (3) The act was objectively dangerous.

  (4) The act caused the death of the victim.

- The act must amount to a criminal offence: *Franklin* (1883), *Lamb* (1967).

- The act must be objectively dangerous, such that 'all sober and reasonable people would inevitably recognise must subject the other person to, at least, the risk of some harm resulting therefrom, albeit not serious harm': *Church* (1966).

- The reasonable man is deemed to have the knowledge that the defendant had, or should have had, at the time of the offence: *Dawson* (1985). Where the risk of harm becomes obvious to the reasonable person present at the scene of the crime, the defendant's unlawful act becomes dangerous: *Watson* (1989).

- Gross negligence manslaughter requires proof of four ingredients:

  (1) The defendant owed a duty of care to the victim.

  (2) The defendant breached that duty.

  (3) The breach caused the death of the victim.

  (4) The defendant's conduct amounted to gross negligence.

- In determining whether the defendant's conduct was grossly negligent, the jury must consider whether, having regard to the risk of death involved, the conduct of the defendant was so bad in all the circumstances as to amount in their judgement to a criminal act or omission: *Adomako* (1995).

The bigger picture

- For detail about the reforms on involuntary manslaughter proposed by the Law Commission, see the Law Commission Report, *Legislating the Criminal Code: Involuntary Manslaughter* (Law Com. No. 237, 1996).

- For a more detailed discussion about the liability of one-punch killers for unlawful act manslaughter and moral culpability, see Mitchell (2008 and 2009).

- For more information about corporate manslaughter, you might wish to consider these recent cases:

  Cotswold Geotechnical Holdings Ltd [2012] 1 Cr App R (S) 26

  JMW Farms Ltd (Belfast Crown Court, unreported, May 2012)

  Lion Steel Equipment Ltd (Manchester Crown Court, unreported, July 2012) (T20117411)

  J Murray & Sons (Belfast Crown Court, unreported, October 2013)

  Cavendish Masonry Ltd (Oxford Crown Court, unreported, May 2014)

  Pyranha Mouldings Ltd (Liverpool Crown Court, unreported, January 2015)

  Peter Mawson Ltd (Preston Crown Court, unreported, December 2015)

? Questions

Self-test questions

1. Explain the difference between involuntary manslaughter, murder, and voluntary manslaughter.

2. Name the four ingredients of unlawful act manslaughter. Cite an authority to support this.

3. What is the test for dangerousness? Cite an authority to support this.

4. What constitutes an unlawful act for the purposes of unlawful act manslaughter?

5. Will an omission be sufficient as a basis of liability for: *(a)* unlawful act manslaughter; *(b)* gross negligence manslaughter?

6. Will a defendant be guilty of unlawful act manslaughter if he supplies drugs to the victim who then consumes the drugs and dies? Cite an authority to support this.

7. Name the four ingredients of gross negligence manslaughter. Cite an authority to support this.

8. Define gross negligence.

9. Does reckless manslaughter exist? Explain your answer.

10. Explain how a corporation might be liable for manslaughter.

 For suggested approaches, please visit the Online Resource Centre.

Exam questions

1. At a showbiz party, John and Carol, two famous actors, ask Richard to supply them with some heroin. Richard prepares two syringes of heroin which he hands to John and Carol. John injects himself with one syringe. Carol asks Richard to hold a tourniquet around her arm while she injects herself with the other syringe. Unfortunately, the dose of heroin which Richard has prepared proves too strong for John and Carol, and they both die from a drug overdose.

    Afraid of getting into trouble, Richard attempts to leave the party. He goes to the cloakroom in order to retrieve his expensive, designer jacket. However, he is unable to find his cloakroom ticket. Jacqui, the cloakroom attendant and a senior citizen, refuses to give Richard his jacket unless he produces his ticket. Richard becomes very angry and shouts at Jacqui whilst punching the desk. Jacqui, who suffers from a serious heart condition, has a heart attack and dies.

    Discuss Richard's liability for the deaths of John, Carol, and Jacqui.

2. To what extent is the law relating to gross negligence manslaughter uncertain and circular? Refer to case law in your answer.

 For suggested approaches, please visit the Online Resource Centre.

Further reading

Books

Ashworth, A. and Mitchell, B. *Rethinking English Homicide Law* (2000), Oxford: Oxford University Press

Matthews, R. *Blackstone's Guide to the Corporate Manslaughter and Corporate Homicide Act 2007* (2008), Oxford: Oxford University Press

Journal articles

Antrobus, S. 'The Criminal Liability of Directors for Health and Safety Breaches and Manslaughter' [2013] Crim LR 309

Dobson, A. 'Shifting Sands: Multiple Counts in Prosecutions for Corporate Manslaughter' [2012] Crim LR 200

Heaton, R. 'Dealing in Death' [2003] Crim LR 497

Herring, J. and Palser, E. 'The Duty of Care in Gross Negligence Manslaughter' [2007] Crim LR 24

Leigh, L. 'Duty of Care and Manslaughter' (2009) 173 JPN 296

Mitchell, B. 'Being Really Stupid: The Meaning and Place of Gross Negligence in English Criminal Law' (2002) 7 Coventry Law Journal 12

Mitchell, B. 'Minding the Gap in Unlawful and Dangerous Act Manslaughter: A Moral Defence for One-Punch Killers' (2008) 72 JCL 537

Mitchell, B. 'More Thoughts about Unlawful and Dangerous Act Manslaughter and the One-Punch Killer' [2009] Crim LR 502

Price, L. 'Finding Fault in Organisations—Reconceptualising the Role of Senior Managers in Corporate Manslaughter' (2015) 35 Legal Studies 385

Quick, O. 'Medicine, Mistakes and Manslaughter: A Criminal Combination?' (2010) 69 Cambridge Law Journal 186

Williams, G. 'Gross Negligence Manslaughter and Duty of Care in "Drugs" Cases: *R v Evans*' [2009] Crim LR 631

Woodley, M. 'Bargaining over Corporate Manslaughter—What Price a Life?' (2013) 77 JCL 33

Reports

Law Commission Report, *Legislating the Criminal Code: Involuntary Manslaughter* (Law Com. No. 237, 1996)

Law Commission Report, *Murder, Manslaughter and Infanticide* (Law Com. No. 304, 2006)

7 Non-fatal offences against the person

░ **LEARNING OBJECTIVES**

By the end of this chapter, you should be able to:

● identify the elements of the main non-fatal offences against the person;

● explain the difference between these offences;

● apply the law relating to these offences to a problem scenario; and

● understand the law relating to and the application of the defence of consent.

Introduction

Offences against the person encompass a wide range of offences from fatal offences, such as murder, to sexual offences, such as rape. The most common fatal offences are dealt with in chapter 5 and chapter 6, and the sexual offences are covered in chapter 8. There are many non-fatal offences against the person which range from well-known offences such as wounding or causing grievous bodily harm with intent, assault occasioning actual bodily harm, attempted murder, and threats to kill, to less commonly used offences such as impeding a person endeavouring to save himself or another from shipwreck. This chapter will explore the main non-fatal offences against the person; consequently we will deal with issues such as whether a person who deliberately or recklessly transmits HIV or a sexually transmitted disease to another person might be guilty of a criminal offence, and the extent to which the law permits a person to consent to the infliction of harm (you might consider how the law deals with the application of a tattoo, getting your hair cut and dyed, a boxer or rugby player sustaining injury in the course of a match, or a married couple who decide to engage in sado-masochistic practices in their bedroom). If the reckless transmission of HIV or a sexually transmitted disease can constitute an offence, you might also want to consider whether this principle should also be extended to the transmission of influenza or tuberculosis.

Non-fatal offences against the person deal with the infliction of unlawful harm on a person. The harm may range from serious injuries to mental harm, or to the mere apprehension of harm or the simple violation of bodily autonomy. In this chapter, we will begin by considering the five main non-fatal offences against the person. In order of increasing severity, these offences are assault (also referred to as 'common assault'), battery, assault occasioning actual bodily harm, maliciously wounding or inflicting grievous bodily harm, and wounding or causing grievous bodily harm with intent. The sentences for these offences range from an absolute discharge to a discretionary sentence of life imprisonment. In June 2011, the Sentencing Council announced new sentencing guidelines for the non-fatal offences against the person (these can be found on the Sentencing Council's website at http://sentencingcouncil.judiciary.gov.uk/docs/ Assault_definitive_guideline_-_Crown_Court.pdf).

Assault and battery, the least serious of the five offences, are summary only offences, charged under s.39 of the Criminal Justice Act 1988. They carry a maximum sentence of 6 months' imprisonment and/or a fine. Assault occasioning actual bodily harm and maliciously wounding or inflicting grievous bodily harm are more serious and are either way offences, charged under ss.47 and 20 of the Offences Against the Person Act (OAPA) 1861, respectively. These offences carry a maximum sentence of 5 years' imprisonment. The final offence of wounding or causing grievous bodily harm with intent is the most serious of these offences and is an indictable only offence, charged under s.18 of the Offences Against the Person Act 1861. This offence carries a maximum sentence of life imprisonment.

Figure 7.1 provides an illustration of the hierarchy of these five main offences with the most serious offence (causing grievous bodily harm with intent) at the top of the pyramid and the least serious offence (assault) at the bottom. This hierarchy is a useful tool for identifying the offence with which a defendant may be charged. It is a good idea to begin with the most serious offence and work your way down the hierarchy, using this as a mental checklist against the facts in a problem scenario.

In this chapter, we will also examine the defence of consent, and the two poisoning offences which are indictable only: maliciously administering poison or a noxious thing so as to endanger life or inflict grievous bodily harm under s.23 of the Offences Against the Person Act 1861, and maliciously administering poison or a noxious thing with intent to injure, aggrieve, or annoy, contrary to s.24 of the same Act (table 7.1). Other defences which may apply to the non-fatal offences against the person include self-defence and lawful chastisement. Self-defence will be dealt with in chapter 14 (Defences II).

Figure 7.1 Hierarchy of the non-fatal offences against the person

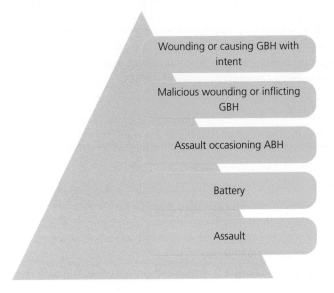

Wounding or causing GBH with intent

Malicious wounding or inflicting GBH

Assault occasioning ABH

Battery

Assault

Table 7.1 Classification of non-fatal offences against the person

Summary offences	Either way offences	Indictable only offences
• Assault	• Assault occasioning ABH	• Wounding or causing GBH with intent
• Battery	• Malicious wounding or inflicting GBH	• Maliciously administering a poison, etc. with intent to injure or annoy
		• Maliciously administering a poison, etc. so as to endanger life or inflict grievous bodily harm

7.1 Assault

Assault is charged contrary to s.39 of the Criminal Justice Act 1988. In *DPP v Taylor; DPP v Little* [1992] 1 QB 645, the Divisional Court held that assault and battery are statutory offences, despite the fact that their elements are defined under the common law. However, in *Haystead v Chief Constable of Derbyshire* [2000] 2 Cr App R 339, the Divisional Court held *obiter* that battery was a common law offence. Although these authorities conflict on this point, the statute contains no definition of the offences, which are defined under the common law. Section 39 of the Criminal Justice Act 1988 does little more than confirm the offences as summary offences triable in the magistrates' court and provide the maximum sentence.

 STATUTE

Section 39, Criminal Justice Act 1988

Common assault and battery shall be summary offences and a person guilty of either of them shall be liable to a fine not exceeding level 5 on the standard scale, to imprisonment for a term not exceeding six months, or to both.

In *Collins v Wilcock* [1984] 1 WLR 1172, Goff LJ stated that the law draws a distinction between assault and battery. An assault has been defined by James J as 'any act which intentionally—or . . . recklessly—causes another person to apprehend immediate and unlawful personal violence': *Fagan v Metropolitan Police Commissioner* [1969] 1 QB 439.

> **CROSS REFERENCE**
> Refer to 2.4.4 for a discussion of *Fagan v MPC* (1969).

7.1.1 *Actus reus*

The *actus reus* of an assault is causing another person to apprehend immediate and unlawful personal violence.

An assault can be committed in a variety of ways, such as by raising an arm as if to strike someone, by pointing a knife at a victim, by shouting threats of violence at a person, by sending a threatening text message or letter, making threats over the phone or even by making silent telephone calls to a victim. The *actus reus* element of an assault is subjectively assessed. The victim must apprehend immediate personal violence.

THINKING POINT

Using the definition of assault from *Fagan v Metropolitan Commissioner* (1969), consider whether the following might constitute the *actus reus* of an assault:

(1) Pointing a knife in V's face.

(2) Raising a fist to the back of V's head.

(3) Opening a drawer to show V a gun.

(4) Shouting at V, 'I'd hit you if the police weren't over the road'.

(5) Threatening to push V, a martial arts expert.

7.1.1.1 Apprehension

If the victim does not apprehend immediate personal violence, there is no assault. In the case of *Lamb* [1967] 2 QB 981, the defendant pointed a revolver at the victim during a game of Russian roulette. The victim, who was a willing participant in the practical joke, did not think that any harm would come to him and, thus, did not apprehend any immediate personal violence. Consequently, there could be no assault.

> **CROSS REFERENCE**
>
> The case of *Lamb* (1967) is an involuntary manslaughter case and was discussed at 6.1.2.

In order to satisfy the physical element of an assault, the victim must perceive the conduct and/or words which cause the apprehension of immediate and unlawful personal violence. If the victim does not so perceive the conduct and/or words in question, there is no assault. Consequently, raising a fist to the back of the victim's head will not be sufficient if the victim does not actually see the threatening gesture. Equally, merely speaking the threatening words is not sufficient: the victim must have heard the threat and apprehend immediate personal violence (although, see 7.1.1.3 for a discussion of whether silent telephone calls can amount to assault). Only an apprehension of such violence is required. It is not necessary for the victim to suffer actual personal violence. The defendant in *Logdon v DPP* [1976] Crim LR 121, committed an assault where he opened a drawer and showed the victim a replica pistol. The victim asked whether the pistol was loaded and the defendant answered that it was. He then stated that he intended to kidnap the victim. The Divisional Court held that assault was committed where by some physical act the defendant intentionally or recklessly caused the victim to believe that unlawful force was about to be inflicted on him.

Although it is often present, fear is not a necessary requirement of an assault. It is enough that the victim anticipated the use of personal violence, even if they were not actually afraid. If I raise my arm up to strike a professional heavyweight boxer, I have committed the *actus reus* of an assault if he thinks that I might strike him, even though he is not afraid of me, and indeed he laughs at me.

7.1.1.2 Unlawful

The anticipated personal violence must be 'unlawful'. The conduct of the defendant might be deemed lawful for a number of reasons, including: if the defendant is acting in self-defence or the defence of another; if the conduct is consented to; or if the defendant is using a reasonable degree of force in the lawful chastisement of a child; or in order to effect a lawful arrest.

> **CROSS REFERENCE**
>
> The lawful use of force is further mentioned in 7.2.1 and 7.7. Self-defence and the defence of another are discussed in detail in chapter 14.

7.1.1.3 Assault by words or silence

An assault may be committed by words alone, although this has not always been the case. In the case of *Meade and Belt* (1823) 1 Lew CC 184, in which a group of people gathered around the victim's house 'singing songs of menace, and using violent language, indicating that they had come with no friendly or peaceable intention', Holroyd J directed the jury that 'no words or singing are equivalent to an assault'. By contrast, in *Wilson* [1955] 1 WLR 493, Lord Goddard CJ stated that calling out 'Get out knives' would amount to an assault. However, these comments were made *obiter*. The law on this issue was finally settled by the House of Lords in *Ireland; Burstow* [1998] AC 147.

🔍 CASE CLOSE-UP

Ireland; Burstow [1998] AC 147

The defendant in *Ireland* made repeated silent telephone calls to three women over a period of 3 months. The calls were generally made at night and sometimes the women could hear heavy breathing. The three women suffered psychiatric illness as a result of receiving these telephone calls. The defendant was convicted of three counts of assault occasioning actual bodily harm contrary to s.47 of the Offences Against the Person Act 1861.

The defendant in *Burstow* harassed a woman over an 8-month period. He made some silent and some abusive telephone calls to her, distributed offensive cards in the street where she lived, turned up uninvited at her home and place of work, surreptitiously took photographs of her, and sent her a menacing note. The woman was diagnosed with a severe depressive illness and the defendant was convicted of unlawfully and maliciously inflicting grievous bodily harm contrary to s.20 of the OAPA 1861.

The House of Lords considered whether words alone might amount to an assault. Lord Steyn stated that, '[t]he proposition that a gesture may amount to an assault, but that words can never suffice, is unrealistic and indefensible. A thing said is also a thing done.' In fact, Lord Steyn went further and suggested that silent telephone calls may also amount to an assault because the silent caller 'intends by his silence to cause fear and he is so understood'. However, His Lordship stated that whether or not an assault is committed by silence would depend upon the facts of the case and be a matter for the jury.

Just as words may amount to an assault, words can negate an assault. This is demonstrated by the authority of *Tuberville v Savage* (1669) 1 Mod Rep 3. In this case, the defendant put his hand on his sword and said, 'If it were not assize-time, I would not take such language from you.' There was no assault here as, there being no intention to assault, the victim could not have apprehended immediate personal violence. This type of situation must be distinguished from a conditional threat which may constitute an assault. In the civil case of *Read v Coker* (1853) 13 CB 850, the defendant told the claimant that he would break his neck if he did not leave a work premises. This was held to amount to an assault as the threat of violence was immediate and accompanied by an intention to assault.

7.1.1.4 **Immediacy**

The apprehension must be one of *immediate* personal violence. Since the case of *Constanza* [1997] 2 Cr App R 492, the immediacy element has been very widely construed. In *Smith v Chief Superintendent of Woking Police Station* (1983) 76 Cr App R 234, the defendant looked through the windows of the victim's bedroom at night. The victim, who was in her nightclothes at the time, was scared. The Divisional Court held that, despite the closed window between the defendant and victim, there was sufficient apprehension of immediate and unlawful violence in this case. The victim did not know what the defendant was going to do next, but the personal violence that she apprehended was held to be sufficiently immediate.

The Court of Appeal also gave 'immediacy' a wide interpretation in *Constanza* (1997). This case involved a defendant who, amongst other things, followed the victim home from work, made numerous silent telephone calls to the victim and telephone calls in which he spoke, sent over 800 letters to her home, and sat outside her house in his car in the early hours of the day. Schiemann LJ held that there would be an assault where the apprehension was of violence 'at some point not excluding the immediate future'. The immediacy requirement was satisfied in this case as the victim thought that something could happen at any time. Similarly, in *Ireland; Burstow* (1998), Lord Steyn held that the immediacy requirement might even be satisfied in a situation involving a silent caller, because the victim may fear that the silent caller is outside the door. It is sufficient that the victim fears the possibility of immediate personal violence. It would seem then that immediacy is very widely defined and could cover making silent phone calls, sending threatening letters, or even text messages. It is worth noting that this type of conduct is more likely to be charged today as an offence of harassment (under s.2 of the Protection from Harassment Act 1997) or stalking (under s.2A of the Protection from Harassment Act 1997 as introduced by s.111 of the Protection of Freedoms Act 2012). However, these offences are beyond the scope of this textbook.

7.1.1.5 Positive act

The courts have stated that assault and battery can only be committed by a positive act and not by an omission. In the case of *Fagan v MPC* (1969), the Divisional Court avoided basing the liability of the defendant on an omission to act by creating the 'continuing act' theory. The defendant's positive act was driving onto the police officer's foot. When he failed to move the car from his foot, the act was continuing. The Court based the defendant's liability upon this positive act. The issue of whether an omission can constitute an assault was raised again in the case of *DPP v Santana-Bermudez* [2003] EWHC 2908 (Admin) (discussed at 2.4.2.3). The appeal to the Divisional Court arose out of the trial judge's decision to accept a submission of no case to answer ruling that an omission to act could not form the basis of an assault or battery. The prosecution appealed against this decision by way of case stated. In the Divisional Court, Maurice Kay J, relying on *Miller* [1983] 2 AC 161, *Roberts* (1971) 56 Cr App R 95, and *DPP v K (a minor)* (1990) 91 Cr App R 23, held that 'where someone (by act or word or a combination of the two) creates a danger and thereby exposes another to a reasonably foreseeable risk of injury which materialises, there is an evidential basis for the *actus reus* of an assault occasioning actual bodily harm'. The Court circumvented the question as to whether or not an assault or battery can be committed by omission. Maurice Kay J stated that '[a] great deal of undesirable complexity has bedevilled our criminal law as a result of quasi-theological distinctions between acts and omissions'. Instead, the Court held that liability in such a situation could be based on the *Miller* principle.

CROSS REFERENCE
Refer to 2.4.2.3 for a discussion of *Santana-Bermudez* (2003) and *Miller* (1983).

7.1.2 *Mens rea*

The *mens rea* of an assault is intention or recklessness in relation to the ingredients of the *actus reus* of an assault, i.e., intentionally or recklessly causing another person to apprehend immediate and unlawful personal violence. It is not sufficient simply to state that the *mens rea* is intention or recklessness in the abstract without attributing those states of mind to the *actus reus* of an assault. The Court of Appeal confirmed in *Venna* [1976] 1 QB 421 that an assault

CROSS REFERENCE
Refer to 3.4 to remind yourself of the meaning of recklessness.

(and a battery) can be committed recklessly. In this case, the defendant kicked out during a struggle with police officers and fractured the hand of an officer. He was convicted of assault occasioning actual bodily harm on the basis that he had recklessly applied force to the police officer. Recklessness was given its subjective *Cunningham* meaning in *Venna* (1976), but in *DPP v K (a minor)* (1990), the Divisional Court applied the objective *Caldwell* test of recklessness. This case was overruled by the Court of Appeal in *Spratt* [1990] 1 WLR 1073, holding that the subjective standard of recklessness is applied to non-fatal offences against the person. The House of Lords confirmed this decision in *Savage; Parmenter* [1992] 1 AC 699.

7.2 Battery

Battery (also described as 'assault by beating': see *DPP v Taylor; DPP v Little* [1992] 1 QB 645) is a statutory offence which is charged contrary to s.39 of the Criminal Justice Act 1988. The definition of battery is found in common law. A person commits a battery if he intentionally or recklessly inflicts unlawful force on another person: *Collins v Wilcock* (1984).

7.2.1 *Actus reus*

The *actus reus* of a battery is the infliction of unlawful force on another person. Battery differs greatly from an assault because it requires force to actually be inflicted on the victim and there is no requirement that the victim apprehend that they are about to be struck. Thus, the elements of an assault are not inherent within a battery. This in turn means that where the defendant has been charged with battery, the jury cannot return an alternative verdict of assault under s.6(3) of the Criminal Appeals Act 1967 (unless assault has specifically been included on the indictment): see *Nelson* [2013] EWCA Crim 30.

 THINKING POINT

Using the definition of battery from *Collins v Wilcock*, consider whether the following might constitute the *actus reus* of a battery:

(1) Punching V in the back of the head.

(2) Bumping into V in a public place.

(3) Giving V an unwanted kiss or embrace.

(4) Spitting at V.

7.2.1.1 Force

A battery requires the actual application of physical force to the victim; in other words, 'the blow has to land' (*per* Keith J in *Nelson* [2013] EWCA Crim 30 at [3]). Unlike an assault, a battery does not require the victim to apprehend violence, so the victim need not perceive the application of force before it occurs: a blow from behind is sufficient *actus reus* for battery but would not be for an assault. The degree of force required for a battery is very slight and no harm to the person is necessary. In *Cole v Turner* (1705) 6 Mod Rep 149, Holt CJ stated that 'the least touching of another in anger' was sufficient. However, in *Faulkner v Talbot* [1981] 3

All ER 468, Lane LCJ stated that battery 'need not be hostile, or rude, or aggressive, as some of the cases seem to indicate'. In *Brown* [1994] 1 AC 212, the House of Lords held that hostile contact was required for battery. Imagine that you attend a Christmas party and, whilst standing under some mistletoe, someone kisses you. The kiss is unwanted but not hostile. Should this amount to a battery? It is arguable that a requirement of hostility is too strict. Such a requirement would lead to an acquittal in the above scenario, even if the kiss were a passionate one, accompanied by physical bodily contact. According to Robert Goff LJ in *Collins v Wilcock* [1984] 1 WLR 1172, the principle underlying the criminalisation of battery is 'that every person's body is inviolate . . . The effect is that everybody is protected not only against physical injury but against any form of physical molestation.' This view suggests that conduct should be criminalised, irrespective of a lack of hostility, where it goes beyond acceptable standards of behaviour.

No harm is required for a battery to be committed. However, where injury is caused the CPS Charging Standards provide guidance to Crown Prosecutors on suitable charges. The Charging Standards state that although any injury that is more than transient or trifling can be classified as actual bodily harm and can thus be subject to a more serious criminal charge, battery (or common assault) will be the appropriate charge where either no injury or injuries which are not serious occur. The Charging Standards state that '[i]n determining the seriousness of injury, relevant factors may include, for example, the fact that there has been significant medical intervention and/or permanent effects have resulted'.

7.2.1.2 Unlawful

As the *actus reus* of battery is so widely drawn, there are inevitably a number of exceptions to the general principle of liability for the least touching of another. For example, the infliction of force is deemed 'lawful' where a police officer lawfully arrests a person, where a child is subjected to reasonable punishment, and where reasonable force is used in self-defence or the prevention of crime. In addition to these specific exceptions, consent is a defence to battery. The law would be absurd if every instance of touching resulted in a conviction for battery. The case of *Collins v Wilcock* (1984) provides that this defence includes implied consent which, according to Robert Goff LJ, allows for 'the exigencies of everyday life'.

Q CASE CLOSE-UP

***Collins v Wilcock* [1984] 1 WLR 1172**

This case involved a police officer, Wilcock, who took hold of a woman's arm in order to detain her for questioning. The woman, Collins, scratched the police officer's arm and was arrested for assaulting a police officer in the execution of her duty. Collins argued that Wilcock had not been acting in the execution of her duty, as she had gone beyond the scope of that duty in grabbing her arm. The Divisional Court considered that the conduct of the police officer was unlawful and amounted to a battery as it went beyond the generally acceptable standards of physical contact. Robert Goff LJ stated:

> Generally speaking, consent is a defence to battery; and most of the physical contacts of ordinary life are not actionable because they are impliedly consented to by all who move in society and so expose themselves to the risk of bodily contact. So nobody can complain of the jostling which is inevitable from his presence in, for example, a supermarket, an underground station or a busy street; nor can a person who attends a party complain if his hand is seized in friendship, or even if his back is, within reason, slapped.

Consequently, physical contact of everyday life is not sufficient to amount to a battery. Only touching which goes beyond generally acceptable standards of conduct is subject to punishment.

7.2.1.3 **Direct or indirect application of force**

Whilst it is clear that the *actus reus* of battery may be committed by direct bodily contact between two people, for example by striking a person's body with a fist, such close physical contact is not always necessary. For instance, a battery may also be committed by striking another person with an instrument or by throwing an object at a person. The precise extent to which the word 'infliction' can be stretched is a matter of debate. There are authorities which suggest that a wide interpretation of this concept is adequate for a battery. In the case of *Martin* (1881–2) LR 8 QBD 54, the defendant, intending to cause terror and alarm, ran out of a theatre, extinguishing the lights. He placed an iron bar across the exit to the theatre. The audience panicked and rushed to the exit. A large number of people were seriously injured in the crush and the defendant was convicted of maliciously wounding or inflicting GBH, contrary to s.20 of the Offences Against the Person Act 1861. Although the defendant in this case was not charged with battery, the authority demonstrates that the *actus reus* requirement of infliction of force may be widely construed. Similarly, in *Thomas* (1985) 81 Cr App R 331, where the defendant touched the bottom of a girl's skirt and rubbed it, the Court of Appeal took the view that 'if you touch a person's clothes whilst he is wearing them that is equivalent to touching him' (*per* Ackner LJ). Another example is the case of *DPP v K (a minor)* [1990] 1 WLR 1067. The defendant in this case was a school-boy who took some sulphuric acid to the toilets in order to test the reaction of the acid with toilet paper. On hearing footsteps outside, he panicked and threw the acid in a hand drier, the nozzle of which was pointing upwards. When another pupil used the hand drier, acid was blown into his face. The Divisional Court held that the defendant was guilty of assault occasioning actual bodily harm, contrary to s.47 of the Offences Against the Person Act 1861.

These authorities may be cited to illustrate that the infliction of force may be widely construed and that the defendant does not need to physically touch the body of the victim with his own body in order for a battery to result. The requirement of the direct application of force was the immediate issue in the case of *Haystead v Chief Constable of Derbyshire* (2000), in which the defendant punched a woman while she was holding a 12-month-old child. As a result of the punches, the woman dropped the child, who hit his head on the floor. The Divisional Court held that the offence of battery was available in such circumstances, demonstrating that the defendant need not have bodily contact with the victim through his body, but it is sufficient that he have direct physical contact with the victim through a medium controlled by his action. In this case, the medium in question was in fact another person: the woman holding the child. The force applied to the victim was the result of the defendant punching the woman.

7.2.2 *Mens rea*

The *mens rea* of battery is intention or recklessness in relation to the infliction of unlawful force on another person (*Venna* (1976) and *Savage; Parmenter* (1992)). Just as with assault, the subjective *Cunningham* standard of recklessness is applied. However, for a conviction for battery to result, the defendant must have intended or foreseen the actual infliction of force, not just the victim's apprehension of force.

7.3 Assault occasioning actual bodily harm (ABH)

Assault occasioning actual bodily harm (ABH) is a statutory offence which is charged contrary to s.47 of the Offences Against the Person Act 1861. It is an either way offence which carries a maximum sentence of 5 years' imprisonment.

> **STATUTE**
>
> **Section 47, Offences Against the Person Act 1861**
>
> Whosoever shall be convicted upon an indictment of any assault occasioning actual bodily harm shall be liable to be imprisoned for any term not exceeding 5 years.

7.3.1 Assault or battery

This offence is an aggravated form of assault or battery which requires proof that an assault or a battery has been committed. However, this offence is more serious than assault or battery as, it actually requires harm to be caused to the victim.

Since the offence of assault occasioning ABH is an aggravated form of assault or battery, the offence requires both the *actus reus* and the *mens rea* of either an assault or a battery to be proved. It must then also be shown that the assault or battery 'occasioned' (or caused) harm amounting to actual bodily harm. The *actus reus* of assault occasioning actual bodily harm contains three elements and the *mens rea* contains just one (table 7.2).

7.3.2 Which 'occasions' (causes)?

The first *actus reus* element of this offence requires the *actus reus* of an assault or battery to be established. The second *actus reus* element is causation: factual and legal causation need to be satisfied.

The chain of causation will be broken, absolving the defendant of liability, where the victim's act is not reasonably foreseeable. The case of *Roberts* (1971) involved a victim who, in a bid to escape from the sexual advances of the defendant, jumped out of a moving car. The Court

> **CROSS REFERENCE**
>
> Refer to 2.5 to remind yourself of the rules on causation. In particular, remind yourself of the facts of and principle from *Roberts* (1971) 56 Cr App R 95.

Table 7.2 Assault occasioning actual bodily harm (s.47, OAPA 1861)

Actus reus	Mens rea
• AR of assault or AR of battery	• corresponding MR of assault or MR of battery
• which causes ('occasions')	
• ABH	

of Appeal held that the defendant would still be liable for the injuries sustained by the victim where her reaction was something that could reasonably have been foreseen as a result of the defendant's conduct. Stephenson LJ stated that the chain of causation would only be broken where the victim's actions could be shown to be 'daft'.

7.3.3 'Actual bodily harm'?

The offence of assault occasioning actual bodily harm is more serious than assault and battery as it requires the proof of harm. 'Actual bodily harm' is interpreted widely, such that it 'includes any hurt or injury calculated to interfere with health or comfort' (Lynskey J in *Miller* [1954] 2 WLR 138).

THINKING POINT

Consider whether the following would amount to 'actual bodily harm':

(1) Clinically recognised psychiatric injury.

(2) Distress.

(3) Loss of consciousness.

(4) Cutting V's hair.

(5) Putting paint in V's hair.

This wide interpretation of actual bodily harm was also held to encompass any injury to a person's state of mind. The Court of Appeal in *Chan-Fook* [1994] 1 WLR 689 held that any physical or psychiatric injury need not be permanent in nature, but it 'should not be so trivial as to be wholly insignificant' (*per* Hobhouse LJ). It was also stated that the phrase 'actual bodily harm' could include a clinically recognised psychiatric injury where properly proved by medical evidence, but it does not include mere emotions, such as fear, distress, or panic. This was confirmed by the House of Lords in *Ireland; Burstow* (1998) and applied by the Court of Appeal in *Morris* [1998] 1 Cr App R 386, in which it was emphasised that expert psychiatric evidence would be required to prove that the symptoms amounted to a psychiatric illness and that such was the result of the assault. In *T v DPP* [2003] EWHC 266 (Admin), the Divisional Court held that a temporary loss of consciousness was sufficient to amount to actual bodily harm.

CASE CLOSE-UP

***DPP v Smith* [2006] 1 WLR 1571**

In *DPP v Smith*, it was held that cutting off a substantial part of a person's hair without consent amounted to actual bodily harm. The defendant in this case pushed his ex-girlfriend onto a bed, sat on top of her, and cut off her ponytail and some hair from the top of her head. His actions left no mark and did not break her skin. Sir Igor Judge (who later became LCJ), giving the leading judgment in the Divisional Court, likened cutting the victim's hair to putting paint on a person's hair or putting some unpleasant substance on it which marked or damaged it without causing injury elsewhere. The Court held that 'actual' means that the bodily harm must be more than trivial or trifling, 'bodily' is concerned with the body and applies to 'all parts of the body', and the meaning of 'harm' was not limited to 'injury' and extended to 'hurt' or 'damage'. Sir Igor Judge stated:

> In my judgment, whether it is alive beneath the surface of the skin or dead tissue above the surface of the skin, the hair is an attribute and part of the human body. It is intrinsic to each individual and to the identity of each individual.... it remains part of the body and is attached to it. While it is so attached...it falls within the meaning of 'bodily'...

We have seen earlier that an omission is not sufficient to amount to an assault, and that the courts have adopted the 'continuing act' theory in order to circumvent this issue.

CROSS REFERENCE
Remind yourself of the authority of *DPP v Santana-Bermudez* (2003) from 2.4.2.3 and 7.1.1.5.

As with battery, the CPS Charging Standards provide guidance to prosecutors as to what constitutes 'actual bodily harm'. The Charging Standards suggest that s.47 of the OAPA 1861 should be charged where the injuries 'exceed those that can suitably be reflected as Common Assault—namely where the injuries are serious'. This new version of the Charging Standards no longer lists the types of injuries which might constitute actual bodily harm and suggests that prosecutors should only charge a defendant under s.47 where the injuries are serious. The Charging Standard continues: '[i]n determining whether or not the injuries are serious, relevant factors may include, for example, the fact that there has been significant medical intervention and/or permanent effects have resulted. Examples may include cases where there is the need for a number of stitches (but not the superficial application of steri-strips) or a hospital procedure under anaesthetic.'

7.3.4 *Mens rea*

The *mens rea* of assault occasioning actual bodily harm is often misstated by students. The only *mens rea* element which needs to be established is that of the assault or battery which resulted in the actual bodily harm, that is, the intention or recklessness as to causing the victim to apprehend immediate unlawful violence, or intention or recklessness as to the infliction of unlawful force. It is not necessary to prove any additional *mens rea* requirement in relation to the actual bodily harm which resulted. This was confirmed by the House of Lords in *Savage; Parmenter* (1992) (overruling the earlier Court of Appeal decision in *Spratt* (1990)). In the case of *Savage*, the defendant intended to throw a pint of beer over the victim, but the glass also left her hand and broke, and a piece of glass cut the victim's wrist. Although the defendant was charged with maliciously wounding the victim, contrary to s.20 of the OAPA 1861, the *mens rea* of the offence of assault occasioning actual bodily harm was considered in the House of Lords. Lord Ackner stated that:

> The verdict of assault occasioning actual bodily harm may be returned upon proof of an assault together with proof of the fact that actual bodily harm was occasioned by the assault. The prosecution are not obliged to prove that the defendant intended to cause some actual bodily harm or was reckless as to whether such harm would be caused.

 SUMMARY OF ELEMENTS

Assault occasioning actual bodily harm = *AR* and *MR* of assault or battery + causation + ABH.

7.4 Maliciously wounding or inflicting grievous bodily harm

The offence of unlawfully and maliciously wounding or inflicting GBH is a statutory offence which is charged under s.20 of the Offences Against the Person Act 1861. This offence is an either way offence which carries a maximum sentence of 5 years' imprisonment.

 STATUTE

Section 20, Offences Against the Person Act 1861

Whosoever shall unlawfully and maliciously wound or inflict any grievous bodily harm upon any other person, either with or without any weapon or instrument, shall be guilty of an offence, and being convicted thereof shall be liable to imprisonment for a term not exceeding 5 years.

7.4.1 *Actus reus*

The *actus reus* of the offence under s.20 of the OAPA 1861 is unlawfully wounding or inflicting grievous bodily harm on another person. As mentioned at 7.1.1.2 and 7.2.1.2 in relation to assault and battery, 'unlawfully' means that there is no lawful justification for the wound or GBH: see *Horwood* [2012] EWCA Crim 253 at [7] (i.e., the harm was not inflicted in self-defence or in the defence of another). The *actus reus* of this offence may be committed in one of two ways: by the defendant wounding the victim or by inflicting grievous bodily harm on the victim.

 THINKING POINT

Would the following amount to a wound or 'grievous bodily harm' or neither:

(1) A scratch?

(2) Pricking V's finger with a pin and drawing blood?

(3) A rupture of internal blood vessels?

(4) Transmitting HIV to another person?

7.4.1.1 **Wounding**

A wound requires the continuity of the skin to be broken: *Moriarty v Brookes* (1834) 6 C & P 684. In *Wood; McMahon* (1830) 1 Mood CC 278, the victim's collarbone had been broken, but there was no break in the continuity of the skin and, hence, no wound. In *R v Beckett* (1836) 1 Mood & R 526, a 'slight scratch' was not sufficient to constitute a wound. The continuity of the whole skin must be broken, it is not enough that just the cuticle or upper skin (epidermis) is broken, both layers of the skin (both the epidermis and the dermis) must be broken:

M'Loughlin (1838) 8 C & P 635. In *C (a minor) v Eisenhower* [1984] QB 331, it was held that a bruise or internal rupturing of blood vessels is not sufficient. This case involved an injury caused by the victim being struck in his left eye by a pellet from an air pistol. The injury in question was a bruise just below the left eyebrow with fluid filling the front part of his left eye for a while afterwards which unusually contained blood. These injuries were not sufficient to constitute a wound as there was no 'break in the continuity of the skin'. However, the skin which is broken need not be external skin: in *Smith* (1837) 8 C & P 173, a cut to the inside of the mouth was sufficient, and in *Waltham* (1849) 3 Cox CC 442, a rupture to the lining membrane of the urethra amounted to a wound.

7.4.1.2 Inflicting grievous bodily harm

In *DPP v Smith* (1961), the House of Lords held that 'grievous bodily harm' should be given its ordinary and natural meaning. Harm would be 'grievous' if it was 'really serious'. The Court of Appeal in *Saunders* [1985] Crim LR 230 took the view that the word 'really' was unnecessary; 'grievous' means 'serious'.

It is necessary that the GBH be 'inflicted' under s.20 of the OAPA 1861. It used to be thought that this required proof of an assault. Consequently, in *Clarence* (1889) LR 22 QBD 23, it was held that a husband could not 'inflict' GBH on his wife by knowingly exposing her to the risk of contracting gonorrhoea through sexual intercourse. By contrast, in the earlier case of *Martin* (1881–2), it was held that the defendant could be convicted of inflicting GBH where by extinguishing the lights in a theatre and placing a bar across the exit people sustained injuries when they panicked. In *Wilson (Clarence)* [1984] AC 242, the House of Lords held that the infliction of GBH did not require an assault. The meaning of 'inflict' was more recently considered by the House of Lords in *Ireland; Burstow* (1998), when the House compared the *actus reus* of s.20 (wounding or *inflicting* GBH) with that of s.18 (wounding or *causing* GBH). It was argued by counsel for Burstow, that 'inflict' had a narrower meaning than 'cause' and that an offence under s.20 required the application of force to the body (a battery). Lord Steyn held that although the words 'cause' and 'inflict' are not 'synonymous', the difference in language was 'not a significant factor' because of the fact that the OAPA 1861 was a consolidating Act containing provisions taken from different Acts passed at different times. His Lordship held that it would be 'absurd' to differentiate between ss.20 and 18 in this way, and that as the criminal law now recognises psychiatric injury as capable of constituting GBH, the word 'inflict' can embrace the infliction of psychiatric injury on a person. To this extent, Lord Steyn took the view that the 'troublesome authority' of *Clarence* 'no longer assists'. Lord Hope held that 'for all practical purposes there is, in my opinion, no difference between these two words' and that they 'may be taken to be interchangeable'.

Just under 7 years later, the Court of Appeal overruled *Clarence* in the case of *Dica* [2004] QB 1257.

CASE CLOSE-UP

Dica [2004] QB 1257

Dica involved facts comparable to those in *Clarence*. The defendant, who knew that he was HIV positive, had unprotected consensual sexual intercourse with two women, who did not know that he was HIV positive and who later tested positive for HIV. The defendant was charged with two counts of inflicting GBH, contrary to s.20 of the OAPA

> 1861. The prosecution case was that he had recklessly transmitted the disease to them. The defendant appealed against his convictions. The Court of Appeal held that where a defendant, knowing that he was HIV positive, recklessly transmitted the virus to someone else, he could be guilty of inflicting GBH, and that by consenting to sexual intercourse the complainants were not to be taken as consenting to the risk of disease. Judge LJ stated that *Clarence* 'has no continuing relevance' and 'is no longer authoritative'. However, the Court held that the defendant would have a defence to s.20 if the victim did consent to the risk of a sexually transmitted disease.

Similarly, in the case of *Konzani* [2005] EWCA Crim 706, the defendant, knowing that he was HIV positive, had unprotected consensual sexual intercourse with three women. He knew that there was a risk of him passing the HIV virus on to them, yet he did not inform them that he was HIV positive. Each of the three women subsequently contracted the virus and the defendant was convicted of inflicting GBH, contrary to s.20 of the OAPA 1861. In the Court of Appeal, Judge LJ took the opportunity to emphasise that the defence of consent is only available where such consent is informed consent, such that the complainant, knowing of the risks of having unprotected sexual intercourse with the defendant, consented to taking those risks. The Court recognised that the defendant's honest (albeit mistaken) belief in the complainant's consent would also provide a defence. Judge LJ acknowledged the conflicting public policy considerations at stake, namely, the public interest in avoiding the spread of catastrophic illness, and maintaining the principle of personal autonomy in adult non-violent sexual relationships. The defendant's conviction was upheld.

Dica has also since been applied in a case of transmission of the sexually transmitted disease of genital herpes. The defendant in *Golding* [2014] EWCA Crim 889 was convicted of inflicting GBH after he infected his partner with an incurable genital herpes virus. The complainant suffered from recurrent symptoms for which there was no cure and the initial infection was debilitating. The defendant pleaded guilty to the offence and admitted that he should have informed his partner of his condition. The Court of Appeal considered that but for the defendant's guilty plea, there was sufficient evidence for the jury to consider that the harm caused by the defendant was 'really serious bodily harm', and held that the harm need not be permanent or dangerous'.

The CPS Charging Standards also provide guidance on what would usually amount to wounding or grievous bodily harm. The Charging Standards recognise that the technical definition of a wound may encompass minor injuries such as a small cut, but suggest that in order to equate this part of the s.20 offence with the second part (inflicting grievous bodily harm), s.20 should be reserved for really serious wounds. The Charging Standards state that grievous bodily harm means 'really serious harm'. Examples include: injury resulting in permanent disability; loss of sensory function or visible disfigurement; broken or displaced limbs or bones, including fractured skull, compound fractures, broken cheek bone, jaw, ribs, etc.; injuries which cause substantial loss of blood, usually necessitating a transfusion or result in lengthy treatment or incapacity; and serious psychiatric injury.

7.4.2 *Mens rea*

The *mens rea* of this offence is also often misstated. Section 20 of the OAPA 1861 provides that maliciously wounding or inflicting GBH is an offence. The *mens rea* element here is contained in the word 'maliciously', which has been deemed to mean 'intentionally or recklessly': *Mowatt* [1967] 3 WLR 1192 and *Savage; Parmenter* (1992). As with all the offences in this chapter, the subjective *Cunningham* test of recklessness is applied. The question then arises as to the degree of harm which needs to be intended or foreseen in order to be guilty under this section. According to the Court of Appeal in *Mowatt* (1967), the defendant must intend to or be reckless as to causing *some* harm. Lord Diplock stated that:

> It is quite unnecessary that the accused should have foreseen that his unlawful act might cause physical harm of the gravity described in the section, i.e., a wound or serious physical injury. It is enough that he should have foreseen that some physical harm to some person, albeit of a minor character, might result.

This was approved by the House of Lords in *Savage; Parmenter* (1992). The defendant in *Parmenter* caused serious injuries to his 3-month-old baby by handling him roughly. He was convicted of maliciously wounding or inflicting GBH contrary to s.20 of the OAPA 1861. This conviction was quashed as the defendant had not foreseen that some harm might occur by his handling of the baby and a conviction of assault occasioning ABH contrary to s.47 of the OAPA 1861 was substituted. The House of Lords confirmed that foresight of some harm is necessary for a conviction under s.20.

7.5 Wounding or causing grievous bodily harm with intent

The offence of unlawfully wounding or causing GBH is a statutory offence which is charged under s.18 of the Offences Against the Person Act 1861. This offence is indictable only and carries a maximum sentence of life imprisonment.

 STATUTE

Section 18, Offences Against the Person Act 1861

Whosoever shall unlawfully and maliciously by any means whatsoever wound or cause any grievous bodily harm to any person with intent to do some grievous bodily harm to any person or with intent to resist arrest or prevent the lawful apprehension or detainer of any person, shall be guilty of an offence, and being convicted thereof shall be liable to imprisonment for life.

7.5.1 *Actus reus*

The *actus reus* of this offence is unlawfully wounding or causing GBH to a person. These elements are similar to those under s.20 and have the same meaning as they do for that offence. One notable difference in the *actus reus* of s.18 is that GBH must be 'caused'.

Although, on the face of it, the word 'cause' implies a wider scope than 'inflict' (the *actus reus* of s.20), the House of Lords has held that these words are 'interchangeable' (*Ireland; Burstow* (1998)) and in practice it seems to make little difference. This is discussed in more detail at 7.4.1.2.

7.5.2 *Mens rea*

The *mens rea* of the offence under s.18 is slightly more complicated than mere 'intention'. A detailed reading of s.18 shows that there are several possible forms of *mens rea* that may be charged. The early part of s.18 mentions the word 'maliciously', and the latter part of the section requires one of a number of alternative forms of *mens rea* to be proved:

- intention to cause GBH; or
- intention to resist arrest; or
- intention to prevent the lawful apprehension of a person; or
- intention to prevent the lawful detainer of a person.

7.5.2.1 Intention to cause grievous bodily harm

Where a defendant is charged with wounding or causing GBH with intention to cause GBH, the offence is relatively straightforward. This is a specific intent offence, so mere recklessness is not sufficient for this form of the offence: *Belfon* [1976] 1 WLR 714. The interpretation given to intention in the law of murder also applies with respect to this offence. As such, a defendant will have direct intent in relation to causing GBH if it is his aim or his purpose to do so, or his intention may be oblique where GBH was virtually certain to occur and the defendant appreciated this: *Nedrick* (1986) and *Woollin* (1999). We saw earlier in relation to s.20, that 'maliciously' means 'intentionally or recklessly'. However, recklessness is not sufficient for an offence under s.18. Hence, where a defendant is charged with maliciously wounding or causing GBH with intent to cause GBH, the word 'maliciously' is effectively redundant. According to Diplock LJ (*obiter*) in the Court of Appeal in *Mowatt* (1967), 'the word "maliciously" adds nothing' to s.18.

CROSS REFERENCE
Refer to 3.3.2 for a detailed discussion on oblique intent.

7.5.2.2 Intention to resist arrest or to prevent the lawful apprehension or detainer of a person

Where a defendant is instead charged with wounding or causing GBH *with intention to resist arrest or to prevent the lawful apprehension or detainer of a person*, the *obiter* statement in *Mowatt* (1967) that 'the word "maliciously" adds nothing' to s.18 does not seem to be satisfactory. For this form of the offence, it should not be sufficient that a mere intention to resist arrest, etc. be proved. The defendant should only be convicted of an offence under s.18 where, in accordance with the requirement of 'maliciously', he also foresaw (i.e., was reckless in relation to) the causing or at least some harm but not necessarily GBH. Thus, this form of the offence requires proof of two *mens rea* elements:

- an intention to resist arrest or to prevent the lawful apprehension or detainer of a person; and
- recklessness as to whether some harm was caused, albeit not serious harm.

Table 7.3 summarises the main non-fatal offences against the person.

Table 7.3 Summary of main non-fatal offences against the person

Offence	Source of law	*Actus reus*	*Mens rea*
Assault	Defined in common law but charged contrary to s.39, CJA 1988	Causing the apprehension of immediate unlawful violence (*Fagan v MPC* (1969))	Intention or recklessness as to causing such apprehension (*Venna* (1976))
Battery	Defined in common law but charged contrary to s.39, CJA 1988	Inflicting unlawful force (*Fagan v MPC* (1969))	Intention or recklessness as to the infliction of force (*Venna* (1976))
Assault occasioning actual bodily harm	s.47, OAPA 1861	(i) *Actus reus* of an assault or battery (ii) which causes (*Savage; Parmenter* (1992)) (iii) actual bodily harm (*Miller* (1954) and *Chan-Fook* (1994))	The *mens rea* of the assault or battery (i.e., intention or recklessness as to causing apprehension of immediate force, or intention or recklessness as to the infliction of force) (*Savage; Parmenter* (1992))
Wounding or inflicting grievous bodily harm	s.20, OAPA 1861	Wounding (*Moriarty v Brookes* (1834)) or inflicting GBH ('really serious harm', *DPP v Smith* (1961))	Intention or recklessness as to causing some harm (*Savage; Parmenter* (1992))
Wounding or causing grievous bodily harm with intent	s.18, OAPA 1861	Wounding (*Moriarty v Brookes* (1834)) or causing GBH ('really serious harm', *DPP v Smith* (1961))	Intention to cause GBH (*Belfon* (1976))

7.6 Administering a noxious thing

In addition to the five main non-fatal offences against the person already discussed, the Offences Against the Person Act 1861 provides two offences of 'poisoning' under ss.23 and 24. The offence under s.23 is the more serious one and carries a maximum sentence of 10 years' imprisonment, while the s.24 offence carries a maximum of 5 years' imprisonment.

 STATUTE

Section 23, Offences Against the Person Act 1861

Whosoever shall unlawfully and maliciously administer or cause to be administered to or taken by any other person any poison or other destructive or noxious thing, so as thereby to endanger the life of such person, or so as thereby to inflict upon such person any griev-ous bodily harm, shall be guilty of [an offence], and being convicted thereof shall be liable to [imprisonment] for any term not exceeding ten years.

 STATUTE

Section 24, Offences Against the Person Act 1861

Whosoever shall unlawfully and maliciously administer or cause to be administered to or taken by any other person any poison or other destructive or noxious thing, with intent to injure, aggrieve, or annoy such person, shall be guilty of [an offence], and being...con-victed thereof shall be liable to [imprisonment for a term not exceeding five years].

7.6.1 *Actus reus*

The *actus reus* of both offences is very similar: both require the defendant to unlawfully admin-ister (or cause to be administered or taken) a poison or noxious thing. The significant distinc-tion between the *actus reus* of these offences is that the more serious offence under s.23 also requires life to be endangered or GBH to be inflicted by the administration.

7.6.1.1 **Administer, cause to be administered or taken**

▶ CROSS REFERENCE

Refer to 6.1.5 for a detailed discussion of the 'drugs cases'.

The poison must be taken by or administered to the victim: 'taken' requires the poison to have been absorbed, for example by eating or drinking it. 'Administer or cause to be administered' includes bringing the noxious thing into contact with the body of the victim. In *Gillard* (1988) 87 Cr App R 189, this was held to encompass the spraying of CS gas into the victim's face. Whether or not a substance has been administered to or taken by the defendant is a question of law for the trial judge: *Gillard*. There are a number of drugs cases involving a defendant who has either injected the victim with heroin or prepared and handed the victim a syringe so that the victim can inject the drugs into himself. Where this conduct results in the death of the victim, the defendant is usually charged with manslaughter and the prosecution is brought on the basis of unlawful act manslaughter. As we have already seen in chapter 6, unlawful act manslaughter requires a criminal offence to have been committed: *Lamb* (1967). The unlawful act is obvious where the defendant injects the drugs into the victim's body and would con-stitute an offence under s.23. However, the issue has until recently been less clear where the victim self-injects.

 THINKING POINT

Consider whether the following would constitute an offence under s.23 or s.24 of the OAPA 1861 (assume that V is an adult unless otherwise stated):

(1) Putting bleach in V's drink.

(2) Lacing V's orange juice with alcohol.

(3) Would your answer to (2) differ if V were a child?

(4) Feeding a child excessive amounts of salt.

(5) Cooking a dinner including poisonous mushrooms for V.

(6) Lacing V's drink with sleeping tablets.

(7) Preparing a syringe of heroin and handing it to V so that he can inject himself with the drug.

 CASE CLOSE-UP

Kennedy (No. 2) [2007] UKHL 38

In this case, the victim asked the defendant to give him something to help him sleep. The defendant prepared a syringe with heroin and handed it to the victim, who injected himself with the drug. The victim died within an hour and the defendant was convicted of unlawful act manslaughter (the unlawful act being the offence under s.23, OAPA 1861). The conviction was upheld by the Court of Appeal, but the case was referred back to the Court of Appeal by the Criminal Cases Review Commission and renamed *Kennedy (No. 2)* [2007] UKHL 38. The defendant appealed against the decision of the Court of Appeal to dismiss his second appeal. The House of Lords allowed the appeal and held that the defendant had not committed an offence under s.23. Lord Bingham stated that he had not caused the drug to be administered to the victim as the victim's voluntary act of self-injection as a 'fully-informed and responsible adult' was an intervening act which broke the chain of causation.

7.6.1.2 Poison or noxious thing

Whether or not a substance amounts to a poison or noxious thing is a question of fact to be determined by the jury. Some substances are inherently noxious, such as heroin: *Cato* [1976] 1 WLR 110 (this was reiterated by Lord Bingham in *Kennedy (No. 2)* (2007)). In *Cato*, the defendant injected the victim, a drug addict, with heroin and was charged with unlawfully and maliciously administering a noxious thing contrary to s.23 of the OAPA 1861. The Court of Appeal held that a substance which was 'liable to cause injury in common use' was a noxious thing for the purposes of s.23. Consequently, heroin was a noxious thing and the fact that it was administered to a person who had a high tolerance to heroin was not relevant. Other substances are only noxious in certain circumstances. In determining whether or not such a substance is noxious, the jury will be directed to consider the circumstances in which such a substance was administered, including its quality and quantity, and the characteristics of the victim.

In the case of *Marcus* (1981) 73 Cr App R 49, the Court of Appeal gave 'noxious' a very wide meaning. The defendant put eight sedative and sleeping tablets into a bottle of milk delivered to her neighbour. She was convicted of an attempt to commit the offence under s.24 of the OAPA 1861 (i.e., attempting maliciously to cause to be taken by the victim or another, a noxious thing with intent to injure, aggrieve, or annoy). At trial, the judge directed the jury in accordance with the definition of 'noxious' from the *Shorter Oxford English Dictionary*: 'injurious, hurtful, harmful, unwholesome'. The Court of Appeal held that whether a substance was a noxious thing was a matter of 'fact and degree'. Tudor Evans J stated:

> A substance which may have been harmless in small quantities may yet be noxious in the quantity administered . . . for example, to lace a glass of milk with a quantity of alcohol

might not amount to administering a noxious thing to an adult but it might do so if given to a child.

The Court acknowledged that the meaning of noxious is very wide, such that placing an obnoxious, objectionable, or unwholesome thing into food or drink with the intention to annoy the victim would be sufficient to constitute an offence under s.24 of the OAPA 1861. The Court stated that the famous example of a snail in a ginger-beer bottle (adapting the facts of the case of *Donoghue v Stevenson* [1932] AC 562) would also be sufficient if accompanied by an intention to injure, aggrieve, or annoy.

7.6.2 *Mens rea*

Both the s.23 and the s.24 offences require the administration to be malicious. 'Maliciously' here means intention or recklessness in relation to the administration of a noxious thing and the subjective *Cunningham* test of recklessness is applied. No further element of *mens rea* is required under s.23 in relation to endangering life or inflicting GBH: *Cato*. However, the offence under s.24 requires an additional element of *mens rea*: an intention to injure, aggrieve, or annoy. The presence of such intention may depend upon the purpose for which the noxious thing is administered.

 CASE CLOSE-UP

Hill (1986) 83 Cr App R 386

In this case, the defendant gave slimming tablets to two boys, aged 11 and 13, in order to stimulate and excite the boys. He admitted unlawfully administering a noxious thing, but denied any intention to injure the boys. In the House of Lords, Lord Griffiths held that the trial judge was correct to direct the jury that injury includes causing harm to the body. His Lordship stated that it was reasonable to infer that the defendant's intention was to 'injure the boys in the sense of causing harm to the metabolism of their bodies by overstimulation' so that they would stay awake for an unnatural period of time, and that his likely motive was to render them susceptible to his sexual advances. However, the House declined to answer the certified question: whether s.24 is committed where the intention is only to keep the victim awake, because the answer would depend upon the factual background of the case. Lord Griffiths gave the following examples: where the noxious thing is administered for a purely benevolent purpose such as keeping a pilot of an aircraft awake, no offence is committed.

On the other hand, if it is administered for a malevolent purpose such as a prolonged interrogation, the necessary intention is likely to be present. This approach was adopted in the case of *Gantz* [2004] EWCA Crim 2862. During a flight, the defendant put Ecstasy in the drink of a woman he had met at the check-in desk. He appealed against his conviction under s.24 of the OAPA 1861. The trial judge had directed the jury in accordance with *Hill*, to consider the defendant's motive in spiking her drink. If the jury were satisfied that the defendant had the intention of causing harm to the metabolism of her body by overstimulation, and if his motive was to render her more susceptible to his advances, then the offence would have been committed. The Court of Appeal held that the judge had been right to so direct the jury, as a purely benevolent motive would have negated any apparent intention to injure.

7.7 Consent

An assault or battery will be rendered lawful by the valid consent of the 'victim'. Thus, consent is a justificatory defence, which negates an *actus reus* element of the offence, that is the element of unlawfulness. There are two issues to be addressed in this section: *(a)* the offences to which consent is available as a defence (see 7.7.1 and 7.7.2); and *(b)* when consent is deemed to be valid (see 7.7.3).

7.7.1 General rule

Consent as a defence to battery has already been considered briefly at 7.2.1.2. We are deemed to impliedly consent to the inevitable physical contact that occurs as part of everyday life: *Collins v Wilcock* (1984).

CROSS REFERENCE
Refer back to 7.2.1.2 for a discussion on implied consent.

The general rule is that consent is only a defence to assault and battery. Consent is no defence to any injury amounting to actual bodily harm: *Donovan* [1934] All ER 207 and *Attorney General's Reference (No. 6 of 1980)* [1981] 2 All ER 1057. The defendant in *Donovan* beat a 17-year-old girl with a cane for his sexual pleasure. The girl was a willing participant. Swift J in the Court of Appeal stated that 'it is an unlawful act to beat another person with such a degree of violence that the infliction of bodily harm is a probable consequence, and when such an act is proved, consent is immaterial'. In *Attorney General's Reference (No. 6 of 1980)*, the defendant had a fist fight with a 17-year-old boy in a public street. The boy sustained bruises to his face and a bleeding nose. The Court of Appeal considered what would be in the interest of the general public and concluded that consent was no defence where a victim sustained injuries amounting to ABH. Lord Lane CJ stated that 'it is not in the public interest that people should try to cause, or should cause, each other actual bodily harm for no good reason'. His Lordship added that it was immaterial whether the act occurred in public or in private. This principle was approved by the House of Lords in *Brown and others* [1994] 1 AC 212 (discussed further at 7.7.2.3).

THINKING POINT

Discuss whether any offence has been committed where:

(1) D fractures X's jaw during a rugby match.

(2) D pierces X's ears.

(3) D flogs X's back at his request during a religious ceremony.

(4) D whips his wife's (X's) buttocks for sexual pleasure, wounding her.

(5) Would your answer to (4) be different if D and X were not married, but cohabiting, or if D and X were homosexual and had been living together for 20 years?

7.7.2 Exceptions

In *Attorney General's Reference (No. 6 of 1980)*, Lord Lane CJ stated that there were a number of exceptions to the general rule that consent is no defence to harm amounting to ABH or

GBH, including injuries sustained during properly conducted sports, lawful chastisement or correction, reasonable surgical interference, and dangerous exhibitions. These exceptions are governed by policy considerations, namely the public interest. One obvious exception to the general rule is where a qualified medical professional causes bodily harm to a patient as part of a consensual and legitimate surgical operation. Such an exception is clearly necessary in the public interest and in order to avoid the absurd situation of a surgeon being held criminally liable for conducting an operation and saving an individual's life. The exception applies similarly to acts of body modification such as cosmetic surgery, ritual circumcision, body piercing, and tattooing. As it has been held that the act of cutting a person's hair may amount to ABH (*DPP v Smith* (2006)), consenting to having one's hair cut must also fall into the list of exceptions. Lord Mustill in *Brown* stated that consensual injuries sustained during religious flagellation also fall under these exceptions. This exception is necessary to avoid a conflict with Article 9 of the European Convention on Human Rights which provides for freedom of religion. Some of the exceptions are discussed in further detail in 7.7.2.1 to 7.7.2.3.

7.7.2.1 **Sports**

The rationale behind the inclusion of properly regulated sports as an exception to the general rule lies in the social utility that sporting activity provides, through the encouragement of physical exercise and as a source of entertainment. Generally speaking, where the sport or game being played is properly regulated and the injury occurs accidentally while the parties are acting within the rules of the game, or from conduct which the participants can reasonably be regarded as having consented to, the perpetrator will not normally be held criminally liable for the harm caused. However, this will not be the case if the rules of the game permit unacceptable conduct, or if the injuries are intentionally inflicted. In such cases, the law would not allow the defendant to avail himself of the defence of consent. Despite this, boxing, a sport which involves the participants intentionally inflicting serious harm on one another, remains a lawful activity.

Where the sport being played does not involve the necessary infliction of harm, no defence of consent will be available where the defendant intentionally inflicts ABH or GBH on another participant. However, if the injury is unintentionally caused, the tribunal of fact will need to consider whether the victim impliedly consented to that level of injury, taking into account the circumstances in which it was caused. The Court of Appeal considered the availability of consent as a defence in relation to sporting injuries in the case of *Barnes* [2004] EWCA Crim 3246. In this case, the defendant broke an opponent's leg during an amateur football match. He was charged with unlawfully and maliciously inflicting GBH contrary to s.20 of the OAPA 1861. The Court of Appeal held that criminal prosecutions should be reserved for particularly grave conduct which is sufficiently serious to be regarded as criminal. This is partly due to the fact that in most sports, disciplinary procedures and civil remedies are available where players do not abide by the rules of the sport. Where a criminal prosecution is brought, the tribunal of fact must objectively evaluate whether such conduct could reasonably be regarded as having been consented to by considering the circumstances in which the injury was sustained. Circumstances which might be taken into account include: the type of sport being played; the level at which it is played; the nature of the conduct; whether the conduct occurred during play or in the heat of the moment when play was not in progress; the degree of force used; the extent of the risk of injury; and the state of mind of the defendant.

7.7.2.2 **'Rough horseplay'**

Consent is available as a defence where injuries amounting to ABH or GBH are sustained during 'rough horseplay'. This exception applies where injuries are caused as a result of rough and undisciplined horseplay which is not intended to cause injury, for example in the school playground. In the case of *Jones and others* (1986) 83 Cr App R 375, a group of school boys were playing, throwing their schoolmates into the air and catching them. Two boys sustained serious injuries. The defendants were charged with unlawfully and maliciously inflicting GBH contrary to s.20 of the OAPA 1861. Their convictions were quashed by the Court of Appeal, which held that consent was available as a defence because the boys were willing participants and they did not intend to cause injury. Similarly, in the case of *Aitken and others* [1992] 1 WLR 1006, newly qualified RAF officers set fire to each other's fire-resistant suits during drunken celebrations. The victim sustained serious burns and the defendants were convicted of unlawfully and maliciously inflicting GBH contrary to s.20 of the OAPA 1861. Their convictions were quashed on appeal because the defence of consent had been rejected by the trial judge at first instance, who refused to leave the issue of consent to the jury. The Court of Appeal held that if the victim had consented, or if the defendant honestly believed that he had consented, the defence of consent was available and should be left for the tribunal of fact to consider.

7.7.2.3 Sexual gratification

THINKING POINT

Consider whether consent should be a defence to the infliction of harm for sexual pleasure?

Should your right to bodily autonomy be absolute?

When, if at all, should the law be allowed to intervene for your protection?

CASE CLOSE-UP

Brown [1994] 1 AC 212

The case of *Brown* involved a group of sado-masochistic homosexual men who willingly and enthusiastically participated in committing acts of violence against one another for sexual pleasure. Their acts of violence took place in private and with the consent of every person there and involved the giving and receiving of pain, including branding each other with hot metal wire and applying stinging nettles to their genitalia. They sustained injuries amounting to ABH and GBH, although none of the injuries were permanent. The defendants were charged with offences under ss.47 and 20 of the OAPA 1861, but pleaded guilty after the trial judge ruled that the prosecution did not have to prove the absence of consent. The Court of Appeal dismissed their appeals against conviction and held that consent was no defence in this case as the injuries were not merely transient or trifling and there was no 'good reason' for allowing the defence of consent. The House of Lords also upheld their convictions by a 3:2 majority (Lords Mustill and Slynn dissenting). The House considered policy and the public interest and held that consent is no defence to ABH or GBH where such injuries have been inflicted in the course of sado-masochistic encounters. Lord Templeman stated that sex was no excuse for violence and that pleasure derived from the infliction of pain was an evil thing. His Lordship took the view that society had to protect itself against 'a cult of violence':

> In principle there is a difference between violence which is incidental and violence which is inflicted for the indulgence of cruelty. The violence of sado-masochistic encounters

> involves the indulgence of cruelty by sadists and the degradation of victims. Such violence is injurious to the participants and unpredictably dangerous. I am not prepared to invent a defence of consent for sado-masochistic encounters which breed and glorify cruelty and result in offences under sections 47 and 20 of the Act of 1861.
>
> The defendants in *Brown* appealed to the European Court of Human Rights, arguing that their right to a private life under Article 8 of the ECHR had been violated. The Court gave judgment in the case of *Laskey v UK* (1996) 24 EHRR 39 and held that there had been no violation as Article 8 is not an absolute right and it can be interfered with where necessary in a democratic society for the protection of health.

Brown applies to the deliberate infliction of ABH or GBH and was distinguished on this basis in *Slingsby* [1995] Crim LR 570, in which the victim sustained cuts when the defendant inserted his hand into her vagina and anus with her consent. The cuts were caused accidentally by a signet ring that the defendant had been wearing. The victim failed to recognise the severity of her injuries and she contracted septicaemia from which she later died. The defendant was charged with unlawful and dangerous act manslaughter, which required proof of a battery that caused her death. It was held that as the injuries had been accidentally caused as a result of consensual sexual activity between the parties, the defendant should not be criminally liable. *Brown* was also distinguished in the case of *Wilson* [1997] 1 QB 47.

In *Wilson* [1997] 1 QB 47, the Court of Appeal held that the defence of consent should have been available where the defendant branded his initials into his wife's buttocks with a hot knife. This act was performed at the express request of his wife (she had originally asked her husband to tattoo his name on her breasts but the defendant talked her out of this idea). Nevertheless, the trial judge directed the jury to convict the defendant of assault occasioning ABH contrary to s.47 of the OAPA 1861. The conviction was quashed on appeal. Russell LJ, who read the judgment of the Court of Appeal, stated 'we cannot detect any logical difference between what the appellant did and what he might have done in the way of tattooing'. Although tattooing is an activity which involves causing ABH, it is rendered lawful by valid consent which prevents any criminal liability. The Court distinguished this case from *Brown*, which the Court said involved 'a sado-masochistic encounter', and held that it was not in the public interest that activities such as those in *Wilson* should amount to criminal behaviour. Russell LJ stated that:

> Consensual activity between husband and wife, in the privacy of the matrimonial home, is not, in our judgment, normally a proper matter for criminal investigation, let alone criminal prosecution.

The Court of Appeal went so far as to criticise the CPS for bringing the prosecution which served no useful purpose yet involved considerable expense. The Court was also concerned that the law should be left to develop on a case-by-case basis.

 THINKING POINT

To what extent do you agree with the Court of Appeal's decision in *Wilson* to distinguish the case of *Brown*?

Both *Wilson* and *Brown* involved the infliction of injuries at the request of or with the full consent of the victim. The injuries sustained in both cases were of comparable severity and they occurred in private. One factual difference between the two cases is that the injuries in *Brown* were inflicted for sexual pleasure which was not the case in *Wilson*; Mrs Wilson wanted to be adorned with the initials of her husband. However, sexual pleasure aside, neither case involved hostility or aggression in the infliction of the injuries. Another difference which is implicitly significant in the judgments of the courts is the fact that *Brown* involved a group of homosexual men, while *Wilson* involved a married heterosexual couple. This begs the question whether the Court of Appeal decision in *Wilson* would have been different if the couple had been unmarried or homosexual. The case of *Emmett* (1999), *The Times*, 15 October, assists us here. This case involved an unmarried heterosexual couple who engaged in consensual sexual acts in the privacy of their bedroom. The defendant tied a plastic bag over his fiancée's head in order to increase her sexual excitement. He then poured lighter fluid over her breasts and set fire to it. The victim sustained a burn measuring 6 cm by 4 cm on her breasts. The Court of Appeal upheld the defendant's convictions for assault occasioning ABH and held that no distinction should be drawn between homosexual and heterosexual sadomasochistic activity. The Court distinguished *Wilson* on the basis that the injuries in this case went far beyond those in *Wilson*.

7.7.3 When is consent valid?

Consent is only valid if it is freely given by a fully informed and competent adult. Consent obtained from a minor is invalid: in *Burrell v Harmer* [1967] Crim LR 196, it was held that two boys aged 12 and 13 were incapable of giving valid consent to having a tattoo. Consent is invalid if it is obtained by fraud as to the identity of the defendant or fraud as to the nature and quality of the act.

The defendant in *Richardson* [1998] 2 Cr App R 200, was a dentist who was suspended from practice. She continued to treat her patients who did not know that she had been suspended. The Court of Appeal held that the consent of the patients was not valid if it had been obtained by fraud as to the identity of the defendant, but this did not extend to lying about one's qualifications. In this case, there was no fraud as to the identity of the defendant and the consent of the patients negated any criminal liability for assault. However, in *Tabassum* [2000] 2 Cr App R 328, the defendant, purporting to be carrying out a study into breast cancer, carried out examinations of the breasts of three women. The women only consented to the touching because they believed the defendant and thought that he was medically qualified. In fact, he was not. He was convicted of three counts of indecent assault and his convictions were upheld in the Court of Appeal. The Court distinguished *Richardson* and held that in this case, the complainants had consented to the nature of the act (the touching) because they thought that it was for a medical purpose, but they had not consented to its quality as indecent behaviour.

Hence, consent is only valid if it is given by a fully informed and competent adult. Consent must be freely given and is rendered invalid if it is obtained by fraud as to the identity of the defendant (but not if he lies about his qualifications) or by fraud as to the nature and quality of the act.

The Court of Appeal in *Dica* held that, although consenting to sexual intercourse did not equate to consenting to the risk of disease, a defendant would have a defence to s.20 if the victim did consent to the risk of a sexually transmitted disease. In *Konzani*, the Court of Appeal held that informed consent would be a defence, i.e., where the complainant, knowing of the risks of having unprotected sexual intercourse with the defendant, consents to taking those risks.

CROSS REFERENCE
For discussion of *Dica* and *Konzani*, see 7.4.1.2.

Table 7.4 The hierarchy of offences in the draft Bill

Clause	Offence	Notes	Sentence
1(1)	Intentionally causing serious injury to another.	Indictable only offence. Can be committed by omission (cl.1(2)).	Maximum life imprisonment.
2(1)	Recklessly causing serious injury to another.	Either way offence.	Maximum 7 years' imprisonment.
3(1)	Intentionally or recklessly causing injury to another.	Either way offence. Injury includes physical and mental injury (cl.15) but does not include anything caused by disease (except in relation to an offence under cl.1).	Maximum 5 years' imprisonment.
4(1)(a)	Intentionally or recklessly applying force to or causing an impact on the body of another.	Summary only offence. Implied consent is still a defence (cl.4(2)).	Maximum 6 months' imprisonment and/or a fine not exceeding £5,000.
4(1)(b)	Intentionally or recklessly causing another to believe that such force or impact is imminent.	Summary only offence.	Maximum 6 months' imprisonment and/or a fine not exceeding £5,000.

7.7.4 Reform

The current law is in need of reform. The existing hierarchy of offences is confusing and lacks coherence. On 3 November 2015, the Law Commission published a report recommending reforms to the existing hierarchy of offences against the person and proposing that a modern statute based on the Draft Bill of 1989 should replace the OAPA 1861.

Summary

- Assault is an offence which is charged under s.39 of the Criminal Justice Act 1988. It is defined as intentionally or recklessly causing the apprehension of unlawful and immediate personal violence: *Fagan v MPC* (1969). Assault may be committed by words alone: *Wilson* (1955), or by silence: *Ireland; Burstow* (1998). Fear is not required. Immediacy is widely construed: *Ireland; Burstow* (1998) and *Constanza* (1997).

- Battery is an offence which is charged contrary to s.39 of the Criminal Justice Act 1988. It is defined as intentionally or recklessly inflicting unlawful force without consent: *Collins v Wilcock* (1984). Only the least touching of another is required: *Cole v Turner* (1705) and no harm is necessary. We impliedly consent to physical contact of everyday life: *Collins v Wilcock* (1984).

- Assault occasioning ABH is a statutory offence under s.47 of the OAPA 1861. It requires the proof of an assault or a battery which causes 'actual bodily harm'. ABH 'includes any hurt or injury calculated to interfere with health or comfort': *Miller* (1983). It includes a clinically recognised psychiatric injury: *Chan-Fook* (1994). The *mens rea* element required is that of the assault or battery. No additional *mens rea* element is required in relation to the degree of harm caused: *Savage* (1992).

- Unlawfully and maliciously wounding or inflicting GBH is a statutory offence under s.20 of the OAPA 1861. A wound requires a break in the continuity of the skin: *Moriarty v Brookes* (1834), *C (a minor) v Eisenhower* (1984). GBH means 'really serious harm': *DPP v Smith* (1961), or 'serious harm': *Saunders* (1985). The *mens rea* requires intention or recklessness as to causing *some* harm: *Savage; Parmenter* (1992).

- Unlawfully wounding or causing GBH with intent is a statutory offence under s.18 of the OAPA 1861. The only real difference to s.20 lies in the *mens rea*. The *mens rea* is intention to cause GBH. Recklessness is not sufficient: *Belfon* (1976).

- There are two offences of unlawfully and maliciously administering a noxious thing under ss.23 and 24 of the OAPA 1861. Section 23 requires life to be endangered or the infliction of GBH. Section 24 requires the intention to injure, aggrieve, or annoy.

- Consent is only a defence to assault and battery and not to intentionally inflicted ABH or GBH: *Donovan* (1934). There are a number of exceptions to this general rule.

The bigger picture

- In order to gain an appreciation of how the non-fatal offences against the person operate in practice and the sorts of injuries that are likely to lead to prosecutors charging the more serious offences, you should read the CPS Charging Standards, Offences Against the Person in full: http://www.cps.gov.uk/legal/l_to_o/offences_against_the_person/.

- For a more detailed discussion on criminal liability for the transmission of sexually transmissted diseases and HIV, see Mawhinney (2013).

- The non-fatal offences against the person is an examinable topic and you should ensure that you are able to answer both essay and problem questions in this area.

- For some guidance on how you might approach essay questions on these topics, you should visit the Online Resource Centre.

? Questions

Self-test questions

1. What is the *actus reus* of an assault?

2. How is 'immediate' interpreted by the courts? Support your answer with case law.

3. What is the significance of *Tuberville v Savage* (1669)?

4. What is the *mens rea* of assault occasioning ABH?

5. Define 'wound' and 'grievous bodily harm'. Support your answers with case law.

6. What is the *mens rea* of the offence under s.20 of the OAPA 1861?

7. In what circumstances may consent be relied upon as a defence?

8. John receives threatening text messages and silent telephone calls from his neighbour, Suzy. As a result, John suffers sleepless nights and becomes severely depressed. Discuss Suzy's criminal liability.

9. Whilst racing around a supermarket with their trolleys, Owen and David deliberately strike each other with their trolleys, causing severe bruising to their legs. Owen accidentally bumps into another shopper, Anna. Angrily, Anna pushes Owen hard in the back. Owen slips over and hits his head on the floor, fracturing his skull. Discuss the criminal liability of the parties.

10. Raj puts a quantity of laxatives into a drink which Bill consumes. Has Raj committed any offence?

 For suggested approaches, please visit the Online Resource Centre.

Exam questions

1. The provisions of the Offences Against the Person Act 1861 are out of date and no longer correspond with the application of the law in practice. To what extent do you agree with this statement? Discuss with reference to case law.

2. Carl and Daniel, two professors of philosophy, are on their way to watch a charity football match organised by their university. In their rush to catch the bus to the match, they push other passengers, causing them to lose their balance. When they arrive at the football stadium, Carl and Daniel sing songs with abusive lyrics, scaring Emma, who is sitting in the row behind. During the match, one of the football players goes to tackle the centre forward. He misses the ball, so he kicks the centre forward in the head in anger, knocking him unconscious. After the match, Carl and Daniel go to the pub, where they become embroiled in a philosophical debate with Frank, a professor of history at the university. Frank throws his drink over Carl, but the glass slips out of his hand and breaks, cutting Daniel. Later that evening, Daniel sends Frank a text message which reads, 'this isn't over'.

    Discuss the criminal liability of the parties.

 For suggested approaches, please visit the Online Resource Centre.

☰ Further reading

Books

Malcolm, T. 'How Far is too Far? The Extent to which Consent is a Defence to Non-Fatal Offences Against the Person: Lord Mustill in *R v Brown* [1994] 1 AC 212' in N. Geach and

C. Monaghan (eds) *Dissenting Judgments in the Law* (2012), London: Wildy, Simmonds and Hill, pp. 317–41

Journal articles

Anderson, J. 'No Licence for Thuggery: Violence, Sport and the Criminal Law' [2008] Crim LR 751

Cooper, S. and James, M. 'Entertainment—The Painful Process of Rethinking Consent' [2012] Crim LR 188

Elliott, C. and de Than, C. 'The Case for a Rational Reconstruction of Consent in Criminal Law' (2007) 70 MLR 225

Gardner, J. 'Rationality and the Rule of Law in Offences Against the Person' (1994) 53 CLJ 502

Jefferson, M. 'Offences Against the Person: Into the 21st Century' (2012) 76 JCL 472

Mawhinney, G. 'To be Ill or to Kill: The Criminality of Contagion' (2013) 77 JCL 202

Murphy, P. 'Flogging Live Complainants and Dead Horses: We May No Longer Need to be in Bondage to *Brown*' [2011] Crim LR 758

Padfield, N. 'Reform of Offences Against the Person' [2015] Crim LR 175

Reed, A. 'Offences Against the Person: The Need for Reform' (1995) 59 JCL 187

Ryan, S. 'Reckless Transmission of HIV: Knowledge and Culpability' [2006] Crim LR 981

Withey, C 'Biological GBH: Overruling *Clarence*?' (2003) 153 NLJ 1698

Other sources

CPS Charging Standards, *Offences Against the Person*, http://www.cps.gov.uk/legal/l_to_o/offences_against_the_person/#P48_1458

Law Commission Report, *Reform of Offences Against the Person* (Law Com. No. 361, 2015)

8 Sexual offences

☐ **LEARNING OBJECTIVES**

By the end of this chapter, you should be able to:

● identify and explain the elements of the main sexual offences;

● apply the law relating to these offences to a problem scenario;

● understand the law relating to and the application of the defence of consent in sexual offences; and

● explain the elements of the main sexual offences against children.

Introduction

The law relating to sexual offences can be complicated, especially where the issue of consent arises. Consider whether a complainant who gives in to pressure to have sexual intercourse consents? Will the answer to this depend upon the nature of the pressure involved? At what stage does a complainant who is intoxicated lose the capacity to consent to sexual intercourse? While the Sexual Offences Act 2003 does provide some guidance on consent, this is a difficult concept to define. This chapter considers the main sexual offences under the 2003 Act and the meaning of consent.

In 1999, the law on sexual offences underwent a comprehensive review, resulting in significant reforms brought in by the Sexual Offences Act 2003. Prior to the 2003 Act, the law relating to sexual offences was located in a variety of statutes, principally the Sexual Offences Act 1956. The 1956 Act was largely a consolidating statute and many of its provisions dated back as far as the nineteenth century. The Act was described in the White Paper of 2002 as 'archaic, incoherent and discriminatory' and was criticised for its failure to 'reflect the changes in society and social attitudes' and for being 'inadequate and out of date'. In July 2000, the Home Office published the results of its review of the law on sexual offences in its paper, *Setting the Boundaries: Reforming the Law on Sex Offences*. The review contained 62 recommendations, most of which were incorporated in the White Paper of 2002 entitled, *Protecting the Public: Strengthening Protection Against Sex Offenders and Reforming the Law on Sexual Offences*.

The Sexual Offences Act 2003, which came into force on 1 May 2004, is now the main piece of legislation on sexual offences. The Act repeals most of the previous law on rape, whilst also placing much of the prior case law on a statutory footing. The aims of the 2003 Act were to modernise the law and make it more coherent. It created a number of offences, such as assault by penetration, sexual assault, and causing a person to engage in sexual activity. It redefined the law on rape and introduced for the first time a definition of consent. The 2003 Act also created four sexual offences against children under the age of 13: rape of a child under 13 (s.5); assault of a child under 13 by penetration (s.6); sexual assault of a child under 13 (s.7); and causing or inciting a child under 13 to engage in sexual activity (s.8). Finally, the Act includes various child sex offences under ss.9–15 which apply to sexual acts committed against complainants under the age of 16. The offences which are committed against children under the age of 13 are the most serious offences, and these are severely punished accordingly.

The first part of this chapter will explore the four main sexual offences committed against adults, namely rape, assault by penetration, sexual assault, and intentionally causing a person to engage in sexual activity. The defence of consent in sexual offences will be considered in 8.2, immediately after the offence of rape. The second part of this chapter will cover sexual offences committed against children.

8.1 Rape

Rape is a serious sexual offence. It is indictable only and carries a discretionary maximum sentence of life imprisonment. The offence of rape is now provided for by s.1(1) of the Sexual Offences Act 2003 (SOA 2003). This section replaces the old rape provision under s.1(1) of the Sexual Offences Act 1956 which simply stated, '[i]t is an offence for a man to rape a woman [or another man]'. The 2003 Act is gender-neutral, in its use of 'A' and 'B' rather than the words 'man' and 'woman', and it is far more specific, actually explicitly setting out precisely the elements of rape. The offence of rape under s.(1) of the SOA 2003 can only be committed by a man as a principal, although a woman can be an accessory to rape.

 STATUTE

Section 1(1), Sexual Offences Act 2003

A person (A) commits an offence if—

   (a) he intentionally penetrates the vagina, anus or mouth of another person (B) with his penis,

   (b) B does not consent to the penetration, and

   (c) A does not reasonably believe that B consents.

There are two *actus reus* elements of rape and two *mens rea* elements. In order to secure a conviction for rape, the prosecution must prove all the elements of rape. It is important to note at this stage that consent is relevant to both the *actus reus* and the *mens rea* of rape: the *actus reus* of rape requires the penetration to be non-consensual and the *mens rea* requires that the defendant does not reasonably believe that the complainant consents (table 8.1).

Table 8.1 Elements of rape

Actus reus	Mens rea
• Penetration of the vagina, anus, or mouth of B with A's penis • Absence of consent	• Intention to penetrate • No reasonable belief in consent

8.1.1 *Actus reus*

The *actus reus* of rape requires the non-consensual penetration of the vagina, anus, or mouth of another person with the penis of the defendant.

8.1.1.1 Penetration

Penetration is defined under s.79(2) of the SOA 2003 as 'a continuing act from entry to withdrawal'.

> **THINKING POINT**
>
> Consider the following scenario: D has consensual sexual intercourse with C, however, at some stage after penetration, C changes her mind and communicates this to D, also telling him to withdraw. Can D be convicted of rape if he omits to withdraw?

Section 79(2) of the SOA 2003 places the decisions of *Cooper v Schaub* [1994] Crim LR 531 and the Privy Council decision in *Kaitamaki* [1985] AC 147 on a statutory footing.

> **CASE CLOSE-UP**
>
> **_Kaitamaki_ [1985] AC 147**
>
> The defendant in *Kaitamaki* appealed against his conviction of rape in New Zealand. It was alleged that he had broken into the complainant's house and raped her twice. In his defence, he argued that she had been consenting or that he honestly believed that she had been consenting (an honest belief in consent would have been sufficient as a defence in 1985). During the second occasion of sexual intercourse, the defendant stated that he realised that the complainant was not consenting after he penetrated her, but he did not withdraw. The Privy Council held that penetration is a continuing act, so if he continued with the act of intercourse knowing that she was not consenting, he was guilty of rape.

The slightest degree of penetration is sufficient for rape. This is evident from the definition of vagina in s.79(9) of the SOA 2003 as including 'vulva'—full penetration is not a requirement of rape. Additionally, s.44 of the Sexual Offences Act 1956 remains good law. This provides that the emission of seed is not required, the prosecution only need prove that penetration occurred.

❯ CROSS REFERENCE

Remind yourself of the case of *Fagan v MPC* (1969) in 2.4.4. The 'continuing act' theory was adopted here in relation to the offence of assault in order to avoid the issue of whether an assault could be committed by omission.

8.1.1.2 '... of the vagina, anus or mouth'

Under s.1(1)(a) of the SOA 2003, penetration must be of the vagina, anus, or mouth of the complainant. It is clear that a woman may be a victim of vaginal, anal, or oral rape, and a man may be a victim of anal or oral rape. As the SOA 2003 is gender-neutral and as s.79(3) states that references to parts of the body include references to surgically constructed parts of the body, a male to female transsexual who has undergone gender reassignment surgery and has a surgically constructed vagina may be the victim of vaginal rape.

By including penile penetration of the mouth as rape, the SOA 2003 has widened the scope of the *actus reus* of the offence. Prior to the SOA 2003, where a man forced a person to perform non-consensual oral sex on him, this amounted only to indecent assault and not to rape.

> **THINKING POINT**
>
> Do you think that the inclusion of non-consensual oral sex under the definition of rape is an improvement to the old law or not?

8.1.1.3 Penile penetration

The offence of rape may only be committed where the penetration occurs with the penis of the defendant: s.1(1)(a) of the SOA 2003. Non-consensual penetration with an object or any other part of the body will not amount to rape, but may fall under the offence of assault by penetration, contrary to s.2 of the SOA 2003.

As the offence of rape requires penetration with the penis, it is quite obvious that a man may be guilty of rape (provided all the other elements of the offence are established).

> **THINKING POINT**
>
> Can a woman ever be convicted of rape?
>
> Consider whether a female to male transsexual who has undergone gender reassignment surgery can be convicted of rape.

In a significant departure from previous legislation relating to sexual offences, the SOA 2003 was drafted in gender-neutral terms. Nevertheless, a woman cannot be convicted of rape as a principal offender because the offence requires penile penetration. However, a woman who acts as an accomplice to a rapist may be guilty of the offence of causing a person to engage in sexual activity without consent, contrary to s.4 of the SOA 2003. Alternatively, she might be convicted of rape as an accessory if she aids, abets, counsels, or procures the rape as in the case of *DPP v K and B* [1997] 1 Cr App R 36. The defendants in this case were two girls who bullied the victim, a 14-year-old girl, into having sexual intercourse with a boy. The Divisional Court held that the defendants could be convicted of rape as accessories as they procured the offence.

> ❯ CROSS REFERENCE
> See chapter 16 on accessorial liability.

Section 79(3) of the Act states that references to parts of the body include references to surgically constructed parts of the body. Thus, a transsexual who has undergone gender reassignment surgery from female to male and has a surgically constructed penis may be guilty of rape.

8.1.1.4 Absence of consent

▶ CROSS REFERENCE

Read 8.2 for a detailed discussion on consent.

Under s.1(1)(b) of the SOA 2003, the offence of rape requires proof that the complainant did not consent to the penetration. As stated at 8.1, the absence of consent is part of the *actus reus* of rape. Consent will be discussed in detail at 8.2 as it is also an element of the other sexual offences.

8.1.1.5 Marital rape

Where a husband has non-consensual sexual intercourse with his wife, he may be guilty of rape. Surprisingly, it was not until 1991 that the House of Lords finally held in *R v R* [1991] 3 WLR 767 that rape within marriage was an offence. Before this ruling, the offence of rape applied to 'unlawful' sexual intercourse, which was intercourse which took place outside of marriage. This decision was put onto a statutory footing by s.142 of the Criminal Justice and Public Order Act 1994 which first removed the word 'unlawful' from the offence of rape. The 2003 Act maintains this position.

8.1.2 *Mens rea*

The *mens rea* of rape comprises of two elements: an intention to penetrate the vagina, anus, or mouth of a person and no reasonable belief in consent.

8.1.2.1 Intentional penetration

The penetration of the vagina, anus, or mouth of the complainant by the defendant's penis must be intentional. This is a subjective element. It is unlikely to be a common issue of contention in rape cases, unless perhaps a defendant is intoxicated to the extent that he did not form such an intention.

 THINKING POINT

Consider the following scenario:

D has consensual vaginal intercourse with his girlfriend, C. They have always agreed not to have anal intercourse. At one stage, D, intending to penetrate C's vagina, accidentally penetrates her anus. Is D guilty of rape?

The *mens rea* of rape requires an intention to penetrate a particular orifice. Where the defendant accidentally penetrates an orifice, he cannot be convicted of rape in relation to that orifice.

8.1.2.2 No reasonable belief in consent

Under s.1(1)(c) of the SOA 2003, the offence of rape requires proof that the defendant did not reasonably believe that the complainant was consenting. A defendant will have the *mens rea* of rape if he intended there to be or knew that there was no consent to the penetration. He will also satisfy the *mens rea* for rape if he recognised a risk that the complainant might not be consenting but went ahead with the act anyway (i.e., he was subjectively reckless); or, if he did not care whether or not the complainant was consenting; or, if he held an unreasonable belief that the complainant was consenting. A defendant who has sex with the complainant intending that the complainant should not be consenting has the *mens rea* of rape, irrespective of whether or not the complainant is actually consenting. However, he will not be guilty of rape if the complainant is actually consenting at the time of intercourse because the *actus reus* of rape will not be present. The approach under the SOA 2003 is a significant departure from the law prior to the Act which was to be found in the House of Lords' decision of *DPP v Morgan* [1976] AC 182.

CASE CLOSE-UP

DPP v Morgan [1976] AC 182

In this case, Mr Morgan, a senior officer in the RAF, invited three junior officers back to his house to have sex with his wife. He told them that she was 'kinky' and that if she put up any resistance they should ignore it as it would be mere pretence on her part. The junior officers did not believe him at first, but they were persuaded otherwise when Morgan provided them with condoms. All four men then had sexual intercourse with Mrs Morgan, despite her screams and protestations. The three junior officers were convicted of rape and aiding and abetting rape, while Mr Morgan was convicted of aiding and abetting rape. Mr Morgan was not charged with rape, as marital rape was not held to be an offence until 1991. The three junior officers argued that they honestly believed that Mrs Morgan was consenting to the intercourse.

The House of Lords held that an honest but mistaken belief in consent is sufficient as defence to a charge of rape. The belief only had to be honestly held and it did not need to be a reasonable one. Consequently, if the junior officers had honestly believed that Mrs Morgan was consenting, they should have been acquitted. The reasonableness of their belief was only relevant to their credibility. However, the House upheld the convictions of the defendants on the basis that a properly directed jury would, nevertheless, have convicted the defendants. Their story was so unbelievable, that the House took the view that a jury would not have considered the defendants' beliefs to be honestly held. The prosecution had not proved that the defendants had honestly believed Mrs Morgan to be consenting.

The test under *DPP v Morgan* was purely a subjective one which was severely criticised by some academics. By contrast, the test under the SOA 2003, that the defendant's belief must be reasonable contains both subjective and objective elements.

SUMMARY

The defendant will have a defence if he reasonably believes that the complainant is consenting. This is a question for the jury which involves the assessment of two questions:

(1) Did D honestly believe that C was consenting?

(2) If the answer to (1) is yes, was his belief a reasonable one?

By including an element of reasonableness, the *mens rea* of rape is partly objectively assessed. Criminal law traditionally requires a subjective assessment of *mens rea*. Evidence of the trend towards subjectivity in recent years can be found in the House of Lords' opinion in the case of *R v G* [2003] UKHL 50 (see chapter 3 on *mens rea*).

Section 1(2) of the SOA 2003 provides guidance in relation to the question of whether or not a belief was reasonable.

STATUTE

Section 1(2), Sexual Offences Act 2003

Whether a belief is reasonable is to be determined having regard to all the circumstances, including any steps A has taken to ascertain whether B consents.

Thus, any steps that the defendant has taken (or has not taken, as the case may be) will be considered by the jury in deciding whether or not his belief was a reasonable one although this section does not impose a duty on the defendant to expressly ascertain whether or not the complainant was consenting.

In *B* [2013] 1 Cr App R 36, the Court of Appeal held that where the defendant held delusional beliefs that the complainant was consenting, such beliefs were by definition irrational, and thus, were unreasonable. In this case, the defendant suffered from a mental disorder which was thought to be paranoid schizophrenia, but expert evidence showed that the defendant had the ability to understand whether the complainant was consenting or not. The Court held that where the defendant's beliefs in consent arose from a mental or personality disorder (other than insanity in law), that belief still had to be judged by the objective standard of reasonableness.

The prosecution may alternatively rely on the conclusive or evidential presumptions under s.76 and s.75, respectively, in proving this *mens rea* element of rape. These sections are discussed at 8.2.

SUMMARY

Law pre-Sexual Offences Act 2003: *DPP v Morgan* (1976)—an *honest* belief in consent is a defence to rape.

Law post-Sexual Offences Act 2003: s.1(1)(c), Sexual Offences Act 2003—a *reasonable* belief in consent is a defence to rape.

8.1.3 Reform

Despite the reforms to the law on rape, in 2008 the Rape (Defences) Bill sought to amend the SOA 2003 to prohibit the use of sleepwalking as a defence to rape. This Private Member's Bill proposed the insertion of a new s.1(3A) into the SOA 2003. If it were ever enacted, s.1(3A) would read:

STATUTE

Section 1(3A), Rape (Defences) Bill 2008

It shall not be a defence for a defendant accused of an offence under this section to claim he was—

(a) sleepwalking, or

(b) suffering from non-insane automatism or other similar condition when the offence was alleged to have taken place.

The Rape (Defences) Bill was proposed in order to deal with a supposed 'loophole' in the law which allows a defendant to escape liability for rape through a plea that he was sleepwalking or suffering from non-insane automatism at the time of the offence. Harry Cohen MP proposed the Bill after hearing about a case in Australia in which a defendant, Leonard Spencer, was acquitted of rape after pleading that he was sleepwalking during the act of intercourse. Concerned that this precedent might be abused by defendants, Mr Cohen proposed the Rape (Defences) Bill and commented that, '[s]leepwalking is not a reasonable excuse for rape that should lead to acquittal' (House of Commons Hansard Debates, 15 October 2008, at col. 800). The Bill did not progress beyond its first reading in the House of Commons on 15 October 2008 and it thus seems unlikely to ever be enacted.

8.2 Consent

Consent is a controversial and complicated area of law. The provisions which will be discussed here apply not just to the offence of rape, but also to the other sexual offences explored in this chapter. It has been mentioned at 8.1 that consent is relevant to both the *actus reus* and the *mens rea* of rape (and, indeed, to those elements of other sexual offences): the prosecution must prove that the complainant did not, in fact, consent (the *actus reus* element); and that the defendant did not reasonably believe that the complainant was consenting (the *mens rea* element) (figure 8.1).

Figure 8.1 Consent in rape

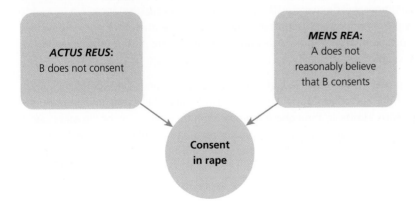

There is clearly no consent when a complainant expressly communicates his/her unwilling-ness or refusal to have sexual intercourse. The situation is less clear where there is no such express refusal or where the complainant submits to sexual intercourse.

THINKING POINT

Consider whether consent has been given in the following scenarios:

(1) A agrees to sexual intercourse because D threatens him with violence if he does not agree.

(2) D has sexual intercourse with B while B is asleep.

(3) D has sexual intercourse with C while C is extremely intoxicated.

(4) E submits to sexual intercourse with D because he threatens to break off their engagement if she refuses to have sex with him.

(5) F is completely indifferent to whether or not D has sexual intercourse with him.

There will also be no consent where the complainant does not have the capacity to consent, for example due to his/her age or mental condition. Neither will consent be present where the complainant does not have the freedom to choose to consent, for example due to being detained or threatened with violence. The SOA 2003 introduced a definition of consent into the law on sexual offences. The definition is contained in s.74 of the Act and is the first definition of consent to be introduced in this area either by case law or by statute. Under s.74, 'a person consents if he or she agrees by choice and has the freedom and capacity to make that choice'. Section 75 sets out two evidential presumptions:

(i) that the complainant was not consenting, and

(ii) that the defendant had no reasonable belief in consent.

These presumptions will be made by the jury where certain circumstances are proved and the defendant knew of the existence of such circumstances. These presumptions are rebuttable by evidence to the contrary (therefore, they are termed 'evidential presump-tions'). If the defendant does not raise evidence to rebut the presumptions under s.75(1), he will be convicted of rape. Section 76 sets out two conclusive presumptions: (i) that the complainant was not consenting; and (ii) that the defendant had no belief in consent. These presumptions will be made by the jury where certain circumstances are proved to exist. These presumptions are irrebuttable by any evidence (therefore, they are termed 'conclusive presumptions') and a conviction will result where all the other elements of rape are satisfied.

When these provisions were enacted, questions were raised about their compatibility with Article 6.2 of the European Convention on Human Rights which sets out the presump-tion of innocence. However, throughout a prosecution for rape or any of the other sexual offences in this chapter, the legal burden remains on the prosecution to prove the guilt of the defendant beyond reasonable doubt. The defendant bears only an evidential burden in relation to consent, which is not a burden to prove anything (and thus not a burden of proof). An evidential burden is merely a burden to adduce some evidence to raise an issue (or to make an issue a 'live' one). Consequently, where the evidential presumptions under s.75(1) are triggered, the defendant only has an evidential burden to adduce some evidence to counter the presumptions. The burden of proof remains with the prosecution to prove beyond reasonable doubt that there was no consent and that the defendant did not reasonably believe that the complainant was consenting. For example, if the prosecution case was that the defendant used violence against the complainant immediately before or during sexual intercourse, the defendant would bear an evidential burden to raise some evidence to rebut the presumption that the complainant was not consenting. In rebuttal of the allegation, the defendant might claim that he and the complainant consensually participated in sado-masochistic sex. By making this a live issue, the defendant will have discharged his evidential burden. The defendant would not have to prove his claim as the legal burden of proof remains on the prosecution to disprove this beyond reasonable doubt. The Court of Appeal rejected an argument that s.75 reverses the burden of proof in *Ciccarelli* [2011] EWCA Crim 2665 and held that s.75 is an evidential provision. Lord Judge CJ stated: 'It was suggested that section 75 of the 2003 Act reverses the ordinary principles relating to the burden of proof in criminal cases. We do not agree. Section 75 is an evidential provision. It relates to matters of evidence, and in particular evidential presumptions about consent in circumstances where, as we have already indicated, as a matter of reality and common sense, the strong likelihood is that the complainant will not, in fact, be consenting. If, however, in those circumstances there is sufficient evidence for the jury to consider, then the burden of disproving them remains on the prosecution. Therefore, before the question of the appellant's reasonable belief in the complainant's consent could be left to the jury, some evidence beyond the fanciful or speculative had to be adduced to support the reasonableness of his belief in her consent' (at [18]).

Despite the definition under s.74, the issue of consent is much more easily approached by starting with the conclusive presumptions under s.76. If s.76 does not apply, the evidential presumptions under s.75 should be considered. If s.75 does not apply, then the definition of consent under s.74 may be considered. The next section of this chapter will explore these provisions in this order (figure 8.2).

Figure 8.2 Flowchart on ss.75 and 76

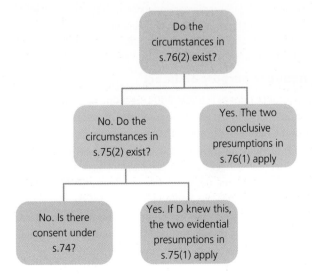

Figure 8.3 Conclusive presumptions under s.76

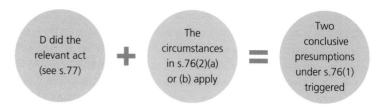

8.2.1 Conclusive presumptions about consent

Where the prosecution prove that the defendant did the relevant act (defined under s.77 as the penetration, touching, or causing a person to engage in sexual activity, depending upon which offence is charged), and one of the circumstances in s.76(2) applies, then the two con-clusive presumptions set out in s.76(1) will be triggered. It will be conclusively presumed that the complainant did not consent and that the defendant did not believe that the complainant was consenting. In such circumstances, the defendant will be guilty of the offence in question and no evidence may be called in rebuttal (figure 8.3).

As the effect of the conclusive presumptions under s.76(1) is so severe, the circumstances which trigger the presumptions are themselves serious and both involve the defendant intentionally deceiving the complainant, either as to the nature and purpose of the act or by impersonating a person known personally to the complainant. Note that the conclusive presumptions will only be triggered in these two situations and no other: *Jheeta* [2007] EWCA Crim 1699.

 STATUTE

Section 76(2), Sexual Offences Act 2003

The circumstances are that—

(a) the defendant intentionally deceived the complainant as to the nature or purpose of the relevant act;

(b) the defendant intentionally induced the complainant to consent to the relevant act by impersonating a person known personally to the complainant.

8.2.1.1 Deception as to the nature or purpose of the act

Section 76 adopts the case law in existence prior to the SOA 2003. Section 76(2)(a) deals with situations where the defendant has intentionally deceived the complainant into having sexual intercourse with him by lying about the nature or purpose of the penetration. The defendant in *Flattery* (1877) 2 QBD 410 had sexual intercourse with a young girl, telling her that he was performing a surgical procedure on her. It was held that the complainant's consent was not valid as the defendant had deceived her as to the nature of the act. Similarly, the defend-ant in *Williams* [1923] 1 KB 340 was a vocal coach. He had sexual intercourse with a young student, persuading her that intercourse would improve her breathing and hence her voice. It was held that the complainant's consent was invalid as it had been obtained by fraud as to the nature of the act. If similar cases were to come before the courts today, they would fall under s.76(2)(a) and the conclusive presumptions under s.76(1) would apply. The case of

Tabassum (2000) was discussed at 7.7.3. In this case, although the complainants did consent to the nature of the act (the touching of their breasts), they did not consent to its quality (as indecent behaviour) as they had been deceived into thinking that the touching was for the purposes of medical research. The word 'quality' as used by the Court of Appeal in *Tabassum* has been superseded by the word 'purpose' in the SOA 2003. Nevertheless, the effect in a case such as *Tabassum* would be the same. In *B* [2013] 2 Cr App R 29, the Court of Appeal considered the scope of the word 'purpose' and held that it should not be construed too widely. In this case, the defendant was charged with causing sexual activity without consent contrary to s.4 of the Sexual Offences Act 2003 after he used two different false identities and made his girlfriend perform sexual acts over the Internet. The Court held that s.76(2)(a) did not apply here because the complainant had not been deceived as to the purpose of the acts, and his deception as to his identity was not sufficient. The Court was concerned to ensure that the word 'purpose' was not construed too widely so that s.76 would cover situations never contemplated by Parliament. Following *Jheeta* [2007] EWCA Crim 1699, the Court stated that where a statutory provision removes the defendant's only line of defence to a serious criminal charge, the provision must be strictly applied.

8.2.1.2 Impersonating a person known personally to the complainant

Section 76(2)(b) deals with situations where the defendant has intentionally induced the complainant to consent to the relevant act by impersonating a person known personally to the complainant. This means that intentionally inducing the complainant to consent to sexual intercourse by pretending to be a famous Hollywood star or footballer would not trigger the conclusive presumptions under s.76(1), although pretending to be someone the complainant knows, such as his/her boyfriend or husband would. This section places the case of *Elbekkay* [1995] Crim LR 163 onto a statutory footing.

 CASE CLOSE-UP

Elbekkay [1995] Crim LR 163

In this case, the complainant went out drinking with her boyfriend and his friend, the defendant. The complainant went upstairs to bed, leaving the defendant downstairs with her boyfriend. At some point during the night, the defendant climbed into bed with the complainant and proceeded to have sexual intercourse with her. The complainant assumed that her boyfriend had come upstairs and climbed into bed with her. Consequently, she willingly participated in the sexual intercourse in a half-asleep state. The defendant continued to have sexual intercourse with the complainant, despite realising that she had assumed he was her boyfriend. The complainant's consent in this case was not deemed to be valid.

8.2.2 Evidential presumptions about consent

Where the prosecution prove that the defendant did the relevant act (defined under s.77 as the penetration, touching, or causing a person to engage in sexual activity, depending upon which offence is charged), and one of the circumstances in s.75(2) applies, and the defendant knew that those circumstances existed, then the two evidential presumptions set out in s.75(1) will be triggered. It will be presumed that the complainant did not consent and that the defendant

Figure 8.4 Evidential presumptions under s.75

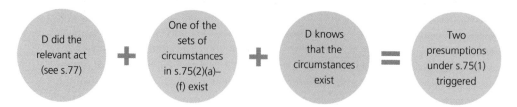

did not reasonably believe that the complainant was consenting. In such circumstances, the defendant will be guilty of the offence in question unless he calls evidence in rebuttal such that the prosecution cannot prove these elements beyond reasonable doubt (figure 8.4).

There are six circumstances which may trigger the evidential presumptions under s.75(1). These are less serious than those under s.76(2) and it must be proved that the defendant knew of the existence of the circumstances under s.75(1) (this requirement is not necessary in relation to s.76(1) as the deception practised under that section must be intentional).

> 📖 **STATUTE**
>
> **Section 75(2), Sexual Offences Act 2003**
>
> The circumstances are that—
>
> (a) any person was, at the time of the relevant act or immediately before it began, using violence against the complainant or causing the complainant to fear that immediate violence would be used against him;
>
> (b) any person was, at the time of the relevant act or immediately before it began, causing the complainant to fear that violence was being used, or that immediate violence would be used, against another person;
>
> (c) the complainant was, and the defendant was not, unlawfully detained at the time of the relevant act;
>
> (d) the complainant was asleep or otherwise unconscious at the time of the relevant act;
>
> (e) because of the complainant's physical disability, the complainant would not have been able at the time of the relevant act to communicate to the defendant whether the complainant consented;
>
> (f) any person had administered to or caused to be taken by the complainant, without the complainant's consent, a substance which, having regard to when it was administered or taken, was capable of causing or enabling the complainant to be stupefied or overpowered at the time of the relevant act.

8.2.2.1 Violence or fear of violence

Section 75(2)(a) and (b) deals with situations where the complainant was, at the time of the relevant act or immediately prior to it, being subjected to violence or feared the immediate use of violence, or where the complainant feared that such violence was being used or would be used against a third person. The violence or threat of violence need not come from the defendant but may emanate from 'any person', for example where the defendant's friend threatened or used violence against the complainant before or during sexual intercourse between the defendant and complainant. Under s.75(2)(a), where the complainant is threatened with violence or actually subjected to violence immediately before or at the time of penetration, the evidential presumptions under s.75(1) will be triggered. Equally, under s.75(2)(b), if violence is threatened or used against the complainant's child, partner, another family member, or even a stranger, prior to or at the time of penetration, the presumptions will also be triggered.

 THINKING POINT

Consider whether the presumptions under s.75(1) are triggered in the following scenarios:

(1) A holds a knife to B's throat and demands sex.

(2) A threatens to harm B unless B has sex with C.

(3) A threatens to kill B's child if B does not have sex with C.

(4) A punches B in the head during sexual intercourse.

The presumption is likely to be much more difficult to rebut where the violence is used or threatened against the complainant's child than an adult man. 'Violence' is not defined in the SOA 2003 but this word implies that some harm must be inflicted or feared greater than the simple use of force. Section 75(2)(a) and (b) is justified by the argument that a complainant does not have the freedom to agree by choice where the complainant is subjected to violence or the fear of violence. A complainant in such a position is likely to consent because of the violence or fear of violence. However, such circumstances only trigger an evidential presumption as it might be possible that a complainant might be consenting (agreeing by choice) to the relevant act, for example where that person consensually participates in sado-masochistic sex.

8.2.2.2 Unlawful detention

Section 75(2)(c) covers situations where the complainant was unlawfully detained at the time of the relevant act. Where the defendant falsely imprisons the complainant and then performs a sexual act against the complainant, the evidential presumptions under s.75(1) will be triggered, that the complainant did not consent and the defendant did not reasonably believe that the complainant was consenting. The defendant must not have been unlawfully detained at the time of the act. This would cover situations where a defendant who is also unlawfully detained is forced to perform a sexual act against the complainant who is unlawfully detained. In such a situation, no presumptions are made against the defendant. Once again, the justification behind this paragraph is that unlawful detention might remove the complainant's freedom to agree by choice to participate in the relevant act. However, the resulting presumptions are only evidential and may be rebutted. This allows for situations where the complainant has formed a close relationship with his/her kidnapper.

8.2.2.3 Asleep or unconscious

Section 75(2)(d) deals with the situation where the complainant is asleep or otherwise unconscious at the time of the relevant act. A person who is asleep or unconscious cannot agree by choice to participate in the relevant act. This paragraph would cover a complainant who has fallen asleep or become unconscious due to intoxication, whether through drink or drugs.

Thus, it would cover a complainant who has been rendered unconscious by the consumption of a 'date rape' drug. This paragraph reflects the law prior to the SOA 2003. In the case of *Larter and Castleton* [1995] Crim LR 75, the defendant had sexual intercourse with a 14-year-old girl who was asleep. The Court of Appeal held that force was not a requirement of the offence of rape, and that a person who was asleep would be unable to consent to sexual intercourse. Thus, the *actus reus* of rape would be present. A sleeping or unconscious complainant will only trigger evidential presumptions of an absence of consent and no reasonable belief in consent. Consequently, a defendant who does not realise that the complainant was asleep or unconscious may call evidence in rebuttal, or such evidence may be called where the complainant consented in advance to the relevant act taking place while the complainant was asleep.

8.2.2.4 Inability to communicate due to physical disability

Section 75(2)(e) covers situations where the complainant suffers a physical disability which meant that the complainant would not have been able to communicate consent, or lack thereof, to the defendant at the time of the relevant act. This is justified by the complainant's inability to communicate whether or not the complainant is consenting. It is open to the defendant to rebut the presumptions under s.75(1).

8.2.2.5 Substance capable of stupefying or overpowering complainant

Section 75(2)(f) deals with situations where a person administered to or caused to be taken by the complainant a substance capable of causing or enabling the complainant to be stupefied or overpowered at the time of the relevant act. The defendant does not have to be the person administering or causing the substance to be administered. This might be done by 'any person'. This paragraph does not actually require the complainant to be stupefied or overpowered by the substance, but the substance must be 'capable' of stupefying or overpowering the complainant. The substance must be administered or taken without the complainant's consent. Although this provision clearly covers situations where the complainant's drink is spiked by a 'date rape' drug, it is not limited to drugs. The substance in question might commonly be alcohol.

 THINKING POINT

Consider whether s.75(2)(f) will apply where D plies C with alcohol which renders C more likely to willingly participate in sexual intercourse when she would normally have refused.

Imagine that D has sexual intercourse with C who is so drunk that she is unable to speak or walk properly. C is too intoxicated to physically resist or communicate consent. Do the evidential presumptions under s.75(1) apply here?

The defendant in *Malone* [1998] 2 Cr App R 447 had sexual intercourse with a 16-year-old girl who was so drunk that she was unable to walk and was drifting in and out of consciousness. He was convicted of rape and appealed on the grounds that there was no evidence that she was not consenting because she did not refuse to sleep with him or communicate her lack of consent, neither did the defendant use force. The Court of Appeal held that it was not necessary for the complainant to demonstrate or expressly communicate her lack of consent, neither was it a requirement of rape that the complainant put up a fight, nor that she physically resist the intercourse. The Court stated that the existence or absence of consent was a matter of common sense. Where the complainant has consented to the consumption of alcohol, s.75(2)(f) would not apply. If the complainant was completely unconscious,

Figure 8.5 Consent under s.74

s.75(2)(d) would clearly apply. However, it is less clear whether s.75(2)(d) would apply where the complainant was drifting in and out of consciousness. Consequently, the jury would have to consider the definition of consent under s.74.

8.2.3 Definition of consent

As stated at 8.2, the SOA 2003 introduced for the first time, a definition of consent (figure 8.5). This provision will be relied upon by the prosecution where the conclusive and evidential presumptions under ss.76 and 75 respectively do not apply. In such cases, the question of whether the complainant consented to the sexual activity or touching will be considered on a case-by-case basis. Section 74 focuses on whether the complainant made a positive choice to consent, but a complainant's consent will only be valid if the complainant had the freedom and capacity to make that choice to consent to the sexual activity or touching. Section 74 reads:

 STATUTE

Section 74, Sexual Offences Act 2003

For the purposes of this Part, a person consents if he agrees by choice, and has the freedom and capacity to make that choice.

Where the complainant's capacity to consent is an issue in the case (such as in the recent cases involving intoxicated complainants), the jury should be directed to consider first, whether the complainant was capable of making a choice whether to have sexual intercourse or not, and only if she was capable should they go on to consider whether the complainant was consenting to sexual intercourse (see *Kamki* [2013] EWCA Crim 2335).

8.2.3.1 Agreeing by choice

The first part of the definition requires the complainant to agree by choice to participate in the relevant act. If the complainant agrees by choice to have sexual intercourse with the defendant, no offence of rape is committed. If the complainant does not agree by choice to have intercourse with the defendant, the *actus reus* of rape is satisfied. This definition of consent requires positive agreement by the complainant. The prosecution need to prove that the complainant did not actively agree to the act of intercourse. The prosecution do not need to prove that the complainant resisted intercourse or that the defendant used force: see *Larter and Castleton* (1995). In the case of *Malone* (1998), mentioned at 8.2.2.5, it was clear that the complainant did not actively agree to the act of intercourse where she was so drunk that she could not walk and was drifting in and out of consciousness. The issue of consent and intoxicated complainants is considered at 8.2.3.2 under the heading 'freedom and capacity to choose', as intoxication could affect the complainant's capacity to consent to sexual activity or touching.

In *Linekar* [1995] 2 WLR 237, the complainant was a prostitute who agreed to have sexual intercourse with the defendant on the basis that he promised to pay her £25. The defendant never actually intended to pay and, in fact, did not pay after intercourse. The Court of Appeal held that although consent was obtained by misrepresentation, there was no rape as she had, nonetheless, consented to have sexual intercourse with the defendant. There had been no fraud as to the nature of the act or the identity of the defendant, so if such a scenario was to arise today, the presumptions under ss.75(1) and 76(1) would not apply. However, could it be said that the complainant had consented in accordance with the definition under s.74? Has she agreed by choice to the intercourse?

> **CROSS REFERENCE**
>
> Refer back to the cases of *Dica* (2004) and *Konzani* (2005) in paragraph 7.4.1.2.

In the case of *B* [2006] EWCA Crim 2945, the defendant was not guilty of rape where he failed to disclose that he was HIV positive before having consensual sexual intercourse with the complainant. The conclusive presumptions under s.76(1) would not apply in this case because there was no deception as to the nature of the act as an act of sexual intercourse. The act of sexual intercourse was consensual, although the complainant had not consented to the quality of the act, i.e., the risk of contracting HIV. There was no question of any deception being practised in this case since the defendant had not actively misled the complainant as regards his HIV status. A defendant in such a case is not a rapist, but may be convicted of maliciously inflicting GBH contrary to s.20 of the OAPA 1861. Where the defendant deceives the complainant in relation to the nature or purpose of the act, he will be guilty of rape (the conclusive presumptions under s.76(1) will be triggered). However, if the deception is to some other aspect of the sexual activity, s.76(1) will not apply, so the prosecution will need to prove that the complainant did not freely agree to the intercourse, in accordance with the definition of consent under s.74.

In *Assange v Swedish Prosecution Authority* [2011] EWHC 2849 (Admin), the Divisional Court emphasised the importance of choice in determining whether the complainant consented to sexual intercourse. This was a case involving active deception, in which the complainant only agreed to sexual intercourse with a condom, but the defendant had sexual intercourse with the complainant without a condom. The Court held that in these circumstances the presumptions under s.76(1) would not be triggered because there was no deception as to the nature and purpose of the act. However, the Court observed that the prosecution could rely on s.74 to prove that the complainant had not consented to unprotected sexual intercourse.

This was further confirmed in *R (F) v DPP* [2013] EWHC 945 (Admin), in which the Divisional Court held that 'choice' is crucial to consent and must be approached in a commonsense way. This case involved an application for judicial review of the DPP's decision not to prosecute the claimant's partner (A) for rape after he deliberately ejaculated inside the claimant's vagina despite the claimant stating that she was only consenting to sexual intercourse on the basis that he would not ejaculate in her vagina. The Court had regard here to the history of the sexual relationship between the parties in which A abusively dominated the claimant. There was evidence in this case that A had made up his mind before sexual intercourse took place that he would ejaculate in the claimant's vagina. The Court pointed out that it was not dealing with situations in which sexual intercourse occurs consensually, but the man, intending to withdraw in accordance with his partner's wishes, accidentally ejaculates prematurely. However, the Court held that '[i]f before penetration began [A] had made up his mind that he would penetrate and ejaculate within the claimant's vagina, or even, because "penetration is a continuing act from entry to withdrawal" (see s.79(2) of the 2003 Act) he decided that he would not withdraw at all, just because he deemed the claimant subservient to his control, she was deprived of choice relating to the crucial feature on which her original consent to sexual intercourse was based. Accordingly her consent was negated' (at [26]).

Where an issue arises as to whether deception vitiates consent, there is no requirement that the deception must be relevant to the definition or features of the sexual act. In *McNally* [2013] EWCA Crim 1051, the Court of Appeal held that deception as to gender can vitiate consent. The defendant in this case was a girl who, while pretending to be a boy, conducted an online relationship with the complainant girl. After 3 or 4 years, the complainant and defendant met and sexual activity took place between them, including penetration of the complainant's vagina. The defendant was convicted of several counts of assault by penetration contrary to s.2 of the Sexual Offences Act 2003 and appealed against her convictions on the basis that consent could not be vitiated by deception as to the gender of the defendant. The Court of Appeal dismissed the appeal and held that s.74 of the Sexual Offences Act 2003 should be applied in a broad commonsense way. The Court held that an act of assault by penetration was different when the defendant deliberately deceived the complainant into believing that the defendant was a male. While some deceptions would not vitiate consent, the complainant's consent here had been vitiated because the deliberate deception removed the complainant's freedom to choose whether or not to have a sexual relationship with a girl.

8.2.3.2 Freedom and capacity to choose

This section deals with two issues: namely whether the complainant has the freedom to choose to consent to the relevant act; and whether he/she has the capacity to choose to consent to the act. If the complainant does not have the freedom to make that choice or does not have the capacity to do so, then there will be an absence of consent for the purposes of the offences under the SOA 2003. Freedom and capacity will be dealt with separately in the following paragraphs.

Freedom to choose to consent

The complainant must have the freedom to choose to consent to the intercourse. Clearly, a complainant who agrees to have sexual intercourse with a defendant under threats of violence does not have the freedom to choose to have intercourse (such a case would fall under s.75(2)(a), and if so, the presumptions under s.75(1) might very well apply). However, the position is less clear where the threats do not involve explicit threats of violence. The leading case on submission and consent is the pre-Sexual Offences Act 2003 case of *Olugboja* [1982] QB 320.

 CASE CLOSE-UP

Olugboja [1982] QB 320

In this case, the complainant submitted to sexual intercourse with the defendant through fear. She had been raped by the defendant's friend, who then went to rape her friend. The defendant told the complainant that he was going to have sex with her and told her to remove her trousers. He did not threaten her with violence. The complainant complied through fear and she did not resist the intercourse. The defendant was convicted of rape and his conviction was upheld by the Court of Appeal. The Court held that consent should be given its ordinary commonsense meaning. There was clearly no consent in this case.

> The Court held that consent covers a wide range of states of mind, from actual desire to have sexual intercourse to reluctant acquiescence. The key question is whether or not the complainant genuinely consented to the intercourse. The SOA 2003 is silent on the issue of if or when submission equates to consent.

It is not clear whether less serious threats which induce sexual intercourse will negate consent (see Gardiner (1996) for an interesting discussion on this point).

Where there are no threats of violence, but the complainant 'felt unable to resist' a demand for sexual intercourse, it does not automatically follow that she did not have the freedom to consent to sexual intercourse. The courts have acknowledged that a person might 'submit to a demand which he or she feels unable to resist, but without lacking the capacity or freedom to make a choice. That is an example of reluctant consent' (W [2015] EWCA Crim 559 at [34]). Whether the complainant had the freedom to choose to consent to sexual intercourse is a question of fact for the jury to determine.

Capacity to choose to consent

The complainant must also have the capacity to choose to consent to the intercourse. The complainant might not have the capacity to consent due to the complainant's mental capacity or because the complainant is intoxicated whether by drink or by drugs. While there is no definition of 'capacity' in the Act guidance might be taken from s.30(2) which defines 'unable to refuse' in the context of the offence of sexual activity with a person with a mental disorder impeding choice. Consequently, in deciding whether a person has the capacity to choose to have sexual intercourse, consideration is likely to be given to that person's ability to understand the nature and possible consequences of consenting to the act of intercourse.

Many of the cases in which capacity to consent has become an issue are cases involving a complainant who is intoxicated. It is clear that an intoxicated complainant who is unconscious does not have the capacity to choose to consent to sexual intercourse (such a situation would inevitably fall under s.75(2)(d) and the presumptions under s.75(1) may be applicable). It is also clear that just because a complainant is intoxicated, it does not automatically follow that she lacks the capacity to consent to choose to have sexual intercourse; an intoxicated complainant may very well have such capacity. However, the courts have acknowledged that there are degrees of consciousness and that a person might lose the capacity to consent to sexual intercourse before they lose consciousness completely: 'there are of course . . . various stages of consciousness . . . from being wide awake to having a dim awareness of reality. In a state of dim and drunken awareness, a person may not be in a condition to make choices' (per HHJ Adrian Smith (trial judge) and approved by the Court of Appeal in Kamki [2013] EWCA Crim 2335 at [17]). Thus, an intoxicated complainant who suffers memory lapses but does not completely lose consciousness may or may not have the capacity to choose to consent to sexual intercourse. Whether she does have such capacity or not is a question of fact which should be left to the jury to decide on consideration of all of the evidence: Hysa [2007] EWCA Crim 2056.

The leading case on intoxicated complainants is Bree [2007] EWCA Crim 804. In this case, the defendant was charged with the rape of a student. Both the defendant and the complainant had been out drinking with a group of friends and the defendant walked the complainant back to her flat. The complainant was very drunk and was extremely sick. They had sexual intercourse. The Court of Appeal held that if, through drink, the complainant had temporarily lost her capacity to choose to consent to intercourse, she was not consenting. However, where the complainant had consumed a substantial amount of alcohol yet remained capable of choosing whether or not to consent, her consent was valid. A complainant might lose her capacity to consent to sexual intercourse well before she lost consciousness. However, whether the complainant had the capacity to consent depends on the facts of the case and must be determined on a case-by-case basis.

As already stated, problems arise where, due to intoxication, the complainant is unable to remember whether or not she consented to the sexual intercourse. In such a scenario, the prosecution will only be able to rely upon the evidential presumptions under s.75(1) if it can be established that the complainant was unconscious at the time of intercourse or that perhaps her drink had been 'spiked'. If neither of these circumstances apply, the prosecution will be forced to rely upon s.74 to try to prove that the complainant did not have the capacity to consent. However, where the jury are not satisfied so that they are sure that the complainant was not consenting, they should acquit the defendant.

One case in which the complainant suffered memory lapses was *Hysa* [2007] EWCA Crim 2056. The complainant in this case was intoxicated and suffered memory lapses of the night in question. She stated that she did not think that she consented to sexual intercourse, but said that she could not remember what she said to the defendant when he asked her for sex. The Court of Appeal stated that the fact that she did not say 'no' to sexual intercourse was 'not...fatal to the prosecution case' (at [31]) and held that the trial judge should have left the issue of consent to the jury:

It was for the jury, not the judge, to decide, on the basis of the evidence called, whether, on these facts, in this case, the complainant had the capacity to consent and/or in fact consented to intercourse or not...Issues of consent and capacity to consent to intercourse in cases of alleged rape should normally be left to the jury to determine (at [32] and [34]).

This issue arose again more recently in the case of *Tambedou* [2014] EWCA Crim 954. The complainant in this case had consumed alcohol, but there was no evidence that she had lost consciousness. She could not remember having sex with the defendant and recalled little of the evening. She stated that she would not have consented to sexual intercourse with the defendant, although, because of her absence of memory of the intercourse, she accepted that she could not exclude the possibility that she might or could have consented to sex. The Court of Appeal held that this evidence from the complainant was not sufficient to prompt the judge to withdraw the case from the jury. In fact, the jury 'was entitled to consider absence of consent and to distinguish it from evidence of absence of memory' (at [16]). The Court stated that this was a classic case for the jury which turned on a consideration of all of the evidence. Thus, case law demonstrates that a trial judge should not withdraw the case from the jury where a complainant is intoxicated and suffers from memory lapses. Rather, issues of whether the complainant had the capacity to consent, and indeed did in fact consent, are questions of fact which should be left to the jury to determine.

8.3 Assault by penetration

Assault by penetration is an offence which was created by s.2 of the SOA 2003. It is an indictable only offence and carries a maximum sentence of discretionary life imprisonment. By its sentence, then, it is deemed to be as serious as the offence of rape. In fact, assault by penetration may be just as serious, if not more serious than rape.

STATUTE

Section 2(1), Sexual Offences Act 2003

A person (A) commits an offence if—

(a) he intentionally penetrates the vagina or anus of another person (B) with a part of his body or anything else,

(b) the penetration is sexual,

(c) B does not consent to the penetration, and

(d) A does not reasonably believe that B consents.

All of the elements of assault by penetration must be proved by the prosecution beyond reasonable doubt in order to secure a conviction. Some of the elements of assault by penetration are the same as those in the offence of rape, but there are, of course, significant differences between the two offences (table 8.2).

8.3.1 *Actus reus*

The *actus reus* of assault by penetration is the penetration of the vagina or anus of the complainant with part of the defendant's body or with anything else.

8.3.1.1 **Penetration of the vagina or anus with part of D's body or anything else**

Penetration has the same meaning as it does for rape. Penetration of the mouth is not sufficient for an offence of assault by penetration. Penetration must be of the vagina or anus. Consequently, a man or a woman might be a victim of this offence. Although the penetration does not need to be with the penis of the defendant, this would clearly be sufficient for assault by penetration as the penis is a part of the body. Thus, there is a significant overlap between this offence and rape. This means that where a complainant is unsure as to whether penetration was by penis or another part of the defendant's body or by an object, the defendant might still be convicted of the serious offence of assault by penetration (which carries a discretionary life sentence). As penetration may be with any part of the body or anything else, a man or woman may be convicted of this offence. This offence would include

Table 8.2 Elements of assault by penetration

Actus reus	*Mens rea*
• Penetration of the vagina or anus of B with part of A's body or anything else	• Intention to penetrate
• The penetration is sexual	• No reasonable belief in consent
• Absence of consent	

penetration of the vagina or anus by finger or the tongue, or by an object such as a bottle or barrel of a gun.

8.3.1.2 Penetration must be sexual

The test for whether or not the penetration is 'sexual' is objective and is found in s.78 of the SOA 2003. This element is discussed in detail at 8.4.1.2 in relation to the offence of sexual assault.

8.3.1.3 Absence of consent

The prosecution must prove that the complainant did not consent to the penetration. Section 2(3) states that ss.75 and 76 also apply to s.2. This element has been discussed in detail at 8.1.1.4 in relation to rape.

8.3.2 *Mens rea*

There are two *mens rea* elements of assault by penetration: the penetration must be intentional; and the defendant must not reasonably believe that the complainant is consenting to the penetration. Section 2(2) states that whether a belief is reasonable is to be determined having regard to all the circumstances, including any steps A has taken to ascertain whether B consents. These elements have been discussed in detail at 8.1.2 in relation to rape.

8.4 Sexual assault

Sexual assault is an offence created by s.2 of the SOA 2003 and which was designed to replace the old offence of indecent assault. It is an either way offence and it carries a maximum sentence of 10 years' imprisonment upon conviction in the Crown court.

 STATUTE

Section 3(1), Sexual Offences Act 2003

A person (A) commits an offence if—

(a) he intentionally touches another person (B),

(b) the touching is sexual,

(c) B does not consent to the touching, and

(d) A does not reasonably believe that B consents.

All of the elements of sexual assault must be proved by the prosecution beyond reasonable doubt in order to secure a conviction (table 8.3). Some of the elements of sexual assault are the same as those in the offences of rape and assault by penetration and these have been discussed earlier.

8.4.1 *Actus reus*

The *actus reus* of sexual assault is sexual touching without consent.

Table 8.3 Elements of sexual assault

Actus reus	*Mens rea*
• A touches B	• Intention to touch
• The touching is sexual	• No reasonable belief in consent
• Absence of consent	

8.4.1.1 Touching

Despite sexual 'assault' being the title of the offence, an assault is not sufficient. Actual touching is required. The offence thus requires a battery to be committed which is sexual in nature. Section 79(8) of the SOA 2003 provides that 'touching' includes touching with any part of the body, with anything else, through anything, and it includes touching amounting to penetration. Consequently, where the complainant is unsure whether or not penetration actually took place (do not forget that penetration need only be slight), then sexual assault may be charged. The touching may involve direct bodily contact or touching the complainant with an object. It also includes touching the complainant on the outside of their clothes. This is in line with the offence of battery (see *Thomas* (1985) discussed at 7.2.1.3) and was confirmed by the Court of Appeal in the case of *H* [2005] EWCA Crim 732.

 CASE CLOSE-UP

H [2005] EWCA Crim 732

In this case, the defendant was convicted of sexual assault. He approached the complainant and said, 'Do you fancy a shag?' She walked away and he asked her if she was shy before taking hold of her jogging bottoms and attempting to pull her towards him. The Court of Appeal held that touching included the touching of a person's clothing.

In relation to s.79(8), Lord Woolf CJ stated:

> We have no doubt that it was not Parliament's intention . . . to make it impossible to regard as a sexual assault touching which took place by touching what the victim was wearing at the time.

8.4.1.2 The touching must be 'sexual'

Whether or not the touching (or the penetration if assault by penetration is charged) is 'sexual' is a question for the jury. Guidance on the meaning of 'sexual' is provided under s.78 of the SOA 2003. This section derived largely from the House of Lords' decision of *Court* [1988] 2 All ER 221. In this case, the defendant took a 12-year-old girl over his knee and spanked her 12 times on the bottom over her clothes. He was charged with the old offence of indecent assault (which would now be sexual assault) and admitted that he had a 'buttock fetish'. He denied that his actions had been indecent because his motive had been a secret one which was not communicated to the complainant. The House of Lords stated that 'indecent' should be objectively assessed according to whether or not right-minded persons would think the conduct was indecent. Lord Griffiths stated that, 'By indecency is meant conduct that right-thinking people will consider an affront to the sexual modesty of a woman.' This objective approach has been followed in s.78 of the SOA 2003.

STATUTE

Section 78, Sexual Offences Act 2003

...penetration, touching or any other activity is sexual if a reasonable person would consider that—

(a) whatever its circumstances or any person's purpose in relation to it, it is because of its nature sexual, or

(b) because of its nature it may be sexual and because of its circumstances or the purpose of any person in relation to it (or both) it is sexual.

Section 78(a) covers touching which is obviously sexual (i.e., which the reasonable person would regard as sexual by its very nature). The defendant's purpose and the circumstances of the touching are irrelevant. Thus, touching the complainant's foot would not be sexual under s.78(a), even if the defendant has a foot fetish, as the touching itself is not inherently sexual in nature. However, penetrating the complainant's anus with an object in order to scare and harm the complainant, will be sexual under s.78(a), even though the defendant's motive is not sexual.

Section 78(b) covers touching which is rendered sexual by its circumstances and/or purpose. In *H* (2005), the facts of which are mentioned at 8.4.1.1, the Court of Appeal held that where touching was not inherently sexual by its very nature, s.78(b) applied and the jury had to consider whether the circumstances of the touching or the defendant's purpose renders the touching sexual. Lord Woolf CJ stated that there are two requirements in s.78(b): (i) that the touching because of its nature may be sexual; and (ii) that the touching because of its circumstances or the purpose of any person in relation to it (or both) is sexual.

THINKING POINT

Would an unlawful intimate search conducted by a police officer or prison officer be sexual under s.78?

His Lordship identified two distinct questions for the jury:

> First, would they, as 12 reasonable people . . . , consider that because of its nature the touching that took place in the particular case before them could be sexual? If the answer to that question was 'No', the jury would find the defendant not guilty. If 'Yes', they would have to go on to ask themselves (again as 12 reasonable people) whether in view of the circumstances and/or the purpose of any person in relation to the touching (or both), the touching was in fact sexual. If they were satisfied that it was, then they would find the defendant guilty. If they were not satisfied, they would find the defendant not guilty.

These were the facts of the case of *George* [1956] Crim LR 52. Under the old law, this act did not amount to indecent assault, irrespective of how sexually pleasing the defendant found the act. However, such a case might be caught under s.78(b) today.

THINKING POINT

Consider a defendant who derives sexual pleasure from removing the shoe from a young girl's foot. Would this act be sexual under s.78?

8.4.1.3 Absence of consent

The prosecution must prove that the complainant did not consent to the touching. Section 3(3) states that ss.75 and 76 also apply to s.2. This element has been discussed in detail at 8.2 in relation to rape.

8.4.2 *Mens rea*

There are two *mens rea* elements of sexual assault: the touching must be intentional; and the defendant must not reasonably believe that the complainant is consenting to it. Section 3(2) states that whether a belief is reasonable is to be determined having regard to all the circumstances, including any steps A has taken to ascertain whether B consents. These elements have been discussed in detail at 8.1.2 in relation to rape.

8.5 Intentionally causing a person to engage in sexual activity

Causing sexual activity without consent is an offence which was created by the SOA 2003. It is an either way offence which carries a maximum sentence of 10 years' imprisonment upon conviction in the Crown court. However, where s.4(4) applies, the offence is indictable only and carries a maximum discretionary life sentence of imprisonment. Section 4(4) applies where the sexual activity involved the penetration of the anus or vagina of the complainant with any part of the defendant's body or anything else; the penile penetration of the mouth; the penetration of another person's anus or vagina with part of the complainant's body or with anything else where the penetration is performed by the defendant; or the penetration of another person's mouth with the defendant's penis.

The elements of the offence of intentionally causing a person to engage in sexual activity are set out in s.4(1) of the SOA 2003.

STATUTE

Section 4(1), Sexual Offences Act 2003

A person (A) commits an offence if—

  (a) he intentionally causes another person (B) to engage in an activity,

(b) the activity is sexual,

(c) B does not consent to engaging in the activity, and

(d) A does not reasonably believe that B consents.

All of the elements of causing another to engage in sexual activity must be proved by the prosecution beyond reasonable doubt in order to secure a conviction (table 8.4). Some of the elements of this offence are the same as those in the other sexual offences and these have been discussed earlier.

8.5.1 *Actus reus*

The *actus reus* of this offence requires the prosecution to prove that the defendant caused the complainant to engage in sexual activity without consent.

8.5.1.1 **Causing a person to engage in an activity**

This offence was created in order to criminalise compelling a person to commit a sexual act against their wishes. In the case of *Sergeant* [1997] Crim LR 50, the defendant forced a boy to masturbate into a condom. He was convicted under the old offence of indecent assault. Such an incident could not be covered by the offence of sexual assault as there was no touching. However, it would today fall under the offence of causing another to engage in sexual activity without consent. In fact, since the complainant in this case was a child, the equivalent child sex offence would apply on these facts today. This offence would also cover situations where the defendant has forced the complainant to have sexual intercourse with another person. As the offence is gender-neutral, both men and women may be convicted of this offence. Thus, the female defendants in the case of *DPP v K and B* (1997) (see 8.1.1.3) could today be convicted of this offence as principals.

The prosecution must prove that the defendant *caused* the complainant to engage in the sexual activity. It is not enough that the activity be merely encouraged. Both causation in fact and causation in law must be established.

8.5.1.2 **The activity must be 'sexual'**

The prosecution must prove that the activity was sexual. 'Sexual' takes the same meaning as it does for the offences of assault by penetration and sexual assault. This element has been discussed at 8.4.1.2.

Table 8.4 Elements of intentionally causing a person to engage in sexual activity

Actus reus	Mens rea
• A causes B to engage in an activity	• Intention to cause B to engage in an activity
• The activity is sexual	• No reasonable belief in consent
• Absence of consent	

CROSS REFERENCE

Re-read 2.5 to remind yourself of the elements of causation.

8.5.1.3 **Absence of consent**

The prosecution must prove that the complainant did not consent to engaging in the activity. Section 4(3) states that ss.75 and 76 also apply to s.2. This element has been discussed in detail at 8.2 in relation to rape.

8.5.2 *Mens rea*

There are two *mens rea* elements of causing a person to engage in sexual activity: the defendant must intend to cause the complainant to engage in an activity; and the defendant must not reasonably believe that the complainant is consenting to it. Section 4(2) states that whether a belief is reasonable is to be determined having regard to all the circumstances, including any steps A has taken to ascertain whether B consents. These elements have been discussed in detail at 8.1.2 in relation to rape.

8.6 Sexual offences against children under 13

More serious forms of the four main sexual offences (which have already been considered in relation to adults) apply in respect of children under the age of 13. Thus, s.5 of the SOA 2003 provides for an offence of rape of a child under 13, s.6 for the offence of assault of a child under 13 by penetration, s.7 for the offence of sexual assault of a child under 13, and s.8 for the offence of causing or inciting a child under 13 to engage in sexual activity. The main factor that differentiates the offences under ss.5–8 from those under ss.1–4 is that of consent. While the presence of consent and a reasonable belief in consent may provide a defence where a sexual offence under ss.1–4 is committed against an adult, consent and/or any belief in consent is never a defence in respect of an offence committed against a child under the age of 13. A child under 13 is deemed not to have the capacity to consent to any sexual activity. The elements of each of the offences under ss.5–8 will be explored in the sections that follow.

8.6.1 **Rape of a child under 13, s.5**

Section 5 of the SOA 2003 provides for the offence of rape of a child under 13. This is the most serious of the sexual offences against children. It is triable on indictment only and carries a maximum sentence of life imprisonment.

 STATUTE

Section 5, Sexual Offences Act 2003

(1)　A person commits an offence if—

　(a)　he intentionally penetrates the vagina, anus or mouth of another person with his penis, and

　(b)　the other person is under 13.

The prosecution must prove all of the elements of the offence of rape of a child under 13 in order for the defendant to be convicted of this offence. Some of the elements of this offence are the same as those required for the offence of rape against an adult under s.1 of the SOA 2003, but as you will see, there major differences between the s.1 and s.5 offences as regards consent.

8.6.1.1 *Actus reus*

The *actus reus* of the offence of rape of a child under 13 contrary to s.5 is performed where the defendant penetrates the vagina, anus, or mouth of a person with his penis, and that person is under the age of 13 (see table 8.5). As stated earlier, this is similar to the *actus reus* for the offence of rape in respect of an adult under s.1 (see 8.1.1), but there are two major differences. First, the offence under s.5 can only be committed against a child under the age of 13. Thus, if the complainant is aged 13 or over at the time of the alleged offence, s.5 will not apply and the defendant should be charged with the offence of rape under s.1 instead. Secondly, there is no reference within s.5 to consent, so the prosecution need not prove an absence of consent as is required for s.1. This is because the law deems a child under the age of 13 to be incapable of consenting to sexual intercourse: 'children under 13 cannot validly or even meaningfully consent to sexual intercourse' (*per* Lord Hoffmann in *R v G* [2009] 1 AC 92 at [12]), '[h]e or she is legally disabled from consenting' (*per* Baroness Hale in *R v G* [2009] 1 AC 92 at [44]). Thus, it will be no defence for a defendant to say that the complainant was consenting, and even if the complainant admits to being a willing participant to the sexual intercourse, this will not constitute consent in law. The rationale for this is to protect children from 'predatory adult paedophiles' and from 'premature sexual activity' (*per* Baroness Hale in *R v G* [2009] 1 AC 92 at [45]).

8.6.1.2 *Mens rea*

There is only one element of *mens rea* for the offence of rape of a child under 13 contrary to s.5 and that is that the penetration is intentional. Since a child under 13 cannot consent to sexual intercourse and the prosecution need not prove the absence of consent as part of the *actus reus* of the offence, there is no corresponding *mens rea* requirement in relation to consent. Thus, the prosecution need not prove that the defendant had a reasonable belief in consent, and a defendant's assertion that he believed that the complainant was consenting will not provide any defence to the offence under s.5. Neither is there any *mens rea* require-ment in relation to the age of the complainant, so it is no defence for the defendant to say that he reasonably believed that the complainant was aged 13 or over. Proof of the age of the complainant is only part of the *actus reus* of the offence, and since there is no corresponding *mens rea* element in respect of the complainant's age, this is a strict liability offence. The case of *R v G* [2009] 1 AC 92, HL is the leading authority on the s.5 offence. This case confirmed that this is an offence of strict liability and held that this does not violate Article 6 of the European Convention on Human Rights.

 CASE CLOSE-UP

***R v G* [2009] 1 AC 92, HL**

The defendant was 15 years old at the time of the offence. He had sexual intercourse with the complainant, who was aged 12 at the time. Initially, the complainant claimed that she had not agreed to have sexual intercourse with the defendant. The defendant offered to plead guilty to the offence charged on the basis that the complainant did indeed agree to sexual intercourse and that he believed that she was 15 years old. At this point, the complainant changed her account and said that she was content with the basis of the defendant's plea. Consequently, the defendant was convicted of rape of a child under 13 contrary to s.5, SOA 2003.

The defendant appealed against his conviction on two grounds, namely that the conviction violated his right to a fair trial and the presumption of innocence under Article 6 of the European Convention on Human Rights, and that it violated his right to privacy under Article 8 of the European Convention on Human Rights because it was disproportionate to charge him with rape under s.5 when he could have been charged with the less serious offence of child sex offences committed by children or young persons under s.13. The Court of Appeal dismissed the appeal and certified two questions as being of general public importance:

> (1) May a criminal offence of strict liability violate article 6(1) and/or 6(2)...

> (2) Is it compatible with a child's rights under article 8 to convict him of rape contrary to section 5...in circumstances where the agreed basis of plea establishes that his offence fell properly within the ambit of section 13...?

The House of Lords dismissed the appeal and held that:

> (1) In relation to the first certified question, the presumption of innocence under article 6(2) is concerned with procedural fairness rather than substantive law. Thus, the offence under s.5 does not violate article 6.

Lord Hoffmann reiterated the *mens rea* element for this offence is simply that the penetration must be intentional. His Lordship further stated that 'there is no requirement that the accused must have known that the other person was under 13. The policy of the legislation is to protect children. If you have sex with someone who is on any view a child or young person, you take your chance on exactly how old they are. To that extent the offence is one of strict liability and it is no defence that the accused believed the other person to be 13 or over' (at [3]).

Outlining the *mens rea* of the offence, Baroness Hale stated that 'there is not strict liability in relation to the conduct involved. The perpetrator has to intend to penetrate' (at [46]). Thus, the conduct element of the offence (the penetration) has a corresponding *mens rea* element (an intention to penetrate). In this respect the offence is not one of strict liability. However, the offence is one of strict liability in respect to the complainant's age:

> Every male has a choice about where he puts his penis. It may be difficult for him to restrain himself when aroused but he has a choice. There is nothing unjust or irrational about a law which says that if he chooses to put his penis inside a child who turns out to be under 13 he has committed an offence...He also commits an offence if he behaves in the same way towards a child of 13 but under 16, albeit only if he does not reasonably believe that the child is 16 or over. So in principle sex with a child under 16 is not allowed. When the child is under 13, three years younger than that, he takes the risk that she may be younger than he thinks she is. The object is to make him take responsibility for what he chooses to do with what is capable of being, not only an instrument of great pleasure, but also a weapon of great danger (at [46]).

(2) On the second certified question, the majority in the House (3:2 majority comprising Lord Hoffmann, Baroness Hale, and Lord Mance, with Lord Hope and Lord Carswell dissenting) held that a conviction under s.5 was compatible with Article 8, even though the defendant's basis of plea meant that his conduct fell within the lesser offence under s.13.

Lord Hoffmann stated that despite the defendant's basis of plea, '"Rape of a child under 13" still accurately described what [he] had done. Parliament decided to use this description because children under 13 cannot validly or even meaningfully consent to sexual intercourse' (at [12]).

Baroness Hale held that the defendant's 'real complaint is that [he] has been convicted of an offence bearing the label "rape". Parliament has very recently decided that this is the correct label to apply to this activity. In my view this does not engage the article 8 rights of the appellant at all, but if it does, it is entirely justified' (at [54]).

Her Ladyship then went on to state that even if the defendant's Article 8 rights were engaged, 'it cannot be an unjustified interference with that right to label the offence which he has committed "rape". The word "rape" does indeed connote a lack of consent. But the law has disabled children under 13 from giving their consent. So there was no consent. In view of all the dangers resulting from under age sexual activity, it cannot be wrong for the law to apply that label even if it cannot be proved that the child was in fact unwilling' (at [55]).

In dissenting, Lord Hope stated that a prosecutor's choice as to which offence to charge a defendant with 'must be exercised compatibly with the Convention rights' (at [34]). His Lordship held that s.5 was designed for a much more serious situation, namely where the defendant is over the age of 18. While he acknowledged that s.5 may be appropriate where the defendant is under 18, His Lordship stated that 'the lower the age, the less appropriate it will be' and in such a case, the question to be asked is, given the choice of offences available, whether in all the circumstances proceeding under s.5 would be proportionate (at [39]).

However, Baroness Hale (in the majority in the House of Lords) emphasised that the objective of the statute was to protect children from sexual conduct and focused on the potential long-term harm done to a child under 13 who engages in sexual activity prematurely. Her Ladyship questioned what difference it makes where the defendant is under 16 and drew attention to the policy reasons for conveying to both adults and children that sexual activity with a child under 13 is an offence.

Table 8.5 Elements of rape of a child under 13

Actus reus	*Mens rea*
• Penetration of the vagina, anus, or mouth of B with A's penis	• Intention to penetrate
• B is under 13	

8.6.2 **Assault of a child under 13 by penetration, s.6**

Section 6 of the SOA 2003 provides for the offence of assault of a child under 13 by penetration. This is also an indictable only offence which carries a maximum sentence of life imprisonment.

 STATUTE

Section 6, Sexual Offences Act 2003

(1) A person commits an offence if—

(a) he intentionally penetrates the vagina or anus of another person with a part of his body or anything else,

(b) the penetration is sexual, and

(c) the other person is under 13.

In order to convict the defendant of assault of a child under 13 by penetration, the prosecution must prove all of the elements of the offence. This offence is also similar to the offence of assault by penetration against an adult under s.2 of the SOA 2003, with the two important differences in respect of the age of the complainant and consent.

8.6.2.1 *Actus reus*

The *actus reus* of the offence of assault of a child under 13 by penetration contrary to s.6 requires proof that the defendant penetrated the vagina or anus of the complainant with a part of his body or anything else, that the penetration was sexual, and that the complainant is under the age of 13 (see table 8.6). The *actus reus* elements are similar to those required for the offence of assault by penetration under s.2 and the word 'sexual' carries the same meaning (set out under s.78) as it does for the s.2 offence. The two *actus reus* elements of this offence which distinguish it from the s.2 offence are that the complainant must be under 13, and there is no requirement that the prosecution prove that the complainant did not consent to the penetration. As with the offence of rape of a child under 13 contrary to s.5, it is no defence for the defendant to argue that the complainant was consenting, as a child under the age of 13 is incapable of consenting to sexual activity.

8.6.2.2 *Mens rea*

The only *mens rea* element requirement is that the penetration must be intentional. As with the s.5 offence, there is no *mens rea* requirement in relation to consent, thus it is no defence for the defendant to say that he reasonably believed that the complainant was consenting.

Table 8.6 **Elements of assault of a child under 13 by penetration**

Actus reus	*Mens rea*
• Penetration of the vagina or anus of B with part of A's body or anything else	• Intention to penetrate
• The penetration is sexual	
• B is under 13	

8.6.3 Sexual assault of a child under 13, s.7

Section 7 of the SOA 2003 provides for the offence of sexual assault of a child under 13. This is an indictable only offence which carries a maximum sentence of 14 years' imprisonment.

 STATUTE

Section 7, Sexual Offences Act 2003

(1) A person commits an offence if—

    (a) he intentionally touches another person,

    (b) the touching is sexual, and

    (c) the other person is under 13.

The offence of sexual assault of a child under 13 requires that the prosecution prove that all of the elements of this offence are satisfied. This offence is similar to the offence of sexual assault against an adult under s.3 of the SOA 2003, with the same two differences in respect of the age of the complainant and consent as feature in s.5 and s.6.

8.6.3.1 *Actus reus*

The *actus reus* elements of the offence of sexual assault of a child under 13 contrary to s.7 are that the defendant touches the complainant, the touching is sexual, and the complainant is under 13 (see table 8.7). As with the offences under s.5 and s.6, the only difference between this offence and the offence of sexual assault against an adult under s.3 are that under s.7 the complainant must be under 13 and there is no requirement that the prosecution prove an absence of consent.

8.6.3.2 *Mens rea*

The only *mens rea* requirement is that the touching is intentional.

8.6.4 Causing or inciting a child under 13 to engage in sexual activity, s.8

Section 8 of the SOA 2003 provides for the offence of causing or inciting a child under 13 to engage in sexual activity. This is an indictable only offence which carries a maximum

Table 8.7 Elements of sexual assault of a child under 13

Actus reus	Mens rea
• A touches B	• Intention to touch
• The touching is sexual	
• B is under 13	

sentence of 14 years' imprisonment, unless the sexual activity involved any of the activities listed under s.8(2), in which case the maximum sentence is life imprisonment.

 STATUTE

Section 8, Sexual Offences Act 2003

(1) A person commits an offence if—

   (a) he intentionally causes or incites another person (B) to engage in an activity,

   (b) the activity is sexual, and

   (c) B is under 13.

(2) A person guilty of an offence under this section, if the activity caused or incited involved—

   (a) penetration of B's anus or vagina,

   (b) penetration of B's mouth with a person's penis,

   (c) penetration of a person's anus or vagina with a part of B's body or by B with anything else, or

   (d) penetration of a person's mouth with B's penis,

is liable, on conviction on indictment, to imprisonment for life.

A defendant will be convicted of the offence of causing or inciting a child under 13 to engage in sexual activity if all of the elements of the offence are proved. This offence is similar to the offence of causing a person to engage in sexual activity under s.4 of the SOA 2003, with the same two differences in respect of the age of the complainant and consent as feature in ss.5–7, and an additional difference in the *actus reus* (see 8.6.4.1).

8.6.4.1 *Actus reus*

The *actus reus* of this offence requires that the defendant causes or incites a person under the age of 13 to engage in an activity which is sexual (see table 8.8). An aggravated form of this offence applies to the activities listed under s.8(2), namely penetration of the complainant's anus or vagina, penetration of the complainant's mouth with a person's penis, penetration of a person's anus or vagina with a part of the complainant's body or by the complainant with anything else, or penetration of a person's mouth with the complainant's

Table 8.8 Elements of causing of inciting a child under 13 to engage in sexual activity

Actus reus	Mens rea
• A causes B to engage in an activity	• Intentionally causes B to engage in an activity
• The activity is sexual	
• B is under 13	

penis. As with the offences under ss.5–7, the differences between this offence and the offence of causing a person to engage in sexual activity under s.4 are that under s.7 the complainant must be under 13 and there is no requirement that the prosecution prove an absence of consent. There is an additional difference under s.8 as this offence can be committed by either causing *or inciting* a child under 13 to engage in sexual activity. Thus, this offence is broader than the offence under s.4 in this respect. In *Walker* [2006] EWCA Crim 1907, the defendant was convicted of inciting a child under 13 to engage in sexual activity. He made phone calls to a telephone box while sitting in his car watching the phone box. He spoke to an 11-year-old girl who answered the phone and he said, 'Show me your fanny'. In *Jones* [2007] EWCA Crim 1118, the Court of Appeal held that the incitement need not be directed at a particular child (applying *R v Most* (1881) 7 QBD 244 on incitement: see 15.3.1.3). In this case, the defendant wrote graffiti in train and station toilets looking for girls aged 8 to 13 for sex in return for payment. The fact that his message was not aimed at a specific individual was not relevant.

8.6.4.2 *Mens rea*

The only *mens rea* of this offence is an intention to cause or incite the complainant to engage in an activity. The prosecution need not prove that the defendant intended the sexual activity that he incited to happen (*Walker* [2006] EWCA Crim 1907).

8.7 Sexual offences against children under 16

In addition to the sexual offences against children under the age of 13, there is a range of offences which apply where the complainant is under 16 years old. A separate category of offences was created for children under the age of 16 because this is the age at which a person may lawfully give his/her consent to sexual activity in England and Wales.

8.7.1 Sexual activity with a child, s.9

The offence of sexual activity with a child under s.9(1) is triable either way. If tried on indictment, it carries a maximum sentence of 14 years' imprisonment. The offence requires that the defendant is aged 18 or over and that he intentionally touches the complainant, the touching is sexual, and either the complainant is under 16 and the defendant does not reasonably believe that the complainant is 16 or over, or the complainant is under 13. The sexual activity has been held to include passionate kissing and embracing: *Lister* [2005] EWCA Crim 1903.

Section 9(2) provides for an aggravated form of the offence which is triable only on indictment and carries a maximum sentence of 14 years' imprisonment. The aggravated form of the offence has a further requirement in relation to the touching, which must involve penetration of the complainant's anus or vagina with a part of the defendant's body or anything else, penetration of the complainant's mouth with the defendant's penis, penetration of the defendant's anus or vagina with a part of the complainant's body, or penetration of the defendant's mouth with the complainant's penis.

8.7.2 **Causing or inciting a child to engage in sexual activity, s.10**

The offence of causing or inciting a child to engage in sexual activity under s.10(1) is also triable either way and, if tried on indictment, carries a maximum sentence of 14 years' imprisonment. The defendant must be aged 18 or over and must intentionally cause or incite a person to engage in an activity which is sexual (as defined under s.78), and either the complainant is under 16 and the defendant does not reasonably believe that the complainant is 16 or over, or the complainant is under 13. Examples of cases involving this offence include *ED* [2005] EWCA Crim 1962, in which the complainant's father held the defendant's erect penis towards the complainant's mouth as the complainant resisted, and *Jordan* [2006] EWCA Crim 3311, in which the defendant asked a prostitute to arrange for him to see young girls under the age of 16 and asked her to pass his number on to a girl aged 13 or 14.

There is also an aggravated form of the offence under s.10(2) which is indictable only and which carries a maximum sentence of 14 years' imprisonment. This aggravated offence has as a further requirement that the activity caused or incited involved either the penetration of the complainant's anus or vagina, penetration of the complainant's mouth with a person's penis, penetration of a person's anus or vagina with a part of the complainant's body or by the complainant with anything else, or penetration of a person's mouth with the complainant's penis.

8.7.3 **Engaging in sexual activity in the presence of a child, s.11**

This offence is triable either way and carries a maximum sentence of 10 years' imprisonment if tried on indictment. It can only be committed by a defendant who is aged 18 or over and who intentionally engages in an activity which is sexual (within the meaning under s.78), and for the purpose of obtaining sexual gratification, he engages in it when a child is present or is in a place from which the defendant can be observed, and the defendant knows or believes that the child is aware of the sexual activity, or the defendant intends that the child should be aware of it. The child in whose presence the sexual activity is performed must either be under 16 and the defendant does not reasonably believe that the child is 16 or over, or the child is under 13. Examples of cases involving this offence include *WH* [2005] EWCA Crim 1917, in which the defendant masturbated in front of an 8-year-old girl, and *Bowling* [2008] EWCA Crim 1148, in which the defendant drove his car close to the kerb to attract the attention of girls aged between 9 and 14 and then exposed his penis and masturbated.

8.7.4 **Causing a child to watch a sexual act, s.12**

This offence is also triable either way and it carries a maximum sentence of 10 years' imprisonment if tried on indictment. It is committed by a defendant who is aged 18 or over and who, for the purpose of obtaining sexual gratification, intentionally causes a child to watch a third person engaging in a sexual activity, or to look at an image of any person engaging in a sexual activity. 'Sexual' has the meaning given under s.78. This offence also requires that the child is either under 16 and the defendant does not reasonably believe that the child is 16 or over, or the child is under 13. An example of a case involving a conviction for this offence is *Abdullahi* [2006] EWCA Crim 2060, in which the defendant plied a 13-year-old boy with alcohol and showed him a pornographic film for the purpose of obtaining sexual gratification either by enjoying the complainant watching the film or with a view to putting the complainant in the mood to sexually please the defendant later.

8.7.5 Child sex offences committed by children or young persons, s.13

Section 13 provides an offence for defendants under the age of 18 who commit any of the offences under ss.9–12. The offence under s.13 is triable either way and carries a maximum sentence of 5 years' imprisonment upon conviction on indictment.

8.8 Other child sexual offences

There are also a wide variety of other child sex offences under the SOA 2003, including arranging or facilitating the commission of a child sex offence under s.14, meeting a child following sexual grooming under s.15, offences involving abuse of a position of trust under ss.16–19, familial child sex offences under ss.25 and 26, indecent photographs of persons aged 16 or 17 under s.45, and abuse of children through prostitution and pornography under ss.47–50.

For a summary of the main sexual offences, see table 8.9.

Table 8.9 Summary of sexual offences

Offence	Source of law	*Actus reus*	*Mens rea*
Rape	s.1, SOA 2003	• A penetrates the vagina, anus, or mouth of B • with A's penis • B does not consent	• Intentional penetration • No reasonable belief in consent
Assault by penetration	s.2, SOA 2003	• A penetrates the vagina or anus of B • with part of A's body or anything else • The penetration is sexual • B does not consent	• Intentional penetration • No reasonable belief in consent
Sexual assault	s.3, SOA 2003	• A touches B • The touching is sexual • B does not consent	• Intentional touching • No reasonable belief in consent
Causing a person to engage in sexual activity without consent	s.4, SOA 2003	• A causes B to engage in an activity • The activity is sexual • B does not consent	• Intentionally causes B to engage in an activity • No reasonable belief in consent
Rape of a child under 13	s.5, SOA 2003	• A penetrates the vagina, anus, or mouth of B • with A's penis • B is under 13	• Intentional penetration

(Continued)

Table 8.9 Continued

Offence	Source of law	Actus reus	Mens rea
Assault of a child under 13 by penetration	s.6, SOA 2003	• A penetrates the vagina or anus of B • with part of A's body or anything else • The penetration is sexual • B is under 13	• Intentional penetration
Sexual assault of a child under 13	s.7, SOA 2003	• A touches B • The touching is sexual • B is under 13	• Intentional touching
Causing or inciting a child under 13 to engage in sexual activity	s.8, SOA 2003	• A causes or incites B to engage in an activity • The activity is sexual • B is under 13	• Intentionally causes or incites B to engage in an activity

Summary

- Rape is the non-consensual intentional penetration of the vagina, anus, or mouth of the complainant with the defendant's penis. The defendant must have no reasonable belief that the complainant is consenting. This is an offence contrary to s.1(1) of the SOA 2003. Rape of a child under 13 is an offence under s.5 of the SOA 2003. This is a strict liability offence re the age of the complainant and consent is no defence to this charge.

- Penetration need only be slight and is a continuing act (s.79(2) and *Kaitamaki* (1985)).

- Consent is part of the *actus reus* and the *mens rea*.

- Whether a belief is reasonable is to be determined having regard to all the circumstances, including any steps A has taken to ascertain whether B consents (s.1(2)).

- If the circumstances in s.76(2) apply, then the conclusive presumptions under s.76(1) are triggered. If the circumstances in s.75(2) apply and the defendant knew of their existence, then the evidential presumptions under s.75(1) are triggered. Otherwise, the definition of consent under s.74 is applied.

- Assault by penetration is the non-consensual intentional penetration of the vagina or anus of the complainant with any part of the defendant's body or anything else. The penetration must be sexual. The defendant must have no reasonable belief that the complainant is consenting. This is an offence contrary to s.2(1) of the SOA 2003. Assault of a child under 13 by penetration is an offence under s.6 of the SOA 2003. This is a strict liability offence re the age of the complainant and consent is no defence to this charge.

- The word 'sexual' is objectively assessed under s.78 (see *H* (2005)).

- Sexual assault is the non-consensual intentional touching of the complainant. The touching must be sexual. The defendant must have no reasonable belief that the complainant is consenting. This is an offence contrary to s.3(1) of the SOA 2003. Sexual assault of a child under 13 is an offence under s.7 of the SOA 2003. This is a strict liability offence re the age of the complainant and consent is no defence to this charge.

- The offence under s.4(1) of the SOA 2003 requires the defendant to intentionally cause the complainant to engage in an activity without their consent. The activity must be sexual. The defendant must have no reasonable belief that the complainant is consenting. Causing or inciting a child under 13 to engage in sexual activity is an offence under s.8 of the SOA 2003. This is a strict liability offence re the age of the complainant and consent is no defence to this charge.

The bigger picture

- For a discussion about the developing concept of 'conditional consent' in sexual offences which arose in the case of *R (F) v DPP* [2013] EWHC 945 (Admin), see Doig and Wortley (2013).
- As intoxication and capacity to consent feature in an increasing number of cases, this is a topic which could be preferred by examiners. Consequently, you should be prepared to be able to answer an essay question on this topic, incorporating recent case law and academic opinion.
- In order to fully appreciate why the law on sexual offences was the subject of radical reform in 2003, you need to have an understanding of the old law and the problems inherent within it. You should read the following papers:

   Home Office Review, *Setting the Boundaries: Reforming the Law on Sex Offences* (2000), London: Home Office

   White Paper, *Protecting the Public: Strengthening Protection Against Sex Offenders and Reforming the Law on Sexual Offences* (Cm 5668, 2002), London: The Stationery Office.

? Questions

Self-test questions

1. Explain how rape differs from the offence of assault by penetration.
2. Can rape be committed by omission?
3. Explain how consent is relevant to the *mens rea* of rape.
4. How may the prosecution prove the absence of consent?
5. How is 'touching' defined?
6. What does 'sexual' mean under the SOA 2003?

7. Sam persuades Betty to have sexual intercourse with him by persuading her that he is a famous footballer. Is Sam guilty of rape?

8. Andy has been claiming benefits to which he is not entitled. Oliver threatens to tell the authorities unless Andy has sex with him. Is Oliver guilty of rape?

9. Sarah has a shoe fetish. She strokes Ruth's shoes. Is Sarah guilty of any offence?

10. Elizabeth, a 35-year-old woman, persuades Jason, a 15-year-old boy, to have sexual intercourse with her after plying him with alcohol. Is Elizabeth guilty of any offence?

For suggested approaches, please visit the Online Resource Centre.

Exam questions

1. Discuss the criminal liability of the parties in the scenarios below:

    (a) Graham has sexual intercourse with his wife, Sandra, while Sandra is asleep. He claims that she likes to be woken up in this way.

    (b) On a night out with Michelle, Joseph places a sedative in Michelle's drink. Brian sees this and rescues Michelle from Joseph. Brian then takes Michelle home and has anal sex with her.

    (c) Simon persuades Helen to perform oral sex on him by telling her that he is a famous actor and that he could get her a part in his latest film.

    (d) Kevin has sexual intercourse with Norman, who is extremely intoxicated at the time.

    (e) Jane kidnaps Pamela and tells Steven to have sex with Pamela.

2. To what extent has the Sexual Offences Act 2003 improved the law relating to rape?

For suggested approaches, please visit the Online Resource Centre.

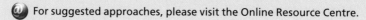

Further reading

Books

Temkin, J. *Rape and the Legal Process* (2002), Oxford: Oxford University Press

Journal articles

Bantekas, I. 'Can Touching Always be Sexual When There is No Sexual Intent?' (2008) 73 JCL 251

Cherkassky, L. 'Being Informed: The Complexities of Knowledge, Deception and Consent When Transmitting HIV' (2010) 74 JCL 242

Doig, G. and Wortley, N. 'Conditional Consent? An Emerging Concept in the Law of Rape' (2013) 77 JCL 286

Gardiner, S. 'Appreciating *Olugboja*' (1996) 16 Legal Studies 275

Laird, K. 'Rapist or Rogue? Deception, Consent and the Sexual Offences Act 2003' [2014] Crim LR 492

Leahy, S. ' "No Means No", But Where's the Force? Addressing the Challenges of Formally Recognising Non-Violent Sexual Coercion as a Serious Criminal Offence' (2014) 78 JCL 309

Rogers, J. 'Further Developments under the Sexual Offences Act 2003' (2013) 7 Archbold Review 7

Rumney, P. and Fenton, R. 'Intoxicated Consent in Rape: *Bree* and Juror Decision-Making' (2008) 71 MLR 279

Sjolin, C. 'Ten Years On: Consent under the Sexual Offences Act 2003' (2015) 79 JCL 20

Slater, J. 'HIV, Trust and the Criminal Law' (2011) 75 JCL 309

Spencer, J. R. 'The Sexual Offences Act 2003: [2] Child and Family Offences' [2004] Crim LR 347

Temkin, J. and Ashworth, A. 'The Sexual Offences Act 2003 (1): Rape, Sexual Assaults and the Problems of Consent' [2004] Crim LR 328

Wallerstein, S. '"A Drunken Consent is Still Consent"—Or Is It? A Critical Analysis of the Law on a Drunken Consent to Sex following *Bree*' (2009) 73 JCL 318

Withey, C 'Female Rape—An Ongoing Concern: Strategies for Improving Reporting and Conviction Levels' (2007) 71 JCL 54

Reports and other sources

Home Office Review, *Setting the Boundaries: Reforming the Law on Sex Offences* (2000), London: Home Office

White Paper, *Protecting the Public: Strengthening Protection Against Sex Offenders and Reforming the Law on Sexual Offences* (Cm 5668, 2002), London: The Stationery Office

9 Theft

LEARNING OBJECTIVES

By the end of this chapter, you should be able to:

- define the offence of theft;
- identify and explain the elements of theft using statute and case law;
- understand the relationship between the *actus reus* and *mens rea* of the offence; and
- apply the law relating to these elements to a problem scenario.

Introduction

This chapter deals with the offence of theft. Theft is one of many offences against property which is found under the Theft Act 1968. Chapter 10 will deal with other common offences against property, such as robbery, burglary, aggravated burglary, blackmail (all also found in the Theft Act 1968), and criminal damage (which is found in the Criminal Damage Act 1971). The offence of fraud under the Fraud Act 2006 will be considered in chapter 11.

The law relating to theft is governed by the Theft Act 1968. Prior to 1968, the law relating to theft was governed by the Larceny Act 1916, a complicated and problematic statute. In 1966, the Criminal Law Revision Committee delivered the Eighth Report: *Theft and Related Offences* (Cmnd 2977). This report led to radical reforms to the old law relating to theft and the enactment of the Theft Act 1968. The 1968 Act aimed to simplify the law on theft by creating a clearer and comprehensive statutory framework. However, the provisions of the Act have been subject to much judicial analysis and interpretation, resulting in a vast mass of complicated case law which it has been stated is 'in urgent need of simplification and modernisation' (Beldam LJ in *Hallam* (1994), *The Times*, 27 May). In studying the law on theft, it is important to gain an understanding of both the Theft Act 1968 and the case law. As you read this chapter, you might want to consider whether the provisions of the Theft Act 1968 and the interpretation given to those provisions have resulted in an offence of theft that is too broad You should also consider when a defendant should be deemed to be dishonest and whether the test for dishonesty from *Ghosh* is satisfactory.

The Theft Act 1968 came into force on 1 January 1969. Theft is an offence which is triable either way and carries a maximum sentence of 7 years' imprisonment upon conviction in the Crown court (under s.7, Theft Act 1968). (On the classification of offences, refer to 1.7.)

The definition of theft is found within s.1(1) of the Theft Act 1968.

 STATUTE

Section 1(1), Theft Act 1968

A person is guilty of theft if he dishonestly appropriates property belonging to another with the intention of permanently depriving the other of it...

There are five elements of the offence of theft. Three are *actus reus* elements: *(a)* appropriation, *(b)* property, and *(c)* belonging to another. There are two *mens rea* elements: *(a)* dishonesty and *(b)* intention to permanently deprive (table 9.1).

Each element will be examined independently, but the prosecution must prove all five elements in order for a conviction of theft to be successful (*Lawrence v Metropolitan Police Commissioner* [1972] AC 626). If one of the elements is missing, any prosecution for theft will fail (figure 9.1).

9.1 *Actus reus*

The three *actus reus* elements of theft which must be proved by the prosecution will be explored in this section. These are: *(a)* appropriation; *(b)* property; and *(c)* belonging to another. The *actus reus* elements of theft are very widely defined. In particular, the scope of what constitutes 'appropriation' has been increased over the years. As a result, Professor Smith argued that the *actus reus* of theft has been 'reduced to vanishing point' (Smith, case commentary to *Gomez* [1993] Crim LR 304 at 306 and Ormerod and Williams 2007: 20).

Table 9.1 Elements of theft

Actus reus	*Mens rea*
• Appropriation	• Dishonesty
• Of property	• Intention to permanently deprive
• Belonging to another	

Figure 9.1   Flowchart in order to determine liability for theft

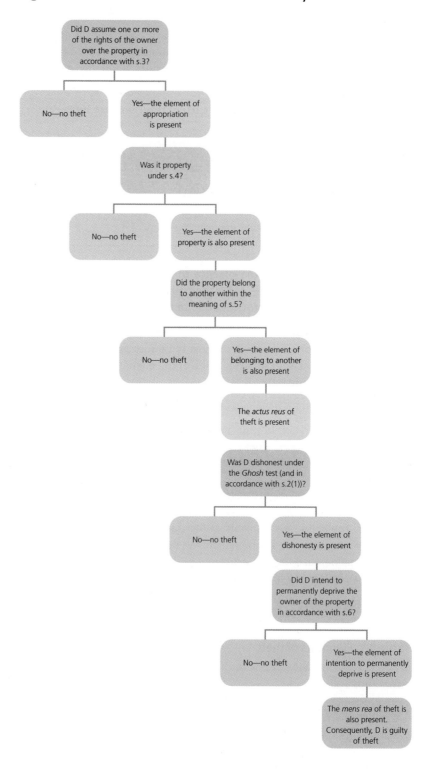

9.1.1 **Appropriation**

The first *actus reus* element of theft is appropriation: the prosecution must prove that the defendant appropriated the property. Appropriation is partially defined under s.3(1) of the Theft Act 1968.

STATUTE

Section 3(1), Theft Act 1968

Any assumption by a person of the rights of an owner amounts to an appropriation, and this includes, where he has come by the property (innocently or not) without stealing it, any later assumption of a right to it by keeping or dealing with it as owner.

According to s.3(1), appropriation involves assuming the rights of the owner of the property; i.e., doing something with the property that the owner has the right to do. It encompasses acts such as taking possession of, using, selling, lending, giving away, and destroying the property, as well as omissions such as failing to return or keeping the property. Section 1(2) of the Act states that in order to be guilty of theft the defendant does not need to appropriate the property with a view to gain or benefit from it. Consequently, a person who takes money from a company in order to donate it to a charity has still appropriated the property, irrespective of the fact that he will not gain or benefit from it himself.

9.1.1.1 **A 'later appropriation'**

The final words of s.3(1) deal with the issue of a 'later appropriation'. A later appropriation occurs 'where [the defendant] has come by the property (innocently or not) without stealing it, any later assumption of a right to it by keeping or dealing with it as owner'. This provision may be used to find a defendant guilty of theft where he does not have the *mens rea* of theft when he initially appropriates the property (i.e., he comes by the property (innocently or not) without stealing it), but at a later stage he does form the *mens rea* of theft, and at that time he also does something (or omits to do something) with the property by which he assumes the rights of the owner over that property. In these circumstances, he is deemed to have appropriated the property and can be convicted of theft (provided that all five elements of theft are present). According to s.3(1), a later appropriation could include deciding to keep the owner's property which he initially borrowed innocently, or dealing with the property as the owner. If the other four elements of theft are present at the moment of the later appropriation, the offence of theft will be complete.

THINKING POINT

Kim agrees to lend Jane Series 1 of a courtroom drama on DVD for a month. Jane keeps the DVDs by her television so that she can watch them. After 2 weeks, Jane has watched all of the DVDs and she really enjoyed the series. Is there an appropriation in the following alternative circumstances?

(1) After 2 weeks, Jane decides to keep the DVDs so she puts them in her DVD cabinet.

(2) After the loan period is up, Jane decides to keep the DVDs.

(3) Jane sells the DVDs to buy Series 2 of the courtroom drama.

9.1.1.2 **Any single right**

Although s.3(1) refers to appropriation as an assumption of *the rights* of the owner, the defendant does not need to assume all of the rights of the owner over the property. The element of appropriation will be satisfied if the defendant assumes *any single* right of the owner over the property. This principle of law is derived from the House of Lords' decision in *Morris* [1984] AC 320.

 CASE CLOSE-UP

***Morris* [1984] AC 320**

This appeal to the House of Lords involved two separate cases in which the defendants swapped the price labels on goods in a supermarket with price labels showing a lower price. The defendants intended that the lower price be charged and paid at the checkout. Lord Roskill gave the leading speech in the House of Lords and stated that that act alone or in conjunction with other acts would be sufficient for the element of appropriation to be satisfied. According to Lord Keith in *DPP v Gomez* [1993] AC 442, it is quite clear that the defendants in *Morris* had assumed a right of the supermarket over the property— that of pricing the goods. His Lordship stated that, '[n]o one but the owner has the right to remove a price label from an article or to place a price label upon it'. Consequently, it is enough to prove that the defendant appropriated the property by proving that he assumed any single right of the owner over it.

9.1.1.3 **Appropriation and consent**

One issue which has troubled the courts is the question of whether or not the assumption of the owner's rights must be unauthorised in order to amount to an appropriation.

 THINKING POINT

Consider whether D appropriates property in the following situations:

    (1) D removes a loaf of bread from a supermarket shelf.

    (2) D borrows X's pen, planning to return it.

    (3) D throws a brick at X's window, breaking the glass.

    (4) D keeps £20 given to him by his mother for his birthday.

    (5) D sells X's television to Y.

The confusion surrounding this issue has historical origins, as prior to the Theft Act 1968, the offence of larceny under s.1(1) of the Larceny Act 1916 required that the property stolen be taken without the consent of the owner. After the enactment of the Theft Act 1968, the issue of consent came before the House of Lords in the notable case of *Lawrence v Metropolitan Police Commissioner* [1972] AC 626. The defendant in this case was a taxi driver who picked up an Italian student who could not speak much English. On reaching the destination, the defendant stated that the £1 note the student had given him was not enough (although the journey should only have cost approximately 50 pence). The student presented his wallet to the defendant, who took a further £5. The defendant's conviction for theft was affirmed in the Court of Appeal and he appealed to the House of Lords on the ground there was no appropriation where the student had consented to him taking money out of his wallet. The House of Lords unanimously dismissed the appeal and held that the absence of consent was not a necessary requirement of appropriation and that the element of appropriation may be satisfied where the owner has consented to the property being taken. Viscount Dilhorne stated, in relation to s.1(1) of the Theft Act 1968, that there was:

> no ground for concluding that the omission of the words 'without the consent of the owner' was inadvertent and not deliberate, and to read the subsection as if they were included is, in my opinion, wholly unwarranted. Parliament by the omission of these words has relieved the prosecution of the burden of establishing that the taking was without the owner's consent. That is no longer an ingredient of the offence.

This unambiguous decision that consent is irrelevant to the element of appropriation should have been the final word on the matter. However, in *Morris* [1984] AC 320, the House of Lords revisited this issue and, noting that there existed a number of conflicting authorities on the point, Lord Roskill concluded that appropriation 'involves not an act expressly or impliedly authorised by the owner but an act by way of adverse interference with or usurpation of those rights'. This was an *obiter dictum* statement which conflicted directly with the principle set forth by the House of Lords 12 years earlier in *Lawrence*, thus adding much confusion to the law on appropriation. This conflict was resolved by the House of Lords 9 years later in the case of *DPP v Gomez* [1993] AC 442.

 CASE CLOSE-UP

DPP v Gomez [1993] AC 442

The defendant in this case was the assistant manager at a shop selling electrical goods. His friend asked him to supply £17, 000 worth of electrical goods and to accept two stolen cheques in payment. The defendant agreed and deceived the manager of the shop into accepting the cheques. The defendant was convicted of theft but this conviction was quashed by the Court of Appeal, following *Morris*. The Crown appealed to the House of Lords against this decision. The House reviewed the authorities with a view to exploring whether a reconciliation of the decisions in *Lawrence* and *Morris* might be possible.

The House decided by a majority (Lord Lowry dissenting) that a reconciliation of the two cases would not be possible, but that appropriation did not require the absence of consent, consequently, *Lawrence* should be followed. Lord Keith agreed with Lord Roskill's opinion in *Morris* that appropriation involved an act by way of adverse interference with or usurpation of the owner's right, but stated that it did not necessarily follow that an act expressly or impliedly authorised by the owner could never amount to appropriation. His Lordship held that '*Lawrence* must be regarded as authoritative and correct.' Lord Browne-Wilkinson agreed, stating 'I regard the word "appropriation" in isolation as being an objective description of the act done irrespective of the mental state of either the owner or the accused.' It is a neutral word which must be established regardless of whether or not the defendant had any dishonest intent.

So, in establishing the elements of theft, appropriation must be examined independently from the *mens rea* elements of dishonesty and intention. As a result of the decisions in *Lawrence* and *Gomez*, appropriation is very widely construed. Professor Smith states that these decisions mean that '[a]nyone doing anything whatever to property belonging to another, with or without the authority or consent of the owner, appropriates it' (Ormerod and Williams 2007: 20). This means that even an act such as taking goods from a supermarket shelf, which is impliedly consented to by the supermarket, amounts to an appropriation. So, when you go shopping in your supermarket, you automatically have the *actus reus* of theft (you are appropriating property belonging to another). If you formed the dishonest intention to permanently deprive the owner of the property at the time that you picked it up, you would be guilty of theft. However, practically speaking, you are unlikely to be caught without doing more.

THINKING POINT

What is the effect on the *mens rea* of having a wide *actus reus* of theft? Which element of theft will be of the most significance in a prosecution?

As the *actus reus* is now so wide, it is further argued by Professor Smith that '[t]he effect is that the *actus reus* of theft is reduced to vanishing point' (Smith, case commentary to *Gomez* [1993] Crim LR 304 at 306 and Ormerod and Williams 2007: 20). Consequently, a defendant's liability for theft will depend largely on whether or not the prosecution can prove that the defendant had the requisite *mens rea*. This in turn elevates the importance of ensuring clear and precise definitions of the *mens rea* elements.

SUMMARY

A defendant only needs to assume any single right of the owner over the property: *Morris*.

Property may be appropriated, irrespective of whether or not the defendant had the consent of the owner to take (or otherwise so treat) the property: *Lawrence* and *Gomez*.

9.1.1.4 *Inter vivos* gifts

Once the courts had decided that property may be appropriated irrespective of the consent of the owner, a new related issue arose: that of whether or not an *inter vivos* gift might be appropriated. The leading case on this issue is now the case of *Hinks* [2000] 4 All ER 833, but two similar cases which raised the issue should be mentioned prior to *Hinks*. The first such case was *Mazo* [1997] Cr App R 518. In this case, the defendant was a maid who was convicted of theft from her employer, Lady S. The convictions related mainly to cheques which she cashed, totalling £37,000. The defendant argued that the cheques were gifts from her employer, but the prosecution's case was that she had dishonestly taken advantage of her employer who was suffering from short-term memory lapses and was vulnerable and suggestible. The Court of Appeal quashed her conviction on the basis that *Gomez* had decided that it was possible to appropriate property given to the defendant by consent if that consent had been obtained by fraud. This narrow interpretation of *Gomez* led the Court to conclude that there could be no conviction for theft where the defendant had received a valid gift *inter vivos*.

However, less than a year later, *Mazo* was criticised by the Court of Appeal in *Hopkins and Kendrick* [1997] Crim LR 359. The facts of this case were similar to those in *Mazo*. The Court of Appeal applied a wider interpretation of the meaning of appropriation, stating that it is a neutral word to be looked at in isolation from any *mens rea* concepts, such as dishonesty and fraud.

CASE CLOSE-UP

Hinks [2000] 4 All ER 833

The final authority on this issue is the House of Lords' decision in *Hinks*. The defendant in this case befriended a 53-year-old man of limited intelligence, who was also extremely naive and gullible. The prosecution case was that the defendant encouraged the man to give her £60,000 and a television set. The defendant was convicted of theft of the money and the television set and appealed. The Court of Appeal dismissed her appeal, holding that a gift could be appropriated, and thus could be the subject of a charge of theft. The Court pointed out that the validity of the gift was not a question for the jury to determine and was not relevant to the question of whether or not the property had been appropriated. Appropriation is looked at independently from the other elements of theft. The House of Lords confirmed, by a 4:1 majority, that a valid gift can be the subject of an appropriation. Lord Steyn stated that applying the principle of law in *Gomez* to property given as a valid gift was necessary to avoid 'plac[ing] beyond the reach of the criminal law dishonest persons who should be found guilty of theft'. His Lordship took the view that a narrow interpretation of appropriation 'would unwarrantably restrict the scope of the law of theft and complicate the fair and effective prosecution of theft'. His Lordship justified the decision of the House by stating that it was in the interests of justice and confirming the faith placed in judges and juries to apply the legal principle in *Gomez* 'in a way which...does not result in injustice'.

The decision in *Hinks* can be criticised for various reasons. The expansion of the scope of appropriation to such a degree creates a conflict between criminal law and civil law. As a result of the decision in *Hinks*, a defendant who is the recipient of a valid gift may be guilty of theft, even though he has a perfect right to the property in civil law. Lord Hobhouse gave a powerful dissenting speech in the House of Lords, arguing that it would be 'simplistic and erroneous' to disregard the civil law when interpreting the elements of theft. In fact, His Lordship pointed out the importance of civil law in relation to the *actus reus* element, belonging to another. Lord Hobhouse stated:

> The truth is that theft is a crime which relates to civil property and, inevitably, property concepts from the civil law have to be used and questions answered by reference to that law...[T]he Act at times expressly requires civil law concepts to be applied.

Despite this, Lord Steyn took the view that the decision in *Hinks* was 'a great advantage' as it meant that there would be no need to explain 'overly complex' matters of civil law to a jury. It would appear that the majority of the House prioritised the accessibility of the law to a lay tribunal of fact over any potential conflict between civil law and criminal law. However, the decision may be defended on the grounds that it serves to protect the vulnerable.

THINKING POINT

Do you consider the House of Lords' decision in *Hinks* a satisfactory one?

The House of Lords' decision has rendered the *mens rea* of theft of pivotal importance. The House could have decided to restrict the decision in *Gomez* to situations involving consent obtained by fraud (because the certified question in *Gomez* related specifically to such cases). However, Lord Steyn confirmed that the principle of law in *Gomez* is of general application, thus expanding the scope of appropriation even further. As the *actus reus* of appropriation is now given such a wide interpretation, the *mens rea* take on more importance—liability is, as a result, largely dependent upon proof of the *mens rea* elements of theft.

Another problem is that the decision requires the defendant to assume his own rights over the property. This anomaly arises because where a person receives a valid gift, the donor gives up his title and rights over the property, and the recipient acquires title to the property. Appropriation involves assuming the rights of the owner over property. It is difficult to see how the recipient of a valid gift can assume the rights of the owner over the property which is the subject of a valid gift if he *is* the owner of the property—he is assuming his own rights over that property. In addition, it is difficult to see how the *actus reus* element of 'belonging to another' is satisfied where the recipient is given a valid gift. Lord Hobhouse (dissenting) stated, '[w]here the defendant has been validly given the property he can no longer appropriate property belonging to another'. His Lordship also highlights a problem with applying s.2(1). Under s.2(1)(a), the defendant will not be guilty of theft if he honestly believes that he had a right in law to the property. If a defendant has been given a valid gift, he will indeed have an honest belief that he had a right in law to the property. Under s.2(1)(b), the defendant will not be guilty of theft if he honestly believes that he had the owner's consent to appropriate the property. As the owner himself, it is difficult to see how he would not have such a belief. Lord Hobhouse disagreed with the approach taken in *Gomez* and by the majority of the House of Lords in *Hinks* of considering the element of appropriation in isolation, as a neutral word. His Lordship preferred to consider 'dishonest appropriation' as a composite phrase, commenting that 'sections 1 to 6 of the Theft Act 1968 should be read as a cohesive whole and that to attempt to isolate and compartmentalise each element only leads to contradictions'. This is particularly true when considering valid gifts.

 CROSS REFERENCE

Section 2(1) on dishonesty will be discussed in detail at 9.2.1.1. You might wish to re-read this section after you have read 9.2.1.

9.1.1.5 **A physical act**

The case of *Briggs* [2003] EWCA Crim 3662 is authority for the principle that appropriation connotes a physical act. In this case, the defendant caused the proceeds of her elderly relatives' house sale to be transferred into her bank account by deceiving them. Her conviction for theft was quashed by the Court of Appeal, holding that appropriation requires a physical act rather than a remote act triggering the payment.

9.1.1.6 *Bona fide* **purchasers**

> 📖 **STATUTE**
>
> **Section 3(2), Theft Act 1968**
>
> Where property or a right or interest in property is or purports to be transferred for value to a person acting in good faith, no later assumption by him of rights which he believed himself to be acquiring shall, by reason of any defect in the transferor's title, amount to theft of the property.

Where a person purchases property in good faith but it later transpires that ownership of the property did not pass to the purchaser (e.g., if it was stolen property), the purchaser will not have appropriated the property. If the purchaser does something with the property assuming the rights of the owner (which he believed he was) over the property, there will be no appropriation. So, a *bona fide* purchaser in good faith cannot be guilty of theft.

9.1.1.7 Appropriation as a continuing act

Appropriation may occur in an instant, and providing that the other four elements of theft are present at that instant, the defendant will be guilty of theft. There is authority to suggest that appropriation is a continuing act. In *Atakpu* [1994] QB 69, the Court of Appeal stated, *obiter*, that theft 'can also involve a course of dealing with property lasting longer and involving several appropriations before the transaction is complete'. It is for the jury to decide when the appropriation is complete and an appropriation may last for as long as the thief is regarded as being 'on the job'.

 SUMMARY

Key House of Lords' Decisions on Appropriation

Morris—only need to assume any single right of the owner.

Lawrence v MPC—appropriation is still present when the victim has consented to or authorised D taking the property.

Morris (*obiter*)—an authorised usurpation of the owner's rights cannot amount to appropriation (overruled by *Gomez*).

DPP v Gomez—confirmed *MPC v Lawrence* that consent is irrelevant to appropriation and held that appropriation is an objective term.

Hinks—further held that a valid gift can be appropriated.

9.1.2 Property

The prosecution must also prove that the defendant appropriated *property*, i.e., something capable of being stolen under the Theft Act 1968. Property is defined under s.4(1) of the Act.

 STATUTE

Section 4(1), Theft Act 1968

'Property' includes money and all other property, real or personal, including things in action and other intangible property.

The definition of property is extremely wide and covers land and all tangible property. Money is specifically mentioned in the definition of property under s.4(1) and refers to coins and bank notes, including foreign currencies. Real property refers to freehold land, although there are a number of exceptions to this under s.4(2), and personal property refers to lease-hold land and chattels (examples of which include objects such as a laptop, iPod, wallet, or

CROSS REFERENCE

See 9.1.2.5 for a more detailed discussion on things in action.

car). Intangible property (property which has no physical existence) is also included. A 'thing in action' (or a 'chose in action') is an example of intangible property—it has no physical existence but it does entitle the owner to bring an action in law. Examples of a thing in action include a share in a company, a debt, a copyright, a trademark, a credit in a bank account, and an agreed overdraft. Other intangible property also covers patents (which are not classified as a thing in action) and export quotas (*Attorney General of Hong Kong v Nai Keung* [1987] 1 WLR 1339). In *Smith, Plummer and Haines* [2011] EWCA Crim 66, the Court of Appeal held that there is nothing in the provisions of the Theft Act 1968 that suggests that 'property' under s.4 ceases to be property for the purposes of theft if its possession or control is unlawful or illegal or prohibited (at [7]). This was a case involving the theft of a quantity of heroin from the victim. The defendants argued in the Court of Appeal that they could not be convicted of stealing something which it was unlawful for a person to possess, such as a controlled Class A drug. Lord Judge CJ rejected the argument, stating that '[c]arried to its logical conclusion, the argument would suggest that the drug-misusing community is permitted to conduct itself in the context of what would otherwise be theft from each other with impunity. The public interest would hardly be secured by the inevitable public warfare which would ensue' (at [9]). His Lordship further stated that the Criminal Division of the Court of Appeal was not the appropriate forum to consider the impact of civil law concepts on the law of theft, and thus notwithstanding that the victim had been in possession of a prohibited drug, 'the appropriation of the drugs by those who attacked him constituted theft' (at [11]).

As the definition of property is so wide, it is easier to examine what is excluded from the definition of property. There are exceptions to the definition of property under both statute and case law. The case law exceptions cover confidential information, electricity, corpses and body parts, and services.

9.1.2.1 Confidential information

Confidential information is not property and cannot be the subject of a charge of theft if dishonestly appropriated. This means that trade secrets are not property for the purposes of the offence of theft. This principle of law is illustrated in the case of *Oxford v Moss* [1979] Crim LR 119. The defendant in this case, Mr Moss, was an undergraduate student studying civil engineering at Liverpool University. He managed to obtain an examination paper for an examination he was due to sit. He copied the questions down and then returned the paper. At first instance, the magistrate dismissed the charge of theft of confidential information. The university authorities prosecuting Mr Moss then appealed to the Divisional Court. However, the Court dismissed the appeal and held that confidential information did not amount to intangible property for the purposes of the Theft Act 1968 and could not be the subject of a conviction for theft.

THINKING POINT

Do you think that the charge of theft against Mr Moss could have been successfully prosecuted on another basis?

Would the elements of theft have been satisfied if Mr Moss had photocopied the examination paper and kept the copies? Would it make a difference if he had paid for the photocopying from his university account?

It has been suggested that Mr Moss might have been convicted if he had been charged with theft of the physical piece of paper. It is argued that the *mens rea* element of intention to permanently deprive might be satisfied because the examination paper had lost all of its goodness or virtue when he returned it (see Ormerod and Williams 2007: 73; and *Lloyd* [1985] QB 829).

CROSS REFERENCE

Intention to permanently deprive is discussed at length at 9.2.2. At this point, you might wish to read the reference to *Lloyd* at 9.2.2.2.

9.1.2.2 Electricity

Whereas gas and water are property and may be stolen, electricity does not amount to property and cannot be stolen (*Low v Blease* [1975] Crim LR 513, DC). Where a person dishonestly uses electricity which another person is paying for, for instance by charging up a mobile phone, iPod, or laptop, they will not be guilty of theft. Such an act may be covered by a separate offence of abstracting electricity, under s.13 of the Theft Act 1968.

9.1.2.3 Corpses and body parts

Under case law, a corpse and body parts are not property and thus cannot be the subject of a charge of theft (*Sharpe* (1857) Dears & B 160). This principle was confirmed in the case of *Kelly and Lindsay* [1999] QB 621, subject to the exception of a corpse or body parts which had acquired different attributes through preservation for purposes of medical or scientific examination, including for educational purposes.

In *Kelly and Lindsay* (1999), body parts used for educational purposes at the Royal College of Surgeons were stolen by Lindsay so that Kelly, a sculptor, could use them to make casts from. The defendants were convicted of theft and their convictions were upheld in the Court of Appeal. Rose LJ held that the body parts had 'acquired different attributes by virtue of the application of skill, such as dissection or preservation techniques, for exhibition or teaching purposes'. However, the Court of Appeal was keen to point out that the law does not stand still and countenanced the possibility that in the future, body parts could amount to property without acquiring different attributes, for example if they were required for use in an organ transplant.

THINKING POINT

If D cuts off V's hair and keeps it, is he guilty of theft?

Where a defendant cuts off a person's hair, an offence against the person will have been committed (unless the act is consented to, of course). In the case of *DPP v Smith* [2006] 1 WLR 1571, the Divisional Court held that cutting off a substantial amount of a person's hair without their consent amounted to assault occasioning actual bodily harm under s.47 of the Offences Against the Person Act 1861. Dishonestly keeping the hair would surely amount to the offence of theft. The hair is tangible property which must belong to the person from whom it was originally taken.

9.1.2.4 Services

Services, for example a bus ride, a driving lesson, and private tuition, do not amount to property under s.4(1), and, therefore, cannot be stolen. This means that where a person dishonestly travels on a bus without buying a ticket, he has not appropriated any property and cannot be guilty of theft. He could, however, be guilty of obtaining services dishonestly under s.11 of the Fraud Act 2006.

CROSS REFERENCE

For a more detailed discussion on the offences under the Fraud Act 2006, see chapter 11.

9.1.2.5 **Things in action**

As mentioned at 9.1.2, a 'thing in action' or 'chose in action' is a form of intangible property, for example a share in a company, a debt, a copyright, a trademark, a credit in a bank
account, and an agreed overdraft. A thing in action is a right which can be enforced by legal
action, and as property under s.4(1) it may be the subject of a charge of theft. If the thing
in action belongs to another and is dishonestly appropriated with the intention to permanently deprive the other of it, the offence of theft will be made out.

Cheques and bank accounts

A credit in a bank account is a thing in action. We use the phrase 'money in the bank' loosely,
but a person does not actually have money in the bank. In the case of *Davenport* [1954] 1
All ER 602, Lord Goddard CJ stated that where a person pays cash into his bank account, the
money becomes the money of the banker and the relationship between banker and customer
is that of debtor and creditor. Assuming that a person's bank account is in credit by £50, he
has a right to sue the bank for the sum of £50 if the bank refuses to give it to him. This right is
the thing in action which amounts to property for the purposes of the Theft Act 1968, and, as
such, this right is capable of being stolen.

 THINKING POINT

Consider whether there is an appropriation of property in the following scenarios:

(1) Your wealthy flatmate gives you a blank cheque and tells you to fill out the cheque
to cover payment for his share of the electricity bill. You calculate his share to be
£20, but instead you draw £200 on his account (i.e., you fill out the cheque for £200
and pay it into your bank account). You know that he has the money in his account.

(2) Would your answer to (1) above be any different if your flatmate did not have the
money in his account?

(3) You forge a cheque from your grandmother's chequebook and present this cheque
to the bank.

In the case of *Kohn* (1979) 69 Cr App R 395, the defendant was convicted of various counts
of theft after he drew cheques on the bank account of his employer. At some times the
employer's account was in credit or overdrawn within an agreed overdraft limit, but at other
times the account was overdrawn beyond the agreed overdraft limit.

Financial position of employer's account at time of drawing cheques

(1) In credit.

(2) In overdraft, but within the limits of the agreed overdraft facility.

(3) In overdraft, but exceeding the limits of the agreed overdraft facility.

The Court of Appeal held that, whilst the account was in credit or overdrawn but within the
limits of the agreed overdraft facility (i.e., in situations (1) or (2) above), the defendant appropriated a thing in action when the cheques were paid into the defendant's account. In this

situation, the bank had an obligation to honour the cheques. So, the 'thing in action' was the legal right to enforce the debt against the bank. The defendant's convictions relating to instances when the employer's account was in credit or within the limits of the agreed over-draft facility were upheld.

However, one of the defendant's convictions for theft was quashed. This conviction related to a cheque that was presented to the bank by the defendant when the employer's account was over the overdraft limit agreed between the bank and the employer (i.e., in situation (3) above). This conviction was quashed because the employer did not have a right to sue the bank when the account was over the agreed overdraft limit—there was no relationship of debtor and creditor at this moment. The bank had no legal obligation to honour a cheque when the account exceeded the agreed overdraft limit. Hence, there was no 'thing in action' to be appropriated, i.e., the property element of theft was not satisfied. Under today's law, the defendant would, nevertheless, be convicted of the offence of fraud under the Fraud Act 2006.

The Court of Appeal followed *Kohn* in *Williams (Roy)* [2001] Cr App R 362. In this case, the defendant was a builder who initially charged customers reasonable prices in order to gain their trust. He then increased the prices, charging far above the market value for work done. The customers (who were elderly householders) paid by cheques which were presented to the bank by the defendant. The defendant was convicted of theft of a thing in action and his con-viction was upheld in the Court of Appeal. The Court of Appeal held that the act of presenting a cheque to the bank and causing a decrease in the credit balance of the victim's bank account was an appropriation of a thing in action. The thing in action (credit balance) which belonged to the victim was destroyed once the defendant presented the cheque to the bank and it was honoured by the bank.

The theft is complete when the cheque is dishonestly presented at the bank, not when the account is actually debited: *Governor of Pentonville Prison, ex parte Osman* [1989] 3 All ER 701.

The case of *Chan Man-Sin v Attorney General of Hong Kong* [1988] 1 All ER 1 deals with the issue of forged cheques. In this case, the defendant drew forged cheques on his employer's bank accounts and paid the cheques into his own account. Forged cheques are null and void and the bank must not honour them. So, in this instance, the employer does not lose the money, but the bank does. Nevertheless, the Privy Council held that this amounted to theft of a thing in action from his employer, namely, the right to draw money on the account.

The piece of paper which represents the cheque is clearly tangible property. However, in the case of *Preddy* [1996] AC 815, the House of Lords held (*obiter*) that a conviction could not be based on theft of this tangible cheque form as the *mens rea* of theft would not be satisfied. There would be no intention to permanently deprive the owner of the cheque because on presentation of the cheque by the payee, the cheque form would be returned to the account holder, via his bank. For a summary, see table 9.2.

9.1.2.6 Statutory exceptions: land, animals, and plants

There are also a number of statutory exceptions to the wide definition of property under s.4(2) to s.4(4) of the Theft Act 1968.

Land

Although land amounts to property under s.4(1) of the Theft Act 1968, s.4(2) imposes limitations on when land can be stolen. A person cannot steal land or things forming part

Table 9.2 Summary re cheque and bank accounts

Financial state of the account	Is it theft?	Explanation
(i) Cheque is drawn on an account in credit	Theft (if all five elements of theft are present)	The bank is obliged to honour the cheque. D appropriates a thing in action: the debt owed by the bank to the employer.
(ii) Cheque is drawn on an account within the limit of an agreed overdraft	Theft (if all five elements of theft are present)	The bank is obliged to honour the cheque. D appropriates a thing in action: the debt owed by the bank to the employer.
(iii) Cheque is drawn on an account which has exceeded the limit of an agreed overdraft	No theft (the property element of theft is not satisfied)	The bank is not obliged to honour the cheque. There is no thing in action as there is no debt owed by the bank to the employer (no relationship of debtor and creditor).
(iv) Forged cheques	Theft (if all five elements of theft are present)	The bank must not honour the cheque. D appropriates a 'thing in action': the employer's right to enforce the debt owed by the bank.

of land and severed from it by him or by his directions unless one of the situations in s.4(2)(a) to (c) exists.

Under s.4(2)(a), where a trustee or personal representative, or someone otherwise authorised to sell or dispose of land, deals with the land in breach of confidence, he may be guilty of theft. Under s.4(2)(b), a person not in possession of land may be guilty of theft of that land if he appropriates something which forms part of the land by severing it or causing it to be severed, or if it has already been severed. This would cover a defendant who enters another's land and removes a birdbath which has been fixed to the land. Under s.4(2)(c), a tenant in possession of land will be guilty of theft where he appropriates a fixture or structure on the land. For example, a tenant who removes a garden shed which is fixed to the land, or even sells the garden shed without severing it, will be guilty of theft.

Wild plants

Section 4(3) imposes limitations on when things growing wild on land can be stolen. A defendant is not guilty of theft if he picks wild mushrooms, or flowers, fruit, or foliage from a plant growing wild. However, he will be guilty of theft if he picks these in order to sell them, or if he completely uproots a whole plant (other than a mushroom).

Wild animals

Section 4(4) imposes limitations on when wild animals can be stolen. Tamed animals (such as a dog or a cat) or animals ordinarily kept in captivity (such as animals kept at London Zoo) are property and can be stolen. Untamed animals or animals not ordinarily kept in captivity cannot be stolen, unless the animal has been, or is in the course of being, reduced into the possession of a person.

9.1.3 **Belonging to another**

The final *actus reus* element which must be proved by the prosecution is that at the time of appropriation, the property belonged to another. It is not necessary to prove to whom the property belonged, as long as it is proved that it belonged to another person. A wide definition is given to 'belonging to another' under s.5(1) of the Theft Act 1968.

 STATUTE

Section 5(1), Theft Act 1968

Property shall be regarded as belonging to any person having possession or control of it, or having in it any proprietary right or interest (not being an equitable interest arising only from an agreement to transfer or grant an interest).

It is clear from s.5(1) that property not only belongs to its owner, but it also belongs to any person who has possession or control of it, or a proprietary interest in it.

9.1.3.1 **Can you steal your own property?**

It is not possible to steal property from yourself. If you are the sole person with any proprietary interest in a piece of property, you cannot be guilty of stealing it. However, it is possible to steal property you own if somebody else has possession or control of it or a proprietary right or interest in it at the moment of appropriation.

 CASE CLOSE-UP

Turner (No. 2) [1971] 2 All ER 441

In the case of *Turner (No. 2)* the defendant was convicted of the theft of his own car. He had left his car at a garage to be repaired, but he later returned and took the car, dishonestly intending to avoid paying the repair bill. The issue in the case was whether the garage had possession or control of the car. The Court of Appeal upheld his conviction because, although he was the owner of the vehicle, the garage had possession or control over the car at the time of appropriation. The idea that you can be guilty of stealing your own property from somebody who is merely in possession of it seems very strange.

By contrast, however, there was held to be no theft in the case of *Meredith* [1973] Crim LR 253, in which the defendant took his car from a police yard after it had been impounded by the police. The trial judge in the Crown court directed the jury to acquit the defendant after ruling that the police had no right to keep the vehicle from the owner. This case conflicts directly with *Turner (No. 2)* and was decided after that case. However, it is merely a first instance decision, so *Turner (No. 2)* carries more authoritative weight.

9.1.3.2 **Abandoned property**

If property has been abandoned, it belongs to no one and cannot be stolen. This begs the question: when is property abandoned?

> ### THINKING POINT
>
> Consider whether property is abandoned in the following scenarios:
>
> (1) You drop a £20 note on Oxford Street in London without realising.
>
> (2) You accidentally leave your pencil in the lecture theatre.
>
> (3) You throw an empty sweet wrapper in a dustbin.
>
> (4) You lose your mobile phone at a music festival.

It is actually very difficult to abandon property. Property is only abandoned if the owner is completely indifferent as to what happens to it and intends to give up his proprietary rights and interests in the property without conferring an interest on another person.

Where property is no longer wanted by the owner and is left out as refuse for the local authority to collect, it is not abandoned and does belong to another. In *Williams v Phillips* (1957) 41 Cr App R 5, the Divisional Court held that, as refuse is left outside for a specific purpose (to be collected) it remains the property of the householder until it has been taken away. When employees of the local authority collect the refuse and place it in their dust carts, the refuse becomes the property of the local authority. Therefore, the refuse belongs to somebody at all times and is not abandoned.

This issue came before the courts in the case of *R (Rickets) v Basildon Magistrates' Court* [2011] 1 Cr App R 15. The claimant in this case was filmed on CCTV in the early hours of the morning, taking items which had been left outside charity shops. He was seen to take items which had been left outside a British Heart Foundation shop and items from bins which were in close proximity to the rear of an Oxfam shop. He was charged with theft and committed for trial. The claimant brought proceedings for judicial review of the court's decision and argued that there was no evidence to prove that the property that he had appropriated actually belonged to another. His application was dismissed and it was held that there was sufficient evidence for a prosecution for theft. In relation to the British Heart Foundation, it was held that it was open to the court to reach the conclusion that even though the charity had not yet acquired a proprietary interest in the property, it had not been abandoned. In the Divisional Court, Wyn Williams J stated (at [13]) that:

> The obvious inference on the bare facts before the magistrates was that persons unknown had intended the goods to be a gift to the British Heart Foundation. Those persons had an intention to give; they had also attempted to effect delivery. Delivery would be complete, however, only when the British Heart Foundation took possession of the items. Until that time, although the unknown would-be donor had divested himself of possession of the items, he had not given up his ownership of the items.

In relation to the Oxfam shop, it was assumed (in the absence of any other evidence) that the bins from which the items were taken belonged to or were controlled by Oxfam. On this assumption, Wyn Williams J held (at [16]) that:

> it would be open to a court to infer that Oxfam had taken delivery of the items once placed within the bin. Alternatively, it could infer that Oxfam had taken possession of the items and had then placed them in the bin for disposal. Either way, Oxfam were in possession of the items at the time of the appropriation by the claimant.

Property belongs to the person in possession or control of it, irrespective of whether or not they are also the owner. In the case of *Woodman* [1974] QB 754, the defendant was charged with theft of scrap metal from a disused factory yard. A quantity of scrap metal had been sold by the company that owned the factory to X. X collected most of the scrap metal but left a small amount on site which X deemed to be uneconomical to collect. The company that owned the factory was unaware that any scrap metal had been left behind. It sought to exclude trespassers from its site by erecting a barbed-wire fence around it and exhibiting signs prohibiting trespassers. The defendant entered the factory yard and removed the remaining scrap metal. The Court of Appeal held that this metal belonged to the company that owned the factory because, by demonstrating an intention to exclude other people from the site, the company was in control of the land and all property on it.

9.1.3.3 Lost property

Property which is merely lost is not abandoned, even if the owner gives up the search for it.

 CASE CLOSE-UP

Hibbert v McKiernan [1948] 2 KB 142

In *Hibbert v McKiernan* (a case decided prior to the Theft Act 1968), the appellant trespassed on land belonging to a golf club and took lost golf balls. He was arrested by a police officer who had been placed on special duty at the golf club in order to prevent trespassers from stealing golf balls. His conviction for simple larceny (for stealing the balls) under s.2 of the Larceny Act 1916 was upheld in the Divisional Court. Humphreys J stated that since the golf club had intended to exclude others from interfering with the balls, there was a clear intention on the part of the members of the golf club to exercise control over the balls.

A case with comparable facts arose in 2003. The defendant in *Rostron* [2003] EWCA Crim 2206 was similarly convicted of theft of golf balls after he retrieved a number of golf balls from the bottom of a lake on a golf course. On appeal, he argued that the balls had been abandoned by their owners (previous golfers) who had long since given up the search for the balls. However, the Court of Appeal followed *Hibbert v McKiernan* and held that there was sufficient evidence for the jury to find that the golf balls belonged to the golf club.

The civil case of *Parker v British Airways* [1982] QB 1004 involved a passenger who found a gold bracelet in the British Airways Executive lounge. It was held that the passenger in taking the bracelet into his care and control acquired rights of possession except against the true owner. British Airways could only displace the passenger's rights if they could show as occupiers an obvious intention to exercise control over the lounge and things in it, for instance by placing notices to this effect around the lounge.

9.1.3.4 Property of the deceased

Where property is stolen from a corpse, proving that the property 'belonged to another' is problematic. The prosecution must prove that the property belonged to someone who was alive. The case of *Sullivan and Ballion* [2002] Crim LR 758 involved two defendants who removed £50,000 from the dead body of a drug dealer. The trial judge at Maidstone Crown court ruled that the property did not belong to another at the time of the act of appropriation and directed an acquittal on the charge of theft.

Who did the money belong to?

The issue of whom the money belonged to was not satisfactorily resolved in this case. Despite the trial judge's ruling that the money did not belong to another for the purposes of the Theft Act 1968, somebody must have been the owner of it or had at least a proprietary interest in the money.

- It is clear that the money could not belong to a person deceased.
- As the proceeds of an illegal transaction, it did not belong to 'the Firm' (the local drug dealers for whom the deceased had been working).
- The trial judge ruled that the money could not be shown to belong to the estate of the deceased because this would necessitate proving that the estate of a deceased person was capable of having possession of money that was: *(a)* not owned by the deceased when he was alive; *(b)* was the proceeds of criminal activity; and *(c)* was being held on behalf of others at the time of death.
- The judge suggested that the money might belong to the Crown as *bona vacantia* (a doctrine under which ownerless property passes to the Crown), but this argument was not adopted by Crown counsel. It is submitted that this is the most appropriate alternative if the property did not belong to the 'employer' of the deceased or his estate.

THINKING POINT

Who do you think the money belonged to?

9.1.3.5 Equitable interest

Property may also belong to a person who has an equitable interest in the property. Where property is the subject of a trust, the trustee holds a legal interest over the property and the beneficiary holds an equitable interest. The property 'belongs to' both the trustee and the beneficiary for the purposes of theft. Thus, the property can be stolen from the beneficiary, just as it can be stolen from the trustee. Section 5(1) provides an exception, under which property will not 'belong to' a person who has an equitable interest in the property which arose only from an agreement to transfer or grant an interest.

9.1.3.6 Property held on trust

Section 5(2) provides that property which is subject to a trust belongs to the beneficiaries of the trust for the purposes of theft. So, a trustee may be guilty of stealing the trust property from the beneficiaries.

STATUTE

Section 5(2), Theft Act 1968

Where property is subject to a trust, the persons to whom it belongs shall be regarded as including any person having a right to enforce the trust, and an intention to defeat the trust shall be regarded accordingly as an intention to deprive of the property any person having that right.

9.1.3.7 **Property received for a particular purpose**

Where title to the property passes to the defendant before the dishonest appropriation of the property, the property does not belong to another and there can be no conviction for theft. However, s.5(3) and (4) deal with two specific situations where the property is deemed to belong to another.

> **STATUTE**
>
> **Section 5(3), Theft Act 1968**
>
> Where a person receives property from or on account of another, and is under an obligation to the other to retain and deal with that property or its proceeds in a particular way, the property or proceeds shall be regarded (as against him) as belonging to the other.

There must be an obligation on the defendant to deal with the property in a particular way. In the case of *Hall* [1973] QB 126, the defendant was a travel agent who received money from customers as deposits for flights to America. He paid the money into the company account but did not supply the customers with their flights. He was convicted of theft of the money, but the Court of Appeal held that although he was under a legal obligation to provide the flights to America, he was under no legal obligation to deal with the money in a particular way. Consequently, the money did not belong to another under s.5(3).

The obligation to deal with the property in a particular way must be a *legal* one (under civil law). A moral or social obligation to do so is not sufficient. There was such a legal obligation in *Davidge v Bunnett* [1984] Crim LR 297, a case in which the defendant had been given money by his flatmate to pay the gas bill. The question of whether such a legal obligation exists is one for the jury to determine: *Foster* [2011] EWCA Crim 1192.

Where a person is given money to pass on to another, there is an obligation to deal with the money in a particular way. The defendant in *Wain* [1995] 2 Cr App R 660 raised money for charity. He spent the proceeds and was charged with theft. The Court of Appeal upheld his conviction because he was under a legal obligation to keep the proceeds and deal with them in a particular way.

9.1.3.8 **Property obtained by mistake**

Section 5(4) is designed to deal with situations where a defendant obtains property by mistake, typically overpayments of wages or in a shop. If there is an obligation on the defendant to restore the money, then despite title in the property passing to the defendant, it is deemed to belong to another for the purposes of the Theft Act 1968.

> **STATUTE**
>
> **Section 5(4), Theft Act 1968**
>
> Where a person gets property by another's mistake, and is under an obligation to make restoration (in whole or in part) of the property or its proceeds or of the value thereof,

> then to the extent of that obligation the property or proceeds shall be regarded (as against him) as belonging to the person entitled to restoration, and an intention not to make restoration shall be regarded accordingly as an intention to deprive that person of the property or proceeds.

The defendant in *Attorney General's Reference (No. 1 of 1983)* [1985] QB 182 was a police officer who received an overpayment of £74.74 by her employer. Her wages were paid into her bank account via direct debit. When she realised she had been overpaid, she did nothing. The Court of Appeal held that the property (the thing in action against her bank for the amount of £74.74) belonged to another under s.5(4) of the Theft Act 1968. The defendant had obtained this money by her employer's mistake and she was obliged to repay it.

It has also been held that where property is transferred to another person under a mistake of fact, the transferor retains an equitable interest in the property: *Shadrokh-Cigari* [1988] Crim LR 465. The property belongs to the transferor under s.5(1). To this degree, s.5(1) and (4) overlap.

There must be a *legal* obligation to restore the money under civil law. In *Gilks* [1972] 3 All ER 280, there was no such legal obligation. This case involved a defendant who placed a bet at a bookmaker's. He was mistakenly paid money in winnings by the bookmaker, which he knew he was not entitled to. Title to the money passed when he took possession of it: at this stage it belonged to the defendant. As the transaction was a wager, there was no legal obligation on the defendant to return this money in civil law. Consequently, s.5(4) did not apply, the money belonged to the defendant and he could not be guilty of stealing it.

9.2 *Mens rea*

There are two *mens rea* elements of theft, both of which have to be proved by the prosecution if the offence of theft is to be made out. The *mens rea* elements are dishonesty and an intention to permanently deprive the other of the property. As the *actus reus* elements of theft are so widely defined, a defendant's liability for the offence will largely depend upon proof of these *mens rea* elements. Consequently, it is important that dishonesty and intention to permanently deprive are clearly and precisely defined by law.

9.2.1 Dishonesty

The first *mens rea* element of theft to be discussed is dishonesty. Different people have different views of what does and what does not amount to dishonest conduct. The prosecution will need to prove to a jury, beyond reasonable doubt, that the defendant was dishonest at the time of appropriation. The element of dishonesty has increased in importance in theft as the scope of the *actus reus* of the offence (in particular, appropriation) has widened. Dishonesty is arguably now the most important element and the vast majority of prosecutions for theft will depend upon its proof. Dishonesty is only partially and negatively defined within the Theft Act 1968, so it is necessary to draw further guidance on this concept from case law. The leading authority on dishonesty is *Ghosh* [1982] QB 1053, which provides a positive test of dishonesty. The Court of Appeal has recently confirmed that the decision in *Ghosh* remains good law: *Cornelius* [2012] EWCA Crim 500. In deciding whether or not a defendant is dishonest, it is first appropriate to consider the negative aspect of dishonesty under s.2(1) of the Theft Act 1968.

9.2.1.1 Negative aspect: s.2(1), Theft Act 1968

The Theft Act 1968 provides a partial, negative definition of dishonesty. Section 2(1) sets out three situations in which a defendant will not be dishonest.

STATUTE

Section 2(1), Theft Act 1968

A person's appropriation of property belonging to another is not to be regarded as dishonest—

    (a) if he appropriates the property in the belief that he has in law the right to deprive the other of it, on behalf of himself or of a third person; or

    (b) if he appropriates the property in the belief that he would have the other's consent if the other knew of the appropriation and the circumstances of it; or

    (c) (except where the property came to him as trustee or personal representative) if he appropriates the property in the belief that the person to whom the property belongs cannot be discovered by taking reasonable steps.

Each of these three situations is self-explanatory and depends upon the defendant having an *honest belief* in the existence of a circumstance. The defendant's belief does not need to be reasonable. However, the reasonableness of the belief is a factor which can be taken into account in deciding whether or not the belief is honest: *Small* (1988) 86 Cr App R 170. Section 2(1)(a) requires the defendant to honestly believe he has a right in law to the property, s.2(1)(b) requires an honest belief that he would have the owner's consent, and s.2(1)(c) requires an honest belief that the owner could not be found by taking reasonable steps. It is important to note that s.2(1)(c) does not actually require the defendant to *take* reasonable steps to find the owner, he only needs an honest belief that the owner would not be found if he did (figure 9.2).

9.2.1.2 Positive aspect: the *Ghosh* test

If none of the situations in s.2(1) apply, the jury will need to consider whether the defendant was dishonest. As 'dishonesty' is an ordinary word, the jury will not usually be directed in relation to its meaning. However, where further direction is required, the trial judge should direct the jury in accordance with the case of *Ghosh* [1982] QB 1053. In *Feely* [1973] QB 530, the Court of Appeal held that dishonesty is a question of fact for the jury to decide and that jurors should apply the current standards of ordinary decent people. This objective approach was modified by the Court of Appeal in the case of *Ghosh* [1982] QB 1053, to include a second, subjective limb. So, the *Ghosh* test is part objective and part subjective.

The *Ghosh* test

The jury must consider:

    (i) whether what the defendant did was dishonest according to the ordinary standards of reasonable and honest people (the objective limb).

If so,

    (ii) whether the defendant realised that reasonable and honest people would regard it as dishonest (the subjective limb).

Figure 9.2 Flowchart on negative aspect of dishonesty: s.2(1), Theft Act 1968

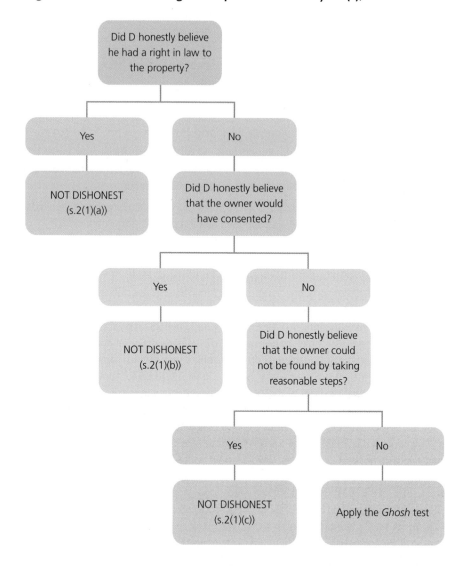

The first limb of the *Ghosh* test is purely objective: the defendant's conduct is judged according to the standards of the honest and reasonable man. The second limb is subjective, requiring the defendant to recognise that his conduct was dishonest according to the objective standard. If both questions are answered positively, the defendant is dishonest (figure 9.3).

The approach adopted in *Feely* was a purely objective one. A jury directed in accordance with this would simply be required to decide whether or not the defendant's conduct was dishonest by the standards of ordinary men. The problem with adopting a purely objective approach was highlighted by Lord Lane CJ in *Ghosh*. Lord Lane CJ gave the following example of:

> a man who comes from a country where public transport is free. On his first day here he travels on a bus. He gets off without paying. He never had any intention of paying. His mind is clearly honest; but his conduct, judged objectively by what he has done is dishonest.

Figure 9.3 Flowchart on positive aspect of dishonesty: the *Ghosh* test

His Lordship stated that 'dishonesty is something in the mind of the accused' and noted that all the situations in s.2(1) of the Theft Act 1968 relate to the belief of the defendant. Consequently, the Court of Appeal rejected the purely objective approach. Lord Lane CJ then considered the criticism levelled at adopting a purely subjective approach to dishonesty:

> There remains the objection that to adopt a subjective test is to abandon all standards but that of the accused himself, and to bring about a state of affairs in which 'Robin Hood would be no robber'.

THINKING POINT

Is the *Ghosh* test a satisfactory way of determining dishonesty?

What are the advantages and disadvantages of having a part-objective and part-subjective approach?

The 'Robin Hood defence' would absolve every defendant who honestly believed that their conduct was honest from liability for theft. Robin Hood, who stole from the rich to give to the poor, would not be dishonest under such an approach. Lord Lane CJ stated that this objection 'misunderstands the nature of the subjective test'. His Lordship held that a defendant would have a defence if he said 'I did not know that anybody would regard what I was doing as dishonest.' This is the *Ghosh* test—a hybrid of subjective and objective approaches. The *Ghosh* test is a compromise between the two extremes of a purely subjective and a purely objective approach, but even this test may be criticised. First, it is quite a complicated test to expect juries to apply, but this argument can also be made of other directions in criminal law, such as the *Nedrick/Woollin* test of oblique intent. Secondly, as standards of dishonesty vary from person to person, similarly there will be a variation of standards of dishonesty between different jurors and different juries. This could lead to inconsistent verdicts. It is entirely possible that two different juries trying the same case might come to different decisions as to whether or not the defendant was dishonest.

The *Ghosh* test has been criticised by many academics, most notably Professor Griew, who argues that the *Ghosh* test is based upon a 'fiction of norms' since there is no ordinary standard of honesty. He criticises the test for confusing state of mind with dishonesty. He takes the view that dishonesty should be a question of law for the judge and suggests that removing the determination of dishonesty from the remit of the jury would lead to more consistent verdicts and certainty in the law (Griew 1985).

9.2.1.3 Willingness to pay

Demonstrating a willingness to pay for the property appropriated does not automatically render the defendant honest; he may still be dishonest.

 THINKING POINT

Consider whether D is dishonest in the following situations:

(1) D, a student, picks up and keeps a £5 note that he finds on the floor outside his lecturer's office.

(2) D travels abroad on a business trip and works extra hours unpaid. In lieu of this, she claims extra expenses to which she is not entitled.

(3) D, in a long queue in a coffee shop at a train station, notices that her train is soon to depart and takes a bottle of water leaving the money for it on the counter.

(4) D finds an iPod on the table in a pub. There are no other customers around, so, after checking with the staff behind the bar, D decides to keep the iPod.

(5) D borrows his brother's new, expensive digital camera to take on holiday without asking.

 STATUTE

Section 2 (2), Theft Act 1968

A person's appropriation of property belonging to another may be dishonest notwithstanding that he is willing to pay for the property.

Section 2(2) might be applied in scenario (3) of the last thinking point. The fact that D has paid for the water by leaving the money for it on the counter, does not automatically render her honest. She may still be convicted of theft if the prosecution can prove that she was dishonest. She might argue that she had an honest belief that the owner of the property would have consented under s.2(1)(b), but whether she did have such belief, and, indeed, whether the jury would believe her, are another matter. If s.2(1) does not apply, the jury would need to apply the *Ghosh* test.

9.2.2 Intention to permanently deprive

The final *mens rea* element of theft under s.1(1) is an intention to permanently deprive the other of the property. As this is a *mens rea* element, it need not be proved that the defendant actually permanently deprived the owner of the property, such as by disposing of it. An intention to permanently deprive also does not require that the defendant intended to profit from the appropriation: '[i]t is immaterial whether the appropriation is made with a view to gain, or is made for the thief's own benefit' (s.1(2), Theft Act 1968). The prosecution must merely prove that the defendant had the intention to permanently deprive the owner of the property at the moment of appropriation.

Intention to permanently deprive is not defined under the Theft Act 1968. The term 'intention' has the same meaning as it does in other offences in criminal law. An intention to permanently deprive may be clear on the facts of the case. For example, if you eat your boss's lunch which he left in the fridge at work, you intend to permanently deprive him of his lunch, and if the other elements of theft are also present, you will be guilty of theft. Similarly, if you take your friend's ticket to a music festival and attend the festival yourself, or if you sell the ticket, you will have intended to permanently deprive your friend of the thing in action (the right to attend the music festival) which the ticket represented. You will also be guilty of theft here if the other elements of theft are satisfied.

Generally speaking, an intention to deprive the owner of the property for only a temporary period of time (i.e., an intention to return the property shortly) does not amount to theft. For instance, if you pick up your friend's textbook in the library to read a page or two, you will have no intention to permanently deprive your friend of the book and you will not be guilty of theft. Similarly, if you pick up your friend's pen to use temporarily, you will not intend to permanently deprive your friend of the pen (however, in this example you will intend to permanently deprive her of the ink that you use).

Section 6(1) of the Theft Act 1968 deals with the issue of when a mere intention to temporarily deprive the other of the property will amount to an intention to permanently deprive the other of it.

 STATUTE

Section 6(1), Theft Act 1968

A person appropriating property belonging to another without meaning the other permanently to lose the thing itself is nevertheless to be regarded as having the intention of permanently depriving the other of it if his intention is to treat the thing as his own to dispose of regardless of the other's rights; and a borrowing or lending of it may amount to so treating it if, but only if, the borrowing or lending is for a period and in circumstances making it equivalent to an outright taking or disposal.

At first glance, this subsection appears quite complicated. Indeed, it has been described by Professor Glanville Williams as 'gobbledygook' (1983: 713). However, on a second reading, you should notice that there are two parts to it, divided by a semicolon. The first part states that a defendant intends to permanently deprive the other of it if he intended to treat the thing as his own to dispose of, regardless of the other's rights. The second part deals with the specific illustration of where the property is borrowed or lent for a period and in circumstances amounting to an outright taking. In *Fernandes* [1996] 1 Cr App R 175, the Court of Appeal held that the important question in s.6(1) is whether the defendant treated the property as his own to dispose of, regardless of the other's rights; the remainder of the section simply provides examples of this. According to the Court of Appeal in the case of *Lloyd* [1985] QB 829, s.6(1) should only be referred to in exceptional cases.

9.2.2.1 Intention to treat the thing as his own to dispose of, regardless of the other's rights

Where a defendant demonstrates an intention to treat the property as his own to dispose of, regardless of the other's rights, he will be regarded as having an intention to permanently deprive the other of the property. In a couple of cases, the Court of Appeal has considered the meaning of the phrase 'to dispose of'. In *Cahill* [1993] Crim LR 141, the Court applied a narrow meaning to 'to dispose of' (which it had taken from the *Shorter Oxford Dictionary*) holding that it meant: 'To deal with definitely; to get rid of; to get done with, finish. To make over by way of sale or bargain, sell.' However, in *DPP v Lavender* [1994] Crim LR 297, a wider meaning was applied as the Court held that 'to dispose of' meant 'to deal with'. The defendant in this case took the doors from a council property in order to put them on his council property. The Divisional Court held that he had intended to treat the doors as his own to dispose of, regardless of the council's rights. Although it is quite clear that the defendant intended to treat the doors as his own, it is less clear how he disposed of them, regardless of the other's rights. The Court concluded that 'to dispose of' meant 'to deal with', thus the defendant did have the intention to dispose of the doors as he had an intention to deal with them, regardless of the other's rights.

In the case of *Marshall* [1998] 2 Cr App R 282, the Court of Appeal had to consider how s.6(1) applied in a case involving defendants who asked commuters for their used one-day London Underground travel cards and sold them on to other commuters. The defendants were charged with theft of the tickets from London Underground as only London Underground had the right to sell the travel cards. The Court of Appeal held that by intending to sell the tickets on to further commuters, the defendants had intended to treat the tickets as their own to dispose of, regardless of the rights of London Underground, and thus they had an intention to deprive London Underground of the tickets. They had intended to deprive London Underground of the revenue they would have made from selling tickets at the full price to new customers. The tickets were held to belong at all times to London Underground, in accordance with the condition on the reverse of the ticket to that effect. The Court held that it was not fatal to the convictions that London Underground might get the tickets back at the end of the day (with their value or worth exhausted).

The Court of Appeal considered the meaning of s.6(1) more recently in *Vinall* [2012] 1 Cr App R 29 and *Zerei* [2012] EWCA Crim 1114, two cases involving the abandonment of property which the defendant had forcibly taken from the victim earlier that day.

CASE CLOSE-UP

Q

Vinall [2012] 1 Cr App R 29

In this case, one of the defendants punched a young man on a bicycle, before the defendants then chased him and took his bicycle. The bicycle was later found abandoned at a nearby bus shelter. While the defendants were actually charged with robbery, the prosecution also had to establish the offence of theft because theft is an element of robbery (see 10.1).

The Court of Appeal explained that s.6(1) requires 'a state of mind in the defendant which Parliament regards as the equivalent of an intention to permanently deprive, namely "his intention to treat the thing as his own to dispose of regardless of the other's rights" ' (at [16]). In establishing the elements of theft, the Court of Appeal held that the appropriation and intention to permanently deprive must coincide. Thus, in order to establish the elements of theft, the prosecution had to prove that the defendant intended to permanently deprive the victim of the bicycle either at the time that he took the bicycle, or at the time of the later appropriation of the bicycle when the defendant abandoned it.

The Court held that it need not be proved that the defendant intended to dispose of the property in a particular way (although evidence of such disposal or of an intention to dispose of the property in a particular way is evidence of the defendant's state of mind from which an intention to permanently deprive can be inferred).

In *Zerei* [2012] EWCA Crim 1114, the defendant forcibly and violently took a car from the victim. The car was found abandoned about half an hour later. His conviction for robbery was quashed on appeal because the trial judge misdirected the jury by failing to distinguish between an intention to permanently deprive and the act of taking possession of the car for a short period of time. The Court of Appeal held that 'taking the car by violence, irrespective of the rights of the owner, is completely different to an intention to permanently deprive' (at [13]). The Court held that the trial judge failed to deal adequately with the important fact that the car had been abandoned; which, applying *Vinall*, could provide evidence of the state of mind of the defendant at the time that he took the car.

Finally, where a defendant attaches a condition to the return of an item which would not be fulfilled or not be fulfilled in the foreseeable future, then this may amount to an intention to permanently deprive. In *Waters* [2015] EWCA Crim 402, the defendant took a mobile phone from the victim and told the victim that he would return it if another person, H, was persuaded to come and speak to the defendant and her friend. Jackson LJ in the Court of Appeal stated that 'if the condition attached to the return of the item is one which would not be fulfilled or not be fulfilled in the foreseeable future, then the circumstances may well amount to an intention permanently to deprive. On the other hand if the condition can readily be fulfilled and may be fulfilled in the near future, the jury may well conclude that intention to deprive has not been made out' (at [18]).

9.2.2.2 Borrowing or lending property

Borrowing property belonging to another is generally not sufficient to constitute theft. However, the second part of s.6(1) states that a borrowing or lending may amount to theft if it is for a period and in circumstances making it equivalent to an outright taking or disposal. This is easily satisfied in some situations, mainly where the property in question is a consumable item. For example, if you borrow a spoonful of your friend's coffee, intending to buy them a new jar, you have the intention to permanently deprive your friend of it. The fact that you intended to replace the coffee you used is not relevant (unless you are going to return the very granules which you took in the first place!).

 CASE CLOSE-UP

Lloyd [1985] QB 829

This part of s.6(1) has been given a very narrow interpretation by the Court of Appeal. In the case of *Lloyd*, the defendant removed films from a cinema, copied them illegally, and then returned the original film reels to the cinema. He was convicted of theft and appealed, arguing that he only intended to borrow the films to copy them, so he did not have any intention to permanently deprive the cinema of the films. He further argued that his taking of the films was not for a period and in circumstances making it equivalent to an outright taking or disposal. The Court of Appeal quashed his conviction for theft. Lord Lane CJ held that a mere borrowing is 'never enough to constitute the necessary guilty mind unless the intention is to return the thing in such a changed state that it can truly be said that all its goodness or virtue was gone'.

According to Lord Lane CJ, there does not strictly need to be an intention to permanently deprive at the moment of appropriation. It is enough that the defendant intended to return the property without any of its goodness or virtue left. As the film reels in *Lloyd* had been returned with some of their goodness or virtue intact, there could be no intention to permanently deprive. This is so, despite the fact that by being copied illegally, they had lost some of their goodness or virtue, their exclusivity.

 THINKING POINT

When does property become so changed that it can truly be said that all of its goodness or virtue has gone?

Consider whether the property in the following situations can truly be said to have lost all of its goodness or virtue:

(1) D borrows V's car without V's permission in order to take it for a joyride. D returns the car with a large dent at the front.

(2) Would your answer to (1) above differ if D dumped the car which he had written off?

(3) D borrows V's pen without permission and returns it with a small amount of ink left in it.

(4) D borrows V's one-month cinema pass (which entitles the person to watch unlimited films for free for one month) without permission. D returns the pass on the day of expiry.

(5) D borrows V's Criminal Law textbook and revision notes without permission a week before V's Criminal Law exam. D returns the textbook and notes on the day after the exam.

(6) D borrows V's digital camera and returns it once the rechargeable battery has died.

(7) Would your answer to (6) above be different if the camera took disposable batteries?

9.2.2.3 Borrowing money

The act of borrowing money (notes and/or coins) which is then spent will usually satisfy the requirement of an intention to permanently deprive. This is true, even where the borrower intends to replace the money borrowed with money of equivalent value. The borrower has deprived the owner of the specific thing which he appropriated. In the case of *Velumyl* [1989] Crim LR 299, the defendant borrowed money from his employer's safe, intending to return money of the same value. This was held to amount to an intention to permanently deprive as the defendant intended to replace the money taken with *different* notes. If exactly the same notes and coins that were taken are returned, then there will be no intention to permanently deprive. However, this is unlikely to occur where money is borrowed.

9.2.2.4 Parting with property under a condition as to its return

Section 6(2) of the Theft Act 1968 deals with situations such as where a person pawns property which belongs to another person without the other's consent. If he may not be able to buy back the property, he will be deemed to be treating the property as his own to dispose of, regardless of the other's rights. Hence, he will have an intention to permanently deprive the other of the property and, provided the other elements of theft are satisfied, he will be guilty of theft.

 STATUTE

Section 6(2), Theft Act 1968

Without prejudice to the generality of subsection (1) above, where a person, having possession or control (lawfully or not) of property belonging to another, parts with the property under a condition as to its return which he may not be able to perform, this (if done for purposes of his own and without the other's authority) amounts to treating the property as his own to dispose of regardless of the other's rights.

There is some question as to whether or not s.6(2) applies when the defendant is convinced that he will be able to perform the condition for return. Professor Richard Card et al. argue that s.6(2) still applies where a defendant is so convinced if, in fact, he may not be able to perform the condition for return (Card 2014: 439). However, Professor Smith took the view that where the defendant is honestly convinced that he would be able to meet the condition for return of the property, he does not fall under s.6(2) (see Ormerod and Williams 2007: 123–4).

9.2.2.5 Conditional intention

If a person intends to permanently deprive the owner of property only if a certain condition is met, he has no intention to permanently deprive.

The defendant in *Easom* [1971] 2 QB 315 was charged with theft of a handbag and the specific items of property which were in the handbag (namely, cosmetics, tissues, etc.). The defendant was in a cinema. He picked up the victim's handbag from the floor in order to see if there was anything worth stealing in it. He intended to steal anything that might have been worth taking. Unfortunately for the defendant, the handbag was attached by a piece of string, to the hand of the victim, who was a police officer. The defendant's conviction for theft was quashed in the Court of Appeal because the defendant had no intention to permanently deprive and a conditional intention to steal something worth stealing was not sufficient. Edmund-Davies LJ stated that:

> What may be loosely described as a 'conditional' appropriation will not do. If the appropriator has it in mind merely to deprive the owner of such of his property as, on examination, proves worth taking and then, finding that the booty is valueless to the appropriator, leaves it ready to hand to be repossessed by the owner, the appropriator has not stolen.

Similarly, in the case of *Husseyn* (1977) 67 Cr App R 131, the defendant and his friend were seen tampering with the back door of a van. Inside the van, there was a holdall containing valuable sub-aqua equipment. The defendant and his friend were both convicted of attempted theft and the defendant appealed to the Court of Appeal against his conviction. The Court quashed his conviction and approved the judgment in *Easom*, holding that a conditional intention was not sufficient for a conviction for theft. Lord Scarman stated that, 'it cannot be said that one who has it in mind to steal only if what he finds is worth stealing has a present intention to steal'. The Court held that the intention to steal (the requisite *mens rea* of attempted theft) must accompany the step taken which constitutes the attempt (the *actus reus* of attempted theft is taking a step which is more than merely preparatory towards the commission of the full offence of theft).

By analogy to the offence of theft, an intention to permanently deprive the owner of the property must accompany the appropriation. Hence, a conditional intention is not sufficient. Although *Attorney General's Reference (Nos 1 and 2 of 1979)* [1980] QB 180 was a case involving burglary, the Court of Appeal made reference to the cases on conditional intention and theft. The Court held that a conditional intention was sufficient for a conviction for burglary, and, consequently, it would be no defence that the trespasser intended to steal only if he found something worth stealing. The Court also explained the decisions in *Easom* and *Husseyn* by holding (*obiter*) that in relation to a charge of theft, the indictment need not specify the items to be stolen, or it may describe the items generically (such as 'the contents of a handbag').

Provided the indictment was drafted appropriately and in accordance with *Attorney General's Reference (Nos 1 and 2 of 1979)*, it would seem that a conviction would be possible today in a case which was based on the same facts as those in *Easom*. The defendant in *Easom* had been charged with the theft of the handbag itself (of which he had no intention of permanently depriving the woman), and the specific items of property which were in the handbag, such as tissues and cosmetics. The defendant had no intention to permanently deprive the victim of these items, so he could not be guilty of theft of them, and neither could he be guilty of attempted theft of them (table 9.3).

Table 9.3 Summary of the elements of theft

Element	Section	Case law
Dishonesty (*mens rea*)	s.2(1)—not dishonest if **D honestly believed** (subjective test): (a) he had a right in law to the property, (b) the owner consented or would have consented had he known, or (c) the owner would not be found even if all reasonable steps were taken	*Ghosh*—(i) would the honest and reasonable person regard what D did as dishonest (objective limb), and (ii) did D realise that the honest and reasonable person would regard it as dishonest (subjective limb)?
Appropriation (*actus reus*)	s.3(1)—any assumption of the rights of the owner	*Morris*—only need to appropriate any single right of the owner *Gomez*—consent is irrelevant (also, *MPC v Lawrence*) *Hinks*—can appropriate a valid gift
Property (*actus reus*)	s.4(1)—includes money and all other property, real or personal, including things in action and other intangible property	*Oxford v Moss*—confidential information cannot amount to property *Low v Blease*—electricity does not amount to property There is no property in a corpse, but there is in body parts used for educational purposes—*Kelly*
Belonging to another (*actus reus*)	s.5(1)—property belongs to a person who has possession or control or any proprietary right or interest in it s.5(3)—property received from another for a particular purpose (where there is a legal obligation to deal with it in that way) belongs to the other s.5(4)—property obtained by another's mistake (where there is a legal obligation to restore) belongs to the other	*Turner (No. 2)*—it is possible to steal property you own It is difficult to abandon property *Williams v Phillips*—even refuse belongs to the householder or the local authority *Hibbert v McKiernan*—lost property is not abandoned Control over land and property on it can be effected by express notice (*Parker v BA Board*) or the exclusion of trespassers (*Woodman*)

(Continued)

Table 9.3 Continued

Element	Section	Case law
Intention to permanently deprive (*mens rea*)	s.6(1)—there will be an intention to permanently deprive if the defendant intends to treat the thing as his own to dispose of regardless of the owner's rights	Key question is whether the defendant treated the property as his own to dispose of regardless of the other's rights: *Fernandes*; s.6(1) should only be referred to in exceptional cases: *Lloyd*.
	s.6(1)—borrowing may amount to theft if it is for a period and in circumstances making it equivalent to an outright taking or disposal	Borrowing will only be sufficient if the intention is to return the thing in such a changed state that it can truly be said that all its goodness or virtue is gone: *Lloyd*
		Borrowing money will satisfy intention to permanently deprive if money is replaced with different notes/coins: *Velumyl*

Summary

- There are five elements of theft under s.1(1) of the Theft Act 1968. The *actus reus* is the appropriation of property belonging to another. The *mens rea* is dishonesty and intention to permanently deprive.

- Appropriation requires any assumption of any single right of the owner: s.3(1) of the Theft Act 1968 and *Morris* (1984).

- Property can be appropriated, even if the assumption of the right of the owner occurs with the consent or authorisation of the owner: *MPC v Lawrence* (1972), *DPP v Gomez* (1993).

- Property is partially defined under s.4 of the Theft Act 1968. It includes money and tangible property, as well as intangible property and things in action.

- Belonging to another is not solely concerned with ownership. Property also belongs to a person in possession or control of it, or someone who has a proprietary right or interest in the property: s.5(1) of the Theft Act 1968.

- A partial, negative definition of dishonesty is given in s.2(1) of the Theft Act 1968 which is based on the honest belief of the defendant (a subjective test). A defendant who holds an honest belief that he has a right in law to the property (s.2(1)(a)), an honest belief that the owner would have consented had he known of the circumstances (s.2(1)(b)), or an honest belief that the owner could not be found if reasonable steps were taken to find him (s.2(1)(c)).

- The positive test of dishonesty is the *Ghosh* (1982) test. This is a two-limbed test which is part objective and part subjective. The first limb asks whether the honest and reasonable person would regard what the defendant did as dishonest (objective limb). If the answer is yes, it must be questioned whether the defendant realised that his conduct would be judged dishonest according to such standards (subjective limb).

- Intention to permanently deprive is given its ordinary meaning. An intention to borrow does not amount to theft unless s.6(1) of the Theft Act 1968 is satisfied. There must be an intention to treat the thing as your own to dispose of, regardless of the other's rights.

- A borrowing may be sufficient for theft if it is for a period and in circumstances making it equivalent to an outright taking or disposal. It must be returned in a changed state such that it can truly be said that all of its goodness or virtue has gone: *Lloyd* (1985).

The bigger picture

- For a more detailed discussion and analysis of the *Ghosh* test for dishonesty, you might like to refer to the following key sources:

    Griew (1985)

    Spencer (1982)

    Halpin (1996)

- In analysing and applying the offence of theft, you should also consider the extent to which there is an overlap between theft and fraud. When considering the liability of a defendant in a problem question for theft, you might also want to consider his/her liability for fraud, unless the question specifically requires you to consider the offence of theft only. You should read chapter 11 on fraud for more detail on this offence.

- Theft is an examinable topic and you should ensure that you are able to answer both essay and problem questions in this area.

 For some guidance on how you might approach essay questions on these topics, you should visit the Online Resource Centre for this book.

? Questions

Self-test questions

1. Identify the *actus reus* and *mens rea* elements of theft.

2. How is appropriation defined under the Theft Act 1968? Under which section?

3. Does an authorised taking of property amount to appropriation? Refer to case law in your answer.

4. Explain the effect of the decision in *Hinks* on the law of theft.

5. How is property defined and under which section of the Theft Act 1968?

6. What is a thing in action?

7. Explain how s.5(3) and (4) operate within the law of theft.

8. What is the negative aspect of dishonesty?

9. What are the two limbs of the *Ghosh* test?

10. When does an intention to temporarily deprive the owner of property amount to theft? Explain with reference to case law.

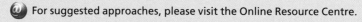 For suggested approaches, please visit the Online Resource Centre.

Exam questions

1. Richard's aunt gives him a cheque for £10,000 which she tells him is to help him get a start in life. She tells him to 'sort out his finances' and put the money towards a deposit on a house. Richard, who is heavily in debt, banks the cheque and then uses £6,000 of the money to pay off his credit cards.

    While Richard's flatmate is on holiday, Richard borrows his car to go on a weekend driving break around the English countryside. In the past, his flatmate had allowed Richard to take the car out for short trips when he wanted to, but Richard had not asked his flatmate on this occasion. He also takes his flatmate's 'pay as you go' mobile phone. Over the weekend, he uses the phone, spending £10 worth of credit. At the end of the weekend, Richard fills up the car with petrol and leaves £10 in his flatmate's room to replace the phone credit he used.

    Discuss Richard's liability for theft.

2. The scope of the *actus reus* of theft is currently so wide that it renders the *mens rea* elements pivotal in assessing the liability of a defendant for theft.

    To what extent do you agree with the statement above? Support your answer with case law.

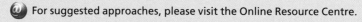 For suggested approaches, please visit the Online Resource Centre.

Further reading

Books

Card, R. *Card, Cross & Jones: Criminal Law* (21st edn, 2014), Oxford: Oxford University Press

Herring, J. 'Theft and Theory' in *Criminal Law: Text, Cases, and Materials* (6th edn, 2014), Oxford: Oxford University Press, pp. 542–64

Monaghan, C. 'Restricting the Meaning of Appropriation under the Theft Act 1968—A Cool, Calm and Rational Approach to the Issue of "Stealing" a Perfectly Valid Gift: Lord Hobhouse in *R v Hinks* [2001] 2 A.C. 241' in N. Geach and C. Monaghan (eds) *Dissenting Judgments in the Law* (2012), London: Wildy, Simmonds and Hill, pp. 289–315

Ormerod, D. and Williams, D. H. *Smith's Law of Theft* (9th edn, 2007), Oxford: Oxford University Press

Williams, G. *Textbook of Criminal Law* (2nd edn, 1983), London: Stevens and Son

Journal articles

Campbell, K. 'The Test of Dishonesty in *Ghosh*' (1994) 43 CLJ 349

Elliott, D. W. 'Dishonesty in Theft: A Dispensable Concept' [1982] Crim LR 395

Glover, R. 'Can Dishonesty be Salvaged? Theft and the Grounding of the MSC Napoli' (2010) 74 JCL 53

Griew, E. 'Dishonesty: The Objections to *Feely* and *Ghosh*' [1985] Crim LR 341

Halpin, A. 'The Test for Dishonesty' [1996] Crim LR 283

Heaton, R. 'Cheques and Balances' [2005] Crim LR 747

Shute, S. 'Appropriation and the Law of Theft' [2002] Crim LR 445

Smith, J. C. Case commentary to *Ghosh* [1982] Crim LR 608

Smith, J. C. Case commentary to *Gomez* [1993] Crim LR 304

Spencer, J. R. 'The Metamorphosis of Section 6 of the Theft Act' [1977] Crim LR 653

Spencer, J. R. 'Dishonesty: What the Jury Thinks the Defendant Thought the Jury would have Thought' (1982) 41 CLJ 222

Thomas, S. 'Do Freegans Commit Theft?' (2010) 30 Legal Studies 98

10 Other offences against property

☐ LEARNING OBJECTIVES

By the end of this chapter, you should be able to:

- distinguish between the various offences against property;
- identify the *actus reus* and *mens rea* elements of these offences; and
- apply the elements of these property offences to problem scenarios.

Introduction

This chapter will explore other offences against property such as robbery, burglary, aggravated burglary, blackmail, handling stolen goods, and criminal damage. The first four of these offences are found in the Theft Act 1968 and criminal damage is found in the Criminal Damage Act 1971. While spraying graffiti on another person's property is usually considered to be an act of criminal damage, you might want to consider the images created by the famous artist Banksy; these images often appear on property belonging to another person and without their consent. They lead to excited publicity and they reach extremely high prices when sold. Is Banksy committing criminal damage by creating these images?

While the offences considered in this chapter primarily seek to protect property or economic interests, some also provide protection to the well-being of the individual. For instance, robbery requires the use or threat of force and burglary may include the infliction of GBH or attempted GBH. In fact, the average lay person probably doesn't realise that the offence of burglary may be committed where, for instance, the defendant's intention upon entering a building as a trespasser is to commit criminal damage inside the property or to inflict GBH upon a person in the building. Thus, burglary does not necessarily involve stealing or an intention to steal. In light of this, it is important to remember that while the offences in this chapter have been labelled as 'property offences', there is some degree of overlap with offences against the person.

10.1 Robbery

Robbery is a statutory offence found under s.8 of the Theft Act 1968. It is an indictable only offence which carries a maximum sentence of life imprisonment: s.8(2).

 STATUTE

Section 8, Theft Act 1968

A person is guilty of robbery if he steals, and immediately before or at the time of doing so, and in order to do so, he uses force on any person or puts or seeks to put any person in fear of being then and there subjected to force.

Theft is a requisite part of the offence of robbery: the word 'steals' in s.8 refers to the commission of the offence of theft under s.1 (see *Raphael* [2008] EWCA Crim 1014). In fact, robbery is an aggravated form of the offence of theft. All five of the elements of theft must be proved for robbery to be satisfied. If one of the elements of theft is missing or cannot be proved, there is no theft, and therefore no robbery. This is illustrated by the case of *Robinson* [1977] Crim LR 173, in which the Court of Appeal held that there was no robbery where the defendant honestly believed that he had a right to the property in question. The defendant had a defence to theft under s.2(1)(a) of the Theft Act 1968, and therefore could not be guilty of robbery.

In addition to the elements of theft, robbery involves the actual use of force or the threat of force. According to the wording of s.8 of the Theft Act 1968, the force or threat of force is required immediately before the theft takes place or at the same time as the theft. A further requirement is that the force must be used or threatened in order to carry out the theft. This is a *mens rea* requirement that the defendant has an intention to steal. (figure 10.1).

 THINKING POINT

What interests does the offence of robbery seek to protect?

Figure 10.1 Elements of robbery

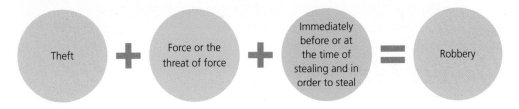

10.1.1 **Theft**

▶ CROSS REFERENCE

Refer to 9.1.1 for a more detailed discussion of the meaning of appropriation.

The robbery is complete when the theft is complete. When the defendant dishonestly appropriates property belonging to another with the intention to permanently deprive and uses force or threatens force on a person in order to do so, he is guilty of robbery. We have already seen in chapter 9 that, as a result of cases such as *DPP v Gomez* [1993] AC 442 and *Hinks* [2000] 4 All ER 833, appropriation in theft is very widely construed.

It is sufficient under s.3(1) of the Theft Act 1968 and *Morris* [1984] AC 320, that the defendant assumes any single right of the owner over the property. It is not necessary for robbery that the defendant actually take the property away. The robbery is complete when the appropriation takes place. Consequently, in *Corcoran v Anderton* (1980) 71 Cr App R 104, the Divisional Court held that tugging at or snatching the victim's handbag causing it to fall from her grasp to the ground was an appropriation and was sufficient for a conviction for robbery. The defendant could be convicted, even though he did not take the handbag away. The Court also held, even if the woman had kept hold of the handbag, the tugging of it may be sufficient for robbery where the defendant gains a sufficient degree of control over the property as to amount to an assumption of the rights of the owner, and thus an appropriation of the property.

In the recent case of *Vinall* [2012] 1 Cr App R 29 (discussed at 9.2.1), the Court of Appeal held that the intention to permanently deprive the victim of his property (namely a bicycle in this case) could be inferred from either the defendant's act of taking the bicycle or from his conduct in abandoning it. However, there could only be a conviction for robbery if the intention to permanently deprive arose at the time of taking the bicycle. If the intention was formed when the bicycle was abandoned, then the theft would have occurred at this point and thus the use or threat of force would not have occurred immediately before or at the time of stealing the property and in order to steal it. Similarly, in *Zerei* [2012] EWCA Crim 1114, the defendant's conviction for robbery was quashed because the trial judge had failed to direct the jury regarding the distinction between an intention to permanently deprive for the purposes of theft and merely taking possession of a car (albeit forcibly) for a short period of time before abandoning it (refer to 9.2.2).

 THINKING POINT

Consider whether robbery is committed in the following scenarios:

(1) D snatches V's handbag from her grasp, causing her to lose her balance.

(2) D stealthily steals V's wallet from his coat pocket.

(3) Would your answer to (2) above be any different if, when V notices that D has taken his wallet, D punches V in the face?

(4) D tells V to hand over his mobile phone or he will burn down V's house.

10.1.2 **Use or threat of force**

The defendant must either use force or put or seek to put any person in fear of being then and there subjected to force in order to carry out the theft. There is no definition of the word 'force' within the Theft Act 1968.

CASE CLOSE-UP

Dawson and James (1977) 64 Cr App R 170

In *Dawson and James*, the Court of Appeal held that 'force' was an ordinary word and its interpretation was to be left to the jury. In this case, the defendants' convictions for robbery were upheld when they stole the victim's wallet after nudging him and causing him to lose his balance. This slight degree of force was sufficient force for the offence of robbery to be left to the jury.

Some force is required, but the amount of force sufficient for a conviction is left to the jury to determine. However, where only the least touching is used, for example in order to pick a person's pocket, the defendant should be charged with theft rather than robbery. Consequently, where a defendant simply snatched a cigarette from the victim's hand without making physical contact with the victim's hand, there was no robbery: see *P v DPP* [2013] 1 Cr App R 7.

If no force is actually applied to any person, it is sufficient if force is threatened. Section 8(1) requires that the defendant puts a person in fear of force being applied, or that the defendant seeks to put any person in fear of being subjected to force. Thus, it does not matter that the person threatened is not actually fearful of such force; what is relevant is that the defendant sought to put any person in fear of force (see *Codsi* [2009] EWCA Crim 1618). The threat of force does not need to be made against the person from whom the property is stolen. It is sufficient that a third party is threatened with force. Additionally, a threat of force being used at some point in the future is not sufficient. The threat must be one of then and there being subjected to force.

The use or threat of force must be directed at a person if the defendant is to be liable for robbery. The defendant in *Clouden* [1987] Crim LR 56 could be guilty of robbery where he grabbed the victim's shopping bag from her grasp. The Court of Appeal held that there was no distinction between force being applied to the actual person and force being applied to property causing force on the person. If force is used against property but it does not cause force on a person, the defendant may be guilty of criminal damage under s.1 of the Criminal Damage Act 1971. Criminal damage required property belonging to another to be destroyed or damaged (see 10.6). A threat of force directed at property might amount to blackmail, for instance if D threatened to destroy V's property unless V gives him money, D will be guilty of blackmail under s.21 of the Theft Act 1968 (see 10.4).

10.1.3 Immediately before or at the time of stealing

The force must be used or threatened immediately before or at the time of stealing. Force used or a threat of force made after the act of stealing may amount to another offence, for example one of assault or battery.

 CASE CLOSE-UP

Hale (1979) 68 Cr App R 415

In the case of *Hale*, the defendants forced their way into the victim's house, put a hand over her mouth to stop her screaming, and stole various items of jewellery. They then tied the victim up and threatened what would happen to her young son if she informed the police within five minutes of their leaving. The Court of Appeal upheld the defendants' convictions and rejected their argument that there could be no robbery because the force had been used after the theft. The Court held that the act of appropriation is a continuous act which does not suddenly cease. It is for the jury to decide whether the appropriation has finished when the force is used. There will be no robbery if the force is used or threatened after the theft is complete. In this particular case, the Court of Appeal held that the jury could have found that the defendants were guilty of robbery by relying upon the force used when a hand was put over the victim's mouth, or by relying on the acts of tying the victim up.

10.1.4 In order to steal

The force must be used or threatened in order to carry out the theft. Thus, the purpose of the force is theft. This is a *mens rea* element—the defendant must have an intention to steal (see *Codsi* [2009] EWCA Crim 1618). There is no robbery if the force is used for a different purpose.

10.1.5 Assault with intent to rob

The offence of assault with intent to rob is found under s.8(2) of the Theft Act 1968. It is an indictable only offence which carries a maximum sentence of life imprisonment. This offence involves the commission of an assault upon a person while intending to steal. It will be charged where the defendant does not actually commit theft but does assault the victim while attempting to steal.

10.2 Burglary

Burglary is a statutory offence found under s.9(1)(a) and (b) of the Theft Act 1968. It is an either way offence which carries a maximum sentence of 10 years' imprisonment: s.9(3). The maximum sentence is 14 years' imprisonment in the case of burglary of a dwelling: s.9(3).

 STATUTE

Section 9, Theft Act 1968

(1) A person is guilty of burglary if—

    (a) he enters any building or part of a building as a trespasser and with intent to commit any such offence as is mentioned in subsection (2) below; or

    (b) having entered any building or part of a building as a trespasser he steals or attempts to steal anything in the building or that part of it or inflicts or attempts to inflict on any person therein any grievous bodily harm.

(2) The offences referred to in subsection (1)(a) above are offences of stealing anything in the building or part of a building in question, of inflicting on any person therein any grievous bodily harm . . . therein, and of doing unlawful damage to the building or anything therein.

Table 10.1 Elements of burglary under s.9(1)(a), Theft Act 1968

Actus reus	Mens rea
• Entry	• Intention to enter
• Of a building or part of a building	• Intentional or reckless trespass
• As a trespasser	• Intention to steal, do GBH, or do unlawful damage therein

The layperson often typically imagines burglary to involve the entry of a building as a trespasser accompanied by theft or, at the very least, an intention to steal. However, burglary does not necessarily involve an intention to steal or the commission of theft. There are two offences of burglary under s.9(1) of the Theft Act 1968.

10.2.1 Burglary under s.9(1)(a)

Section 9(1)(a) of the Theft Act 1968 provides that a person is guilty of burglary if he enters a building or part of a building as a trespasser with the intention of stealing anything, inflicting grievous bodily harm on any person, or doing unlawful damage to the building or anything therein. The *actus reus* of this offence is the entry of a building or part of a building as a trespasser. The *mens rea* elements are an intention to enter, intentional or reckless trespass, and an intention to do one of the three acts mentioned in s.9(2) of the Theft Act 1968 (intention to steal, inflict grievous bodily harm, or do unlawful damage) (table 10.1).

10.2.1.1 Entry

The first key element of burglary is the defendant's entry into the building or part of a building. The *actus reus* of burglary requires the physical act of entry and the *mens rea* requires an intention to enter. Authorities suggest that a defendant's entry must be 'effective and substantial'. The most well-known authority on entry is the case of *Collins* [1973] QB 100.

 CASE CLOSE-UP

Collins [1973] QB 100

The defendant in this case saw the complainant asleep in her bedroom. He removed his clothes (with the exception of his socks, which he claimed he left on just in case he needed to effect a quick exit) and climbed a ladder to her bedroom window intending to rape her. While he was on the windowsill, the complainant awoke and, assuming that the defendant was her boyfriend, invited the defendant into her room. They had consensual sexual intercourse. The defendant was charged with burglary (note that, in 1973, the entry of a building as a trespasser with the intention to rape amounted to burglary. This was repealed by the Sexual Offences Act 2003 which created a new offence of trespass with intent to rape under s.63 of that Act). The issue in the case was whether the defendant had entered the room as a trespasser or whether he had, in fact, entered as a visitor, having been invited in by the complainant. Consequently, as stated by Edmund Davies LJ, a key question in the case was:

> where exactly Collins was at the moment when, according to him, the girl manifested that she was welcoming him. Was he kneeling on the sill outside the window or was he already inside the room, having climbed through the window frame, and kneeling upon the inner sill?

If the defendant had not yet entered the room (i.e., he was on the sill outside) when the complainant invited him in, then he had not entered as a trespasser and so could not be guilty of burglary. However, if he had entered the room (i.e., he was on the inner sill) when she invited him in, then he had entered as a trespasser with the intention to rape and could be guilty of burglary under s.9(1)(a) of the Theft Act 1968. The Court of Appeal held that the defendant should not be convicted unless the jury were satisfied that he had made 'an effective and substantial entry' into the room.

This principle was followed in the case of *Brown* [1985] Crim LR 212. The defendant in this case broke a shop window and leant in through it with the top half of his body. His feet remained on the floor outside, but he used his arms to rummage around looking for property to steal. The Court of Appeal dismissed the defendant's appeal against conviction and held that the defendant's entry was 'effective' and 'substantial'.

In the case of *Ryan* [1996] Crim LR 320, however, the Court of Appeal held that the word 'substantial' did not add anything and that entry only has to be 'effective'. However, the Court did not define 'effective'. The defendant in *Ryan* leant in through a window and got stuck. He was unable to move his head and one arm and had to be removed by the fire brigade. He was convicted of burglary under s.9(1)(a) of the Theft Act 1968 and appealed on the basis that he could not be said to have entered the building as he was unable to actually steal anything due to being trapped. The Court upheld his conviction and held that he had entered the building whether he was able to steal anything or not.

It would appear from case law that entry of the entire body into the building is not necessary. Neither is it necessary that the defendant be capable of stealing. The law seems to have taken a step back in the direction of the old common law position prior to the Theft Act 1968. Prior to the Theft Act 1968, the insertion of any part of the body into the building amounted to entry. Thus, a defendant who inserted the forepart of his forefinger through a window had entered the building: *Davis* (1823) Russ & Ry 499. Whether or not the insertion of a small part of the body, such as a finger, will be enough to constitute entry today remains to be seen. The law is also unclear in relation to the insertion of objects into a building. There is no recent authority on whether or not inserting an inanimate object, such as a fishing pole or a wire hanger, will constitute entry. There is also some confusion over whether the introduction of an animate object, such as a small child under the age of 10 or a monkey, into a building in order to steal constitutes entry and whether a prosecution for burglary could be based on the doctrine of innocent agency (see the case of *Michael* (1840) 9 C & P 356 in the introduction to chapter 16 (accessorial liability)). Under the common law such a prosecution would have been possible (see Professor Glanville Williams (1983: 840)). However, while the view taken by Professor Ormerod and Karl Laird (2015) is that this rule probably no longer applies, Professor Griew is of the opinion that the doctrine should be available (1986: 92).

10.2.1.2 **Building or part of a building**

There is only a partial definition of 'building' under the Theft Act 1968. Case law suggests that a building is a structure of considerable size with some degree of permanence. Examples include a house, a shop, a garage, a factory, a garden shed, or a greenhouse. However, temporary shelters, such as a tent, are not. In *B and S v Leathley* [1979] Crim LR 314, it was held that a freezer container which was 25 feet long, 7 feet high, and 7 feet deep and weighed 3 tons, was a building. The freezer had not been moved for over 2 years and was intended to be permanent or at least to remain where it was for a considerable time. These characteristics were sufficient to render the freezer a building. By contrast, in *Norfolk Constabulary v Seekings and Gould* [1986] Crim LR 167, unhitched lorry trailers on wheels which were being used for temporary storage were not of sufficient permanence to amount to buildings.

Whether a structure qualifies as a building is a question of fact to be determined by the jury. Most buildings will have walls and a roof. It seems clear that a structure with four walls but no roof will not amount to a building. Lush LJ stated in *Manning and Rogers* (1871) LR 1 CCR 338, 'it is sufficient that is should be a connected and entire structure. I do not think four walls erected a foot high would be a building'.

As 'building' is an ordinary word in everyday usage, the Theft Act 1968 only partially defines it. Section 9(4) of the Theft Act 1968 states that, 'building . . . shall apply also to an inhabited vehicle or vessel, and shall apply to any such vehicle or vessel at times when the person having a habitation in it is not there as well as at time when he is'. So, a caravan, a houseboat, or a mobile home will also amount to a building for the purposes of the Act.

A defendant who enters a building lawfully (i.e., not as a trespasser), but then enters another part of that building with the necessary ulterior intent will be guilty of burglary under s.9(1)(a). A room will clearly amount to a part of a building. So, a student who lawfully enters the house he shares with other students becomes a burglar if he then enters his housemate's bedroom as a trespasser intending to steal. Equally, a customer who goes behind a counter in a department store intending to steal is guilty of burglary.

Q CASE CLOSE-UP

Walkington [1979] 1 WLR 1169

In the case of *Walkington*, the defendant did exactly that. He entered a Debenhams department store shortly before closing time and went behind a three-sided, moveable counter into an area reserved for staff. His intention there was to steal from the till, but the till was empty. He was charged with burglary under s.9(1)(a) of the Theft Act 1968. The Court of Appeal held that whether the defendant had entered a part of a building as a trespasser was a question of fact to be determined by the jury. Geoffrey Lane LJ held that the counter was 'a physical demarcation', but whether it was sufficient to amount to a part of a building from which the public were clearly excluded was a matter for the jury.

The defendant in *Laing* [1995] Crim LR 395 similarly entered a department store with permission. However, after the store was closed, the defendant was found in an area of the building which was closed to the public. The defendant's conviction for burglary under s.9(1)(a) of the Theft Act 1968 was quashed on appeal. The Court of Appeal held that there was no evidence that the defendant was a trespasser when he was found as he was not a trespasser when he entered the building. Perhaps the prosecution could have brought their case on the basis that the defendant became a trespasser when he moved to another part of the building as a trespasser, but they did not.

10.2.1.3 **As a trespasser**

In order to be guilty of burglary under s.9(1)(a), the defendant must be a trespasser on entry. Trespass is a civil law concept. It is defined in the law of tort as the intentional, reckless, or negligent entry into a building which is in the possession of another person, where that person does not consent to the entry. The *mens rea* of burglary also requires the defendant to know he is trespassing or be reckless as to whether he is trespassing or not: *Collins* (1973). The subjective *Cunningham* test of recklessness is applied, so the defendant must recognise a risk that he might be trespassing but enter the building anyway.

Where a person enters a building knowing or being reckless as to whether he is in excess of the permission granted to him, he enters as a trespasser.

 CASE CLOSE-UP

Jones and Smith [1976] 1 WLR 672

The defendants in the case of *Jones and Smith*, entered Smith's father's house and stole two television sets. They were charged with burglary under s.9(1)(b), that having entered a building as trespassers they did steal. The Court of Appeal held that they would be trespassers if they entered the house knowing that they were entering in excess of the permission that had been given to them, or being reckless as to whether they were entering in excess of such permission. Although Smith had a general permission to enter the house, he exceeded that permission when he entered with the intention to steal the television sets.

10.2.1.4 **With an ulterior intention**

Section 9(1)(a) of the Theft Act 1968 requires the defendant to have an intention to commit one of the offences under s.9(2). The defendant must have either an intention to steal, to inflict grievous bodily harm, or to do unlawful damage (an intention to commit rape used to be an alternative ulterior intent, but this element was repealed by the Sexual Offences Act 2003). The defendant must have this ulterior intention on entry. A conditional intention to steal only if there is something worth stealing is no defence to the charge of burglary: *Attorney General's Reference (Nos 1 and 2 of 1979)* (1980).

CROSS REFERENCE

Refer to 9.2.2.5 for a more detailed discussion on conditional intention.

An intention to inflict grievous bodily harm refers to an intention to commit an offence under s.18 of the Offences Against the Person Act 1861. An intention to do unlawful damage refers to an intention to commit criminal damage under s.1 of the Criminal Damage Act 1971.

10.2.2 **Burglary under s.9(1)(b)**

Section 9(1)(b) of the Theft Act 1968 provides that a person is guilty of burglary if, having entered any building or part of a building as a trespasser, he steals or attempts to steal anything in the building or that part of it or inflicts or attempts to inflict on any person therein any grievous bodily harm. As with the offence under s.9(1)(a), the *actus reus* of the offence

Table 10.2 Elements of burglary under s.9(1)(b), Theft Act 1968

Actus reus	Mens rea
• Having entered	• Intention to enter
• A building or part of a building	• Intentional or reckless trespass
• As a trespasser	• *Mens rea* of the ulterior offence
• *Actus reus* of the ulterior offence (theft or inflicting GBH or attempted theft or attempted GBH)	

under s.9(1)(b) is the entry of a building or part of a building as a trespasser. The *mens rea* elements are an intention to enter and intentional or reckless trespass. Burglary under s.9(1)(b) also requires the commission of an ulterior offence: theft, inflicting grievous bodily harm, or an attempt to do one of these (table 10.2).

THINKING POINT

Comment upon the scope of the offences of burglary under s.9(1) of the Theft Act 1968. Do you think that the offences are too widely or too narrowly drafted, or neither?

Consider the impact of the scope of the offences on the promotion of fair labelling.

All of the elements of the ulterior offence must be proved. If one of the elements is missing, any prosecution for burglary under s.9(1)(b) will fail. In respect of the infliction of grievous bodily harm, the prosecution must prove the offence under s.20 of the Offences Against the Person Act 1861. The defendant must be a trespasser on entry, but under s.9(1)(b), no intention to commit an ulterior offence is required on entry. It is enough that the defendant actually commits the full offence of theft of grievous bodily harm, or attempts to, once in the building (figure 10.2).

THINKING POINT

Consider whether D may be guilty of burglary under s.9(1)(a) or s.9(1)(b) of the Theft Act 1968 in the following scenarios:

(1) While climbing through the window of a house in order to beat up the occupier, D is caught with one leg on the inner windowsill and one leg outside.

(2) D visits a public house and hides in the toilets until closing time. After the landlord has gone to bed, D helps himself to drinks at the bar.

(3) While walking along the canal, D sees a barge with an open window. After checking that no one is home, D sticks his arm through the window to see if there is anything worth stealing.

(4) D, a plumber, is given permission to enter V's house in order to fix a leak. D enters the house intending to steal from V.

Figure 10.2 Flowchart on liability for burglary

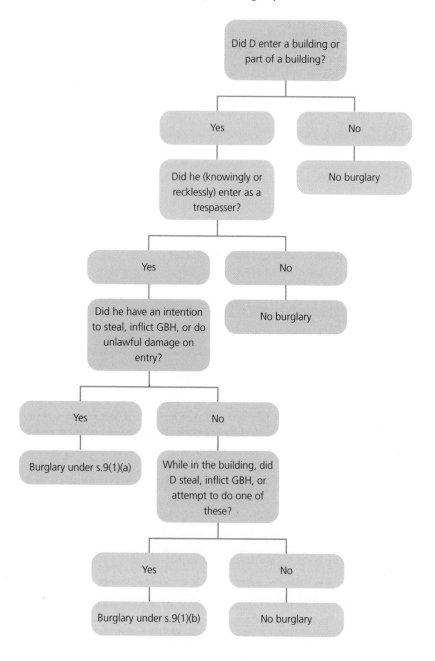

10.3 Aggravated burglary

The offence of aggravated burglary is found under s.10(1) of the Theft Act 1968. It is an indictable only offence which carries a maximum sentence of life imprisonment: s.10(2).

STATUTE

Section 10(1), Theft Act 1968

A person is guilty of aggravated burglary if he commits any burglary and at the time has with him any firearm or imitation firearm, any weapon of offence, or any explosive; and for this purpose—

(a) 'firearm' includes an airgun or air pistol, and 'imitation firearm' means anything which has the appearance of being a firearm, whether capable of being discharged or not; and

(b) 'weapon of offence' means any article made or adapted for use for causing injury to or incapacitating a person, or intended by the person having it with him for such use; and

(c) 'explosive' means any article manufactured for the purpose of producing a practical effect by explosion, or intended by the person having it with him for that purpose.

This offence requires proof of the elements of burglary under s.9(1)(a) or s.9(1)(b) (both the *actus reus* and the *mens rea*) and that at the time of the burglary the defendant was in possession of one of the objects listed in s.10(1) (see figure 10.3).

10.3.1 'At the time'

The defendant must have the weapon with him 'at the time' of the burglary. The crucial time at which the defendant must have the weapon with him is dependent upon which offence of burglary is proved. If burglary has been committed under s.9(1)(a), the defendant must have the weapon with him at the time of entry. If burglary has been committed under s.9(1)(b), the defendant must have the weapon with him when he commits the ulterior offence (i.e., at the time of the dishonest appropriation if he steals or at the moment he inflicts grievous bodily harm or when he takes steps which are more than merely preparatory to the commission of the full offence). In the case of *Francis* [1982] Crim LR 363, the defendants had gained entry to a house armed with sticks. They then discarded the sticks and stole property from the house. The Court of Appeal quashed their convictions for aggravated burglary. The Court held that unless they intended to steal when they entered the house (which the prosecution had not proved), they were only guilty of aggravated burglary if they had a weapon with them at the moment when they stole. In the case of *O'Leary* (1986) 82 Cr App R 341, the defendant entered the

Figure 10.3 Elements of aggravated burglary

house as a trespasser. He took a knife from the kitchen, went upstairs, and used it to confront the occupiers, demanding cash and jewellery. He was convicted of aggravated burglary under s.10(1) of the Theft Act 1968 because, at the time of committing the burglary under s.9(1)(b), he had with him a weapon of offence. In this case, it was not necessary to prove that the defendant had the weapon with him at the time of entry.

10.3.2 Firearm, weapon of offence, or explosive

These weapons are further defined within s.10(1) of the Theft Act 1968. Section 10(1) covers imitation firearms as well as firearms. An explosive is defined as any article which has been manufactured for the purpose of producing an explosion, or an article which is intended for that purpose. A 'weapon of offence' means any article which is made for causing injury or incapacitating a person, or adapted for use for causing injury to or incapacitating a person, or intended by the person having it with him for such use. An article made for injuring or incapacitating a person might include a knuckleduster, a flick knife, or handcuffs. An article adapted for such use might include a baseball bat which has had a nail put through it or a bottle which had been broken in order to injure. There is a wide interpretation on the types of articles intended for such use and might include a screwdriver, a razor blade, or sleeping pills.

Where it is alleged that the defendant has with him an article intended for causing injury to or incapacitating a person, it must be proved that he intended to use the article for that purpose at the time of the actual theft.

 CASE CLOSE-UP

Kelly (1993) 97 Cr App R 245

The defendant in the case of *Kelly* used a screwdriver to break into a house. He was disturbed during the burglary while holding the screwdriver. The Court of Appeal held that he was guilty of aggravated burglary because it had been proved that the defendant had used the screwdriver at the time of the theft with the requisite intent, namely the intention to injure if the need arose.

10.3.3 Knowledge

The defendant must know that he has the weapon with him. However, there is no need to prove that the defendant intended to use the weapon to cause injury during the burglary. The defendant in the case of *Stones* [1989] 1 WLR 156 was found in possession of a knife which he claimed he carried for self-defence. He was convicted of aggravated burglary, as any intention not to use the knife was irrelevant.

10.4 Blackmail

Blackmail is a statutory offence found under s.21(1) of the Theft Act 1968. It is an indictable only offence which carries a maximum sentence of 14 years' imprisonment: s.21(3).

STATUTE

Section 21(1), Theft Act 1968

A person is guilty of blackmail if, with a view to gain for himself or another or with intent to cause loss to another, he makes any unwarranted demand with menaces; and for this purpose a demand with menaces is unwarranted unless the person making it does so in the belief—

(a) that he has reasonable grounds for making the demand; and

(b) that the use of the menaces is a proper means of reinforcing the demand.

The *actus reus* of blackmail involves making a demand with menaces. The *mens rea* requires an intention to make a demand with menaces, the demand must be unwarranted and it must be made with a view to gain for himself or another or with intent to cause loss to another.

10.4.1 *Actus reus*

10.4.1.1 **A demand**

A demand may be made in writing, orally, or by conduct. In *Collister and Warhurst* (1955) 39 Cr App R 100, the Court of Appeal held that the demand may be express or implied. The Court approved the direction given to the jury by Pilcher J, who stated that it would be sufficient to prove that, 'the demeanour of the accused and the circumstances of the case were such that an ordinary reasonable man would understand that a demand...was being made upon him...'. It does not matter what is demanded. Section 21(2) of the Theft Act 1968 states: 'The nature of the act or omission demanded is immaterial, and it is also immaterial whether the menaces relate to action to be taken by the person making the demand.' However, the demand must be made with a view to gain or intent to cause loss (this *mens rea* element will be discussed further at 10.4.2.2).

The House of Lords held in *Treacy v DPP* [1971] AC 537 that the demand need not actually be communicated to the victim. Where the demand is contained within a letter it is made when posted. The demand does not need to reach the victim.

CASE CLOSE-UP

Treacy v DPP [1971] AC 537

In the case of *Treacy v DPP*, the defendant's conviction for blackmail was upheld (by a 3:2 majority in the House of Lords) when he posted a letter in England which was addressed to a woman in Germany. The demand was held to have been made in England when the letter was posted. In the Court of Appeal, John Stephenson J summarised the position in respect of oral and written demands:

> When the demand is made by word of mouth it is usually made at one time and place. If the intended victim is too deaf to hear it or unable to understand it, it is nonetheless made. Or a demand may be made orally over the telephone. In that case it is made and received simultaneously and it may be right to regard it as made at one time but in two

> places…When the demand is made in writing…it will usually be made at one time and place and received at another time and place. If the intended victim is blind or illiterate, the demand is nonetheless made…not when it reaches the victim but when it leaves the demander beyond recall on its way to the intended victim whom it will reach in the ordinary course of things.
>
> Lord Diplock in the House of Lords stated that the issue could be resolved by asking the question, 'Are the circumstances of this case such as would prompt a man in ordinary conversation to say: "I have made a demand"?' The majority in the House of Lords held that the Court of Appeal rightly decided that the demand need not be communicated.

This principle could also be applied to more modern modes of communication, such as email, text messaging, or social networking websites such as Facebook. A demand would be made when sent via email or text message. The email or text message would not need to be read or received by the victim, as it does not need to be communicated. However, the position could be slightly different with regards to social networking websites such as Facebook, as a message which is posted on a person's profile page can be deleted by the person posting it. As such, it is not 'beyond recall on its way to the intended victim whom it will reach in the ordinary course of things' and, thus, may only amount to a demand when communicated to the victim. However, this issue has not yet arisen before the courts.

10.4.1.2 With menaces

The demand must be accompanied by menaces. In the case of *Thorne v Motor Trade Association* [1937] AC 797, Lord Wright in the House of Lords stated that 'the word "menace" is to be liberally construed and not…limited to threats of violence but…including threats of any action detrimental to or unpleasant to the person addressed'. His Lordship also held that it may include a warning that in certain events such action is intended. Menaces is 'an ordinary English word', so a trial judge will not usually be required to give the jury any further direction as to its meaning: *Lawrence & Pomroy* (1971) 57 Cr App R 64. Jurors will be expected to use their common sense and knowledge of the world in deciding whether a demand had been made with menaces.

In *Collister and Warhurst*, it was stated that menaces might be 'not perhaps direct, but veiled menaces—so that [the victim's] ordinary balance of mind was upset…' In *Clear* [1968] 1 QB 670, the Court of Appeal held that menaces would be 'threats or conduct of such a nature and extent that the mind of an ordinary person of normal stability and courage might be influenced or made apprehensive so as to accede unwillingly to the demand'. It does not matter that the person to whom the threat is made is not actually afraid.

A threat must be more than trivial. The case of *Harry* [1974] Crim LR 32 involved a student organisation, Rag, which was raising money for charity. The treasurer of the Rag committee sent letters to 115 shopkeepers, offering to exclude them from any 'inconvenience' that might be caused by their activities. The defendant was charged with blackmail, but only a few of the shopkeepers had complained. Applying the case of *Clear*, the trial judge ruled that this was not a menace because the threat was not 'of such a nature and extent that the mind of an ordinary person of normal stability and courage might be influenced or made apprehensive so as to accede unwillingly to the demand'. The majority of shopkeepers had

not complained about the letters, showing that they were not influenced or made apprehensive by them.

As already mentioned, *Lawrence and Pomroy* confirms that jurors will usually require no
direction as to the meaning of menaces. However, in the case of *Garwood* [1987] 1 WLR
319, the Court of Appeal held that further direction might be necessary where the threats
would not have affected the mind of a person of normal stability but did, in fact, affect
the mind of the victim. The jury should be directed that this could amount to menaces,
provided that the defendant was aware of the likely effect of his actions on the victim.
Hence, where the threats might have affected an ordinary person of normal stability but
did not affect the victim, the threats are clearly menaces. Where the threats affected
the victim but would not affect a person of normal stability, the threats are menaces
if the defendant was aware of the likely effect (i.e., if the defendant was aware of the
victim's timidity).

10.4.2 *Mens rea*

The *mens rea* of blackmail includes an intention to make a demand with menaces, the demand
must be unwarranted and it must be made with a view to gain for himself or another or with
intent to cause loss to another. An intention to make a demand with menaces is relatively
self-explanatory. The latter two elements will be considered below.

10.4.2.1 **Unwarranted demand**

Any demand is unwarranted unless s.21(1)(a) and (b) of the Theft Act 1968 applies. Under
s.21(1), any demand with menaces is unwarranted, unless the person making it does so in
the belief that: *(a)* he has reasonable grounds for making the demand; and *(b)* the use of the
menaces is a proper means of reinforcing the demand. Whether or not a demand is unwarranted is based upon the defendant's belief and, thus, is subjectively assessed. Section 21(1)(a)
includes an objective element as the defendant must believe that he has reasonable grounds
for making the demand. Section 21(1)(b) requires that the defendant believes that the menaces are a proper means of enforcing the demand.

The case of *Harvey, Uylett and Plummer* (1980) 72 Cr App R 139 narrowed the scope of this
definition. The defendants paid £20,000 to the victim, who promised to supply them with cannabis. The victim had no intention of supplying the cannabis and kept the money. When the
defendants realised that he had done so, they threatened to maim, rape, and kill the defendant's wife and child unless the money was repaid. They kidnapped the victim's wife and child.
The defendants were convicted of blackmail under s.21(1) of the Theft Act 1968. They claimed
that their demand for repayment was warranted due to an honest belief that there were reasonable grounds for making the demand, namely the money owed to them which had not
been paid. However, the Court of Appeal held that the means used to make the demand were
clearly not proper. It could not be proper to threaten to do something known to be unlawful
or morally wrong.

10.4.2.2 **With a view to gain or intent to cause loss**

The offence of blackmail protects economic interests and, thus, also requires the defendant
to make the unwarranted demand with menaces with a view to gain for himself or another
or with intent to cause loss to another. The terms 'gain' and 'loss' are further defined under
s.34(2)(a) of the Theft Act 1968.

STATUTE

Section 34(2), Theft Act 1968

For purposes of this Act—

(a) 'gain' and 'loss' are to be construed as extending only to gain or loss in money or other property, but as extending to any such gain or loss whether temporary or permanent; and—

(i) 'gain' includes a gain by keeping what one has, as well as a gain by getting what one has not; and

(ii) 'loss' includes a loss by not getting what one might get, as well as a loss by parting with what one has.

THINKING POINT

To what extent is the element 'with a view to gain for himself or another or with intent to cause loss to another' widely construed under the Theft Act 1968?

Consider this question again in light of the case law mentioned later in the chapter.

The view to gain or to cause loss extends only to money or other property, so where the defendant threatens to reveal that the victim is a drug addict unless she sleeps with him, the defendant is not guilty of blackmail. However, property is widely construed. In the case of *Bevans* (1988) 87 Cr App R 64, the Court of Appeal held that there was a 'view to gain' where the defendant, at gunpoint, demanded that a doctor give him an injection of morphine to relieve his pain. The morphine amounted to the property that the defendant had a view to gain. The defendant's motive in getting the morphine, i.e., the relief of pain, was irrelevant. Under s.34(2)(a), the gain or loss may be temporary or permanent. The defendant in the case of *Parkes* [1973] Crim LR 358 demanded money owed to him by the victim. The trial judge held that 'gain' includes gaining money which is owed to the defendant through a lawful debt. The defendant intended to obtain hard cash from the victim rather than a mere thing in action (a debt in this case). This was sufficient for the offence of blackmail as 'gain' includes 'getting what one has not'. At that point in time, the defendant had a mere right of action, so by seeking cash from the victim, he was getting more than he had.

THINKING POINT

Consider whether Susan has committed the offence of blackmail under s.21(1) of the Theft Act 1968 in the following scenarios:

(1) Susan threatens James that she will reveal to their employer that James is an alcoholic unless he has sex with her.

(2) Susan posts a message on William's profile page on a social networking site saying, 'Give me the money you owe me or I'll send Derek round to deal with you'. Susan then deletes the message before William reads it.

> **(3)** Susan sends Matt a text message which reads, 'I'll tell your wife about our affair unless you give me £1,000.'
>
> **(4)** On 31 October, Susan knocks on her neighbours' front doors and says 'Trick or treat?'

10.5 Handling stolen goods

The offence of handling stolen goods is found under s.22(1) of the Theft Act 1968. It is an either way offence which carries a maximum sentence of 14 years' imprisonment upon conviction on indictment: s.22(2).

 STATUTE

Section 22(1), Theft Act 1968

A person handles stolen goods if (otherwise than in the course of the stealing) knowing or believing them to be stolen goods he dishonestly receives the goods, or dishonestly undertakes or assists in their retention, removal, disposal or realisation by or for the benefit of another person, or if he arranges to do so.

The *actus reus* of the offence requires the defendant to receive, undertake, assist, or arrange for the retention, removal, disposal, or realisation of goods which are stolen by or for the benefit of another person. The handling must occur otherwise than in the course of stealing. The *mens rea* of the offence requires proof of dishonesty and the defendant must know or believe the goods to be stolen.

10.5.1 *Actus reus*

The *actus reus* of the offence is extremely wide and encompasses most acts which a defendant might commit after the theft. It includes activities such as keeping, storing, hiding, selling, transporting, destroying, or receiving stolen goods after the theft. The goods must be stolen at the time of the act of handling. The handling must occur otherwise than in the course of stealing. Thus, the theft must be complete prior to the act of handling. It is sometimes difficult to determine where the theft ends and the handling begins. In the case of *Pitham and Hehl* (1976) 65 Cr App R 45, the Court of Appeal held that the theft is complete at the moment of appropriation, which is an instantaneous act. However, this approach conflicts with the case of *Atakpu* [1994] QB 69, in which appropriation was deemed to be a continuing act.

The word 'goods' is defined under s.34(2)(b) of the Theft Act 1968 so as to include 'money and every other description of property except land, and includes things severed from the land by stealing'. This definition is similar to that given for property under s.4(1) of the Theft Act 1968. There is a further definition of 'stolen goods' under s.24(2), which extends the definition to parts of the original goods as well as any proceeds of sale. Thus, where the original stolen goods have been sold, a defendant may be guilty of handling the proceeds of that sale, provided the *mens rea* of the offence is proven.

10.5.2 *Mens rea*

▶ CROSS REFERENCE

Refer to 9.2.1 for further discussion of the definitions of dishonesty in theft.

The *mens rea* of the offence requires the prosecution to prove that the defendant was dishonest and that he knew or believed the goods to be stolen. The partial, negative definition of dishonesty under s.2(1) of the Theft Act 1968 applies, as does the positive definition under *Ghosh* [1982] QB 1053.

The requirement that the defendant knew or believed the goods to be stolen is a subjective one. Thus, it is irrelevant whether or not a reasonable person would have known or believed the goods to be stolen. What is important is whether the defendant himself had that knowledge or belief. Belief is a less culpable state of mind than knowledge, but is more culpable than mere suspicion (see *Moys* (1984) 79 Cr App R 72). Belief has been defined by the Court of Appeal in *Hall* (1985) 81 Cr App R 260 as:

> something short of knowledge. It may be said to be the state of mind of a person who says to himself: 'I cannot say I know for certain that these goods are stolen, but there can be no other reasonable conclusion in the light of all the circumstances, in the light of all that I have heard and seen' (*per* Boreham J).

10.5.3 **Proving the *mens rea***

Section 27(3) of the Theft Act 1968 provides the prosecution with some assistance in proving the *mens rea* of the offence of handling stolen goods. Under s.27(3)(a), evidence that the defendant has handled stolen goods within the last 12 months may be adduced in court in support of the prosecution's case that the defendant knew or believed the goods to be stolen. This does not require evidence of a conviction for handling stolen goods. Under s.27(3)(b), evidence that the defendant has been convicted of theft or handling stolen goods within the past 5 years may also be adduced in court for the same reason.

10.6 Criminal damage

There are two offences of destroying or damaging property under the Criminal Damage Act 1971. Simple criminal damage falls under s.1(1) of the Act, an aggravated form of the offence is provided for under s.1(2). If either of these two offences of criminal damage is committed by fire (i.e., arson), it is charged under the relevant section for the offence (i.e., s.1(1) or (2), depending upon whether simple or aggravated criminal damage has been committed) and s.1(3) of the Criminal Damage Act 1971.

10.6.1 **Simple criminal damage**

The simple form of the offence of criminal damage under s.1(1) of the Criminal Damage Act 1971 is triable either way. It carries a maximum sentence of 10 years' imprisonment if tried in the Crown court, according to s.4(2) of the Criminal Damage Act 1971.

Table 10.3 Elements of criminal damage under s.1(1), CDA 1971

Actus reus	Mens rea
• Destroys or damages	• Intention or recklessness as to destroying or damaging such property
• Property	
• Belonging to another	
• Without lawful excuse	

 STATUTE

Section 1(1), Criminal Damage Act 1971

A person who without lawful excuse destroys or damages any property belonging to another intending to destroy or damage any such property or being reckless as to whether any such property would be destroyed or damaged shall be guilty of an offence.

The *actus reus* elements of the offence are that property belonging to another is destroyed or damaged without lawful excuse. The *mens rea* is intention to destroy or damage property or being reckless as to whether or not property is destroyed or damaged (table 10.3).

10.6.1.1 Destroy or damage

The defendant must destroy or damage property. The damage need not be permanent. It has been held that trampling down grass amounts to damage. The respondent in *Gayford v Chouler* [1898] 1 QB 316 trespassed onto a field of knee-deep grass and walked across it, causing damage to the value of 6d. The Divisional Court held that actual damage had been done to the grass. However, the damage to property must be more than merely trivial or nominal. In *A (a juvenile) v R* [1978] Crim LR 689, the appellant's conviction for criminal damage was quashed in the Crown court. The appellant spat on a police officer's raincoat. There was a faint mark in the general area where the spittle was alleged to have landed. This was held not to be sufficient damage as the spittle could probably have been wiped away with a damp cloth, leaving no mark. The coat had not been rendered imperfect or inoperable. This case involved a garment designed to be waterproof. Perhaps the decision would have been different if the material of the garment was such that it might have been stained or marked.

The Divisional Court has held that what constitutes damage is a matter of fact and degree. In *Roe v Kingerlee* [1986] Crim LR 735, the defendant smeared mud graffiti onto the walls of a police cell. The cost of cleaning the walls was £7. The Divisional Court held that this could amount to criminal damage and that the magistrates were wrong at first instance to state that it could not amount to damage as a matter of law. Whether or not this would amount to criminal damage is a question of fact to be determined by the tribunal of fact (the magistrates or jury, depending upon the court of trial). The tribunal of fact will consider the degree of the graffiti. Similarly, in *Hardman v Chief Constable of Avon & Somerset* [1986] Crim LR 330, the defendants were held to be guilty of criminal damage where they had painted human silhouettes on the pavement in water-soluble paint. This was held to amount to damage even though it could be washed away, because it had caused expense and inconvenience to the local authority. The court approved of the approach of Walters J in *Samuels v Stubbs* (1972) 4 SASR 200, a case in which a police officer's cap which had been stamped on was held to have been damaged, even though it could be pushed back into shape:

> It seems to me that it is difficult to lay down any very general and, at the same time, precise and absolute rule as to what constitutes 'damage'. One must be guided in a great degree by the circumstances of each case, the nature of the article, and the mode in which it is affected or treated. Moreover, the meaning of the word 'damage' must . . . be controlled by its context. The word may be used in the sense of 'mischief done to property'.

The facts of the cases of *Lloyd v DPP* [1992] RTR 215 and *Mitchell* [2003] EWCA Crim 2188 are similar. Both defendants damaged clamps which had been placed on their cars, which were illegally parked. The defendants were both convicted of criminal damage.

Erasing or altering computer programs or data on computer discs has in the past also been held to constitute damage for the purposes of the Criminal Damage Act 1971. The defendant in *Cox v Riley* (1986) 83 Cr App R 54 was an employee who deliberately erased a computer program from a printed circuit card at his workplace. The programs on the card operated a computerised saw when the card was inserted into the saw. The saw was rendered inoperable due to the defendant having erased the programs and he was convicted of criminal damage of the circuit card under s.1(1) of the Criminal Damage Act 1971. The Divisional Court held that this could amount to damage. The card was tangible property within the meaning of s.10(1) of the Criminal Damage Act 1971, and the damage to it put the saw out of operation such that time, labour, and money had to be spent on restoring the relevant programs.

In the case of *Whiteley* (1991) 93 Cr App R 25, the defendant was a computer hacker who gained unauthorised access to a computer network. He altered data on discs within the system and caused computers in the network to fail. He was convicted of criminal damage under s.1(1) of the Criminal Damage Act 1971, on the basis that he had altered the state of the magnetic particles on the discs containing information, so as to delete and add files. Although the discs themselves had not been physically damaged, once the magnetic particles containing information were written onto the disc, they formed part of the disc. The discs and the particles being one entity were therefore capable of being damaged. The defendant's conviction was upheld in the Court of Appeal. Lord Lane CJ stated that, 'What the Act requires to be proved is that tangible property has been damaged, not necessarily that the damage itself should be tangible.' The Court held that there would be damage where the particles had been altered 'in such a way as to cause an impairment of the value or usefulness of the disc to the owner'. Lord Lane CJ continued, 'The fact that the alteration could only be perceived by operating the computer did not make the alterations any the less real, or the damage, if the alteration amounted to damage, any the less within the ambit of the Act.'

Cases such as these would today be prosecuted under s.3(1) of the Computer Misuse Act 1990 (as amended by s.36 of the Police and Justice Act 2006). This section provides for the offence of unauthorised acts with intent to impair, or with recklessness as to impairing, the operation of the computer and would cover erasing or altering computer programs or infecting programs with a virus.

The principle that property is damaged if its value or usefulness is impaired also applies to other types of property. The case of *Morphitis v Salmon* [1990] Crim LR 48 involved damage to a scaffold bar. The appellant removed the scaffold bar and clip from an upright. He was charged with damaging the scaffold bar by scratching it. However, the Divisional Court quashed his conviction for two reasons. First, it had not been proved that the appellant had scratched the bar. Secondly, even if he had, there was no impairment of the value or usefulness of the bar as scratching was a usual incident of scaffolding components. It was suggested by the Court that a charge of criminal damage to the whole barrier would have succeeded. In his commentary of the case in the *Criminal Law Review*, Professor Smith argued that a structure of a machine could be damaged by the removal, however carefully, of one of its parts. This approach is in line with that in the case of *Fisher* (1865) LR 1 CCR 7. Professor Smith states that, 'If a malicious person were to remove the doors from my house, I should certainly consider that the house had been damaged even if the removal had been effected with the greatest possible care and the doors, hinges and screws were left in perfect condition. The parts had not been damaged, but the house as a whole had.'

The case of *Fiak* [2005] EWCA Crim 2381 provides a more recent example of the application of the principle that an impairment of value or usefulness of property constitutes damage. The defendant in this case had been arrested, taken to the police station, and placed in a cell. He had been provided with a blanket which he placed down the lavatory in his cell, before flushing the lavatory repeatedly, flooding his own cell, two adjoining cells, and a passageway. The blanket was wet, but the water was clean, so the blanket was not soiled. However, the blanket was rendered unusable as it had to be cleaned and dried, and the cells had to be cleaned by a contract cleaner before they could be used. The defendant's appeal against his conviction for criminal damage was dismissed. Sir Igor Judge (later the Lord Chief Justice) took the view that there was a case to answer against the defendant:

> while it is true that the effect of the appellant's actions in relation to the blanket and the cell were both remediable, the simple reality is that the blanket could not be used as a blanket by any other prisoner until it had been dried out (and, we believe, also cleaned) and the flooded cells remained out of action until the water was cleared. In our judgment it is clear that both sustained damage for the purposes of the 1971 Act.

 THINKING POINT

Do any of the following amount to damage for the purposes of the Criminal Damage Act 1971?

(1) Andy paints a small graffiti tag on the side of Brian's house in washable paint.

(2) Carlos spills water over Denise's cashmere scarf.

(3) Eric uses ingredients in his mother's kitchen to bake a cake.

(4) Francis removes the plug from her boyfriend's games console.

(5) Gareth deletes Helen's criminal law lecture notes from her USB stick.

10.6.1.2 Property

Section 10(1) of the Criminal Damage Act 1971 defines property which may be damaged.

STATUTE

Section 10(1), Criminal Damage Act 1971

In this Act 'property' means property of a tangible nature, whether real or personal, including money...

CROSS REFERENCE
Refer to 9.1.2 and 9.1.2.6 for a more detailed discussion of the meaning of property under the Theft Act 1968.

This definition shares similarities to the definition of property under the Theft Act 1968, but there are significant differences between the two definitions. For instance, the definition of property under the Criminal Damage Act 1971 only applies to tangible property and so is narrower than that under the Theft Act 1968. While the Theft Act 1968 applies to intangible property, the Criminal Damage Act 1971 does not. So a thing in action such as a credit in a bank account can be stolen but cannot be damaged. However, in relation to land, the scope of property which can be damaged is wider than that which can be stolen. Land is property for the purposes of criminal damage, but the exceptions which apply under s.4(2) of the Theft Act 1968 to the theft of land do not apply to the Criminal Damage Act 1971. So, where land can always be damaged, it may not always be stolen. Lastly, the Criminal Damage Act 1971 expressly excludes as property mushrooms growing wild on any land or flowers, fruit, or foliage of a plant growing wild on any land. Such property may not be damaged, but may be stolen (see s.4(3) of the Theft Act 1968) (see table 10.4).

10.6.1.3 **Belonging to another**

A person cannot be guilty of criminal damage of their own property. You are perfectly entitled to destroy your mobile phone or to knock down your garden shed without liability for simple criminal damage. However, if the property also belongs to another, you will be guilty of criminal damage. The prosecution must prove that the defendant destroyed or damaged property belonging to another as defined under s.10(2) of the Criminal Damage Act 1971.

Under s.10(2), property belongs to another if somebody else has custody or control of the property you own, or they have a proprietary right or interest in it, or a charge on it. Thus, if the property falls under any of these categories, you will be guilty of criminal damage if you destroy that property.

Table 10.4 Table comparing meaning of property in criminal damage and theft

Property under the Criminal Damage Act 1971	Property under the Theft Act 1968
Applies to tangible property	Applies to tangible property
Excludes intangible property and things in action	Applies to intangible property and things in action
Applies to land	Applies to land but note the exceptions under s.4(2), Theft Act 1968
Excludes mushrooms growing wild on any land or flowers, fruit, or foliage of a plant growing wild on any land	Includes mushrooms growing wild on any land or flowers, fruit, or foliage of a plant growing wild on any land (see s.4(3), Theft Act 1968)

The meaning of belonging to another under s.10(2) of the Criminal Damage Act 1971 is also similar to that under the Theft Act 1968, albeit slightly different terminology is used. While the Theft Act 1968 provides that property belongs to a person having 'possession' of it, the Criminal Damage Act 1971 uses the word 'custody' instead. Both Acts provide that property belongs to a person having control of property or a proprietary right or interest in it. Under s.10(3) of the Criminal Damage Act 1971, property under a trust belongs to any person having a right to enforce the trust. Under s.10(4) of the Act, property of a corporation solely belongs to the corporation even though there may be a vacancy in the corporation.

10.6.1.4 **Without lawful excuse**

The offence of criminal damage is not committed where the defendant had lawful excuse for destroying or damaging the property. The prosecution must prove that the defendant did not have lawful excuse for the destruction or damage. Depending upon the offence charged, lawful excuse may come from a general defence or from within the statute. Section 5(2) of the Criminal Damage Act 1971 sets out the instances in which a person will be deemed to have lawful excuse for the damage or destruction. This section applies to the offence of simple criminal damage under s.1(1) of the Criminal Damage Act 1971, but does not apply to the aggravated form of the offence under s.1(2) of the Act.

Under s.5(2)(a), a person will have lawful excuse if he honestly believed that he had the consent of the owner of the property or that he would have had the consent of that person to destroy or damage the property, had he known of the circumstances.

Section 5(2)(a) is similar to s.2(1)(b) of the Theft Act 1968 and is subjectively assessed. It is immaterial whether that belief is justified or not, as long as it is honestly held: s.5(3). Consequently, a person who harbours a mistaken belief may avail themselves of the defence of lawful excuse, provided their mistake is an honest one. The reasonableness of the defendant's belief is not relevant. In the case of *Denton* [1982] 1 All ER 65, the defendant was an employee who set fire to his work premises in the belief that his employer had asked him to burn the property down in order to make a fraudulent insurance claim. He successfully appealed against his conviction for arson under s.1(1) and s.1(3) of the Criminal Damage Act 1971, arguing that he had lawful excuse under s.5(2)(a).

It has also been held that a belief induced by voluntary intoxication may be sufficient. In *Jaggard v Dickinson* [1981] QB 527, the defendant had been staying with a friend who gave her permission to treat the house as her own. The defendant returned drunk one evening and broke a window of what she thought was her friend's house in order to gain entry. The defendant appealed against her conviction for criminal damage. The Divisional Court held that she could rely upon the defence of lawful consent under s.5(2)(a) as she honestly believed that her friend would have consented. Thus, an honest mistake is sufficient for the defence of lawful excuse, even if that mistake was not justified or was made due to voluntary intoxication.

Under s.5(2)(b), a defendant will have lawful excuse if he acted in order to protect property in the honest belief it was in immediate need of protection and that the means of protection adopted were or would be reasonable having regard to all the circumstances.

Although the defendant's belief must be honest, there is an objective element to this section, in that the means of protection adopted must be reasonable in the circumstances. In the case of *Hunt* (1978) 66 Cr App R 105, the defendant set fire to a guest room in an old people's home. He claimed that he did it in order to draw attention to the defective fire alarm system. He was convicted of arson under s.1(1) and (3) of the Criminal Damages Act 1971 and appealed, arguing that the defence of lawful excuse under s.5(2)(b) should be available to him. The Court of Appeal applied an objective test to 'in order to protect property' under s.5(2)(b). Roskill LJ held that the defendant's act 'was not done in order to protect property; it was done in order to draw attention to the defective state of the fire alarm. It was not an act which in itself did protect or was capable of protecting the property.'

🔍 CASE CLOSE-UP

Hill; Hall [1989] Crim LR 136

The Court of Appeal confirmed the decision in *Hunt* in the case of *Hill; Hall*. This case involved two defendants who had been convicted of possession of an article with intent to damage property under s.3 of the Criminal Damage Act 1971. Hill had been in possession of a hacksaw blade, intending to use it to cut the fence at a US military base in order to enter the site and protest against the presence of US nuclear weapons in the UK. The defendants relied upon the defence of lawful excuse under s.5(2)(b), in that they were acting in order to protect the property of those living nearby, whose houses would be destroyed in the event of an attack. The Court of Appeal held that the trial judge must ask himself:

(i) did the defendant honestly believe that he was protecting property (the subjective test);

(ii) on the facts as the defendant believed them to be, could the act amount to something done to protect property (the objective test)?

The Court of Appeal rejected the defence of lawful excuse because the proposed act of demonstration was too remote from the threat of harm and the proposed aim. Additionally, there was no evidence to justify the defendant's belief that there was need to protect from immediate danger.

This test was applied in *Blake v DPP* (1992) 93 Cr App R 169. The defendant in this case was a vicar who, in protest against the use of military force by the US and UK in Iraq and Kuwait, wrote a Biblical quotation on a concrete pillar outside the Houses of Parliament. He appealed against his conviction, arguing that he had lawful excuse because he believed that he had God's consent to write on the pillar. The Divisional Court held that the defence of lawful excuse could not apply. The defendant could not rely on s.5(2)(a) because an honest belief in God's consent is not sufficient. Neither could the defendant rely on s.5(2)(b) because the defendant's act was not capable of protecting property in Iraq and Kuwait as it was too remote.

In order to rely on lawful excuse under s.5(2)(b), the defendant must believe that the property in question is in immediate need of protection. There was no such belief in the case of *Johnson v DPP* [1994] Crim LR 673, in which the defendant changed the locks on the doors of a house he was squatting in. He argued that he had done this in order to protect his property under s.5(2)(b). The Divisional Court rejected this and held that the damage had not been done in order to protect property (the objective test), and even if it had been, the defendant had no belief that the property was in immediate need of protection (the subjective test). A belief in an unspecified danger at some point in the future was not sufficient.

The defendant in *Kelleher* [2003] EWCA Crim 3525 went into an art gallery and knocked the head off a statue of Lady Thatcher. His act caused damage to the value of £150,000. He appealed against his conviction for criminal damage, arguing that his actions were a political protest against globalisation. He believed that Margaret Thatcher's policies had made the world a dangerous place to live in and would lead to the destruction of the planet. He claimed that his actions were motivated by fears about his baby son's future. The Court of Appeal held that there was no lawful excuse for his conduct and that s.5(2)(b) of the Criminal Damage Act 1971 was not applicable. The defendant did not act in order to protect property belonging to another, he had acted in order to gain publicity for his views.

10.6.1.5 *Mens rea*

In order to secure a conviction for criminal damage under s.1(1) of the Criminal Damage Act 1971, the prosecution must also prove the *mens rea* of the offence. The prosecution must show either that the defendant intended to destroy or damage such property or that he was reckless as to whether the property would be destroyed or damaged.

Intention carries its ordinary meaning. Even where the defendant intends to destroy or damage property, he has a defence if he mistakenly but honestly believes that he is damaging his own property. In *Smith* [1974] QB 354, the defendant had fixed panels to the walls of his flat during his tenancy. When he did so, the panels became the property of the landlord under civil law. At the end of his tenancy, he took down the panels and destroyed them. His conviction for criminal damage under s.1(1) of the Criminal Damage Act 1971 was quashed because his mistaken belief that the panels belonged to him negated his intention. Although he intended to destroy the property, he honestly believed that the panels belonged to him. His mistake as to the civil law was a valid defence to the *mens rea*.

Where there is no intention to damage property, a prosecution may be brought on the basis of recklessness. A defendant will be guilty of criminal damage under s.1(1) of the Act where he was reckless as to whether or not property would be damaged or destroyed by his act. The House of Lords has held that a subjective test of recklessness applies. In *R v G and another* [2003] UKHL 50, the House overruled its previous decision of *MPC v Caldwell* [1982] All ER 341 and adopted the definition of recklessness set out in clause 18 of the Draft Criminal Code 1989:

> A person acts 'recklessly' within the meaning of section 1 of the Criminal Damage Act 1971 with respect to—
>
> (I)   a circumstance when he is aware of a risk that exists or will exist;
>
> (II) a result when he is aware of a risk that it will occur;
>
> and it is, in the circumstances known to him, unreasonable to take the risk.

❯ CROSS REFERENCE

Refer to 3.4 for a more detailed discussion on the case of *R v G and another* [2003] UKHL 50 and the development of the law on recklessness in relation to criminal damage.

10.6.2 **Aggravated criminal damage**

The aggravated form of the offence of criminal damage under s.1(2) of the Criminal Damage Act 1971 is indictable only. It carries a maximum sentence of life imprisonment under s.4(1) of the Criminal Damage Act 1971.

STATUTE

Section 1(2), Criminal Damage Act 1971

A person who without lawful excuse destroys or damages any property, whether belonging to himself or another—

(a) intending to destroy or damage any property or being reckless as to whether any property would be destroyed or damaged; and

(b) intending by the destruction or damage to endanger the life of another or being reckless as to whether the life of another would be thereby endangered;shall be guilty of an offence.

Table 10.5 Elements of aggravated criminal damage under s.1(2), CDA 1971

Actus reus	Mens rea
• Destroys or damages	• Intention or recklessness as to destroying or damaging such property
• Property	
• Belonging to the defendant or another	• Intention or recklessness as to thereby endangering the life of another
• Without lawful excuse	

The *actus reus* elements of the offence are that property belonging to the defendant or another is destroyed or damaged without lawful excuse. There are two *mens rea* elements of the offence under s.1(2), namely: an intention to destroy or damage property or recklessness as to whether or not property is destroyed or damaged; and an intention by the destruction or damage to endanger the life of another or recklessness as to whether the life of another would be thereby endangered (table 10.5).

10.6.2.1 *Actus reus*

The *actus reus* elements of the offence of aggravated criminal damage are generally the same as those for simple criminal damage. One difference in the *actus reus* is that aggravated criminal damage requires that some property be damaged, but it does not require that the property belong to another; thus, the defendant may be guilty of aggravated criminal damage in respect of property which he owns (whether as sole or joint owner). It seems quite peculiar that a defendant who damages his own property can be guilty of a criminal offence in respect of this. The offence of aggravated criminal damage may serve to protect the property rights of another person where the defendant damages property belonging to another person or property that he jointly owns with another person. However, the rationale is less clear where a defendant damages or destroys property that he is the sole owner of, such as if he burns his own house down. It would appear that a conviction for aggravated criminal damage in this situation seeks to protect against the endangerment of the life of another, even though this is not part of the *actus reus* of the offence and it is not really the purpose of the statute, which aims to deal with actual or threatened damage to property. Thus, in *Merrick* [1996] 1 Cr App R 130, the defendant was employed by a householder to remove a television cable belonging to the householder, and in the process of doing so he exposed a live electrical cable for six minutes. The defendant was held to be guilty of aggravated criminal damage (despite the fact that he deliberately damaged the cable with the consent of the owner) because he was reckless as to whether the life of another was endangered. This strange result has been criticised on the basis that 'the gravamen of the conduct in a case like *Merrick* has nothing to do with damage to property' (see Ormerod and Laird 2015: 1167–8). Professor Ormerod and Karl Laird then go on to ask, 'Why should it be different if the danger arose not from cutting old cable but from the installation of new?' and they comment that 'The implications of the result are "absurd and alarming"' (Ormerod and Laird 2015: 1168).

Lawful excuse is also a defence to the offence under s.1(2), but the instances set out in s.5(2) do not apply to s.1(2). Lawful excuse is not defined for the purposes of s.1(2). As the offence under s.1(2) involves intention or recklessness as to the endangerment of life, any lawful excuse would have to be exceptional to be a defence. For instance, acting to prevent a danger to the defendant's own life.

 THINKING POINT

The offence under s.1(2) of the Criminal Damage Act 1971 is often referred to as 'aggravated' criminal damage. What is the 'aggravation' that the law seeks to criminalise?

10.6.2.2 *Mens rea*

The most significant difference between the two offences lies in the *mens rea* elements. Proof of aggravated criminal damage under s.1(2) requires proof of two *mens rea* elements:

(i) there must be an intention to destroy or damage property or recklessness as to whether property would be destroyed or damaged; and

(ii) there must be an intention by the destruction or damage to endanger life or recklessness as to whether or not life would be endangered.

Once again, intention carries its ordinary meaning and recklessness is subjectively assessed under *R v G and another* [2003] UKHL 50.

There is no requirement that life actually be endangered because this is not an *actus reus* element, but is a *mens rea* element. The prosecution must prove that the defendant had the intention to endanger the life of another or was subjectively reckless as to whether another person's life was endangered. Thus, if a defendant intended only to endanger his own life by the damage to property, and did not foresee any endangerment of the life of another person, such as where he drives to a secluded area and sets fire to his own car in a bid to commit suicide, he will not be guilty under s.1(2): *Thakar* [2010] EWCA Crim 2136. However, if the defendant sets fire to his own house in a suicide bid, he may be guilty of aggravated criminal damage if he foresaw the risk to the lives of his neighbours who live in an adjoining property (see *Brewis* [2004] EWCA Crim 1919).

The defendant must intend or be reckless as to endangering life *by* the damage or destruction he caused. This was confirmed by the House of Lords in *Steer* [1986] 1 WLR 1286. The defendant in this case fired a rifle at the bedroom window of his ex-business partner's house at night. His conviction for aggravated criminal damage under s.1(2) of the Act was quashed because the danger to life had been caused by the gunshot, rather than by the damage to the window. *Steer* was distinguished in the case of *Dudley* [1989] Crim LR 57. In *Dudley*, the defendant threw a firebomb at a house, causing a high sheet of flame outside the door which was quickly extinguished. Only a small amount of damage resulted. The defendant was convicted of arson under s.1(2) and s.1(3) of the Criminal Damage Act 1971. The fact that the actual damage caused was not sufficient to endanger life was no defence. What was important was the damage or destruction that the defendant envisaged. If he was intending by the destruction or damage to endanger the life of another or being reckless by the destruction or damage as to whether the life of another was endangered, he could be guilty.

These cases were applied in *Asquith, Webster and Seamans; Warwick* (1995) 1 Cr App R 492.

CASE CLOSE-UP

Asquith, Webster and Seamans; Warwick (1995) 1 Cr App R 492

Asquith, Webster and Seamans and *Warwick* were two separate cases which were tried together in the Court of Appeal. In *Asquith, Webster and Seamans*, the defendants pushed a heavy stone from a railway bridge onto a train which was passing below. The stone landed on the roof of a carriage and passengers were showered with debris from the roof, including fibreglass, however, the stone did not go through the roof into the carriage. The passengers were not physically injured.

In *Warwick*, the defendant was in a stolen car that was being chased by the police. The defendant threw bricks from the stolen car. One brick smashed the window of the police car, showering the police officers with glass, and another struck a police officer.

The Court of Appeal held that s.1(2)(b) of the Act relates to the damage *envisaged* by the defendant, not the actual damage caused by the defendant. Thus, a defendant would only be convicted of this offence if he intended or was reckless about endangering the life of another by the damage that he envisaged he would cause. Lord Taylor CJ stated that:

> Otherwise, the gravamen of an offence involving damage by missile would depend not on the defendant's intention but on whether he was a good shot in seeking to carry it out. Thus, if a defendant throws a brick at the windscreen of a moving vehicle, given that he causes some damage to the vehicle, whether he is guilty under section 1(2) does not depend on whether the brick hits or misses the windscreen, but whether he intended it to hit and intended that the damage therefrom should endanger life or whether he was reckless as to that outcome.

The cases of *Steer* [1986] 1 WLR 1286 and *Asquith, Webster and Seamans; Warwick* (1995) 1 Cr App R 492 were considered more recently in *Wenton* [2010] EWCA Crim 2361. The defendant in this case smashed a window of a house and threw a canister of petrol in through the window with a piece of paper that had been lit. The petrol did not ignite and the occupants of the house were unharmed. The defendant's appeal against his conviction for aggravated criminal damage was quashed on appeal because the act of damage (smashing the window) and the act causing the endangerment to life (throwing in the canister) were two unrelated acts. The defendant could only have been guilty had he either (i) intended or foreseen the endangerment to life caused by the damage to the window, or (ii) caused damage by throwing in the canister which he thereby intended or foresaw would endanger life. This case is consistent with the earlier cases and the Court of Appeal drew attention to the fact that those prosecuting similar cases need to be careful when drafting the indictment upon which the prosecution is based. The prosecution in this case was based upon the damage to the window and there was no evidence that the defendant had intended to or foreseen any endangerment to life resulting from this damage.

 THINKING POINT

John throws a brick at a passing train. The brick smashes through the window and hits the driver on the head, causing him a serious head injury and knocking him unconscious. Has John committed an offence under s.1(1) and/or s.1(2) of the Criminal Damage Act 1971?

10.6.3 **Arson**

Arson is criminal damage by fire. It is an indictable only offence which carries a maximum sentence of life imprisonment under s.4(1) of the Criminal Damage Act 1971. Arson is provided by s.1(3) of the Criminal Damage Act 1971.

A defendant will be guilty of arson if he commits an offence of criminal damage under either s.1(1) or s.1(2) of the Criminal Damage Act 1971 by fire. If he commits simple criminal damage by fire he will be charged under s.1(1) and s.1(3) of the Act. If he commits aggravated criminal damage by fire he will be charged under s.1(2) and s.1(3) of the Act.

10.6.4 **Threats to destroy or damage property**

Under s.2 of the Criminal Damage Act 1971, it is an offence to threaten to commit an offence under s.1 of the Act (i.e., to destroy or damage property). It is an either way offence which carries a maximum sentence of 10 years' imprisonment.

There must be a threat to destroy or damage property belonging to another (s.2(a)) or a threat to destroy or damage the defendant's own property in a way which he knows is likely to endanger life (s.2(b)). The threat to destroy or damage the property may be written, verbal, or by conduct. The threat is considered objectively: *Cakmak* [2002] 2 Cr App R 158. There must be words or actions which, objectively speaking, constitute a threat, and it must be a threat which, objectively considered, amounts to a threat to damage any property: *Ankerson* [2015] EWCA Crim 549. It does not matter that the actual listener perceived the words or action to be a threat if it would not objectively be considered a threat: *Ankerson*. The defendant must also intend that the other person would fear that the threat would be carried out. According to the Court of Appeal in *Ankerson*,

> there is no material difference between a defendant who intends that the listener should fear that the threat will be carried out and one who intends that the listener should fear that it might be carried out … the critical word is 'fear'. To fear something will happen is not to be equated with a belief that it will happen … it is enough if the intention is to create in the mind of an objective listener the genuine fear that the threat might be carried out. (At [11])

The instances of lawful excuse under s.5(2) apply to the offence under s.2(a) but not to that under s.2(b) of the Criminal Damage Act 1971.

10.6.5 **Possession of articles**

Under s.3 of the Criminal Damage Act 1971, it is an offence to be in possession of an article intending it to be used to commit an offence under s.1 of the Act (i.e., to destroy or damage property). It is an either way offence which carries a maximum sentence of 10 years' imprisonment.

A conditional intention to use the article in question should it prove necessary to do so is sufficient for this offence: *Buckingham* (1976) 63 Cr App R 159. In this case, the defendant was stopped by police while carrying a jemmy (an iron bar used for breaking into properties). He claimed that he worked for a squatters' association and admitted that he had the jemmy with him in case he needed to use it to break into a property. His conviction under s.3 was upheld. The instances of lawful excuse under s.5(2) apply to the offence under s.3(a) but not to that under s.3(b) of the Criminal Damage Act 1971.

10.6.6 **Racially or religiously aggravated criminal damage**

Racially or religiously aggravated criminal damage is an offence under s.30 of the Crime and Disorder Act 1998 (as amended by s.39 of the Anti-terrorism, Crime and Security Act 2001). It is an either way offence which carries a maximum sentence of 14 years' imprisonment.

 Summary

- Under s.8 of the Theft Act 1968, robbery involves the use or threat of force immediately before or at the time of stealing and in order to steal.

- There are two offences of burglary under s.9(1)(a) and (b) of the Theft Act 1968. The offence under s.9(1)(a) requires a defendant to enter a building or part of a building as a trespasser with the intention of stealing, inflicting grievous bodily harm, or doing unlawful damage. The defendant must be a trespasser on entry and must have an intention to steal, inflict grievous bodily harm, or do unlawful damage on entry.

- The offence under s.9(1)(b) requires a defendant who has entered a building or part of a building as a trespasser to steal or inflict grievous bodily harm or attempt to steal or inflict grievous bodily harm. The defendant must be a trespasser on entry. While in the building, the defendant must then commit the full offence of theft or grievous bodily harm, or attempt to do so.

- Under s.10(1) of the Theft Act 1968, aggravated burglary involves burglary and at the time the defendant has with him a firearm or imitation firearm, or a weapon of offence or an explosive.

- Blackmail is an offence under s.21(1) of the Theft Act 1968. Blackmail involves making an unwarranted demand with menaces, with a view to gain for himself or another, or with intent to cause loss to another.

- Handling stolen goods is an offence under s.22 of the Theft Act 1968 and requires the defendant to be dishonest and to know or believe that the goods are stolen.

- There are two main offences of destroying or damaging property: simple criminal damage under s.1(1) of the Criminal Damage Act 1971; and aggravated criminal damage under s.1(2) of the Act. Arson is criminal damage by fire under s.1(3).

 The bigger picture

- For a more detailed discussion of the property offences under the Theft Act 1968 (and the offence of fraud under the Fraud Act 2006), you could consult the authoritative work by Ormerod and Williams, *Smith's Law of Theft* (2007).

- You might want to consider how the offence of criminal damage applies to graffiti art, such as the very valuable artwork created by the artist known as Banksy. For a more detail discussion on this issue, you should read Edwards (2009).

- For more information about offences under the Computer Misuse Act 1990, such as the offence of unauthorised acts with intent to impair, or with recklessness as to impairing, the operation of a computer under s.3(1) of the Computer Misuse Act 1990 (as amended by s.36 of the Police and Justice Act 2006) mentioned at 10.6.1.1, you might want to read the following:

  Fafinski (2009)

  Fafinski (2008)

  McEwan (2008)

? Questions

Self-test questions

1. Identify the elements of robbery.

2. Explain the degree of entry which is required for burglary. Cite authorities to support your answer.

3. Identify the *mens rea* of burglary under s.9(1)(a) of the Theft Act 1968.

4. Identify the *actus reus* of burglary under s.9(1)(b) of the Theft Act 1968.

5. Explain when the defendant must have the weapon with him for the purposes of aggravated burglary under s.10(1) of the Theft Act 1968.

6. What are 'menaces' for the purposes of the offence of blackmail?

7. When is a demand unwarranted?

8. What constitutes damage under the Criminal Damage Act 1971? Cite authorities to support your answer.

9. Explain when a defendant might have lawful excuse to damage.

10. What is the *mens rea* of aggravated criminal damage under s.1(2) of the Criminal Damage Act 1971?

@ **For suggested approaches, please visit the Online Resource Centre.**

Exam questions

1. Critically evaluate the extent to which the criminal law seeks to protect the well-being of individuals as well as property through the criminalisation of robbery, burglary, blackmail, and criminal damage.

2. Answer *both* parts (a) and (b) below:

   (a) While walking along the canal bank after a day of fishing, Paul notices a canal barge with an open window. He feeds his fishing net through the window, hoping to catch something worth stealing. As his efforts are unsuccessful, Paul decides to climb in through the window. He is spotted by the owner of the barge, Johnny, who shouts, 'Stop, thief!' Paul grabs a laptop from a table on the barge and tries to leave. He knocks over a vase in his panic, breaking it. As he tries to leave, he is confronted by Johnny. Paul hits Johnny round the head with the laptop and flees.

And

(b) In protest against their use of animals in testing their products, Charlotte sends a letter to the head office of a cosmetics company threatening to burn down their premises unless they stop this practice. Receiving no reply from the company, Charlotte decides to set fire to the premises at head office. Late at night, when the employees have gone home, she approaches the building. She sees a light on in reception but notices that the desk is empty. Unbeknown to Charlotte, the night security guard is laying on a sofa in reception having a nap. She throws a petrol bomb towards the reception area which explodes and the building catches fire.

What offences, if any, have Paul and Charlotte committed?

 For suggested approaches, please visit the Online Resource Centre.

 Further reading

Books

Fafinski, S. *Computer Misuse: Response, Regulation and the Law* (2009), Cullompton: Willan Publishing

Griew, E. *The Theft Acts 1968 and 1978* (1986), London: Sweet & Maxwell

Herring, J. 'Burglary and Blackmail: Theory' in *Criminal Law: Text, Cases, and Materials* (6th edn, 2014), Oxford: Oxford University Press, pp. 606–15

Herring, J. 'Theoretical Issues on Criminal Damage' in *Criminal Law: Text, Cases, and Materials* (6th edn, 2014), Oxford: Oxford University Press, pp. 629–34

Ormerod, D. and Laird, K. *Smith and Hogan: Criminal Law* (14th edn, 2015), Oxford: Oxford University Press

Ormerod, D. and Williams, D. *Smith's Law of Theft* (9th edn, 2007), Oxford: Oxford University Press

Williams, G. *Textbook of Criminal Law* (2nd edn, 1983), London: Stevens & Sons

Journal articles

Ashworth, A. 'Robbery Reassessed' [2001] Crim LR 851

Edwards, I. 'Banksy's Graffiti: A Not-So-Simple Case of Criminal Damage?' (2009) 73 JCL 345

Elliott, D. W. 'Endangering Life by Destroying or Damaging Property' [1997] Crim LR 382

Fafinski, S. 'Computer Misuse: The Implications of the Police and Justice Act 2006' (2008) 72 JCL 53

Laird, K. 'Conceptualising the Interpretation of "Dwelling" in Section 9 of the Theft Act 1968' [2013] Crim LR 656

McEwan, N. 'The Computer Misuse Act 1990: Lessons from its Past and Predictions for its Future' [2008] Crim LR 955

11 Fraud

LEARNING OBJECTIVES

By the end of this chapter, you should be able to:

- understand the background to the Fraud Act 2006;
- define the offence of fraud;
- identify the three ways in which fraud can be committed;
- demonstrate an understanding of other offences under the Fraud Act 2006;
- demonstrate an understanding of the offence of making off without payment; and
- apply the law relating to these offences to a problem scenario.

Introduction

This chapter explores the offence of fraud, which was created by the Fraud Act 2006. While the introduction of the Fraud Act 2006 undoubtedly improved the law by replacing the complicated deception offences (see 11.1 for the background to the Fraud Act 2006) with a single offence of fraud, the offence of fraud is also subject to criticism. You will see as we explore the offence that there is a degree of overlap between the offences of theft (see chapter 9) and fraud. The offence of fraud has been very widely drafted to mitigate the problems created by the narrow construction of the previous deception offences. In light of the scope of the *actus reus* and in a similar vein to the offence of theft, a conviction for the offence of fraud is dependent upon proof of the *mens rea* requirement of dishonesty. This in itself is also problematic, as it is not always easy to determine whether a jury will find that a person is dishonest within the scope of *Ghosh*. As you read this chapter, you might want to consider the type of situations in which the offence could potentially apply in practice, as well as whether the broad *actus reus* is appropriate or whether the offence is too widely drafted.

11.1 Background to the Fraud Act 2006

The law relating to deception and fraud was the subject of extensive reform in 2007. The old deception offences under the Theft Acts of 1968 and 1978 were repealed and replaced by a single offence of fraud under the Fraud Act 2006. These reforms were the result of recommendations made by the Law Commission in their report entitled *Fraud* which was published in 2002 (Law Com. No. 276, Cm. 5560). In 1998, the former Home Secretary, Jack Straw, asked the Law Commission:

> to examine the law on fraud, and in particular to consider whether it: is readily comprehensible to juries; is adequate for effective prosecution; is fair to potential defendants; meets the need of developing technology including electronic means of transfer; and to make recommendations to improve the law in these respects with all due expedition. In making these recommendations to consider whether a general offence of fraud would improve the criminal law. (Written Answer, House of Commons Hansard, 7 April 1998, vol. 310, at cols 176–7.)

In its report, the Law Commission recommended that all of the old deception offences under the Theft Acts of 1968 and 1978 be repealed and that the common law offence of conspiracy to defraud be abolished. The Law Commission also recommended the creation of two new offences: one of fraud which could be committed in three different ways; and one of obtaining services dishonestly. The objective of these extensive reforms was to simplify and improve the law, making it comprehensible to juries and more accessible to citizens. In May 2004, the Government published its Consultation Paper entitled 'Fraud Law Reform' with a view to obtaining views from lawyers and academics on the Law Commission's proposals. The Government response to these views was published on 24 November 2004. The Fraud Bill was introduced into the House of Lords on 25 May 2005. The Fraud Act 2006 received Royal Assent on 8 November 2006 and came into force on 15 January 2007 (Fraud Act 2006 (Commencement) Order (SI 2006/3200)).

The Fraud Act 2006 did not abolish the common law offence of conspiracy to defraud, but many of the old deception offences under the Theft Acts of 1968 and 1978 were repealed. These offences included:

- obtaining property by deception (s.15, Theft Act 1968);
- obtaining a money transfer by deception (s.15A, Theft Act 1968);
- obtaining a pecuniary advantage by deception (s.16, Theft Act 1968);
- procuring the execution of a valuable security by deception (s.20(2), Theft Act 1968);
- obtaining services by deception (s.1, Theft Act 1978); and
- evading liability by deception (s.2, Theft Act 1978).

The old deception offences were problematic for a number of reasons. The following issues were highlighted to the Law Commission by the Home Secretary:

- There were many different deception offences which were too specific and there was no general definition of fraud. The Home Secretary and the Law Commission took the view that reform would 'make the law more comprehensible to juries, especially in serious fraud trials'.

- The old deception offences were quite narrowly defined; Professor Ormerod (2007) described them as 'notoriously technical and 'over-particularised'. This meant that the wrong offence could sometimes be charged where another was more suitable, resulting in 'unjustified acquittals and costly appeals'.

- One single offence of fraud would simplify the law of fraud. The law needs to be clear and simple in order to be accessible and capable of being understood by citizens.

- A general all-encompassing offence of fraud would not focus on the particular manner in which the fraud was committed. Thus, 'it should be better able to keep pace with developing technology', such as the use of email, text messaging, and electronic transfers.

11.2 The offence of fraud

The Fraud Act 2006 replaced the old deception offences with one single offence of fraud which can be committed in three ways. Repealing the many complicated deception offences and replacing these with a single offence of fraud immediately simplified the law. However, as Professor Ormerod has stated, 'Having been seven years in gestation and heralded in debates... As one of the best Bills from the Home Office in recent years it has much to live up to' (Ormerod 2007: 193). Ormerod is particularly critical of the Fraud Act 2006 because while the Act has simplified the law, it has done so at a cost by producing 'a general offence that is overbroad, based too heavily on the ill-defined concept of dishonesty, too vague to meet the obligation under Art.7...And otherwise deficient in principle' (Ormerod 2007: 219).

Like the offence of theft, fraud is an either way offence, triable in the Crown court or the magistrates' court. Upon summary conviction, the offence carries a maximum sentence of 12 months' imprisonment or a fine not exceeding the statutory maximum or both. If the defendant is convicted on indictment, the maximum sentence is 10 years' imprisonment or a fine or both.

Section 1(1) of the Fraud Act 2006 provides for the offence of fraud. There is no definition of fraud under the Act, instead s.1(2) sets out three different ways in which this offence may be committed (figure 11.1).

Figure 11.1 Fraud

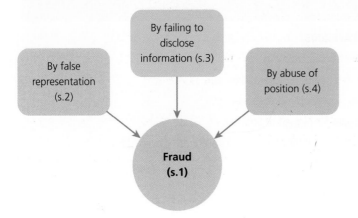

STATUTE

Section 1, Fraud Act 2006

(1) A person is guilty of fraud if he is in breach of any of the sections listed in subsection (2) (which provide for different ways of committing the offence).

(2) The sections are—

   (a) section 2 (fraud by false representation),

   (b) section 3 (fraud by failing to disclose information), and

   (c) section 4 (fraud by abuse of position).

THINKING POINT

To what extent do you think that ss.2, 3, and 4 of the Fraud Act 2006 overlap? Can you think of examples of where a defendant might be guilty of fraud by more than one of the methods in ss.2, 3, and 4?

There are no references to 'deception' within the Fraud Act 2006; this term has been discarded in favour of 'fraud'. Oddly, however, there is no definition of 'fraud' under the Act. Section 1(2) sets out the ways in which the offence of fraud may be committed and ss.2, 3, and 4 define these methods in more detail, but without defining fraud itself. Unlike the old deception offences, the offence of fraud does not require the defendant to have actually obtained anything, such as goods or services. The offence focuses instead on the *mens rea* elements of dishonesty and intention to make a gain or cause loss. These are common requirements of the general offence of fraud, irrespective of the method by which the fraud is committed.

11.2.1 Fraud by false representation

Under s.1(2)(a) of the Fraud Act 2006, a person is guilty of fraud if he breaches s.2. Section 2 of the Act provides that it is an offence to commit fraud by making a false representation.

STATUTE

Section 2(1), Fraud Act 2006

A person is in breach of this section if he—

   (a) dishonestly makes a false representation, and

   (b) intends, by making the representation—

     (i) to make a gain for himself or another, or

     (ii) to cause loss to another or to expose another to a risk of loss.

The *actus reus* of this form of the offence of fraud is making a false representation. The *mens rea* elements are: dishonesty, knowledge that the representation is or might be false, and an

Table 11.1 Elements of fraud by false representation

Actus reus	Mens rea
• Making a false representation	• Dishonesty
	• Knowledge that the representation is or might be false
	• Intention to make a gain for himself or another, or to cause loss to another, or to expose another to a risk of loss

intention (by making the representation) to make a gain for himself or another, or to cause loss to another or to expose another to a risk of loss (table 11.1).

This is a very wide form of the offence of fraud since the defendant need simply make a false representation with the requisite *mens rea*. It is not necessary for the prosecution to prove that the victim relied upon the representation, nor that the representation actually resulted in the defendant gaining anything or causing any loss. The offence of fraud thus differs from many of the old deception offences which required a defendant to actually *obtain* property, services, a pecuniary advantage, or a money transfer *by* the deception practised. Thus, a defendant is convicted on the basis of the representation that they make, rather than on the basis of whether they were actually successful in making an actual gain or causing an actual loss. Professor Ormerod states that 'it is worth emphasising how dramatic is the shift from a result-based deception to a conduct-based representation offence' (Ormerod 2007: 196).

However, Professor Ormerod goes on to criticise this offence for being too wide and for effectively criminalising lying:

> Should lying be a sufficient basis for criminal liability? What is the wrong which D performs which warrants the criminal sanction? It is not one derived from intentionally harming V's interests directly—there need be no such harm . . . The wrong seems to be the act of lying or misleading with intent to gain or cause loss . . . Even if this is sufficient to warrant criminalisation, is it properly called fraud? (Ormerod 2007: 196).

11.2.1.1 Dishonesty

The offence of fraud by false representation under s.2 of the Fraud Act 2006 requires the false representation to be made dishonestly and since the *actus reus* elements of the offence of fraud have been so broadly defined, the *mens rea*, and particularly dishonesty, is 'the principal determinant of criminal liability' (Ormerod 2007: 200). Dishonesty is not defined under the Fraud Act 2006, yet it is also an element of the offence of fraud committed by failure to disclose information under s.3 or fraud by abuse of position under s.4 of the Act.

The definition of dishonesty which was developed for the offence of theft applies to the offence of fraud. The test comes from the cases of *Feely* [1973] QB 530 and *Ghosh* [1982] QB 1053 (recently confirmed to be good law in *Cornelius* [2012] EWCA Crim 500) and is discussed in more detail in chapter 9. In *Feely*, it was held that whether or not the defendant was dishonest is a question for the jury. The test of dishonesty contains two limbs, one of which is objective and the other is subjective. The first limb is purely objective: the defendant's conduct is judged according to the standards of the honest and reasonable man. The second limb is subjective, requiring the defendant to recognise that his conduct was dishonest according to the objective standard.

SUMMARY

According to *Ghosh*, the jury must consider:

(1) whether what the defendant did was dishonest according to the ordinary standards of reasonable and honest people (the objective limb).

If so,

(2) whether the defendant realised that reasonable and honest people would regard it as dishonest (the subjective limb).

> **CROSS REFERENCE**
> Refer to 9.2.1.2 for a detailed discussion on dishonesty.

Although the *Ghosh* test has been used in the context of the offence of theft for around 30 years, it is not without problems itself. The test can be criticised for many reasons. For instance, it is a complex test which we expect jurors to be able to understand and apply, and it leads to inconsistent verdicts as individual jurors have different views on what conduct is dishonest. Professor Ormerod highlights the fact that the *Ghosh* test has been criticised for requiring the jury to define what constitutes dishonesty and that 'it has been suggested that *Ghosh* may fall foul of Art. 7' because this element is defined after the defendant has acted (Ormerod 2007: 201). Ormerod also criticises the test because it 'increases the chances that more cases will go to trial as defendants have little to lose by "trying their luck"'. He argues that 'a lack of certainty in the substantive law and inefficiency in the criminal justice system render this undesirable' (Ormerod 2007: 201).

As we saw in chapter 9, a defendant charged with theft can absolve himself of liability by arguing that he honestly believed that he had a right in law to the property, or that the owner would have consented, or that the owner could not be found if all reasonable steps were taken to locate him. This is the negative aspect of dishonesty which is provided for under s.2(1) of the Theft Act 1968. Section 2(1) does not apply to the offence of fraud.

11.2.1.2 Making a false representation

Section 2(1) of the Fraud Act 2006 requires a defendant to make a false representation. Whether the defendant has made a false representation is a question of fact to be determined by the jury. Making a false representation encompasses both an *actus reus* element and a *mens rea* element. Under s.2(2) of the Fraud Act 2006:

 STATUTE

Section 2(2), Fraud Act 2006

representation is false if—

(a) it is untrue or misleading, and

(b) the person making it knows that it is, or might be, untrue or misleading.

When is a representation 'false'?

The *actus reus* element requires that a representation is made which is false. Section 2(2)(a) of the Act explains that a false representation is one that is 'untrue or misleading'. The inclusion of the word 'misleading' ensures that the offence is wide in scope. Section 2(2)(b) of the Act sets out the *mens rea* required in relation to the false representation: the defendant must know that it is untrue or misleading, or know that it might be untrue or misleading.

What is a 'representation'?

The meaning of representation is dealt with in s.2(3) to (5) of the Fraud Act 2006. A representation is defined in s.2(3) of the Act. Under s.2(3), a representation may be made about a fact, or about law. A representation includes a representation about a person's state of mind. Section 2(4) of the Act states that a representation may be express or implied. An express representation will usually present no problems, whereas implied representations have been the subject of extensive examination in the courts. A representation may be made by words or by conduct. It may be made in writing or orally.

This aspect of the Fraud Act 2006 is similar to the old law, under which deception could be by words or conduct. In the case of *Barnard* (1837) 7 C & P 784, the defendant entered a shop in Oxford wearing a university cap and gown. By an express representation that he was a member of Oxford University, he induced the shopkeeper to sell him goods on credit. The court held that this amounted to deception and made an *obiter* comment to the effect that the defendant would also have been guilty if he had said nothing. However, silence alone was not thought to be sufficient to constitute a deception under s.15(4) of the Theft Act 1968 which also referred to 'words or conduct'. By contrast, s.2(4) of the Fraud Act 2006 does not refer to 'words or conduct'.

Where the defendant's silence means that he has failed to disclose information that he was under a legal duty to disclose, the defendant will be guilty of fraud by failing to disclose information, dealt with under s.3 of the Fraud Act 2006. However, as this section applies only where there was a legal duty to disclose information, it remains to be seen whether silence where there is only a moral duty to disclose information will be capable of being deemed a 'representation'. This may, however, prove to be an unnecessary issue for the courts to determine. In its report, the Law Commission gave an example of an antique dealer who 'calls on vulnerable people and buys their heirlooms at unrealistically low prices, making no misrepresentation as to the value of the items but exploiting the victims' trust'. The Law Commission took the view that although there is no *legal* duty to disclose the truth in such a scenario, there is clearly a *moral* duty to do so and 'If the dealer's failure to do so is regarded by the fact-finders as dishonest, we see no reason why he should not be guilty of fraud' (at paragraph 7.24). Under the Fraud Act 2006, such a scenario would be covered by fraud by abuse of a position of financial trust under s.4.

An interesting example of a false representation arose in the case of *Idrees v DPP* [2011] EWHC 624 (Admin), in which the defendant, who had failed his theory driving test 15 times previously, had another person (who was unknown to the court) impersonate him to sit the test. Another example is the case of Farrakh Nizzar, a shop worker in a convenience store, who pleaded guilty to fraud by false representation after he informed a woman who had a £1 million winning lottery ticket that she had won nothing on the lottery (*Nizzar*, Oldham Magistrates' Court, unreported, July 2012). Finally, in *O'Leary* [2013] EWCA Crim 1371, the defendant, who was a self-employed roofer, was convicted of fraud by false representation after he visited elderly victims who suffered from dementia and demanded money from them for work which he said he had carried out for them. In fact, the work had never been carried out and the prosecution case was that the defendant had 'preyed upon the vulnerability of [his] two elderly victims who suffered from dementia in order to extract money from them'.

Implied representations

It was also the case under the old law that a representation could be implied. In *Harris* (1975) 62 Cr App R 28, it was held that a customer who books into a hotel makes an implied representation that he intends to pay his bill at the end of his stay. Similarly, a customer who enters a restaurant and orders food makes implied representations that he intends to pay for his meal and that he has the means to do so. The defendant in the case of *DPP v Ray* [1974] AC 370 went to a restaurant with four friends. When they first entered the restaurant, the defendant did so intending to pay for his meal. However, after finishing his food, he dishonestly decided to leave without paying. He waited for the waiter to leave the room then ran off. The House of Lords held that by entering the restaurant and ordering food, the defendant made an implied representation that he was an honest customer intending to pay for his meal. When the defendant changed his mind about paying after the meal was served and eaten, the representation was falsified. Lord Reid stated that the implied representation that a customer intends to pay for his meal is a continuing representation—it continues until the customer leaves the restaurant in the normal course of events. Lord MacDermott held that the implied representation was 'a continuing representation which remained alive and operative' up to and including payment for the meal.

Applying the new offence of fraud to this scenario, if the defendant knew when he entered the restaurant and ordered his food that he did not intend to pay, his representation would have been a false one when made. On the other hand, if he changed his mind at some stage before leaving the restaurant, the prosecution would need to prove that the representation was still continuing at that moment, following the approach taken in *DPP v Ray*.

Under the old law, cases where the defendant had obtained property, etc. by the unauthorised use of a cheque card or a credit card caused some problems for the courts. This issue was considered in the case of *Metropolitan Police Commissioner v Charles* [1976] 1 All ER 659.

🔍 CASE CLOSE-UP

Metropolitan Police Commissioner v Charles [1976] 1 All ER 659

In this case, the defendant's bank account was overdrawn, so his bank manager told him not to cash any more than one cheque per day and for no more than £30. However, the defendant visited a casino and used his cheque card to guarantee 25 cheques for £30 each. He was convicted of obtaining a pecuniary advantage by deception under s.16 of the Theft Act 1968. The House of Lords held that by using his chequebook and cheque guarantee card, he was making an implied representation that he had an account with the bank and that he was authorised to use the chequebook and cheque guarantee card. Although it was true that the defendant had an account with the bank, the second representation as to his authority to draw on the account to the extent that he did, was false. It was also clear that the defendant knew that his second representation was false as he had been told by his bank manager to cash no more than one cheque for £30 per day. This would amount to a false representation under the Fraud Act 2006. Thus, such a defendant might be tried for the offence of fraud by false representation today.

The case of *Metropolitan Police Commissioner v Charles* was followed in *Lambie* [1981] 3 WLR 88. *Lambie* was a similar case involving a credit card. The defendant had exceeded her credit limit, yet she used the card to obtain property. She was also convicted of obtaining a pecuniary advantage by deception under s.16 of the Theft Act 1968 (although she should have been charged with obtaining property by deception under s.15 of the Theft Act 1968). The House of Lords held that the same principle applies to credit cards as applies to cheques. When a credit card is presented at a till, there is an implied representation that the holder has an account with the credit card provider and is authorised to use the card. This would also amount to a false representation under the Fraud Act 2006 today.

The Fraud Act 2006 also deals with the practice of 'phishing'. In the Explanatory Notes to the Fraud Act 2006, 'phishing' is described as a practice by which 'a person disseminates an email to large groups of people falsely representing that the email has been sent by a legitimate financial institution. The email prompts the reader to provide information such as credit card and bank account numbers so that the "phisher" can gain access to others' assets.' Where a defendant sends an email to the victim purporting to be from the victim's bank, he is making a false representation. He also knows that the representation is false and intends to gain for himself and/or cause a loss to another. If it can also be proved that the defendant was dishonest, the offence of fraud by false representation has been committed. As an illustration, in *Agrigoroaie and Savoae* [2015] EWCA Crim 50, two defendants were convicted (on guilty pleas) of fraud by false representation after a search of their flats revealed a laptop containing the details of 150 bank accounts obtained via a phishing exercise.

When is a representation 'made'?

Under the old law, proof of actual deception was required. However, this is not necessary under the Fraud Act 2006. For the offence of fraud by false representation to be committed, it is enough that the prosecution prove that the false representation was *made*. Section 2(5) of the Fraud Act 2006 specifies when a representation may be regarded as 'made' for the purposes of fraud.

 STATUTE

Section 2(5), Fraud Act 2006

For the purposes of this section a representation may be regarded as made if it (or anything implying it) is submitted in any form to any system or device designed to receive, convey or respond to communications (with or without human intervention).

Under the old law, it was not possible to deceive a machine, the deception required a human victim: see the case of *Davies v Flackett* (1972) 116 SJ 526. Section 2(5) of the Fraud Act 2006 makes it clear that the false representation can be made to a machine as well as a person. Thus, the Fraud Act 2006 is appropriately drafted to encapsulate fraudulent conduct committed through the use of modes of modern technology, including through the Internet. The Act does not specify that the representation needs to be communicated, but simply that it must be 'submitted'. Hence, a representation by email will be made when the email is sent, irrespective of whether or not the victim has read it. Liability for fraud by false representation may ensue from a representation made to a machine, even where there is no human intervention. This is particularly relevant to the use of modern technology to commit fraudulent behaviour. The Explanatory Notes to the Act give an example of such a representation of a person entering a number into a 'Chip and PIN' machine. This subsection may also be relied upon where fraudulent transactions are conducted over the Internet.

11.2.1.3 Intention to gain or cause loss

In order to be guilty of fraud, the defendant must intend by making the representation, to make a gain for himself or another, or to cause loss to another or to expose another to a risk of loss. This is a *mens rea* element which applies generally to the offence of fraud, so it will also be required for fraud by failing to disclose information under s.3 of the Fraud Act 2006 and fraud by abuse of a position of financial trust under s.4 of the Act. Intention will take its ordinary meaning and will also cover foresight of consequences as virtually certain to occur (refer back to the case of *Woollin* [1998] AC 82 in chapter 3). The terms 'gain', 'loss', and 'property' are defined under s.5 of the Fraud Act 2006.

 STATUTE

Section 5, Fraud Act 2006

(1) 'Gain' and 'loss'—

    (a) extend only to gain or loss in money or other property;

    (b) include any such gain or loss whether temporary or permanent;

    and 'property' means any property whether real or personal (including things in action and other intangible property).

(2) 'Gain' includes a gain by keeping what one has, as well as a gain by getting what one does not have.

(3) 'Loss' includes a loss by not getting what one might get, as well as a loss by parting with what one has.

The definitions of the terms 'gain' and 'loss' under the Fraud Act 2006 are the same as the definitions of those words under s.34(2) of the Theft Act 1968 which apply in relation to the offence of blackmail under s.21 of the Theft Act 1968. 'Property' is also defined under s.5(2) of the Fraud Act 2006. It bears the same definition as that given to property under s.4(1) of the Theft Act 1968.

The defendant must also intend to make such a gain or cause such a loss *by* making the false representation. In *Gilbert* [2012] EWCA Crim 2392, the Court of Appeal held that a causative link must be established between the intention to make a gain for himself or another, or to cause loss to another or to expose another to a risk of loss and the false representation made by the defendant. The Court also held that it is a matter for the jury to determine whether the causative link is established. The defendant's intention must not be too remote from his making the false representation. Professor Ormerod questions how remote the defendant's intentions can be: 'Suppose that D makes false representations to induce V, a wealthy banker, to marry him. Is he guilty of the s.2 offence if one intention is to enrich himself? Presumably such matters will be left to the jury to determine' (Ormerod and Laird 2015: 998).

Chris Monaghan (2010a) questions whether parents who lie on school application forms in order to secure a school place for their child could or should be prosecuted for fraud. He argues that the Fraud Act 2006 is 'inappropriate to be used to prosecute in these circumstances' since the Act leaves 'too much discretion in the hands of the tribunal of fact'.

THINKING POINT

Consider whether the offence of fraud by false representation under s.2 of the Fraud Act 2006 has been committed in the following scenarios:

(1) Graham visits a petrol station, intending not to pay. He fills up his car and drives away without paying.

(2) Sam sends an email to all students at his university stating, 'You have won a £1,000 university prize. Reply with your bank account details in order to receive the money by transfer today.'

(3) Hoping to obtain a chocolate bar, Walter puts a foreign coin into a vending machine. The machine accepts the coin and dispenses a chocolate bar.

(4) Would your answer to (3) above be any different if the machine did not dispense a chocolate bar?

(5) Keen to ensure that her son receives a place at a particular grammar school, Jenny puts down her mother's address on the application form. Her mother lives within the school catchment area.

11.2.2 Fraud by failing to disclose information

Under s.1(2)(b) of the Fraud Act 2006, a person is guilty of fraud if that person breaches s.3. Section 3 of the Act provides that it is an offence to commit fraud by failing to disclose information.

STATUTE

Section 3, Fraud Act 2006

A person is in breach of this section if he—

(a) dishonestly fails to disclose to another person information which he is under a legal duty to disclose, and

(b) intends, by failing to disclose the information—

(i) to make a gain for himself or another, or

(ii) to cause loss to another or to expose another to a risk of loss.

The *actus reus* of this form of the offence of fraud is failing to disclose information which that person is under a legal duty to disclose. The *mens rea* elements are: dishonesty and intention (by failing to disclose the information) to make a gain for himself or another, or to cause loss to another, or to expose another to a risk of loss (table 11.2).

Some of the elements of this form of the offence (namely, the *mens rea* elements) have been explored already in this chapter. The *Ghosh* test applies in respect of dishonesty and s.5 of the Fraud Act 2006 deals with the element of intention (by failing to disclose the information) to make a gain for himself or another, or to cause loss to another or to expose another to a risk of loss.

CROSS REFERENCE
Refer to 11.2.1.1 and 11.2.1.3 for a discussion of dishonesty and intention to make a gain or cause loss.

Table 11.2 Elements of fraud by failing to disclose information

Actus reus	Mens rea
• Failing to disclose information which he has a legal duty to disclose	• Dishonesty • Intention to make a gain for himself or another, or to cause loss to another, or to expose another to a risk of loss

The remaining element is the failure to disclose information which the defendant has a legal duty to disclose. The Fraud Act 2006 does not define a 'legal duty', but the Explanatory Notes state that it includes 'duties under oral contracts as well as written contracts'. In its report on fraud, the Law Commission took the view that:

> 7.28—Such a duty may derive from statute (such as the provisions governing company prospectuses), from the fact that the transaction in question is one of the utmost good faith (such as a contract of insurance), from the express or implied terms of a contract, from the custom of a particular trade or market, or from the existence of a fiduciary relationship between the parties (such as that of agent and principal).

> 7.29 For this purpose there is a legal duty to disclose information not only if the defendant's failure to disclose it gives the victim a cause of action for damages, but also if the law gives the victim a right to set aside any change in his or her legal position to which he or she may consent as a result of the non-disclosure. For example, a person in a fiduciary position has a duty to disclose material information when entering into a contract with his or her beneficiary, in the sense that a failure to make such disclosure will entitle the beneficiary to rescind the contract and to reclaim any property transferred under it.

This form of fraud would also cover situations such as that in the case of *Firth* (1989) 91 Cr App R 217. In this case, the defendant was a consultant at a hospital who deliberately failed to disclose that patients he had treated were private patients, intentionally depriving the hospital of revenue. There is an employer–employee relationship in this case and such a defendant would be convicted of fraud by failure to disclose information if tried today.

Whether or not there is a legal duty to disclose information is a question of civil law. The courts have often struggled to apply the civil law in the context of criminal offences, for example in the offence of theft (see chapter 9). Fraud will be committed by a failure to disclose information where a statute provides that there is a legal duty to do so, such as where there is a contractual duty to do so, including in contracts of insurance or where there is a fiduciary relationship between the parties. The Explanatory Notes give as an example a person who fails to disclose information relating to his heart condition when making an application for life insurance. There will also be a legal duty on a solicitor to disclose relevant information to his client because there is a fiduciary relationship between these two parties. However, this last example will also fall under fraud by abuse of position under s.4.

11.2.3 Fraud by abuse of position

Under s.1(2)(c) of the Fraud Act 2006, a person is guilty of fraud if he breaches s.4. Section 4 of the Act provides that it is an offence to commit fraud by abuse of position of financial trust.

STATUTE

Section 4(1), Fraud Act 2006

A person is in breach of this section if he—

    (a) occupies a position in which he is expected to safeguard, or not to act against, the financial interests of another person,

    (b) dishonestly abuses that position, and

    (c) intends, by means of the abuse of that position—

        (i) to make a gain for himself or another, or

        (ii) to cause loss to another or to expose another to a risk of loss.

The *actus reus* of this form of the offence of fraud is the occupation of a position in which the defendant is expected to safeguard, or not to act against, the financial interests of another person and the abuse of such a position. The *mens rea* elements are: dishonesty and an intention (by means of the abuse of that position) to make a gain for himself or another, or to cause loss to another or to expose another to a risk of loss (table 11.3).

> **CROSS REFERENCE**
>
> Refer to 11.2.1.1 and 11.2.1.3 for a discussion of dishonesty and intention to make a gain or cause loss.

Some of the elements of this form of the offence of fraud (namely, the *mens rea* elements) have been explored already in this chapter. The *Ghosh* test applies in respect of dishonesty and s.5 of the Fraud Act 2006 deals with the element of intention (by abuse of position of financial trust) to make a gain for himself or another, or to cause loss to another, or to expose another to a risk of loss.

This form of the offence of fraud requires the existence of a position of financial trust between the defendant and the victim. Under s.4(1)(a), a position of financial trust is one in which the defendant is expected to safeguard or not to act against the financial interests of another person. This type of fraudulent conduct also requires that position of trust to be abused. The Fraud Act 2006 does not define the word 'position', but the Law Commission took the view (at paragraph 7.38 of its report) that:

> The necessary relationship will be present between trustee and beneficiary, director and company, professional person and client, agent and principal, employee and employer, or between partners. It may arise otherwise, for example within a family, or in the context of voluntary work, or in any context where the parties are not at arm's length. In nearly all cases where it arises, it will be recognised by the civil law as importing fiduciary duties, and any relationship that is so recognised will suffice. We see no reason, however, why the existence of such duties should be essential. This does not of course mean that it would be entirely a

Table 11.3 Elements of fraud by abuse of position

Actus reus	Mens rea
• Occupying a position in which the defendant is expected to safeguard, or not to act against, the financial interests of another person • Abuse of that position	• Dishonesty • Intention to make a gain for himself or another, or to cause loss to another, or to expose another to a risk of loss

matter for the fact-finders whether the necessary relationship exists. The question whether the particular facts alleged can properly be described as giving rise to that relationship will be an issue capable of being ruled upon by the judge and, if the case goes to the jury, of being the subject of directions.

In *Valujevs* [2015] 3 WLR 109, the Court of Appeal held that s.4 is not restricted to situations in which the defendant owes a fiduciary duty to the victim, but there must be either a fiduciary duty or an obligation which is akin to a fiduciary duty. There will be a suitable relationship between a trustee and beneficiary, a director and company, a solicitor and client, a banker and client, and an employer and employee, etc. An employer necessarily grants an employee access to the employer's premises, equipment, records, and customers in order for the employee to carry out his contractual duties. An employer trusts an employee to use these in an appropriate manner and for the benefit of the employer, and any abuse of such trust may fall under the offence of fraud by abuse of position. In *Rouse* [2014] EWCA Crim 1128, this offence was applied to a defendant who was the deputy manager of a care home. He had access to residents' bank cards, credit cards, and account information, and thus could be said to have been in a position in which he was expected to safeguard, or not to act against, the financial interests of the residents. However, he abused that position by using residents' bank cards to withdraw money from a cash machine which he then used for his own purposes, and by using their credit cards to pay his personal bills. He pleaded guilty to four offences of fraud by abuse of position.

This type of fraud was also covered in some respects by the old deception offences. The defendant in the case of *Silverman* [1987] Crim LR 574 was a workman who had previously carried out work for the family of two elderly sisters. The two sisters engaged his services in reliance upon his honesty. However, the defendant deceived the sisters into paying a grossly excessive sum for work that he did on their central-heating system and electrical work. The Court held that this amounted to deception because there was an implied representation that the price that he set was fair and reasonable. This representation existed because there was clearly a relationship of trust in existence between the two sisters and the defendant. This type of scenario would now fall under fraud by abuse of position of trust (s.4), but it could also still fall under fraud by false representation (s.2).

The term 'abuse' is not defined under the Act, but s.4(2) states that abuse of position may be committed by an omission as well as by a positive act.

 THINKING POINT

Consider whether the offence of fraud under s.1 of the Fraud Act 2006 has been committed in the following scenarios:

(1) Billy fills out an application form for his car insurance. He declares on the form that he has not been involved in an accident in the past year and that he does not have any motoring offences. In fact, Billy was convicted of dangerous driving after being involved in a car crash 3 months ago.

(2) Sarah is a university lecturer. She obtains prospective students' personal details from university records and contacts them, offering private tuition of an introduction to their degree course for a fee as an alternative to a foundation course run by

the university. She uses an empty classroom at the university in which to carry out the private tuition.

(3) Joe, a computer specialist, is engaged by Saul to carry out repairs on Saul's laptop. Joe accesses Saul's bank details from the laptop and transfers £3,000 from Saul's account into his own.

11.3 Obtaining services dishonestly

The old offence of obtaining services by deception under s.1 of the Theft Act 1978 was repealed by the Fraud Act 2006. Section 11 of the Fraud Act 2006 creates a new offence of obtaining services dishonestly.

 STATUTE

Section 11, Fraud Act 2006

(1) A person is guilty of an offence under this section if he obtains services for himself or another—

    (a) by a dishonest act, and

    (b) in breach of subsection (2).

(2) A person obtains services in breach of this subsection if—

    (a) they are made available on the basis that payment has been, is being or will be made for or in respect of them,

    (b) he obtains them without any payment having been made for or in respect of them or without payment having been made in full, and

    (c) when he obtains them, he knows—

        (i) that they are being made available on the basis described in paragraph (a), or

        (ii) that they might be,

    but intends that payment will not be made, or will not be made in full.

 THINKING POINT

To what extent does the offence under s.11 of the Fraud Act 2006 overlap with the offence of fraud by false representation under s.2 of the Act?

Obtaining services dishonestly is an either way offence, triable in the Crown court or the magistrates' court. Upon summary conviction, the offence carries a maximum sentence of

Table 11.4 Elements of obtaining services dishonestly

Actus reus	Mens rea
• Obtaining services by an act	• Dishonesty
• The services must be available on the basis that payment has been, is being, or will be made for or in respect of them	• Knowledge that payment is required
• D obtains the services without any payment having been made for or in respect of them or without payment having been made in full	• Intention that payment will not be made, or will not be made in full

12 months' imprisonment or a fine not exceeding the statutory maximum or both. If the defendant is convicted on indictment, the maximum sentence is 5 years or a fine or both.

The elements of this offence are slightly more complicated than those required for the offence of fraud. The defendant must actually obtain a service (this is not a requirement for the offence of fraud) (table 11.4).

There must be a positive act—this offence cannot be committed by omission. The defendant must do an act dishonestly to obtain services which he knows should be paid for, intending not to pay for those services. Unlike the offence of fraud, this is a result offence—a service must be obtained. There is no definition of the word 'service' under the Fraud Act 2006.

This offence would cover using a credit card which has been reported as stolen to obtain a service on the Internet, such as the use of a travel website (which is a service) in order to buy a ticket (which is property) or downloading music or films illegally. This situation would also be covered by fraud by false representation under s.2 of the Act. Examples given in the Explanatory Notes to the Act include climbing over a wall to watch a football match without paying the entrance fee and attaching a decoder to one's television set in order to obtain satellite television channels without paying.

11.4 Possession of articles for use in frauds

Section 6(1) of the Fraud Act 2006 creates an offence of being in possession or control of an article for use in frauds. This is an either way offence, triable in the Crown court or the magistrates' court. Upon summary conviction, the offence carries a maximum sentence of 12 months' imprisonment or a fine not exceeding the statutory maximum or both. If the defendant is convicted on indictment, the maximum sentence is 5 years or a fine or both.

This offence has been used to prosecute a defendant who was caught in possession of a phone that he was using for recording films in the cinema which he then uploaded onto a website for people to download (*Nimley* [2010] EWCA Crim 2752), a defendant who was in possession of black paper which was the same size as currency and which he intended to sell to people along with chemicals which he claimed could convert the paper into money (*Kazi* [2010] EWCA Crim 2026), and defendants who were in possession of a bank card and false driving licences along with photographs to be used to make further false driving licences (*Montague* [2013] EWCA Crim 1781).

An 'article' is partially defined under s.8(1) of the Act as including 'any program or data held in electronic form'. Examples given in the Explanatory Notes to the Act include computer programs which generate credit card numbers, computer templates of blank utility bills, and computer files containing lists of people's credit card details.

In *Sakalauskas* [2014] 1 WLR 1204, it was held that the offence under s.6 is intended to prevent the possession of articles intended for use in the present or future. Thus, a conviction cannot be based upon the possession of articles which have been used in the past.

11.5 Making or supplying articles for use in frauds

Section 7(1) of the Fraud Act 2006 creates an offence of making or supplying an article for use in frauds. This is an either way offence, triable in the Crown court or the magistrates' court. Upon summary conviction, the offence carries a maximum sentence of 12 months' imprisonment or a fine not exceeding the statutory maximum or both. If the defendant is convicted on indictment, the maximum sentence is 10 years or a fine or both.

This offence makes it an offence to make, adapt, supply, or offer to supply an article for use in connection with fraud (the *actus reus*). The defendant must know that the article is designed or adapted for use in connection with fraud or intend that it be so used (the *mens rea*). An article is defined under s.8(1) of the Act (see 11.4).

The case of *Nimley* [2010] EWCA Crim 2752 also involved a conviction for the offence of making or supplying articles for use in fraud under s.7, namely the recording of the films which the defendant uploaded onto a website for people to download for free.

11.6 Conspiracy to defraud

This is a common law offence which was preserved by s.5(2) of the Criminal Law Act 1977 when most other common law conspiracies were abolished. The Law Commission recommended the abolition of this common law offence. However, the Government decided to retain the offence after receiving the responses to its Consultation Paper with a view to reassessing its position after the enactment of the Fraud Act 2006 and the publication of the Law Commission's report into inchoate liability: *Inchoate Liability for Assisting and Encouraging Crime* (Law Com. No. 300, Cm. 6878, 2006). It remains to be seen whether this offence will be abolished at a future date.

11.7 Making off without payment

Making off without payment is provided for in s.3(1) of the Theft Act 1978. It can be distinguished from the offence of theft because ownership of the property passes to the defendant prior to the formation of any dishonesty. The defendant does not dishonestly appropriate property belonging to another and cannot be convicted of theft. Similarly, making off without payment did not sit neatly with the old deception offences because there was no requirement that the goods or services were obtained by deception. Nevertheless, making off is an offence of dishonesty which involves the defendant obtaining goods or services but failing to pay for them. For these reasons, the offence is most appropriately placed within this chapter.

Making off is an either way offence which carries a maximum sentence of 2 years' imprisonment where the defendant is convicted in the Crown court.

 STATUTE

Section 3, Theft Act 1978

(1) ...a person who, knowing that payment on the spot for any goods supplied or service done is required or expected from him, dishonestly makes off without having paid as required or expected and with intent to avoid payment of the amount due shall be guilty of an offence.

(2) For purposes of this section 'payment on the spot' includes payment at the time of collecting goods on which work has been done or in respect of which service has been provided.

(3) Subsection (1) above shall not apply where the supply of the goods or the doing of the service is contrary to law, or where the service done is such that payment is not legally enforceable.

The *actus reus* of this offence requires the defendant to make off from the spot without having paid when payment was required or expected. The *mens rea* requires: the defendant to know that payment is required or expected from him, dishonesty, and an intention to avoid payment (table 11.5).

Table 11.5 Elements of making off without payment

Actus reus	Mens rea
• Makes off from the spot	• Knowledge that payment was required or expected
• Without having paid as required or expected	• Dishonesty
	• Intention to avoid payment

11.7.1 *Actus reus*

11.7.1.1 **Makes off from the spot**

The location of the 'spot' has been the subject of some debate. There are conflicting authorities as to where the 'spot' is in a restaurant. There is authority to suggest that a defendant must leave a restaurant in order to be guilty of making off under s.3 of the Theft Act 1978, but there is also authority to suggest that simply passing the point where payment is required is sufficient (i.e., the till). The defendant in the case of *McDavitt* [1981] Crim LR 843, walked towards the exit of a restaurant without having paid. The 'spot' was held to be the actual restaurant itself. So, the defendant could only be guilty of attempting to make off. He would have been guilty of the full offence of making off without payment once he had left the restaurant. By contrast, in the case of *Brooks and Brooks* (1982) 76 Cr App R 66, it was held that making off meant 'to depart'. Thus, according to this authority, the offence of making off is complete when the defendant passes the cash register (which is 'the spot where payment is required'), rather than the restaurant door. These authorities are difficult to reconcile and it is unclear which is preferred.

> **THINKING POINT**
>
> What would be the position in a restaurant where it is usual practice to pay at the table at the end of a meal?

Provided the *mens rea* is present at the time of the *actus reus*, applying *Brooks and Brooks*, it could be said that the defendant has made off when he leaves the table. However, on the *McDavitt* approach, the defendant would have to leave the restaurant entirely.

11.7.1.2 **Without having paid as required or expected**

The defendant must make off from the spot without having paid as required or expected for goods supplied or service done. The Act does not define 'goods' or 'service'. The point in time at which payment is required or expected is obvious in some scenarios. For instance, it is clear that payment is required or expected in a restaurant at least at the end of the meal, or at a petrol station after filling up with petrol but before driving away. However, in some cases, the point at which payment is required or expected has been in dispute.

> **CASE CLOSE-UP**
>
> ***Troughton v The Metropolitan Police*** [1987] Crim LR 138
>
> In the case of *Troughton v The Metropolitan Police*, the defendant, who was drunk, took a taxi. He gave the driver directions as far as Highbury, where the driver stopped to obtain further directions from the defendant. However, an argument broke out between the defendant and the driver, in which the defendant accused the driver of taking an unnecessarily long route to Highbury.
>
> The defendant did not give the driver any more directions, so the driver took the defendant to the police station. The defendant tried to leave the taxi and was charged with making off without payment under s.3 of the Theft Act 1978. His conviction was quashed on appeal because the time at which payment was required or expected had not been

> reached. The driver was contracted to complete the journey and he did not do so. By departing from the contracted journey to the defendant's home, the taxi driver had in fact breached his contract with the defendant. As the driver's side of the contract had not been performed, the driver was not in a position to be able to demand the fare and the defendant was under no legal obligation to pay it. Thus, payment was not required or expected at the moment when the defendant tried to leave the taxi.

The case of *Aziz* [1993] Crim LR 708 also involved a dispute over a taxi fare. The defendant took a taxi and, upon reaching his destination, he disputed the fare, refusing to pay. The taxi driver then started to drive back towards a police station, but the defendant jumped out of the taxi and ran off without paying. He was convicted of making off without payment under s.3 of the Theft Act 1978 and his conviction was upheld on appeal. The Court of Appeal held that the payment was required or expected once the driver and passenger had reached the destination. This was the 'spot' from which the defendant had made off. The offence was complete once the destination had been reached and payment was required or expected. The fact that the driver had then turned around and headed towards a police station did not negate the offence which was already complete.

THINKING POINT

Do you think the decision in this case was correct?

11.7.2 *Mens rea*

11.7.2.1 **Knowledge that payment was required or expected**

The *mens rea* of the offence of making off without payment requires that the defendant knew that payment was required or expected for goods or services supplied.

11.7.2.2 **Dishonesty**

▶ CROSS REFERENCE
Refer to 9.2.1.2 and 11.2.1.1 for a detailed discussion on dishonesty.

Dishonesty is a question of fact for the jury to determine: *Feely*. The *Ghosh* test of dishonesty also applies to making off without payment. Thus, the jury must consider whether what the defendant did was dishonest according to the ordinary standards of reasonable and honest people (this is the objective limb which was adopted in *Feely*). If the jury are satisfied that it was, they must consider whether the defendant realised that reasonable and honest people would regard it as dishonest (this is the subjective limb added to the test by the case of *Ghosh*). The negative aspect of dishonesty under s.2(1) of the Theft Act 1968 does not apply to the offence of making off without payment.

11.7.2.3 **Intention to avoid payment permanently**

The defendant must intend to avoid payment permanently. It has been held that it is not enough to simply intend to delay payment. This is clear from the House of Lords' authority of *Allen* [1985] 2 All ER 641. In this case, the defendant left a hotel without paying his bill. The Court of Appeal quashed his conviction because he had a valid defence, namely that he did intend to pay the bill at some point. Hence, he had no intention to permanently avoid payment. This decision was upheld by the House of Lords.

THINKING POINT

Consider whether the offence of making off without payment under s.3 of the Theft Act 1978 had been committed in the following scenarios:

(1) Kensie visits a coffee shop and orders a slice of blueberry cheesecake and a coffee. The waitress brings these over to him. Whilst in the coffee shop, Kensie receives a phone call which distracts him. He rushes out of the coffee shop without paying.

(2) Annie goes to a petrol station at which the customer has a choice whether to pay by card at the petrol pump before filling up or pay in the petrol station shop after filling up. Annie pretends to put her card into the reader at the petrol pump and fills up her car with petrol. She then drives off without having paid for the petrol.

(3) Robert takes a group of friends to a wine bar to celebrate the end of their criminal law exam. He orders four bottles of their finest champagne which is brought over to their table. After finishing the champagne, Robert and his friend leave the wine bar. Robert calls out to the waitress, 'I'll pay another time.'

 # Summary

- There is a general offence of fraud under s.1 of the Fraud Act 2006.

- There are three ways in which fraud may be committed. Section 2 of the Fraud Act 2006 provides for fraud by false representation; s.3 provides for fraud by failing to disclose information; and s.4 provides for fraud by abuse of a position of financial trust.

- Dishonesty is common to all three of these ways of committing fraud. The *Ghosh* (1982) test of dishonesty applies, namely: *(i)* was what the defendant did dishonest according to the ordinary standards of reasonable and honest people? If so, *(ii)* did the defendant realise that reasonable and honest people would regard it as dishonest?

- The defendant must intend, by making the representation, to make a gain for himself or another, or to cause loss to another or to expose another to a risk of loss. 'Gain' and 'loss' are defined under s.5 of the Fraud Act 2006. This is also an element common to all three ways of committing fraud.

- In order to be guilty of fraud by false representation (s.1(2)(a), Fraud Act 2006), the representation must be a false one: i.e., it must be 'untrue or misleading' (s.2(2)(a)). Additionally, the defendant must know that it is untrue or misleading, or know that it might be untrue or misleading (s.2(2)(b)).

- In order to be guilty of fraud by failing to disclose information (s.1(2)(b), Fraud Act 2006), there must be a legal duty to disclose the information (s.3(a)).

- In order to be guilty of fraud by abuse of position of financial trust (s.1(2)(c), Fraud Act 2006), there must be a position of financial trust. Such a position is one in which the defendant is expected to safeguard or not to act against the financial interests of another person (s.4(1)). This position must be dishonestly abused (s.4(1)(b)).

The bigger picture

- In order to fully appreciate why the deception offences were replaced with the single offence of fraud, you need to have an understanding of the old law and its problems. You should read the following:

    Law Commission Report, *Fraud* (Law Com. No. 276, 2002)

    Smith (1997)

    R v Preddy [1996] 3 All ER 735, HL

    Explanatory Notes to the Fraud Act 2006.

- Since the *Ghosh* test on dishonesty applies to both theft and fraud, you should refer to 9.2.1.2 on the application of the *Ghosh* test and why the test has both objective and subjective limbs.

- Fraud is an examinable topic and you should ensure that you are able to answer both essay and problem questions in this area.

    For some guidance on how you might approach essay questions on these topics, you should visit the Online Resource Centre.

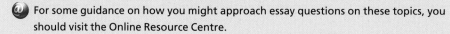

? Questions

Self-test questions

1. Explain the main objective behind the reforms of the law of fraud.

2. What are the three ways in which the offence of fraud can be committed?

3. What is the test for dishonesty? Refer to case law in your answer.

4. How does the Fraud Act 2006 define 'gain' and 'loss'?

5. What is a 'representation'?

6. When is a representation 'false'?

7. Can fraud be committed against a machine?

8. Give examples of when there might be a duty to disclose information.

9. What type of 'positions' does s.4 apply to?

10. Identify the elements of the offence of making off without payment.

    For suggested approaches, please visit the Online Resource Centre.

Exam questions

1. Answer *all* parts below:

    (a) Margaret applies for a mortgage and life insurance. She states on the mortgage application form that she has an income of £40,000 and she does not fill out the section relating to credit card debts held. In fact, Margaret's income is £25,000 and she owes £3,000 on various credit cards. In relation to the life insurance application, Margaret does not declare on the form that her family has a history of heart disease.

And

(b) Geoffrey, a solicitor, receives £100,000 from Tony, a client. Instead of transferring the money into the business account, he transfers the money into his personal account.

And

(c) Holly drives to a car wash which is operated by tokens purchased from a shop. Instead of buying a token, Holly uses a fake token which she has made herself. She places the fake token into the machine. The machine accepts it and washes Holly's car.

What offences, if any, have Margaret, Geoffrey, and Holly committed?

2. The Fraud Act 2006 has been a great success. The general offence of fraud created by the Act is simple, accessible, and has the flexibility to deal with future developments.

To what extent to you agree with this statement? Explain your answer.

 For suggested approaches, please visit the Online Resource Centre.

 Further reading

Books

Farrell QC, S., Yeo, N., and Ladenburg, G. *Blackstone's Guide to The Fraud Act 2006* (2007), Oxford: Oxford University Press

Ormerod, D. and Laird, K. *Smith and Hogan: Criminal Law* (14th edn, 2015), Oxford: Oxford University Press

Ormerod, D. and Williams, D. H. *Smith's Law of Theft* (9th edn, 2007), Oxford: Oxford University Press

Smith, J. C. *The Law of Theft* (8th edn, 1997), Butterworths

Journal articles

Collins, J. 'Fraud by Abuse of Position: Theorising Section 4 of the Fraud Act 2006' [2011] Crim LR 513

Monaghan, C. 'Fraudsters? Putting Parents in the Dock' (2010a) 174 JPN 581

Monaghan, C. 'To Prosecute or Not to Prosecute? A Reconsideration of the Over-Zealous Prosecution of Parents under the Fraud Act 2006' (2010b) 74 JCL 259

Ormerod, D. 'The Fraud Act 2006—Criminalising Lying?' [2007] Crim LR 193

Wilson, G. and Wilson, S. 'Can the General Fraud Offence "Get the Law Right"? Some Perspectives on the "Problem" of Financial Crime' (2007) 71 JCL 36

Withey, C. 'The Fraud Act 2006—Some Early Observations and Comparisons with the Former Law' (2007) 71 JCL 220

12 Drugs offences

□ **LEARNING OBJECTIVES**

By the end of this chapter, you should be able to:

● distinguish between the main drug offences under the Misuse of Drugs Act 1971;

● identify and explain the elements of these offences;

● understand the applicability of the various defences to the drug offences; and

● apply the elements of these drug offences to problem scenarios.

Introduction

You may have seen recent headlines in the news which call for 'legal highs' to be banned. 'Legal highs' are psychoactive substances which mimic the effects of some controlled drugs. The call for the possession, supply, production, etc. of these 'legal highs' to be banned is based upon the recent increase in the emergence of these substances and concern that they lead to criminal conduct and harm to individuals. While this proposal for reform continues to make its way though Parliament, the current main piece of legislation governing drugs offences with which this chapter is concerned is the Misuse of Drugs Act 1971. The offences under the 1971 Act aim to protect people from the misuse of dangerous and harmful drugs by punishing drug misuse. This chapter will explore the main drug offences under the Misuse of Drugs Act 1971, including possession of controlled drugs, possession with intent to supply controlled drugs, the supply and production of controlled drugs, and the offence of an occupier or a person concerned in the management of any premises permitting drug-related activities to take place on those premises. Each of these offences will be discussed in turn in this chapter.

As you can see from the titles of these offences, the Misuse of Drugs Act 1971 applies to activities relating to 'controlled drugs'; this term applies to the list of drugs which feature under Schedule 2 to the Act. Controlled drugs are divided into three main classes: Class A, Class B, and Class C; Class A drugs being the most harmful (and therefore offences involving these drugs are more serious and carry higher sentences), and Class C drugs being the least harmful (and the offence is correspondingly less serious and carries a lower maximum sentence) and this is considered at 12.1.2.

Finally, the chapter also explores the recent proposals in respect of other psychoactive drugs ('legal highs'—it should be noted that this term has been criticised by the Government as 'inappropriate given that the chemicals in them are often neither legal nor safe for human consumption' (see the Explanatory Notes to the Psychoactive Substances Bill 2015, para. 7)).

12.1 Possession of controlled drugs

It is an offence to be in possession of a controlled drug. The rationale for the inclusion of possession of a controlled drug in the Misuse of Drugs Act 1971 was explained by Lord Morris in *Warner v Metropolitan Police Commissioner* [1969] 2 AC 256:

> It is a declared purpose of the Act to prevent the misuse of drugs. If actual possession of particular substances which are regarded as potentially damaging is not controlled there will be danger of the misuse of them by those who possess them. They might be harmfully used: they might be sold in most undesirable ways. (At 295)

The offence of possession of a controlled drug is provided for by s.5(2) of the Misuse of Drugs Act 1971.

 STATUTE

Section 5, Misuse of Drugs Act 1971

(1) Subject to any regulations under section 7 of this Act for the time being in force, it shall not be lawful for a person to have a controlled drug in his possession.

(2) Subject to section 28 of this Act and to subsection (4) below, it is an offence for a person to have a controlled drug in his possession in contravention of subsection (1) above.

This offence is triable either way and the maximum sentence available to the court upon conviction varies according to the class of drug in question: s.25 and Schedule 4 (see table 12.1). The more serious offence is possession of a Class A drug and the least serious offence is possession of a Class C drug.

This offence simply requires the defendant 'to have a controlled drug in his possession'. The *actus reus* of this offence does not require any conduct on the part of the defendant, thus the offence does not require the defendant to *obtain* the controlled drug or to *consume* the controlled drug, rather this is a 'state of affairs' crime which is committed when the defendant is *in possession* of a controlled drug. The meaning of 'possession' is explored at 12.1.1.

⟩ CROSS REFERENCE

For the guidance given to prosecutors on the possession of cannabis for personal use, see 12.1.2.

Table 12.1 Maximum penalties for possession of a controlled drug, s.5(2)

Classification of drug	Maximum sentence if tried summarily	Maximum sentence if tried on indictment
Class A	6 months' imprisonment and/or a fine	7 years' imprisonment and/or a fine
Class B	3 months' imprisonment and/or a fine	5 years' imprisonment and/or a fine
Class C	3 months' imprisonment and/or a fine	2 years' imprisonment and/or a fine

12.1.1 Meaning of possession

The term 'possession' is not defined within the Misuse of Drugs Act 1971. The only provision which partially provides for the term is s.37(3), which states that for the purposes of the Act: 'the things which a person has in his possession shall be taken to include any thing subject to his control which is in the custody of another'. This is far from a comprehensive explanation of the meaning of possession and an examination of the common law is required for a more helpful explanation of the term. The leading case on the meaning of possession is the House of Lords' decision in *Warner v Metropolitan Police Commissioner* [1969] 2 AC 256. This is a case which was decided before the enactment of the Misuse of Drugs Act 1971, but the opinion of the House on the meaning of possession is applicable to the 1971 Act: *McNamara* (1988) 87 Cr App R 246.

🔍 CASE CLOSE-UP

***Warner v Metropolitan Police Commissioner* [1969] 2 AC 256**

The defendant in this case had been driving in his van when he was stopped by a police officer. Three cases were found in the back of the van; one case contained bottles of perfume and another case held a plastic bag containing 20,000 amphetamine sulphate tablets. The defendant stated that he had picked up these two cases from a café where he usually went to collect boxes of perfume from an associate called Bill. He had been told by the café owner that a parcel from Bill was under the counter, and the defendant found the two cases there, which he took. The defendant claimed that he did not know that one of the cases contained drugs. He was convicted of having drugs in his possession without being duly authorised, contrary to s.1(1) of the Drugs (Prevention of Misuse) Act 1964 and he appealed against his conviction. The appeal was dismissed by the Court of Appeal, but the defendant appealed to the House of Lords on a certified point of law of general public importance, namely:

> Whether . . . a defendant is deemed to be in possession of a prohibited substance when to his knowledge he is in physical possession of the substance but is unaware of its true nature.

The House of Lords held that the offence of possession of a drug under s.1(1) of the Drugs (Prevention of Misuse) Act 1964 was an offence of 'absolute' liability. The question of whether the defendant was in possession of the drugs with a guilty intention or not was deemed to be irrelevant to his liability. Thus, the prosecution did not need to prove that the defendant intended to be or knew that he was in possession of a controlled drug.

However, the House drew a distinction between merely being in physical custody or control of an object and being in possession of an object, and held that knowledge is an essential element of possession because a person cannot be in possession of something if he is unaware that it exists.

Lord Pearce stated that:

the term 'possession' is satisfied by a knowledge only of the existence of the thing itself and not its qualities and that ignorance or mistake as to its qualities will not excuse. This would comply with the general understanding of the word 'possess'. Though I reasonably believe the tablets which I possess to be aspirin, yet if they turn out to be heroin I am in possession of heroin tablets. This would be so, I think, even if I believed them to be sweets. It would be otherwise if I believed them to be something of a wholly different nature. At this point a question of degree arises as to when a difference in qualities amounts to a difference in kind. That is a matter for a jury . . .

The situation with regard to containers presents further problems. If a man is in possession of the contents of a package, prima facie his possession of the package leads to the strong inference that he is in possession of its contents. (At 305)

Thus, the prosecution was required to prove that the defendant knew that he was in possession of the case containing the drug (i.e., proof of possession of the container) and that he knew that the case contained something (i.e., proof of possession of the contents). It did not matter that the defendant did not know that the case contained controlled drugs.

Lord Pearce continued:

But can this be rebutted by evidence that he was mistaken as to its contents? As in the case of goods that have been 'planted' in his pocket without his knowledge, so I do not think that he is in possession of contents which are quite different in kind from what he believed. (At 305–6)

Lord Pearce also relied upon the question of whether the defendant had a reasonable opportunity to inspect the contents of the case he picked up:

a man takes over a package or suitcase at risk as to its contents being unlawful if he does not immediately examine it (if he is entitled to do so). As soon as may be he should examine it and if he finds the contents suspicious reject possession by either throwing them away or by taking immediate sensible steps for their disposal. (At 307)

THINKING POINT

Read the extracts from the opinion of Lord Pearce in the case close-up box for *Warner v Metropolitan Police Commissioner* [1969] 2 AC 256. What do you think Lord Pearce was referring to by 'contents which are quite different in kind from what he believed' (at 306)?

Since this case raised an issue of social concern, the decision is grounded in policy considerations: the objective of the courts being the prevention of the misuse of drugs. Consequently, the courts imputed knowledge to the meaning of the term 'possession', such that knowledge is an essential element of possession. So, possession requires more than just being in custody or control of an object, but the defendant must also know that he has the object.

> **CROSS REFERENCE**
> Knowledge is a *mens rea* element which is subjectively assessed. See 3.5 for further discussion on this point.

THINKING POINT

Imagine that you share a house with three other people and a package containing cocaine is found in a chest of drawers in the living room. Are you in possession of the cocaine for the purposes of s.5(2) of the Misuse of Drugs Act 1971?

12.1.2 'Controlled drugs'

The offence of possession under s.5(2) requires that the drugs which form the subject of the charge are 'controlled drugs'. Section 37(1) of the Misuse of Drugs Act 1971 states that '"controlled drug" has the meaning assigned by section 2 of this Act'. Section 2 of the Act states that a 'controlled drug' is a drug on the list in Schedule 2 to the Act or in a Temporary Class Drug Order.

Schedule 2 to the Act provides a list of controlled drugs. These are divided into three classes, A, B, and C, in accordance with the harmful and/or dangerous nature of the drug.

12.1.2.1 Class A drugs

Class A drugs are the most harmful and/or dangerous drugs and these form the basis of a more serious offence and harsher sentence; these include cocaine, methadone, opium, and morphine. 'Cocaine' within Schedule 2 includes cocaine in its natural form, its derivatives, and stereoisomeric forms: '"cocaine" as used in paragraph 1 is a generic word which includes within its ambit both the direct extracts of the coca leaf, the natural form, and whatever results from a chemical transformation' (*per* Lawton LJ in *R v Greensmith* [1983] 1 WLR 1124 at 1127). Ecstasy (or 'MDMA') is also a Class A drug (para. 1(c), Schedule 2), as is LSD (known as 'acid'). Magic mushrooms are a Class A drug under the Misuse of Drugs Act 1971 since they constitute a '[f]ungus (of any kind) which contains psilocin or an ester of psilocin' (inserted by s.21, Drugs Act 2005). Methylamphetamine (known as 'crystal meth' or 'ice') was reclassified from a Class B drug to a Class A drug in 2007 (by article 2(1) of the Misuse of Drugs Act 1971 (Amendment) Order 2006 (SI 2006/331)).

12.1.2.2 Class B drugs

Class B drugs are deemed to be slightly less harmful and/or dangerous; these include cannabis, cannabis resin, amphetamine, barbiturates, ketamine, methylphenidate (or 'ritalin'), and codeine. The Crown Prosecution Service will usually bring a prosecution against a defendant who is charged with possession of more than a minimal quantity of a Class B or Class C drug (CPS Charging Standards Drug Offences available at http://www.cps.gov.uk/legal/d_to_g/drug_offences/#a01). Where the defendant has been found in possession of a small amount of cannabis for personal use, the CPS Charging Standards advise prosecutors to consider the guidance provided by the National Police Chief's Council (formerly the Association of Chief Police Officers). This guidance suggests that where this is the defendant's first offence, he should be given a 'cannabis warning' unless there are aggravating features, no admission by the defendant, or the defendant is a repeat or persistent offender. If any of these circumstances exist, the defendant should instead be charged or issued with a Penalty Notice for Disorder. Where this is the defendant's second offence and he admits the offence or there is sufficient evidence that the offence has been committed, a Penalty Notice for Disorder is the suggested disposal. Where this is the third or subsequent offence, the suggestion is that the defendant should be arrested and charged (see CPS Charging Standards Drug Offences).

12.1.2.3 **Class C drugs**

Finally, the least harmful and/or dangerous drugs which fall under the Act are Class C drugs; these include ketamine, diazepam, temazepan, and khat.

12.1.2.4 **Temporary Class Drug Orders**

Where a drug falls under a Temporary Class Drug Order, it is a 'controlled drug' for the purposes of the Misuse of Drugs Act 1971. Under s.2A, a drug may be made the subject of a Temporary Class Drug Order by the Secretary of State, provided that the drug in question 'is being, or is likely to be, misused, and…that misuse is having, or is capable of having harmful effects' (s.2A(4)). Unless the substance is subsequently listed within Schedule 2, the Temporary Class Drug Order lasts for 1 year (s.2A(6)).

12.1.3 **Defences**

Sections 5(4) and 28 of the Misuse of Drugs Act 1971 contain defences to some of the offences under the Act. Each of these provisions will be dealt with separately at 12.1.3.1 and 12.1.3.2 respectively.

12.1.3.1 **Section 5(4) defences**

Section 5(4) of the Misuse of Drugs Act 1971 provides two defences to the offence under s.5(2) (possession of a controlled drug). These defences are specific defences in the sense that they only apply to the offence of possession of a controlled drug under s.5(2) and will not apply where a defendant is charged with the more serious offence of possession of a controlled drug with intent to supply under s.5(3).

 STATUTE

Section 5(4), Misuse of Drugs Act 1971

In any proceedings for an offence under subsection (2) above in which it is proved that the accused had a controlled drug in his possession, it shall be a defence for him to prove—

(a) that, knowing or suspecting it to be a controlled drug, he took possession of it for the purpose of preventing another from committing or continuing to commit an offence in connection with that drug and that as soon as possible after taking possession of it he took all such steps as were reasonably open to him to destroy the drug or to deliver it into the custody of a person lawfully entitled to take custody of it; or

(b) that, knowing or suspecting it to be a controlled drug, he took possession of it for the purpose of delivering it into the custody of a person lawfully entitled to take custody of it and that as soon as possible after taking possession of it he took all such steps as were reasonably open to him to deliver it into the custody of such a person.

These defences apply where the defendant took possession of the drug, knowing or suspecting it to be a controlled drug, and:

- his/her purpose in doing so was to prevent someone else from committing an offence in connection with that drug, and as soon as possible after taking possession of it he took all such steps as were reasonably open to him to destroy the drug or to deliver it into the custody of someone lawfully entitled to take custody of it (s.5(4)(a)); or

- his/her purpose was to deliver the drug into the custody of a person lawfully entitled to take custody of it, and as soon as possible after taking possession of it he took all such steps as were reasonably open to him to deliver it into the custody of such a person (s.5(4)(b)).

⟩ CROSS REFERENCE

Refer back to 1.10.3 to remind yourself of the difference between the legal burden and the evidential burden.

Since the House of Lords' decision in *R v Lambert* [2001] 2 WLR 211, it would seem that the defences under s.5(4) only place an evidential burden on the defendant, as opposed to a legal burden. This was the decision reached by the House in respect of the defence under s.28 of the Misuse of Drugs Act 1971 in order to ensure that the provision is compatible with the presumption of innocence under Article 6.2 of the European Convention on Human Rights (see particularly the opinion of Lord Slynn at [17]). The same must also apply to s.5(4).

While the defences in s.5(4) apply specifically to s.5(2), s.5(6) also provides that a defendant is open to raise any other defence that might apply to him. Thus, a defendant charged under s.5(2) is not restricted only to the defences under s.5(4) and may indeed raise any other defence that applies in his circumstances.

12.1.3.2 Section 28 defences

A defendant charged with an offence under s.5(2) (or indeed, for the purposes of this chapter, under s.5(3), 4(2), or 4(3)) may rely on the defence under s.28 of the Misuse of Drugs Act 1971.

 STATUTE

Section 28, Misuse of Drugs Act 1971

(2) Subject to subsection (3) below, in any proceedings for an offence to which this section applies it shall be a defence for the accused to prove that he neither knew of nor suspected nor had reason to suspect the existence of some fact alleged by the prosecution which it is necessary for the prosecution to prove if he is to be convicted of the offence charged.

(3) Where in any proceedings for an offence to which this section applies it is necessary, if the accused is to be convicted of the offence charged, for the prosecution to prove that some substance or product involved in the alleged offence was the controlled drug which the prosecution alleges it to have been, and it is proved that the substance or product in question was that controlled drug, the accused—

　(a) shall not be acquitted of the offence charged by reason only of proving that he neither knew nor suspected nor had reason to suspect that the substance or product in question was the particular controlled drug alleged; but

　(b) shall be acquitted thereof—

　　(i) if he proves that he neither believed nor suspected nor had reason to suspect that the substance or product in question was a controlled drug; or

　　(ii) if he proves that he believed the substance or product in question to be a controlled drug, or a controlled drug of a description, such that, if it had in fact been that controlled drug or a controlled drug of that description, he would not at the material time have been committing any offence to which this section applies.

Under s.28(2), the defendant will have a defence if he did not know of, nor suspected, nor had reason to suspect the existence of some *fact* alleged by the prosecution that the prosecution must prove in order to establish the offence charged. For instance, if, unbeknown to the defendant, another person places a quantity of cocaine into the defendant's pocket, such that the defendant is not aware that he is in possession of the substance, he may raise a defence under s.28(2):

> a man does not have possession of something which has been put into his pocket or into his house without his knowledge: in other words something which is 'planted' on him, to use the current vulgarism. (*McNamara* (1988) 87 Cr App R 246 at 250–1)

If the defendant is aware that he is in possession of a controlled drug, but is mistaken about the precise controlled drug that he is in possession of, he will have no defence (s.28(3)(a)).

Section 28(3)(b) provides that where the prosecution have to prove that a substance is a controlled drug, the defendant will have a defence if he neither believed, nor suspected, nor had reason to suspect that the substance or product in question was a controlled drug (s.28(3)(b)(i)), or if he believed the substance or product in question to be a controlled drug, such that, if it had in fact been that controlled drug, he would not at the material time have been committing the offence charged (s.28(3)(b)(ii)). For instance, if the defendant is charged with possession of cocaine, but he thought he was in possession of a substance that was not a controlled drug, such as sugar, he raises the defence under s.28(3)(b)(i). If the defendant knew that he was in possession of a controlled drug, but he believed that he was in possession of a drug which he was lawfully permitted to be in possession of, such as a doctor, dentist, or veterinary practitioner acting within the authorisation provided by s.7 of the Act, he may raise the defence under s.28(3)(b)(ii) if he is actually in possession of a controlled drug which he is not authorised to take possession of.

The defences under s.28 only place an evidential burden on the defendant: *R v Lambert* [2001] 2 WLR 211.

Section 28(4) provides that any other general defence which falls outside this Act might be relied upon by the defendant.

12.2 Possession with intent to supply

It is an offence to be in possession of a controlled drug with the intention to supply that drug to another. This offence is provided for by s.5(3) of the Misuse of Drugs Act 1971. This offence is rendered more serious than the simple offence of possession by virtue of the additional requirement that the defendant must intend to supply the drug to another person.

 STATUTE

Section 5(3), Misuse of Drugs Act 1971

Subject to section 28 of this Act, it is an offence for a person to have a controlled drug in his possession, whether lawfully or not, with intent to supply it to another in contravention of section 4(1) of this Act.

Table 12.2 Maximum penalties for possession of a controlled drug with intent to supply, s.5(3)

Classification of drug	Maximum sentence if tried summarily	Maximum sentence if tried on indictment
Class A	6 months' imprisonment and/or a fine	Life imprisonment and/or a fine
Class B	6 months' imprisonment and/or a fine	14 years' imprisonment and/or a fine
Class C	3 months' imprisonment and/or a fine	14 years' imprisonment and/or a fine

This offence is also triable either way and the maximum sentence available to the court upon conviction also varies according to the class of drug in question. The maximum sentences set out within Schedule 4 are higher than those for the simple offence of possession to reflect the increased seriousness of this offence (see table 12.2).

The prosecution must not only prove that the defendant was in possession of the controlled drug, but must also prove that he intended to supply the drug. 'Supplying' is partially defined under s.37(1) as 'including distributing'. An intention to supply may be proved by adducing evidence of a large quantity of drugs in the defendant's possession and asking the tribunal of fact to infer from that quantity that the defendant did not merely intend to use the drug for personal use, but intended to supply it to other persons. Such an intention may also be inferred from the existence of drugs paraphernalia, such as scales, small plastic bags, and quantities of cash.

The defences under s.5(4) do not apply to a charge under s.5(3), but a defendant charged under s.5(3) may rely on a defence under s.28 (see 12.1.3.2).

12.3 Production and supply of controlled drugs

This paragraph deals with the offences of the production of controlled drugs and the supply of controlled drugs under s.4(2) and (3) of the Misuse of Drugs Act 1971 respectively.

 STATUTE

Section 4, Misuse of Drugs Act 1971

(1) Subject to any regulations under section 7 of this Act [or any provision made in a temporary class drug order by virtue of section 7A] for the time being in force, it shall not be lawful for a person—

(a) to produce a controlled drug; or

(b) to supply or offer to supply a controlled drug to another.

(2) Subject to section 28 of this Act, it is an offence for a person—

  (a) to produce a controlled drug in contravention of subsection (1) above; or

  (b) to be concerned in the production of such a drug in contravention of that subsection by another.

(3) Subject to section 28 of this Act, it is an offence for a person—

  (a) to supply or offer to supply a controlled drug to another in contravention of subsection (1) above; or

  (b) to be concerned in the supplying of such a drug to another in contravention of that subsection; or

  (c) to be concerned in the making to another in contravention of that subsection of an offer to supply such a drug.

Each of these offences will be considered under 12.3.1 and 12.3.2.

12.3.1 Production of controlled drugs

Section 4(2) provides that it is an offence to produce a controlled drug, or to be concerned in the production of such a drug by another. This offence is triable either way and the maximum sentence available to the court upon conviction varies according to the class of drug in question (see table 12.3).

The prosecution must prove that the defendant did one of two activities, either that he:

- produced a controlled drug (s.4(2)(a)); or
- was concerned in the production of such a drug by another person (s.4(2)(b)).

'Produce' is defined under s.37(1) as 'producing it by manufacture, cultivation or any other method'. This is only a partial definition, so, if the defendant has manufactured or cultivated the controlled drug in question, he may be charged under this offence. However, the Act also includes the production of a controlled drug by 'any other method', such as by stripping the leaves from a cannabis plant, discarding the parts which were not usable, and putting together those parts which were (see *R v Harris; R v Cox* [1996] 1 Cr App R 369). Alternatively, the defendant could be charged with this offence if another person produces the drug, but the defendant is concerned in the production of that drug. The words 'being concerned in' require proof that the defendant participated in the enterprise: *R v Akinsete and Prempah* [2012] EWCA Crim 2377 at [24]. Thus,

Table 12.3 Maximum penalties for production, or being concerned in the production, of a controlled drug, s.4(2)

Classification of drug	Maximum sentence if tried summarily	Maximum sentence if tried on indictment
Class A	6 months' imprisonment and/or a fine	Life imprisonment and/or a fine
Class B	6 months' imprisonment and/or a fine	14 years' imprisonment and/or a fine
Class C	3 months' imprisonment and/or a fine	14 years' imprisonment and/or a fine

for a conviction under s.4(2)(b), it must be shown that the defendant has participated in the production of the drug. In *Dunn* [2008] EWCA Crim 2308, the Court of Appeal held that by performing the role of cleaner in premises in which there is a production of cannabis on a large scale, knowing what was going on there, the defendant was capable of being a participant in the production of the drug: '[t]he clearing of rooms at the appropriate part of the production cycle was an integral part of the process of production' (at [36]).

A defendant charged with the production of a controlled drug under s.4(2) may rely on a defence under s.28 (see 12.1.3.2).

12.3.2 Supply of controlled drugs

Section 4(3) provides that it is an offence to supply or offer to supply a controlled drug to another, or to be concerned in the supplying of such a drug to another, or to be concerned in the making to another of an offer to supply such a drug. This offence is triable either way and the maximum sentence available to the court upon conviction varies according to the class of drug in question (see table 12.4).

The prosecution must prove that the defendant did one of four activities, either that he:

- supplied a controlled drug to another person (s.4(3)(a));
- offered to supply a controlled drug to another person (s.4(3)(a));
- was concerned in supplying such a drug to another person (s.4(3)(b)); or
- was concerned in making an offer to supply such a drug to another person (s.4(3)(c)).

'Supplying' is partially defined under s.37(1) as 'including distributing'. The Court of Appeal has recently held that '"supply" is a broad term' which is not confined to '"actual delivery" or "past supply"', but rather '[i]t refers to the entire process of supply', and includes the current transportation of drugs from one place to another: *Martin (Dwain) and another* [2015] 1 WLR 588.

The leading authority on the elements that need to be proved for a conviction under s.4(3)(b) or (c) is *R v Hughes* (1985) 81 Cr App R 344. Robert Goff LJ held (at 348) that for such an offence to be committed, the prosecution must prove:

(1) the supply of a drug to another, or the making of an offer to supply a drug;

(2) participation by the defendant in an enterprise involving such supply; and

Table 12.4 Maximum penalties for supplying or offering to supply a controlled drug, or being concerned in the doing of either activity by another, s.4(3)

Classification of drug	Maximum sentence if tried summarily	Maximum sentence if tried on indictment
Class A	6 months' imprisonment and/or a fine	Life imprisonment and/or a fine
Class B	6 months' imprisonment and/or a fine	14 years' imprisonment and/or a fine
Class C	3 months' imprisonment and/or a fine	14 years' imprisonment and/or a fine

(3) knowledge by the defendant of the nature of the enterprise, i.e., that it involved supply or the offer to supply a drug.

This approach has been followed more recently in *R v Akinsete and Prempah* [2012] EWCA Crim 2377 (see [23]), in which it was also held that the words 'being concerned in' require proof that the defendant participated in the enterprise (at [24]). It has been held that the offence of being concerned in the offer to supply a controlled drug to another person 'has been particularly widely drawn to involve people who may be at some distance from the actual making of the offer': *R v Blake; R v O'Connor* (1979) 68 Cr App R 1 at 3. 'Being concerned in the supply' of a controlled drug includes a situation in which the defendant has introduced someone wanting to obtain drugs to someone who could supply those drugs, and together they obtain the heroin on the understanding that the defendant will pay for his share: *Baker* [2009] EWCA Crim 535.

A defendant charged with the supply of a controlled drug under s.4(3) may rely on a defence under s.28 (see 12.1.3.2).

12.4 Occupier permitting drug-related activities on premises

Under s.8 of the Misuse of Drugs Act 1971, it is an offence for an occupier or someone concerned in the management of premises to knowingly permit the premises to be used for certain drug-related activities.

 STATUTE

Section 8, Misuse of Drugs Act 1971

A person commits an offence if, being the occupier or concerned in the management of any premises, he knowingly permits or suffers any of the following activities to take place on those premises, that is to say—

(a) producing or attempting to produce a controlled drug in contravention of section 4(1) of this Act;

(b) supplying or attempting to supply a controlled drug to another in contravention of section 4(1) of this Act, or offering to supply a controlled drug to another in contravention of section 4(1);

(c) preparing opium for smoking;

(d) smoking cannabis, cannabis resin or prepared opium.

This offence is triable either way and the maximum sentence available to the court upon conviction varies according to the class of drug in question (see table 12.5).

Table 12.5 Maximum penalties for being the occupier, or concerned in the management, of premises and permitting or suffering certain activities to take place there, s.8

Classification of drug	Maximum sentence if tried summarily	Maximum sentence if tried on indictment
Class A	6 months' imprisonment and/or a fine	14 years' imprisonment and/or a fine
Class B	6 months' imprisonment and/or a fine	14 years' imprisonment and/or a fine
Class C	3 months' imprisonment and/or a fine	14 years' imprisonment and/or a fine

The object of s.8 is to 'punish those persons who are able to exclude from their premises potential offenders who wish to smoke cannabis in those premises, but do not do so': per Roskill LJ in *Tao* [1977] QB 141 at 144. The offence requires proof of three main elements:

1. the defendant must be the occupier of the premises in question, or must be concerned in the management of those premises;

2. he must knowingly permit or suffer an activity listed below to take place on those premises; and

3. one of the following activities must have taken place, namely:

    • producing or attempting to produce a controlled drug,

    • supplying or attempting to supply a controlled drug to another or offering to supply a controlled drug to another,

    • preparing opium for smoking, or

    • smoking cannabis, cannabis resin, or prepared opium.

12.4.1 Occupier or concerned in the management of the premises

The term 'occupier' is given a 'common sense interpretation', such that an occupier is 'someone who, on the facts of the particular case, could fairly be said to be "in occupation" of the premises in question, so as to have the requisite degree of control over those premises to exclude from them those who might otherwise intend to carry on . . . forbidden activities': *Tao* [1977] QB 141 at 144. Thus, 'occupier' covers owners of premises (including lessees) as well as licensees who do not have exclusive possession but who have 'sufficient exclusivity of possession' over and above a mere right to use the premises: *Tao* [1977] QB 141 at 146. Thus, in *Tao* the defendant had an exclusive contractual licence to use a room in his college, and thus he constituted an occupier.

A person who is 'concerned in the management of the premises' is someone who is 'managing them in the sense of running them, organising them and planning them' and he need not have any legal right to the premises; in fact, even a squatter or trespasser may fall within this category: *R v Josephs; R v Christie* (1977) 65 Cr App R 253.

12.4.2 Knowingly permits or suffers a specified activity to take place

The prosecution must also prove that the defendant knowingly permitted or suffered one of the specified activities to take place on those premises. This means that it must be proved that the defendant knew that the activity was taking place and he did nothing to stop it. In *R v Thomas; R v Thomson* (1976) 63 Cr App R 65, the Court of Appeal held that the word 'knowingly' adds nothing to this section; it is superfluous since knowledge is inherent within the word 'permits' (and 'permits' and 'suffers' mean the same thing). The Court held that suspicion is not the same as knowledge and is not sufficient on its own to constitute permission (see also *Souter* [1971] 1 WLR 1187), but that knowledge can be inferred from a person shutting their eyes to suspicious circumstances: *R v Thomas; R v Thomson* (1976) 63 Cr App R 65 at 69. The term 'permits' also requires proof that the defendant was unwilling to prevent the prohibited act from taking place on the premises: *Souter* [1971] 1 WLR 1187.

12.5 Reform: 'legal highs'

There are currently proposals to criminalise the use of 'legal highs'. These are psychoactive drugs which do not at present fall within the list of 'controlled drugs' under the Misuse of Drugs Act 1971. The term 'legal highs' has been criticised by the Government as 'inappropriate given that the chemicals in them are often neither legal nor safe for human consumption' (see the Explanatory Notes to the Psychoactive Substances Bill 2015, para. 7)). These substances mimic the effects of some controlled drugs and there is concern at the recent and sudden surge in the emergence of these substances which are causing an increase in anti-social and criminal behaviour, as well as harm to individuals, and sometimes fatalities (see the Explanatory Notes at paras. 11 to 13). The Psychoactive Substances Bill 2015 was introduced into the House of Lords in 2015. It will make it an offence to produce, supply, offer to supply, possess with intent to supply, import, or export psychoactive substances. At the time of writing, the Bill is awaiting a date for its second reading in the House of Commons. The scope of the Bill as presented to the House of Lords introduces a blanket ban on any substance 'capable of producing a psychoactive effect': clause 2(1)(a). The Bill has been the subject of some criticism for being so broad as to have to specifically exclude from its application substances such as food, caffeine, alcohol, medicines, and nicotine (Schedule 1), and it has been labelled a 'knee-jerk legislative response to a passing public mood': Robins (2015).

 THINKING POINT

Is it right that the production, supply, possession with intent to supply, etc. in relation to 'legal highs' should be criminalised?

To what extent is the Psychoactive Substances Bill 2015 far too reactionary?

Summary

- The offence of possession of a controlled drug is provided for by s.5(2), Misuse of Drugs Act 1971. 'Possession' requires 'a knowledge only of the existence of the thing itself': *Warner v Metropolitan Police Commissioner* [1969] 2 AC 256.

- A 'controlled drug' is a drug on the list in Schedule 2 to the Act (Classes A, B, and C) or in a Temporary Class Drug Order: s.2, Misuse of Drugs Act 1971.

- Section 5(4), Misuse of Drugs Act 1971 provides two defences to the offence of possession of a controlled drug under s.5(2), and s.28(2), (3)(a), and (3)(b) provide three defences to the offences under ss.5(3), 4(2), and 4(3).

- It is an offence under s.5(3), Misuse of Drugs Act 1971 to be in possession of a controlled drug with the intention to supply that drug to another.

- Section 4(2), Misuse of Drugs Act 1971 provides that it is an offence to produce a controlled drug, or to be concerned in the production of such a drug by another.

- Section 4(3), Misuse of Drugs Act 1971 provides that it is an offence to supply or offer to supply a controlled drug to another, or to be concerned in the supplying of such a drug to another, or to be concerned in the making to another of an offer to supply such a drug.

- Under s.8, Misuse of Drugs Act 1971, it is an offence for an occupier or someone concerned in the management of premises to knowingly permit the premises to be used for certain drug-related activities.

 The bigger picture

- You might want to consider how the drugs offences featured in this chapter fit in with other areas of criminal law, particularly unlawful act manslaughter in chapter 6 and the issue of causation (also see chapter 2). You should refer back to the 'drugs cases' on unlawful act manslaughter at 6.1.5.

- For more information on the proposed reforms regarding psychoactive substances, you should read the Psychoactive Substances Bill 2015 and the Explanatory Notes to the Bill. You can find these documents and follow the process of the Bill through Parliament on Parliament's website at http://services.parliament.uk/bills/2015-16/psychoactivesubstances.html.

- For a more detailed discussion of the drugs offences featured in this chapter and other drugs offences, you should consult the authoritative work by Rudi Fortson (2012).

? **Questions**

Self-test questions

1. What is the meaning of 'possession' under s.5(2), Misuse of Drugs Act 1971?

2. What is a 'controlled drug' for the purposes of the Misuse of Drugs Act 1971?

3. Explain when the defences under s.5(4), Misuse of Drugs Act 1971 apply.

4. Who bears the burden of proof where the defence under s.28 is raised?

5. Explain the meaning of 'produce' for the purposes of s.4(2), Misuse of Drugs Act 1971.

6. Identify the elements of the offences under s.4(3)(b) and (c), Misuse of Drugs Act 1971.

7. Who is an 'occupier' for the purposes of s.8, Misuse of Drugs Act 1971?

8. Define the term 'permits' for the purposes of s.8, Misuse of Drugs Act 1971.

9. Explain the rationale for the offence under s.8, Misuse of Drugs Act 1971.

10. What is a 'legal high' and what are the current proposals for reform in relation to these?

Exam questions

1. Aiden is a university student who sets up a business making methylamphetamine (known as 'crystal meth'). He perfects the manufacturing process in his bedroom in the university halls of residence and often stays up late into the night making the methylamphetamine. Beryl, a postgraduate student who is the warden of the halls of residence, hears rumours that Aiden is using the university halls of residence for something illegal. Late one night, she goes down to Aiden's room to investigate and she notices a strange smell coming from the room. Not wishing to get involved, she decides not to report the rumours or her own observations to anybody.

   Carol is a cleaner who works at the university. She cleans the bedrooms in the halls of residence three times a week. She cleans Aiden's room and disposes of the chemical waste produced by the manufacturing process. She hears a rumour that Aiden is involved in some criminal activity but she does not report the nature of the waste that she finds in Aiden's room to anybody. One day, Carol notices a box by the waste containers in Aiden's room. She picks up the box and puts it in her car. The box contains a large quantity of methylamphetamine. Carol is arrested by the police after they search her car and find the box containing the methylamphetamine. She claims that she was suspicious that Aiden was 'up to no good' and that she was taking the box to the police station to hand it in.

   Aiden supplies a quantity of the methylamphetamine to Damian in order that Damian can distribute the drug to drug users. When Damian is caught by the police with the drugs in his car, he tells the police that he thought that the drug was amphetamine sulphate (or 'speed').

   Aiden asks Edgar if he is interested in making some money distributing methylamphetamine. When Edgar tells Aiden that he is not interested in doing anything illegal, Aiden plants a quantity of methylamphetamine in Edgar's backpack. Edgar is arrested after the police stop and search him in the street.

   Discuss the criminal liability of the parties.

2. Critically evaluate the meaning given to the term 'possession' by the House of Lords in *Warner v Metropolitan Police Commissioner* [1969] 2 AC 256.

 ## Further reading

Books

Fortson, R., *Misuse of Drugs and Drug Trafficking Offences* (6th edn, 2012), London: Sweet & Maxwell

Journal articles

Jason-Lloyd, L. 'The Reclassification of Methylamphetamine' (2007) 168 Criminal Lawyer 5

Jason-Lloyd, L. 'More Intervention on Legal Highs' (2011) 205 Criminal Lawyer 3

Jason-Lloyd, L. 'Continuing Intervention to Control "Legal Highs" ' (2012) 209 Criminal Lawyer 3

Robins, J. 'Legal Highs' (2015) 179 Criminal Law and Justice Weekly 444

Shiels, R. 'Controlled Drugs and Premises of Multiple Occupancy' [1998] Crim LR 404

Walsh, C. 'Magic Mushrooms and the Law' [2005] Crim LR 773

Reports and other sources

CPS Charging Standards, Drug Offences: http://www.cps.gov.uk/legal/d_to_g/drug_offences/#a10

Explanatory Notes to the Psychoactive Substances Bill 2015

Home Office, *New Psychoactive Substances Review: Report of the Expert Panel*, September 2014: https://www.gov.uk/government/uploads/system/uploads/attachment_data/file/368583/NPSexpertReviewPanelReport.pdf

13

Defences I: incapacity and negating the elements of the offence

☐ **LEARNING OBJECTIVES**

By the end of this chapter, you should be able to:

● explain the presumption of *doli incapax*;

● understand the procedure surrounding fitness to plead;

● distinguish between the defences of insanity and automatism;

● explain the rules relating to voluntary and involuntary intoxication; and

● understand the law relating to mistake.

Introduction

When a defendant is charged with a criminal offence, the defendant will decide whether to plead guilty and admit liability or to plead not guilty and contest liability. If the defendant pleads not guilty, he may challenge the prosecution case in one of three ways:

(1) by challenging the factual basis of the charge, by arguing that the facts are not as the prosecution allege them to be;

(2) by arguing that one or more of the *actus reus* or *mens rea* elements of the offence charged have not been proved; or

(3) by pleading a substantive defence to the charge, i.e., by arguing that there is a legal reason why he should not be held liable for the offence charged.

This chapter and chapter 14 consider the general defences that a defendant might seek to rely upon in order to escape criminal liability. This chapter focuses on the defences which either bear upon the defendant's capacity to commit the offence charged, or which negate an element of the offence charged. We will answer questions such as: Can an 8-year-old be guilty of a criminal offence? Will a defendant who commits an offence whilst drunk be absolved of liability? What about a defendant who is not in control of their actions because they are sleepwalking at the time of the offence, or one who crashes their car while sneezing?

In chapter 1, we saw that the burden of proof in a criminal trial rests with the prosecution (confirmed by Viscount Sankey LC in *Woolmington v DPP* [1935] AC 462). The prosecution bring the case and the prosecution have to prove each element of the offence charged. The standard of proof in a criminal trial is high. The prosecution must prove beyond reasonable doubt that the defendant is guilty. (Refer to 1.10 for a discussion of the burden and standard of proof.) While the defendant does not usually have to prove anything, there are some rare circumstances in which the burden of proving the elements of a defence rests with the defendant. One example where this occurs is with the defence of insanity, which is discussed in this chapter at 13.4. Under the law, every man is presumed to be sane. A defendant who pleads insanity bears the legal burden of proving the elements of the defence. The rationale behind this is ease of proof—the defence are in a better position to provide evidence as to the defendant's mental condition, as the defence may instruct an expert to undertake a psychiatric assessment of the defendant.

Occasionally, the defendant will bear an evidential burden in relation to a defence. An evidential burden is not a burden of proof and, consequently, does not have a standard of proof. It is merely a burden to raise some evidence in order to make an issue a 'live' one. The defendant will bear an evidential burden if the defendant raises defences such as automatism (discussed in this chapter at 13.5), self-defence, and duress (both discussed in chapter 14). Thus, in order to rely upon such a defence, either some evidence of the relevant defence would have to be adduced by a prosecution witness, or the defendant would have to raise some such evidence. However, the defendant does not bear a legal burden, thus the defendant does not have to prove the elements of the relevant defence. The prosecution bear the legal burden of proving that the elements of the defence are not present. (Refer to 1.10.1 and 1.10.3 for a discussion on the distinction between a legal burden of proof and an evidential burden.)

13.1 General and specific defences

This chapter is the first of two chapters on general defences. A general defence is one which a defendant may plead in relation to any criminal offence. Examples of general defences include insanity, automatism, self-defence, and mistake. A special defence may only be pleaded in relation to specific offences. Examples include loss of control and diminished responsibility which may only be raised by a defendant charged with murder.

13.1.1 Complete and partial defences

At this stage, it is also necessary to distinguish between complete defences and partial defences. Where a defendant successfully pleads a complete defence, he will be acquitted of the offence charged. By contrast, where a partial defence is successfully pleaded, a defendant will be acquitted of the offence charged, but may still be convicted of a lesser offence. For instance, loss of control is a partial defence which may only be pleaded in respect of a charge of murder. If successfully pleaded, the defendant will be acquitted of murder, but convicted of manslaughter.

13.1.2 Capacity and negating the elements of the offence

This chapter specifically explores situations in which a defendant does not have the capacity to be held liable for a criminal offence or has a defence which negates the definitional elements of the offence (*actus reus* or *mens rea*). Issues such as infancy (*doli incapax*), insanity, automatism, and intoxication will be examined. The issue of a defendant's capacity to stand trial, his fitness to plead, is also examined. These are not defences as such, but they are pleas that the defendant does not have the capacity to be, or that due to his mental condition he should not be, criminally liable for an offence. For the purposes of this chapter, they will be referred to as defences. Upon a successful plea of some of the defences discussed in this chapter, the defendant will be acquitted (see infancy at 13.2 and automatism at 13.5). The defence of insanity (at 13.4) leads to a special verdict (upon conviction on indictment) of not guilty by reason of insanity, which confers on the judge special powers of disposal. Evidence of intoxication may result in the acquittal of the defendant in relation to some offences, but his conviction for other, lesser offences.

13.2 Infancy

13.2.1 Children under the age of 10

In England and Wales, a child under the age of 10 lacks the capacity to commit a criminal offence. Section 50 of the Children and Young Persons Act 1933 provides a conclusive presumption that children under the age of 10 cannot be held criminally liable.

Hence, children under 10 are presumed to be *doli incapax* (incapable of committing a criminal offence), no matter how serious their conduct. The rationale behind this presumption is that young children lack the moral capacity to commit a criminal offence because their knowledge and ability to reason are still in the process of developing and they are unable to fully understand the consequences of their actions or of what is right and wrong. This presumption cannot be rebutted under any circumstances. So, if an adult persuades a child aged 9 to steal from a shop, the child cannot be held liable for theft. However, the adult could be convicted of theft through an innocent agent.

Children aged 10 or over can be held liable for any criminal offence. This is often referred to as the 'age of criminal responsibility'. Those aged 10 or above cannot rely upon the defence of infancy (or *doli incapax*).

> **CROSS REFERENCE**
> Refer to chapter 16 for further discussion of liability through innocent agency.

13.2.2 The age of criminal responsibility in Europe

The age of criminal responsibility varies from country to country and with the passing of time. For instance, in Scotland, a child may be criminally liable at the age of 12. (In March 2011, the age of criminal responsibility was increased from 8 to 12 by s.41A, Criminal Procedure (Scotland) Act 1995 (as amended by s.52, Criminal Justice and Licensing (Scotland) Act 2010).) In Ireland, a child can only be guilty of a criminal offence when he reaches 12 years of age (increased from 7 years old in October 2006), and in France the age is 13. In Denmark, Norway, and Sweden the age of criminal responsibility is 15, and in Belgium it is as high as 18 years old

Table 13.1 Current ages of criminal responsibility in Europe

England, Wales, Northern Ireland	10
Scotland	12
Republic of Ireland	12
France	13
Germany, Italy	14
Denmark, Norway, Sweden	15
Poland, Spain	16
Belgium	18

(table 13.1). At the time of writing, the Age of Criminal Responsibility Bill 2015–16 (a Private Member's Bill started in House of Lords by Lord Dholakia) has had its first reading in the House of Lords. The Bill proposes to increase the age of criminal responsibility in England and Wales from 10 to 12. However, the second reading of the Bill has yet to be scheduled, so it is unlikely that these proposals will become law in the near future.

13.2.3 Abolishing the rebuttable presumption for children aged 10 to 13

There used to be a rebuttable presumption of *doli incapax* for children aged 10 to 13. This could be rebutted by the prosecution proving (in addition to the *actus reus* and *mens rea* for the offence in question) that the child knew that their conduct was seriously wrong or that they had 'mischievous discretion'. The rebuttable presumption of *doli incapax* was abolished by s.34 of the Crime and Disorder Act 1998. In the recent House of Lords' decision of *R v JTB* [2009] UKHL 20, Lord Phillips confirmed that s.34 abolished the defence of *doli incapax*. Thus, the defence of *doli incapax* is not available to those aged 10 or over.

13.3 Fitness to plead

In order to be tried for a criminal offence, a defendant must be 'fit to plead', i.e., the defendant must have the mental capacity to stand trial. If the defendant is deemed to be unfit to plead at the time of the trial, he will not be tried for the criminal offence charged. Fitness to plead is concerned with the defendant's mental state at the time of *trial*, not his mental state at the time that the offence was allegedly committed. The separate and distinct defence of insanity concerns the mental state of the defendant at the time of the relevant offence. Insanity is discussed at 13.4.

The procedure relating to fitness to plead is found in ss.4, 4A, and 5 of the Criminal Procedure (Insanity) Act 1964. This Act was amended in 1991 by the Criminal Procedure (Insanity and Unfitness to Plead) Act 1991 and again in 2005 by the Domestic Violence, Crime and Victims Act 2004. The provisions outlined below refer to the amended version of the 1964 Act.

13.3.1 **Is the defendant fit to plead?**

Section 4 of the Criminal Procedure (Insanity) Act 1964 applies where a defendant is suffering from a disability which constitutes a bar to the defendant standing trial (s.4(1)). The issue of fitness to plead is determined as soon as it arises, provided the jury have not already returned a verdict of not guilty (ss.4(3) and 4(4), Criminal Procedure (Insanity) Act 1964).

Whether a defendant is fit to plead used to be determined by a jury, but is now determined by the judge (see s.4(5), Criminal Procedure (Insanity) Act 1964, as amended by s.22(2), Domestic Violence, Crime and Victims Act 2004). The judge may only rule upon the issue of a defendant's fitness to plead where the written or oral evidence of two or more registered medical practitioners is before the court (s.4(6), Criminal Procedure (Insanity) Act 1964).

THINKING POINT

What factors do you think a judge might consider in determining whether or not a defendant is fit to plead?

The factors to be considered in determining whether the defendant is fit to plead were established back in 1836 in the case of *Pritchard* (1836) 7 C & P 303. More recently, in the case of *John M* [2003] EWCA Crim 3452, the trial judge identified six factors to consider in determining whether or not the defendant was fit to plead. These were the defendant's ability to: *(a)* understand the charges; *(b)* decide whether to plead guilty or not; *(c)* exercise his right to challenge jurors; *(d)* instruct solicitors and counsel; *(e)* follow the course of the proceedings; and *(f)* give evidence in his own defence. The Court of Appeal considered the trial judge's approach to be 'admirable' (figure 13.1).

In the case of *Podola* (1959) 43 Cr App R 220, the defendant argued that he was unfit to stand trial for murder due to amnesia. He claimed that he had suffered memory loss of the events prior to and at the time of the alleged murder. The Court of Appeal held that amnesia in relation to the events surrounding the offence did not, by itself, render the defendant unfit to plead. The Court also held that where the defendant raises the issue of fitness to plead, he bears the legal burden of proving that he is unfit to plead on a balance of probabilities. Where the prosecution raise the issue and the defendant disputes it, the burden of proof rests with the prosecution to prove beyond reasonable doubt that the defendant is unfit to plead.

13.3.2 **Did the defendant do the act or make the omission charged?**

Where the judge decides that the defendant is fit to plead, the defendant will stand trial for the offence charged in the usual way. If the judge decides that the defendant is not fit to stand trial, then the trial should not proceed any further. At this stage, a jury must be empanelled in order to determine if the defendant 'did the act or made the omission charged against him as the offence' (s.4A(2), Criminal Procedure (Insanity) Act 1964).

If the jury decides that the defendant did not do the act or make the omission charged against him, they must acquit him (s.4A(4), Criminal Procedure (Insanity) Act 1964). However, if the jury decide that the defendant did do the act or make the omission charged against him, the judge will then decide upon an appropriate disposal for that particular defendant under

Figure 13.1 Fitness to plead: factors to consider

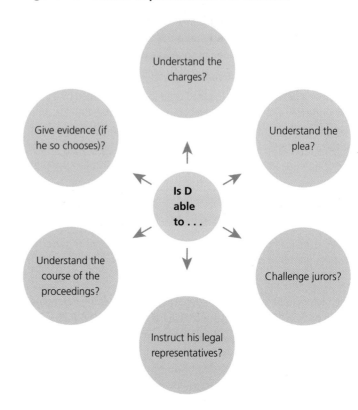

s.5 of the Criminal Procedure (Insanity) Act 1964. Under s.5(2), the judge may impose upon the defendant:

(a) a hospital order (with or without an order restricting his discharge from hospital);

(b) a supervision and treatment order; or

(c) an order for his absolute discharge.

Under s.5(3) of the Criminal Procedure (Insanity) Act 1964, where the offence is one for which the sentence is fixed by law (i.e., murder), and the court has the power to make a hospital order, then the court shall make a hospital order with a restriction order, forbidding the defendant's release from hospital without the consent of the Secretary of State (figure 13.2).

The procedure under s.4A for deciding whether a defendant who is unfit to stand trial did the act or made the omission charged has been held to be compatible with Article 6 of the European Convention on Human Rights. In *H* [2003] UKHL 1, the House of Lords held that although the procedure under s.4A could lead to an acquittal of the defendant, it could not lead to a conviction of a criminal offence and did not involve the determination of a criminal charge.

13.3.3 Summary trial

It should also be noted that the provisions of the 1964 Act do not apply to summary trials. Where the issue of fitness to plead arises in relation to a defendant being tried summarily for an offence which is punishable by imprisonment, the court must first determine the issue of whether the defendant did the act or made the omission charged against him. If the court

Figure 13.2 Flowchart of fitness to plead procedure

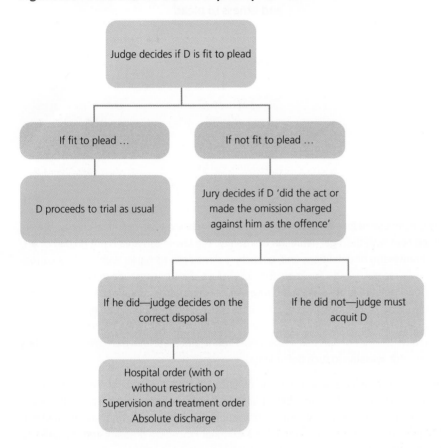

finds that the defendant did the act, it may adjourn proceedings for an inquiry into the mental condition of the defendant prior to deciding how to deal with the offender (under s.11(1) of the Powers of Criminal Courts (Sentencing) Act 2000). Alternatively, the magistrates' court may make a hospital or guardianship order without convicting the defendant (s.37(3), Mental Health Act 1983).

13.3.4 **Reform**

The tests relating to fitness to plead and the rules on insanity are currently being considered by the Law Commission with a view to identifying better and more up-to-date legal tests and rules in this area. The Law Commission is currently writing a final report on 'Unfitness to Plead' which it is anticipated will be published in 2016.

13.4 Insanity

The defence of insanity (or insane automatism) is concerned with the mental condition of the defendant at the time that the offence was committed. A defendant who is insane at the time of trial will argue that he is unfit to plead (figure 13.3).

Figure 13.3 Distinguishing between insanity and fitness to plead

Insanity is a general defence which may be pleaded in relation to any criminal charge. We are concerned here with the legal definition of insanity. The law in this area is not guided by any medical knowledge or definitions and, as such, is difficult to reconcile with medical equivalents, such as 'mental disorder' or 'mental illness'. In fact, it will become apparent in this section that the legal definition of insanity controversially encompasses conditions such as epilepsy and sleepwalking. A defendant who commits a criminal offence during an epileptic seizure or whilst sleepwalking may only rely upon the defence of insanity (aka insane automatism). The alternative defence of automatism (aka non-insane automatism) which covers involuntary behaviour is not available to such defendants.

The defence of insanity is not a popular defence: defendants understandably prefer to avoid the social stigma of being labelled 'insane'. Where a defendant successfully pleads the defence of insanity, a special verdict of 'not guilty by reason of insanity' is returned (s.1, Criminal Procedure (Insanity) Act 1964). The Criminal Procedure (Insanity and Unfitness to Plead) Act 1991 amended the Criminal Procedure (Insanity) Act 1964 in order to increase the disposal options available to a judge upon the return of such a verdict. Under s.5 of the 1964 Act, the judge may make one of three orders (also specified at 13.3.2):

(a) a hospital order (with or without an order restricting his discharge from hospital);

(b) a supervision and treatment order; or

(c) an order for his absolute discharge.

As with fitness to plead, where a defendant is charged with an offence where the penalty is fixed by law (i.e., murder) and he successfully pleads insanity, the court will impose a hospital order with restriction on the defendant (s.5(3), Criminal Procedure (Insanity) Act 1964). This means that the defendant may only be discharged from hospital with the permission of the Secretary of State.

13.4.1 The distinction between insanity and automatism

It is important to be able to distinguish between insanity and automatism because they lead to significantly different outcomes if pleaded successfully. We have already seen that a successful plea of insanity results in a special verdict of 'not guilty by reason of insanity'. By contrast, a successful plea of automatism will result in a complete acquittal. For this reason, the defence of automatism is favoured by defendants.

Figure 13.4 Distinguishing between automatism and insanity

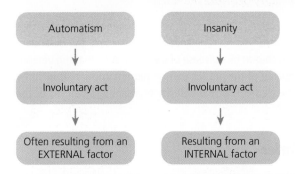

THINKING POINT

How does the law determine whether a defendant may plead insanity or automatism?

The defence of insanity requires proof of an internal factor, a 'disease of the mind'. Where there is no such disease of the mind, the defendant may plead automatism. Where the defendant acts as an automaton, there is often an external factor acting upon him at the time of the *actus reus*. Although, it is important to note that this will not always be the case. For instance, where a defendant suffers a stroke whilst driving and crashes his car, he will be able to plead automatism, even though there was no external factor acting upon him (figure 13.4).

Another important difference between insanity and automatism relates to the burden of proof. Where insanity is raised as a defence, the legal burden is reversed. Hence, the defence bear the burden of proving (on a balance of probabilities) the elements of insanity. However, if the defence of automatism is raised, the legal burden is not reversed. The defence bears the evidential burden (not a burden of proof, but a burden to raise some evidence of automatism) in relation to the defence, but the legal burden remains with the prosecution. Hence, the prosecution must prove (beyond reasonable doubt) that the defendant was not acting due to automatism.

> **CROSS REFERENCE**
> Refer to 1.10.1 for a discussion of *Woolmington v DPP* (1935) and the burden and standard of proof.

13.4.2 Burden and standard of proof

THINKING POINT

Why do you think that the defendant bears the legal burden of proving that he is insane? Refer to the Introduction for guidance.

The *M'Naghten Rules* govern the defence of insanity. These rules state that every man is presumed to be sane. If a defendant wishes to rely on the defence of insanity, he must rebut this presumption. Thus, the burden of proving the elements of the defence of insanity rests with the defence. It is unusual in criminal proceedings for the burden of proof to be upon the defence. The exception in relation to insanity is specifically provided for by Viscount Sankey LC in the leading authority, *Woolmington v DPP* [1935] AC 462.

CROSS REFERENCE

Refer to 1.10.1 and 1.10.3 to ensure that you are fully aware of the distinction between a legal burden of proof and an evidential burden.

Where the burden of proof is on the defence, a lower standard of proof applies: 'on a balance of probabilities'. The defence must prove that on a balance of probabilities, the defendant was suffering from 'a defect of reason caused by a disease of the mind, such that the defendant did not know the nature and quality of the act, or that he did not know that what he was doing was wrong'. These are the elements of the defence of insanity as defined by the *M'Naghten Rules*.

13.4.3　The *M'Naghten Rules*

The *M'Naghten Rules* govern the defence of insanity. These rules are derived from the leading authority of *M'Naghten* (1843) 10 Cl & F 200.

 CASE CLOSE-UP

M'Naghten (1843) 10 Cl & F 200

The defendant in this case was charged with the murder of Sir Robert Peel's private secretary. He shot the victim by mistake, having instead intended to kill Sir Robert Peel. The defence called medical evidence to show that he was suffering from morbid delusions at the time of the offence. These delusions meant that he was not capable of controlling his actions and he had no moral perceptions of right and wrong. The defendant was found to be insane and was acquitted. This result was highly controversial at the time and led to the House of Lords revisiting the law on insanity.

The *M'Naghten Rules* were laid down by the House of Lords and have become the leading rules on insanity. The Rules state that the defendant must prove that at the time he committed the act he was 'labouring under such a defect of reason, from disease of the mind, as not to know the nature and quality of the act he was doing, or if he did know it, that he did not know he was doing what was wrong'.

The *M'Naghten Rules*

(a) there is a presumption that every man is sane;

(b) this presumption can be rebutted by the defendant who must prove, on a balance of probabilities, that at the time of the offence:

　(i) he was suffering from a defect of reason,

　(ii) which was caused by a disease of the mind, and

　(iii) that he did not know the nature and quality of the act, or

　(iv) that he did not know that what he was doing was wrong.

The question of whether the defendant was suffering from a defect of reason caused by a disease of the mind is a question of law to be determined by the trial judge. The issue of whether the defendant knew the nature and quality of the act, or if he did know it, whether he knew that his conduct was wrong, is a question of fact to be determined by the jury (figure 13.5).

Figure 13.5 Elements of insanity

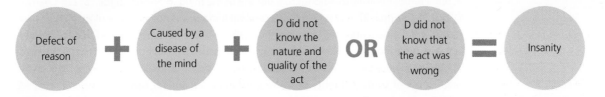

13.4.4 **Defect of reason**

In order to plead insanity, a defendant must prove that, at the time of the offence, he was suffering from a defect of reason which was caused by a disease of the mind. This is a question of law for the judge to determine.

It is difficult to define a defect of reason with any precision. At the time of the offence, the defendant must be unable to use his power of reasoning. This must occur due to a disease of the mind. Authority shows that mere absentmindedness does not constitute a defect of reason.

The defendant in *Clarke* [1972] 1 All ER 219 was charged with the theft of various products from a supermarket. She had placed these items into her bag and did not present them at the checkout to be paid for. The defendant argued that she had acted absentmindedly and that she had not intended to steal the items. There was medical evidence that the defendant had been suffering from depression. The trial judge ruled that her absentmindedness amounted to insanity. Not wishing to plead insanity, the defendant changed her plea to one of guilty and appealed to the Court of Appeal. The Court quashed the defendant's conviction on the basis that the trial judge had been wrong to rule that absentmindedness amounted to insanity. The defendant was not suffering from a defect of reason because she was not 'deprived of the power of reasoning'. Ackner J stated that the *M'Naghten Rules* 'do not apply and never have applied to a momentary failure by someone to concentrate'.

13.4.5 **Disease of the mind**

The defence must also prove that the defendant was suffering from a disease of the mind at the time of the offence. The disease of the mind must cause the defect of reason. The disease must affect the 'mind', rather than the brain in the physical sense. The disease must affect the ordinary mental faculties of 'reason, memory and understanding' (*per* Devlin J in *Kemp* [1957] 1 QB 399). In the case of *Hennessy* [1989] 1 WLR 287, Lord Lane CJ stated that disease of the mind, 'does not mean any disease of the brain. It means a disease which affects the proper functioning of the mind.' Various conditions have been held to amount to a disease of the mind, including schizophrenia, epilepsy, sleepwalking, and hyperglycaemia (diabetes). Some of these medical conditions are considered below.

 THINKING POINT

To what extent do you think that the terminology 'disease of the mind' and the meaning attached to it in *Kemp* are satisfactory?

Would you make any changes to the Rules? If so, what would they be?

13.4.5.1 Cerebral tumour

A brain tumour is likely to amount to a disease of the mind. However, in the case of *Charlson* (1955) 39 Cr App R 37, it was held that a cerebral tumour was not a disease of the mind. In this case, the defendant attacked his son with a mallet. Medical evidence showed that the defendant was suffering from a cerebral tumour which made him liable to motiveless outbursts of impulsive violence over which he would have no control. This decision was disapproved in the later House of Lords' authority of *Bratty v Attorney General for Northern Ireland* [1963] AC 386, in which Lord Denning took the view that a brain tumour was a disease of the mind. The case of *Charlson* is not likely to be followed today.

▶ **CROSS REFERENCE**

See reference to *Bratty v Attorney General for Northern Ireland* (1963) at 13.4.5.3.

13.4.5.2 Arteriosclerosis

Arteriosclerosis is a hardening of the arteries which leads to a congestion of blood in the brain and a temporary lack of consciousness. Arteriosclerosis was held to amount to a disease of the mind in the case of *Kemp* [1957] 1 QB 399.

The defendant in this case had launched a motiveless attack on his wife with a hammer. Medical evidence showed that he was suffering from arteriosclerosis. Due to his condition, the defendant had suffered a temporary loss of consciousness, during which the attack occurred. Doctors agreed that the defendant did the act not knowing anything about it. They took the view that at the time he did the act, he was not conscious that he had picked up the hammer or that he was striking his wife with it. The defence pleaded automatism, but Devlin J left the defence of insanity to the jury which returned a verdict of not guilty by reason of insanity. Devlin J rejected an argument that the disease at this stage was purely physical and that it would only become a disease of the mind when it interferes with the brain cells so that they degenerate. His Lordship held that the 'mind' did not refer to the 'brain'.

Devlin J stated that:

> The law is not concerned with the brain but with the mind, in the sense that 'mind' is ordinarily used, the mental faculties of reason, memory and understanding . . . In my judgment the condition of the brain is irrelevant and so is the question of whether the condition of the mind is curable or incurable, transitory or permanent . . . Temporary insanity is sufficient.

In *Bratty*, Lord Denning approved of the decision of Devlin J to leave insanity to the jury. His Lordship also took the view that arteriosclerosis amounted to a disease of the mind.

13.4.5.3 Epilepsy

Epilepsy is classed as a disease of the mind. For this reason, a defendant who commits an offence during an epileptic seizure may only plead the defence of insanity, rather than the more favourable defence of automatism.

In the case of *Bratty v Attorney General for Northern Ireland* [1963] AC 386, the House of Lords held that epilepsy amounted to insanity. The defendant was charged with murder after he strangled a young girl with her stocking. He claimed that he did not know what he was doing and that 'a blackness' came over him. There was medical evidence to suggest that he was suffering from psychomotor epilepsy. Medical experts who were called all agreed that psychomotor epilepsy is a defect of reason due to a disease of the mind. The trial judge refused to leave the defence of automatism to the jury, but instead left the defence of insanity to them. The jury rejected the defence of insanity and convicted the defendant of murder. The defendant appealed on the ground that the defence of automatism should have been left to the jury.

Both his appeals to the Court of Criminal Appeal of Northern Ireland and the House of Lords were dismissed. It was held that, as the jury had rejected the theory that the defendant had been acting unconsciously during the course of an epileptic attack, there was no evidence that he had been acting unconsciously from any other cause.

In the House of Lords, Lord Denning defined a disease of the mind as: 'any mental disorder which has manifested itself in violence and is prone to recur'. However, this statement is misleading. A disease of the mind might manifest itself in ways other than violence, for instance through theft or criminal damage. Thus, a manifestation of violence is an inaccurate barometer by which to measure a disease of the mind. Similarly, as stated in *Quick and Paddison* [1973] QB 910, although diabetes might manifest itself in violence and be prone to recur, 'no mental hospital would admit a diabetic merely because he had a low blood sugar reaction'.

The finding that epilepsy amounts to insanity was followed by the House of Lords in *Sullivan* [1984] AC 156.

 CASE CLOSE-UP

Sullivan [1984] AC 156

The defendant in this case was charged with causing GBH with intent, contrary to s.18 of the Offences Against the Person Act 1861 and inflicting GBH, contrary to s.20 of the same Act.

These charges arose out of an incident during which he attacked his friend, repeatedly kicking him in the head and the body. The defendant pleaded the defence of automatism and claimed that he had carried out the attack during an epileptic fit. The trial judge rejected this defence and ruled that the only defence available to the defendant would be insanity. As a result, the defendant changed his plea to guilty to the lesser charge of assault occasioning ABH, contrary to s.47 of the Offences Against the Person Act 1861.

He appealed on the grounds that the defence of automatism should have been left to the jury. In the Court of Appeal, Lawton LJ ruled that epilepsy amounted to insanity as it affects the mind, i.e., the mental faculties of reason, memory, and understanding. Lawton LJ stated that:

> the special verdict has to be returned whenever there is evidence of a total lack of understanding and memory due to a morbid inherent condition of the brain. Epilepsy brings about such total lack of understanding and memory as can other morbid inherent conditions of the brain.

The defendant in *Sullivan* had suffered a defect of reason during his epileptic state. It did not matter that his defect of reason was only a temporary state. The defendant appealed further to the House of Lords. There, despite being sympathetic to Mr Sullivan's position, Lord Diplock reluctantly confirmed that epilepsy amounted to insanity in law. His Lordship stated that the purpose of the law relating to the defence of insanity has always been 'to protect society against recurrence of the dangerous conduct'. In defining a 'disease of the mind', Lord Diplock cited with approval, Devlin J in *Kemp*.

Lord Diplock stated:

> that 'mind' in the M'Naghten Rules is used in the ordinary sense of the mental faculties of reason, memory and understanding. If the effect of a disease is to impair these

> faculties so severely as to have either of the consequences referred to in the latter part
> of the rules, it matters not whether the aetiology of the impairment is organic, as in
> epilepsy, or functional, or whether the impairment itself is permanent or is transient
> and intermittent, provided that it subsisted at the time of commission of the act.
>
> Lord Diplock's reluctance to categorise epilepsy as insanity is apparent:
>
> it is natural to feel reluctant to attach the label of insanity to a sufferer from psy-
> chomotor epilepsy of the kind to which Mr. Sullivan was subject, even though the
> expression in the context of a special verdict of 'not guilty by reason of insanity' is a
> technical one which includes a purely temporary and intermittent suspension of the
> mental faculties of reason, memory and understanding resulting from the occurrence
> of an epileptic fit. But the label is contained in the current statute, it has appeared in
> this statute's predecessors ever since 1800. It does not lie within the power of the
> courts to alter it. Only Parliament can do that. It has done so twice; it could do so
> once again.

Research by Mackay and Reuber demonstrates that between 1975 and 2001, the special
verdict of not guilty by reason of insanity was returned 179 times. Epilepsy accounted for
just 13 of these verdicts (see Mackay and Reuber 2007). The rationale behind the defence of
insanity appears to be the protection of society against the recurrence of dangerous conduct.
However, the definition of a disease of the mind has become too wide. Classifying epileptic
defendants as 'insane' is surely improper and offensive. Mackay and Reuber argue that reform
of the defence of insanity is necessary and that it is 'surely no longer acceptable to use the
label "insanity" for any case of epileptic automatism or indeed for any other conditions which
give rise to the special verdict' (see Mackay and Reuber 2007: 793). They ask 'is it not time
for the Law Commission to take up this challenge and to rid the law of an insanity defence
which in its current form has no place in the 21st century?' The law on insanity is clearly in
need of reform and the Law Commission is reviewing the law in this area, with a view to
recommending reforms.

13.4.5.4 Sleepwalking

Sleep-related violence is also classed as insanity in law. Hence, where a defendant commits a
criminal offence whilst sleepwalking, he will only have the defence of insanity available to him.
This was established in the case of *Burgess* [1991] 2 QB 92, in which the defendant attacked
his girlfriend while she was sleeping. He struck her with a bottle and a video recorder, before
putting his hand around her throat. He was charged with causing GBH with intent, contrary
to s.18 of the Offences Against the Person Act 1861. He claimed that he had been sleepwalking and that this amounted to the defence of automatism. However, the trial judge refused to
leave automatism to the jury, ruling that there was evidence of insanity. He directed the jury
in accordance with the *M'Naghten Rules*. The jury returned a special verdict of not guilty by
reason of insanity. The defendant appealed against the trial judge's ruling that automatism
should not be left to the jury. The Court of Appeal dismissed the appeal and held that where a
defendant commits a criminal offence while sleepwalking, insanity is the appropriate defence.
The Court adopted Lord Denning's definition of a disease of the mind from *Bratty*. The Court
categorised sleepwalking as a disease of the mind due to the danger of it recurring and the
fact that it is caused by an internal factor. Lord Lane CJ gave the leading judgment in the Court
of Appeal and stated:

> It seems to us that . . . the judge was right to conclude that this was an abnormality or dis-
> order, albeit transitory, due to an internal factor, whether functional or organic, which had

manifested itself in violence. It was a disorder or abnormality which might recur, though the possibility of it recurring in the form of serious violence was unlikely.

13.4.5.5 Diabetes: hyperglycaemia

A defendant who suffers from diabetes and who commits a criminal offence whilst in a hyperglycaemic state may only rely upon the defence of insanity. Hyperglycaemia is a condition where the blood sugar level in the body is high and is caused by diabetes. Diabetics regulate their blood sugar level by taking insulin. A failure to take insulin will result in a high blood sugar level and hyperglycaemia. The case of *Hennessy* [1989] 1 WLR 287 provides authority for the principle that a defendant who commits an offence in a hyperglycaemic state may only plead insanity.

> ### 🔍 CASE CLOSE-UP
>
> ***Hennessy* [1989] 1 WLR 287**
>
> The defendant was a diabetic. He had failed to take his insulin due to stress, anxiety, and depression. He was arrested after being seen getting into and driving off in a car which had been reported as stolen. He was charged with taking a conveyance without consent, contrary to s.12(1) of the Theft Act 1968 and driving whilst disqualified, contrary to s.99(b) of the Road Traffic Act 1972.
>
> The defendant argued that, at the time of the offence, he had been suffering from hyperglycaemia caused by his failure to take his insulin. The defendant sought to plead automatism at trial, but the trial judge refused to leave this defence to the jury, ruling that the appropriate defence was that of insanity. As a result of this decision, the defendant changed his plea to guilty and appealed. He argued that his stress, anxiety, and depression were external factors which superseded the lack of insulin such that the defendant should have had the defence of automatism available to him.
>
> The Court of Appeal dismissed the appeal. Lord Lane CJ stated that:
>
> > hyperglycaemia, high blood sugar, caused by an inherent defect, and not corrected by insulin is a disease, and if, as the defendant was asserting here, it does cause a malfunction of the mind, then the case may fall within the M'Naghten Rules.
>
> The Court held that hyperglycaemia amounted to a disease of the mind because it was caused by an internal factor: the condition of diabetes itself. Thus, insanity was the appropriate defence. The Court also held that although the stress, anxiety, and depression suffered by the defendant were caused by external factors, they were not themselves external factors. According to Lord Lane CJ, they did not 'come within the scope of the exception of some external physical factor such as a blow on the head or the administration of an anaesthetic'. They could not themselves, either separately or together, form the basis of a plea of automatism.

A defendant who commits a criminal offence whilst in a hypoglycaemic state (low blood sugar level) may rely upon the defence of automatism if the hypoglycaemia is caused by an external factor, rather than the condition of diabetes itself. Thus, where the hypoglycaemia is caused by an injection of insulin which leads to excess insulin in the blood, the defence of automatism may be raised. However, if the hypoglycaemic state is due to natural factors, the defence will not be available (figure 13.6).

▶ CROSS REFERENCE
Refer to 13.5.2.3 for a discussion on hypoglycaemia and automatism.

Figure 13.6 Insanity and automatism: distinguishing between hyperglycaemia and hypoglycaemia

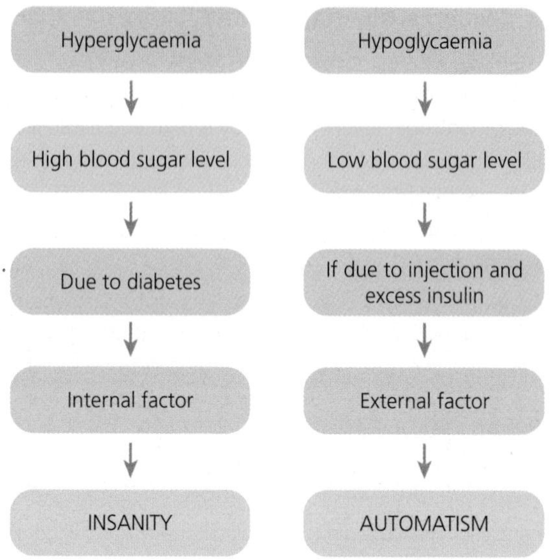

13.4.6 Did not know the nature and quality of the act

Once the defendant has proved that at the time of the offence he was suffering from a defect of reason caused by a disease of the mind, the defendant must further prove either:

(i) that he did not know the nature and quality of the act; or

(ii) that he did not know the act was wrong.

Proof that the defendant did not know the nature and quality of the act or did not know that the act was wrong is proof that the defendant did not have the *mens rea* of the relevant offence. According to the Court of Appeal in *Codere* (1917) 12 Cr App R 21, the 'nature and quality' of the act refers to the physical nature of the act, not the moral or legal nature of the act. Hence, the defendant must not know the physical nature of the act. The issue here is not whether or not the defendant knows that the act he is doing is wrong, but whether the defendant knows what he is doing. For example, did the defendant know that he was stabbing a person or striking a person, or that he was burning down a building or taking property which belongs to another, or that he was having sexual intercourse with a person? In relation to this last example, the Rape (Defences) Bill (if enacted) will prevent a defendant from relying upon sleepwalking or non-insane automatism as a defence to rape. Thus, the Bill will mean that such a defendant will not be able to claim that he did not know what he was doing.

CROSS REFERENCE

Refer to 8.1.3 for a discussion relating to the Rape (Defences) Bill.

13.4.7 Did not know the act was wrong

If the defendant did know the physical nature of the act he was doing, the defendant may still prove insanity if he can prove that he did not know that the act was wrong. It must be proved that the defendant did not know that the act was legally wrong, rather than merely morally wrong. This was confirmed by the Court of Appeal in the case of *Windle* [1952] 2 QB 826.

THINKING POINT

Do you think 'wrong' should mean legally wrong or morally wrong?

CASE CLOSE-UP

Windle [1952] 2 QB 826

The defendant in this case was a 40-year-old man of weak character. He was unhappily married and the defendant's wife often talked about committing suicide. The defendant gave his wife 100 aspirins, killing her. He was heard to say to a police officer, 'I suppose they will hang me for this?' Despite evidence that the defendant suffered from a defect of reason caused by a disease of the mind, the trial judge refused to leave the defence of insanity to the jury. The defendant was convicted of murder and appealed on the ground that insanity should have been left to the jury.

The Court of Appeal considered the meaning of the word 'wrong' and concluded that it meant 'contrary to law', rather than morally wrong. The defendant's appeal was dismissed: there was evidence that he was suffering from a defect of reason caused by a disease of the mind, but his comment to the police officer clearly demonstrated that he knew that his act was legally wrong.

This strict approach was confirmed in the case of *Johnson* [2007] EWCA Crim 1978, where the issue of the meaning of 'wrong' arose again before the Court of Appeal. The defendant suffered from paranoid schizophrenia. He stabbed the victim with a kitchen knife. The trial judge refused to leave the defence of insanity to the jury because the defendant had known that what he was doing was against the law. The defendant was convicted of wounding with intent to cause GBH, contrary to s.18 of the Offences Against the Person Act 1861. He appealed against his conviction, arguing that insanity should have been left to the jury because, although he knew what he was doing was against the law, he felt that his actions were morally justified. The Court of Appeal considered the strict approach in the case of *Windle* and the conflicting wider approach in the authority of *Stapleton* (1952) 86 CLR 358 from the High Court of Australia. The Court dismissed the appeal. Applying *Windle*, the Court confirmed that 'wrong' means 'contrary to law'. Thus, the issue is whether the defendant knew that the act was legally wrong. The wider issue of whether he thought the act was morally justified or whether the reasonable man would have thought that the act was morally justified is irrelevant. The Court took the view that this was an issue ripe for debate in the House of Lords. The Court invited counsel to ask the Court to certify a question of public importance for consideration by the House of Lords.

Professor Mackay has explored this limb of the *M'Naghten Rules* (Mackay 2009). He noted that most common law jurisdictions incorporate an aspect of 'moral' wrongness into the defence of insanity. He welcomed the Law Commission's plans to review the law on unfitness to plead and insanity and called for a reconsideration of the decision in *Windle* and whether a test of 'wrongness' should be retained at all in the reforms.

13.4.8 **No defence of 'irresistible impulse'**

It is no defence for a defendant to argue that he acted under an impulse which he could not control due to a defect of reason caused by a disease of the mind. This defence was rejected by the Court of Appeal in the case of *Kopsch* (1927) 19 Cr App R 50. The defendant in this case killed a relative by strangling her. The defendant argued that at the time of the offence he had lost his conscious mind and acted subconsciously. The Court of Appeal rejected the defence of uncontrollable impulse. Similarly, in the case of *Sodeman v R* [1936] 2 All ER 1138, the Privy Council rejected the defence of 'irresistible impulse'. The *M'Naghten Rules* are clear that where the defendant understands the nature and quality of his act and knows that his act is legally wrong, he will not be able to rely upon the defence of insanity. Where the defendant is charged with murder, he could plead the partial defence of diminished responsibility under s.2 of the Homicide Act 1957.

13.4.9 **Reform**

The *M'Naghten Rules* have been subject to criticism and there have been many calls for reform of the law in this area. The Rules were created by the judiciary, rather than those in the medical profession who perhaps would have been better placed to define the defence. Dating from 1843, the Rules are 170 years old and the terminology is archaic. In its *Report of the Butler Committee on Mentally Abnormal Offenders* in 1975, the Butler Committee proposed reform of the law and the creation of a new defence of mental disorder with a verdict of 'not guilty on evidence of mental disorder', when argued successfully. This new terminology was designed to move away from the stigma currently attached to the defence of insanity of being labelled 'insane'. This proposal was incorporated into the Law Commission's Draft Criminal Code, but Parliament has yet to give effect to any proposed reforms. It is clear that the law on insanity is in need of reform and the Law Commission is currently reviewing the *M'Naghten Rules* with a view to identifying a more modern test. The Law Commission published a discussion paper on 'Insanity and Automatism' in July 2013 setting out provisional proposals for reform of these defences.

13.5 Automatism

Automatism (also known as non-insane automatism) is a general defence: it is available in relation to any criminal charge. Insanity (aka insane automatism) and automatism are similar defences as both involve situations where a defendant is unable to control his actions or is unaware of what he is doing. In the case of *Bratty v Attorney General for Northern Ireland* [1963] AC 386, Lord Denning defined automatism as:

> an act which is done by the muscles without any control by the mind, such as a spasm, a reflex action or a convulsion; or an act done by a person who is not conscious of what he is doing, such as an act done whilst suffering from concussion or whilst sleepwalking.

In chapter 2, we saw that the *actus reus* of a criminal offence must be performed voluntarily (see 2.3). Where the defendant is compelled or forced to perform the *actus reus* due to some external factor, his conduct is involuntary. Such a defendant will usually have the defence of automatism (non-insane automatism) open to him.

Defence of automatism

Thus, the defence of automatism is available where:

(1) the defendant is not in control of his actions; or

(2) the defendant is unaware of what he is doing.

We have already seen that committing an offence whilst sleepwalking amounts to insanity, rather than automatism (see *Burgess* (1991)). Thus, Lord Denning's reference to sleepwalking in the quote cited earlier must be ignored.

CROSS REFERENCE

Refer to 13.4.5.4 and the case of *Burgess* (1991).

13.5.1 Total loss of voluntary control

For the defence of automatism to be successful, the defendant must suffer a total loss of voluntary control. Where the defendant retains some degree of control, the defence will fail. This is illustrated in the case of *Broome v Perkins* (1987) 85 Cr App R 321, in which the defendant retained enough control to drive himself home during a hypoglycaemic attack. The defendant was a diabetic. He was charged with driving without due care and attention (contrary to s.3 of the Road Traffic Act 1972) after he was seen driving erratically and he caused damage to other vehicles. He raised the defence of automatism, arguing that he had suffered a hypoglycaemic attack during the journey. The magistrates dismissed the case against the defendant, but the prosecution appealed to the Divisional Court by way of case stated. The Divisional Court held that automatism required a total loss of control. There was evidence that the defendant had swerved to avoid other vehicles and that he braked violently to avoid hitting a queue of traffic. Therefore, the defendant had retained some control when he succeeded in negotiating his way home, negating the defence of automatism.

Similarly, in the case of *Attorney General's Reference (No. 2 of 1992)* [1994] QB 91, the defence of automatism was not available to the defendant because evidence showed that he had some voluntary control. The defendant was driving a lorry on the hard shoulder of the motorway when he collided with a car which had broken down, killing the driver of the car. He was charged with causing death by reckless driving. Expert evidence that the defendant had been 'driving without awareness' was adduced. The trial judge left the defence of automatism to the jury and the defendant was acquitted. On appeal by the prosecution, the Court of Appeal held that the defence of automatism should not have been left to the jury. The defendant had some voluntary control: he was able to steer straight and responded to bright lights. Consequently, the defendant did not suffer a total loss of voluntary control. The Court held that impaired or reduced control was not sufficient for automatism.

13.5.2 Involuntary conduct due to an external factor

The involuntary conduct of the defendant may be due to an external factor. If the factor which causes the involuntary conduct is classed as a disease of the mind (an internal factor), the defence of insanity will be available instead. We have seen in 13.4 that internal factors include schizophrenia, arteriosclerosis, epilepsy, sleepwalking, and hyperglycaemic attacks. Such internal factors will usually constitute a disorder or condition which causes prohibited conduct which is likely to recur. External factors include muscle spasms, reflex actions, convulsions, concussion, physical force, sudden unconsciousness (such as through a blackout), the administration of a drug, including an anaesthetic, and hypoglycaemic attacks. Where an external factor is operating on the defendant at the time of the criminal offence, he will have the defence of automatism available to him. External factors usually involve a one-off incident and, as such, the prohibited conduct is not likely to recur. Some of these external factors are considered below.

 THINKING POINT

The law distinguishes between insanity and automatism by reference to internal and external factors. Is this approach a satisfactory one?

13.5.2.1 Reflex action or muscle spasm

A defendant who involuntarily commits a criminal offence through a reflex action or muscle spasm will have the defence of automatism available to him. In the case of *Hill v Baxter* [1958] 1 QB 277, Lord Goddard CJ cited an example of a driver who temporarily lost control of the car due to being attacked by a swarm of bees. His Lordship took the view that the hypothetical defendant in such a case could not be held liable for any criminal offence which resulted from his reflex action. Where the defendant's conduct was the result of a muscle spasm, the defendant would not be liable for any criminal offence which ensues. For instance, if the defendant suffered a muscle spasm in his foot, causing his foot to press the accelerator in a car rather than the brake, he will be able to plead automatism to any criminal offence which results. However, if the conduct of the defendant was a voluntary one, not caused by a reflex or spasm, no defence of automatism is available. The case of *Attorney General's Reference (No. 4 of 2000)* [2001] EWCA Crim 780 illustrates this point. The defendant in this case accidentally put his foot down on the accelerator rather than the brake, causing the vehicle to move forwards. The Court of Appeal held that the defence of automatism was not available to the defendant because his action was a voluntary physical movement.

13.5.2.2 Physical force

Where the conduct of the defendant is physically forced or compelled by another, the defendant will be able to plead automatism to any criminal offence which results. For example, if the defendant is pushed into a glass window which breaks, the defendant will not be liable for criminal damage because his conduct was not voluntary.

13.5.2.3 Diabetes: hypoglycaemia

A defendant who suffers from diabetes and who commits a criminal offence whilst in a hypoglycaemic state may rely upon the defence of automatism. Hypoglycaemia is a condition where the blood sugar level in the body is low and is caused by excess insulin. The case of *Quick and Paddison* [1973] QB 910 confirms that hypoglycaemia amounts to automatism.

Similarly, in the case of *Bingham* [1991] Crim LR 433, the Court of Appeal confirmed that the defence of automatism was available to a defendant who commits a criminal offence during a hypoglycaemic attack. The defendant in this case was charged with theft after he placed items in a bag in a supermarket and then left without paying for them. He claimed that he had been suffering from hypoglycaemia at the time of the offence and he wanted to raise automatism. The trial judge ruled that he could only plead insanity. However, the Court of Appeal confirmed that the defendant should have been able to plead automatism.

Contrast this to the defendant in *Hennessy* (1989) (discussed at 13.4.5.5) who suffered a hyperglycaemic attack caused by his failure to take insulin. As the defendant's hyperglycaemia was caused by an internal factor (the condition of diabetes), rather than an external factor (the insulin), the defendant could only plead insanity.

 CASE CLOSE-UP

***Quick and Paddison* [1973] QB 910**

The defendants in this case were nurses at a psychiatric hospital who were charged with assaulting a patient thereby occasioning him actual bodily harm, contrary to s.47 of the Offences Against the Person Act 1861. Quick was a diabetic. He claimed that at the time of the offence, he had a low blood sugar level and was suffering from hypoglycaemia. The trial judge refused to leave automatism to the jury and ruled that the defendant's hypoglycaemic state amounted to insanity. As a result, the defendant changed his plea to guilty and appealed against his conviction.

The Court of Appeal quashed the defendant's conviction. The Court held that the defendant's state was a result of an external factor, excess insulin, and this did not amount to a disease of the mind (as required for insanity under *M'Naghten*). Consequently, the Court held that the defendant should have been afforded the opportunity of running automatism at trial.

13.5.2.4 Post-traumatic stress disorder causing a disassociative state

It has also been held that a defendant suffering from a disassociative state caused by an external factor may plead automatism. The defendant in the case of *T* [1990] Crim LR 256 had been raped 3 days prior to committing an offence. Medical evidence was adduced that the defendant was suffering from post-traumatic stress disorder due to the physical trauma of rape which caused the defendant to be in a disassociative state at the time of the offence. The trial judge held that the rape could be an external factor which caused a 'malfunctioning of the mind' and that there was a total loss of control because the defendant was acting as though she were in a dream. As such, the trial judge held that the defence of automatism should be left to the jury. For examples of external and internal factors, see table 13.2.

13.5.3 Dangerous and non-dangerous drugs

Self-induced automatism is no defence for a defendant who is deemed to be at fault. The courts have drawn a distinction between dangerous drugs and non-dangerous drugs. A drug is 'dangerous' if it is common knowledge that the drug may cause the defendant to become aggressive or do dangerous things.

Table 13.2 Examples of external factors and internal factors

External factors (automatism)	Internal factors (insanity)
• Muscle spasm	• Arterioscleosis: *Kemp* (1957)
• Reflex action: *Hill v Baxter* (1958)	• Epilepsy: *Sullivan* (1984)
• Convulsion	• Sleepwalking: *Burgess* (1991)
• Concussion	• Hyperglycaemia: *Hennessy* (1989)
• Physical force	• Schizophrenia
• Administration of a drug	
• Hypoglycaemia: *Quick and Paddison* (1973)	
• Post-Traumatic Stress Disorder: *T* (1990)	

If the defendant's automatism is caused by a dangerous drug, the defendant will have no defence to a crime of **basic intent**, although he may use evidence of his intoxication to negate the *mens rea* for a **specific intent** crime. If the automatism is caused by a non-dangerous drug, the defence of automatism will be available to the defendant, provided he was unaware of the risk of becoming an automaton.

13.5.3.1 Dangerous drugs

If the automatism is caused by the voluntary consumption of drink or dangerous drugs, the rules relating to the defence of intoxication apply, as set out by the House of Lords in *DPP v Majewski* [1977] AC 443. This means that automatism will not be a defence to a basic intent crime, although it may be a defence to a crime of specific intent.

In the case of *Lipman* [1970] 1 QB 152, the defendant was charged with the murder of his girlfriend after she was found dead in a hotel room. The defendant had taken LSD and experienced a 'trip'. He claimed that he was under the delusion that he was descending to the centre of the earth and fighting snakes that were attacking him. During this delusion, he struck his girlfriend on the head and stuffed bed sheets into her mouth, suffocating her. He claimed that he did not know what he was doing at the time, but that he discovered his girlfriend was dead when he recovered from his 'trip'. The Court of Appeal upheld his conviction for manslaughter (a basic intent offence). The fact that he was unaware of what he was doing was no defence to a basic intent offence because the defendant's automatism had been self-induced through his voluntary and deliberate consumption of a dangerous drug. The Court took the view that by taking the drug, the defendant had run the risk of (i.e., been subjectively reckless in relation to) losing control or acting violently. Such recklessness precluded the defendant from relying upon the defence of automatism in respect of a basic intent offence.

13.5.3.2 Non-dangerous drugs

Where the automatism is caused by a non-dangerous drug, the defendant will be able to plead automatism, provided he was unaware of the risk of becoming an automaton (figure 13.7).

🔍 CASE CLOSE-UP

Bailey [1983] 1 WLR 760

In the case of *Bailey*, the defendant, a diabetic, attacked his ex-girlfriend's boyfriend with a length of lead piping. He claimed that he had a low blood sugar level and suffered a hypoglycaemic attack at the time of the offence, causing him to lose control. He had taken insulin but, through his own fault, he had not eaten, causing the hypoglycaemic attack. The trial judge refused to leave automatism to the jury because the defendant had been at fault by failing to eat sufficient food after taking insulin. The defendant was convicted of causing GBH with intent, contrary to s.18 of the Offences Against the Person Act 1861 and appealed.

The Court of Appeal held that

> the trial judge's direction to the jury had been wrong. Self-induced automatism (when it is not caused by drink or dangerous drugs) may be a defence where the defendant's conduct is not reckless. In considering whether the defendant's conduct was reckless, the jury should take into account the defendant's knowledge of the likely consequences of his conduct.

---

basic intent

a crime of 'basic intent' is one which can be committed with a lesser form of *mens rea* than intention (i.e., recklessness)

specific intent

a crime of 'specific intent' is one which requires intention as the *mens rea*

⬤ CROSS REFERENCE

See 13.6.2.2 for an explanation of the difference between a crime of basic intent and one of specific intent.

⬤ CROSS REFERENCE

See 13.6 for further discussion on intoxication and liability.

Thus, in *Bailey*, the defendant would have had a defence if he was not aware that failing to eat sufficient food after taking insulin might cause the defendant to lose control and attack someone. He would have no defence if he did recognise such a risk, but he went on to take that risk, i.e., if he was subjectively reckless.

The jury should consider:

(i) whether the defendant appreciated the risk that his failure to take adequate food after taking insulin might lead to aggressive, unpredictable, and uncontrollable conduct; and

(ii) whether he, nevertheless, deliberately ran the risk or otherwise disregarded it.

If the defendant was aware of the risk or disregarded it, he is reckless and may not rely upon the defence of automatism.

If he was unaware of the risk, the defence of automatism is available to him.

Figure 13.7 Flowchart on the defences of automatism and insanity

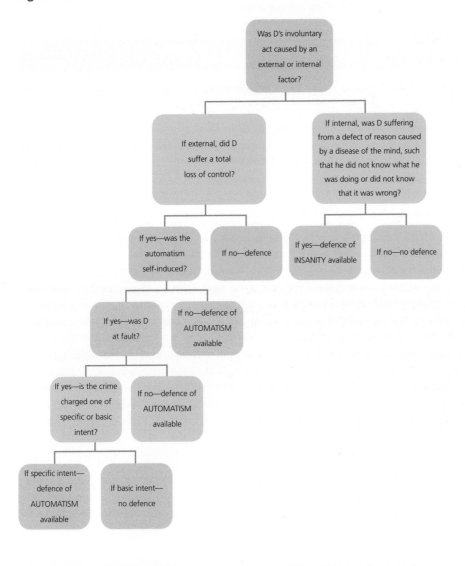

13.6 Intoxication

Technically speaking, intoxication is not a defence as such. For policy reasons, the courts frown upon the use of intoxication (in particular, voluntary intoxication) as a means of escaping criminal liability. However, a defendant may argue that due to his intoxicated state, he did not have the *mens rea* for the offence charged. Hence, intoxication is evidence which may negate the *mens rea* of an offence and, thus, may be evidence in support of a defence, rather than constituting a defence in itself. Nevertheless, most textbooks and courses on criminal law deal with intoxication within a chapter on general defences and refer to intoxication as a defence. This chapter will follow that same approach.

There are two types of intoxication: involuntary and voluntary. Voluntary intoxication arises most commonly in case law, but we will deal with involuntary intoxication first.

13.6.1 **Involuntary intoxication**

Involuntary intoxication may be a defence to any offence provided that the defendant does not have the *mens rea* for the offence in question.

 THINKING POINT

Try to think of examples of involuntary intoxication.

Intoxication will be deemed involuntary where the defendant is not aware that he is consuming alcohol or drugs, or the defendant, who is not at fault in taking a drug, is unaware of the effect it will have on him. An example of the former includes situations where the defendant's drink is spiked. In relation to the latter, the defendant will be involuntarily intoxicated where he takes a drug prescribed for him in accordance with the prescription or where he is not at fault in taking a non-dangerous drug.

Even where the defendant is involuntarily intoxicated, his intoxication will only provide a defence where he does not have the *mens rea* for the offence. If there is clear evidence of the *mens rea*, the defendant will have no defence. For instance, in the case of *Kingston* [1995] 2 AC 355, the defendant was charged with indecent assault against a 15-year-old boy. He claimed that his drink had been laced and that he remembered nothing other than seeing the boy on a bed. The trial judge directed the jury that they should convict the defendant if they were sure that despite his intoxicated state, he intended to commit indecent assault. The defendant appealed against his conviction. The House of Lords confirmed the trial judge's direction and held that a drugged intent is still an intent. Thus, if the defendant intended to commit indecent assault, he had the requisite *mens rea* for the offence and this could not be negated by his involuntary intoxication. This same principle was applied in the earlier case of *Sheehan and Moore* [1975] 1 WLR 739, in which the Court of Appeal held that a drunken intent is still an intent.

Where the defendant voluntarily takes a prescribed or non-dangerous drug and is not reckless in doing so, he will be able to rely on his involuntary intoxication to negate his *mens rea*, provided there is no compelling evidence that he, nonetheless, formed the necessary *mens rea*. This principle was laid down by the Court of Appeal in the case of *Hardie* [1985] 1 WLR 64.

Hardie [1985] 1 WLR 64

The defendant in this case took some valium tablets in order to calm his nerves. The tablets had been prescribed to his girlfriend. The defendant fell asleep and was unable to remember periods of time after this. He later set fire to a wardrobe in the bedroom. He was charged with aggravated criminal damage contrary to s.1(2) of the Criminal Damage Act 1971. The defendant argued that he did not have the *mens rea* of the offence because he was involuntarily intoxicated by the valium and he could not remember setting the wardrobe on fire. The defendant's conviction was quashed on appeal due to a misdirection by the trial judge.

The Court of Appeal stated that the important question to determine was whether the defendant's conduct in taking the valium was reckless. To this end, the jury should consider the nature of the drug as a lawful one in prescribed quantities, the fact that the defendant was unaware of the effect that the drug would have on him (in fact, he had been informed by his girlfriend that the tablets would be harmless), and the usual effect of the drug which is used as a sedative.

Where a defendant voluntarily consumes an alcoholic drink, but believes the alcohol content of the drink to be lower than it is, the defendant will not be able to argue that he was involuntarily intoxicated. In the case of *Allen* [1988] Crim LR 698, the defendant drank some wine, believing it to have a lower alcohol content that it actually did. The Court of Appeal held that the defendant's lack of awareness of the level of alcohol content of the wine did not render his intoxication involuntary. He had voluntarily consumed a drink he knew to be alcoholic. However, the situation would probably have been different if the defendant's glass of wine had been spiked, for example with shots of vodka or a drug. This issue did not arise in *Allen*, but it is likely that the courts would regard this as involuntary intoxication.

13.6.2 **Voluntary intoxication**

Where the intoxication is not involuntary it will be voluntary and the rules laid down in the leading House of Lords' authority of *DPP v Majewski* [1977] AC 443 will apply. According to this case, voluntary intoxication is no defence to a basic intent offence. However, a defendant may use evidence of his voluntary intoxication at the time of the offence to negate the *mens rea* of a specific intent offence (by arguing that due to his intoxication he did not, in fact, form the necessary intention and thus is not liable).

13.6.2.1 **The rule in *DPP v Majewski***

DPP v Majewski [1977] AC 443

The defendant was involved in an altercation in a pub, during which he punched a customer in the face, cut the landlord with a piece of broken glass, and struck a police officer. He was charged with assault occasioning actual bodily harm, contrary to s.47 of the Offences Against the Person Act 1861, and assaulting a police officer in the execution of his duty. The defendant had taken a mixture of drugs and alcohol prior to the incident. He argued that due to his intoxication, he did not know what he was doing and he did not form the *mens rea* for the offences charged. The trial judge rejected intoxication as a defence and the defendant was convicted. On appeal, the case reached the House of Lords.

The House held that evidence of voluntary intoxication cannot be used as a defence to a crime of basic intent. However, evidence of voluntary intoxication may be used as a defence to a specific intent crime if the intoxication negates the *mens rea* of the offence (i.e., intention). The decision in *DPP v Majewski* was largely based upon policy reasons. The House was concerned that allowing intoxication as a defence would 'undermine the criminal law', one of the prime purposes of which is the protection of the public from violent behaviour. Thus, in order to protect the community, the *mens rea* of a basic intent offence will not be negated through proof of voluntary intoxication. Lord Elwyn-Jones LC gave the leading opinion in the House of Lords. His Lordship took the view that a defendant who voluntarily becomes intoxicated should be criminally liable for his conduct while he is in such a condition.

Lord Elwyn-Jones LC famously stated:

> If a man of his own volition takes a substance which causes him to cast off the restraints of reason and conscience, no wrong is done to him by holding him answerable criminally for any injury he may do while in that condition. His course of conduct in reducing himself by drugs and drink to that condition in my view supplies the evidence of *mens rea*, of guilty mind certainly sufficient for crimes of basic intent. It is a reckless course of conduct and recklessness is enough to constitute the necessary *mens rea* in assault cases...

His Lordship took the view that a defendant's voluntary intoxication in fact provides the necessary *mens rea* of any offence of basic intent, which he commits whilst in such a state. According to this view, the defendant's conduct in becoming drunk is itself reckless. Thus, the defendant automatically has the *mens rea* of a basic intent offence. If the defendant then commits the *actus reus* of such an offence, he will be liable for that offence. In *DPP v Majewski*, the defendant had been charged with basic intent offences and, as such, his voluntary intoxication could afford him no defence.

 THINKING POINT

What is your understanding of the extract from the opinion of Lord Elwyn-Jones above?

Where a defendant uses evidence of his voluntary intoxication to negate his intention in relation to a specific intent offence, he will automatically be liable for any lesser offence of basic intent which may exist. For instance, if the defendant is charged with murder and successfully argues that due to his intoxicated state he did not form the necessary intention to kill, he will nevertheless be guilty of the lesser, basic intent offence of manslaughter. Similarly, if the defendant is charged with causing GBH with intent under s.18 of the Offences Against the Person Act 1861 and argues that he did not form the necessary intention due to his voluntary intoxication, he will automatically be guilty of the lesser and basic intent offence of maliciously inflicting GBH under s.20 of the same Act. Thus, a defendant is ill-advised to plead voluntary intoxication to even an offence of specific intent.

13.6.2.2 'Specific intent' and 'basic intent' offences

As the decision in *DPP v Majewski* focused heavily on the nature of the offence charged as one of 'specific intent' or one of 'basic intent', some understanding of the distinction between these terms is necessary.

 THINKING POINT

Explain your understanding of the difference between 'specific intent' offences and 'basic intent' offences.

Unfortunately, however, there is no clear authority on their meaning. The term 'specific intent' was first used by Lord Birkenhead in the House of Lords' decision of *DPP v Beard* [1920] AC 479. However, it is doubtful that His Lordship intended the phrase to take on the importance and focus that it did in the later authority of *DPP v Majewski* and since that case.

Offences of 'specific intent' and 'basic intent'

As stated in chapter 3, and earlier in this chapter, a crime of 'specific intent' is one which requires intention as the *mens rea*. For example, murder is a crime of specific intent as the *mens rea* is intention to kill or cause GBH. Intention must be proved; recklessness would not be sufficient.

Examples of offences capable of being specific intent offences include murder, wounding, or causing GBH with intent (s.18), theft, robbery, and all attempts.

A crime of 'basic intent' is one which can be committed with a lesser form of *mens rea* than intention (i.e., recklessness). For example, criminal damage is a crime of basic intent as the *mens rea* requires intention *or recklessness* to destroy or damage property. Thus, a defendant can be convicted if he is merely reckless as to whether property would be destroyed or damaged.

Examples of offences capable of being basic intent offences include manslaughter, maliciously wounding or inflicting GBH (s.20), assault occasioning ABH (s.47), assault, battery, sexual assault (and other sexual offences), and criminal damage.

Since the decision in *DPP v Majewski* was based heavily upon public policy considerations, it is clear that the use of and distinction between the terms 'specific intent' and 'basic intent' did not create a logical framework upon which the law on voluntary intoxication could rest. Lord Salmon conceded that the distinction between specific and basic intent offences was illogical:

> If voluntary intoxication by drink or drugs can…negative the special or specific intention necessary for the commission of crimes such as murder and theft, how can you justify in strict logic the view that it cannot negative a basic intention, e.g., the intention to commit offences such as assault and unlawful wounding? The answer is that in strict logic this view cannot be justified. But this is the view that has been adopted by the common law of England, which is founded on common sense and experience rather than strict logic.

However, Lord Salmon was prepared to accept a 'degree of illogicality' in order for the law to protect individuals against physical violence.

The practical utility of the terms 'specific intent' and 'basic intent' has also been questioned by the Court of Appeal. Difficulties arise with classifying an offence which requires proof of two elements of *mens rea*: one of intention and one of recklessness. For example, consider the offence of sexual assault contrary to s.3 of the Sexual Offences Act 2003. The *mens rea* of this offence requires *(a)* intentional touching, and *(b)* that the defendant has no reasonable belief in consent. The intentional touching is a specific intent element, while the requirement of lack of reasonable belief is one of basic intent. Similarly, rape requires intentional penetration (specific intent) and no reasonable belief in consent (basic intent). So, are these offences ones of specific intent or basic intent?

Precisely this question arose in the case of *Heard* [2007] EWCA Crim 125. At trial, the judge ruled that sexual assault was an offence of basic intent. Thus, voluntary intoxication provides no defence to sexual assault. The Court of Appeal took the view that the use of the terms 'specific intent' and 'basic intent' to categorise offences might not be appropriate in every case. Hughes LJ stated that 'it should not be supposed that every offence can be categorised simply as either one of specific intent or of basic intent . . . [D]ifferent elements of it may require proof of different states of mind.' In this case, the Court held that the touching had to be intentional and this required no more than basic intent, such that the defendant's voluntary intoxication could not be relied upon to negate it. Although this authority would seem to apply to offences such as rape and sexual assault under the Sexual Offences Act 2003, it is unlikely that the judgment will have much more impact than this. The case has been criticised by academics for rejecting the specific and basic intent distinction. The case also creates further confusion in the law by allowing crimes which can only be committed intentionally to be treated as basic intent offences. Some commentators have pointed out that the application of this case leaves murder in an uncertain state. Murder has always been regarded as a specific intent offence, but as no 'ulterior intent' (i.e., an intent to do more than the simple act, but an intent to bring about a specified consequence) is required, it could be treated as a basic intent offence if *Heard* is applied. The Court attempted to redefine offences of 'specific intent' as offences which require proof of purpose or consequence, but this was merely an *obiter* comment which conflicts with the more straightforward approach adopted in *DPP v Majewski*.

13.6.2.3 **Criticisms of *DPP v Majewski***

The House of Lords' decision in *DPP v Majewski* has been criticised for a number of reasons, some of which were put forward by counsel for the appellant in the House of Lords.

The criticism is largely aimed at the decision of the House to compromise fundamental principles of criminal law for reasons of policy. Although it is undoubtedly important that the law is not seen to condone drunken behaviour which is harmful to society, the decision in *DPP v Majewski* arguably violates fundamental principles of criminal liability by imposing a presumption of recklessness upon a defendant who becomes voluntarily intoxicated. This is evident from the opinion of Lord Elwyn-Jones who stated that evidence of intoxication 'supplies the evidence of *mens rea*, of guilty mind, certainly sufficient for crimes of basic intent'. The criticism of the decision is examined in more detail in the following paragraphs.

 THINKING POINT

What do you think are the main criticisms of the decision of the House of Lords in *DPP v Majewski*?

Violation of the maxim 'actus non facit reum nisi mens sit rea'

One of the fundamental principles of criminal law is that no man is guilty of a crime unless he has a guilty mind (with the exception of strict liability offences, discussed in chapter 4). This principle is derived from the Latin maxim: *actus non facit reum nisi mens sit rea*. It can be argued that the rule in *DPP v Majewski* violates this principle by imposing liability for basic intent offences on a defendant who commits the *actus reus* of an appropriate offence whilst voluntarily intoxicated. Applying the decision in *DPP v Majewski*, the law does not require proof of the defendant's state of mind because his *mens rea* (recklessness) is presumed. Thus, even if, at the time of the offence, the defendant (who is not insane) does not know what he is doing due to his voluntary intoxication, he will be liable for any basic intent offence which ensues.

Contravention of s.8 of the Criminal Justice Act 1967

The presumption of recklessness derived from *DPP v Majewski* contravenes s.8 of the Criminal Justice Act 1967. This provision requires a jury to take into account all of the evidence before concluding that the defendant foresaw the consequences of his actions. Counsel for the appellant argued that it is 'logically and ethically indefensible' to convict a defendant who commits the *actus reus* of assault whilst in a state of automatism (whether induced voluntarily through drink or not) of assault.

No coincidence of *actus reus* and *mens rea*

Coincidence of *actus reus* and *mens rea* is another fundamental principle of criminal law that is compromised by the decision in *DPP v Majewski*.

According to Lord Elwyn-Jones, a defendant's course of conduct in reducing himself through drink or drugs to a condition which causes the defendant to 'cast off the restraints of reason and conscience' amounts to recklessness. Thus, the recklessness is in existence before the *actus reus* of the offence takes place. As recklessness involves the defendant recognising the risk of certain specified consequences amounting to the *actus reus* of the offence, there can be said to be no coincidence of *actus reus* and *mens rea*. The 'recklessness' of the defendant which is presumed under *DPP v Majewski* is not related to the defendant's *actus reus* as it arises prior to his performance of the *actus reus*.

> **CROSS REFERENCE**
> Refer to 3.7.1 for a more detailed explanation of the principle of coincidence of *actus reus* and *mens rea*.

Too much reliance on policy

The decision in *DPP v Majewski* was largely based upon policy considerations, namely the protection of the public. Whilst it is important that the law is not seen to condone drunken behaviour, the common law must be founded upon principles of law. The decision of the House compromises some of the fundamental principles of criminal law.

An alternative approach

Although much of the discussion above has been based on the premise that *DPP v Majewski* imposes a presumption of recklessness upon a defendant who becomes voluntarily intoxicated, an alternative approach has been taken by the Court of Appeal in some more recent authorities. Rather than impose a presumption of recklessness, this alternative approach regards evidence of intoxication as irrelevant and requires the jury to question whether the defendant would have had the *mens rea* had he not been intoxicated.

This approach was adopted in the case of *Wood* (1981) 74 Cr App R 312, in which the defendant was charged with rape. His defence was that he was so drunk that he did not realise that the complainant was not consenting. The Court of Appeal held that his intoxication was not relevant and should be disregarded. Similarly, in *Aitken* [1992] 1 WLR 1006, the Court of

Figure 13.8 Flowchart on intoxication

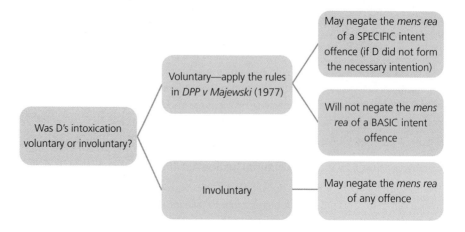

Appeal stated that the defendant would be guilty of unlawfully and maliciously inflicting GBH contrary to s.20 of the Offences Against the Person Act 1861 if he foresaw the risk of causing some harm to the victim, or he would have done but for his intoxicated state. A more recent example of this approach is the case of *Richardson and Irwin* [1999] 1 Cr App R 932. In this case, the defendants were university students who, whilst drunk, held the victim over a balcony. They were convicted of unlawfully and maliciously inflicting GBH contrary to s.20 of the Offences Against the Person Act 1861 after the victim fell and sustained several broken bones. Their convictions were quashed on appeal. The Court of Appeal held that the jury should have been directed that they could only convict if they were sure that the defendants recognised the risk of the victim falling and sustaining some harm, or that they would have recognised it had they not been drinking (figure 13.8).

13.6.3 Dutch courage

A defendant who deliberately consumes alcohol or drugs in order to gain the confidence to commit a criminal offence may not rely upon evidence of his intoxication in order to negate the *mens rea* of the offence. This was confirmed by the House of Lords in the case of *Attorney General for Northern Ireland v Gallagher* [1963] AC 349. In this case, Lord Denning stated that '[t]he wickedness of [the defendant's] mind before he got drunk is enough to condemn him, coupled with the act which he intended to do and did do'. Such a defendant clearly has the intention to commit the offence and cannot evade liability by pleading intoxication which was induced to give him the courage to do so. The defendant's intoxication provides no defence, even to a crime of specific intent.

13.6.4 Intoxication and defences

It is important to consider the impact of intoxication upon the defences in criminal law. Where a defendant who is drunk wishes to raise a defence, how will his intoxicated state affect his defence? In order to answer this question, we need to consider each of the defences separately.

13.6.4.1 Mistake

A defendant's intoxicated mistake will not negate the defence of lawful excuse under s.5(2) of the Criminal Damage Act 1971 to a charge of criminal damage. The defendant will still have the defence available to him. The authority for this is the case of *Jaggard v Dickinson* [1981] QB 527, in which the defendant, whilst drunk, broke into somebody's house, believing that it was her friend's house. Her friend had given her permission to treat his home as her own, and after a night of drinking, the defendant tried to break into what she thought was her friend's house. The defendant's defence was that she held a mistaken but honest belief that her friend would have consented to the damage she caused if she had targeted his house. The Divisional Court held that the defendant could rely upon her mistaken, but honest, belief in her defence even though her mistake was induced by intoxication.

13.6.4.2 **Self-defence**

Where a defendant mistakenly acts in self-defence, but that mistake is induced by the defendant's intoxicated state, self-defence will be no defence: *O'Grady* [1987] QB 995 and *O'Connor* [1991] Crim LR 135. This principle has been subject to criticism because where an intoxicated defendant who kills V may escape liability for murder if he lacked the relevant *mens rea* for that offence, an intoxicated defendant who kills due to a mistaken belief that he is acting in self-defence may not rely upon his intoxicated mistake in his defence.

CROSS REFERENCE
Refer to 14.2.3.4 for further discussion of intoxication and self-defence.

13.6.4.3 **Duress**

Duress requires that the defendant has reasonable grounds for believing that there is a threat to his life or one of serious physical injury to him. If that belief is induced by intoxication, the defence of duress will not be available to the defendant.

13.6.4.4 **Automatism and insanity**

Where the defendant's intoxication induces a state of automatism, the defendant may not rely upon automatism. The relevant defence is intoxication (see *Lipman* (1970)). According to the Court of Appeal in *Coley; McGhee; Harris* [2013] EWCA Crim 223, the law has long recognised the distinction between intoxication and a disease of the mind induced by intoxicants (see *DPP v Beard* [1920] AC 479 and *Davis* (1881) 14 Cox CC 563). The law is clear that a temporary state of insanity is treated in the same way as insanity, thus, where the intoxication induces a disease of the mind, the defendant may have the defence of insanity available to him. This will be dependent upon satisfaction of the remainder of the *M'Naghten Rules* (1843). The Court of Appeal has recently stated that while intoxication may lead to a disease of the mind in some cases, '[d]irect acute effects on the mind of intoxicants, voluntarily taken' do not constitute a disease of the mind: *Coley; McGhee; Harris*.

13.6.4.5 **Loss of control**

While the statutory provisions on loss of control make no specific reference to a mistaken belief induced by intoxication, it is thought that whether the defendant will still be able to rely on the defence of loss of control will depend upon the qualifying trigger applied. The Explanatory Notes to the Coroners and Justice Act 2009 indicate that the fear trigger under s.55(3) is to be subjectively applied (para. 345), thus, the defendant must have a genuine fear of serious violence and that fear need not be reasonable. Consequently, if the defendant honestly, but mistakenly, believes that he has cause to fear serious violence, he will still have the defence of loss of control available to him (although, it has been argued that '[i]f the fear is irrationally based as a product of mental abnormality,...diminished responsibility...is the appropriate defence' (see Alan Reed and Nicola Wake, 'Anglo-American Perspectives on Partial Defences: Something Old, Something Borrowed, and Something New' in Reed and Bohlander 2011: 204). Where the mistake is induced by voluntary intoxication, it has been argued that the intoxication may be relevant to the issue of intention in murder (as a crime of specific intent: as per *DPP v Majewski*), but it would not be relevant in relation to the defendant's fear of serious violence (see Reed and Bohlander 2011: 205).

The Explanatory Notes on the anger trigger under s.55(4) indicate that whether a defendant's sense of being seriously wronged is justifiable is an objective question. This would suggest that a defendant who mistakenly believed that things were said or done which amounted to circumstances of an extremely grave character and caused the defendant to have a justifiable sense of being seriously wronged would need to show that his mistake was not only honest, but also reasonable (for a more detailed discussion on this point, see Jesse Elvin, 'Killing in Response to "Circumstances of an Extremely Grave Character": Improving the Law on Homicide' in Reed and Bohlander 2011: 142–4). Where the mistake is induced by voluntary intoxication, it is unlikely to be a reasonable one, and thus loss of control will be unlikely to afford the defendant any defence.

In relation to the final limb of loss of control under s.54(1)(c) of the Coroners and Justice Act 2009 (whether a person of the defendant's age and sex, with a normal degree of tolerance and self-restraint and in the circumstances of the defendant, might have reacted in the same or in a similar way to the defendant), voluntary intoxication is not a factor to be taken into account. In *Asmelash* [2013] EWCA Crim 157, the Court of Appeal held that:

> It does not mean that the defendant who has been drinking is deprived of any possible loss of control defence: it simply means . . . that the loss of control defence must be approached without reference to the defendant's voluntary intoxication. If a sober individual in the defendant's circumstances, with normal levels of tolerance and self-restraint might have behaved in the same way as the defendant confronted by the relevant qualifying trigger, he would not be deprived of the loss of control defence just because he was not sober. (At [25])

The Court went on to state that the situation would be different if the defendant suffered from alcoholism or an addiction to drugs and he was taunted about that condition: 'to the extent that it constituted a qualifying trigger, the alcohol or drug problem would then form part of the circumstances for consideration' (at [25]).

13.6.4.6 Diminished responsibility

The impact of intoxication upon the defence of diminished responsibility was explored in chapter 5.

13.6.5 Reform

On 15 January 2009, the Law Commission published a report on *Intoxication and Criminal Liability* (Law Com. No. 314) and produced a Draft Bill, the Draft Criminal Law (Intoxication) Bill. Whilst satisfied with the general approach of the law, the Law Commission identified the current lack of clarity surrounding the use of the terms 'specific intent' and 'basic intent'. Thus, the Law Commission made recommendations to clarify the terminology used to make it more 'comprehensible, logical and consistent'.

13.7 Mistake

Generally speaking, ignorance of the law is no defence to a criminal charge. So a defendant's mistake as to the criminal law will not usually absolve him of liability. For example, if a defendant, unaware of the speed limit in England, drives up the M1 at 100 mph, it is no defence for him to claim that he mistakenly believed that the speed limit was 100 mph.

However, mistake may provide a defence in three scenarios: *(a)* where the mistake relates to civil law and negates the *mens rea* of the offence; *(b)* where it relates to a fact and negates the *mens rea* of the offence; and *(c)* where the mistake relates to a defence element. These will be explored in turn.

13.7.1 Mistake as to civil law

A defendant's mistake as to civil law may provide a defence if it negates the *mens rea* of the offence. This is illustrated in the case of *Smith* [1974] QB 354. The defendant in this case was renting a flat. He was given permission by his landlord to install roofing material and wall panels, and to lay floorboards in the flat. At the conclusion of his tenancy, the defendant damaged the roofing, wall panels, and flooring in order to access some electric wiring he had installed for his music system. He was charged with criminal damage, contrary to s.1(1) of the Criminal Damage Act 1971. Under civil law, the roofing, wall panels, and flooring had become the property of the landlord upon being fixed to the flat. The defendant was unaware of this and claimed that he thought he was damaging his own property. His conviction was quashed by the Court of Appeal. The Court held that the defendant's mistake as to the civil law negated his *mens rea* as he did not intend to damage property belonging to another.

13.7.2 Mistake as to fact

A defendant's honest mistake as to fact may provide a defence by negating the *mens rea* of the offence. For example, where a defendant appropriates property belonging to another, mistakenly believing it to be his own, he is not guilty of theft provided his mistake is an honest one. His mistake as to fact here negates the *mens rea* of theft: the defendant is not dishonest if he honestly believes that he has a right in law to the property (s.2(1)(a), Theft Act 1968). The leading authority on mistake as to fact is *DPP v Morgan* [1976] AC 182.

> **CROSS REFERENCE**
> Refer to 8.1.2.2 for a discussion of *DPP v Morgan* (1976).

In this case, the House of Lords held that an honest but mistaken belief in consent is sufficient as a defence to a charge of rape. The belief only had to be honestly held and it did not need to be a reasonable one. Thus, the defendant's mistaken belief as to an *actus reus* element of the offence negates the *mens rea* of the offence. However, in relation to sexual offences, a defendant's mistake as to consent must be both honest and reasonable (see the Sexual Offences Act 2003).

Although a mistake generally only has to be honestly held in order to negate the *mens rea* of the offence, the case of *Tolson* (1889) 23 QBD 168 required a mistake to be both honest and reasonable. However, this authority has been disapproved by the House of Lords in the case of *B (A minor) v DPP* [2000] 2 AC 428, in which the House of Lords held that the defendant's mistake as to the complainant's age was a defence if it was honestly held. The mistake did not also have to be a reasonable one.

> **CROSS REFERENCE**
> Refer to 4.1.3 for a discussion of B *(A minor) v DPP* (2000).

13.7.3 Mistake as to a defence element

This paragraph deals with situations where a defendant makes a mistake as to a defence element. For instance, where a defendant would have had a defence had the facts been as he believed them to be. The question of whether his defence is still valid despite the mistake depends upon the defence relied upon and whether the mistake is honestly and/or reasonably held.

As will be seen at 14.1, defences may be divided into justifications and excuses. Justificatory defences negate the *mens rea* of the offence. Excusatory defences do not negate the *mens rea* of the offence, but they excuse the conduct of the defendant.

> **CROSS REFERENCE**
> For further discussion on the distinction between justifications and excuses see 14.1.

13.7.3.1 **Self-defence**

Self-defence is a justificatory defence. Where the mistake is made as to a justificatory defence, the mistake need only be honestly held. Hence, a defendant who mistakenly believes that he needs to use force to defend himself will still be able to rely upon self-defence, provided his mistake was an honest one: see *Williams (Gladstone)* [1987] 3 All ER 411 at 14.2.3.4. The defendant is judged on the facts as he honestly believed them to be.

13.7.3.2 **Duress**

Duress is an excusatory defence. Where the mistake is made as to an excusatory defence, the mistake must be both honest and reasonable. A defendant who intentionally commits an offence under the mistaken belief that he is being coerced into doing so, will still be able to rely upon duress. According to the case of *Graham* (1982) 74 Cr App R 235, the defendant's belief in the existence of the threat of death or serious injury needed to be both honest and reasonable. This was approved by the House of Lords in *Howe* [1987] AC 417, but both statements were *obiter dicta*. More recently, in *Hasan* [2005] UKHL 22, Lord Bingham stated that the defendant's belief in the threat must be both honest and reasonable.

 ## Summary

- A general defence is one which a defendant may plead in relation to any criminal offence (e.g., insanity, automatism, self-defence, and mistake). A special defence may only be pleaded in relation to specific offences (e.g., provocation and diminished responsibility).

- Children under the age of 10 are conclusively presumed to be *doli incapax*.

- Insanity (insane automatism) is concerned with the mental condition of the defendant at the time that the offence was committed. It leads to a special verdict of 'not guilty by reason of insanity'.

- The defendant must prove (on a balance of probabilities) that at the time he committed the act, he was 'labouring under such a defect of reason, from disease of the mind, as not to know the nature and quality of the act he was doing, or if he did know it, that he did not know he was doing what was wrong': *M'Naghten Rules* (1843).

- Automatism is available where the defendant suffers a total loss of control over his actions or he is unaware of what he is doing. Automatism is dependent upon some external factor acting upon the defendant at the time of the *actus reus*, whereas insanity requires proof of an internal factor, a 'disease of the mind'.

- Involuntary intoxication may be a defence to any offence provided that the defendant does not have the *mens rea* for the offence in question. A drugged intent still amounts to intention: *Kingston* (1995).

- Voluntary intoxication is no defence to a basic intent offence. It may be used to negate the *mens rea* of a specific intent offence if, due to his intoxication, the defendant did not form the necessary intention: *DPP v Majewski* (1977).

- A mistake as to civil law may provide a defence by negating the *mens rea* of the offence charged: *Smith* (1974). A mistake as to fact may negate the *mens rea* of an offence if it is honestly held: *DPP v Morgan* (1976) and *B (A minor) v DPP* (2000).

The bigger picture

- For more information on the Law Commission's provisional proposals on reforming the law on insanity and automatism, you should read the Law Commission Discussion Paper, *Insanity and Automatism* (July 2013). The Law Commission is also currently looking at unfitness to plead. You can follow the developments on the Law Commission website (http://www.lawcom.gov.uk/project/unfitness-to-plead/). You should look out for the Law Commission Report, *Unfitness to Plead*, which is due to be published in 2016.

- You might want to also consider how intoxication affects the defendant's ability to raise another defence, such as self-defence (see 14.2.3.4), automatism (see 13.5.3), loss of control (see 5.4.5), and diminished responsibility (see 5.5.6). You should also consider the impact of intoxication upon a complainant's capacity to consent to sexual activity (see 8.2.3.2).

- Insanity, automatism, and intoxication are examinable topics which could arise individually, together, or within the context of particular offences. You should ensure that you are able to answer both essay and problem questions on these defences.

ⓦ **For some guidance on how you might approach such questions, you should visit the Online Resource Centre.**

? Questions

Self-test questions

1. What is the age of criminal responsibility?

2. What are the elements of insanity? Cite an authority for this.

3. What is a 'disease of the mind'? Cite an authority.

4. When may a defendant plead non-insane automatism?

5. What defence is available to a defendant who commits an offence whilst in a hypoglycaemic state?

6. What defence is available to a sleepwalking defendant?

7. Explain the key differences between insanity and automatism.

8. Is self-induced automatism a defence?

9. Explain the rule in *DPP v Majewski* (1977).

10. When is mistake a defence?

ⓦ **For suggested approaches, please visit the Online Resource Centre.**

Exam questions

1. Jacques and Saul celebrate the end of their exams by attending a party at a friend's house. After several pints of beer, Jacques has sexual intercourse with Belinda in one of the bedrooms, believing that she is consenting. In fact, she was not consenting. Jacques falls asleep on the bed. Belinda's friend, Tomas, goes to the bedroom to

confront Jacques about having sex with Belinda. Whilst sleepwalking, Jacques strikes Tomas over the head with a lamp, causing him serious injury. Saul is on antibiotics which means that he should not drink alcohol. He drinks orange juice all night, but he tells a friend that he feels 'a bit funny'. Suddenly, Saul throws his glass of orange juice at a window, breaking the window and the glass. A friend encourages him to sit down and gets him a brandy to 'calm his nerves'. However, after drinking the brandy, Saul strikes his friend, believing that he is fighting off demons.

Discuss which defences may be available to Jacques and Saul.

2. The law relating to intoxication is in need of reform because it is confusing, illogical, and is not founded upon principles of criminal law.

    To what extent do you agree with this statement? Give reasons for your answer.

 For suggested approaches, please visit the Online Resource Centre.

 Further reading

Books

Reed, A. and Bohlander, M. *Loss of Control and Diminished Responsibility Domestic, Comparative and International Perspectives* (2011), Farnham: Ashgate

Journal articles

Ashworth, A. 'Insanity and Automatism: A Discussion Paper' [2013] Crim LR 787

Child, J. J. and Sullivan, G. R. 'When Does the Insanity Defence Apply? Some Recent Cases' [2014] Crim LR 788

Hathaway, M. 'The Moral Significance of the Insanity Defence' (2009) 73 JCL 310

Horder, J. 'Pleading Involuntary Lack of Capacity' (1993) 52 CLJ 298

Mackay, R. D. 'Righting the Wrong? Some Observations on the Second Limb of the M'Naghten Rules' [2009] Crim LR 80

Mackay. R. D. 'Ten More Years of the Insanity Defence' [2012] Crim LR 946

Mackay, R. D. and Reuber, M. 'Sleepwalking, Automatism and Insanity' [2006] Crim LR 901

Mackay, R. D. and Reuber, M. 'Epilepsy and the Defence of Insanity—Time for a Change' [2007] Crim LR 782

Peay, J. 'Insanity and Automatism: Questions From and About the Law Commission's Scoping Paper' [2012] Crim LR 927

Simester, A. 'Intoxication is Never a Defence' [2009] Crim LR 3

Williams, R. 'Voluntary Intoxication—A Lost Cause?' (2013) 129 LQR 264

Reports

Butler Committee, *Report of the Butler Committee on Mentally Abnormal Offenders* (Cmnd 6244, 1975)

Law Commission Report, *Intoxication and Criminal Liability* (Law Com. No. 314, 2009)

14 Defences II: general defences

	LEARNING OBJECTIVES

By the end of this chapter, you should be able to:

- understand the difference between a justification and an excuse;
- explain the defences of self-defence and prevention of crime;
- distinguish between the defences of duress, necessity, and duress of circumstances; and
- explain the elements of the defence of duress.

Introduction

We began chapter 13 by looking at some of the terminology relating to defences and distinguishing between complete and partial defences, and general and special defences. Chapter 13 dealt with defences which are linked to capacity or negate either an *actus reus* or *mens rea* element of an offence. This chapter explores the remaining general defences of self-defence and the prevention of crime, duress, necessity, duress of circumstances, and marital coercion.

What if someone threatens you that unless you commit a robbery, your family will suffer serious harm? Will you have the defence of duress open to you? What about if the offence you are told to commit is a murder instead of robbery? This chapter explores the elements of the defence of duress and when it is available to a defendant. Occasionally the media fixate on issues such as whether a householder is permitted to strike or kill a burglar who enters his home, often citing the old proverb, 'an Englishman's home is his castle' as support for the rights of the householder. Imagine that you interrupt a burglar in your house in the middle of the night who approaches you with his fist clenched while uttering violent threats. If you instinctively grab a cricket bat and strike the burglar, causing him serious injury, will you be able to rely on self-defence to escape criminal liability? This chapter considers the elements of the defence of self-defence and how they apply specifically to householders.

Table 14.1 Defences as justifications and excuses

Justification	Excuse
Self-defence or defence of another	Duress
Prevention of crime	Duress of circumstances
Necessity	Marital coercion

14.1 Justification or excuse?

Most of the defences discussed in this chapter can be categorised by the terms 'justification' and 'excuse'. Much theoretical debate surrounds this area and academic opinion differs as to how we should distinguish between justifications and excuses or, indeed, as to whether such a distinction is of any practical use. If you wish to delve further into the theories of justification and excuse, you may wish to read some of the literature referred to in the list of further reading at the end of this chapter (see Horder 2004; and Smith 1989).

The conduct of the defendant is justified where the law permits the conduct to take place. A justificatory defence makes the defendant's conduct lawful, and thus negates the unlawfulness of the *actus reus* of the offence. Defences such as self-defence and consent are justifications for this reason. A defendant is excused from liability where, in the circumstances, he is not held to be to blame for his conduct. An excuse does not negate an element of the offence. Duress is an excusatory defence (table 14.1).

14.2 Self-defence and the prevention of crime

It is a complete defence to use reasonable force against another in self-defence, in the defence of another person, or for the prevention of crime. These defences are justificatory defences. The use of reasonable force in the defence of oneself, of another person, or for the prevention of crime, is justified and negates the unlawfulness of the criminal offence charged. Self-defence and the defence of another are private defences defined under the common law (explored at 14.2.2). Both defences have been clarified by s.76 of the Criminal Justice and Immigration Act 2008 (see 14.2.5). Prevention of crime is a public defence provided for by s.3 of the Criminal Law Act 1967.

 STATUTE

Section 3(1), Criminal Law Act 1967

A person may use such force as is reasonable in the circumstances in the prevention of crime, or in effecting or assisting in the lawful arrest of offenders or suspected offenders or of persons unlawfully at large.

There is a significant overlap between these three defences and the common law rules relating to self-defence generally also apply to the statutory defence under s.3 of the Criminal Law Act 1967. For the sake of convenience, these three defences will be dealt with collectively within this section of the chapter and will be referred to as 'self-defence'.

14.2.1 The legal and evidential burden

Where the defendant wishes to rely on self-defence, the defence bear an evidential burden to raise or point to some evidence of self-defence. This evidence may come from the defendant himself or even from a prosecution witness. However, the burden of proving that the defendant did not act in self-defence, defence of another, or the prevention of crime rests with the prosecution (beyond reasonable doubt): *Lobell* [1957] 1 QB 547.

> **CROSS REFERENCE**
>
> Refer to 1.10.1 and 1.10.3 to ensure that you are fully aware of the distinction between a legal burden of proof and an evidential burden.

14.2.2 Self-defence: the common law

The leading authority on self-defence is the case of *Palmer v R* [1971] AC 814, in which the Privy Council confirmed that self-defence is available to a defendant who honestly believes that it is necessary to use force, and uses force which is proportionate to the circumstances as he believed them to be. The test can be broken down into two questions, one subjective and the other objective.

The *Palmer v R* test:

(1) Did the defendant honestly believe that the use of force was necessary? (A subjective test.)

(2) Did the defendant use a reasonable amount of force in the circumstances as he believed them to be? (An objective test with a subjective element.)

Thus, a defendant will be able to rely on self-defence where he honestly believes that the facts are such that he must use force in order to protect himself and he uses reasonable force to do so. The defendant is to be judged according to the circumstances as he believed them to be, regardless of whether his belief is reasonable or not, or mistaken or not: see *Williams (Gladstone)* [1987] 3 All ER 411 at 14.2.3.4.

In the later case of *Oatridge* (1992) 94 Cr App R 367, the Court of Appeal confirmed the existing law on self-defence using different wording. Mustill LJ stated that in cases of self-defence, the following questions must be asked:

(1) Was the defendant under actual or threatened attack by the victim (or did he honestly believe that he was)?

(2) If yes, did the defendant act to defend himself against this attack?

(3) If yes, was his response commensurate with the degree of danger created by the attack (or with the degree of risk which the defendant believed to be created by the attack under which he believed himself to be)?

The first of these questions from the judgment of Mustill LJ in *Oatridge* is subjective, similar to the first question from *Palmer v R*. The second question in *Oatridge* is designed to filter out those cases where the defendant is acting for some reason other than in defence of himself or another. For instance, where a defendant is acting out of revenge or anger, the defence of self-defence should clearly not be available, and any plea would fail on question (2). The third question relates to the amount of force used, which must be objectively reasonable in

Figure 14.1 Elements of self-defence

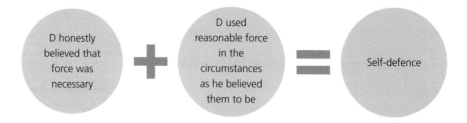

the circumstances as the defendant subjectively believed them to be. It is essentially the same as the second question from *Palmer v R*. The next paragraphs will explore further these two questions (see, also, figure 14.1):

(1) Was force necessary? (The subjective question.)

(2) Was the amount of force used reasonable? (The objective question.)

14.2.3 Did D believe force was necessary?

The first question in the *Palmer v R* test asks whether the defendant believed that the use of force was necessary. A defendant may not rely on self-defence if he uses force on another person out of revenge or in retaliation. A defendant may only lawfully use force on another person if the use of force is necessary to defend himself or another from attack or to prevent the commission of a criminal offence. This question is subjectively assessed, so the important issue is whether the defendant himself believed that the use of force was necessary. The defendant's belief does not need to be reasonably held. There are a number of issues to consider in determining whether the defendant believed that the use of force was necessary.

14.2.3.1 Pre-emptive strikes

A defendant may strike his 'attacker' first in order to defend himself, provided he honestly believed that the use of force was necessary to ward off an attack. A pre-emptive strike does not preclude a defendant from relying upon self-defence.

🔍 **CASE CLOSE-UP**

***Beckford v R* [1988] AC 130**

In the case of *Beckford v R*, the defendant was a police officer who shot and killed a man who was running away from a house in which it had been alleged that an armed man had been terrorising his family. The defendant was charged with murder, but argued that he should have a defence available to him if he honestly believed that he was in danger. The Privy Council quashed his conviction and confirmed that the defendant would have a defence if he used force due to an honest belief that he was in danger. The fact that the defendant's act was pre-emptive did not preclude the defence of self-defence.

Lord Griffiths stated that:

a man about to be attacked does not have to wait for his assailant to strike the first blow or fire the first shot: circumstances may justify a pre-emptive strike.

More recently, in the case of *Rashford* [2005] EWCA Crim 3377, it was held that where the defendant goes looking for the victim in order to exact revenge, he is not precluded from relying upon self-defence if the victim retaliates violently and the defendant honestly believes that the use of force is necessary in self-defence.

14.2.3.2 Danger must be sufficiently imminent

The danger to the defendant must be sufficiently imminent in order to justify the defensive action taken by the defendant. In the case of *Devlin v Armstrong* [1971] NI 13, Lord MacDermott CJ held that 'the anticipated attack must be imminent'. His Lordship stated that the danger that the defendant anticipates must be 'sufficiently specific or imminent to justify the actions she took as measures of self-defence'. Under the common law, the anticipation of a future danger is not sufficient for self-defence because the threat must be imminent.

However, in some circumstances it would appear to be possible to lawfully make preparations in order to defend oneself in respect of future attacks. In *Attorney General's Reference (No. 2 of 1983)* [1984] AC 456, the defendant could not rely upon self-defence after he made preparations for future attacks which he feared. He owned a shop which had been attacked and damaged by rioters previously. Fearing further attacks, the defendant made petrol bombs to use in self-defence as a last resort. He was charged with the offence of making an explosive substance in such circumstances as to give rise to a reasonable suspicion that he had not made it for a lawful object, contrary to s.4 of the Explosive Substances Act 1883. The defendant was acquitted by the jury after pleading that his 'lawful object' was self-defence. The Attorney General referred the case to the Court of Appeal which held that self-defence was sufficient as a lawful object.

Despite the decision in *Attorney General's Reference (No. 2 of 1983)* (1984), most preparatory acts performed in order to protect oneself from future attack will not be lawful. For instance, where a person decides to carry a knife in anticipation of a future attack he will be guilty of possession of an offensive weapon, contrary to s.1 of the Prevention of Crime Act 1953. Self-defence is unlikely to be a defence to this offence where it is committed in advance of any attack.

14.2.3.3 No duty to retreat

There is no duty on the defendant to retreat from the scene before using force. This was confirmed by the Court of Appeal in the case of *Bird* [1985] 2 All ER 513. In this case, the defendant was charged with unlawfully and maliciously wounding, contrary to s.20 of the Offences Against the Person Act 1861 after she hit her ex-boyfriend in the face with a glass, causing him to lose an eye. She argued that she had been acting in self-defence. They had had an argument, during which she claimed that he held her up against a wall. The trial judge directed the jury that before the defence of self-defence would be available to the defendant, she would have to demonstrate an unwillingness to fight. The defendant was convicted and appealed. The Court of Appeal quashed the conviction and held that this had been a misdirection. The Court held that there was no duty on a defendant to retreat prior to using force. Similarly, in the earlier case of *McInnes* [1971] 1 WLR 1600, it was held that there was no duty to retreat. However, a demonstration of unwillingness to fight could amount to evidence that the use of force was necessary and that the amount of force used was reasonable and may be taken into account by the jury when considering whether the defendant was acting in self-defence or out of a desire for revenge or retaliation.

14.2.3.4 Mistaken belief in self-defence

Where the defendant acts in self-defence due to a mistaken belief that the use of force is necessary, his mistake will not preclude him from relying upon the defence, provided his belief was honestly held. This principle was confirmed in the leading authority of *Williams (Gladstone)* [1987] 3 All ER 411.

 CASE CLOSE-UP

Williams (Gladstone) [1987] 3 All ER 411

The defendant in this case saw a man wrestle a youth to the floor and twist his arm behind his back. The man told the defendant that he was a police officer, arresting the youth. When the defendant asked to see a warrant card, the man could not produce one. In fact, he was not a police officer. The defendant punched the man, believing that the use of force was necessary to protect the youth. He was charged with assault occasioning actual bodily harm, contrary to s.47 of the Offences Against the Person Act 1861. In fact, the man had chased the youth and knocked him to the ground after witnessing him snatch a woman's handbag. Although the defendant honestly believed that he was defending the youth from attack, in fact the man was apprehending the youth for robbery. The defendant raised the defence of protection of another and argued that his mistaken belief that the use of force was necessary to protect the youth did not preclude the defence. His conviction was quashed by the Court of Appeal. It was held that the defendant's mistaken belief that the use of force was necessary did not preclude self-defence, provided the defendant's belief was honestly held.

Lord Lane CJ held that:

> where self-defence or the prevention of crime is concerned, if the jury came to the conclusion that the defendant believed, or may have believed, that he was being attacked or that a crime was being committed, and that force was necessary to protect himself or to prevent the crime, then the prosecution have not proved their case. If however the defendant's alleged belief was mistaken and if the mistake was an unreasonable one, that may be a powerful reason for coming to the conclusion that the belief was not honestly held and should be rejected...Even if the jury come to the conclusion that the mistake was an unreasonable one, if the defendant may genuinely have been labouring under it, he is entitled to rely upon it.

The defendant's honest belief justified his behaviour and negated the element of unlawfulness in the offence.

However, where the mistake was induced by the voluntary intoxication of the defendant, self-defence will not be available to the defendant. This principle was confirmed in the case of *O'Grady* [1987] QB 995. In this case, the defendant fell asleep after drinking heavily with a friend. He claimed that he woke up to find his friend hitting him, so he struck his friend with a piece of glass, killing him. The Court of Appeal distinguished the case of *Williams (Gladstone)*. Lord Lane CJ stated that:

> where the defendant might have been labouring under a mistake as to the facts he must be judged according to that mistaken view, whether the mistake was reasonable or not. It is then for the jury to decide whether the defendant's reaction to the threat, real or imaginary, was a reasonable one. The court was not in that case [*Williams (Gladstone)*] considering

what the situation might be where the mistake was due to voluntary intoxication by alcohol or some other drug.

His Lordship concluded that:

> where the jury are satisfied that the defendant was mistaken in his belief that any force or the force which he in fact used was necessary to defend himself and are further satisfied that the mistake was caused by voluntarily induced intoxication, the defence must fail.

This statement in *O'Grady* was merely an *obiter* comment, but the same approach was adopted in the case of *O'Connor* [1991] Crim LR 135 and in the more recent case of *Hatton* [2005] EWCA Crim 2951.

14.2.4 Was the amount of force used reasonable?

The second question in the *Palmer v R* test asks whether the amount of force used by the defendant was reasonable. If the defendant uses excessive force, the defence will fail. According to *Oatridge*, the question is: was his response commensurate (or proportionate) with the degree of danger created by the attack? This question is objectively assessed and is a matter for the jury. The jury may take into account a number of factors such as the size and strength of the respective parties, the number of people involved, the nature and degree of the force used, the seriousness of the evil to be prevented, the possibility of preventing it by alternative means, and any unwillingness to fight.

The objective nature of this test was doubted in the case of *Scarlett* [1993] 4 All ER 629, in which the defendant, a landlord of a pub, ejected a customer from his pub. The customer died after falling down the stairs in the pub. The Court of Appeal quashed the defendant's conviction for unlawful act manslaughter and held that the trial judge had failed to properly direct the jury. The Court held that the defendant should not be guilty if he believed that the circumstances called for the degree of force he used, irrespective of whether that belief was reasonable or not. This subjective approach was rejected in the case of *Owino* [1996] 2 Cr App R 128. The test of whether or not the force used was reasonable is an objective one, although it does contain a subjective element (the defendant is to be judged on the facts as he believed them to be).

14.2.4.1 The 'heat of the moment'

The law gives the defendant some leeway by acknowledging that, sometimes, the defendant may have very little time to consider his response. In *Palmer v R*, Lord Morris expressed this by stating that in the 'heat of the moment', the defendant will not be expected to 'weigh to a nicety the exact measure of his necessary defensive action'. In *Palmer v R*, Lord Morris stated that:

> If a jury thought that in a moment of unexpected anguish a person attacked had only done what he honestly and instinctively thought was necessary, that would be most potent evidence that only reasonable defensive action had been taken.

In the Court of Appeal judgment in *Whyte* [1987] 3 All ER 416, Lord Lane CJ explained the 'reasonable force' element of the defence further:

> A man who is attacked may defend himself, but may only do what is reasonably necessary to effect such a defence. Simply avoiding action may be enough if circumstances permit. What is reasonable will depend upon the nature of the attack. If there is a relatively minor attack, it is not reasonable to use a degree of force which is wholly out of proportion to the demands of the situation. But if the moment is one of crisis for someone who is in imminent danger, it may be necessary to take instant action to avert that danger.

In *Owino* (1996), the Court of Appeal again confirmed that the second question in *Palmer v R* is an objective test which contains a subjective element. Collins J held that:

> A person may use such force as is (objectively) reasonable in the circumstances as he (subjectively) believed them to be.

14.2.4.2 Excessive force

The greater the danger to the defendant, the more force a defendant may use to repel an attack. However, the force used must be reasonable in the circumstances as the defendant believed them to be. If the defendant uses excessive force, he will not be able to rely upon self-defence.

In the case of *Clegg* [1995] 1 AC 482, the House of Lords held that a defendant who kills using excessive force is guilty of murder and will not be able to avail himself of the defence of self-defence. The defendant in this case was a British soldier serving in Northern Ireland. He fired four shots at a car which broke through a checkpoint, killing a passenger. The defendant was convicted of murder. Although the first three shots fired had been fired in self-defence, the final shot was fired after the car had broken through the checkpoint and the danger had passed. This final shot was excessive. The House of Lords held that killing by using excessive force does not constitute self-defence and may not even offer a partial defence to a defendant.

14.2.4.3 Defendant's psychiatric condition not relevant

Recent authority demonstrates that a defendant's psychiatric condition is not relevant to whether or not the defendant has used reasonable force in self-defence.

Q | CASE CLOSE-UP

Martin (Anthony) [2001] EWCA Crim 2245

In *Martin (Anthony)*, the defendant was a farmer in Norfolk. He lived alone in an isolated farmhouse called 'Bleak House'. He had been the victim of burglary on several occasions. One night, the two victims broke into the defendant's house. The defendant armed himself with a shotgun and fired at the victims, killing one and wounding the other. The defendant was charged with various offences, including murder of one victim and wounding with intent of the other. At trial, he claimed to have been acting in self-defence, but the jury rejected this and he was convicted.

The Court of Appeal considered that the defendant had used excessive force. The defendant had adduced fresh evidence on appeal that he had, in fact, been suffering from a paranoid personality disorder. The defence argued that this disorder meant that at the time of the killing, the defendant would have perceived a much greater danger to himself than the average person. The Court of Appeal held that the defendant's psychiatric condition should not be taken into account when determining whether the amount of force used by the defendant was reasonable. The defence of diminished responsibility was held to be available to the defendant and his conviction for murder was quashed and replaced by one of manslaughter due to diminished responsibility.

This decision that the defendant's psychiatric condition cannot be taken into account conflicts with the subjective element in this limb, that the force used must be reasonable in the circumstances *as the defendant believed them to be* (see *Owino* (1996)). In *Sean Oye v R* [2013]

EWCA Crim 1725, the Court of Appeal confirmed that the defendant's psychiatric condition was not relevant to the question of whether the force used by the defendant was reasonable in the circumstances as the defendant believed them to be. In this case, the defendant suffered from insane delusions that evil spirits were intent on harming him. The Court rejected the appellant's argument that the prosecution could not prove that the degree of force used was unreasonable *in the circumstances as the defendant believed them to be*. The Court concluded that '[a]n insane person cannot set the standards of reasonableness as to the degree of force used by reference to his own insanity' (at [47]). Public policy considerations were paramount here because if the law were otherwise, '[i]t could mean that the public is exposed to possible further violence from an individual with a propensity for suffering insane delusions' (at [45]).

 THINKING POINT

Compare this approach in *Martin (Anthony)* (2001) to the one taken in *Attorney General for Jersey v Holley* [2005] UKPC 23 in respect of the old defence of provocation. Are these cases reconcilable?

14.2.5 The Criminal Justice and Immigration Act 2008

In response to repeated media campaigns about the use of reasonable force by householders, clarification of the law on the use of force in self-defence or the prevention of crime has been provided by s.76 of the Criminal Justice and Immigration Act 2008, which came into force on 14 July 2008. This provision has since been amended by s.148 of the Legal Aid, Sentencing and Punishment of Offenders Act 2012 and s.43 of the Crime and Courts Act 2013. The Explanatory Notes to the Criminal Justice and Immigration Act 2008 state that the section is 'intended to improve understanding of the practical application of these areas of the law'. The provision incorporates established principles from case law, but does not change the existing law. The most recent amendments create a separate, more generous test for the degree of force that is deemed to be reasonable in cases involving householders.

14.2.5.1 General principles

Sections 76(1) and 76(2) explain that the section applies where an issue arises as to whether the defendant can rely on self-defence, the defence of property, or the prevention of crime and whether the force used was reasonable in the circumstances. Section 76(3) confirms that the question of whether the force used was objectively reasonable is to be judged according to the circumstances as the defendant subjectively believed them to be. This is in accordance with the common law position as set out in the cases of *Palmer v R* (1971), *Oatridge* (1992), and *Owino* (1996).

 STATUTE

Section 76(3), Criminal Justice and Immigration Act 2008

The question whether the degree of force used by D was reasonable in the circumstances is to be decided by reference to the circumstances as D believed them to be, and subsections (4) to (8) also apply in connection with deciding that question.

Subsections (4) to (8) confirm further principles decided under the common law. The defendant's use of force must be reasonable in the circumstances as the defendant believed them to be. When taking into account the defendant's belief in the existence of any such circumstances, s.76(4) states that the defendant's belief need only be honest. It does not need to be reasonable. Thus, where the defendant makes a mistake as to the circumstances, he will still be able to rely on self-defence, provided his belief was honestly held. Section 76(4) is based on the principle in the case of *Williams (Gladstone)* (1987) (see 14.2.3.4).

Section 76(5) states that the defendant will not be able to rely on self-defence if his mistaken belief has been induced by voluntary intoxication. This places the decisions in *O'Grady* (1987), *O'Connor* (1991), and *Hatton* (2005) on a statutory footing (see 14.2.3.4).

Sections 76(5A) (discussed at 14.2.5.2) and 76(6) elaborate on the second, objective question from the test in *Palmer v R* (1971) and deal with the degree of force that it is permissible to use. Generally speaking, the use of force is not reasonable if it is disproportionate in the circumstances as the defendant believed them to be. These subsections follow the approach taken in *Owino* (1996) in the sense that the test is an objective one with a subjective element. These two subsections distinguish between cases involving householders and cases involving non-householders. Section 76(6) deals with cases other than householder cases.

 STATUTE

Section 76(6), Criminal Justice and Immigration Act 2008

In a case other than a householder case, the degree of force used by D is not to be regarded as having been reasonable in the circumstances as D believed them to be if it was disproportionate in those circumstances.

Section 76(5A) is a new subsection inserted into the Act by s.43(2) of the Crime and Courts Act 2013. This subsection makes specific provision for cases involving householders, which are now to be treated differently to other cases (see 14.2.5.2).

Section 76(6A) confirms the position in *Bird* [1985] 2 All ER 513 that there is no duty to retreat, but provides that the possibility that the defendant could have retreated is a factor to take into consideration if relevant.

Section 76(7) places on a statutory footing the consideration highlighted in *Palmer v R*, that a defendant acting in self-defence in the heat of the moment may not always have time to 'weigh to a nicety the exact measure of any necessary action' (s.76(7)(a)) and that 'evidence of a person's having only done what the person honestly and instinctively thought was necessary for a legitimate purpose constitutes strong evidence that only reasonable action was taken by that person for that purpose' (s.76(7)(b)) (see 14.2.4.1).

Section 76(8) provides that other matters may also be taken into account and s.76(9) simply states the purpose of the new provision is to clarify the law relating to self-defence (except in relation to householder cases, in which different provision is made). Section 76(10) defines various terms used in s.76.

14.2.5.2 Cases involving householders

As stated at 14.2.5.1, s.76(5A) is a new subsection (inserted into the Act by s.43(2), Crime and Courts Act 2013) which provides specifically for cases involving householders. This amendment makes it clear that cases of self-defence by householders within a dwelling are to be treated differently to other cases. It provides that the degree of force used by a defendant in a householder case is not to be regarded as having been reasonable in the circumstances as the defendant believed them to be if it was grossly disproportionate in those circumstances. Thus, a greater degree of leniency is offered towards a householder who will only use more than reasonable force if the force used was *grossly* disproportionate.

A 'householder' case is defined in s.76(8A) as a case in which:

* the defendant raises the common law defence of self-defence;
* he uses force while in or partly in a building or part of a building that is a dwelling or forces accommodation, or both ('building' includes a vehicle or vessel (s.76(8F));
* he is not trespassing at the time the force is used; and
* he believed the victim to be in, or entering, the building or part of a building as a trespasser.

It is worth noting here that the statute expressly refers to self-defence and does not mention the defence of property or the prevention of crime. Thus, it would appear that the leniency granted to householders only applies where the defendant acts to defend himself, and not if he is acting in defence of his property or the prevention of crime. Section 76(8B) further extends the operation of s.76(5A) to parts of a building which are used as a place of work by the defendant or another person, provided that the defendant or other person dwells in another part of the building, and that the part of the building used for work is internally accessible from the part containing the dwelling. Section 76(5A) also applies to the part of the building providing internal access between the place of work and the dwelling.

14.2.6 Defence of another

As stated in 14.2, a defendant may use reasonable force in the defence of another person. In the case of *Rose* (1884) 15 Cox CC 540, the defendant shot his father whilst acting in defence of his mother. The defendant was acquitted of murder. It was held that where a defendant acts in defence of his mother, his conduct is excusable.

The defence extends to the use of reasonable force in the defence of any person in order to prevent the commission of an offence. In the case of *Duffy* [1967] 1 QB 63, while acting in defence of her sister, the defendant struck the victim with a bottle. The defendant was convicted of unlawfully and maliciously wounding the victim, contrary to s.20 of the Offences Against the Person 1861. The defendant appealed against her conviction on the grounds that the trial judge had wrongly directed the jury that the defence of another was not available to the defendant. The Court of Appeal held that it was unnecessary in this case to determine whether or not a person could act in the defence of a sibling because '[q]uite apart from any special relations between the person attacked and his rescuer, there is a general liberty even as between strangers to prevent a felony'. This defence has now been put onto a statutory footing by s.3(1) of the Criminal Law Act 1967 and it also falls within the ambit of the statutory clarification offered by s.76 of the Criminal Justice and Immigration Act 2008.

14.2.7 **Defence of property**

▶ **CROSS REFERENCE**

Refer to 10.6 and 10.6.1.4 for further discussion of criminal damage and the defences available under the Criminal Damage Act 1971.

A defendant may act in defence of his property. The defence of property was a valid defence under the old common law prior to the Criminal Law Act 1967: *Hussey* (1925) 18 Cr App R 160. This defence has most recently been recognised in the amendments to s.76 of the Criminal Justice and Immigration Act 2008 made by s.148 of the Legal Aid, Sentencing and Punishment of Offenders Act 2012 (by the inclusion of the new s.76(2)(aa)). Thus, the principles of self-defence contained within s.76 of the Criminal Justice and Immigration Act 2008 also apply to the common law defence of property.

Although the defence of property exists, it is very unlikely that the defence would extend to killing a person in defence of property. It was not accepted that the defendant in the case of *Martin (Anthony)* [2001] EWCA Crim 2245 had acted in defence of property when he killed and seriously injured two burglars on his property. This was largely due to the fact that the Court of Appeal considered the defendant to have used excessive force (following the decision of the jury) because he shot the victim in the back. Nevertheless, it is a valid defence to act in defence of one's property.

There is another form of the defence of property contained within a statute designed specifically to protect property, namely the Criminal Damage Act 1971. Thus, where the defendant is charged with damaging or destroying property belonging to another under the Criminal Damage Act 1971 and he damages such property in defence of his own property, the defence of lawful excuse under s.5 of the Criminal Damage Act 1971 applies.

Similarly, where a defendant is charged with an offence against the person after trying to protect his property from being taken from him, the defendant may plead that he was acting in defence of his property; this would be covered by the prevention of crime under s.3(1) of the Criminal Law Act 1967.

14.2.8 **Lethal force**

Where the defendant kills another person while using reasonable force to defend himself, the defendant will be able to rely upon self-defence and will be acquitted of any charge of murder or manslaughter. Where the force used is excessive, this defence will not be available to the defendant. The jury will determine whether or not the amount of force used was reasonable, taking into account the factors mentioned in 14.2.4.

> **THINKING POINT**
>
> Consider whether the use of lethal force in self-defence is compatible with the European Convention on Human Rights.

Under Article 2 of the European Convention on Human Rights every person has a right to life. Article 2.2 provides for certain circumstances in which a person may lawfully be deprived of their right to life. These circumstances include the use of force in the defence of a person from unlawful violence; in order to effect a lawful arrest or prevent the escape of a person lawfully detained; and in action lawfully taken to quell a riot. Article 2.2 provides that the degree of force used in such circumstances must be no more than is absolutely necessary in the circumstances. If in such circumstances, the use of force which is no more than absolutely necessary results in the death of a person, there is no violation of Article 2.

CASE CLOSE-UP

McCann and others v UK (1996) 21 EHRR 97

The issue of the compatibility of our domestic law on self-defence with the European Convention on Human Rights arose in the case of *McCann and others v UK* (1996) 21 EHRR 97. In this case, three men, who were members of the IRA, were shot and killed in Gibraltar by members of the SAS. The three men had been suspected of being involved in planning a terrorist attack on Gibraltar by detonating a car bomb. The intelligence gathered by the SAS was, in fact, inaccurate. The families of the three men who were killed complained to the European Court of Human Rights, arguing that there had been a violation of the human rights of the deceased men. In particular, the applicants argued that there had been a violation of Article 2 of the European Convention on Human Rights, the right to life.

The European Court of Human Rights held that there had been a violation of Article 2. The Court was of the view that the use of lethal force had been more than was absolutely necessary in the circumstances. The Court held that where a person holds a mistaken belief that the use of force is necessary, that belief must be an honest belief held for good reasons.

Thus, there is a conflict between our domestic law which requires a mistaken belief merely to be honestly held, and the view of the European Court of Human Rights which requires good reasons for that honest belief (see *Leverick* [2002] Crim LR 347 for further argument that our law on self-defence is incompatible with Article 2 and *Smith* [2002] Crim LR 958 for a counter-argument).

14.3 Duress

Duress has been described as a 'concession to human frailty': *Howe* [1987] AC 417. The issue of duress arises where the defendant is threatened that he must commit a criminal offence or suffer physical injury or injury to his family (e.g., 'commit theft or else'). This type of duress is often referred to as duress by threats. A defendant who commits a criminal offence because his will is overborne by threats of violence may plead duress. Duress is an excusatory defence. A defendant who commits a criminal offence under duress is excused from liability because he is not held to be blameworthy enough to warrant criminal sanction. The defence of duress does not negate an element of the offence. It is a complete defence. Thus, if pleaded successfully the defendant is acquitted. The defendant bears an evidential burden in relation to duress: he must adduce some evidence of duress in order to make the issue a live one. The burden of proof is on the prosecution to disprove duress beyond reasonable doubt: *Bone* [1968] 1 WLR 983.

> **CROSS REFERENCE**
> Refer to 1.10.1 and 1.10.3 to ensure that you are fully aware of the distinction between a legal burden of proof and an evidential burden.

14.3.1 Which offences is duress a defence to?

Duress is a general defence. It is available in respect of most offences. However, duress is no defence to charges of treason, murder (*Howe* [1987] AC 417), or attempted murder (*Gotts* [1992] 2 AC 412). Duress is no defence to a defendant who is charged with murder, either as a principal (*Abbott v R* [1977] AC 755) or as a secondary party (*Howe* [1987] AC 417, HL, overruling the House of Lords' decision in *Lynch v DPP for Northern Ireland* [1975] AC 653).

The rationale behind limiting the application of duress to offences other than murder and attempted murder relates to the importance that the law places on the sanctity of life and the protection of the lives of individuals. Thus, the law does not excuse a defendant from committing murder or attempting to do so, even where he was under severe pressure of threats to his own life or those of his family.

The House of Lords ruled definitively on the issue of duress and murder in the case of *Howe* [1987] AC 417. Prior to *Howe*, there were two conflicting authorities on this matter. In *Abbott v R*, the Privy Council ruled that duress could not be a defence to a principal offender charged with murder. A year or so earlier, in *Lynch v DPP for Northern Ireland*, the House of Lords had ruled that duress was a defence to a secondary party to murder. The House resolved this apparent conflict in the case of *Howe*. In this case, the defendants participated in one killing as secondary parties, but were the principals in another killing. They claimed that they acted out of fear that they would be seriously harmed or killed by a man named Murray, who organised the killings. The defendants wished to plead duress. The trial judge ruled that duress was a defence to secondary parties to murder, but was no defence to principals to murder. The House of Lords ruled that duress was no defence to murder, irrespective of whether the defendant was a principal or a secondary party to murder. In the House of Lords, Lord Brandon stated that:

> so far as the defence of duress is concerned, no valid distinction can be drawn between the commission of murder by one who is a principal in the first degree and one who is a principal in the second degree.

Thus, the House overruled the previous decision of the House in *Lynch v DPP for Northern Ireland*.

In the case of *Gotts* [1992] 2 AC 412, the defendant was charged with the attempted murder of his mother, contrary to s.1(1) of the Criminal Attempts Act 1981. He claimed that his father had threatened to shoot him unless he killed his mother, and he wished to plead duress. The trial judge ruled that duress was not available to a charge of attempted murder. As a result of this ruling, the defendant pleaded guilty and appealed on the ground that the trial judge's direction had been wrong. The House of Lords dismissed the appeal and confirmed that duress is no defence to a charge of attempted murder. While the *mens rea* for attempted murder is an intention to kill, a lesser intention to cause GBH is sufficient for a charge of murder. Lord Jauncey questioned whether there is, 'logic in affording the defence to one who intends to kill but fails, and denying it to one who mistakenly kills intending only to injure'. His Lordship gave two examples to illustrate his point.

THINKING POINT

Attempted murder is a less serious offence than murder because no death results. Why do you think duress is also not available in respect of attempted murder?

Example 1

(1a) A stabs B in the chest intending to kill him and leaves him for dead. By good luck B is found whilst still alive and rushed to hospital where surgical skill saves his life.

(1b) C stabs D intending only to injure him and inflicts a near identical wound. Unfortunately D is not found until it is too late to save his life.

His Lordship commented:

> I see no justification of logic or morality for affording a defence of duress to A who intended to kill when it is denied to C who did not so intend.

Example 2

(2a) E plants in a passenger aircraft a bomb timed to go off in mid-flight. Owing to bungling it explodes while the aircraft is still on the ground with the result that some 200 passengers suffer physical and mental injuries of which many are permanently disabling, but no one is killed.

(2b) F plants a bomb in a light aircraft intending to injure the pilot before it takes off but in fact it goes off in mid-air killing the pilot who is the sole occupant of the airplane.

His Lordship commented:

> It would in my view be both offensive to common sense and decency that E if he established duress should be acquitted and walk free without a stain on his character notwithstanding the appalling results which he has achieved, whereas F who never intended to kill should, if convicted in the absence of the defence, be sentenced to life imprisonment as a murderer.

Thus, the rationale for precluding a defendant charged with attempted murder from relying upon duress is that the state of mind of the defendant may, indeed, be more serious and inexcusable than that of a defendant charged with murder. In *Howe*, Lord Griffiths also dealt with this question in an *obiter* statement:

> It cannot be right to allow the defence to one who may be more intent upon taking a life than the murderer. This leaves, of course, the anomaly that duress is available for the offence of wounding with intent but not to murder if the victim dies subsequently. But this flows from the special regard that the law has for human life, it may not be logical but it is real and has to be accepted.

Lord Griffiths acknowledges here that the law is not entirely logical, in that it allows duress as a defence to a charge of wounding or causing GBH with intent, but does not allow it as a defence to murder. Nevertheless, the line must be drawn somewhere. Focusing on the aim of the law of duress, the protection of life, the law prohibits the defence where a defendant intends to kill and where he does kill, coupled with at least an intention to cause GBH.

14.3.2 Duress: the test

A defendant may plead duress if he commits a criminal offence because his will is overborne by threats by another of death or physical injury. In the case of *Lynch v DPP for Northern Ireland* [1975] AC 653, Lord Simon described duress:

> I take it for present purposes to denote such [well-grounded] fear, produced by threats, of death or grievous bodily harm [or unjustified imprisonment] if a certain act is not done, as overbears the actor's wish not to perform the act, and is effective, at the time of the act, in constraining him to perform it.

The test for duress is derived from two important decisions: the Court of Appeal decision in *Graham* (1982) 74 Cr App R 235 and the House of Lords' decision in *Howe* [1987] AC 417. These cases were approved by the House of Lords' in the case of *Hasan* [2005] UKHL 22.

> ## ↻ SUMMARY
>
> The following two questions must be asked:
>
> **(1)** Was D impelled to act as he did because he reasonably feared that, if he did not so act, X would kill him or cause him serious physical injury?
>
> **(2)** Would a sober person of reasonable firmness, sharing the characteristics of the defendant, have responded to D's belief by taking part in the killing?

The defendant in *Graham* (1982) was living with his wife and a homosexual man, King, with whom the defendant was also in a relationship. King was a violent man who was jealous of the defendant's wife. He suggested that they kill her. King placed electrical flex around the wife's neck and told the defendant to pull on the other end. He did so and the wife died. The defendant was charged with murder and pleaded duress. He argued that he only acted out of fear of King. He was convicted of murder and appealed, but the Court of Appeal upheld his conviction because the threat to the defendant was not sufficiently grave to raise duress. Lord Lane CJ gave the leading judgment of the Court of Appeal. His Lordship stated that the jury should have been directed to consider two questions:

(1) Was the defendant, or may he have been, impelled to act as he did because, as a result of what he reasonably believed King had said or done, he had good cause to fear that if he did not so act King would kill him, or (if this is to be added), cause him serious physical injury?

(2) If so, have the prosecution made the jury sure that a sober person of reasonable firmness, sharing the characteristics of the defendant, would not have responded to whatever he reasonably believed King said or did by taking part in the killing?

The first of these questions is subjective and asks whether the defendant acted because he feared that he would be killed or suffer serious physical injury. This question also contains an objective element: the defendant's fear must be reasonably held. The second question is objectively assessed and asks whether a reasonable person would have acceded to the threat as the defendant did. This question also contains a subjective element as some of the characteristics of the defendant may be taken into account. Both of these questions will be looked at in more detail at 14.3.3 and 14.3.4.

In the more recent authority of *Hasan* [2005] UKHL 22, the House of Lords revisited the law on duress. This case is the most recent example of the increasingly restrictive approach adopted by the judiciary in relation to the defence of duress (see, also, figure 14.2).

Figure 14.2 Test for duress

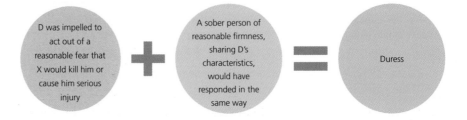

CASE CLOSE-UP

Hasan [2005] UKHL 22

The defendant in this case worked as a driver for a woman who was involved in prostitution. The woman's boyfriend, S, was a drug dealer and a violent man. The defendant was charged with aggravated burglary, contrary to s.10 of the Theft Act 1968. He claimed that he had acted under duress, having been coerced into committing the burglary by S. Following previous authorities (see 14.3.5), the trial judge directed the jury that the defence of duress would not be available to the defendant if they found that by associating with S he had voluntarily put himself in a position in which he knew that he was likely to be subjected to threats. The defendant was convicted and appealed. The Court of Appeal allowed the defendant's appeal and certified a point of law to be considered by the House of Lords. The House of Lords restored the defendant's conviction and remitted the matter to the Court of Appeal.

The House of Lords confirmed the test for duress from *Graham* and *Howe*. Lord Bingham examined the defence of duress in some detail and identified the limitations of the defence. His Lordship held that:

(1) duress is no defence to murder, attempted murder, and some forms of treason;

(2) the threat relied on must be to cause death or serious injury;

(3) the threat must be directed against the defendant or his immediate family or someone close to him;

(4) the test for duress is largely objective;

(5) duress is only available where the criminal offence has been directly caused by the threats which are relied upon;

(6) duress is only available if there was no evasive action he could reasonably have been expected to take;

(7) the defendant may not rely on duress to which he has voluntarily laid himself open.

The next part of this chapter explores each of these questions in turn.

14.3.3 The subjective question

The first question in the *Graham/Howe* test asks whether the defendant was impelled to act as he did out of a reasonable fear that if he did not so act, he would be killed or suffer serious physical injury. This is a subjective question which concerns the defendant's belief in such a threat. However, there is an objective element to this question as the defendant's belief in the threat must be a reasonable one. A number of factors relating to this question must be considered.

14.3.3.1 Who must the threat be directed towards?

In the case of *Wright* [2000] Crim LR 510, the Court of Appeal confirmed that the defence of duress was not confined to threats to the defendant himself, but also extended to threats of death or serious violence towards a person for whose safety the defendant would reasonably regard himself as responsible. In *Hasan*, the House of Lords confirmed that the threats of death or serious injury to which the defendant accedes may be directed towards the defendant himself, his immediate family, or someone close to him. Lord Bingham stated that the decision in *Wright* was also consistent with the rationale of the duress exception. Thus, it would appear that it would even be possible for a defendant to plead duress successfully where the threat has been directed towards a stranger, provided the defendant reasonably regards himself as responsible for that stranger. Consider, for example, a defendant who is compelled to commit a criminal offence by threats towards the child he is babysitting for the first time. The child would be a relative stranger, but would certainly be someone for whom the defendant reasonably regards himself as responsible.

14.3.3.2 Cumulative threats

The defendant must act as a result of threats of death or serious injury. However, threats of death or serious injury do not need to be the sole threats which cause the defendant to act. The defence of duress is still available to a defendant who acts as a result of an accumulation of different threats, provided he would not have acted had it not been for the threats of death or serious injury. This is illustrated in the case of *Valderrama-Vega* [1985] Crim LR 220. The defendant in this case was charged with being knowingly concerned in the fraudulent evasion of the prohibition on the importation of cocaine from Columbia, contrary to s.170 of the Customs and Excise Management Act 1979. He smuggled cocaine into the UK for members of a Mafia-type organisation who had threatened him with death or serious injury. The defendant claimed that he committed the offence due to these threats as well as threats to disclose his homosexuality and financial pressure. The defendant appealed against his conviction. The Court of Appeal held that duress was available, even if the defendant acted as a result of the cumulative effect of all the threats, provided that he would not have acted but for the threats of death or serious injury.

14.3.3.3 Threat must be of immediate harm

The House of Lords in *Hasan* confirmed that the threat of death or serious injury must be immediate, such that the defendant could not reasonably have been expected to take evasive action. In doing so, the House disapproved the case of *Hudson and Taylor* [1971] 2 QB 202.

A wider approach had been taken by the Court of Appeal in the case of *Hudson and Taylor* (1971). The Court held that the threat would be imminent simply if it were operating on the defendant's mind at the time of the offence. The defendants in this case were two young girls who were charged with perjury after they gave evidence in respect of an incident they witnessed in a pub. Both defendants were called to give evidence against the man charged, X, but both failed to identify him in court. They argued that Hudson had been approached by X's friends who threatened her with physical injury if they gave evidence. The trial judge ruled that duress was not available because there was no immediate threat to the defendants. The threats could not be carried out as the defendants had the protection of the police and the judge while giving evidence in court. The defendants were convicted and appealed. The Court of Appeal quashed their convictions and held that the defence of duress was available to the defendants. The Court took the view that the threats were 'no less compelling, because their execution could not be effected in the court room, if they could be carried out in the streets of Salford the same night'. The Court stated that the trial judge should have left the jury to decide whether the threats had overborne the will of the appellants at the time when they gave the false evidence.

This approach was also followed in the case of *Abdul-Hussain* [1999] Crim LR 570. In this case, the defendants were Shia Muslims from Iraq. They sought refuge in Sudan after fleeing from the Iraqi regime. They feared that they would be deported back to Iraq and that they would be subjected to violence or death. They hijacked an aeroplane bound for Jordan and diverted it to London. They were charged with hijacking, contrary to s.1(1) of the Aviation Security Act 1982. They argued that they had committed the offence in order to escape deportation back to Iraq where they feared they would lose their lives. The trial judge ruled that the defence of duress of circumstances was not available to the defendants because the threat of violence or death was not sufficiently immediate—the defence required an almost spontaneous reaction to the threats. The defendants were convicted and appealed. The Court of Appeal quashed their convictions and held that duress was available. Even though the reaction to the threats was not spontaneous and thus not immediate, they were imminent and had operated on the minds of the defendants at the time of the offence so as to overbear their will. The Court held that in order to rely on duress, the defendant must have had no reasonable opportunity to take evasive action.

The wide approach taken in these cases to the immediacy element of duress was disapproved by the House of Lords in *Hasan*. The House held that the threatened act must be immediate or almost immediate upon the defendant's failure to comply with the threat and the defendant must have no opportunity to take evasive action. Lord Bingham stated that:

> if the retribution threatened against the defendant...is not such as he reasonably expects to follow immediately or almost immediately on his failure to comply with the threat, there may be little if any room for doubt that he could have taken evasive action, whether by going to the police or in some other way, to avoid committing the crime with which he is charged.

14.3.3.4 Nexus between threat and offence

The defence of duress is only available where there is a sufficient nexus between the threat and the offence committed. The defendant must essentially be told, 'commit this crime or else'. In the case of *Cole* [1994] Crim LR 582, the defendant owed money to some people who threatened to harm him, his girlfriend, and his baby unless he paid off his debts. As a result of these threats, the defendant committed two robberies on building societies. He tried to plead duress, but the trial judge ruled that it was not available to him. This decision was approved by the Court of Appeal because the threats to the defendant and his family were not sufficiently linked to the offences he committed. The defendant had not been told that he should commit robbery in order to pay the money back. The moneylenders merely demanded the money and did not insist upon the method by which the defendant should acquire the money. The defendant could have pursued other lawful options in order to pay off his debts.

14.3.3.5 Mistaken belief in a threat

The first question in the *Graham/Howe* test for duress requires the defendant to reasonably believe that there is a threat of death or serious physical injury. However, no threat need actually exist. The question then arises as to whether the mistaken defendant's belief need only be honest, or whether it must also be reasonably held.

In *Safi* [2003] EWCA Crim 1809, the Court of Appeal approved the approach in *Graham*, that the defendant must have a reasonable belief in the existence of a threat, but that the threat itself need not actually exist. An objective approach was followed by the House of Lords in *Hasan*. Lord Bingham stated that:

> It is of course essential that the defendant should genuinely, i.e. actually, believe in the efficacy of the threat by which he claims to have been compelled. But there is no warrant for relaxing the requirement that the belief must be reasonable as well as genuine.

However, a subjective approach was followed in the earlier case of *Martin (David Paul)* [2000] 2 Cr App R 42. The Court of Appeal took a subjective approach to the issue of the defendant's mistaken belief in threats and held that the defendant's psychiatric condition would be relevant. This approach is similar to that taken in relation to mistake and self-defence (see the case of *Williams (Gladstone)* at 14.2.3.4).

The words of Lord Bingham in *Hasan* must surely be authoritative on this issue. The House of Lords has confirmed in strong terms the objectivity of the defence of duress. Thus, the defendant must honestly believe that a threat exists and that belief must be a reasonable one.

14.3.4 The objective question

The second question in the *Graham/Howe* test asks whether a sober person of reasonable firmness, sharing the characteristics of the defendant, would have responded to the threats as the defendant did. This is an objective test which requires a defendant to meet the same standard of resilience as the reasonable man. However, there is a subjective element to this question which dilutes the objectivity of duress. The authorities allow some of the defendant's characteristics to be taken into account.

 CASE CLOSE-UP

Bowen [1996] 2 Cr App R 157

The case of *Bowen* is the leading authority on the characteristics which may be taken into account. The defendant in this case was convicted of the offence of obtaining services by deception. He was a man of low IQ, with a reading age of 7 years old, and was abnormally suggestible and vulnerable. The defendant claimed that he had been threatened by two men that they would throw a petrol bomb at his house unless he committed the offence. The trial judge ruled that the defendant's characteristics, which made him more likely to accede to such threats, were not relevant to duress.

The Court of Appeal held that the defendant's low IQ (short of mental impairment), vulnerability, and suggestibility were not relevant characteristics to be taken into account when considering whether the defendant would have acceded to the threats as the defendant did. Stuart Smith LJ stated that:

> The mere fact that the accused is more pliable, vulnerable, timid or susceptible to threats than a normal person are not characteristics with which it is legitimate to invest the reasonable/ordinary person for the purpose of considering the objective test.

The Court also held that characteristics due to self-induced abuse of alcohol or drugs would not be relevant. The only relevant characteristics were the age and possibly the sex of the defendant, pregnancy (where the threat of harm is to the unborn baby), serious physical disability, and a clinically recognised psychiatric condition.

Bowen was followed in *Antar (Kayed Kevin)* [2004] EWCA Crim 2708, in which the trial judge excluded the evidence of a psychologist about the defendant's mental impairment. The Court of Appeal held that this evidence should have been left to the jury because it was for the jury to decide on all the evidence whether the defendant 'fell into a category of persons who were less able to resist pressure than the sober person of reasonable firmness'.

Table 14.2 Duress and characteristics

Relevant characteristics	Irrelevant characteristics
• Age	• Low IQ (short of mental impairment)
• Sex	• Timidity
• Pregnancy	• Vulnerability
• Serious physical disability	• Self-induced abuse (e.g., alcohol, drugs)
• Clinically recognised psychiatric condition	• Emotional instability
	• Possible effects of sexual abuse as a child

Earlier authorities have held that evidence of the defendant's self-induced drug addiction was not a relevant characteristic (*Flatt* [1996] Crim LR 576), nor was evidence of emotional instability and a 'grossly elevated neurotic state' (*Hegarty* [1994] Crim LR 353). The Court of Appeal has also ruled that evidence of the possible effects of sexual abuse as a child is not relevant (*Hurst* [1995] 1 Cr App R 82), and nor is evidence of pliability and vulnerability (*Horne* [1994] Crim LR 584): see table 14.2. However, it has been held that evidence of post-traumatic stress disorder is a relevant characteristic (*Emery* (1993) 14 Cr App R (S) 394) and in *R v GAC* [2013] EWCA Crim 1472, the Court of Appeal recently held that 'learned helplessness', a feature of battered women syndrome, could be of relevance to a defence of duress, although this would depend on a careful analysis of the extent and timing of the domestic abuse, the impact on the person, and their presentation at the relevant time.

14.3.5 **Associating with criminals**

Where the defendant voluntarily associates with criminal individuals or a criminal gang, such that he recognises the risk that he might be forced to commit offences, the defence of duress is not available to him. For instance, in the case of *Fitzpatrick* [1977] NILR 20, the defendant voluntarily joined the IRA, officially recognised as a terrorist organisation. He was pressured into committing a robbery, during which he shot and killed a person. He tried to plead duress to charges of murder and robbery, but this was rejected by the trial judge. The Court of Appeal in Northern Ireland agreed with the decision of the trial judge that duress was not available to this defendant because he had voluntarily joined an organisation which he knew to be officially categorised as a terrorist organisation.

Similarly, in *Sharp* [1987] QB 853, the defendant voluntarily joined a criminal gang, knowing that they committed robberies with firearms. The defendant pleaded duress after he participated in a robbery of a post office at which a man was killed. He claimed that he had tried to withdraw from the robbery when he found out that guns were to be used. However, the trial judge refused to leave duress to the jury and the defendant was convicted of manslaughter. The Court of Appeal agreed that duress was not available to the defendant. Lord Lane CJ concluded the judgment of the Court by stating:

> where a person has voluntarily, and with knowledge of its nature, joined a criminal organisation or gang which he knew might bring pressure on him to commit an offence and was an active member when he was put under such pressure, he cannot avail himself of the defence of duress.

The same principle is applied whether the defendant voluntarily associates with a criminal gang or a criminal individual. In the case of *Ali* [1995] Crim LR 303, the defendant voluntarily associated with a man he knew to be a drug dealer and violent. He agreed to sell drugs for him, but failed to hand over the proceeds of sale. The drug dealer then pressured the defendant into committing a robbery of a building society and gave him a gun. Duress was held not to be available to the defendant because he had voluntarily associated with a man he knew to be violent. Similarly, the defence of duress was not available to the defendant in the case of *Heath* [2000] Crim LR 109. The defendant in this case also voluntarily associated with a drug dealer. He owed the drug dealer money and understood that he had placed himself in a position where he might be subjected to violence or threats of violence. The defendant was charged with possession of cannabis with intent to supply. The Court of Appeal held that duress was not available to the defendant.

By contrast, the defence of duress will be available if the defendant voluntarily associates with a criminal gang not known to use violent methods. For example, the defendant in *Shepherd* (1987) 86 Cr App R 47 voluntarily joined a gang of shoplifters. They were not a violent gang and the defendant did not know them to use violent methods. However, the defendant was threatened with violence, as a result of which he committed a burglary. The trial judge followed previous authorities and refused to leave duress to the jury. On appeal against his conviction, the Court of Appeal ordered a retrial and held that duress should have been available to the defendant in this case. The Court distinguished this case on the grounds that the gang the defendant joined was not known to use violence.

14.4 Necessity

It is unclear whether necessity exists as a general defence. The courts have skirted around the issue of whether necessity may be relied upon to justify a defendant's actions in committing a criminal offence in order to avoid a greater evil. If it does indeed exist, necessity is a justificatory defence: it is a justified choice between two evils. Necessity differs from duress as duress excuses a defendant's behaviour as a concession to human frailty, whereas necessity justifies it. Necessity does not require a threat made by a person of death or physical injury, but merely a choice between two evils. Necessity is similar in nature to duress of circumstances because the threat emanates from circumstances rather than a particular person. Necessity does not require a threat of death or serious injury to the person, whereas duress of circumstances does. However, the courts have used these phrases interchangeably within judgments, adding to the confusion surrounding the existence of necessity.

In the notorious case of *Dudley and Stephens* (1884) 14 QBD 273, it was held that the defendants could not rely upon a defence of necessity. The defendants, along with a third man and a cabin boy named Parker, were shipwrecked in a storm. They spent almost 3 weeks in an open boat and had no food or water for about a week. They decided to kill and eat the cabin boy who was very weak and unlikely to survive. The defendants believed that they would die unless they ate a person on the boat. The cabin boy probably would have died before the defendants. Four days later, they were rescued by a passing ship. The defendants were convicted of murder and sentenced to death. On appeal, their convictions were upheld but the sentence was commuted to 6 months' imprisonment without hard labour. Lord Coleridge CJ rejected necessity as a defence in this case:

> it is admitted that the deliberate killing of this unoffending and unresisting boy was clearly murder, unless the killing can be justified by some well-recognised excuse admitted by the

law. It is further admitted that there was in this case no such excuse, unless the killing was justified by what has been called 'necessity'. But the temptation to the act which existed here was not what the law has ever called necessity. Nor is this to be regretted.

Lord Coleridge CJ was concerned that allowing a defence of necessity to a charge of murder would divorce law from morality. His Lordship acknowledged the duty to preserve one's own life, but also spoke of a duty to sacrifice it in some circumstances. His Lordship recognised the danger of abuse of the law in allowing such a defence:

> Who is to be the judge of this sort of necessity? By what measure is the comparative value of lives to be measured? Is it to be strength, or intellect, or what? It is plain that the principle leaves to him who is to profit by it to determine the necessity which will justify him in deliberately taking another's life to save his own.

Necessity has been relied upon in medical cases. In *F v West Berkshire Area Health Authority* [1989] 2 All ER 545, F was a patient in a mental hospital. She was 36 years old and suffered from a very serious mental disability. She formed a sexual relationship with a male patient. Usual contraceptive methods were considered to be unsuitable for F and evidence was given that pregnancy would be disastrous for F psychologically. F was unable to give her consent to undergo a sterilisation operation and her mother obtained a declaration that the operation would not be unlawful without F's consent. The Official Solicitor appealed to the Court of Appeal and then to the House of Lords. The appeal was dismissed and the operation was held to be lawful as it would be in the best interests of the patient. The operation was deemed necessary to prevent the risk of pregnancy and the disastrous psychological effect on F. Lord Goff put forward the principle of necessity to justify the imposition of medical treatment without consent where such treatment would be in the best interests of the patient.

Following the case of *Re A (Children) (Conjoined Twins: Surgical Separation)* [2001] Fam 147, it would appear that necessity may be used as a defence to murder.

THINKING POINT

Consider how the decision in *Re A (Children) (Conjoined Twins: Surgical Separation)* (2001) has given new life to the defence of necessity.

CASE CLOSE-UP

***Re A (Children) (Conjoined Twins: Surgical Separation)* [2001] Fam 147**

This case involved the surgical separation of conjoined twins, Jodie and Mary. Mary, the weaker twin, was incapable of existence independently of her twin and would certainly have died if they were separated. Jodie had a better chance of surviving the separation, but would be expected to die within 6 months if the separation did not take place because of the strain placed on her heart of oxygenating both her own and Mary's bodies. The Court of Appeal was required to consider whether the operation would be lawful. The Court held that, applying *Woollin*, the operation would involve the intentional killing of Mary: Mary's death was virtually certain to occur as a result of the separation and the doctors recognised this.

❯ CROSS REFERENCE

Refer to chapter 3 for a reminder of the test in *Woollin*.

In order to avoid liability for murder being imposed upon the doctors, the Court sought a justification for the operation. Brooke LJ relied upon the defence of necessity in justifying the intentional killing of Mary. His Lordship stated that there are three requirements of necessity:

(1) the act is needed to avoid inevitable and irreparable evil;

(2) no more should be done than is reasonably necessary for the purpose to be achieved; and

(3) the evil inflicted is not disproportionate to the evil avoided.

Brooke LJ distinguished the case of *Dudley and Stephens* because in *Re A* nature had selected the person who would die, whereas a human made that choice in *Dudley and Stephens*.

However, despite this judgment, there are a number of reasons why *Re A* is not a particularly persuasive case on necessity. The judgments conflict and their Lordships adopted entirely different reasoning in reaching their conclusions. Brooke LJ relied upon necessity to justify the operation. While accepting the arguments regarding necessity, Walker LJ considered there to be no intention to kill Mary on the part of the doctors. Ward LJ explored quasi self-defence, by which the doctors could come to Jodie's defence in separating the twins. However, His Lordship also concluded that 'the law must allow an escape through choosing the lesser of two evils', a phrase undoubtedly associated with the defence of necessity. That the judgments are conflicting and confusing is not surprising. The case was brought before the Court of Appeal at speed and decided very quickly, without much time for the careful drafting of speeches. The case is also really a civil authority, decided in the Civil Division of the Court of Appeal.

Nevertheless, it does seem that the Court was sanctioning the use of necessity as a defence in exceptional and limited circumstances. Ward LJ concluded his judgment by stating:

> Lest it be thought that this decision could become authority for wider propositions...it is important to restate the unique circumstances for which this case is authority. They are that it must be impossible to preserve the life of X without bringing about the death of Y, that Y by his or her very continued existence will inevitably bring about the death of X within a short period of time, and that X is capable of living an independent life but Y is incapable under any circumstances, including all forms of medical intervention, of viable independent existence. As I said at the beginning of this judgment, this is a very unique case.

In recent years, necessity has been rejected as a defence. In the case of *Quayle* [2005] EWCA Crim 1415, the Court of Appeal held that necessity was not available as a defence to offences involving the medicinal use of cannabis to alleviate pain. In *R (on the application of Nicklinson) and another v Ministry of Justice and others* [2015] AC 657, the Supreme Court held that necessity is not available as a defence to assisted suicide.

THINKING POINT

Consider a driver who stops at a red traffic light. An ambulance, sounding its siren on its way to an emergency, pulls up behind the driver's car. While the traffic light is still red, the driver moves his car past the traffic light and pulls over to the left to let the ambulance go.

Should the defence of necessity be available to the driver if he is charged with jumping a red light?

14.5 Duress of circumstances

Duress of circumstances is an excusatory defence. The defence of duress of circumstances may be relied upon by a defendant who is compelled to commit an offence by force of circumstances. It is distinct from duress by threats as the 'threat' does not come from a person, but from the circumstances in which the defendant finds himself. It is narrower than necessity because duress of circumstances requires the defendant to be in reasonable fear of death or serious injury. Nevertheless, the courts have often confused necessity and duress of circumstances and used these two defences interchangeably.

One of the first cases on duress of circumstances was *Willer* (1986) 83 Cr App R 225. The defendant in this case was driving around town with some friends. Their car was set upon by a gang of 20 to 30 youths who were shouting threats and striking the car. One youth managed to open the back door and attempted to climb into the car. In order to escape, the defendant drove over a section of the pavement. He then made his way to a police station to report the incident. He was arrested and charged with reckless driving (an old offence). The trial judge refused to leave the defence of necessity to the jury. The defendant pleaded guilty then appealed. The Court of Appeal quashed his conviction and held that the defendant could rely upon 'duress' as a defence. Watkins LJ held that the trial judge should have left to the jury 'the question whether or not . . . the appellant was wholly driven by force of circumstances into doing what he did and did not drive the car otherwise than under that form of compulsion'. Although the Court referred to the defence of 'duress', this case is a clear example of the application of duress of circumstances.

Similarly, in *Conway* [1989] QB 290, the defence of duress of circumstances applied to another case of reckless driving. The defendant drove recklessly in order to escape two men who came running towards the car. The passenger in the car had been shot at two weeks previously and feared another attack. The two men running towards the car were actually plain-clothed policemen seeking to arrest the passenger, who was the subject of a bench warrant. The defendant appealed against his conviction for reckless driving. The Court of Appeal quashed the defendant's conviction and held that 'a defence of "duress of circumstances" is available only if from an objective standpoint the defendant can be said to be acting in order to avoid a threat of death or serious injury'. At one point, the Court somewhat confusingly referred to the defence as 'necessity'.

The principles governing duress of circumstances were elaborated upon in *Martin* [1989] 1 All ER 652. The defendant's wife had suicidal tendencies. She threatened to commit suicide unless the defendant drove his stepson to work. The defendant genuinely believed that she would carry out her threat, so he drove the son to work. The defendant had been disqualified from driving and was convicted of this offence. The Court of Appeal quashed his conviction and held that duress of circumstances would be available as a defence here. Simon Brown LJ summarised the principles of duress of circumstances:

> first, English law does, in extreme circumstances, recognise a defence of necessity. Most commonly this defence arises as duress, that is pressure on the accused's will from the wrongful threats or violence of another. Equally however it can arise from other objective dangers threatening the accused or others. Arising thus it is conveniently called 'duress of circumstances'.
>
> Second, the defence is available only if, from an objective standpoint, the accused can be said to be acting reasonably and proportionately in order to avoid a threat of death or serious injury.

Figure 14.3 Elements of duress of circumstances

Once again, the court appears to use the words 'necessity' and 'duress of circumstances' inter-changeably. However, there is a more definitive statement in the judgment of Simon Brown LJ, labelling this defence as 'duress of circumstances'. His Lordship then went on to state that the two questions from *Graham/Howe* (see 14.3.2 and figure 14.3) should be applied to this defence. In *Santos v CPS Appeals Unit* [2013] EWHC 550 (Admin), the Divisional Court applied *Martin* [1989] 1 All ER 652 and confirmed that the defence of 'necessity' applies to strict liability offences. The defence was referred to as one of 'necessity' in this case, but it is mentioned here under the heading of duress of circumstances in light of Simon Brown LJ's statement in *Martin*. There appears to be no coherent and rational distinction between the courts' use of the terms 'necessity' and 'duress of circumstances'.

In *Pommell* [1995] 2 Cr App R 607, the Court of Appeal acknowledged that the defence of duress of circumstances is not limited to driving offences, but is of general application. However, the defence does not apply to murder, attempted murder, or treason in the same way that duress by threats does not apply to these offences.

Thus, while duress of circumstances is similar in its nature to necessity, it follows the same principles as duress by threats. It requires the defendant to have a reasonable fear of a threat of death or serious injury and that a reasonable person sharing the defendant's characteristics would act in the same way.

14.6 Marital coercion

Until recently, marital coercion or coercion by a husband was a defence under s.47 of the Criminal Justice Act 1925. However, this provision was abolished by s.177 of the Anti-social Behaviour, Crime and Policing Act 2014, which came into force on 13 May 2014. Section 47 of the Criminal Justice Act 1925 provided that a woman who committed an offence in the presence of her husband and under his coercion had a defence. This was a complete defence, resulting in an acquittal if successfully relied upon. It was a general defence, but could not be relied upon in defence to a charge of murder or treason. This was one of the rare defences where the legal burden shifted onto the defence; thus the burden of proving the defence was on the defendant. Hence, the wife had to prove, on a balance of probabilities, that she committed the offence in the presence of and under the coercion of her husband.

The leading case on marital coercion was *Shortland* [1996] 1 Cr App R 116. In this case, the Court of Appeal held that coercion could be physical or moral and did not require physical force or the threat of physical force. This principle was approved by the Court of Appeal in

Cairns [2002] EWCA Crim 2838. Marital coercion was wider than the defence of duress, which does require the defendant to believe in a threat to her physical well-being. The defendant had to prove, on a balance of probabilities, that her will was so overborne by the wishes of her husband, that she was forced unwillingly to participate in the offence. The Court stated that marital coercion was very different to a situation where a wife willingly participates in a criminal offence out of loyalty to the husband. The defence required unwilling participation in the offence.

Marital coercion was rarely pleaded and, if pleaded, was rarely successful. The defence was unsuccessfully pleaded by Anne Darwin who was convicted of various deception offences along with her husband, John Darwin, after they faked John Darwin's death in order to claim on a life insurance policy and pensions: see *Darwin and Darwin* [2009] 2 Cr App R (S) 115. More recently, the defence was unsuccessfully pleaded by Vicky Pryce who was convicted of perverting the course of justice after she accepted driving licence penalty points which were actually incurred by her husband: *Pryce* (Southwark Crown Court, unreported, 8 March 2013).

It is somewhat surprising that this defence was not abolished until 2014. Marital coercion did not apply to unmarried women, married men, or anyone in a same-sex relationship. It was an outdated defence which was rightly abolished.

 Summary

- A defendant will be able to rely on self-defence where he honestly believes that the use of force is necessary in order to protect him and he uses reasonable force to do so: *Palmer v R* (1971).

- A pre-emptive strike does not preclude self-defence: *Beckford v R* (1988). There is no duty on a defendant to retreat before using force: *Bird* (1985) and s.76(6A) of the Criminal Justice and Immigration Act 2008.

- A defendant's mistaken belief in self-defence does not preclude the defence provided that his belief that force was necessary was honestly held: *Williams (Gladstone)* (1984) and s.76(4) of the Criminal Justice and Immigration Act 2008. However, there is no defence available where the mistake was induced by the voluntary intoxication of the defendant: *O'Grady* (1987), *O'Connor* (1991), and s.76(5) of the Criminal Justice and Immigration Act 2008.

- A defendant acting in the heat of the moment is not expected to weigh to a nicety the exact measure of his defensive response: *Palmer v R* (1971) and s.76(7)(a) of the Criminal Justice and Immigration Act 2008.

- Duress is no defence to murder (whether as a principal or a secondary party) (*Howe* (1987)) or attempted murder (*Gotts* (1992)).

- Test for duress from *Graham/Howe*: *(a)* Did D act because he reasonably feared that he would be killed or suffer serious physical injury or death? And *(b)* would a reasonable person sharing D's characteristics have acceded to the threat as D did?

- The threat must be directed against the defendant or his immediate family or someone close to him: *Hasan* (2005). Duress is only available if there was no evasive action he could reasonably have been expected to take: *Hasan* (2005).

- The defendant may not rely on duress to which he has voluntarily laid himself open: *Fitzpatrick* (1977), *Sharp* (1987), *Ali* (1995), *Hasan* (2005).

- Necessity is a justified choice between two evils.

The bigger picture

- For a more detailed discussion on the provision relating to householders and self-defence under the Criminal Justice and Immigration Act 2008, you should read the recent article by Lydia Bleasdale-Hill (2015).

- For more information on the Law Commission's proposals in relation to duress, duress of circumstances, and necessity, see the Law Commission Report, *Legislating the Criminal Code: Offences Against the Person and General Principles* (Law Com. No. 218, 1993).

- The general defences are examinable either as a stand-alone topic or within the context of a question about the offences to which they might apply. You should ensure that you are able to answer both essay and problem questions in this area.

 For some guidance on how you might approach exam questions on these defences, you should visit the Online Resource Centre.

? Questions

Self-test questions

1. Explain the difference between a justification and an excuse.

2. What is the test for self-defence? Cite an authority for this.

3. Is the test for self-defence objective or subjective or both? Explain your answer using case law.

4. Can a defendant who acts in the mistaken belief that self-defence is necessary still rely on the defence? Explain your answer using case law.

5. When, if at all, might a defendant use lethal force in self-defence?

6. What is the test for duress? Cite two authorities for this.

7. What are the limitations on the defence of duress?

8. To what extent, if at all, are the defendant's characteristics relevant to the defence of duress?

9. Explain the difference between duress and duress of circumstances.

10. Is necessity a defence?

 For suggested approaches, please visit the Online Resource Centre.

Exam questions

1. Mildred and John, two law students, decide to go to the Student Union for a few drinks after their finals. After several drinks, Mildred confesses to John that she cheated in her criminal law exam. John threatens to tell their lecturer unless Mildred steals the takings from behind the bar. Mildred refuses at first, but John makes further threats to reveal Mildred's homosexual inclinations on Facebook and to send someone round to beat her up. Frightened that John will carry out his threats, Mildred steals £100 from behind the bar. On her way out of the Student Union, Mildred is approached by Bert, a security guard, who has witnessed the theft. Fearing that John has sent Bert to find her, Mildred strikes Bert on the head with her textbook, causing him a serious injury.

   Discuss whether Mildred has any defences.

2. Critically evaluate the relationship between duress, necessity, and duress of circumstances.

 For suggested approaches, please visit the Online Resource Centre.

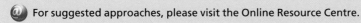

Further reading

Books

Gardner, J. *Offences and Defences: Selected Essays in the Philosophy of Criminal Law* (2007), Oxford: Oxford University Press

Horder, J. *Excusing Crime* (2004), Oxford: Oxford University Press

Simpson, A. W. B. *Cannibalism and the Common Law* (1986), Harmondsworth: Penguin Books

Smith, J. 'Justification and Excuse in the Criminal Law', *Hamlyn Lectures* (1989), London: Stevens and Sons

Journal articles

Arenson, K. 'The Paradox of Disallowing Duress as a Defence to Murder' (2014) 78 JCL 65

Bleasdale-Hill, L. ' "Our Home is our Haven and Refuge—A Place Where We Have Every Right to Feel Safe": Justifying the Use of up to "Grossly Disproportionate Force" in a Place of Residence' [2015] Crim LR 407

Horder, J. 'Occupying the Moral High Ground: The Law Commission on Duress' [1994] Crim LR 334

Leverick, F. 'Is English Self-Defence Law Incompatible with Article 2 of the ECHR?' [2002] Crim LR 347

Padfield, N. 'Duress, Necessity and the Law Commission' [1992] Crim LR 778

Rogers, J. 'Necessity, Private Defence and the Killing of Mary' [2001] Crim LR 515

Smith, J. 'The Use of Force in Public or Private Defence and Article 2' [2002] Crim LR 958

Wake, N. 'Battered Women, Startled Householders and Psychological Self-Defence: Anglo-Australian Perspectives' (2013) 77 JCL 433

15 Inchoate offences

LEARNING OBJECTIVES

By the end of this chapter, you should be able to:

- understand the concept of inchoate liability;
- explain the law relating to the three offences of encouraging or assisting crime under ss.44–46 of the Serious Crime Act 2007;
- briefly explain the old common law offence of incitement;
- define the elements required for liability for conspiracy to commit an offence;
- define the elements required for an attempted offence; and
- identify the various inchoate offences and apply the relevant law to a problem scenario.

Introduction

The preceding chapters have concentrated on the commission of a full offence, requiring proof that the defendant has actually completed the offence charged. However, does this mean that someone who tries to burgle your house but flees when your burglar alarm sounds, or someone who encourages another person to sexually abuse a child, is not criminally liable because they have not themselves performed the *actus reus* elements with the requisite *mens rea*? Criminal liability does not depend upon the completion of the full offence, but a defendant who encourages or assists, conspires, or attempts to commit an offence can be held criminally liable under the principle of inchoate liability. 'Inchoate' means incomplete or undeveloped. This chapter deals with liability for inchoate offences. Traditionally, there were three types of inchoate offence: incitement, conspiracy, and attempt; however, recent reforms by the Serious Crime Act 2007 have abolished the common law offence of incitement and replaced it with three new offences related to encouraging or assisting crime. This chapter will explore the new offences, but will also consider briefly the old common law offence of incitement because the common law offence will still apply to any offence which occurred before the Act came into force on 1 October 2008.

15.1 Criminalising inchoate offences

THINKING POINT

Why does the law criminalise inchoate liability where no harm results?

The rationale behind criminalising inchoate offences is largely the prevention of harm. Criminal law would also be farcical if it required a police officer to wait for an offender to complete the full offence before he could be arrested. Inchoate liability enables such offenders to be convicted and punished if their conduct reaches such a degree that criminalisation is justified in order to protect society and prevent harm, even though they did not complete the full offence.

There are a number of stages which may or may not occur, leading up to the commission of a substantive offence. Some of these stages themselves will result in criminal liability, even if the full substantive offence is not committed.

THINKING POINT

At what stage in the process of committing an offence should a defendant become liable for an inchoate offence?

Deciding that you will commit an offence is not a criminal act. A defendant cannot be convicted of a criminal offence if he only possesses the intention to commit an offence or the *mens rea* of the full offence. For example, if I form an intention to kill X, but do nothing in pursuance of that intention, I am not guilty of any criminal offence. Neither am I guilty of a criminal offence if I formulate my plans to commit the offence in my mind, nor if I begin to prepare for the killing of X. Merely preparing to commit a criminal offence is not in itself a crime. Inchoate liability requires more than just the *mens rea* of the full offence and more than mere preparation to commit the full offence. So, when does a defendant become liable for an inchoate offence? Where the defendant reaches such a stage in his preparation that the safety of the public and society is threatened, the criminal law should intervene to protect the public (table 15.1).

The old common law offence of incitement required the defendant to encourage the commission of an offence. The new offences under the Serious Crime Act 2007 also require encouragement or assistance in the commission of an offence. Conspiracy requires the defendant to agree with another person to commit a criminal offence, and an attempt to commit a criminal offence requires the defendant to take steps that are more than merely preparatory towards the commission of an offence (table 15.2).

Table 15.1 Inchoate liability

No liability	Liability
• Deciding to commit an offence	• Agreeing with X to commit an offence (conspiracy)
• Intending to commit an offence	• Encouraging X to commit an offence (Serious Crime Act 2007 or incitement)
• Mentally planning the offence	• Assisting X to commit an offence (Serious Crime Act 2007)
• Preparing to commit the offence	• Taking steps that are more than merely preparatory towards the commission of an offence (attempt)

Table 15.2 The inchoate offences

Offence	Source	Requirement
Incitement	Common law (abolished from 1 October 2008)	Encouraging
Encouraging or assisting	Serious Crime Act 2007	Act capable of encouraging or assisting
Conspiracy	Criminal Law Act 1977 or common law	Agreeing
Attempt	Criminal Attempts Act 1981	More than mere preparation

As a final note, it should be remembered that a defendant may not be convicted of 'conspiracy', 'incitement', or 'attempt' in the abstract. Students often make the mistake of discussing a defendant's liability for 'conspiracy'. However, liability for these inchoate offences clearly requires the defendant to encourage another person to commit a substantive offence or to conspire or attempt to commit a substantive offence. Thus, a defendant may be guilty of attempted *burglary* or conspiracy *to steal*, but not simply of 'conspiracy'.

15.2 Encouraging or assisting crime

Part 2 of the Serious Crime Act 2007 abolished the common law offence of incitement and created three new offences related to encouraging or assisting crime:

(i) intentionally encouraging or assisting an offence;

(ii) encouraging or assisting an offence believing it will be committed; and

(iii) encouraging or assisting offences believing one or more will be committed.

The Act came into force on 1 October 2008 and was Parliament's response to the Law Commission's Report of 2006, *Inchoate Liability for Assisting and Encouraging Crime* (Law Com. No. 300, Cm. 6878).

The offences created by the Serious Crime Act 2007 criminalise encouraging or assisting another person to commit a criminal offence. A defendant will be liable under the Serious Crime Act 2007 where the person he encouraged or assisted did not actually commit a substantive offence. For instance, if Marie encourages Mick to burgle a house, but Mick does not carry out the burglary, Marie may be convicted under the Serious Crime Act 2007. This is inchoate liability because the substantive offence of burglary was not completed. However, where the person encouraged or assisted does actually commit the substantive offence, the defendant can still be convicted under the Serious Crime Act 2007. Thus, if Mick does actually carry out the burglary, Marie will still be liable under the Serious Crime Act 2007. In fact, as the law currently stands, the Serious Crime Act 2007 overlaps with accessorial liability, so the prosecution will have to choose whether to prosecute such a defendant under this Act or as an accessory under the Accessories and Abettors Act 1861.

> **CROSS REFERENCE**
>
> Read chapter 16 on accessorial liability for further information on liability under the Accessories and Abettors Act 1861.

These offences were used to prosecute those who used social media to encourage rioting and looting in the riots of 2011 which started in Tottenham, London and spread throughout the country. In *Blackshaw and others* [2011] EWCA Crim 2312, two of the ten defendants pleaded guilty to offences under the Serious Crime Act 2007. Blackshaw pleaded guilty to doing an act capable of encouraging the commission of riot, burglary, and criminal damage, believing that one or more of those offences would be committed, contrary to s.46 of the Act. Blackshaw had used Facebook to create a public event page entitled 'Smash Down in Northwick Town'. The event was to begin behind McDonald's at 1 pm the following day, and he posted a message of encouragement: 'we'll need to get on this, kicking off all over' (at [55]). Another defendant, Sutcliffe, pleaded guilty to intentionally encouraging the commission of riot, contrary to s.44 of the Serious Crime Act 2007. He had used Facebook to create a page called 'The Warrington Riots' and he sent a message to 400 contacts on Facebook inviting them to meet him at a carvery in Warrington (at [60]). This page was also open to the general public to view. While *Blackshaw and others* is really an authority on sentencing, it serves as a useful illustration of how the offences under ss.44 to 46 of the Serious Crime Act 2007 were used to prosecute offenders in the riots of 2011.

Parliament's main aim in enacting Part 2 of the Serious Crime Act 2007 was to close a loophole in the law which allowed a person who assisted an offence which did not take place, i.e., assisting an inchoate offence. Prior to the Serious Crime Act 2007, there was no liability in respect of a defendant who assisted an offence which did not actually take place. Such a defendant could only previously be held criminally liable where the full offence he assisted was completed. Although the old law clearly contained a loophole, arguably such extensive reforms were not really necessary. The common law offence of incitement was well established, clear, and unproblematic. The Court of Appeal recently commented '[i]t may well be that the common law offence of inciting someone else to commit an offence was less complex. It may equally be that the purpose of the legislation could have been achieved in less tortuous fashion' (see *Sadique (Omar)* [2013] EWCA Crim 1150 at [30]). It is submitted that Parliament could have easily plugged the loophole by creating a simple, single offence of assisting an offence which does not take place. Instead, Parliament chose to overhaul radically the common law and, as a consequence, we are currently left with an overlap between inchoate and accessorial liability. It remains to be seen whether Parliament will also now reform the law on accessorial liability to conform with the new offences under the Serious Crime Act 2007 (see table 15.3).

The three new offences under the Serious Crime Act 2007 are discussed in 15.2.1 to 15.2.3.

Table 15.3 Comparing the old law and the new law

	Liability under old law	Liability under new law
Encouraging an offence which does not take place	Common law offence of incitement	ss.44–46, SCA 2007
Encouraging an offence which does take place	Abetting or counselling an offence, under s.8, Accessories and Abettors Act 1861	ss.44–46, SCA 2007 or abetting or counselling under s.8, Accessories and Abettors Act 1861
Assisting an offence which does not take place	No liability	ss.44–46, SCA 2007
Assisting an offence which does take place	Aiding an offence, under s.8, Accessories and Abettors Act 1861	ss.44–46, SCA 2007 or aiding under s.8, Accessories and Abettors Act 1861

15.2.1 Intentionally encouraging or assisting an offence

The first new offence is found under s.44(1) of the Serious Crime Act 2007. This section provides for an offence of intentionally encouraging or assisting an offence.

 STATUTE

Section 44(1), Serious Crime Act 2007

A person commits an offence if—

(a) he does an act capable of encouraging or assisting the commission of an offence; and

(b) he intends to encourage or assist its commission.

15.2.1.1 *Actus reus*

The *actus reus* of the offence under s.44(1) requires the defendant to do an act which is capable of encouraging or assisting the commission of an offence: s.44(1)(a). The *actus reus* of this offence is clearly wider than the common law offence of incitement as it includes assisting the commission of an offence which does not ultimately take place—'the anticipated offence': s.49(1). This addition to the law plugs the loophole identified by the Law Commission and Parliament (see 15.2). Thus, if June asks Nick to supply her with a gun so that she can rob a bank and Nick does so, he will be liable for assisting the commission of an offence, whether June carries out the robbery or not.

Section 44(1)(a) requires the defendant to do an *act* capable of encouraging or assisting an offence. However, a positive act is not required: according to s.65(2)(b), this offence may be committed by a failure to take reasonable steps to discharge a duty (i.e., by an omission to act). Section 65(1) provides a partial definition of doing an act capable of *encouraging* the commission of an offence, stating that it 'includes a reference to his doing so by threatening another person or otherwise putting pressure on another person to commit the offence'. Thus, encouragement is widely construed, as it was in respect of the old common law offence of incitement. Under s.66, a defendant may be convicted if he indirectly encourages or assists the commission of an offence by arranging for another person to do an act capable of encouraging or assisting an offence. Thus, using the example given above, if Nick gives Doris a gun to give to June, Nick will be liable, as will Doris if the requisite *mens rea* of the offence is proved.

15.2.1.2 *Mens rea*

Under s.44(1)(b), the *mens rea* is an intention to encourage or assist the commission of the offence. It is sufficient to show that the defendant intended to encourage or assist the doing of an act which would amount to the commission of an offence: s.47(2). It does not matter that the defendant did not know that he was encouraging or assisting an offence or that he did not intend the criminal offence which results. Section 44(2) provides that the defendant 'is not to be taken to have intended to encourage or assist the commission of an offence merely because such encouragement or assistance was a foreseeable consequence of his act'. The drafting of this section renders its precise meaning ambiguous. The Explanatory Notes to the Act state that the section makes it 'clear that foresight of consequences is not sufficient to establish intention'. This suggests that it must be the defendant's purpose to encourage or assist the commission of an offence (i.e., direct intent is required) and oblique or indirect intent is not sufficient (thus, *Woollin* would not apply). However, the section could be interpreted to mean that foresight of the consequences is not to be equated with intention. On such an interpretation, foresight of the consequences may amount to evidence of intention (thus, *Woollin* could apply).

> **CROSS REFERENCE**
>
> Refer to 3.3.2 to remind yourself of oblique intent and the *Woollin* direction.

Despite such ambiguity, the section is likely to be interpreted in line with the Explanatory Notes to the Act. This is because foresight of consequences would be caught by the offence under s.45 which requires the defendant to *believe* that the offence will be committed.

The most complicated section of Part 2 of the Serious Crime Act 2007 is s.47(5) which sets down rules of proof relating to the *mens rea* of the offences under ss.44–46 of the Act. Section 47(5)(a) sets out the requirements of the defendant's state of mind in relation to the *mens rea* of the perpetrator of the anticipated offence. Section 47(5)(b) sets out further requirements of the defendant's state of mind in relation to the circumstances and consequences (*actus reus* elements) of the anticipated offence.

Under s.47(5)(a), the prosecution must prove that the defendant either: *(i) believed* that the act of the person encouraged or assisted would be done with the necessary *mens rea* of the anticipated offence, or *(ii)* that the defendant was *reckless* as to whether or not it would be done with that *mens rea*, or *(iii)* that the defendant himself would have the *mens rea* of the anticipated offence were he to commit it himself. For example, imagine that Neal intentionally encouraged Jerome to commit criminal damage. According to s.47(5)(a), the prosecution must prove that Neal believed that, or was reckless as to whether, Jerome would have the *mens rea* for criminal damage, or the prosecution must prove that Neal would have the *mens rea* of criminal damage were he to do the act of damage himself.

Under s.47(5)(b), the prosecution must prove that the defendant believed that, or was reckless as to whether, if the act were done, it would be done in the circumstances or with the consequences required by the anticipated offence. For example, imagine that Manuel encouraged Sonny to have sexual intercourse with Yasmina. If Manuel was charged with encouraging rape, the prosecution would have to prove that Manuel believed that, or was reckless as to whether,

Yasmina was consenting to sexual intercourse (consent being a circumstance required by the offence of rape).

SUMMARY OF *MENS REA* REQUIREMENTS

(1) Intention to do acts of encouragement or assistance.

(2) Intention to encourage or assist the commission of the offence.

(3) Belief that or reckless as to whether the person encouraged or assisted would have the *mens rea* for the anticipated offence, or D himself would have had the *mens rea* of the anticipated offence.

(4) Belief that or reckless as to whether the circumstances or consequences of the anticipated offence are fulfilled.

15.2.2 Encouraging or assisting an offence believing it will be committed

Section 45 of the Serious Crime Act 2007 provides for the offence of encouraging or assisting an offence believing that the offence will be committed.

STATUTE

Section 45, Serious Crime Act 2007

A person commits an offence if—

(a) he does an act capable of encouraging or assisting the commission of an offence; and

(b) he believes—

(i) that the offence will be committed; and

(ii) that his act will encourage or assist its commission.

15.2.2.1 *Actus reus*

The *actus reus* of this offence is the same as that required for the offence under s.44. It involves doing an act which is capable of encouraging or assisting the commission of an offence: s.45(a). Under s.45(b), the *mens rea* requires that the defendant believes *(i)* that the offence will be committed, and *(ii)* that his act will encourage or assist the commission of the offence.

Section 49(7) provides that in proving s.45(b)(i) (that the defendant believes that the offence will be committed), it is sufficient that the defendant believes that the offence will be committed if certain conditions are met. Imagine, for example, that Louise encourages Tom to ask Anna if he can borrow Anna's iPhone, but Louise tells Tom that he should steal the iPhone if Anna refuses to hand it over. Louise would be guilty of an offence under s.45 because she believes that a theft will be committed if certain conditions are met (i.e., if Anna refuses to hand over the iPhone).

15.2.2.2 *Mens rea*

The offence under s.45 requires proof of a lesser *mens rea* than the offence under s.44(1). The prosecution need only prove the defendant's beliefs, rather than his intention.

Belief is a less common form of *mens rea*. It is a subjective concept and, as with oblique intent, there is a range of degrees of 'belief'. A defendant might consider the consequences to be 'virtually certain' to occur, or he might think that they are 'highly probable' or 'probable', or even 'possible'. It is difficult to know which of these is sufficient to satisfy the requirement of belief. Belief was defined by the Court of Appeal in *Hall* (1985) 81 Cr App R 260 (a case relating to the offence of handling stolen goods) as:

> something short of knowledge. It may be said to be the state of mind of a person who says to himself: 'I cannot say I know for certain that these goods are stolen, but there can be no other reasonable conclusion in the light of all the circumstances, in the light of all that I have heard and seen.' (*Per* Boreham J)

CROSS REFERENCE
Refer to 3.5 for a brief discussion of belief.

Thus, belief is a less culpable state of mind than knowledge. However, belief requires a more culpable state of mind than mere suspicion that something might occur (see *Moys* (1984) 79 Cr App R 72). Recklessness as to the possibility of something occurring is not sufficient. Belief would therefore appear to sit somewhere between intention and recklessness. The courts are likely to leave the interpretation of this ordinary word to the common sense of the jury.

Section 47(5) (discussed in 15.2.1.2) also applies to the offence under s.45.

15.2.3 Encouraging or assisting offences believing one or more will be committed

Section 46(1) provides for the offence of encouraging or assisting the commission of offences, believing that one or more offences will be committed.

 STATUTE

Section 46(1), Serious Crime Act 2007

A person commits an offence if—

(a) he does an act capable of encouraging or assisting the commission of one or more of a number of offences; and

(b) he believes—

(i) that one or more of those offences will be committed (but has no belief as to which); and

(ii) that his act will encourage or assist the commission of one or more of them.

In *Sadique and Hussain* [2012] 1 WLR 1700, the appellants challenged the compatibility of the offence under s.46 with Article 7 of the European Convention on Human Rights, arguing that s.46 was 'too vague and uncertain'. However, while the Court of Appeal commented that the 'provisions creating and defining section 46 are very complex', the Court held that there was no violation of Article 7. The Court provided some procedural guidance on how s.46 should be approached (however, it should be noted that the Court later emphasised the *obiter* nature of this guidance in *Sadique (Omar)* [2013] EWCA Crim 1150). The guidance was as follows:

- Section 46 should only be used if it may be that it was D's belief at the time of doing the act that one or more offences will be committed but he has no belief as to which.

- The prosecution should identify which offences D's act was capable of encouraging and assisting and upon which it wishes to rely.

- There should be a separate s.46 count for each of those offences if there is to be a trial and the particulars of each count should be the same.

In *Sadique (Omar)* [2013] EWCA Crim 1150 (in a later appeal against conviction), the Court of Appeal held that despite the complexity of the Serious Crime Act 2007, the Act created three distinct offences of encouraging or assisting crime and the legislation had to be interpreted to give effect to all three of the offences; thus, it was not open to the Court to set one of the offences (s.46) aside. The Court considered the offence under s.46 to reflect practical reality and highlighted its purpose in providing for cases in which a defendant contemplated that one of a number of offences might be committed as a result of his encouragements as in *DPP for Northern Ireland v Maxwell* [1978] 1 WLR 1350 (see 16.1.2.3). The Court also made specific reference to Virgo (2013: 7–8) here. The Court held that the defendant had to believe that one or more offences would be committed, even though he is unable to specify which one would be committed. The Court further stated that before the defendant in this case could be convicted, the jury had to be satisfied:

(a) that he was involved in the supply of relevant chemicals;

(b) that, if misused criminally, the chemicals were capable of misuse by others to commit offences of supplying or being concerned in the supply of, or being in possession with intent to supply, Class A and/or Class B drugs;

(c) that at the time of supply of the chemicals, S believed that what he was doing would encourage or assist the commission of one or more drug-related offences; and

(d) that he also believed that that was the purpose for which the chemicals would be used by those to whom he supplied them.

15.2.3.1 *Actus reus*

Under s.46(1)(a), the *actus reus* requires that the defendant does an act capable of encouraging or assisting the commission of one or more of a number of offences.

15.2.3.2 *Mens rea*

The *mens rea* under s.46(1)(b) requires the defendant to believe: *(i)* that one or more of those offences will be committed (although the defendant need not have a belief as to which offence will be committed), and *(ii)* that his act will encourage or assist the commission of one or more of them (although he need not have a belief as to which offence will be encouraged or assisted: s.46(2)). In *Sadique and Hussain* [2012] 1 WLR 1700, the Court of Appeal stated, '[a]t the risk of over-simplification, it can be said that the section 46 offence requires proof of "full" *mens rea* on the part of D in relation to the offence which he believed would be committed, nothing less than subjective recklessness will do'. Section 49(7) (mentioned in 15.2.2.1) which relates to conditional belief also applies to this offence.

Section 47(5) (discussed in 15.2.1.2) also applies to the offence under s.46.

THINKING POINT

Consider whether D would be liable for an offence under the Serious Crime Act 2007 in the following scenarios:

(1) D, who has a string of convictions for robbery, asks X if he can borrow his car for a few hours. X suspects that D is 'up to something', but lends him the car anyway.

(2) D, a shopkeeper, sells a knife to X, an aggressive character.

(3) D, aged 12, performs oral sex on an adult male.

(4) D persuades X to rifle through V's handbag and to steal V's USB stick if it is there.

15.2.4 Defence of acting reasonably

Section 50 of the Serious Crime Act 2007 provides for two defences of acting reasonably. The first defence is found under s.50(1) of the Act. This defence requires the defendant to prove that he knew of the existence of certain circumstances and that it was reasonable for him to act as he did in those circumstances. The burden of proof is quite clearly placed on the defendant to prove the elements of the defence on a balance of probabilities. This reverse onus of proof raises the issue of compatibility with the presumption of innocence under Article 6.2 of the European Convention on Human Rights. However, at this early stage of the provision's legislative life, no such challenge has yet been made. The defence is objectively assessed, so the defendant's conduct must be reasonable in the circumstances. It is not sufficient for the defendant to prove that he believed that his conduct was reasonable.

The second defence is found under s.50(2) of the Serious Crime Act 2007. This defence requires the defendant to prove that he believed that certain circumstances existed, that his belief was reasonable, and that it was reasonable for him to act as he did in the circumstances as he believed them to be. The burden of proving this defence also falls on the defendant and this defence is also objectively assessed.

Section 50(3) applies to both defences and sets out a number of factors to be considered in determining whether the defendant's conduct was reasonable. The list is non-exhaustive and includes: the seriousness of the anticipated offence(s), any purpose for which the defendant claims to have been acting, and any authority by which the defendant claims to have been acting. The Law Commission proposed a narrower version of this defence in their report, *Inchoate Liability for Assisting and Encouraging Crime*. The Law Commission gave an example of when the defence might be available. Imagine that Cheryl is driving at the maximum speed limit in the right-hand lane of a motorway, when a second car, driven by Horace, speeds up and sits behind Cheryl's car, very close to her bumper. Cheryl knows, or at least believes that, if she pulls into the left-hand lane to let Horace overtake her, she will be assisting Horace to commit the offence of speeding. Cheryl might plead the defence of acting reasonably in such a situation, however, the success of the defence will depend upon whether the jury consider her conduct to be reasonable.

15.2.5 Protection of the victim

Section 51 of the Serious Crime Act 2007 provides that those who fall within the 'protected category' are not to be held liable for an offence under ss.44–46 of the Act. This provision is designed to put the case of *Tyrell* [1894] 1 QB 710 on a statutory footing in order to protect victims of crime from liability. Thus, if a child encourages an adult man to have sex with her, the child will not be guilty of an offence of encouraging or assisting the criminal offence of child rape (s.5 of the Sexual Offences Act 2003).

15.2.6 Impossibility

Under ss.44–46 of the Serious Crime Act 2007, the defendant's act must be 'capable' of encouraging or assisting the commission of an offence. Consequently, if the defendant's act is incapable of providing such encouragement or assistance, the defendant will not be guilty of an offence. Thus, impossibility is a defence to these offences. For example, if Kevin intends to use poison to kill someone, but Sanjeev mistakenly provides him with a harmless substance instead, Sanjeev cannot be guilty of assisting murder as Sanjeev's act is not capable of assisting murder: the offence of murder is impossible. However, Sanjeev might be convicted of attempting to do an act that would have been capable of assisting Kevin (i.e., attempting to provide Kevin with a poison). Impossibility is no defence to an attempt (see 15.5.3).

15.3 The common law offence of incitement

The common law offence of incitement was abolished by s.59 of the Serious Crime Act 2007. This provision came into force on 1 October 2008. However, as any conduct which occurs before 1 October 2008 and amounts to incitement may still be charged under the common law, the offence will be discussed briefly here.

15.3.1 *Actus reus*

15.3.1.1 Definition

The *actus reus* of the common law offence of incitement involves encouraging, threatening, persuading, commanding, or putting pressure on another person to commit a criminal offence, either by words or by gestures.

In *Applin v Race Relations Board* [1973] QB 815, Lord Denning stated that:

> to 'incite' means to urge or spur on by advice, encouragement, and persuasion. . . . A person may 'incite' another to do an act by threatening or by pressure, as well as by persuasion.

15.3.1.2 Express or implied incitement

Incitements may be express or implied. An example of an implied incitement arose in the case of *Invicta Plastics Ltd v Clare* [1976] RTR 251 in which Invicta Plastics Ltd advertised a device called 'Radatec' for sale. The device gave drivers a warning when a police radar trap had been set up nearby. Although it was not illegal to own the device, a licence was required to operate it. The Divisional Court held that Invicta Plastics Ltd had incited people to commit the offence of using the device without a licence, an offence under s.1(1) of the Wireless Telegraphy Act 1949.

By stating that the virtue of the device was in its operation, Invicta Plastics Ltd had impliedly encouraged people to use the device.

15.3.1.3 Can be addressed to the world

The incitement can be addressed to the world at large and does not have to be directed to one specific person. In the case of *Most* (1881) 7 QBD 244, the defendant published an article in German in a London newspaper, urging people around the world to kill their heads of state. This was held to amount to an incitement to commit murder, a statutory offence under s.4 of the Offences Against the Person Act 1861 (discussed further at 15.3.4). There was no requirement that the incitement be directed towards a particular person.

15.3.1.4 Must be communicated to the incitee

The case of *Ransford* (1874) 13 Cox CC 9 is authority for the principle that the incitement must be communicated to the incitee. The defendant in this case wrote a letter to a 14-year-old boy, encouraging him to meet him in order to have sexual intercourse with him. However, the letter was intercepted by the authorities, so the boy never received it. It was held that there was no incitement to commit buggery here as the words of encouragement had not been communicated to the boy. However, this did amount to an attempt to incite buggery.

15.3.1.5 Must be a criminal offence by the incitee

In *Whitehouse* [1977] 3 All ER 737, it was held that the act incited by the defendant must be one which would amount to a criminal offence if performed by the incitee. The defendant here incited his 15-year-old daughter to have sexual intercourse with him. If they had had sex, the defendant would have been guilty of the full offence of incest, but his daughter would not have been guilty of incest because she was under 16 years of age. The defendant's conviction for inciting the sexual intercourse was quashed because the act incited would not have amounted to a criminal offence by the person incited (the daughter).

15.3.2 *Mens rea*

The *mens rea* requires that the defendant intend that the offence be committed by the incitee. The defendant must also know or believe that the incitee will act with the necessary *mens rea* for the offence incited, but the defendant himself does not need to have the *mens rea* for the offence incited and nor does the person incited: *DPP v Armstrong* [2000] Crim LR 379. This case involved a police officer known as 'John', who received a phone call from the defendant asking to purchase indecent photographs of children. The defendant was charged with inciting the police officer to distribute indecent photographs of children. The Divisional Court held that although it must be proved that the defendant knew or believed that the police officer would have the *mens rea* for the offence incited, it need not be proved that the police officer himself had such *mens rea*.

15.3.3 Impossibility

Under the common law, impossibility was generally a defence to an offence of incitement. A defendant could not be guilty of inciting another person to commit a crime that it was, in the circumstances, impossible to commit: *Fitzmaurice* [1983] QB 1083. For example, D could

Figure 15.1 Types of impossibility

Factual impossibility	Legal impossibility	Impossibility due to inadequate means
E.g., inciting, conspiring, or attempting to: kill a person who is already dead or steal from a handbag which is, in fact, empty	E.g., inciting, conspiring, or attempting to: handle goods which D mistakenly believes to be stolen	E.g., inciting, conspiring, or attempting to: kill V with a harmless substance or break into a house with a pencil

not be guilty of inciting X to handle goods which were not in fact stolen (this is an example of legal impossibility). One exception to this principle arises if the offence was only impossible due to inadequate means. Where the defendant encourages another person to commit an offence using inadequate means, impossibility would be no defence at common law. Contrast this position to that relating to the new offences under the Serious Crime Act 2007. Under the 2007 Act, impossibility due to inadequate means would be a defence because the act of the defendant must be 'capable' of encouraging or assisting the anticipated offence (figure 15.1).

15.3.4 Soliciting murder

The statutory offence of soliciting murder under s.4 of the Offences Against the Person Act 1861 has been retained, despite the reforms of the Serious Crime Act 2007. This offence is rarely prosecuted. One example of a successful prosecution for soliciting murder is that of the radical Islamist cleric, Abu Hamza, in February 2006. The prosecution was based upon encouragements to kill given by Abu Hamza in lectures and sermons at mosques in Finsbury Park (London), Luton, Blackburn, and Whitechapel (London). In November 2006, Abu Hamza lost his appeal against his conviction for six counts of soliciting murder (see *R v Abu Hamza* [2006] EWCA Crim 2918).

15.4 Conspiracy

A conspiracy is an agreement to commit a criminal offence. The offence takes place as soon as the parties enter into an agreement with the requisite *mens rea*. It does not matter whether the agreement is actually acted upon. The defendant is guilty of conspiracy to steal, irrespective of whether any of the conspirators actually do steal any property. Conspiracy is generally a statutory offence, although there are two common law conspiracies still in existence (discussed briefly at 15.4.4). Statutory conspiracy is found under s.1(1) of the Criminal Law Act 1977 and involves an agreement between two or more people to pursue a course of conduct which amounts to a criminal offence.

> **STATUTE**
>
> **Section 1(1), Criminal Law Act 1977**
>
> ..., if a person agrees with any other person or persons that a course of conduct shall be pursued which, if the agreement is carried out in accordance with their intentions, either—
>
> (a) will necessarily amount to or involve the commission of any offence or offences by one or more of the parties to the agreement, ...
>
> he is guilty of conspiracy to commit the offence or offences in question.

15.4.1 *Actus reus*

15.4.1.1 **The elements**

The *actus reus* of conspiracy is set out under s.1(1)(a) of the Criminal Law Act 1977. It requires the prosecution to prove that:

 (i)   there was an agreement;

 (ii) between two or more persons;

 (iii) to pursue a course of conduct;

 (iv) which amounts to a criminal offence.

15.4.1.2 **The agreement**

The prosecution must prove that the defendant agreed with at least one other person, to pursue a course of conduct which amounts to a criminal offence. The co-conspirators must agree to commit the same crime. Thus, in the case of *Taylor* [2002] Crim LR 205, where D1 agreed to import Class A drugs and D2 agreed to import Class B drugs, there was no conspiracy. In *Mehta* [2012] EWCA Crim 2824, the Court of Appeal reviewed the legal principles relating to conspiracy and held that 'a conspiracy requires that the parties to it have a common unlawful purpose or design', and this means 'a shared design', thus it is not sufficient if another person has a similar, but separate, design. This was emphasised in *Shillam* [2013] EWCA Crim 160, in which the Court of Appeal held that a 'conspiracy requires a single joint design between the conspirators within the terms of the indictment'. Thus, two or more persons can only be convicted of a conspiracy if they each have a shared common purpose or design.

The defendant himself does not need to be involved in committing the offence he conspires to commit. In fact, the agreement may involve the anticipated offence being committed by the other person in the conspiracy. The guilty act here is the agreement. Thus, the defendant will be guilty of conspiring to commit the offence irrespective of whether the anticipated offence occurs or not. Once the defendant has entered into the agreement, he is guilty of conspiracy and simply changing his mind will not negate his liability.

15.4.1.3 **The limitations: who can conspire?**

There are some limitations on who can be guilty of a conspiracy to commit an offence. According to s.2(2)(a) of the Criminal Law Act 1977, a husband and wife cannot commit conspiracy if they enter into an agreement, whilst married, to commit a criminal offence. This principle of law is derived from traditional attitudes towards marriage, according to which the stability of marriage is upheld and a husband and wife are regarded as one unit. However, a husband and wife may conspire together with a third person to commit an offence. Thus, if husband and wife, James and Hayley, agree to kill Angelo, neither of them will be guilty of conspiracy to murder. However, if James and Hayley agree with Manisha to kill Angelo, James will be guilty of conspiring with Manisha to commit murder and Hayley will also be guilty of conspiring with Manisha to commit murder. Section 2(2)(a) of the Criminal Law Act 1977 reflects the common law position according to the case of *Mawji v R* [1957] AC 126. This principle has also been extended to civil partnerships, so civil partners cannot commit conspiracy together under s.2(2)(a) of the Criminal Law Act 1977 (as amended by the Civil Partnership Act 2004). Although conspiracy cannot be committed by husband and wife during marriage, if the agreement to commit an offence was entered into prior to marriage, the offence of conspiracy is committed: *Robinson's Case* (1746) 1 Leach 37.

A further limitation on who can be guilty of conspiracy relates to children under the age of criminal responsibility. Under s.2(2)(b) of the Criminal Law Act 1977, it is not possible to conspire with a child under the age of criminal responsibility (10 years old) to commit an offence. Similarly, under s.2(2)(c) of the Criminal Law Act 1977, the intended victim of a conspiracy may not be guilty of the conspiracy.

15.4.2 *Mens rea*

The mental element of conspiracy is confusing and difficult to elucidate. In the second edition of his *Textbook of Criminal Law*, Professor Glanville Williams stated that the Criminal Law Act 1977 'is badly drafted on the mental element, . . . succeeding only in making obscure what was almost entirely plain before' (1983: 429).

The *mens rea* of conspiracy is, essentially, intention. The defendant must:

(i) intend to enter into the agreement; and

(ii) intend that the agreement be carried out and the substantive offence be committed.

There is also a further requirement implicit under s.1(2) of the Criminal Law Act 1977, that the defendant and conspirator:

(iii) intend or know that the facts or circumstances which constitute the *actus reus* of the offence do or will exist.

15.4.2.1 Intention to enter into the agreement

Agreeing to pursue a course of conduct necessarily involves a mental element. Thus, the first element of *mens rea* that the prosecution must prove is that the defendant intended to enter into an agreement to pursue the relevant course of conduct. However, there is no need to prove that the defendant knew that the course of conduct would amount to a criminal offence: *Churchill v Walton* [1967] 2 AC 224.

15.4.2.2 Intention that the agreement be carried out and the substantive offence be committed

The prosecution must prove that the defendant and one other conspirator intended that the agreement be carried out by himself and/or a conspirator and that the full substantive offence be committed. The House of Lords' decision in *Anderson* [1986] AC 27 caused much confusion in this area by, in fact, reaching the opposite conclusion. The defendant in this case was convicted of conspiring to break another person out of prison. The defendant agreed to supply the necessary cutting equipment for a payment of £20,000. However, he argued that he never actually intended the plan to go ahead. His intention was to supply the equipment, take the £20,000, and go abroad. He stated that he did not believe that the plan was capable of succeeding. Nevertheless, the defendant's conviction was upheld. The House of Lords held that there was no need to prove that the defendant intended that the agreement be carried out. It was sufficient that the defendant had simply entered into the agreement. Despite being a decision of the House of Lords, this authority has not been applied by the courts in later cases, such as *McPhillips* [1989] NI 360 and *Yip Chiu-Cheung v R* [1995] 1 AC 111 which are both discussed next.

In *McPhillips* [1989] NI 360, the Court of Appeal of Northern Ireland held that the offence of conspiracy required the prosecution to prove that the defendant intended that the agreement be carried out. The defendant's conviction for conspiracy to murder was quashed because he did not intend that the agreement (to murder) be carried out. In *Yip Chiu-Cheung v R* [1995] 1 AC 111, the Privy Council held that the defendant could be convicted of conspiracy to traffic in drugs where he and a conspirator intended that the agreement be carried out. Thus, there appears to be a conflict between the decision of the House of Lords in *Anderson* and later authorities of the lower courts and Privy Council. As a decision of the highest court in England and Wales, *Anderson* is technically binding until it is overruled by a Supreme Court decision. However, the decision in *Anderson* has also suffered criticism at the hands of academics. It would appear that the cases of *McPhillips* and *Yip Chiu-Cheung v R* reflect the preferred approach.

Although the defendant must intend that the agreement be carried out, it is now clear that he does not need to intend to play any active part in carrying out the agreement. However, this issue was also thrown into confusion by the House of Lords' decision in *Anderson*. In *Anderson*, Lord Bridge stated (*obiter*) that it must be proved that the defendant 'had intended to play some part in the agreed course of conduct'. This implied that the defendant not only had to intend that the agreement be carried out, but that he also must intend to play some part in carrying it out.

In the case of *Siracusa* (1990) 90 Cr App R 340, the Court of Appeal sought to explain the comments made by Lord Bridge in *Anderson*. Giving the judgment of the Court, O'Connor LJ stated that Lord Bridge's dicta 'must be read in the context of that case'. The Court held that '[p]articipation in a conspiracy is infinitely variable: it can be active or passive'. O'Connor LJ stated:

> We think it obvious that Lord Bridge cannot have been intending that the organiser of a crime who recruited others to carry it out would not himself be guilty of conspiracy unless it could be proved that he intended to play some active part himself thereafter.

The Court held that a defendant could demonstrate an intention to 'play some part in the agreed course of conduct' simply by continuing to agree with the proposed unlawful course of conduct or by failing to stop the unlawful activity. O'Connor LJ continued:

> Consent, that is the agreement or adherence to the agreement, can be inferred if it is proved that he knew what was going on and the intention to participate in the furtherance of the criminal purpose is also established by his failure to stop the unlawful activity. Lord Bridge's dictum does not require anything more.

In seeking to clarify the *dicta* of Lord Bridge in *Anderson*, the Court of Appeal in *Siracusa* adopted a loose interpretation of the word 'participation'. Thus, a defendant may passively participate in a conspiracy by failing to stop the substantive offence from occurring. This failure is sufficient evidence of the defendant's intention to participate in the agreed course of conduct.

15.4.2.3 **Intention or knowledge as to the circumstances of the offence**

Section 1(2) of the Criminal Law Act 1977 deals with the mental element required in respect of the circumstances of the substantive offence. This subsection is confusing and is referred to by Professor Glanville Williams as 'mind-twisting' (1983: 429). Where the existence of a particular fact or circumstance is an ingredient of the *actus reus* of the substantive offence only, the prosecution must prove that the defendant knew about or intended those facts or circumstances: s.1(2) of the Criminal Law Act 1977. Mere suspicion that such facts or circumstances existed is not sufficient. This was confirmed in the House of Lords' decision in *Saik* [2006] UKHL 18. The defendant in this case was charged with conspiracy to launder money. The full offence of laundering money required the defendant to have reasonable grounds to suspect that the money was the proceeds of crime. The defendant claimed that he did not know the money was the proceeds of crime, but that he only suspected that it was. The majority in the House of Lords took the view that the offence of conspiracy to launder money required proof that the defendant intended or knew that the money was the proceeds of crime. Mere suspicion or recklessness as to the circumstances that constitute the *actus reus* of the substantive offence were held to be insufficient for a conspiracy.

 THINKING POINT

Consider the liability of the following parties for conspiracy to rape:

(1) Hanz and Frederick agree that they will have sexual intercourse with Natalia. They suspect that Natalia will not consent to having sexual intercourse with them.

(2) Cecil and Robert agree that they will have sexual intercourse with Derek, whether or not Derek consents.

(3) Would your answer to (2) differ if Derek was, in fact, consenting?

You may need to refer to 8.1 to remind yourself of the elements of rape.

 SUMMARY OF *MENS REA*

(1) Intention to enter into the agreement.

(2) Intention that the agreement be carried out and the substantive offence be committed.

(3) Intention or knowledge of the facts or circumstances which constitute the *actus reus* of the offence.

15.4.3 **Impossibility**

According to s.1(1)(b) of the Criminal Law Act 1977, impossibility is no defence to the statutory offence of conspiracy. The position at common law was that impossibility was a defence to conspiracy: *DPP v Nock* [1978] AC 979. This is relevant because two common law conspiracies still exist. Thus, impossibility will be a defence to the common law conspiracies, but not to a charge of conspiracy under the Criminal Law Act 1977.

15.4.4 **Common law conspiracies**

Section 5 of the Criminal Law Act 1977 abolished all common law conspiracies, except for conspiracy to defraud and conspiracy to do acts tending to corrupt public morals and outrage public decency. These are rarely prosecuted offences which are not likely to form a significant part of any criminal law module. However, the reader should be aware of their existence.

Surprisingly, the common law offence of conspiracy to defraud was retained when the Fraud Act 2006 was enacted, despite recommendations by the Law Commission that it should be abolished. The Government was reluctant to abolish the common law offence, opting instead to wait to see how the offences under the Fraud Act 2006 would fare before taking such action. It seems likely that most conspiracies to defraud would now be charged under s.1(1) of the Criminal Law Act 1977.

Conspiracy to do acts tending to corrupt public morals and outrage public decency is rarely prosecuted and will not be considered here. Students who wish to consider this area in more detail are directed to read the House of Lords' decisions in *Shaw v DPP* [1962] AC 220 and *Knuller (Publishing and Printing Promotions) Ltd v DPP* [1973] AC 435.

15.5 Attempt

A defendant may be guilty of attempting to commit a particular offence where he does not complete the full offence, but has taken sufficient steps for his conduct to be classed as criminal by law. An attempt is a statutory offence and is charged under s.1(1) of the Criminal Attempts Act 1981. This provides that a defendant is guilty of attempting to commit an offence if the defendant takes steps which are more than merely preparatory towards the commission of that offence.

 STATUTE

Section 1(1), Criminal Attempts Act 1981

If, with intent to commit an offence to which this section applies, a person does an act which is more than merely preparatory to the commission of the offence, he is guilty of attempting to commit the offence.

Section 1(4) of the Criminal Attempts Act 1981 provides that a defendant may only be convicted under the Act of an attempt of an indictable offence (i.e., an indictable only offence or an offence triable either way). A defendant may not be convicted of an attempt to commit a summary only offence unless the statute providing for that offence creates a specific offence of attempt.

15.5.1 *Mens rea*

15.5.1.1 **Intention as to acts and consequences**

As the *mens rea* of an attempt is the first element mentioned under s.1(1) of the Criminal Attempts Act 1981, it is usual practice to state it first. The *mens rea* of an attempt requires an intention to commit the full offence. The defendant must intend the act which constitutes the more than preparatory steps and he must intend all of the elements of the full offence (*Pace* [2014] EWCA Crim 186). The *mens rea* of attempted theft is an intention to steal; the *mens rea* for attempted GBH is an intention to commit GBH; and the *mens rea* for attempted murder is an intention to kill. The *mens rea* of attempted murder was confirmed in the case of *Whybrow* (1951) 35 Cr App R 141, in which the defendant connected the soap dish in the bathroom to the mains so that his wife suffered an electric shock whilst in the bath. He was charged with the attempted murder of his wife. The Court of Criminal Appeal held that the *mens rea* for this offence was an intention to kill, and an intention to do GBH would not be sufficient.

15.5.1.2 **Recklessness as to circumstances**

Where the full offence requires the defendant to be reckless in relation to circumstances required by the *actus reus* of the full offence, recklessness is sufficient for an attempt to commit that offence. This principle is derived from the case of *Khan* [1990] 1 WLR 815 which involved the offence of attempted rape. This case was heard prior to the enactment of the Sexual Offences Act 2003. Under the old law, the full offence of rape required the defendant to be reckless as to whether or not the complainant was consenting (a circumstance of the *actus reus* of rape). Thus, prior to the enactment of the Sexual Offences Act 2003, the offence of attempted rape only required the defendant to be reckless as to that circumstance.

15.5.1.3 **Is foresight of consequences (oblique intent) sufficient?**

We saw in chapter 3 that the meaning of 'intention' has occupied the courts' time for years. In *Pearman* (1985) 80 Cr App R 259, the Court of Appeal held that 'intent' under the Criminal Attempts Act 1981 means the same as it does under the common law. Thus, in accordance with the cases on oblique intent, the jury might infer the defendant's intention from foresight of the consequences, although foresight was not to be equated with intent. This was also confirmed in the case of *Walker and Hayles* (1990) 90 Cr App R 226, in which the Court of Appeal applied *Nedrick* (1986) 83 Cr App R 267 in a case involving a charge of attempted murder. If death was virtually certain to occur as a result of the defendant's conduct and the defendant appreciated this, the jury could infer that he had the requisite *mens rea* for attempted murder. Whether oblique intent is sufficient for other attempted offences remains to be seen. The Law Commission has recommended that oblique intent should be enough for a conviction for an attempted offence (see Consultation Paper No. 183, *Conspiracy and Attempt* (2007)).

15.5.2 *Actus reus*

Under s.1(1) of the Criminal Attempts Act 1981, the defendant has the *actus reus* of an attempt if he takes steps that are more than merely preparatory towards the commission of an offence. This is a question of fact for the jury to decide: s.4(3) of the Criminal Attempts Act 1981. The trial judge first decides whether the defendant's conduct is *capable* of being more than merely preparatory. If it is, the trial judge then leaves the issue of whether the defendant's conduct *was*, in fact, more than merely preparatory to the jury.

 THINKING POINT

At what stage should the law intervene to criminalise a defendant's conduct as an attempt?

The Criminal Attempts Act 1981 fails to provide any guidance as to what constitutes an attempt. It is therefore difficult to know exactly what amounts to 'steps that are more than merely preparatory' and where the line is drawn between such steps and mere preparation. Consequently, liability for an attempt is determined on a case-by-case basis.

 THINKING POINT

Do you think there has been an attempt in the following scenarios:

(1) Charlotte approaches the back door of a house she intends to burgle. As she takes hold of the door handle, the lights go on inside the house and Charlotte escapes.

(2) Alan arms himself with a gun and enters a bank, intending to commit robbery. The police arrest him before he approaches a cashier.

(3) Intending to kill Lindsay, Robert places arsenic in a cup of tea which he then hands to her. However, before Lindsay can drink the tea, Robert takes the cup away.

(4) Andrew goes to meet Chris and takes a gun with him, intending to kill Chris. As Andrew takes the gun out of his bag and raises it, Chris runs away and escapes.

Prior to the Criminal Attempts Act 1981, the courts struggled to find a test to be applied in determining whether the defendant was guilty of an attempt. In the early case of *Eagleton* (185–55) 169 ER 826, the test applied was the proximity test. Under this test, acts immediately connected with the offence were considered to be attempts, but acts remotely leading towards the offence were not. Thus, the acts had to be proximate to the commission of the offence. In *DPP v Stonehouse* [1978] AC 55, the House of Lords applied the 'last act' test. Under this test, the defendant will have committed an attempt if he has performed the last act required of him. Lord Diplock stated that 'the offender must have crossed the Rubicon and burnt his boats'.

The following cases provide guidance on how the Court of Appeal has interpreted s.1(1) of the Criminal Attempts Act 1981. However, these cases merely serve as illustrations of how the law has been applied and they do not set down any particular rules about how s.1(1) should be applied. The courts have taken the view that the Criminal Attempts Act 1981 is a codifying statute which represents entirely the law relating to attempts. In *Campbell* (1991) 93 Cr App R 350, Watkins LJ stated that:

> It would be unwise of a court to lay down hard and fast rules as to when, in varying circumstances, an attempt has begun. The matter has to be decided on a case by case basis as the issue arises.

15.5.2.1 Acts which are more than mere preparation: attempts

The defendants in *Boyle and Boyle* (1987) 84 Cr App R 270 were charged with attempted burglary. They damaged the door of a house which they intended to burgle. The defendants appealed against their convictions for attempted burglary on the basis that the case should have been dismissed at the close of the prosecution case because there was insufficient or no evidence of the *actus reus* of attempted burglary. The appeal was dismissed and the defendants' convictions were upheld. The Court of Appeal held that there was sufficient evidence for the jury to find that the appellants intended to commit burglary and that in breaking down the door they did more than a merely preparatory act towards committing burglary.

CASE CLOSE-UP

Q

Jones [1990] 1 WLR 1057

In the case of *Jones*, the defendant was convicted of attempted murder. He was a married man who had been having an affair with another woman. She started seeing another man and broke off her relationship with the defendant. The defendant became distraught at this and went to find his mistress's new boyfriend (the victim) with a sawn-off shotgun. The victim took his daughter to school by car. When the daughter left the car, the defendant jumped into the back seat. He was wearing overalls and a crash helmet. He told the victim to drive to a location, then, when the car stopped, the defendant pulled out the shotgun, loaded it, pointed it at the victim and said, 'You are not going to like this.' There was a struggle. The defendant placed a length of cord around the victim's neck. The victim managed to escape. The Court of Appeal upheld the defendant's convictions and held that the judge was right to allow the case to go before the jury as there was evidence of conduct capable of amounting to the *actus reus* of an attempt.

The Court took the view that the Criminal Attempts Act 1981 was a codifying statute which now represents the entire law relating to attempts. Thus, the words of the statute should not be construed by reference to previous case law. Taylor LJ held that:

> the correct approach is to look first at the natural meaning of the statutory words, not to turn back to earlier case law and seek to fit some previous test to the words of the section.

The Court of Appeal broke down the events which took place. Taylor LJ stated that:

> Clearly his actions in obtaining the gun, in shortening it, in loading it, in putting on his disguise, and in going to the school could only be regarded as preparatory acts. But, . . . once he had got into the car, taken out the loaded gun and pointed it at the victim with the intention of killing him, there was sufficient evidence for the consideration of the jury on the charge of attempted murder. It was a matter for them to decide whether they were sure those acts were more than merely preparatory.

The case of *Tosti* [1997] Crim LR 746 involved two defendants who were convicted of attempted burglary. They were seen to approach the door of a barn and examine the padlock, but they ran off when they realised they were being watched. The defendants had hidden some cutting equipment in a hedge nearby. Their appeal against conviction was dismissed. The Court of Appeal reiterated the test set out in *Geddes* [1996] Crim LR 894 (discussed in 15.5.2.2). However, the Court concluded that there was sufficient evidence of an attempt to leave the offence to the jury, despite the fact that the defendants had not got as far as trying to commit the burglary (the defendants were merely examining the padlock while the cutting equipment was in a hedge).

15.5.2.2 **Acts which are mere preparation: not attempts**

However, in the case of *Gullefer* [1990] 1 WLR 1063, the defendant's conviction for attempted theft was quashed on appeal. The defendant went to a greyhound racing track and placed an £18 bet on a dog in the last race. Realising that his dog was losing the race, the defendant climbed down onto the racetrack and waved his arms, attempting to distract the dogs. His aim was to disrupt the race so that it would be declared void and then to claim his £18 stake back. The Court of Appeal quashed the defendant's conviction for attempted theft because the defendant was not in the process of committing theft. The Court held that, by jumping onto the track, the defendant had not gone beyond mere preparation. Lord Lane CJ stated that an attempt 'begins when the merely preparatory acts come to an end and the defendant embarks upon the crime proper'. There were still more steps which had to take place before the defendant could get his money back. At this stage, the defendant was simply hoping that his conduct would force the stewards to declare the race void so that he could go back to the bookmaker and demand the £18 stake. Lord Lane CJ held that s.1(1) of the Criminal Attempts Act 1981 'seek[s] to steer a midway course between the *Eagleton* test and Lord Diplock's "Rubicon test"'. His Lordship stated that 'the words [of the 1981 Act] give as clear a guidance as is possible in the circumstances' on what amounts to the *actus reus* of an attempt.

Similarly, in *Campbell* (1991) 93 Cr App R 350, the defendant's conviction for attempted robbery was quashed on appeal. The defendant was arrested after he had been seen lurking around outside a post office. He was seen riding a motorcycle past the post office and walking up to and away from the post office. He was carrying an imitation firearm and a threatening note. The defendant claimed that he had changed his mind about committing the robbery shortly before being arrested. The Court of Appeal quashed the defendant's conviction on the basis that, at the time of arrest, the defendant had not even gained the place where he could be in a position to carry out the offence. Watkins LJ stated that:

> A number of acts remained undone and the series of acts which he had already performed—namely, making his way from his home or other place where he commenced to ride his motor cycle on a journey to a place near a post office, dismounting from the cycle and walking towards the post office door—were clearly acts which were, . . . indicative of mere preparation.

There were still many more steps to take in order to effect the robbery, such as entering the post office, approaching the counter, making a threat towards the cashier to give him money.

In *Geddes* [1996] Crim LR 894, the defendant's conviction for attempted false imprisonment was quashed. He was found on school premises, in a lavatory block. He had no right to be there. On being confronted by a police officer who happened to be on the premises, the defendant left the school. He discarded a rucksack in some bushes nearby. The rucksack contained a large kitchen knife, some rope, and masking tape. The Court of Appeal acknowledged that there was evidence of intention to kidnap a child, but held that the defendant's conduct amounted to mere preparation. The Court held that there was not sufficient evidence for the judge to leave the charge of attempted false imprisonment to the jury. This decision was largely based upon the fact that the defendant 'had never had any contact or communication with any pupil; he had never confronted any pupil at the school in any way'. Lord Bingham CJ commented on the post-1981 case law:

> The cases show that the line of demarcation between acts which are merely preparatory and acts which may amount to an attempt is not always clear or easy to recognise. There is no rule of thumb test. There must always be an exercise of judgment based on the particular facts of the case.

The Court paraphrased the statutory test in the following way:

> Does the available evidence demonstrate that the defendant has done an act which shows that he has actually tried to commit the offence in question or has he merely got ready or put himself in a position or equipped himself to do so?

For a summary of *actus reus* cases, see table 15.4.

Table 15.4 Summary of *actus reus* cases

Case	Brief facts	Attempt or not?
Boyle and Boyle (1987)	Damaging door of house intending to burgle.	Attempted burglary.
Jones (1990)	Obtaining the gun, shortening it, loading it, putting on disguise, going to the school. Getting into the car, taking out the loaded gun, pointing it at the victim with the intention of killing him.	Would not have been an attempt at this stage, but... ...became an attempt at this stage.
Tosti (1997)	Examining padlock on barn door. Cutting equipment in hedge.	Attempted burglary.
Gullefer (1990)	Jumping on racetrack to disrupt race.	No attempted theft (still had to have race declared void and claim stake back).
Campbell (1991)	Walking backwards and forwards outside post office with threatening note and imitation firearm.	No attempted robbery (still had to enter post office, approach counter, and make threat).
Geddes (1996)	Found in school toilets. Rucksack with knife, rope, and tape.	No attempted false imprisonment (had no contact with any child).

15.5.3 Impossibility

According to s.1(2) of the Criminal Attempts Act 1981, impossibility is no defence to an attempt. Thus, a defendant will be guilty of an attempted offence, even where commission of the full substantive offence was impossible. This applies whether the impossibility is due to inadequate means, factual impossibility, or legal impossibility.

Previously, under the common law, physical or legal impossibility was a defence: *Haughton v Smith* [1975] AC 476. So, a defendant could not be guilty of attempting to handle stolen goods where the goods were not, in fact, stolen. However, impossibility due to inadequate means was no defence. Thus, a defendant who tried to kill a person with a harmless substance could still be convicted of an attempt.

The case of *Anderton v Ryan* [1985] AC 567 threw the law relating to impossibility into confusion. In this case, the House of Lords ruled that a defendant who had purchased a video recorder believing it to be stolen, could not be guilty of attempting to handle stolen goods. The House refused to apply s.1(2) of the Criminal Attempts Act 1981 and applied the old law under *Haughton v Smith* (1975). However, this was overruled by the House of Lords in the case of *Shivpuri* [1987] AC 1. The defendant in *Shivpuri* appealed against his conviction for attempting to be knowingly concerned in dealing with and harbouring prohibited drugs under s.170 of the Customs and Excise Management Act 1979. The drug was, in fact, a harmless vegetable substance. The House of Lords overruled the decision in *Anderton v Ryan* and held that impossibility was no defence to an attempt. The House justified criminalising such behaviour by focusing on the intention of the defendant. Lord Bridge stated that:

> What turns what would otherwise, from the point of view of the criminal law, be an innocent act into a crime is the intent of the actor to commit an offence.

However, if the defendant wrongly believes that he is committing a crime when, in fact, he is not, he is not guilty of attempting to commit any offence. This is evident from the case of *Taaffe* [1984] AC 539, in which the defendant wrongly believed that he was importing currency into England, when the substance he was importing was, in fact, cannabis. The defendant could not be convicted of being knowingly concerned in the fraudulent evasion of the prohibition on the importation of cannabis, contrary to s.170 of the Customs and Excise Management Act 1979. The defendant was judged on the facts as he believed them to be. He believed that he was importing currency into the country—an act which was not, in fact, illegal. The defendant had no knowledge that he was importing cannabis into the country, so could not be guilty of attempting to commit that offence.

15.6 Reform

In 2007, the Law Commission published a Consultation Paper called *Conspiracy and Attempts*, in which the Law Commission recommended the abolition of the Criminal Attempts Act 1981. The proposal was that the Act be replaced by two offences of criminal attempt and criminal preparation. The proposed offence of criminal attempt would be limited to the last acts needed to commit the intended offence. The proposed offence of criminal preparation would be limited to acts of preparation which are properly to be regarded as part of the execution of the plan to commit the intended offence. To date, these proposals have not been introduced.

 Summary

- 'Inchoate' offences are incomplete or undeveloped offences.

- The three main types of inchoate offence now are: encouraging or assisting an offence, conspiracy, and attempt.

- There are three offences of encouraging or assisting an offence under ss.44–46 of the Serious Crime Act 2007.

- Section 44—intentionally encouraging or assisting an offence; s.45—encouraging or assisting an offence believing that the offence will be committed; and s.46—encouraging or assisting the commission of offences, believing that one or more offences will be committed.

- Impossibility is a defence to an offence under Part 2 of the Serious Crime Act 2007.

- The common law offence of incitement was abolished by s.59 of the Serious Crime Act 2007, but still applies to offences committed before 1 October 2008. It involves encouraging another person to commit a criminal offence: *Applin v Race Relations Board* (1973).

- The *actus reus* of statutory conspiracy under s.1(1) of the Criminal Law Act 1977 involves an agreement between two or more people to pursue a course of conduct which amounts to a criminal offence.

- The *mens rea* requires: intention to enter into the agreement; intention that the agreement be carried out and the substantive offence be committed; and intention or knowledge of the facts or circumstances which constitute the *actus reus* of the offence.

- Impossibility is no defence to the statutory offence of conspiracy: s.1(1)(b) of the Criminal Law Act 1977.

- An attempt is committed where the defendant takes steps which are more than merely preparatory towards the commission of an offence with the intention that the full offence be committed: s.1(1) of the Criminal Attempts Act 1981.

- Impossibility is no defence to an attempt: s.1(2) of the Criminal Attempts Act 1981 and *Shivpuri* (1987).

The bigger picture

- Inchoate offences is an examinable topic. A problem question which requires an examination of inchoate offences would necessarily arise within the context of particular substantive offences which the defendant is conspiring, attempting, etc. to commit. Such a question will require you to recognise the relevant substantive offences as well as discuss and apply the elements of the inchoate offences. An essay question might ask you to consider the Serious Crime Act 2007 or the *actus reus* of an attempt.

- For some guidance on how you might approach exam questions on inchoate offences, you should visit the Online Resource Centre.

- For more information on the rationale behind the creation of the offences of encouraging or assisting crime under the Serious Crime Act 2007, you should read the Law Commission Report of 2006, *Inchoate Liability for Assisting and Encouraging Crime* (Law Com. No. 300, Cm. 6878).

- You should consider how the offences of encouraging or assisting crime under the Serious Crime Act 2007 fit in with both inchoate offences and accessorial liability. See 15.2 on inchoate offences and 16.1.4 on accessorial liability.

? Questions

Self-test questions

1. What does 'inchoate' mean?

2. Why does the law seek to criminalise inchoate offences?

3. How might a defendant be liable for an inchoate offence?

4. Identify the three new offences found under the Serious Crime Act 2007.

5. What was the purpose of Part 2 of the Serious Crime Act 2007?

6. When will there be no conspiracy despite an agreement by two people to commit a criminal offence?

7. What is the *mens rea* of statutory conspiracy?

8. What is the *mens rea* of an attempt?

9. When does preparation turn into an attempted offence? Refer to case law in your answer.

10. When is impossibility a defence to an inchoate offence?

 For suggested approaches, please visit the Online Resource Centre.

Exam questions

1. Danielle, an animal rights activist, persuades her friend, Chris, to join her in protest at the opening of a new animal testing laboratory. They decide that they will set the laboratory on fire that evening when all employees have left. They purchase cans of petrol and pieces of cloth, which they hide in bushes nearby. Danielle approaches the building with a view to checking that it is empty. As she reaches the front doors, she triggers an intruder alarm and the building is lit by floodlights. Danielle and Chris escape. It later transpires that the petrol cans actually contained water.

    Discuss the liability of Danielle and Chris for any inchoate offences.

2. The reforms under Part 2 of the Serious Crime Act 2007 were unnecessary and have complicated what was a relatively straightforward area of law.

    To what extent do you agree with this statement?

 For suggested approaches, please visit the Online Resource Centre.

 ## Further reading

Books

Williams, G. *Textbook of Criminal Law* (2nd edn, 1983), London: Stevens and Son

Journal articles

Bohlander, M. 'The Conflict between the Serious Crime Act 2007 and Section 1(4)(b) Criminal Attempts Act 1981—A Missed Repeal?' [2010] Crim LR 483

Child, J. J. 'Exploring the Mens Rea Requirements of the Serious Crime Act 2007 Assisting and Encouraging Offences' (2012) 76 JCL 220

Dennis, I. 'The Rationale of Criminal Conspiracy' [1997] 93 LQR 39

Jarvis, P. and Bisgrove, M. 'The Use and Abuse of Conspiracy' [2014] Crim LR 261

Mirfield, P. 'Intention and Criminal Attempts' [2015] Crim LR 142

Ormerod, D. and Fortson, R. 'Serious Crime Act 2007: The Part 2 Offences' [2009] Crim LR 389

Rogers, J. 'The Codification of Attempts and the Case for "Preparation" ' [2008] Crim LR 937

Spencer, J. R. and Virgo, G. 'Encouraging and Assisting Crime: Legislate in Haste, Repent at Leisure' (2008) 9 Archbold News 7

Sullivan, G. R. 'Inchoate Liability for Assisting and Encouraging Crime—The Law Commission Report' [2006] Crim LR 1047

Virgo, G. 'Part 2 of the Serious Crime Act 2007—Enough is Enough' (2013) 3 Archbold Review 7

Virgo, G. 'R v Sadique: Making Sense of Section 46 of the Serious Crime Act 2007' (2013) 7 Archbold Review 4

Reports

Law Commission Report, *Inchoate Liability for Assisting and Encouraging Crime* (Law Com. No. 300, Cm. 6878, 2006)

Law Commission, Consultation Paper, *Conspiracy and Attempts* (Law Com. CP No. 183, 2007)

16 Accessorial liability

By the end of this chapter, you should be able to:

- distinguish between principals and secondary parties;
- identify the elements of accessorial liability;
- understand the doctrine of joint enterprise; and
- explain when withdrawal from a joint enterprise is a defence.

Introduction

NOTE: The law relating to joint enterprise has been considerably altered by the judgment in *R v Jogee* [2016]. Please see the prelims, page xii, for an update on this case.

This chapter explores the law relating to accessorial liability or parties to crime. It is important to begin by distinguishing between the different parties to crime and the terminology used to describe each participant. A defendant may be convicted as a principal offender or as a secondary party (also known as an accessory) to an offence (table 16.1).

Table 16.1 Terminology

Principal	The principal is the person who performs or causes the *actus reus* of a substantive criminal offence with the necessary *mens rea*.
Joint principals	Where there are two or more people who both perform the *actus reus* of an offence with the necessary *mens rea*, they are joint **principals**.
Innocent agent	A principal may cause the *actus reus* of the offence through an **innocent agent**, such as a child.
Secondary party (or accessory or accomplice)	A **secondary party (or accessory or accomplice)** may assist with the commission of the principal offence in a number of ways (e.g., by standing as lookout or providing a weapon or by encouraging the offence), but he does not directly cause the *actus reus*.

So far, we have seen that a defendant will be held liable for a criminal offence if the prosecution can prove that he performed the *actus reus* of the offence with the appropriate *mens rea* and in the absence of a defence. Such a defendant is the principal offender. This chapter explores the concept of accessorial liability in criminal law and the way in which the law deals with secondary parties (or accessories) to a criminal offence.

Imagine that Nicole and Phil decide to carry out a robbery of a jewellery shop. They agree that Nicole will threaten the shop attendant with a gun and demand the jewellery, while Phil will keep lookout inside the jewellery shop, also with a gun. It is quite clear that Nicole will be guilty of robbery, as she will commit the *actus reus* of robbery with the necessary *mens rea*, but Phil's liability is less straightforward. By keeping lookout, Phil does not actually participate in the *actus reus* of a robbery, which requires the use or threat of force immediately before or at the time of stealing and in order to steal (s.8, Theft Act 1968). Nicole is the principal offender and will be convicted of the full offence of robbery. Phil is an accessory or secondary party to the robbery. He may be convicted as an accessory of aiding the robbery under s. 8 of the Accessories and Abettors Act 1861. Alternatively, even though he did not physically carry out all elements of the *actus reus* of robbery, he may be convicted of the full offence of robbery under the doctrine of joint enterprise. The doctrine of joint enterprise is highly controversial and defendants who are members of criminal gangs may unwittingly find themselves criminally liable for a serious offence, even though they did not physically perform the *actus reus* of that offence, provided it can be shown that they shared a common purpose with the perpetrator. Liability under the Accessories and Abettors Act 1861 will be discussed at 16.1. The doctrine of joint enterprise will be discussed at 16.2.

If Phil also threatens a person in the shop in order to steal jewellery, he will also have performed the *actus reus* of robbery and will also be charged as a principal, provided he also had the relevant *mens rea*. In such a scenario, Nicole and Phil will be joint principals and both may be convicted of the full offence of robbery. The prosecution will have to prove that each defendant committed the *actus reus* of the offence and that they both had the relevant *mens rea*.

Where the principal causes the *actus reus* of the offence through an innocent agent, such as a child, the principal remains liable for the offence, provided he also has the requisite *mens rea*. The innocent agent will not be criminally liable, despite committing the *actus reus*, as he does not have the requisite *mens rea*. In the case of *Michael* (1840) 9 C & P 356, the defendant was convicted of the murder of her baby son through the innocent agency of a 5-year-old child. The defendant gave the nurse a bottle of poison, informing her that it was medicine for the baby. The nurse decided that the baby did not need any medicine and placed the bottle of poison on the mantelpiece. Four days later, while the nurse was out, the nurse's 5-year-old son gave the baby some of the poison. The baby died as a result. The defendant's conviction for murder was upheld on the basis that the administration of poison by the 5-year-old child was 'under the circumstances of the case, as much, in point of law, an administering by the prisoner as if the prisoner had actually administered it with her own hand'.

16.1 Liability under the Accessories and Abettors Act 1861

This paragraph will explore the liability of a secondary party under s.8 of the Accessories and Abettors Act 1861.

STATUTE

Section 8, Accessories and Abettors Act 1861 (as amended by the Criminal Law Act 1977)

Whosoever shall aid, abet, counsel, or procure the commission of any indictable offence, whether the same be an offence at common law or by virtue of any Act passed or to be passed, shall be liable to be tried, indicted, and punished as a principal offender.

Under s.8 of the Accessories and Abettors Act 1861, a defendant may be convicted as a secondary party to an offence if he aids, abets, counsels, or procures the commission of that offence. In order to convict a defendant as a secondary party under s.8 of the Act, the prosecution must prove both *actus reus* and *mens rea* elements. However, the *actus reus* and *mens rea* elements required for liability as a secondary party are different to those required for liability as a principal offender. For instance, imagine that Mick supplies Chris with a sledgehammer which Chris uses to kill George. In order to convict Chris of murder as a principal offender, the prosecution would have to prove that Chris had both the *actus reus* and *mens rea* of murder, i.e., that he unlawfully caused George's death with the intention to kill or cause GBH. However, in order to convict Mick as a secondary party to the murder, the prosecution would have to prove different *actus reus* and *mens rea* elements.

The *actus reus* of secondary liability requires the defendant to aid, abet, counsel, or procure the principal to commit a criminal offence. Thus, the *actus reus* requires the secondary party to assist or encourage the principal offence. The prosecution must also prove *mens rea* elements of secondary liability. This requires the prosecution to prove (as summarised in table 16.2):

(1) that the defendant intended to do the act which assisted or encouraged the principal offence, and

Table 16.2 Elements of secondary liability

Actus reus	Mens rea
• Aiding, abetting, counselling, or procuring an offence	• Intention to do the act of assistance or encouragement
	• Knowledge of the essential matters which constitute the principal offence

(2) that he knew the essential matters which constitute the principal offence (i.e., that he knew the circumstances which form the *actus reus* of the offence which might be committed and that he foresaw the *mens rea* of the principal).

Thus, referring back to our example involving the murder of George, Mick could be convicted as a secondary party if the prosecution prove:

(1) that he aided (i.e., helped) the murder by supplying the sledgehammer;

(2) that he intended to supply the sledgehammer to Chris;

(3) that he knew that Chris might kill; and

(4) that he foresaw that if Chris did kill, he would do so with the requisite *mens rea* for murder (i.e., intention to kill or cause GBH).

16.1.1 *Actus reus*

The *actus reus* under s.8 of the Accessories and Abettors Act 1861 is aiding, abetting, counselling, or procuring the commission of the principal offence. In *Attorney General's Reference (No. 1 of 1975)* [1975] QB 773, Lord Widgery CJ held that the words of s.8 of the Act should be given their ordinary meaning. His Lordship stated:

> We approach the section on the basis…that if four words are employed here, 'aid, abet, counsel or procure', the probability is that there is a difference between each of those four words and the other three, because, if there were no such difference, then Parliament would be wasting time in using four words where two or three would do. Thus, in deciding whether that which is assumed to be done under our reference was a criminal offence we approach the section on the footing that each word must be given its ordinary meaning.

Aiding, abetting, counselling, and procuring are separate and distinct types of act. However, there is a degree of overlap between them. The Court of Appeal confirmed in *Bryce* [2004] EWCA Crim 1231, that prosecutors should use the 'catch-all' phrase 'aid, abet, counsel or procure' when charging secondary parties 'because the shades of difference between them are far from clear' (as stated by Potter LJ).

Aiding may occur either before or during the commission of the principal offence. Abetting occurs during the principal offence, and counselling and procuring occur before the commission of the principal offence. This type of accessory used to be known as an 'accessory before the fact'. We will consider the meaning of aiding, abetting, counselling, and procuring in 16.1.1.1 to 16.1.1.4.

16.1.1.1 **Aiding**

Aiding involves helping, assisting, or supporting the principal offender with the commission of the offence. Aiding occurs before or during the principal offence. Where X helps a principal offender after the commission of the principal offence, for example by disposing of incriminating evidence or hiding the principal, X will not be guilty of an offence under s.8 of the Accessories and Abettors Act 1861. Such an offender would be dealt with by separate offences of participation after the offence (see 16.3).

Examples of aiding include acting as lookout during the commission of the offence, driving the principal to the scene of the crime (as in *DPP for Northern Ireland v Maxwell* [1978] 1 WLR 1350, in which the defendant drove the principals to a pub which they attacked by throwing a bomb inside—see 16.1.2.3), supplying the principal with a weapon or with information which helps him to commit the principal offence (as in *Bainbridge* [1960] 1 QB 129, in which the defendant supplied the principals to a burglary with oxygen cutting equipment—see 16.1.2.3).

16.1.1.2 Abetting

Abetting involves encouraging or inciting the principal to commit the offence. Abetting occurs during the offence. An example would be shouting words of encouragement during the offence.

> **Abetting requires proof that:**
>
> (1) the defendant was present at the scene of the crime;
>
> (2) he wilfully encouraged the commission of the offence; and
>
> (3) he intended to encourage the offence.

The prosecution must prove that the defendant was present at the scene of the principal offence. It must also be proved that the defendant wilfully encouraged the principal to commit the substantive offence.

THINKING POINT

What constitutes 'wilful encouragement'? Consider whether it is possible to abet an offence by inactivity.

In *Coney* (1881–2) LR 8 QBD 534, Hawkins J stated that 'to constitute an aider and abettor some active steps must be taken by word, or action, with the intent to instigate the principal'. Thus, the mere presence of the defendant at the scene of the crime is not sufficient. This was confirmed in the case of *Clarkson & Carroll* [1971] 3 All ER 344. The defendants in this case were two soldiers who, along with a group of other soldiers, gathered outside the door to a room in which an 18-year-old woman was being raped. The door fell open and the soldiers fell into the room. The defendants were charged as secondary parties to the rape on the basis that they had abetted the offence. They were convicted and appealed. The Appeal Court allowed the defendants' appeals against conviction and held that it must be proved that the defendants had wilfully encouraged the principals to commit the offence. There was no evidence in this case that the defendants had done any act to encourage the principals or verbally encouraged the principals. The mere presence of the defendants at the scene was not sufficient, even if that presence had in fact provided encouragement to the principals.

Similarly, in *Coney* (1881–2) LR 8 QBD 534, the defendants' convictions for aiding and abetting an assault at an illegal prizefight were quashed. The Divisional Court held that presence at the scene was not conclusive proof that the defendants had abetted the fight. The prosecution must also prove that the defendants encouraged the fight. Cave J, who gave the leading judgment in the Divisional Court, also stated that mere presence may provide *evidence* of encouragement. Cave J held that:

> Where presence may be entirely accidental, it is not even evidence of aiding and abetting. Where presence is prima facie not accidental it is evidence, but no more than evidence, for the jury.

Thus, mere presence might provide evidence from which it can be inferred that the defendant had encouraged the principal offence, but presence alone does not automatically equate to encouragement.

In the case of *Bland* [1988] Crim LR 41, the defendant's conviction as a secondary party to her boyfriend's possession of drugs was quashed. The mere fact that the defendant shared a room with her boyfriend was not sufficient for a conviction. The prosecution had proved presence but not wilful encouragement. A defendant will not be guilty of abetting an offence if he merely witnesses a fight and does nothing to prevent it from continuing. In *Allan and others* [1965] 1 QB 130, Edmund Davies J held that presence 'remains no more than evidence for the jury even when one adds to presence at an affray a secret intention to help'.

THINKING POINT

Read the facts of *Wilcox v Jeffery* [1951] 1 All ER 464 below.

If mere presence at the scene is not sufficient, why was Mr Wilcox convicted of aiding and abetting Mr Hawkins to breach the conditions of his entry to the country?

CASE CLOSE-UP

Wilcox v Jeffery [1951] 1 All ER 464

An example of a spectator being held guilty of aiding and abetting a crime is to be found in the case of *Wilcox v Jeffery*, in which the case of *Coney* (1882) was applied. This case involved an American saxophone player, named Mr Hawkins, who came to England to play at a jazz club in London. He had been granted entry to the country on the basis that he would not take up employment during his stay in England. Mr Wilcox, a journalist for a music magazine, went to the airport to report the arrival of Mr Hawkins for his magazine. Mr Wilcox knew that Mr Hawkins was in the country illegally. He then attended the concert and wrote an article about it in his magazine. He was convicted of aiding and abetting Mr Hawkins to breach the conditions of his entry to the country under the Aliens Order 1920.

The Divisional Court cited with approval Cave J in *Coney* (1882). The presence of Mr Wilcox was not accidental and thus it could provide evidence of encouragement. Lord Goddard CJ further stated:

> The appellant attended that concert as a spectator. He paid for his ticket. Mr Hawkins went on the stage and delighted the audience by playing the saxophone. The appellant did not get up and protest in the name of the musicians of England that Mr Hawkins ought not to be here competing with them and taking the bread out of their mouths or the wind out of their instruments. It is not found that he actually applauded, but he was there having paid to go in, and, no doubt, enjoying the performance, and then, lo and behold, out comes his magazine with a most laudatory description, fully illustrated, of this concert.

The Divisional Court found evidence of encouragement in the following facts:

- Mr Wilcox had attended the concert.
- He had paid for a ticket.
- He failed to protest against the performance.
- He no doubt enjoyed the concert.
- He reported the concert in his magazine, which was sold for profit.

Another authority in which encouragement was inferred from presence at the scene is the case of *Du Cros v Lambourne* [1907] 1 KB 40. In this case, the defendant was charged with unlawfully driving his motorcar at a speed dangerous to the public. There was a dispute as to whether the defendant himself was driving or whether a woman sitting next to him was driving. The Divisional Court upheld the decision of the Quarter Sessions and held that, even if the woman had been driving, the defendant had been an accessory to her speeding because he must have known that she was driving at a dangerous speed. If the woman had been driving, then it was clear that she was doing so with the 'consent and approval' of the defendant. The defendant was the owner, was sitting by her side, and was in control of the car. Therefore, the Court held that he could and ought to have prevented her driving at such excessive and dangerous speed.

Similarly, in the case of *Tuck v Robson* [1970] 1 WLR 741, the defendant aided and abetted an offence through inactivity. The defendant was a licensee of a pub. He was convicted of aiding and abetting customers to consume alcohol outside licensing hours by allowing them to continue to drink alcohol after hours. The Divisional Court held that the defendant had aided and abetted the customers because he had taken no steps to stop them drinking, despite being in a position of control. Thus, a defendant can abet an offence through inactivity if he is present at the scene and in a position of control or authority.

16.1.1.3 Counselling

Counselling involves advising, soliciting, encouraging, or threatening the principal to commit an offence. Counselling differs from abetting as it occurs before the principal offence, whereas abetting requires proof that the defendant wilfully encouraged the principal offence at the scene of the crime. In the case of *Giannetto* (1997) 1 Cr App R 1, the Court of Appeal cited an example of counselling given to the jury by the trial judge in the case:

> Supposing somebody came up to [the defendant] and said, 'I am going to kill your wife', if he played any part, either in encouragement, as little as patting him on the back, nodding, saying, 'Oh goody', that would be sufficient to involve him in the murder, to make him guilty, because he is encouraging the murder.

A further example of counselling is provided by the case of *Calhaem* [1985] 2 WLR 826, in which the defendant was convicted of counselling a private detective to kill the victim. The victim was a woman who had been having an affair with the defendant's solicitor, who the defendant herself was infatuated with. The private detective killed the victim and was convicted of her murder. The defendant appealed against her conviction for counselling the murder, arguing that counselling required a causal link between the solicitation and the killing. The Court of Appeal upheld the defendant's conviction and held that there need not be any causal connection between the counselling and the principal offence. This last statement no longer seems to represent accurately the law in light of the Court of Appeal decision in *Bryce* (2004). Potter LJ stated that 'for secondary party liability there must be some causal connection between the act of the secondary party relied on and the commission of the offence by the perpetrator'.

16.1.1.4 Procuring

Procuring means 'to produce by endeavour', i.e., making something happen by taking appropriate steps to produce that result. Procuring occurs before the principal offence. The leading authority on the meaning of procuring is *Attorney General's Reference (No. 1 of 1975)* [1975] 2 All ER 684. In this case, the defendant secretly laced his friend's drink with alcohol, knowing that his friend would be driving home. His friend was stopped by the police on his way home and charged with driving whilst over the prescribed limit, contrary to s.6(1) of the Road Traffic Act 1972. The defendant was charged with aiding, abetting, counselling, or procuring this offence under s.8 of the Accessories and Abettors Act 1861. The defendant was acquitted after the trial judge ruled that there was no case to answer because there was no shared intention between the defendant and his friend. The defendant had not been present in the car when his friend drove home, nor did he encourage him to drive. The Attorney General referred the case to the Court of Appeal. Lord Widgery CJ gave the judgment of the Court and held that there was no requirement of such a shared intention. The defendant had procured the offence. His Lordship stated that:

> To procure means to produce by endeavour. You procure a thing by setting out to see that it happens and taking the appropriate steps to produce that happening.

The offence of driving whilst over the prescribed limit had been procured because, unknown to his friend, the defendant had put him in a position in which he committed an offence which he never would have committed otherwise. His Lordship emphasised that proof of causation is important. There must be a causal link between the defendant's act and the commission of the principal offence.

A further example of procuring can be seen in the case of *Cogan and Leak* [1975] 2 All ER 1059 (discussed at 16.1.3). For a summary, see table 16.3.

16.1.2 *Mens rea*

Mens rea of secondary liability

The *mens rea* of secondary liability is a complicated area. Traditionally, the *mens rea* of secondary liability has been expressed as requiring proof of the following:

(1) that the defendant intended to do the act which assisted or encouraged the principal offence; and

(2) that he knew the essential matters which constitute the principal offence.

Table 16.3 Summary

	Explanation	Examples	When?	Causal link required?
Aiding	Helping, assisting, supporting the principal	Lookout, providing weapon or information, driving principal to scene of crime	Before or during principal offence	No
Abetting	Wilfully encouraging the principal at the scene of the crime	Gestures or words of encouragement	During principal offence	No
Counselling	Instigating, soliciting, encouraging the principal offence	Trial judge's example in *Giannetto* (1997): 'I am going to kill your wife'; husband: 'Oh goody'	Before principal offence	No
Procuring	To produce by one's own endeavour	Spiking friend's drink, knowing he is driving home (*Attorney General's Reference (No. 1 of 1975)* (1975))	Before principal offence	Need causal link

Knowledge of the essential matters of the offence means that the prosecution must prove that the defendant knew the circumstances which form the *actus reus* of the offence which might be committed, and that he foresaw that the principal might act with the requisite *mens rea* of the offence.

16.1.2.1 Intention to do act of assistance or encouragement

The first element of *mens rea* which must be proved is that the defendant intended to do the acts of assistance. This was confirmed by the Divisional Court in *National Coal Board v Gamble* [1959] 1 QB 11. This case involved a weighbridge operator who allowed a lorry which had been overloaded with coal to leave the colliery. As a result, the lorry was driven on a road whilst nearly four tons overweight. The National Coal Board, the employer of the weighbridge operator, was convicted of aiding, abetting, counselling, or procuring the offence of unlawfully using an overloaded lorry on a road. The National Coal Board's appeal was dismissed. The Divisional Court held that by allowing the lorry to leave the colliery (through one of its employees), the Board intended to aid the principal offence. Devlin J confirmed that:

> aiding and abetting is a crime that requires proof of *mens rea*, that is to say, of intention to aid as well as of knowledge of the circumstances, and that proof of the intent involves proof of a positive act of assistance voluntarily done.

THINKING POINT

Paul lends Vivek a cricket bat. Paul visits Vivek in order to ask for the cricket bat back. Vivek knows that Paul has a violent streak and becomes worried when Paul states that he wants the cricket bat in order to get his revenge on his neighbour. Vivek hands over the bat and Paul uses it to cause serious injury to his neighbour. Paul is charged with causing grievous bodily harm with intent, contrary to s.18 of the Offences Against the Person Act 1861.

Can Vivek be convicted as an accessory to this crime?

Devlin J went on to consider whether a man who gives to a criminal a weapon which the latter has a right to demand from him, can be held liable as a secondary party for an offence when the criminal then uses that weapon to commit that offence. Although handing over the weapon 'aids in the commission of the crime as much as if he sold or lent the article', Devlin J stated that 'this has never been held to be aiding in law'. Devlin J thought that the reason for this was that the act was a negative one, a failure to prevent the commission of the crime by means of detaining the property. Thus, looking at the example in the thinking point above, where Vivek hands Paul his own property on demand, Vivek would not be guilty of aiding any offence committed by Paul with that article, unless Vivek's act of handing the article over could be deemed to be a positive and voluntary act of assistance.

Devlin J distinguished this from a situation where a man supplies or sells an object (thus, transferring title in it) to someone who then uses it to commit a criminal offence. In this type of scenario, Devlin J thought that the man would be convicted as an accessory to the crime if he has the relevant *mens rea* of an accessory.

Some consideration should also be given to the civil case of *Garrett v Arthur Churchill (Glass) Ltd* [1970] 1 QB 92. In this case, it was held that even where there is a legal duty under civil law to hand the object over to its owner, no civil action would be taken against a party who refused to do so if the handing over of that object would aid the commission of an offence.

> ### THINKING POINT
>
> Is this a contradictory statement? How might these two principles be reconciled?

According to the Court of Appeal in *Bryce* (2004), the secondary party must intend to assist the principal in the act that he was doing, although it is not necessary to prove that the secondary party intended the crime to be committed by the principal.

In the Court of Appeal, Potter LJ drew on previous authorities and academic opinion to support the Court's conclusion that an intention to assist the principal's *acts* was required. The Court appears to have drawn a distinction between an intention to assist the *acts* of the principal and an intention to assist the *offence* committed by the principal. However, Jonathan Herring states that 'it is far from clear exactly what [this] means' (Herring 2011: paragraph 17.5.1). One interpretation provided by Professor David Ormerod and Karl Laird is that the Court has confirmed that oblique intent is sufficient for secondary liability. Thus, 'the jury can "find" an intention to assist from the evidence of D's intended performance of the act of assistance, even though his purpose or desire is not to assist' (Ormerod and Laird 2015: 226).

16.1.2.2 Knowledge of the matters which constitute the offence

The second *mens rea* element that the prosecution must prove is knowledge of the essential matters that constitute the offence. In *Johnson v Youden* [1950] 1 KB 544, Lord Goddard stated that:

> Before a person can be convicted of aiding and abetting the commission of an offence he must at least know the essential matters which constitute that offence. He need not actually know that an offence has been committed, because he may not know that the facts constitute an offence... If a person knows all the facts and is assisting another person to do certain things, and it turns out that the doing of those things constitutes an offence, the person who is assisting is guilty of aiding and abetting that offence...

The 'essential matters which constitute the offence' are the circumstances which amount to the elements of the *actus reus* of the offence (i.e., the act that the principal is going to do) and the *mens rea* of the principal offender (i.e., the principal's state of mind when he commits the *actus reus*).

In *Bryce* (2004), the Court of Appeal held that the secondary party must foresee a 'real risk' that the principal might commit the offence. This requires the secondary party to foresee the type of act that might be committed by the principal and the circumstances which constitute the *actus reus* of the offence. In *Webster* [2006] EWCA Crim 415, the Court of Appeal held that in order to establish secondary liability, the prosecution must prove that the defendant 'foresaw the likelihood' that the principal would perform the *actus reus* of the offence. The Court confirmed that this is a subjective test. Moses LJ stated that:

> It is the defendant's foresight that the principal was likely to commit the offence which must be proved and not merely that he ought to have foreseen that the principal was likely to commit the offence.

16.1.2.3 How much knowledge does an accessory need?

What exactly must the accessory know in order to be convicted as a secondary party to an offence? Does he merely need to suspect that a particular type of crime might be committed? Or must his knowledge be more detailed, including knowledge of the precise details of the principal offence?

 CASE CLOSE-UP

Bainbridge [1960] 1 QB 129

The issue as to the amount of knowledge that a secondary party needs arose in the case of *Bainbridge*. The defendant in this case was charged with being an accessory to office-breaking (an old offence which would be burglary today). He had supplied the principals with oxygen cutting equipment which was used to break into the Midland Bank in Stoke Newington. The defendant admitted that he had suspected that the principals had wanted the equipment for 'something illegal', but claimed that he did not know it would be used to break into a bank, he thought it would be used for breaking up stolen goods. He appealed, arguing that the trial judge had misdirected the jury by directing them that the prosecution must prove that the defendant 'knew that a [crime] of that kind was intended'. The Court of Appeal held that this was a valid direction. Lord Parker CJ stated that:

> there must be not merely suspicion but knowledge that a crime of the type in question was intended.

In the Court of Appeal, Lord Parker CJ held that it is not enough to show that the defendant knew that the equipment would be used for 'some illegal venture', such as disposing of stolen property. However, it is also unnecessary to prove that the defendant knew that the particular crime would be committed, on the particular date, and at the particular premises. Thus, the defendant did not need to know that the principals would break into the Midland Bank in Stoke Newington on the night of 30 October 1958. It was enough that the defendant knew that the principals intended to use the equipment to commit a crime of that type.

Similarly, in *DPP for Northern Ireland v Maxwell* [1978] 1 WLR 1350, the House of Lords applied *Bainbridge* (1960) and held that it is enough that the defendant knows the type of crime that would be committed. The defendant was a member of the UVF, a terrorist organisation in Northern Ireland. A member of the organisation told him to drive his car to a pub and guide another car to the pub. He was followed by a group of terrorists. The defendant then drove away. The terrorists threw a bomb into the pub. Fortunately, the bomb was thrown out again and exploded outside without causing any injury or damage. The defendant was convicted of unlawfully and maliciously doing an act with intent to cause an explosion likely to endanger life, contrary to s.3(a) of the Explosive Substances Act 1883 and possession of a bomb under s.3(b). The defendant claimed that he did not know the nature of the job that he was carrying out, neither did he know about the presence of the bomb. The defendant's appeal against his conviction was dismissed by the Court of Appeal and the House of Lords. In the House of Lords, Viscount Dilhorne stated that:

> [The defendant] knew that a 'military' operation was to take place. With his knowledge
> of the UVF's activities, he must have known that it would involve the use of a bomb or
> shooting or the use of incendiary devices. Knowing that he led them there and so he

aided and abetted whichever of these forms the attack took. It took the form of placing a bomb.

The House held that the defendant had enough knowledge to support a conviction because he must have known that there would be an attack on the pub and the type of crimes that might be committed: bombing was one of the possible offences. As in *Bainbridge* (1960), the fact that the defendant did not know the precise details of the offence does not preclude liability.

This has been confirmed more recently by the Court of Appeal in *Bryce* (2004), in which Potter LJ stated that 'it is sufficient for the accused to have knowledge of the type of crime in contemplation'.

16.1.3 **Issues concerning derivative liability**

16.1.3.1 **Principal must be capable of committing an offence**

Accessorial liability is derivative liability: this means that the liability of the secondary party is derived from the liability of the principal offender. In order for a secondary party to be convicted of aiding, abetting, counselling, or procuring an offence, the principal must be capable of committing the principal offence, i.e., there must be the *actus reus* of a principal offence. Where the principal has not committed the *actus reus* of an offence, there can be no accessorial liability. This is illustrated by the case of *Thornton v Mitchell* [1940] 1 All ER 339, in which the conductor of an omnibus could not be convicted of aiding and abetting an offence which had not been committed by the principal driver. The charge against the driver of driving an omnibus without due care and attention had been dismissed. The driver had reversed the omnibus into two pedestrians. As the driver could not see the road behind him, it was the duty of the conductor to signal that the road was clear. The conductor gave the signal, despite the presence of two pedestrians behind the omnibus. The conductor's conviction for aiding and abetting the offence alleged against the driver was quashed on appeal. Lord Hewart CJ stated that:

> In one breath [the Justices] say that the principal did nothing which he should not have done, and in the next breath they hold that the bus conductor aided and abetted the driver in doing something which had not been done or in not doing something which he ought to have done. I really think that, with all respect to the ingenuity of counsel for the respondent, the case is too plain for argument, and this appeal must be allowed and the conviction quashed.

16.1.3.2 **Can a secondary party be liable when the principal is acquitted?**

The liability of a secondary party is not dependent upon the *conviction* of the principal. Where the *actus reus* of the principal offence is present, but the principal is acquitted because he lacks the *mens rea* for the offence, a secondary party may be liable for aiding, abetting, counselling, or procuring the principal offence.

 CASE CLOSE-UP

Cogan and Leak **[1975] 2 All ER 1059**

An example of the acquittal of the principal but conviction of the secondary party is to be found in *Cogan and Leak*. In this case, Mr Leak took Mr Cogan back to his house to have sex with his wife. Mr Leak told his wife that he was going to see to it that she had sex with Mr Cogan. Mrs Leak did not consent to sexual intercourse with Mr Cogan, but she was afraid of her husband. She did not struggle during intercourse, but was sobbing throughout. Mr Cogan was convicted of rape of Mr Leak's wife. Mr Leak was convicted as a secondary party, having procured the rape. Mr Cogan's conviction for rape was quashed in the Court of Appeal on the ground that he honestly believed that she was consenting (based upon the law as it was decided in the House of Lords' decision of *DPP v Morgan* [1976] AC 182, discussed at 8.1.2.2). Thus, there was no longer a principal offence. Nevertheless, the Court of Appeal upheld the conviction of Mr Leak, the secondary party, on the ground that it would be 'an affront to justice and to the common sense of ordinary folk' to quash his conviction simply because the principal had been acquitted.

As an *obiter* comment, Lawton LJ stated that Mr Leak could have been convicted as a principal offender through the innocent agency of Mr Cogan. However, His Lordship acknowledged that this would amount to 'a legal impossibility as a man cannot rape his own wife during cohabitation'. (Note that, since *R v R* [1991] 3 WLR 767, rape within marriage was confirmed to be an offence.) This suggestion is a controversial one and has been criticised by academics. Notably, *Smith and Hogan* considered this to be 'contrary to principle' because 'it is impossible to say that D has personally committed the conduct required by the definition of the *actus reus*' (see Ormerod and Laird 2015: 211). In this case, it is impossible to say that Mr Leak had personally committed the rape.

Cogan and Leak (1975) was followed in *Millward* [1994] Crim LR 527, a case in which the defendant was convicted as an accessory to the old offence of causing the death of a person by reckless driving. The principal was the driver and employee of the defendant. He drove a tractor and trailer on the road without knowing that the joint between the two was in a dangerous condition (thus, he lacked the *mens rea* for the offence). The trailer became detached from the tractor and hit a car, killing a passenger. The defendant employer was still liable as an accessory to the offence because the *actus reus* of the principal offence was proved.

Similarly, in the case of *DPP v K and B* [1997] 1 Cr App R 36, the defendants were convicted of procuring a rape, despite the fact that the principal had not been apprehended and was *doli incapax*. The defendants were two girls, aged 11 and 14. They threatened and bullied the victim into removing her clothes and having sexual intercourse with a boy. The Divisional Court held that the defendants could be convicted as secondary parties, despite the fact that the principal had not been apprehended. The *actus reus* of the rape was present, even if the capacity of the principal offender was in dispute.

16.1.3.3 Can a secondary party be convicted of a more serious offence than the principal?

It is possible for a secondary party to be convicted of a more serious offence than the principal. In an *obiter* statement, Lord Mackay in the House of Lords has stated that secondary parties do not benefit from a special defence which may be available to a principal. For instance, if a principal can successfully plead diminished responsibility to a charge of murder, his conviction will be reduced to that of manslaughter. However, the secondary party cannot also avail himself of this defence and will remain liable for aiding, abetting, counselling, and procuring murder. In the case of *Howe* [1987] AC 417 (discussed at 14.3.1), the House of Lords referred to an example given by Lord Lane CJ in the Court of Appeal:

> Counsel before us posed the situation where A hands a gun to D informing him that it is loaded with blank ammunition only and telling him to go and scare X by discharging it. The

ammunition is in fact live, as A knows, and X is killed. D is convicted only of manslaughter, as he might be on those facts. It would seem absurd that A should thereby escape conviction for murder (at [1986] Q.B. 626, 641–2).

Lord Mackay in the House of Lords agreed with the reasoning of Lord Lane CJ and confirmed that:

> where a person has been killed and that result is the result intended by another participant, the mere fact that the actual killer may be convicted only of the reduced charge of manslaughter for some reason special to himself does not, in my opinion in any way, result in a compulsory reduction for the other participant.

16.1.4 Serious Crime Act 2007

CROSS REFERENCE

Refer to 15.2 for a more detailed discussion of the offence under the Serious Crime Act 2007.

It will be remembered from the last chapter that the Serious Crime Act 2007 has introduced three new offences of encouraging or assisting crime. These offences overlap considerably with secondary liability under s.8 of the Accessories and Abettors Act 1861 because the offences under the 2007 Act are not restricted to inchoate liability.

16.2 The doctrine of joint enterprise

NOTE: The law in this area has been considerably altered by the judgment in *R v Jogee* [2016]. Please see the prelims, page xii, for an update on this case.

Where two or more people, sharing a common purpose, embark upon the commission of a criminal offence, they are part of a joint enterprise. All parties sharing a common purpose to commit an offence are liable for any offence committed in pursuance of that common purpose. It should be noted that defendants who act as part of a joint enterprise are not necessarily joint principals.

Until recently, the precise place of the doctrine of joint enterprise in the context of secondary liability was unclear. Some commentators, such as Simester, argue that the doctrine of joint enterprise is a separate form of liability, whereas others, such as Professor Ormerod in *Smith and Hogan*, argue that it is part of secondary liability, so that those who are party to a joint enterprise are secondary parties. In the case of *Bryce* (2004), the Court of Appeal appeared to draw some distinction between cases of assistance at the 'preliminary stage' and 'joint enterprise' cases. However, more recently, in *Mendez and another* [2011] 3 WLR 1, the Court of Appeal held that joint enterprise liability does not differ doctrinally from the ordinary principles of secondary liability and is not an independent form of liability, but that joint enterprise liability is instead an aspect of secondary liability which involves the application of ordinary principles (see also *Stringer* [2011] EWCA Crim 1396). The Court approved the view expressed by Professor Ormerod in *Smith and Hogan: Criminal Law* (13th edn, 2011) that the only key difference is that the *actus reus* element of joint enterprise liability is established by proof of the common purpose; there is no need to also prove any assistance or encouragement to commit the offence. Consequently, joint enterprise cases are subject to a separate set of rules in the sense that no acts of aiding, abetting, counselling, or procuring need be proved and they do not require proof of an intention to assist the acts of the principal (compare this to the *mens rea* requirements for secondary liability at 16.1.2.1).

A common purpose may arise due to the parties expressly agreeing to embark upon the commission of an offence. Alternatively, a common purpose may arise out of an implied agreement where, for instance, a fight erupts spontaneously and a number of parties join in to attack an individual. Here, the common purpose is implicit in the conduct of the participants.

Consider our example at the start of this chapter in which Nicole and Phil decide to carry out a robbery of a jewellery shop. They agree that Nicole will threaten the shop attendant with a gun and demand the jewellery, while Phil will keep lookout inside the jewellery shop, also with a gun. Both Nicole and Phil can be convicted of robbery under the doctrine of joint enterprise, even though Phil did not physically carry out all elements of the *actus reus* of robbery. Nicole and Phil shared a common purpose, the robbery of the shop, therefore, they are both liable for the robbery which was committed in pursuance of the common purpose.

In *Gnango* [2011] UKSC 59, the Supreme Court restored the conviction of a defendant who had been involved in a shoot-out which resulted in the death of a passer-by. The defendant and another man (X) engaged in a gunfight with each other during which X shot and killed a passer-by while aiming for the defendant. The defendant was convicted of murder on the basis that they had been acting in a joint enterprise, under a common agreement to have a gunfight, i.e., to shoot at each other and be shot at, in which each would attempt to kill or seriously injure the other, and he appealed against his conviction. The Court of Appeal quashed the defendant's conviction and held that there was no common purpose here because the defendant and X had not been acting together or in concert, but had in fact been acting 'independently and antagonistically'. However, the Supreme Court by a majority of 6:1 held that where two defendants voluntarily engage in fighting each other, each intending to kill or cause grievous bodily harm to the other and each foreseeing that the other has the reciprocal intention, both will be guilty of murder where one of the defendants mistakenly kills V in the course of the fight. The Court considered that it was unnecessary to determine whether Mr Gnango should correctly be described as a principal or an accessory to the murder since this was irrelevant to his guilt and not important in this case.

The Court of Appeal has observed that '[a]lthough the difference in law between principals and accessories is of considerable importance in our system of justice in terms of defining the criminal liability of the individual concerned . . . , in the vast majority of cases—as presented to juries—the distinction tends to be unimportant' (*per* Fulford LJ in *Montague* [2013] EWCA Crim 1781 at [23]). The Court acknowledged that where it is unclear whether the defendant has acted as a principal or an accessory, the issue can be left to the jury on an alternative basis.

16.2.1 Liability for unusual consequences

A secondary party will also be liable for any unusual consequences which result from the common purpose, whether those consequences are foreseen or not: *Anderson and Morris* [1966] 2 QB 110. Imagine that Verity and Rahul decide that Rahul will hold Lee while Verity beats him up. They agree that Verity will only inflict minor injuries upon Lee. The common purpose is probably to commit assault occasioning actual bodily harm. However, if, unbeknown to Verity and Rahul, Lee suffers from a thin skull and dies as a result of the minor injuries, both Verity and Rahul will be liable for his death, because they are liable for any unusual consequences which result from the common purpose and the injuries were inflicted in accordance with the common purpose. Their liability is not precluded by the fact that Lee's death was unforeseeable.

16.2.2 **Departing from the common purpose**

If one person in the joint enterprise departs from the common purpose, the other participants will not be liable for any unforeseen offence which that person commits. In *Anderson and Morris* [1966] 2 QB 110, Lord Parker CJ famously stated that:

> where two persons embark on a joint enterprise, each is liable for the acts done in pursuance of that joint enterprise, that that includes liability for unusual consequences if they arise from the execution of the agreed joint enterprise but...if one of the adventurers goes beyond what has been tacitly agreed as part of the common enterprise, his co-adventurer is not liable for the consequences of that unauthorised act.

His Lordship continued that:

> to say that adventurers are guilty of manslaughter when one of them has departed completely from the concerted action of the common design and has suddenly formed an intent to kill and has used a weapon and acted in a way which no party to that common design could suspect is something which would revolt the conscience of people today.

Refer back to our example involving Nicole and Phil at 16.2. Imagine that Nicole goes beyond the agreement and kills a shop assistant. Clearly, Nicole would be guilty of murder as a principal offender (she would have both the *actus reus* and *mens rea* of murder). Would Phil also be guilty of murder under the doctrine of joint enterprise? The answer to this question depends upon whether Phil foresaw that Nicole might kill and that she might do so with the *mens rea* for murder.

16.2.2.1 **What degree of foresight is required?**

What degree of foresight is necessary in order to convict a secondary party? For instance, does Phil need to foresee that Nicole *might* kill, that she *probably* will kill, or that she is *virtually certain* to kill?

In *Chan Wing-Siu* [1985] AC 168, the Privy Council stated that it is sufficient that the secondary party contemplated the *possibility* that the offence would be committed. Sir Robin Cooke stated that:

> The case must depend rather on the wider principle whereby a secondary party is criminally liable for acts by the primary offender of a type which the former foresees but does not necessarily intend...The criminal culpability lies in participating in the venture with that foresight.

In *Hyde; Sussex; Collins* [1991] 1 QB 134, the Court of Appeal considered the degree of foresight required of a secondary party and held that the secondary party will be guilty under the doctrine of joint enterprise if he realises that the principal *might* kill and continues to take part in the joint enterprise.

Lord Lane CJ summarised the position:

> If B realises (without agreeing to such conduct being used) that A may kill or intentionally inflict serious injury, but nevertheless continues to participate with A in the venture, that will amount to a sufficient mental element for B to be guilty of murder if A, with the requisite intent, kills in the course of the venture.

This decision was approved by the Privy Council in the case of *Hui-Chi Ming* [1992] 1 AC 34.

For over 10 years, the leading case on joint enterprise has been the House of Lords' decision in *Powell and Daniels; English* [1997] 4 All ER 545. In this case, the House of Lords held that where one party (P) departs from the common purpose, other parties to the joint enterprise will be liable for any crimes that P commits provided they foresaw that P might commit those acts with the requisite *mens rea* of the offence. Lord Hutton summarised the position:

> where two parties embark on a joint enterprise to commit a crime, and one party foresees that in the course of the enterprise the other party may carry out, with the requisite *mens*

rea, an act constituting another crime, the former is liable for that crime if committed by the latter in the course of the enterprise.

THINKING POINT

In your own words, what must the prosecution prove in order for a secondary party to be convicted of the crimes of the principal under the doctrine of joint enterprise?

The House of Lords confirmed the degree of foresight required: the defendant must foresee that P *might* commit a different criminal offence. Thus, the House of Lords held that a secondary party will be convicted of murder if: *(1)* he foresees that the principal might kill; and *(2)* he foresees that the principal might have the intention to kill or cause GBH when he does so.

The Court of Appeal summarised the law relating to joint enterprise in *Uddin* [1999] QB 431 and the House of Lords revisited the area in the case of *Rahman and others* [2008] UKHL 45. Both cases applied the law as stated in *Powell and Daniels; English* (1997). More recently, the Court of Appeal has commented on the House of Lords' decision in *Rahman*. In *R v A* [2011] QB 841, the Court of Appeal explained that the case of *Rahman* did not change the law with respect to the requirements of *mens rea* in cases of murder by joint enterprise and reiterated that the law requires proof that the defendant foresaw that the principal offender might act with the intention to kill or with the intention to do grievous bodily harm. In *Jogee* [2013] EWCA Crim 1433, the Court of Appeal held that the principles on joint enterprise from *Rahman* applied in cases in which the secondary party had provided encouragement, as well as in cases of active participation. The Court stated that '[e]ncouragement is a form of participation', thus the *actus reus* of the secondary party is in 'lending support to the primary actor, whether by active participation or encouragement or both'.

Where the defendant does not have the requisite foresight to be convicted of murder under the joint enterprise (i.e., he does not foresee that the principal would use a weapon with the intention to kill or cause really serious harm), he may still be guilty of manslaughter as a secondary party if the principal acted with the intention to kill and the defendant foresaw that the principal would use a particular weapon to cause some harm: see *Carpenter* [2012] QB 722.

16.2.2.2 **Fundamentally different act**

A further issue which arose in the case of *Powell and Daniels; English* [1997] 4 All ER 545, was whether a defendant would still be liable under the doctrine of joint enterprise if P's act was fundamentally different from the act that the defendant foresaw that P might commit.

CASE CLOSE-UP

***English* [1997] 4 All ER 545**

In the case of *English*, the defendant and another person (P) launched a joint attack on a police officer. They beat him with wooden posts intending to cause him injury. However, P then produced a knife and stabbed the police officer to death. It was found that it was reasonably possible that the defendant did not know that P was carrying a knife. The defendant's conviction for murder was quashed because the defendant did not foresee the type of act that P committed. Lord Hutton held that where P kills with a deadly weapon which the defendant does not foresee that P might use, the defendant should not be convicted of murder. He should only be convicted of murder if he foresees 'an act of the type which the principal party committed'. In this particular case, 'the use of a knife was fundamentally different to the use of a wooden post'. Lord Hutton continued:

> if the weapon used by the primary party is different to, but as dangerous as, the weapon which the secondary party contemplated he might use, the secondary party should not escape liability for murder because of the difference in the weapon, for example, if he foresaw that the primary party might use a gun to kill and the latter used a knife to kill, or vice versa.

Thus, if the weapon used by P had been fundamentally different from, but *as dangerous as*, the weapon the defendant contemplated that P might use, the defendant could still be convicted of murder. Lord Hutton provided the example of the use of a knife instead of a gun. In the case of *English*, if the defendant and P had agreed to use a gun to kill the police officer, but P actually produced a knife and killed the officer, the defendant would be guilty of murder, even though he did not know of the existence of the knife.

The question of whether the weapon used was fundamentally different to the one the defendant contemplated might be used is one of fact, for the jury to decide: *Greatrex* [1999] 1 Cr App R 126. In the case of *Uddin* [1999] QB 431, the Court of Appeal applied *Powell and Daniels; English* (1997) and dealt with situations involving spontaneous violence. The Court stated that if a weapon is produced by one participant during a spontaneous attack, the others will be guilty of murder if, knowing that that participant has such a weapon, they continue to participate in the attack and the weapon is used to inflict a fatal injury.

The House of Lords provided some useful guidance on the application of the 'fundamentally different' rule in the case of *Rahman and others* [2008] UKHL 45. The House held that a secondary party will not be guilty of murder if:

(1) he foresaw that the principal might kill with the intention to cause GBH, or

(2) he foresaw that the principal might cause GBH with that intention, or

(3) he himself had that intention,

provided that the act that the defendant contemplated was fundamentally different to the act which did occur (figure 16.1).

The Court of Appeal revisited the 'fundamentally different act' test in *Mendez* (2011) and stated that the directions to the jury must be stated as simply as possible in order to make the directions as comprehensible as possible. Toulson LJ stated that the jury should be directed to consider 'whether P's unforeseen act (if such it was) was of a nature likely to be altogether more life-threatening than acts of the nature which D foresaw or intended' (at [48]). This is merely a simpler and more accessible way of expressing the 'fundamentally different act' test and it does not alter the substance of the law.

16.2.3 Withdrawing from the joint enterprise

This section of the chapter deals with the issue of withdrawal from a joint enterprise. Where a defendant initially shares the common purpose of the other participants in a joint enterprise, but later decides that he no longer wishes to participate in the criminal enterprise,

Figure 16.1 Summary of *Rahman and others* [2008] UKHL 45

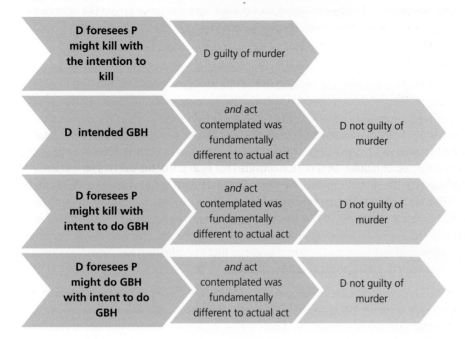

what must he do in order to ensure an effective withdrawal from the enterprise? The answer to this question will depend upon two factors:

(1) the stage at which the defendant has attempted to withdraw; and

(2) the method by which he did so.

 THINKING POINT

Consider whether D has withdrawn from the joint enterprise in the following scenarios:

(1) D agrees to take part in a burglary of a dwelling with P. D knows that P carries a knife and that he would not hesitate to use it as a weapon. During the burglary, the occupant disturbs D and P. P produces the knife and threatens the occupant. D says, 'I've changed my mind. I'm ringing the police' and escapes from the house.

(2) D agrees to take part in an armed robbery of a museum. He knows that his co-conspirators are likely to use violence if necessary. On the morning of the planned robbery, D phones his co-conspirators and tells them that he no longer wants any part in the robbery.

(3) Would your answer to (2) above be any different if, instead of phoning his co-conspirators, D simply failed to turn up to the museum at the designated time?

(4) D and P become embroiled in a fistfight with a group of other people outside a pub. When P produces a knife, D decides that he no longer wants to be involved in the fight and walks away without saying anything.

16.2.3.1 **Withdrawal before the offence begins**

Where the defendant wishes to withdraw from the joint enterprise before the offence has begun, he may do so by communicating his withdrawal.

In the case of *Grundy* [1977] Crim LR 543, the defendant supplied information to two people in order to help them commit a burglary. The information related to the premises which were the subject of the burglary and the occupants of the premises. Two weeks before the burglary was due to take place, the defendant tried to persuade the burglars not to commit the offence. The evidence relating to his withdrawal was not left before the jury and the defendant was convicted of burglary. However, the conviction was quashed on appeal because the defendant had communicated his withdrawal to the burglars and this evidence should have been put before the jury. This case was applied by the Court of Appeal in *Whitefield* (1984) 79 Cr App R 36. The defendant in this case informed his co-conspirators that he no longer wanted to take part in a burglary of a flat that they had planned to commit. His co-conspirators went ahead with the burglary in any event. The defendant's conviction for burglary was quashed on appeal because the jury had not been informed about the possible defence of withdrawal. The Court of Appeal held that there was sufficient evidence that the defendant had served unequivocal notice of his withdrawal on his co-conspirators.

However, a defendant must communicate his withdrawal. Failing to turn up at the scene of the planned crime at the agreed time does not amount to unequivocal communication of withdrawal from the joint enterprise: *Rook* [1993] 1 WLR 1005. A co-conspirator who absents himself from the scene of the crime is deemed to be present unless he has unequivocally communicated his withdrawal from the enterprise.

16.2.3.2 **Withdrawal during the offence (at the scene of the crime)**

Where the defendant decides to withdraw from the joint enterprise after the offence has begun, he must do more than simply communicate his intention to play no further part in the enterprise: *Becerra and Cooper* (1976) 62 Cr App R 212.

CASE CLOSE-UP

Becerra and Cooper (1976) 62 Cr App R 212

This case involved two defendants who, along with a third man, committed a burglary of a house. Becerra used a knife to cut the telephone wires and then passed the knife to Cooper. The defendants were disturbed by a tenant in the property. Becerra said, 'Come on, let's go', and he left through a window along with the third man. Cooper was unable to escape through the back door. When confronted by the tenant, Cooper stabbed him, killing him. Becerra appealed against his conviction for murder, claiming that he had withdrawn from the joint enterprise. However, the Court of Appeal held that Becerra had not effectively withdrawn. Roskill LJ stated that:

> if Becerra wanted to withdraw at that stage, he would have to 'countermand, '...or 'repent' to use another word..., in some manner vastly different and vastly more effective than merely to say 'Come on, let's go,' and go out through the window.

It is unclear exactly what the defendant must do in order to withdraw from a joint enterprise whilst the offence is underway. Merely communicating withdrawal is clearly not sufficient at such a late stage. According to the Court of Appeal, the defendant must 'countermand' or 'repent'. However, exactly what this means is not clear. The defendant is required to act in some way to prevent the offence from occurring. The Court of Appeal suggested that there might come a point in time during a criminal enterprise when 'the only way in which [the defendant] could effectively withdraw...would be physically to intervene'.

The Court gave examples of how the defendant might physically intervene, such as by interposing his own body between them or somehow getting in between them or by some other action. However, it was not necessary in this case for the Court to decide whether that point in time had yet been reached.

Presumably then, the degree of interference required of the defendant will vary depending upon the stage that the joint enterprise had reached. For example, if X decides to withdraw from a burglary on arriving at the scene of the crime but before the crime proper has commenced, might communication of withdrawal as well as a phone call to the police amount to sufficient intervention? On the other hand, if X decides to withdraw when the enterprise is in full progress or close to completion, intervention of a more physical nature is likely to be required (e.g., taking the knife from a co-conspirator or standing in front of the victim to protect him).

16.2.3.3 **Withdrawal from spontaneous violence**

Where the joint enterprise has arisen spontaneously, i.e., through spontaneous violence, unequivocal communication of withdrawal is generally also required: *Robinson* [2000] EWCA Crim 8.

The law took a rather unusual turn in *Mitchell and King* [1999] Crim LR 496, when the Court of Appeal decided that a defendant could withdraw from spontaneous violence without even communicating his withdrawal to the other parties to the joint enterprise. This case involved an unplanned fight in which the defendants and another man, P, had a fight with the owner of a restaurant and his two sons. Mitchell had been inflicting blows upon one man with a weapon, but he threw down his weapon and moved away from the incident. Shortly after this, P used a weapon to beat the victim on the head. The victim died. In his defence, Mitchell relied upon the fact that he had dropped his weapon and moved away as evidence of his withdrawal from the enterprise. The Court of Appeal quashed his conviction for murder and held that communication of withdrawal was not necessary.

In the later case of *Robinson* (2000), the Court of Appeal stated that *Mitchell and King* (1999) was an 'exceptional case' and held that communication was usually required for withdrawal, 'in order to give the principal offenders the opportunity to desist rather than complete the crime'. Where the defendant has initiated the violence, the Court held that simply walking away would not be sufficient to effectively withdraw from the enterprise. Otton LJ stated that:

> it would be a very curious state of our law if a person who had encouraged or incited violence by initiating the attack, could stand aside when he was aware that those who were to continue the violence might form the necessary intention to commit (and did commit) an offence of grievous bodily harm and could thereafter escape all responsibility except for assault occasioning actual bodily from the initial blow. Commonsense and the Common Law go hand in hand.

The Court held that communication was also required in cases of spontaneous violence, 'unless it is not practicable or reasonable so to communicate as in the exceptional circumstances pertaining in *Mitchell* where the accused threw down his weapon and moved away before the final and fatal blows were inflicted'.

Table 16.4 Accessorial liability

Old terminology	Accessory before the fact	Accessory after the fact
Occurs when?	Liability for acts before or during the commission of the principal offence	Liability for acts occurring after the principal offence
Liability for?	• Aiding, abetting, counselling, or procuring under s.8, Accessories and Abettors Act 1861, or • Doctrine of joint enterprise	• Impeding arrest under s.4, Criminal Law Act 1967, or • Compounding an arrestable offence under s.5, Criminal Law Act 1967

16.3 Participation after the offence

An offender who is criminally liable for acts performed either *before or during* the commission of the principal offence is referred to as a secondary party or accessory. Such an offender used to be referred to as an 'accessory *before* the fact'. Where the defendant assists the principal *after* the offence, he may be liable for an offence under s.4 or s.5 of the Criminal Law Act 1967. Such a defendant used to be referred to as an 'accessory *after* the fact' (table 16.4).

Section 4 of the Criminal Law Act 1967 provides for the offence of impeding arrest. A person will be guilty of this offence if, knowing or believing the principal to be guilty of an arrestable offence, he does any act, without lawful authority or reasonable excuse, with intent to impede his apprehension or prosecution. Examples of such an offence include acting as the getaway driver, concealing the offender, destroying evidence relating to the principal offence.

Section 5 of the Criminal Law Act 1967 provides for the offence of compounding an arrestable offence. A person will be guilty of this offence if, knowing or believing the principal to be guilty of an arrestable offence, he accepts or agrees to accept any consideration (other than the making good of loss or injury caused by the offence) for not disclosing information that might be of material assistance in securing the prosecution or conviction of the principal.

16.4 Protection of the victim

CROSS REFERENCE

Refer to 15.2.5 for more information on protection of the victim.

The law protects certain types of victim from prosecution as secondary parties to an offence: *Tyrell* [1894] 1 QB 710. Victims are now also protected from liability under s.51 of the Serious Crime Act 2007.

16.5 Reform

The Law Commission Report, *Murder, Manslaughter and Infanticide* (Law Com. No. 304, 2006) recommends reforms to the law relating to accessorial liability in murder. This report was considered at 5.2.4. In 2007, the Law Commission published their report, *Participating in Crime* (Law Com. No. 305, 2007). This report makes recommendations for a new statutory scheme of liability for those who participate in crime. The report identifies three distinct forms of liability: secondary liability, innocent agency, and the offence of causing another person to commit a no-fault offence.

In relation to secondary liability, the Law Commission recommends that the defendant might be liable in two distinct ways:

(i) D would be liable for a principal offence committed by P if D assisted or encouraged P to perpetrate the conduct element of the principal offence and *intended* that the conduct element should be perpetrated; or

(ii) D would be liable for any offence committed by P provided that its commission was pursuant to a joint criminal venture and fell within the scope of the joint venture.

Summary

- The principal offender is the person who performs or causes the *actus reus* of a substantive criminal offence with the necessary *mens rea*.

- A secondary party may be guilty of aiding, abetting, counselling, or procuring an offence under s.8 of the Accessories and Abettors Act 1861.

- Aiding involves assisting before or during the offence. Abetting requires presence at the scene and wilful encouragement during the crime: *Clarkson & Carroll* (1971). Counselling is soliciting an offence before it occurs: *Calhaem* (1985). Procuring means to produce by one's own endeavour: *Attorney General's Reference (No. 1 of 1975)* (1975).

- The *mens rea* under s.8 of the Accessories and Abettors Act 1861 requires proof that the defendant intended to do the act which assisted or encouraged the principal offence (*National Coal Board v Gamble* (1959)), and that he knew the essential matters which constitute the principal offence (*Johnson v Youden* (1950)).

- The defendant must know the type of crime that will be committed: *Bainbridge* (1960).

- If one person in the joint enterprise departs from the common purpose, the other participants will not be liable for any unforeseen offence which that person commits: *Anderson and Morris* (1966).

- Where P departs from the common purpose, other parties to the joint enterprise will be liable for any crimes that P commits provided they foresaw that P might commit those acts with the requisite *mens rea* of the offence: *Powell and Daniels; English* (1997).

- If the weapon used by P is fundamentally different from, but *as dangerous as*, the weapon the defendant contemplated that P might use, D could still be convicted of murder: *Powell and Daniels; English* (1997).

- Where the defendant wishes to withdraw before the offence has begun, he need simply communicate his withdrawal: *Grundy* (1977). Where the defendant decides to withdraw after the offence has begun, he must do more than this: *Becerra and Cooper* (1976).

☐ The bigger picture

- For more information about the reforms to accessorial liability proposed by the Law Commission, you should read: Law Commission Report, *Participating in Crime* (Law Com. No. 305, 2007) on a new statutory scheme of liability for those who participate in crime, and Law Commission Report, *Murder, Manslaughter and Infanticide* (Law Com. No. 304, 2006) on proposals to reform accessorial liability with respect to murder.

- Accessorial liability is an examinable topic which could arise by way of a problem question or an essay. You should ensure that you are able to answer both essay and problem questions in this area.

  🔞 **For some guidance on how you might approach exam questions on accessorial liability, you should visit the Online Resource Centre.**

- Accessorial liability is a controversial and complicated area of law. In order to gain a further understanding of the issues that arise in this area, you might wish to refer to the following:

  Crewe et al. (2015)

  Sullivan, R. 'Accessories and Principals after *Gnango*' in Reed and Bohlander (2013), Farnham: Ashgate

  Virgo (2012)

  Wilson and Ormerod (2015).

❓ Questions

Self-test questions

1. What is a principal offender?

2. What is a secondary party?

3. Explain how a secondary party might be liable for an offence committed by the principal offender?

4. How much knowledge does an accessory need? Use case law in your answer.

5. Can a secondary party still be liable when the principal has been acquitted? Use case law in your answer.

6. Can a secondary party be tried for a more serious offence than a principal? Use case law in your answer.

7. How might a secondary party be liable under the doctrine of joint enterprise?

8. Explain how a secondary party might be liable under the doctrine of joint enterprise if the principal departs from the common purpose?

9. Explain how a defendant may withdraw from a joint enterprise. Use case law in your answer.

 For suggested approaches, please visit the Online Resource Centre.

Exam questions

1. 'The doctrine of secondary liability has developed haphazardly and is permeated with uncertainty.' (Law Commission Report, *Participating in Crime* (Law Com. No. 305, 2007) at 1.12.)

   To what extent do you agree with the above statement?

2. In order to initiate Jacques into their criminal gang, Alan and Keith decide to encourage Jacques to rape Nina. They entice Nina back to Alan's flat and tell Jacques that he needs to prove his mettle in order to join the gang. Jacques agrees, and the three men take Nina into the bedroom in order to rape her. Alan rapes Nina first, then Keith does so. Alan then produces a knife, which he uses to threaten Nina. Neither Jacques nor Keith knew that Alan was carrying a knife. Keith says, 'This is getting too out of hand', and leaves the flat. Meanwhile, Jacques rapes Nina while Alan holds a knife at Nina's throat. After the rape, Alan stabs Nina and she dies.

   Discuss the liability of the parties for murder.

 For suggested approaches, please visit the Online Resource Centre.

 Further reading

Books

Herring, J. *Criminal Law* (7th edn, 2011), London: Palgrave

Ormerod, D. *Smith & Hogan: Criminal Law* (13th edn, 2011), Oxford: Oxford University Press

Ormerod, D. and Laird, K. *Smith & Hogan: Criminal Law* (14th edn, 2015), Oxford: Oxford University Press

Reed, A. and Bohlander, M. *Participation in Crime Domestic and Comparative Perspectives* (2013), Farnham: Ashgate

Smith, K. *A Modern Treatise on the Law of Criminal Complicity* (1991), Oxford: Oxford University Press

Journal articles

Clarkson, C. 'Complicity, *Powell* and Manslaughter' [1998] Crim LR 558

Crewe, B., Liebling, A., Padfield, N., and Virgo, G. 'Joint Enterprise: The Implications of an Unfair and Unclear Law' [2015] Crim LR 252

Dyson, M. 'The Future of Joint-Up Thinking: Living in a Post-Accessory Liability World' (2015) 79 JCL 181

Forster, S. 'Joint Enterprise Liability' (2009) 173 JPN 501

Freer, E. '*R v Gnango*: The Curious Case of Bandana Man—Part 1' (2012) 175 JPN 181

Green, A. and McGourlay, C. 'The Wolf Packs in our Midst and Other Products of Criminal Joint Enterprise Prosecutions' (2015) 79 JCL 280

Krebs, B., 'Joint Criminal Enterprise' (2010) 73 MLR 578

Parsons, S. 'Joint Enterprise and Murder' (2012) 76 JCL 463

Taylor, R. 'Procuring, Causation, Innocent Agency and the Law Commission' [2008] Crim LR 32

Virgo, G. 'The Doctrine of Joint Enterprise Liability' (2010) 10 Archbold Review 6

Virgo, G. 'Joint Enterprise Liability is Dead: Long Live Accessorial Liability' [2012] Crim LR 850

Wilson, W. 'A Rational Scheme of Liability for Participation in Crime' [2008] Crim LR 3

Wilson, W. and Ormerod, D. 'Simply Harsh to Fairly Simple: Joint Enterprise Reform' [2015] Crim LR 3

Reports

Law Commission Report, *Murder, Manslaughter and Infanticide* (Law Com. No. 304, 2006

Law Commission Report, *Participating in Crime* (Law Com. No. 305, 2007)

17 Study skills

Introduction

While the preceding chapters provide you with the general principles of law required in a criminal law module, this chapter focuses on your study skills with the objective of assisting you in your preparation for your assessments in criminal law. The chapter offers guidance as to how to study effectively and how to approach your assessments and exams. Although this chapter has been written with the study and assessment of criminal law in mind, much of the guidance within the following pages may equally be applied to the study of other subjects on a law degree or graduate diploma in law.

17.1 Manage your time effectively

Managing your time effectively and getting into a routine of regular study and preparation for classes is crucial to your aim of achieving good results (figure 17.1).

Get organised from the very first week of term. You should buy an academic diary during the first week of term and use it throughout the year to write down your timetable of study,

Figure 17.1 Time management

including term dates, exam periods, the classes which you are to attend, and the dates that coursework titles or other assessments will be handed out and their respective deadlines.

17.2 Lectures and seminars/workshops

Criminal law modules are traditionally delivered by means of lectures and seminars (or workshops). A lecture is a large group session led by the lecturer; lectures may be delivered online or in a lecture theatre. Different lecturers may take different approaches to delivering a lecture: some may be interactive, encouraging participation from students, whereas others may prefer to present material to the group, perhaps dealing with any questions from students at the end. Seminars (or workshops) are traditionally the place to test your understanding of the subject. The lecturer will usually lead a small group of students through questions which have been set by the module leader. You should make the most of your seminars/workshops and your tutor by using this time to clarify any problems or areas of confusion which you may have come across during your preparation. Do not be afraid to ask questions and do your best to contribute by answering questions when you can. Students are often nervous about speaking in class in front of classmates and refrain from asking questions for fear of appearing foolish. Remember that your fellow students are in the same position as you, probably feel equally nervous about asking questions, and more than likely wish to ask exactly the same question. Seminars/workshops are a forum for discussion and you should try to leave your nerves at the door of the classroom.

In the following paragraphs there are a few pointers to help you to get the most out of your lectures and seminars/workshops (figure 17.2).

17.2.1 **Preparation before class**

It is important that you prepare for your lectures and seminars/workshops before attending. Your lecturer will be able to advise you on the preparation you should undertake prior to class. You will probably be required to read the relevant chapter of the textbook and answer a set

Figure 17.2 Getting the most out of your classes

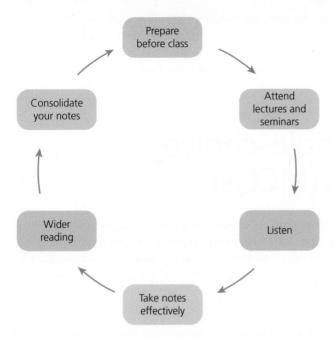

of questions prior to the class. You may also be required to read any key cases and relevant articles from academic journals.

17.2.2 **Attendance!**

It is very easy to underestimate the value of attending lectures and seminars/workshops (or of listening to podcasts of the lectures and/or attending online classes if you are completing your course via distance learning). Do not skip lectures out of complacency, sheer laziness, or lack of organisation. However, if for any reason you are having problems attending your classes, you should make an appointment to see your personal tutor or year tutor, who may be able to offer you some kind of assistance.

17.2.3 **Effective note-taking**

It is difficult to explain how to take notes effectively as this is a skill which you will develop over the course of your studies. You will need to listen carefully to lectures and make use of any podcasts or video recordings of previous lectures that your university provides. When listening to a lecture, you should not write out the entire lecture verbatim, but you must identify the relevant material to take notes of. Similarly, when reading a chapter of the textbook, you should not simply write out the chapter as this is not productive. You need to read in order to gain an understanding of the topic before taking notes of the key legal principles and authorities. You should try to identify and make a note of the key principles of cases, rather than simply the facts of the case. The facts of cases are important to the extent that they provide context to the relevant principle of law. You should try to gain a wider understanding of a particular topic in order to obtain some perspective and a greater appreciation of what is and what is not relevant.

17.2.4 **Consolidating your notes**

After attending your classes for the week, you should get into the habit of consolidating your notes in preparation for the exams. At this stage, you may wish to do some wider reading in order to gain a greater appreciation of the subject. It is a good idea to consolidate your notes immediately after your seminar/workshop because the subject will be fresh in your mind at this time.

17.3 Multiple-choice questions (MCQs)

Some modules in criminal law may include assessment by way of multiple-choice questions (MCQs). These may be MCQs which you are required to answer online after watching an online lecture or during a seminar/workshop. If your module does include assessment by MCQs, you will need to ensure that you are working throughout the year and consolidating your notes immediately after classes in order to ensure that you are able to answer the questions to the best of your ability.

You will also need to ensure that you do attend your classes as any absences may affect your overall grade in the module. If you are unable to attend an exam for a genuine reason, then you should notify your tutor (preferably in advance) as they may be able to make alternative arrangements for you or advise you on how to notify the exam board if necessary.

When answering MCQs you should always make sure that you read the question and options very carefully. The differences between the available options may be very subtle and you will need to read these closely to discover the correct answer. If you are able to answer the question before even looking at the options, then you have made your job easier as you will then need to merely (but carefully) identify the answer that you already know. However, you will only be able to take this approach if you have prepared sufficiently by attending classes and undertaking the necessary reading prior to the assessment. Another possible method of approaching MCQs is to identify the answer by the process of elimination. However, it is likely that the examiner will have drafted the potential options with this in mind—this will therefore call for very careful reading of the options.

17.4 Writing assignments

Depending upon the specific method of assessment of the criminal law module at your university, you may be required to complete a written assessment, such as a piece of coursework. Completing a coursework question is very likely to require you to undertake some wider legal research. You should begin by reading the question and identifying the topic and focus of the question. You should then acquire some basic knowledge about the topic by reading up on that topic in textbooks. Once you have a basic grasp of the relevant area of law, you should undertake further legal research by reading relevant cases, journal articles, and other scholarly writings, such as monographs. You should cite these sources accurately. If you are unsure about how to do this, speak to your tutor. Do not use inappropriate and poor academic

Figure 17.3 Writing an assignment

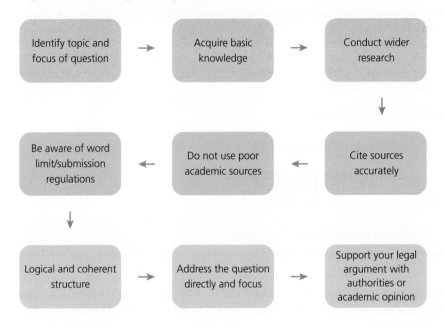

sources. If you wish to use the Internet to conduct your research, you should only use reputable sources recommended by your institution. You should not rely upon user-generated websites as there is no guarantee that the information contained within the site is legally accurate.

You should plan your answer before you begin to write. Be aware of the word limit or page limit of the coursework, any restrictions on the font you should use or the method of submission, and the penalties for breaching the regulations relating to submission (you will usually find these in the programme handbook or you should ask a lecturer). Take great care to ensure that you do not breach the regulations.

Ensure that your answer follows a logical and coherent structure and that you address the question directly. You should remind yourself of the title and focus of your answer throughout the writing process. Support your legal arguments with authorities, whether this is through case law, statute, or academic opinion (figure 17.3).

17.5 The exam

The grade which you achieve in your examination will more likely than not form the greater part, if not the entirety, of your overall grade for the module. You should make sure that you are aware of the weighting of any coursework and examinations. In the following paragraphs, you will find some guidance on how to approach the examination and how to answer problem-scenario questions and essay questions.

17.5.1 **Before the exam**

Make yourself aware of the rubric for the examination well in advance of the exam. There are a number of questions you should find out the answer to before you begin to revise.

Table 17.1 Checklist

Checklist	Answer
How long is your exam?	
Is there additional reading time?	
Is the exam divided into sections?	
How many questions do you need to answer?	
How many questions are there on the exam paper?	
Do the exam questions all carry the same number of marks?	
Work out how long you have to answer each question.	

Most of the answers to these questions should be available to you in your course or module handbooks. If you are unsure of the answers to any of them, you should check with your tutor (table 17.1).

Do not make the mistake of leaving your revision until the last minute. You should begin revising as soon as you can. If you have been consolidating your notes throughout the year, you will have made your task of revising much easier. Plan your revision schedule to ensure that you will have enough time to revise sufficiently.

You should attend any revision classes which are held at the university and make the most of these sessions by preparing for them in advance.

Attempt past examination paper questions and, if possible, show your answer to a tutor. If you find this a daunting task, then try it first with your notes. When you are quite confident with your knowledge of a particular topic, attempt past paper questions without any notes and under timed examination conditions.

Ensure that you are aware of the exact date, time, and location of your exam and arrive at the exam hall in time. However, do not turn up to the exam too early. Many nervous students congregate outside the exam hall well before the start of the exam and try to cram in a last bit of revision. It is best to avoid becoming drawn into the panic of last-minute cramming by keeping away from the exam hall until shortly before the exam.

17.5.2 **In the exam**

Figure 17.4 provides some tips which you should follow in the exam.

17.5.2.1 **Plan your time!**

One of the most common reasons for poor performance in exams is running out of time. This is down to poor time management in the exam. You may have spent months revising hard and know your subject inside out, but if you do not properly plan your exam time, you will not perform as well as you expect and may even fail the examination. You must allow yourself some time to read the exam paper, select the questions you wish to answer,

Figure 17.4 In the exam

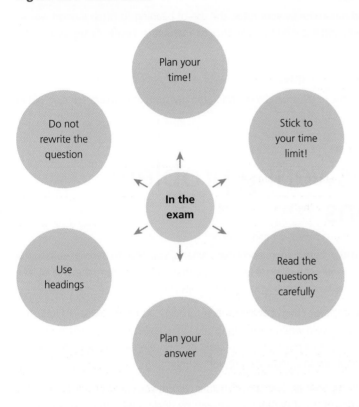

and time to plan your answers. You should already have worked out how long you have to answer each question.

Stick to this time limit and move on to the next question when your allotted time for that question is up, even if you have not finished the question. You are likely to achieve a higher grade if you attempt to answer the number of questions required of you and you do not complete them, rather than if you answer fewer questions but complete them.

17.5.2.2 Read the questions carefully

If you do not read the questions properly, you risk misidentifying the topic and sacrificing a substantial number of marks.

17.5.2.3 Plan your answer (briefly)

You should spend some time planning your answer. Writing structured answers is important.

If you include a brief plan at the start of your answer but put one line through it, it will not be read as part of your answer. However, if you then fail to complete your answer, the examiner is likely to have a look at your plan in order to see where you were going. You may then be given credit for the section of your answer which you did not complete because the examiner would already have a good idea of the level of your knowledge and application of the law.

If you don't finish your answer to each question, you can use the last few seconds of your time limit to make some short bullet points at the end of your question. You can come back to the answer at the end of the exam if you have time.

17.5.2.4 Use headings

Unless you are advised otherwise by your tutor, the use of headings is often a good way of breaking up your answer and ensuring that you stick to a structure. Headings are also helpful in focusing your answer.

17.5.2.5 Do not rewrite the question

Do not waste valuable time in the exam by rewriting the question or problem scenario out in your answer booklet.

17.6 Answering problem questions

When answering a question based upon a problem scenario, you need to demonstrate to the examiner that you can identify the relevant legal issues, that you understand the area of law, and that you can apply the law accurately to a practical situation.

You should avoid rewriting large chunks of the problem scenario as this is a waste of time. It is equally important that you avoid writing everything you know about the relevant area of law. Examiners do not want to read a regurgitation of a set of lecture notes, but want to see that you can apply the relevant law to a particular problem scenario.

Spend some time planning your answer. You should structure your answer in a logical and coherent way. You may wish to structure your answer by dealing with the events chronologically or by assessing the liability of each party in turn, or in another manner. A particular structure may be more appropriate for each topic. For instance, problem questions on theft or non-fatal offences against the person lend themselves more easily to a chronological approach. Take guidance from your seminars/workshops and revision sessions.

Within your answer, you will need to identify legal issues, set out principles of law and authorities, and apply the law numerous times. Thus, each time you identify a legal issue, you should follow this 'mini structure': identify the legal issue, set out the relevant principle of law, support this with an authority, and apply the law (figure 17.5).

Figure 17.5 Answering problem questions

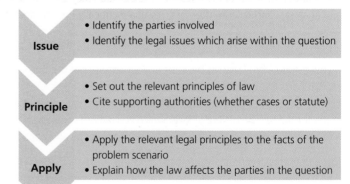

Issue
- Identify the parties involved
- Identify the legal issues which arise within the question

Principle
- Set out the relevant principles of law
- Cite supporting authorities (whether cases or statute)

Apply
- Apply the relevant legal principles to the facts of the problem scenario
- Explain how the law affects the parties in the question

Do not provide lengthy quotations from statutory provisions. An exam is not a memory test and examiners wish to see that you can evaluate and apply the law, rather than recite it verbatim. In many institutions, statute books are allowed in the exam: it is pointless simply copying out sections of law which the examiner knows that you have in front of you. You should structure your answer appropriately, interweaving the law with application. Avoid writing out large chunks of law, then tacking a tiny bit of application onto the end of the paragraph. You should try to apply the law throughout the question. Each time you set out a legal principle, apply it to the facts of the problem question by explaining how it affects the legal position of the parties.

Draw your answer together at the end with a brief conclusion. You should avoid regurgitating your entire answer again, but simply highlight briefly the main issues which impact upon the liability of the parties. It might not be possible to determine definitively whether or not a defendant in a question is guilty. Examiners are looking for your ability to evaluate and apply the relevant law, rather than an unsubstantiated guess as to whether or not the defendant will be convicted. If you feel that further information is required in order to reach a conclusion as to liability, then specify what you would need to know and why.

17.7 Answering essay questions

An essay question is not simply an excuse for you to write everything you know about a particular topic. Examiners are not interested in reading a regurgitation of a set of lecture notes or chapter of a textbook. The most common reason for poor performance on essay questions is a failure actually to address the question asked. If you decide to answer an essay question in the exam, you must ensure that you address the question directly. You must read the question carefully and identify the focus of the question in order to understand what the examiner is looking for.

Plan your answer and stick to your structure. Avoid waffling on about irrelevant material as this simply wastes your valuable exam time and does not earn you extra marks.

You should begin your answer with a brief introduction, in which you demonstrate that you understand the focus of the question; and outline (briefly) what you are going to discuss. In the main body of your answer, you should demonstrate your understanding of the relevant topic and address the focus of the question. The question may ask you to set out the arguments for and against a particular matter, or to evaluate critically the position of the law, including any potential reforms. You should conclude your answer by drawing together your arguments and addressing the question directly.

Good luck!

Glossary

Accessory (or 'secondary party') An accessory aids, abets, counsels, or procures the principal offence.

Actual bodily harm The degree of harm required for the offence under s.47, Offences Against the Person Act 1861.

Actus reus The elements of a criminal offence which do not relate to the state of mind of the defendant.

Anger trigger Applies where something is said and/or done which amounted to circumstances of an extremely grave character and caused the defendant to have a justifiable sense of having been seriously wronged.

Attempt An inchoate offence which involves doing an act which is more than merely preparatory towards the commission of the full offence under s.1, Criminal Attempts Act 1981.

Basic intent A term used to describe an offence which can be committed with a lesser form of *mens rea* than intention (i.e., recklessness). Compare to 'specific intent.

Burden of proof (or 'legal burden') An obligation imposed upon a party in proceedings to prove a fact in issue.

Causation Where the offence is a result crime, the prosecution must prove that the defendant caused the result.

Charge A term used to describe the formal accusation that the defendant has committed a criminal offence. A defendant is charged with a criminal offence at the police station.

Conspiracy An inchoate offence which involves agreeing with another person to commit an offence.

Controlled drug A list of drugs found in Schedule 2 to the Misuse of Drugs Act 1971 or drugs denoted by a Temporary Class Drug Order which are the subject of offences under the Misuse of Drugs Act 1971.

Conviction A term used to indicate that a defendant has either been found guilty of an offence after a trial or has pleaded guilty to an offence.

Diminished responsibility A partial defence to murder under s.2, Homicide Act 1957 (as amended by s.52, Coroners and Justice Act 2009).

Direct intent One's aim or purpose. Compare to 'oblique intent'.

Evidential burden An obligation to adduce some evidence to make an issue a 'live' one.

Fear trigger Applies where the defendant has a fear of serious violence.

Grievous bodily harm (GBH) The degree of harm required for offences under ss.20 and 18, Offences Against the Person Act 1861. Also described as 'really serious harm' or 'serious harm'.

Homicide An umbrella term used to describe offences involving unlawful killing (e.g., murder, manslaughter).

Inchoate Incomplete or undeveloped. Refers to liability for conspiracy, attempt, and encouraging and assisting crime.

Involuntary manslaughter A form of manslaughter which applies where the defendant unlawfully causes the death of the victim but has no intention to kill or cause GBH.

Joint enterprise A doctrine under which two or more people who embark upon the commission of a criminal offence, are liable for any offence committed in pursuance of their common purpose.

Loss of control A partial defence to murder under s.54, Coroners and Justice Act 2009.

Malicious Intentionally or recklessly.

Mens rea The mental element of a criminal offence (e.g., intention and recklessness).

Murder Unlawfully killing a person with the intention to kill or cause GBH.

Objective An objective approach compares the defendant's actions or state of mind with that of a hypothetical reasonable person.

Oblique intent A less common form of intention than direct intent. It requires the consequences of the defendant's actions to be virtually certain to occur and the defendant must appreciate that they are so.

Recklessness A form of *mens rea*. A subjective test of recklessness is applied which requires the defendant to foresee the possibility of a consequence occurring and go ahead and take that (unjustifiable or unreasonable) risk.

Specific intent A term used to describe an offence which requires intention as the *mens rea*. Compare to 'basic intent'.

Standard of proof The degree of certainty that the tribunal of fact must have when deciding upon an issue of fact.

Strict liability A term used to describe offences which lack at least one element of *mens rea*.

Subjective A subjective approach examines what the defendant himself saw or perceived as a consequence of his actions.

Voluntary manslaughter A form of manslaughter which applies where the defendant unlawfully causes the death of the victim and has an intention to kill or cause GBH, but successfully pleads a partial defence, such as loss of control or diminished responsibility.

Index